DISPOSABLE
PATRIOT

Disposable Patriot:

Revelations of a Soldier in America's Secret Wars

By Jack Terrell with Ron Martz

National
Press
Books

Washington, D.C.

Library of Congress Cataloging-in-Publication Data

Jack Terrell, 1941-
Disposable patriot
revelations of a soldier in America's secret wars
by Jack Terrell with Ron Martz
480 pp., 156 x 22.5 cm
ISBN 0-915765-38-1
$24.95
1. Intelligence service--United States.
2. United States Central Intelligence Agency.
I. Martz, Ron, 1947-
II. Title.
JK468.I6T43   1992
327.1'273—dc20
92-32766
CIP

PRINTED IN THE UNITED STATES OF AMERICA

Dedication

Dedicated to John C. Williams, Milton G. Nottingham, Jr., Sharon —
Peggy — Donna, Randy and Kelli Terrell, Caryl Carrico, Del Harris, the
believer, Ron Martz, the master of words

To Robert: I finally finished something.

To Cindy, Chris, Colin and Veronica: With love and thanks for your
patience, understanding and affection.

Acknowledgments

This book would not have been possible without the support and
friendship of Tony Avirgan, Brian Barger, Karen Burns, Leslie Cockburn,
Dr. Margaret Brenman Gibson, Martha Honey, Chris Isham, David Mac-
Michael, Dick McCall, John Mattes, Robert Parry, Peter Dale Scott and
Jonathan Winer.

Contents

1. In Shades of Gray   9
2. Going South   43
3. The Place That Time Forgot   77
4. Begin the Beguine   99
5. Amazing Grace   115
6. Men at War   125
7. A Call to Arms   149
8. Yesterday Once More   165
9. The Casting Call   185
10. A Declaration of Independents   209
11. Disengagement   225
12. Out of the Bubble   241
13. Indian Wars   255
14. Exodus   275
15. Down and Out on Bourbon Street   305
16. Shoot the Messenger   327
17. Government for Sale   365
18. Selective Prosecution   397
19. A Matter of Survival   423
20. In the End   445
Appendices   460
Notes   471
Index   475

1

In Shades of Gray: Death in Nicaragua

The small, green helicopter came across the border into Nicaragua low and fast, closely following three Cessna twin-engine "push-pull" fixed-wing planes. The four aircraft dropped below the ridge lines of the maze of mountains to conceal their flight path and muffle the noise of their engines as they flew south. They dropped even lower when they reached the scrub-covered hills of the Siapali Valley of northern Nicaragua until they were barely skimming the red dirt.

As they approached a Sandinista military school near the village of Santa Clara eleven miles south of the border, the three planes backed off, forcing the helicopter into the lead. Quickly it flared into attack position. A stocky, dark-haired American shifted his weight behind the M-60 machine gun that had been hastily mounted in the door. He jammed the black, plastic stock against his shoulder and began firing short, controlled bursts at the Sandinista soldiers and their Cuban trainers scrambling for cover among the clapboard shacks that made up the camp.

The hulking American sitting at the helicopter's controls manipulated the craft with a finesse that belied his size. His delicate touch kept the overloaded craft dancing and weaving as the Sandinista soldiers slowly recovered from their initial surprise, grabbed their AK-47s and returned fire.

The helicopter carried a third person that afternoon, a Nicaraguan pilot-in-training. Though small compared to the two Americans, the extra pilot's added weight made the overloaded craft even more difficult to handle in the heavy afternoon air. In addition to the three men, the helicopter carried the awkwardly positioned M-60 machine gun with several hundred rounds of ammunition and two external pods, each loaded with 18 2.75-inch rockets.

The extra weight barely mattered to this pilot, though. In one, short, 20-mile run into Nicaragua from the Contra covert military base in Honduras, known as Las Vegas, he had taken nearly 20 years off his life. The smell of cordite, the steady metallic chatter of the M-60 and the lush green foliage took him back to a time when he flew Hueys instead of an overloaded Loach, a time when his back didn't constantly ache from crash-landing too many bullet-riddled helicopters, a time when his door gunner was firing at Vietnamese instead of Nicaraguans and their Cuban trainers, a time when he was convinced that what he was doing was right.

Once again, he was defending the free world against Communism, or so he had been convinced by those who recruited him for this raid. In Vietnam, those Communists had been more than 12,000 miles from home and appeared to pose no immediate threat to the United States. It was easy then for skepticism and cynicism to infect the patriotic ideals with which he first went to war. But these Nicaraguans were different. They seemed to present a real threat. On this day, September 1, 1984, these Nicaraguan Communists were little more than 750 miles from the Texas border.

Romulo Cruz, a local campesino, rushed outside the little wooden shack where he lived across the dirt road from the school and looked up to see the helicopter and three twin-engine planes firing rockets and machine guns into the compound. His peaceful nap on this steamy September afternoon had suddenly become a profusion of noise as rockets exploded inside the base and soldiers screamed curses at the attackers before firing back, their AK-47s rattling on in long-sustained bursts of frustration and anger.

Cruz grabbed his wife and two children and herded them across the road to a trench hidden by trees inside the military school's perimeter wire. A squad of soldiers from the People's Sandinista Army huddled in the trench, cursing and sweating in the heat. Smoke hung lazily in the still air and the smell of fear and gunpowder crowded into the trench with them.

The rocketing and machine-gun fire went on for about 20 minutes before the helicopter turned north and flew low over the trench where Cruz, his family and the soldiers were hiding. The soldiers popped up and unleashed a concentrated barrage of automatic rifle fire. Cruz said later he could see the glass in the Chopper's bubble crack as the bullets smacked into it.[1]

The three push-pulls scrambled for the border, leaving the crew of the damaged helicopter to fend for itself. The chopper struggled gamely into the hostile mountains, but it was too heavy to make it to the border. About three miles short of the border and safety, it crashed. The three men riding in it were killed.

By the next day, the Sandinistas' highly efficient and incredibly strident propaganda machine was trumpeting the news of the deaths of the two Americans through its official newspaper, *La Barricada,* and the sympathetic words of the legion of international correspondents camped out in Managua eagerly awaiting an invasion. As news of the helicopter's shootdown and the deaths of the Americans became public, the U.S. government's private war in Nicaragua using proxy troops began to emerge from the shadows in which it had lurked for several years.

Had the helicopter crashed in Honduras, it is likely that little would ever have been heard of it. The crash site would have been quickly cleaned up, the bodies of the two Americans disposed of or quietly returned to their families, and the Nicaraguan pilot buried in an anonymous grave in Honduras.

But through fate or luck – whether bad or good depends on one's political persuasion – the Sandinistas got to the crash site first and discovered the Americans. Rumors of direct American participation in the war had been rampant throughout Nicaragua, but never before had such indisputable evidence been dropped into their laps.

The three dead men became martyrs in a public relations war being fought by the Sandinistas, the United States government and the rebel army it was sponsoring, the Nicaraguan Democratic Force – FDN by its Spanish initials, but better known as the Contras.

The U.S. government and the Contras piously insisted that the helicopter was on a "mission of mercy," trying to recover some wounded rebels when it was shot down.[2]

That story never carried much weight. Neither did the Contras' claim that the helicopter and the three Cessnas took off from bases inside Nicaragua, not Honduras. At the time, the Hondurans were still vigorously denying they were harboring any counterrevolutionary army.

The Sandinistas' stories were not much more believable. It was widely known that Cuban advisers, the target of the raid, were at Santa Clara. Local residents had nicknamed one steep hill "Cerro Cuba" because of the Cuban trainers' fondness for running the Nicaraguan recruits up and down it. And the locals readily admitted they knew of at least four Cubans who had died in the Santa Clara attack. But the Sandinista government tried to convince the world that only poor, innocent civilians were killed that day.[3]

The Nicaraguans also never let it become public knowledge that the three men on the helicopter were still alive after it crashed. Though injured, the three were taken into custody by Sandinista soldiers and then summarily executed. Their bodies were later doused in gasoline and set afire to make it appear as if they had in fact died in a flaming crash, as the Sandinistas claimed.

Nicaraguan officials said they had problems making positive identification of the remains, and it was nearly a month before the Americans were returned to the U.S. for burial.

The two Americans who died in the raid on Santa Clara were hailed as average, patriotic citizens who had sacrificed their lives to aid the Contras at a time when Congress had decided to cut off aid to them through legislation that became known as the Boland Amendment. In reality, these were anything but average Americans.

At the controls of the helicopter was James Powell III, a 36-year-old Vietnam veteran from Memphis, Tennessee, known to his friends and flying companions as one of the best inter-mountain helicopter pilots they had ever seen.

Firing the machine gun was 37-year-old Dana H. Parker, an intense, dedicated police detective from Huntsville, Alabama. Parker also was a member of the Alabama National Guard's 20th Special Forces Group out of Huntsville and a specialist in low-intensity conflicts.

The pilot-in-training riding with them was Mario Pozo, one of the 15,000 dispossessed and disenfranchised Nicaraguans who fled the ineptitude and corruption of the Sandinista regime and tried to find a home in exile in the counterrevolutionary movement. He was on his first combat mission when he died.

Parker and Powell, according to the story promulgated by the United States government, were part of a shadowy Alabama-based group known as Civilian Military Assistance (CMA). This private group of weekend warriors and Rambo wannabes supposedly had adopted the Contras and was providing non-lethal aid and trainers to the army in exile. The story went that Parker and Powell had gone to Honduras as part of this humanitarian aid package on their own time and at their own expense because they were concerned about the spread of Communism in the hemisphere.

To support this story, CMA leaders handed out portions of a diary Powell supposedly kept during the August trip in which he waxed poetic about the Contras and their struggles.

"They [the Contras] have impressed us with their determination and valor," he wrote. "We have visited both hospitals and saw wounded but resilient soldiers, met [name deleted], heard about Meskito [sic] Indians. These people and the Americans I am with make me proud to be here and [make this] one of the most proud times of my life. I think of my son often, mother and father and all my friends coast to coast. They don't understand why I am here, I'm sure. I'm doing what I think is right."[4]

But while in Honduras, something went terribly wrong. The two let their patriotism get the best of their pragmatism and decided one afternoon to just jump into an armed helicopter and wage their own little war on the Sandinistas. If the official line was to be believed, the little escapade at Santa Clara that cost Parker and Powell their lives was nothing more than a spur-of-the moment joy ride for two thrill-seeking good old Southern boys.

Or so the U.S. government wanted a gullible public and a skeptical Congress to believe. The government denied the raid was sanctioned by the U.S. Army, the Central Intelligence Agency, the Defense Intelligence Agency, the State Department or any other agency that had its fingers stirring the mess that was the heretofore very unpublicized war against Nicaragua.

But civilians don't just drop into a war zone uninvited. They don't just jump into a heavily armed helicopter and cross an international border. They don't just decide to go on a combat mission against the military forces of a foreign government.

It just isn't done.

Dana Parker and Jim Powell had the approval of the United States government to go on this mission. Both were under an "asset" arrangement with the Defense Intelligence Agency, possibly through one of its offices in Huntsville, when they got into that Hughes 500D and led the Cessna push-pulls across the border into Santa Clara. The raid was well-planned and well-financed. But, as were many of the Contras' missions, this one was poorly executed; the Contra pilots didn't have the nerve for a fight and backed off, forcing Powell into the lead in his ill-equipped and quite vulnerable helicopter.

Parker and Powell were on an approved mission, although they had been told not to expose themselves to enemy fire. They did so only because the Contra pilots in the Cessnas, which had come from the New Jersey Air National Guard for this mission that was known as "Project

Elephant Herd," lost their nerve and dropped their bombs on the wrong village because the ground fire was so intense.[5]

After that day, those Cessnas never flew again in a combat mission. They were grounded at the CIA air base at Aguacate for the duration.

What Parker did was an act of war, carried out by a member of the 20th Special Forces Group. Dana Parker was the first U.S. military casualty in the war that to this day the U.S. government will not admit it was fighting.

While alive, Parker and Powell provided the Contras with useful training in helicopter assaults and low-intensity conflicts. These two were to be the vanguard of a legion of private, "plausibly deniable" citizens – those whose participation could be easily denied – that the U.S. government sought to introduce into the war because of Congressional restrictions against overt aid.

But in death, Parker and Powell proved even more valuable to the United States government. Their deaths provided a public relations coup for the White House and the impetus needed to get its efforts to privatize the war off the ground.

The floodgates were opened after Parker and Powell died. Every right-wing nut with a gun and a hatred of Communism was drawn to Central America. The presence of civilians in a war zone fighting what was perceived to be a major Communist threat to the United States was a great gimmick to bludgeon Congress into restoring aid to the heretofore covert insurgents.

Parker was on leave from his job as a police detective in Huntsville when he went to Honduras in the company of Powell, William Courtney, who was another 20th Special Forces member and a full-time employee of the Alabama National Guard in Huntsville, and two other American "volunteers." Some of Parker's friends and relatives believe he had actually been placed on active duty before the August trip.

Powell was a civilian, but apparently he had been lured back into covert government service by the Defense Intelligence Agency, which needed his flying skills and the "plausible deniability" he gave the agency as a civilian.

Powell was among the best anyone had ever seen at navigating offensively blind, aging helicopters through jungle-encrusted mountains crawling with bad guys. He also was chosen for his politically correct beliefs born in Tennessee and honed in Vietnam. Those beliefs maintained that Communism was the scourge of mankind and was making unacceptable inroads into the Western Hemisphere. First Cuba, now Nicaragua. Texas was next. It was the kind of patriotism that played well in the first term of Ronald Reagan and made it easy for government agencies to recruit people like Powell to fight their wars by proxy.

The mindset of this new administration was to take no flak from anybody and to carry out its agenda by bullying any country or any leader who had the audacity to do business with the "evil empire," the Soviet Union. Reagan's California Mafia came to power with what it believed was a mandate from the American people to show the world the United States was back and ready to kick ass after its sobering surrender in Vietnam and years of postwar self-flagellation. The Moral Majority was in charge now and woe be unto those who doubted it or its power.

From top to bottom, the Reagan administration was looking for some Third World country with just enough bravado to challenge it – but not enough to challenge it seriously – so that all the pent up power and frustration could be unleashed in a convincing display of brute force to try to compensate for any misunderstandings left in Saigon. Grenada was just a warm-up. Now, Nicaragua presented a chance to backdoor Castro and send a stiff message to Moscow, although the Kremlin appeared to have little appetite for further expansion in the back yard of the United States. Nicaragua would be the proving ground for the Reagan administration's game of brinkmanship. All bets were off in this little secret war and all leashes were off any government agency or department that might suddenly decide it had some vested interest in this part of the world.

The marriage of Parker and Powell was no accident. They didn't just stumble into one another in Honduras and decide to go kill some Commies. The DIA in Huntsville apparently put the team together, blending Powell's helicopter expertise with Parker's Special Forces skills with weapons and low intensity conflict tactics.

Their service in this quasi-military operation and their cover as civilians were not all that unusual. Parker and Powell were part of a much larger pool of well-trained professional talent into which the government occasionally dips when it wants something done but doesn't want to get its hands dirty.

Since the advent of the Cold War and the ensuing frequent eruptions of Third World conflicts pitting Communism against capitalism, the U.S. government has pulled recruits from this pool on numerous occasions. Usually the recruits are military men, working out of the Army's Special Forces, the Navy's SEALs or the Air Force's Special

Operations Wing (SOW) pilots in what were known as "black" operations.

In a successful textbook black operation, these people are never heard about, the operation is never made public and civilians are not called in to assist. There are dozens of black operations going on around the world at any moment and in virtually all of them civilians are not welcome. A civilian walking into a black operation would be quickly arrested and sent home.

Done successfully, these operations can be lifesavers and government savers. Done wrong, they can become political and military disasters.

The stirrings of a counterrevolutionary army in Honduras and Costa Rica, designed to overthrow the Marxist government of Nicaragua, was to become the largest black operation since the failed Bay of Pigs invasion of Cuba.

The Contra war was a black operation that went wrong. In Central America, the U.S. government stepped outside the classic model following the deaths of Parker and Powell. Their deaths traumatized the government for a while, until some smart guys in gray suits and wing-tip shoes who will draw green government checks for the rest of their lives figured out how to use this to their political advantage.

It went from a black operation to a gray operation because of the congressional restrictions on aid to the Contras that made it necessary and politically expedient to hire civilians to fight Communism in Central America. These restrictions were put in place in August 1984 because the black operation went bad.

When the secrecy surrounding black operations is penetrated by the light of disclosure, it then turns into a gray operation, much like sunlight illuminating the darkness at dawn. But this gray operation was merely a stopgap that never actually slowed the black operation in scope or spirit.

The Central Intelligence Agency had been empowered, through a presidential intelligence "finding," to use its resources to create a military force from the remnants of the old Nicaraguan National Guard, the Guardia Nacionale, for the express purpose of overthrowing the Sandinista regime. Crafted and executed by William Casey, director of Central Intelligence, and Duane Clarridge, CIA chief of counter-terrorism, money and materiel began to flow to Honduras and Costa Rica. Funds were channelled through proprietary banks and military equipment was acquired through various gimmicks from different military establishments.

Casey was one of the prime movers and shakers within the administration who liked the scheme and helped get it implemented, but Clarridge was on the ground and doing it his way. A vehicle like this could bring future rewards of glory to any CIA professional who could pull it off, but Clarridge got carried away with all the money and war toys.

Clarridge was known down south as "Dewey Maroni." More frequently he was referred to as "Mr. *No Problema.*" Whenever any of the Contra leaders wanted something from the CIA, Clarridge's response was "no problem." Ask of Clarridge and ye shall receive. It is generally accepted in the intelligence community that Clarridge ordered the mining of the harbors at Puerto Corinto and Puerto Sandino on Nicaragua's Pacific Coast in early 1984. Not until the Soviet tanker Lugansk struck one of those mines, blowing a hole in its side and injuring five sailors, did the hot line light up in Reagan's office and people start asking, "What the hell is going on in Nicaragua?" That's when people started taking notice of what Dewey had created.

This kind of notoriety was just what the administration wasn't looking for, and when Clarridge's mines-across-the-water scheme suddenly became public knowledge and political ammunition for the media, Congress chimed in with indignant screams about the policy of waging war against our southern neighbor.

So loud was the cry that an obscure congressman from Massachusetts rammed through the first version of what would become the battle standard against every Contra aid package sent up to the Hill by the administration, the Boland Amendment. This little law, although it lacked punishment for any violators of its sanctions, would virtually bring to a halt all official efforts to aid and abet Reagan's south-of-the-border minutemen and their efforts to wage war.

Enactment of the Boland Amendment didn't stop Casey or Reagan, though. By all accounts, the president was determined to aid the Contras and instructed Casey to find a way around Boland. True black operations were out of the question because any government agency found in violation of Boland risked having its budget being trimmed severely in the next fiscal year.

So Reagan and Casey turned to the National Security Council and its gung-ho Marine adviser, Lieutenant Colonel Oliver North. It was North's job to set up a gray operation, to step outside the textbook and establish, at the behest of Reagan and Casey, an extra-agency enterprise utilizing civilians.

The Boland Amendment changed the rules in Central America and the anti-Communist civilian hordes came rushing in with the U.S. government's encouragement and approval. They were allowed in because their presence served a political purpose: It inflamed the right and made all that anti-Communist rhetoric about the Sandinistas being ready to march through Mexico across the Rio Grande and into America's heartland that much more plausible.

Thus arose the need for those self-proclaimed freedom loving cowboys who didn't give a damn about the law of the land when it came to the defense of the nation. What few of these proxy warriors, these gray soldiers, realized was that if they were caught or killed or their actions proved politically embarrassing to the United States, their existence and actions would be publicly denied.

That's exactly what happened to Parker and Powell.

It was superpower versus superpower by proxy using private citizens. Unlike secret black operations, this gray operation was designed to use civilians and attract attention of the public and the media.

The Cessnas had come from the CIA/FDN air base at Aquacate in Honduras. They were being assisted in the attack through radio communications with U.S. military ground control inside Honduras. Claims that they had taken off inside Nicaragua were absurd, since the Contras controlled not a single inch of their native dirt. The helicopter, on loan from the U.S. Army, also came from Honduras, but it had been sent from the big Contra base at Las Vegas, just a few miles north of the border.

In reality, that helicopter nearly made it back across the border after it was hit. Powell, despite his skills as a pilot, was forced to put it down hard about three miles inside Nicaragua.

Confusion reigned at Las Vegas, Aguacate and the big American military base at Palmerola just north of Tegucigalpa as the chatter over military frequencies crackled with disbelief about the shootdown. No one was quite sure how to react, but there were initial, frantic efforts to get an accurate fix on the crash site. A battalion of Honduran troops, the Pumas, was dispatched on a desperate and politically risky rescue attempt and was already several kilometers inside Nicaragua.

Then, as news filtered back to Las Vegas, it was apparent that the Americans still in camp would have to quickly depart the area and eventually the country. When the international press got their teeth into this one, the Honduran government would have trouble denying the existence of the Contras in their country. This messy little covert war had suddenly gone overt.

It quickly became a race to see whether the Pumas or the Sandinistas would get to the crash site first. Unfortunately for Parker, Powell and Pozo, a company of Sandinista soldiers was nearby when the helicopter went down and they got there well ahead of the Hondurans, who were clawing their way through the thick mountainous jungle at a tortuously slow pace.

According to several reports I received, Parker, Powell and Pozo were bruised and beat up by the crash, but were still alive when the Sandinistas arrived. The Sandinistas had no mercy on them. Bullet wounds indicated numerous gunshots wounds from close range.[6]

By the time the Sandinistas had murdered the three injured men, the Hondurans were getting close. The Sandinistas took the bodies and as much of the wreckage as they could carry and moved it farther from the border. The Hondurans, unwilling to risk getting trapped inside Nicaragua despite their numerical superiority at that point and unable to rescue Parker, Powell and Pozo, were forced to hurry back across the border empty-handed.

Although the Sandinistas claimed later that the bodies were burned in the crash, photographs of the wreckage clearly indicate no evidence of a fire.[7]

After much delay because of the ensuing political fallout and much propagandizing by the regime in Managua, the bodies of Parker and Powell were badly burned when returned to the United States for burial at the end of September.

The Hondurans were intent on getting to the crash site first not so much to rescue any survivors, but to sanitize it and prevent it from being used for propaganda purposes. The crash would have been covered up like so many other crashes that happened involving pilots from Task Force 160, the U.S. Army's Special Forces helicopter unit from the 101st Airborne Division (Air Assault), out of Fort Campbell, Kentucky.

Pilots from Task Force 160 later told me during unguarded conversations in moments of frustration: "Jesus Christ, you don't know how many pilots we've lost inside Nicaragua."

It was not surprising that Task Force 160 pilots were dying. They were flying night training missions using night-vision goggles, called NVGs, inside Nicaragua at treetop level. The NVGs were not highly developed and not particularly trustworthy at that time. It was not unusual for pilots wearing NVGs to fly their aircraft straight into the ground.

Task Force 160 pilots had adopted the nickname "Night Stalkers." Their motto was "Death Waits in the Dark." They wore civilian clothes on their missions and carried weapons that could not be traced back to the U.S. government. Most carried several thousand dollars in cash for bribes and a major credit card with at least a $1,000 line of credit.[8]

If the pilots crashed and survived, they were instructed to blow up the aircraft with explosives they carried especially for that purpose and to try to make their way back to Honduras.

If they crashed and were killed, the U.S. military simply said the helicopter went down while on a training mission over water off Norfolk, Virginia, or Panama. Frequently, the families were told, the bodies were not recovered. The system was known as "body washing."

Parker and Powell, while not working for Task Force 160, nevertheless were operating at the behest of the Pentagon through the DIA and would have suffered the same fate had the Hondurans gotten to the crash site first.

News that Parker and Powell had died put the other CMA members who accompanied them to Honduras in a difficult situation. In addition to Courtney, the other Americans at Las Vegas at the time of the shootdown were Walton "Cisco" Blanton, a U.S. Army Special Forces veteran, and Cliff Albright, a parachute jumpmaster and former Republic Airlines pilot.

Courtney, in addition to being one of the founders of CMA, served a special role in the gray operation. He was a warrant officer with the 20th Special Forces Group in charge of logistics and a civilian employee of the Alabama National Guard unit that had access to the unit's supplies and paperwork. Courtney had access to any type of military supplies he wanted, from automatic rifles to ammunition to hand grenades.

Courtney was assisted by Sergeant Ray Potts of the same unit who assisted in acquiring items needed for transportation to the new front. He had placed his retirement pension on the line by doing so and scurried into hiding after Parker and Powell died.

After the shootdown and the roles played by members of the 20th Special Forces became public knowledge, then-Governor George C. Wallace went through the roof. He ordered the adjutant general of the Alabama National Guard to inventory all military supplies and to issue orders that if any guardsman got caught in any act involving the Contras, whether on or off duty, he would be court-martialed and kicked out of the guard. The highest military authority in Alabama got caught by surprise on this and was incensed about being kept in the dark about covert actions utilizing its personnel. Not only was the state's pride at stake, there was the matter of voters and several bereaved families to consider.

By all accounts, Courtney was involved in this particular mission because the DIA planned to use CMA as a conduit to ferry supplies to the Contras and circumvent the Boland Amendment. The use of CMA gave the DIA the plausible deniability it was looking for. Only with CMA, the deniability was more than plausible. It was absolutely believable.

I never realized the extent of the supplies CMA was getting for the Contras until one day several months later, after I had gotten involved with CMA. I went to the home of Tom Posey, the Decatur, Alabama, produce dealer who had been Parker's go-fer but was thrust into the leadership of CMA by the deaths in Nicaragua. Posey took me in one room of his house and my mouth dropped open. Military weapons and ammunition filled the room from the floor to the ceiling.

Posey had new barrels for M-60 machine guns, hand grenades, and boxes and boxes of ammunition for M-16s and M-60s, artillery that not even a licensed firearms dealer would have in this quantity.

Where is a private citizen going to get cases of military ammunition?

These were the kinds of munitions you can't go out to a military surplus store and buy. It came from within. It came from the DIA and from the warehouses of the 20th Special Forces Group, despite repeated denials that anything was missing from the inventory.

Posey became the conduit for these supplies because he could use his produce warehouse by the railroad tracks in downtown Decatur to store them. It was the perfect front. Aided by other guard members, a method known as "surplusing" made ammunition, parts and supplies available from various military facilities throughout Alabama and other southern states.

The DIA's involvement in this was brought home to me one day when I was with Posey in Decatur. A DIA agent who openly identified himself as such drove up in a government vehicle and began unloading military uniforms from the back of the car. He made no secret about what he was doing and promised to come back in a few weeks with additional gear. He had an assignment in California to take care of, but said he would return. This evidently was an arrangement of lengthy duration because Posey and the agent seemed to know each other well.

If Parker and Powell had not been killed, this trickle of supplies would have become a flood. This was the perfect vehicle for the military and the CIA to remain involved at a time when Congress prohibited it. They planned to use private citizens to do their dirty work. Or citizens the government claimed were civilians. It was ingenious.

That's what led me to believe I too could get involved.

Opening the Door

I leaned back in my office chair in Gulf Shores, Alabama, and stared at the late summer thunderstorms brewing out over the tepid waters of the Gulf of Mexico on September 5, 1984. As manager of a condominium service, I didn't have much to do. Most days I just sat and stared out my office window, fantasizing of something that would revitalize my life. I was 43 and going nowhere. I was alone and bitter about my life.

That summer had not been a good one for the tourist business in Gulf Shores. That short stretch of beach that the folks next door in Florida derisively refer to as the "Redneck Riviera" was hit hard by an economic slowdown. Gulf Shores merchants depended on the tourists from Mobile, Birmingham, Atlanta and as far away as Canada to give them enough business from Easter to Labor Day to get through the winter.

The big money didn't come to Gulf Shores that summer. The town was hurting. I was hurting. That's why the news about Powell and Parker caught my attention. The Alabama newspapers were full of stories about the two men and their organization, Civilian Military Assistance. The group had its headquarters in Decatur, near Huntsville in the state's northeastern corner.

Huntsville is home to some of the brightest minds in the National Aeronautics and Space Administration. Nearby Decatur is home to some of the state's most radical Ku Klux Klan members and other factions of the right-wing lunatic fringe. It was not at all surprising that this part of the state had given birth to CMA, whose members espoused virulent anti-communist views.

Politically, philosophically and militarily, CMA struck a chord with me. The thought of traveling to Honduras and Nicaragua and getting involved in what had been a clandestine war suddenly thrust into the public spotlight excited me.

But how would I finagle my way into the organization?

What would I tell the leaders of the group, who I believed were sure to grill me mercilessly about my skills and my background?

I had no real military experience, outside a brief stint some years earlier in Rhodesia with the Grey Scouts. I was largely self-taught, my military skills obtained from reading technical manuals and training unofficially with certain Army Reserve Special Forces groups years earlier. The stories in the papers implied that CMA members were professionals, well-trained and hardened combat veterans of Vietnam and other wars. If they learned what little I had to offer, surely they would reject me outright.

But the lure of quick adventure overcame whatever fear I had of rejection. I picked up the phone and called information in Decatur.

There was no listing for CMA.

I considered calling the newspaper in Decatur, but dismissed that idea. There was a chance some reporter would answer and start asking too many questions I didn't want to answer at that time.

Instead, I called the Decatur Police Department and pretended to be with another law enforcement agency. I told the desk sergeant who answered the phone that we had a prisoner in custody on a weapons charge who claimed to be a member of CMA.

The sergeant immediately launched into a lengthy explanation about the organization and Tom Posey, the local produce dealer who had suddenly become a national celebrity because of the deaths of Parker and Powell. Posey's Howdy Doody face and his cockeyed grin and receding hairline had been in newspapers and on television ever since the two men had been killed. Posey had become the mouthpiece for CMA, a good old boy defender of democracy against the godless Communists.

The sergeant told me that there was some concern among local law enforcement agencies that CMA was being used by some organization to run guns and ammunition to Central America.

What neither he nor I knew at that time was that the organization was the United States government.

I thanked the sergeant and hung up. It didn't make sense. A small-town produce dealer running what appeared to be a major anti-communist organization in support of Ronald Reagan's "freedom fighters"? Out of his produce warehouse in Decatur, Alabama?

As I was to learn later, it was not all that odd or mysterious. It was absolutely brilliant. The good old boys of Alabama, the pure-hearted patriotic defenders of democracy, were providing the perfect cover story for the Reagan administration's privatization of the war in Nicaragua.

I got the number for Posey's produce business from the operator. Patsy Posey, Tom's wife, answered the phone. When I asked for information about CMA she told me I would have to talk to Tom about it, but he was busy with the media. They had been besieging him about the funerals for Powell and Parker. She told me she would send an application for the group and I gave her my address.

When the application didn't arrive after two weeks of waiting, I called back. Patsy answered the phone again. I told her, with more than a hint of irritation in my voice, that I wanted to join the group and wanted an application. She apologized and said she would send one immediately. It arrived three days letter.

The CMA application turned out to be a crudely printed letter filled with the standard right-wing jargon of virtually every anti-communist group. There were the usual pleas for donations to support the "freedom fighters" in Nicaragua and expressions of dire concern that the Communists were ready to march across the Rio Grande into Texas.

I carefully filled out the application to make it appear that I had a military background. I wanted CMA leaders to take notice of me, but I didn't want to draw too much attention to myself. As an added touch, I wrote a cover letter in which I sympathized in the strongest possible terms with Posey's particular strain of anti-Communism. I also wrote that I thought I had certain skills that might be useful to CMA, although I provided no particulars. It was a very sketchy resume, but the cover letter contained all the right buzzwords, at least enough to interest Posey, I hoped.

When I didn't hear from Posey or anyone else in the organization for several days, I called his home. Patsy told me Tom was planning to spend the weekend in New Orleans loading supplies for shipment to the Contras. She said he planned to stay at the Contempra Inn on Williams Boulevard. And, she said, he would be driving a U-Haul truck loaded with supplies.

I decided rather than trying to track Posey down by telephone, which appeared to be a fruitless endeavor, I would go to New Orleans to talk to him face to face.

On Friday, October 5, 1984, I left Gulf Shores for New Orleans in my Chevy S-10 Blazer, arriving late in the afternoon. During the two-hour drive I began adding details to my bogus background, details that included service with the U.S. Army in Vietnam, although what I knew about Vietnam came right out of the pages of *Soldier of Fortune* magazine.

I was the right age to be a Vietnam veteran and despite my lack of firsthand military experience, I had become extremely knowledgeable about a wide variety of tactics, demolitions and weapons, including the Soviet-made weapons being shipped to Nicaragua by Cuba. On paper, I was a low-intensity conflict specialist. In reality, I lacked field experience. I was hoping there wouldn't be too many expert background checkers in CMA.

As it turned out, there weren't too many experts at anything in CMA. CMA was made up primarily of guys who liked to sit around and try to impress one another with their war stories.

Posey had not checked in at the Contempra Inn by the time I arrived, so I went to my room and lay down, still working on my story. The Jack Terrell that I knew was beginning to fade. Another man, another person without a name but with my face, was beginning to emerge from my imagination.

Posey did not show up that night. The next morning, I went to the window and in the parking lot behind the Denny's restaurant next to the motel was the orange U-Haul truck that I assumed Posey had driven from his home in Alabama. I went to the desk and asked for his room number. It was about 6 a.m., but I immediately went to his room and knocked on the door.

I heard someone moving around in the room and then the door opened slightly. There stood Posey, the staunch anti-Communist, the highly visible advocate of the Nicaraguan "freedom fighters," in his Jockey shorts, rubbing his eyes. He looked for all the world like just another sleepy suburbanite rushing into middle age.

I told him who I was and he thanked me for waking him, saying he had to get an early start unloading the supplies. He spoke in a soft, easy drawl. Neither his face nor his voice had any of the hardness to it that one might have expected of this defender of truth, justice and the American way. He told me to go to Denny's, have a cup of coffee and wait for him.

About 30 minutes later, Posey and another man emerged from his room. Posey was about 6-foot-2 and 175 pounds. He had thinning brown hair, slightly stooped shoulders and a sort of bemused, vacant expression on his face. It was the kind of look you see on the faces of farmers in rural Alabama, open and friendly, but unaware of much outside their small universe. He wore a pair of old bluejeans, a denim jacket and brown boots. He looked more like the Alabama farm boy he was than some would-be mercenary on a mission from God to save the country from Communism.

The man with Posey was only slightly taller, but was almost twice as wide. Posey introduced him as "Sailor." Sailor looked like a mountain man with his heavy beard and moustache. He had recessed eyes that cast the gaze of a man who had been in war. He walked with a slight limp from severe wounds received in that war. He wore a bush hat with some sort of insignia, a camouflaged vest, faded blue jeans and combat boots.

Sailor, I learned later, was Jim Turney, a Vietnam veteran, firearms dealer and owner of a military surplus store in Memphis. We shook hands and slid into the booth farthest from the door and other people.

I immediately launched into my story about the difficulty I had linking up with Tom and how I was eager to contact the group. Tom inquired whether I sent in an application and I told him that I had sent it to Decatur weeks ago, but did not get an answer. Because of that I elected to bring my resume to him personally. With much doubt about what might happen next, I pulled the papers from my pocket and presented them to Posey.

He began to scan the fake resume and I could immediately tell by the look in his eyes that he liked what he was reading. When he was finished reading about the Jack Terrell who was still little more than a creature of my imagination, not the man sitting in the booth with Posey and Turney, Posey launched into his anti-Communist, anti-Sandinista spiel. He explained about his role with the FDN (*Fuerza Democratica Nicaraguensa* in Spanish, which Posey couldn't pronounce). He tried to impress on me that CMA was a supply network made up of donors of materiel, money and volunteers. But he also tried to blend in a sense of macho militarism possessed by freedom-loving Americans who were ready to jump off at any border any time to defend against Communism. As he continued to talk, I began to get amused because he talked more like a puppet than a real human being, and his rambling analysis of the war and the situation in Central America demonstrated a total lack of military logic.

Posey was the propaganda-meister. Sailor just sat there nodding in agreement, a kind of Pavlovian response to Posey's buzzwords. It was clear I was dealing with a couple of flaming Ghadaffi-like right-wingers here, if not the Grand Dragon and the Royal High Cyclops of the Ku Klux Klan. These were people who couldn't put together a five-word sentence. They had the collective intelligence of a banana slug. I couldn't figure out how these guys were running in and out of Honduras and doing cross-border operations without getting caught.

One's ideological bent proved to be the most important factor in becoming a member of CMA. It didn't matter if you had no formal military training and no particular skills to do anything related to combat. As long as you loved Jesus and Ronald Reagan and hated Communism, you were accepted.

Posey said he had arrived during the night with a load of 2,000 pairs of boots that were to be shipped to Honduras for distribution to members of the FDN. He invited me to go with him and Sailor to the house of Mario Calero, the brother of FDN head Adolfo Calero, where other CMA members would be gathering with supplies from other cities.

Tom asked me to ride with him in the U-Haul because he didn't want too many vehicles in the area. I thought that was a bit strange, but complied with his request. It was the first indication I had of the paranoia that seemed endemic to CMA members. The second was when we arrived at Mario's house. The name on the mailbox was not Calero. The CMA members inside the house did nothing to dispel that sense of paranoia. They frequently talked in whispers and kept looking out the window. They acted like the Secret Service.

I was probably the only person on the premises not holding some type of piece. The combination of guns and borderline lunatics didn't give me much of a sense of security. The guns, I was to learn, were more of a security blanket for these guys than they were a threat to others. Guns were like dicks to these guys – they had the illusion that bigger is better.

The entire group in Mario's house gave me a warm welcome and acted as if I was being ushered into what I still thought was a credible organization with instant, full membership. The resident Nicaraguans were especially effusive with their greetings, particularly Mario. He strode from the den like a man in total command of the house and all in it. He was a large man, about 6-foot-4 and 250 pounds, with a broad, pitted face and shiny black hair streaked with gray. He wore a *guayabera*, the loose-fitting shirt worn by men in many Latin countries. Mario wore it, I suspect, more to conceal his ample stomach than as a concession to the fashion of his native country.

He was in a big hurry this day and said we would all take time later to talk, but first there was much work to be done. We quickly divided into three groups and left in three cars in three separate directions. I rode with Mario and two other men, a Nicaraguan I didn't know and Tom Stone, a retired Army sergeant major from Memphis. We drove past the entrance to New Orleans International Airport and turned onto a road leading to a group of low, unpainted concrete warehouses next to the general aviation ramp. A small sign on the front of one of the buildings read Behring International.

The place appeared vacant. The two steel doors leading into the warehouse were closed and there were no other cars in the parking lot except for ours. A stack of frames for military LC-1 (ALICE) back-packs lay discarded in front of the doors. I began to wonder exactly what Mario was up to.

Within minutes, the other two vehicles arrived at the loading ramp and Posey backed the U-Haul up to the door. Mario went into the warehouse through a small office door and as Posey backed the truck up the ramp, the main doors began opening. The truck stopped halfway into the main warehouse in front of a large steel shipping pallet. Everyone walked around the truck to the rear and as Posey opened the door, fiberglass sacks with combat boots began tumbling out. The U-Haul was stuffed with bags of new boots. We immediately began tossing them onto the pallet.

As the work progressed, Posey pulled me aside and said he wanted to talk to me in private. It was evident I was important to him. He said that among our group were two journalists from *Eagle* magazine, a pulp publication for right-wing adventurers and armchair commandos, a poor-man's *Soldier of Fortune*. They had volunteered to help unload the truck in exchange for a photo essay of the activity. The writer was James Adair of Houston, a man who would later play an unusual part in certain operations in Honduras. His partner was an Australian photographer and former "para-bat" (parachute battalion) mercenary who felt comfortable in these surroundings.

Posey advised me that Adair and his partner had been given a set of strict guidelines about photographs of CMA members and that I had control over whether they could photograph me or interview me. I told him that under no conditions would I permit my picture to be taken. I said if certain people saw it and identified me it could be fatal because of my participation in recent CIA missions. I said that to build my own image and impress Posey, and he bought my fabrication. It played well on Tom because he had a fantasy about becoming a "spook" or operative for the government and assumed that I might know someone who could put him in contact with the inner circle of agents. I didn't discourage his thinking as it was to work in my behalf.

The warehouse work was hard and no one seemed to be in the physical shape required for doing it for an extended time. My back ached and every muscle felt torn, but outwardly I was showing no pain. I would keep up or do better than the others if it killed me.

The boots we unloaded were part of a deal between the FDN and Genesco, the manufacturer. Genesco specially designed a boot for the Contras because of the unusual terrain in northern Nicaragua. The construction had to be solid because of the rugged, mountainous areas and the sole had to be mud-proof due to monsoon-like rains that turned the valleys into quagmires. Instead of the "Panama lug sole" normally used in jungle terrain, the FDN boot had a "sports tread" that picked up everything from mud to mosquitoes.

Five thousand pairs of these boots had been ordered by the FDN with a guarantee that if they did not hold up Genesco would replace them.

This guarantee put Genesco in the perfect position to be scammed. Once the boots reached their destination in the field – at least that portion that survived Honduran black market tariffs and FDN skimming – the commandantes issued a few pairs to the soldiers. They wore the boots about two weeks before returning them as instructed. The commandantes then separated the soles from the body of the boot and sent them to headquarters complaining that the boots could not take the punishment of battle. A few samples were sent back to the FDN office in New Orleans where they were then presented to Genesco with painful, almost tearful, explanations about the effects on the men and battles as the result of shoddy boots.

Genesco graciously replaced the so-called faulty boots with another, much better boot and forgave the charges. This amounted to the theft of nearly 10,000 pairs of boots that, at the time, sold for nearly $30 a pair. Not a bad deal for the FDN cockroaches who thrived on misrepresentation.

When we were finished with the boots, Mario asked for volunteers to accompany him to another warehouse. I jumped at the opportunity because I wanted to make an impression on him. We drove to a small rented warehouse about two miles from the terminal. Upon opening the doors we saw that rain had leaked through the roof and soaked everything inside. In this building was food, medicine, clothing of all types and military paraphernalia. We were asked to repack everything and load it onto the truck. The temperature was blistering hot and time dragged on. Most of the items I saw appeared to be donated civilian wear. The military items were those for which there was little demand – salt tablets, folding shovels, cots and winter garb. Surely the FDN wasn't paying good money to send this to the front? It wasn't, but its presence in the warehouse made good press.

I was getting to the point to where I wanted to get down to business and leave this tedious chore to some of the other volunteers. The bleak picture painted by Mario of circumstances in Honduras didn't jibe with the absence of his fellow Nicaraguans, who were supposed to be the backstops in the U.S. He constantly complained that no Nicaraguans showed up to help when they were most needed. I was in total agreement by this time, and from what I had observed the only people interested in helping the FDN were the American volunteers who gave up their weekends to do this dirty work. But this dirty work gave a certain luster to those who would use this as a vehicle to get down south where they felt the action was.

Mario finally called it a day around seven o'clock. He had worked with great intensity all day, giving of himself as much as he asked of us and no one had any gripes about how he worked with the group. My adrenaline was still pumping despite my weariness and a strong desire to return to the motel to crash. I saw the opportunity to discuss war and was not going to let it pass.

We arrived back at Mario's house as his wife started to serve a traditional Nicaraguan dinner of beans and rice and lime tea. Mario made it a point to make me taste the tea as part of my introduction to the people of his country and his culture. To my surprise, I found it to be different and refreshing and from then on lime tea became my drink of choice.

The assortment of characters sitting around the small dining table set up in the living room was as bizarre as any I had ever seen. There was Mario, Tom Posey, Sailor and Tom Stone; Jim Adair, the Australian; Robert "Doc" Ohrman, former dust-off medic; Chris Heinz, a Florida arms dealer; and Walton "Cisco" Blanton, a veteran of the original CMA campaign in Honduras, who had arrived late.

Cisco was a very unusual number. He was stocky and wore sleeveless sweat shirts much of the year, khaki pants that fit tightly at the ankles and mountain boots. He combed his reddish-brown hair straight back and sported a bushy mustache. He had blue eyes that were in a perpetual squint, as if he were trying to focus on something in the distance but couldn't quite make it out. Cisco tried to give the impression he was quite knowledgeable, but his constant paranoia quickly dispelled that first take on him. He felt that any telephone he used was tapped and any vehicle that could not be readily identified was carrying agents of some sort who were watching his movements. He drove a van that belonged to Tom and kept a full auto FN-FAL assault rifle on board. He always carried a small equipment bag slung over his shoulder that contained a .45-caliber automatic pistol with extra clips. Mario liked Cisco but often referred to him as "dependably undependable" because he could never be trusted to meet a deadline.

During dinner and the meeting after it, Cisco sat quietly at one end of the table opposite Mario. Tom was on Mario's right and I was on the left. Mario turned to me and asked about the plan I mentioned earlier to him. I started my proposal with a remark about my identity and that I would not divulge it to anyone unless he was on a need to know basis. I felt I should operate under a code name.

Hearing the coolness in my voice and catching a not-so-subtle hint, Mario asked Adair and the Australian to leave. Mario evidently had been given a copy of the resume I submitted to Posey because he said he had to call Miami and talk to a former CIA agent who purchased arms for the FDN. According to Mario, his name was Jim McCoy.

McCoy actually was a retired Army lieutenant colonel who had been an attache at the U.S. Embassy in Managua in 1979 where he came to know Mario's elder brother and Contra leader Adolfo Calero. McCoy was suspected of being an active asset of the CIA and engaged in a secret U.S. military operation involving arms and communications equipment being transported from the Dominican Republic to El Salvador under the code name "Operation Sea Spray."

Mario asked if I knew McCoy and I said I did. Then he got up from the table and walked into the kitchen to make a telephone call. First he spoke softly in Spanish before changing to English. After a few minutes he walked back to the table with the telephone muffled in his hand and asked if I had a code name or could give him the name of a mission that I had participated in for authentication by McCoy.

I looked straight into his eyes, searching for an answer, and suddenly the name Ramses popped into my head.

"Ramses," I told Mario.

He walked back into the kitchen and shortly returned. Adolfo had said everything was okay, he said. At this point I did not know who Adolfo was but figured he was someone important. I had no idea why Adolfo signed off on a bogus operation and have never been able to figure out why he did. His clearance seemed to embed me further in the group and I began to gain confidence. I felt like I controlled the whole room and everyone in it. This clearance appeared to be an outright endorsement of me and my credentials. This later proved to make things quite easy for me and my plans.

Mario told me that he would think about a code name if I couldn't come up with one, but at that point I was more interested in laying out my plan than in obtaining a nom de guerre.

I told those sitting around the table that I had been involved in the Phoenix Project in Vietnam and saw where such a program could be carried off successfully in the war in Nicaragua. The Phoenix Project was implemented by the U.S. in Vietnam, as I explained to them, "to identify the Viet Cong infrastructure, locate, pinpoint and terminate with extreme prejudice."

Under a similar project to be known as "Operation Pegasus," CMA would go into the Honduran-Nicaraguan border area and put together a special strike force made up of Americans and Nicaraguans that I referred to as "spike teams." Each team would consist of fifteen men and would be sent into the interior of Nicaragua and hit all critical targets available to cripple the Sandinistas' ability to wage war. We were to assassinate all key government leaders, including President Daniel Ortega, Foreign Minister Miguel D'Escoto, Tomas Borge and Nora Estorga. No one would be spared, and through Operation Pegasus the FDN could demonstrate its effectiveness to strike deep in Sandinista territory and thereby change world opinion about their fighting ability and will to win.

Operation Pegasus was to be launched in conjunction with a "spectacular" envisioned by Duane Clarridge. Clarridge's "spectacular" included the destruction of one of two major dams north of Managua.[9] Had this been done, thousands of innocent civilians below the dams would have died. I wasn't going to push this thing that far, but in order to become a permanent fixture within this organization being administered by this "dining table general staff," I had to indicate that nothing was out of the question.

It didn't seem to matter to anyone that we were violating federal laws that evening. We were in the United States discussing assassinating foreign heads of state and overthrowing a foreign government with which our country was not at war. It was a clear violation of the Neutrality Act, but none of those sitting around the table in Mario Calero's house apparently knew of, or cared about, the Neutrality Act's prohibition on conversations like this about the overthrow of foreign governments. Laws were for civilians and this group considered itself in a territory between the military and private citizens.

All that mattered to them was driving the "Goddamned Commanists out of Managua before they became any more of a threat to the good old U.S. of A.," as Posey liked to phrase it in his own inimitable way.

The plan for Operation Pegasus was based mostly on my research of the old Phoenix Project. When necessary, I ad-libbed to give an added touch that kept the interest of the men piqued in favor of my concept. Mario asked questions as to the number of men, ratio of Americans to Nicaraguans, time in training and where the supplies were coming from. He also said all this would have to be approved by Adolfo, but with his personal recommendation he thought he could put it through.

CMA had virtually tossed the FDN into the laps of the American public with all of the attention as a result of the deaths of Parker and Powell. Mario wasn't about to let CMA get out of the public eye for long, but he was hesitant about allowing Americans to once again become involved in combat. That could backfire on the FDN and cause more problems with a Congress unwilling to vote more aid and more willing to stop the effort completely.

I requested that myself and one other man, to be named by Mario and Tom, go to Honduras and tour the bases occupied by Contra forces on the border. We would select a site for the new base and begin choosing men from various camps to become the special forces used in the strike team. This would be a two-week assessment and intelligence run with our findings to be reported back to Mario for the development of the project scenario. Mario disagreed with my proposal, saying I should be able to speak the language before entering the region or I would be handicapped when conversing with commandantes. I pressed for permission anyway.

The most likely candidate to make the trip with me was Cisco. He was unemployed and had some knowledge of Hondurans since he had been there when the helicopter was shot down. Tom agreed with this, but Mario was hesitant because he felt the Honduran government would have hard feelings towards those who were recently involved in an incident that made them look like active participants, not neutral observers, in this war.

Honduras was trying to put on a new face for the world to go along with its new armed forces chief of staff, Walter Lopez. The Hondurans did not want to agitate the Sandinistas at this particular time. Honduras wasn't really sure if the U.S. would back it if hostilities broke out over the Contras, despite the ever-growing presence of American troops in the country.

The FDN had good relations with the Honduran secret police and it was pointed out that our presence might not be discovered since we planned to be in country for a short time and would be staying on Contra bases, thus diminishing our chances of being spotted by American press. Mario still had some problems with this issue. While he liked the overall plan, he insisted on Spanish classes before the trip. I was somewhat dismayed at his suggestion, for I did not really know the importance of being able to speak the language at the time. Mario said that no decision would be made at this meeting and we should retire for the evening.

After a day and a night in which I appeared to have been totally and unconditionally accepted into the organization and my plan for Operation Pegasus seriously considered, I suddenly became frustrated. I was really down about the prospects of the project and felt it may not come together, since Mario was calling the shots and was sticking to his guns on the language issue. We left the issue unresolved and returned to the Contempra Inn.

Despite the blessing of Adolfo and Mario Calero and the initial warmth with which they greeted me, the rest of the members of CMA were curious about me and suspicious of me. They didn't know what to make of me. If they had to guess, they probably would have guessed that I had been sent there by the CIA to help them. Most of them, including Posey, kept their distance, except for "Doc Ohrman," who welcomed me to the group and made it clear he was ready to go to the frontier on a moment's notice and stay there for up to six months. Doc told me he was a male nurse in a Memphis hospital and a Vietnam veteran. He was friendly and it was difficult not to like him, even though he was hyper, couldn't sit still and talked too loudly and too much. Doc was devoted to his place in the group and followed orders well.

As we talked, I noticed Cisco had come out of his room and was standing along the guard rail looking out into the parking lot below. I was curious about Cisco because he hadn't had much to say throughout the course of the meeting. In fact, when Posey first broached the possibility of Cisco accompanying me to the border, Cisco tried to wave off the suggestion. I felt that maybe he knew something about this that I didn't and decided at my first opportunity I would cut him away from the rest of the members and talk to him about the mission and whether he would go.

I left Doc and began talking to Cisco, making small talk about the day to see what direction to take the conversation. He quickly started griping about the many weeks he had been moving supplies for Posey and the FDN without a job to make ends meet. He said he had been promised money for his time but had yet to see a dime. Tom had told me that he was footing Cisco's expenses while on the road and that he was a volunteer like the rest of the group. Tom also implied that Cisco would hit anyone up for a loan but that he was bad pay.

Cisco elaborated about his experiences in Honduras with Jim Powell and Dana Parker and tried to impress on me his friendship with Parker. He said the two of them had been close friends and had worked a few police "gigs" around Huntsville. He told one story in which he said he and Dana were involved in a crowd disturbance on a back street in Huntsville when Dana had to shoot one person in the crowd. During the melee, Cisco said, he was shot in the back of the head and rushed to a hospital where he lay unconscious for several days before recovering. I later asked Tom if he knew that Cisco had been shot in the head and Tom cracked up and said Cisco had a tendency to exaggerate a little.

Cisco never changed his story, though, and from his actions on occasion I believed that he had indeed been shot and it had affected his thought patterns.

Cisco appeared to be very agitated about the deaths of Jim and Dana. I told him that if he wanted to be in a position to avenge their deaths and if he wanted to see that they did not die in vain, then he should help me get this project underway and get something going for the Americans participating in the war. I asked Cisco about his feelings on the war. Was he participating for money or to get the Communists out of our hemisphere? He spoke in general terms and went to great lengths to avoid any discussion of money, no matter how hard I tried to lead him in that direction. He said he had been pulled out of Las Vegas when the news broke of the shootdown and he was eager to get back, but he was unsure about a combat role inside Nicaragua. He wanted to think about that for a while.

Despite the setback on the Spanish lessons, I was feeling rather cocky because I felt I had the upper hand on these people. There was a good possibility that my project would be implemented and I was involved in something that got my senses stirring again. I went back to my room for a few minutes rest before joining the group at Denny's for a night of drinking coffee and probing one another for information. After I joined them, I got far more than I gave.

The weekend had been quite productive and I was invited back the next weekend, even though they needed time to allow their heads to stop ringing from the hammer I had hit them with. There were more supplies to be loaded for shipment south and they needed help. Everything seemed to be clicking.

I slept late and left for home on the afternoon of October 7. It was still hot and muggy along the Gulf coast, but it was quiet that Sunday night, as Sundays usually are in Gulf Shores after the tourists have gone home.

I had been home only a few hours when the telephone rang. It was a call that changed not only my life, but the direction of the U.S. government's involvement in Central America.

A Perfect Cutout

"Is your name Jack Reynolds Terrell?" the caller asked.

"Yes, it is," I replied. "Who's this?"

The voice on the telephone was unfamiliar, but sounded firm and formal. Most people who telephoned me called me Pete, Jack or Jackie. No one I knew used my full name.

"That's not important right now," said the voice.

"Are you sure you have the right number?" I asked.

"I assure you I have the right number. Let me explain something to you. I know you just came from New Orleans. I know that you were in the company of Mario Calero and Tom Posey and other members of the organization known as Civilian Military Assistance."

My first reaction was that this was a practical joke. But I didn't know anybody who would play that kind of a joke on me. Then I thought it was a test by the CMA people to see if I was trustworthy.

But the more the stranger talked, the more I realized this was no joke and it certainly was not a voice I recognized from CMA members.

I could feel a knot forming in my stomach. Someone had been watching me and knew exactly what I had been doing for the last few days.

But who was he?

And what did he want with me?

"Do you plan to join them?" the voice asked me, referring to CMA.

"That's why I went over there," I said.

"For what reason?"

"To tell you the truth, at this point I really don't know what reason," I said. "My life's shit here and these people offered me a gig. CMA can probably get me what I want."

"I'm aware of that," the voice said. "How would you like to go to Honduras, have some fun and do something for your country?"

"What do you mean?"

"What I'm about to say is not official U.S. government policy. I'm talking to you person to person."

There was a pause on the line.

"My name is Donald Fortier and I work in a certain part of the U.S. government," he said finally.

The name meant nothing to me. I thought he was just another member of the government's "spook" corps. The truth of the matter was that Donald Fortier was the No. 3 man at the National Security Council.

He had been promoted to that post in 1983, but was relatively invisible in the Reagan administration. He was a paper shuffler, an ideas man, a behind the scenes player. Robert McFarlane, Reagan's national security adviser, had turned to Fortier for assistance in September 1984 when it became apparent Congress was about to cut off aid to the Contras.

"I, along with others," Fortier continued, "are suspect of the motives of this Civilian Military Assistance group and what they are doing in

Honduras as civilians. We're also not sure if they are officially sanctioned, if they are officially working for anyone.

"But there are those here who would like to know what their motives are and whether they run counter to what we believe should be the correct policy of the United States government."

"Exactly what is it you want me to do?" I asked Fortier.

"Let's put it this way: This group [CMA] might be credible. It might be honorable. It might be a lot of things. But we need to know firsthand everything we can about these people, what they're doing, what their motives are and who's behind them."

He stressed that his contact with me was "unofficial," that I would not be protected if I decided to work with the group he represented, that I would be on my own, but that I would be doing a service for my country.

Fortier wanted to know how many members CMA actually had, whether it was a few dozen as he believed, or the several thousand Posey claimed in his numerous public appearances. He wanted to know the infrastructure of the leadership, who the leaders' contacts were, how they procured arms, whether they were shipping arms out of the United States, whether they were connected with drugs and whether they were involved in any other illegalities inside or outside the United States.

"This is a decision you're going to have to make on your own," Fortier said of my involvement.

"I'm going to hang up now, but I'll call back later. I may call back in an hour. I may call back in a day. I may call back in two or three days. But I want you to think very strongly about involving yourself."

There was a soft beep on the line like a secure telephone had been disconnected and the voice was gone.

"Holy fuck! What the hell is this?" I thought to myself as I looked at the telephone.

I lit a cigarette and tried to sort out what was going on. I am suspicious of everyone, but some intuitive sense told me this was a conversation I should not ignore. Although I didn't realize it at the time, Fortier was recruiting me to be a "cutout" for a faction of a very compartmentalized NSC.

When you become a cutout for an intelligence agency, it's like being a condom. You're used, and you might have enjoyed it, but you're thrown away. Being a cutout is totally unlike being an intelligence asset. As an asset, you are given knowledge of an ongoing operation. I was to be given no knowledge. I would simply be told where to go, whom to see and how many hoops to jump through; I would also be provided with enough money to do it all.

I have speculated at length over the years, sometimes to the point of questioning my own sanity, about why I was chosen for this. How did Donald Fortier and the NSC come up with my name?

Was it from my relationship with a Washington contact and old CIA asset, Milton Nottingham?

Was it people I knew from an Army Special Forces Group when I lived in Columbus, Mississippi, several years earlier?

Was it my previous associations with people who made themselves available for mercenary work and filtered in and out of my life on occasion?

Most likely it was the simple fact that I was an Alabamian known to be available for such work and would fit right in with a good old boy group like CMA.

But I've never found out the real reason I was chosen. At the time of Fortier's telephone call, though, it didn't really matter. I was interested in getting involved in the war in Central America and I thought Fortier might be able to supply some form of government sanction that would enable me to do just that.

Neither were Fortier's motives for needing a cutout ever quite clear. My original thoughts were that he represented some group of super-patriots, silent sentinels trying to ensure that a few individuals, or a few powerful agencies within the government, didn't get out of control.

I doubt that it was ever quite that noble. More likely it was a matter of one group of paranoid bureaucrats (the CIA and NSC) trying to figure out what another group of paranoid bureaucrats (the DIA and the Pentagon) had their assets, snitches and cutouts doing down south.

The NSC and the CIA didn't know what the Defense Intelligence Agency or anyone else was doing to aid the Contras. They wanted to make sure who was in the game, and doing what, before they plunged further into the mess down there. I was to be their eyes and ears.

My role in the Contra war was to be far more significant than I realized at the time. It was not until years later that I began to get even the slightest glimmer of the implications of what I did and who I was working for.

The first few conversations with Fortier led me to believe I was being recruited by an intelligence agency. I wasn't sure who. I wasn't sure why. But the CIA opened two files on me, a real file and a dummy one that was displayed when people came snooping around asking about me.[10]

Years later, during a secret deposition for a Senate committee investigating the Contras, I revealed Fortier's name for the first time under oath. I also told of certain details of his life he had given me that would prove he had communicated with me.

When I mentioned Fortier's name during the deposition before a bipartisan group of aides and attorneys for the Senate Foreign Relations Committee, I got the distinct impression from the looks exchanged around the table that it struck home.

That deposition was classified as soon as I finished it. It remains classified to this day.

Why?

No doubt I revealed sensitive information and spoke to subjects that were too much of an embarrassment to the government to be revealed, even by the Senate Foreign Relations Committee.

Despite my natural suspicions about Fortier, at a very early point I was convinced he was real. I began to trust this voice; when I picked up the telephone and started talking to him, it was like talking to someone I had known for 20 years.

People ask me how I could get involved in something like this on the basis of a few telephone calls. It's a sense you develop. When the right person calls with the right information, you know it. If someone called me today and started talking about a gig, I'd know within seconds whether he was for real.

Fortier knew as much about me and what I had done as I did. Maybe more. When he started revealing people I knew and places I had been in my life that I thought were kept confidential on Big Brother's computers, I knew Fortier could be believed.

Besides, what Fortier was asking me to do was not diabolical. He was not asking me to do anything I wouldn't be doing on my own. I was going to find out what CMA was all about on my own, so there was no reason not to help Fortier, especially since he appeared to represent someone, or some group, in the government.

Four days later, on Thursday, October 11, Fortier called back.

"I thought about what you said," I said after we exchanged pleasantries, "but I'm really not aware of what all this involves. Why don't you get down to the nitty-gritty and tell me what you really want?"

"We want you to penetrate Civilian Military Assistance and any other group of people that are involved in this movement," Fortier said. "I will emphasize again that you will not have a sanction. It will not be official. But we will be in contact with you."

"What am I supposed to do for money?"

"That will be arranged."

"Arranged how?"

"We're talking in the neighborhood of $50,000."

I almost laughed into the telephone.

"You're going to pay me $50,000 to go to Honduras?"

"In a manner of speaking. It will be paid in three installments. You will be paid $10,000 at a time of our choosing. You will receive $20,000 at another stage. And you will get $20,000 if you live to tell about it."

"The way you talk, it's a dangerous situation."

"I grant you it's dangerous."

"For what reason?"

"Not because of any combat role," he said. "And I'm warning you now, do not get involved in any combat situation. But you will fall in harm's way through the treachery of other people."

"What do you mean by that?"

"You will figure that out on your own."

"How am I going to get the money?"

"It will be delivered to you in New Orleans."

"What am I going to tell these people about who I am?"

"Take mental notes on what I am about to tell you," he said. "If you take written notes, commit them to memory and then burn them."

It sounded like dialogue from a bad spy movie, but I followed his instructions.

Fortier then began designing a new person, one who looked like me, talked like me and acted like me, but who had a background that was totally untraceable. It was like he read my self-designed script in advance, since I was using the same method on CMA already. The new Jack Terrell that Fortier created was a former U.S. Army major who in 1969 served with the euphemistically named Studies and Observations Group (SOG) in Laos. This supersecret outfit run out of Military Assistance Command Vietnam (MACV) went on reconnaissance missions deep into Laos and Cambodia. And, by most accounts, its members participated in CIA-sponsored assassinations of Pathot Lao, Khmer Rouge and Viet Cong leaders. Many of the details of their missions remain classified.

He told me the names of two operations – Daniel Boone and Prairie Fire – that I was to use to validate my credentials with SOG if that became necessary.

"The reason I'm telling you this," Fortier said, "is that these missions are classified to this day and there is no way on God's earth they can ever be authenticated. You are creating a background nobody can check out."

Fortier said the new Jack Terrell served eight years on detached service to SOG, before getting out and drifting into occasional CIA contract work.

"The important thing is you have to be believable," Fortier said. "Then you've got to offer them something, or you're going to be just another socks toter. You've got to put on the air of someone who has someone behind him."

It didn't seem at all strange to me that a man I had never met, a man I had never even heard of before, called me on the telephone one Sunday night, asked me to go to Honduras and said he would pay me $50,000 to do it. In fact, in made perfect sense to me.

Psychologically and emotionally, I was ripe for his offer. I was ready to do anything, even if it meant disappearing from society, from my family, from everyone I knew, just for the chance to at last serve my country in a manner I had always dreamed of. If it meant going to Nicaragua and frogging some Commies, so be it.

It was the same appeal North and Co. used on those who backed their schemes to fund the war through the private sector, either with donations of money or their talents. We were vulnerable politically and psychologically and were easily taken advantage of.

"How am I going to stay in contact with you people?" I asked Fortier.

"Don't worry about that," Fortier said. "We'll contact you."

"I feel kind of strange. This sounds like 'Mission Impossible.'"

"It is."

Through deception and lying about myself, I had successfully created a nonexistent person and now would have to live this second entity. I was committed to the task now and there just wasn't any way I would back up. In discussing Pegasus, I made suggestions as to weapons, night vision devices and special sniper equipment we must possess. It was also we needed bait for the FDN to go along with the idea because it had plenty of conventional weapons. I was riding high on pushing the special equipment for I knew it would make a big difference in the outcome of Mario's decision, especially if he understood that neither he nor the FDN would have to purchase said strange equipment. Fortier's money would place me in the driver's seat and allow me to dictate some of the rules of this game.

I began to make arrangements for my departure to New Orleans for the weekend ahead. I decided that this must be a one-way trip and that I must dispose of all assets and traces of myself in Gulf Shores and

Mobile in order to disappear into a world that I did not know, but where I was sure that I would find my destiny.

I went to the home of a close personal friend, Teri Cassil, with whom I had confided most of the recent events and who later became a mail drop in the U.S. I told her the details of what had transpired in recent days and asked her to help me get rid of my personal effects and cover for me when my family started wondering what had happened to me.

We laid out an elaborate plan as to how I was going to vanish off the face of the earth without question. My family was to be told that I had gone to Nicaragua and no more. My business partner was to find out through my absence. Since I didn't own the business I could not be stuck with the problems that would ensue from contractors and employees. My small communications business interests would have to remain in limbo or the manufacturer would have to come pick up the equipment. I was in the frame of mind that I was fed up with all of this and looked forward to getting away from the business and the people associated with it. Nothing had happened here to improve my life, so I was going to change it, even if it meant dying in the process.

I took what clothing I thought I needed and the following weekend returned to New Orleans. I went straight to Mario's house. Tom and Cisco arrived about the same time. I had talked to both of them during the week before my departure from Mobile and it was pretty well decided that Cisco would accompany me on the intelligence mission. I had tried to locate a Spanish language school, but wasn't having much success. I continually argued with Mario about the subject, trying to dissuade him from insisting on my learning the language. I told him I would go to school after I returned from the trip. He relented, but wasn't happy with the decision.

My trouble was that I thought I knew everything about the country, the people and the war. As I was to find out, I was out of touch with reality about Nicaragua and the war. But, I had secret backer and a crazy plan, and I was ready to follow the yellow brick road all the way to my own personal Oz.

2

Going South: Civilian Military Assistance Group

Felipe Portocarrero was Mario Calero's brother-in-law.

He was a native Nicaraguan, but stood about 6-foot-4 and spoke English as easily and flawlessly as he spoke Spanish. He was friendly and chatty and let it be known that he felt it was important for all Nicaraguans to do their duty for their country. Felipe seemed like the ultimate patriot, dedicated to ousting the Sandinistas and restoring democracy in Nicaragua. The only problem was that he also was a U.S. Army sergeant on active duty at nearby Fort Polk, Louisiana.

I first met Felipe at Mario's house on Saturday, October 21, prior to another weekend session of preparing supplies for shipment south. I thought he had just come up from Miami or Nicaragua to help out. But Felipe was a key link in the FDN-U.S. government aid chain to the Contras. He later became logistics liaison to the FDN at the American air base at Palmerola, Honduras, and we used him to facilitate the shipment of supplies from the U.S. military to the Contras.

I was determined to stay in New Orleans until I had the opportunity to go to Honduras. There would be no going back to Gulf Shores, no matter how many supplies I had to load before my chance came. That Saturday, there was a DC-6 waiting to be loaded and Felipe was among those doing the loading.

We spent most of the morning stacking supplies on pallets and transferring the pallets to a truck. Just as we finished, Louisiana Congressman Bob Livingston, a staunch backer of the Contras, arrived. Mario quickly convinced him to pose with us for a group picture. I didn't like the idea of being photographed by anyone and tried to hide on the fringes of the group. Mario wanted the picture not so much for a keepsake, but because he needed Livingston much more than Livingston needed us. While Livingston could use his ties to the FDN politically, Mario needed his influence with the Federal Aviation Administration to obtain approval for the flights south. Livingston's political use of the Contras was not unusual. The White House and any number of other politicians used them regularly to demonstrate to their constituents that they truly cared about the poor, downtrodden peasants of Central America. It was good politics using a bad policy.

Livingston wasn't the only government employee interested in us that morning. Mario's car was last in the caravan that had cars fore and aft of the flatbed trailer truck loaded with pallets of supplies when we left Behring and headed for the airport. As we drove slowly along the road to the back entrance of the airport, I could see the ancient DC-6 that had come in from O'Conner Air Service of Miami to ferry the supplies south. Two uniformed pilots were walking around the plane checking the oil-caked engines. I could also see several Jefferson Parish sheriff's cars stopped on the shoulder of the road and an unmarked car with someone in civilian clothes holding a camera with a telephoto lens and shooting everything in sight.

One of the sheriff's cars pulled into line behind us as we moved toward the gate. Just as we cleared it, the car pulled sideways on the road, blocking the exit. There was a small general aviation office on my right and I noticed the employees standing there as if frozen. I looked at Mario and he looked in shock.

"What's going on?" I asked.

Mario didn't have an answer, but he was scared. I could see it in his face. He wasn't expecting this.

In the distance I noticed several other cars moving swiftly toward the plane. No one had made a move to stop us yet and Mario pulled the car under the left wing of the DC-6. But as we got out about 40 uniformed and plain clothes police officers surrounded us. Men with dark glasses and badges on their uniforms or hanging out of the breast pockets of their suits were everywhere. I wasn't sure what was happening, but I certainly didn't want my picture taken. The police had a number of cameramen there, taking pictures of all of us as they separated us from the plane and one another and began interviewing us individually.

While some of the interviews were starting, I slowly moved closer to the edge of the police perimeter. Inside the small general aviation building, I could see a heavily armed SWAT team. I made it a point to stay close behind Felipe to take advantage of his size to shield me from the photographers. I stood very close to him and whispered that I needed him to shadow me from the cameras.

I didn't realize at the time that he probably needed to be shielded more than me since he was active duty military. But Felipe never made a move to hide his face or avoid the cameras. He wasn't at all camera shy.

The crew from the chartered DC-6 wasn't sure what was going on. They stood on the tarmac transfixed by the crowd of police officers. They must have thought it was a drug bust, which was not at all uncommon in these parts.

There were agents from Customs, the FBI, CIA, Bureau of Alcohol, Tobacco and Firearms and Drug Enforcement Administration involved in the raid. A police dog was brought out to sniff through the plane and our supplies. But neither the dog nor the officers found the guns and drugs they apparently expected to find. Instead, this show seemed to have a particular motive not known to us. Mario recognized one of the custom officers and struck up a conversation with him. Mario seemed to be putting distance between himself and the group. I thought that odd.

Finally it was my turn to be interviewed and a plainclothes officer approached me rather intently. I had dodged in every way I knew how, but I was now isolated. I took on the demeanor of an agitated innocent and asked the officer if I was under arrest? He said, "No," but that our group was "challenging the U.S. law," the Neutrality Act, and they had the right and power to investigate. He asked for any identification that could prove who I claimed I was. He was filling out some form as he interrogated me. It started with name, address, telephone and the other essentials. When he got to the remarks section, he asked if I was a member of the Civilian Military Assistance group. I said I was not.

I began explaining that I was a law enforcement officer from Alabama, asked by friend to help a charitable organization load relief supplies bound for Central America. The plainclothes officer looked at me over the top of his sunglasses with an expression on his face that said: "Yeah, piss in my ear and tell me it's raining."

He knew I was trying to cover my ass, but asked to see my credentials. I produced my gold constable's badge from the State of Alabama, which I had earned years before when my life had some meaning. This drew surprised curious glances from the CMA people standing nearby. The officer told me that he was only doing his job and for me not to get upset. I simply walked away and joined Sailor, who was standing near the plane and was visibly angry.

Sailor said he felt this was a giant conspiracy by the U.S. government to put a stop to CMA. Finally, he looked at me with an impish grin and told me he was going to get a Coke from the machine near the aviation building where the SWAT squad was positioned. Two officers quickly approached him and told him that he could not go anywhere. Sailor feigned outraged indignation over not being allowed to get a drink and was making such a scene that finally one of the senior uniformed officers came over and informed him that he could get his drink, as long as he was accompanied by the two officers. Sailor didn't like it, but turned to us and smiled as if to say that he had made his point and had won a minor battle since he was being personally escorted by armed guards to get his Coke.

Sailor's efforts to push the limits of patience of the officers seemed to break the strain evident on both sides. After a few more tense moments, and plenty of photographs, the officers packed up and left, leaving us to the hot, unglamorous work of loading several thousand pairs of combat boots and incidental military gear into the plane.

Our visit from the police was not without benefit to them. They had names, addresses, Social Security numbers and photographs of everybody working with CMA that afternoon. It was a way of finding out a lot about the group in a short period of time.

I always thought Donald Fortier may well have been behind that little episode, either checking on CMA or checking on me, but I never learned for sure. It could also have been the Custom Service's way of making sure all that military gear was actually heading to Honduras and not to some group trying to overthrow a friendly Caribbean nation. In 1981, New Orleans had been the planned launching point for an invasion by American mercenaries of the island of Dominica. It never got off the ground. The plotters were arrested, the coup aborted.[1] But New Orleans officials were rather sensitive to seeing tons of military equipment loaded onto aircraft and wanted to make sure it was going to the right place.

Tom Posey had returned to New Orleans in another U-Haul truck loaded with more supplies. As usual, the civilian articles were culled from the lot and only military items were put on the flight. It was miserable work. The warehouse where the goods had been stored was hot and airless, as was the inside of the DC-6. I originally thought that the FDN was paying CMA members for their time and efforts. I was mistaken. CMA members had to pay their own way. Transportation, meals, hotel rooms, whatever other expenses they might have incurred, came right out of their pockets. The FDN gave them nothing except the opportunity to get involved in this covert war, albeit on a limited basis. The FDN was playing on the patriotic fervor of these poor, misguided souls and making them pay for it.

When we returned to Mario's house after a long, tiring day, Chris Heinz, the arms dealer, was waiting with catalogues and pictures of weapons that could be purchased by the FDN for, as he put it, "cheap prices." Mario had evidently leaked information about Pegasus to Heinz and he had come calling with a variety of "special weapons" deals for the mission.

Heinz was short and thin and had the look a small-time arms dealer should — like a weasel. He tried to make us believe he was a big leaguer in the arms business, but he wasn't particularly convincing. His claim to fame was a lighting device, which he claimed he invented, that could be used as an all-weather beacon for parachute drop zones. But it was far too small to do what he claimed it could and was not very impressive, given the scope of what was planned for Pegasus.

After Chris gave us the dog-and-pony show about his abilities to produce exotic weapons for the mission, Mario asked him to leave. Mario was eager to discuss details of the trip to Honduras.

Mario expressed great reluctance about allowing Cisco and me to go to Honduras on our own, but said the trip might open new vistas once we were able to analyze the conflict firsthand. I had planted that idea with Mario but wanted him to feel it was as much his idea as anyone's. He was never reluctant to take credit for an idea given him by someone else. I also wanted him to feel that he was the titular head of everything, thus pumping up his ego, which wasn't hard to do.

As we discussed more detailed plans about Pegasus, Mario's eyes grew bigger and bigger. It was easy to see he was excited about the possibility of becoming the commander of a group of special forces troops that would take the war to the Sandinistas. I saw the greed in his eyes and I saw how my verbal massage was working on his ego.

He said he would write a personal letter of introduction for me to the supreme commander of the field troops, Commandante 380, Enrique Bermudez, a long and trusted friend of his. He got out a piece of paper with the FDN letterhead and began writing. He no sooner started when he paused, looked up at me and asked what code name he should use for me. He said if the letter fell into the wrong hands, there could be trouble, particularly with the Honduran authorities, who would think nothing of throwing me in jail.

I told him that I had not yet thought of a suitable code name. Mario got up from the table and walked into the kitchen for coffee. He said something to his wife that I couldn't understand, but when he returned from the kitchen he had a big smile on his face.

"Flaco," he said simply.

"What does that mean?" I asked.

"Flaco, the thin one," said Mario.

I certainly fit that description because of my slight build. I liked it. It fit well. To the CMA and the FDN, I was no longer Jack Terrell. I was Flaco, Major Flaco at first, but several weeks later mysteriously and unceremoniously promoted to Colonel Flaco. Jack Terrell was disappearing and this mysterious mercenary named Colonel Flaco was taking his place.

Mario's letter was in Spanish and only a page long, but he said he told Commandante 380 who I was and what my mission was to be. I could not read Spanish so I had to take his word on its contents.

This imprimatur gave me a special status with the group and I felt the power. Although Posey was the nominal head of CMA, I felt as if the power had been transferred to me and I instructed him and the others to begin working on obtaining special supplies for us, because when I returned from Honduras I would probably have a battle plan ready and we would have to act quickly.

I told Sailor to start getting men lined up and checked out, because I did not know just how many people CMA had on file who would volunteer for this type of project or would be able to pull it off.

Cisco seemed excited – he was getting the opportunity to go back to Honduras and see some friends he had made, he now felt like the top trainer for CMA and, most importantly to him, the trip would be paid for by someone else.

There was excitement in Mario's house that night. The CMA members thought they were about to embark on a new and more important role in the war in Nicaragua that would help them fulfill whatever goals and whatever fantasies impelled them to get involved in this mess.

Into the Maze

October passed so quickly I couldn't keep up with time. I had fully committed my mind and soul to the project and didn't care what day of the week it was. The hours and days ran together as I scurried from one task to another. I kept trying to do too much too quickly. I wanted to be finished with all the small tasks and get on the road. The anticipation that this dream was approaching reality kept me nervous and on edge. I was about to sever the umbilical cord that tied me to Jack Terrell and his past life. I was, in that period of stasis, not quite Major Flaco but not quite Jack Terrell either.

Tom, Sailor and the others had to return home, leaving Cisco and me in the Contempra Inn with time on our hands to plan the tactics for our trip and Pegasus. Cisco had not been particularly eager to participate until I told him that I would guarantee his expenses would be paid. He seemed to be involved in CMA more for whatever money he could get out of it than any burning desire to drive the Sandinistas out of the Western Hemisphere.

I filled his head with tales of my time with the Rhodesian Army and with SOG in Cambodia and Laos. Little of it was true, but they were good stories and he believed them as eagerly and as naively as a child.

I told him how during operations we carried "hot shots" of sodium pentothal laced with cyanide and if we were in danger of being captured we were to inject ourselves or one another so that we couldn't give away any secrets under torture. Later, I would instruct Doc Ohrman to prepare syringes with the drug for distribution to everyone who became part of Pegasus. The intent was to give team members a humane alternative to torture and death at the hands of the Sandinistas if they were captured after we crossed the border. I was serious about this part of operations, but in time, knowledge of the plan became a detriment to public perception of me. Information about the "hot shots" was later used to portray me as a brutal commander who was preparing suicide missions into Nicaragua.

This sort of super-macho approach to any problem appealed to Cisco, though. Whether such actions were pragmatic or justified didn't matter. What mattered to him was saving face in front of his friends. How CMA members were perceived by their friends mattered more than just about anything, except their own lives. It was the Southern version of the Latin machismo at work.

A few days later, Donald Fortier called me at the Contempra Inn. The conversation was brief. There was no small talk, no pleasantries, no request for information about CMA, its members or its plans. Fortier simply told me to go to the back parking lot of the Sheraton Inn on Veterans Boulevard behind the Contempra between 8 and 9 o'clock that night. There, I would find a van and a man who would give me "the package."

Fortier did not say if there would be money or a time bomb in "the package," but I assumed it would contain the first installment of the $50,000 he had promised me for assisting him.

Shortly after 8 p.m. I left Denny's and walked around the swimming pool and the trash dumpster into the Sheraton parking lot. There was a metallic blue Ford van waiting there, the only van in the parking light. There were two men in it. Both were well-dressed.

"Are you Jack Terrell?" the driver asked as I approached. He wore a gray tweed sport coat and blue slacks. The other man wore a gray sharkskin suit.

"Yes," I replied.

The driver said nothing, but the passenger got out of the van. He was large and well-built and moved like he had once been a football player. He reached into the pocket of his sport coat and pulled out a brown envelope that had been folded over at the edges. He never asked for identification or for any verification that I was who I claimed to be.

I simply took the envelope, put it in the back pocket of my bluejeans, turned and walked away. I didn't even say "thank you."

When I got back to the room I opened the envelope. Inside were 100 $100 bills, the $10,000 Fortier promised as a first installment. The bills were old and wrinkled. No two were in numerical sequence. I stood and looked at the money for a long time. I felt a great sense of uneasiness. I was not sure exactly what it was Fortier would demand of me for this money, but by accepting it I had sealed the bargain. I knew I was playing in the big leagues now.

That was the last time I had direct contact with anyone I knew who came directly from Donald Fortier and who was acting on his instructions.

In addition to feeling uneasy about the money, I had an overwhelming desire to let someone else in on the secret. I needed someone to share the burden, but Cisco was definitely the wrong person. Posey had returned to the Contempra that day and I decided to confide in him and impress on him, without giving full knowledge of my benefactor, that we had money with which to work. But I also wanted him to know that things would not be as fast and loose as he might suppose because we would probably have to account for the money. I singled him out on the second-floor balcony of the Contempra Inn the night I received the first installment.

"Tom," I said, "I don't really need to tell you this, but believe it or not the money is coming from the Agency. This is money we don't misuse or misappropriate or fuck around with, because these people have a collection agency that would make the Mafia look sick."

Posey said nothing, but he appeared adequately frightened.

I decided not to tell him about Fortier. Posey was ready to believe all manner of conspiracies, but some unknown government agency, perhaps as high as the White House, getting involved in this was a bit too much, even for him. Besides, I still wasn't sure about who Fortier was or what he wanted from me. Fortier paid well though, as was evident by the $10,000 in my suitcase. But that kind of money was small change for this operation, as I later learned.

If anybody bothered to check the arithmetic of my involvement with the Contras, it was clear I was getting big bucks from somewhere, and it wasn't my personal bank account. I didn't have that kind of money. I probably spent close to $100,000 while I was involved with CMA. I was paying all the hotel bills, all the food bills and most of the transportation bills. And I paid for a lot of the equipment.

Some of the money later came from a daffy Texas millionaire named Maco Stewart, who once showed up in Honduras with $9,900 cash in one sock and $9,900 in another sock, intended for expenses to take a group of American Indians and himself into Nicaragua.

Envelopes stuffed with cash showed up at the strangest times. One day I checked into the Maya Hotel in Tegucigalpa under one of my aliases, Frank Winchester.

"Would you like to get your belongings out of the safety deposit box, Mr. Winchester?" the desk clerk asked me.

"What safety deposit box?" I said.

"This one," he said, handing me a claim check for a safety deposit box. It was in the name of Frank Winchester, even though I had not rented it. When I opened the box there was a bulky hotel envelope in it. On the back, near the bottom, someone had scrawled: "Good luck." When I opened the envelope there was $15,000 in crisp $100 bills in it.

It was absolutely crazy. I had money all the time and had no idea where it came from.

My secret benefactors never made it easy to figure out where they were coming from, what their motives were or just who they represented. After Fortier stopped calling me, I talked on the telephone numerous times with all sorts of strange people who claimed to represent his group. I was never sure when someone started asking me specific questions about what I was doing whether he was from Fortier's group, some branch of the CIA, or just plain nosy. It was extremely bizarre.

It got to the point where I wanted to pull people aside and whisper: "Are you working for the government? Do you know Donald Fortier?" But I never did.

I was the only one worried about the group. Everyone else around me saw only the money. Mario began to see me as his way to fame and fortune among the Contras and their backers in and out of the U.S. government. He was also convinced that I had been sent by the CIA and he became even more obsessed with secrecy than he had been before I arrived.

Plans were made for Cisco and me to leave New Orleans for Honduras the third week of October, but there was a problem with the reservations and Mario put the trip off until the 25th. I told Cisco that we should use the time to start getting physically prepared for the terrain in Honduras and Nicaragua. Since I had a vehicle, we could go to a nearby park and jog.

Cisco saw this as an opportunity to dump his personal problems on me. He had been getting more and more nervous about something as our departure date neared, but he wouldn't talk about it. He dropped hints for several days about some problem he was having with the estate of his late father, which had been in limbo for several years, but was coming up for settlement soon. He claimed his sister was opposing him and that if he was not present when the case was heard in court, he would lose a great deal of money.

As we slowly jogged along one of the canals in Kenner in our combat boots, Cisco griped non-stop about having to be in New Orleans wasting time when he could be in Huntsville taking care of his business. I had gotten a gut full of his bitching and finally told him to go home and take care of his "business" if it was that important.

Once we returned to the motel he showered, gathered up his rucksack and personal belongings and loaded them into his car. He was about to leave when he asked if I would lend him $100 to make the trip. I figured, what the hell, I'll be footing his bills on the trip anyway and $100 is nothing. I had plenty more where that came from. The only thing that concerned me about Cisco's absence was whether he would make it back in time for the flight to Honduras.

I called Posey and told him about my conversations with Cisco. Tom said he knew Cisco well enough to know that this was a sign he was having second thoughts about the trip. Cisco had trouble handling pressure, he said, and that he may have agreed to go only for the money.

When I related Cisco's accusations that he had not been paid for any of his trips with CMA, Posey got angry. He said that for three months Cisco got every dime and that he couldn't understand why Cisco would lie about it. Posey was beginning to feel that our trip might be jeopardized because Cisco could not be trusted to do what he said he would.

At the time, this was a surprise to me, but I knew that Mario had to be kept in the dark about the trouble or he would deep-six the trip altogether. My dream was beginning to look like a bad dream.

Over the next few days I tried to put Cisco and his problems out of my mind and spent my time scouring Army-Navy surplus stores in New Orleans for gear. I bought anything I thought I would need and everything I thought the Hondurans would allow into the country. I had a rucksack, uniforms, military emblems, shotguns, ammunition and a variety of survival gear stuffed into seabags. I also bought a Browning 88A 9mm pistol and registered it with Customs in New Orleans. Americans traveling abroad could carry three weapons and up to 1,000 rounds of ammunition into a foreign country, as long as that country did not disapprove.

As I learned later, the Hondurans didn't care if you brought a tank into the country, as long as you were an American.

In the days before leaving for Honduras, I had many occasions to talk with Mario and try to gain some knowledge about the country I was about to invade. I liked Mario as a person. He was friendly and outgoing and had a rather naive, childlike view of war. Mario was more complex than outward appearances would indicate, however. He controlled the logistics for U.S. purchases for the FDN and the shipping of equipment to Honduras. He had access to huge amounts of money through FDN headquarters in Miami and liked to brag about it.

One day we were sitting in his office at his home when he pointed out a three-drawer file cabinet he claimed was the depository for cashier's checks from Miami. He showed me a stack of Visa travelers checks, issued by B.A.C. International Bank in the Grand Cayman Islands, worth $100,000. He pointed out that some would go into the top drawer, some in the second and the balance in the third drawer. Or, as he put it, "the FDN's, their's and mine."

There was no misunderstanding what he meant. Mario was paid a healthy monthly salary, somewhere in the neighborhood of $7,000, and was about to purchase a second home. He certainly didn't live in the same conditions as did his fellow countrymen in Nicaragua, who were being portrayed as suffering from the dual afflictions of Communism and poverty.

Mario went to great lengths to explain that he and his older brother Adolfo were graduates of Notre Dame. He was particularly proud of the fact that Adolfo attended Notre Dame under Father Theodore Hesburgh and was a student aide to him.

Mario also talked frequently and fondly of the days under the Somozas in Nicaragua and what he described as the lack of class differences among the people. Adolfo had been a favorite of former Nicaragua President Anastasio Somoza Debayle, and was among the honored guests invited to the last party given by Somoza in Managua just before he boarded a helicopter and flew into exile in a hail of Sandinista gunfire. Adolfo, Mario liked to recount, had been a millionaire landowner, cattle baron and former general manager of Coca-Cola for all of Nicaragua. One didn't rise to this level of business without being a part of the Somoza inner circle.

Mario also told me of the time he and Adolfo were involved in a rebel movement designed to oust Luis Somoza, Anastasio's predecessor and older brother, with the help of Fidel Castro. According to Mario, Anastasio helped organize an arms shipment into northeastern Nicaragua from Cuba. The night that the arms were to arrive, the rebel group was waiting in the darkness. But instead of planes, the Guardia Nacionale showed up and arrested all the waiting rebels. Either someone had tipped the government, or the Cubans had double-crossed their newfound friends.

Some of the rebels were put in jail and others were deported. Mario believed Castro double-crossed them and vowed he and Adolfo would get even with the Cubans after they came to power in Nicaragua following the ouster of the Sandinistas. He said the FDN would take all the money the Cubans were willing to give, but no free Cuban would ever be in a position to fight with them. One Cuban later told me, "The FDN likes the milk, but they don't like the cow it comes from."

The Cubans had been trying to gain entrance into this war to get at Castro from someone else's real estate, but they were being badly taken advantage of. Miami Cubans were continually being asked to donate money, food, clothing and military equipment and did so willingly. Hubert Matos, a former official of Castro's government, was working feverishly to get into the thick of the fight in Nicaragua and even had relatives in high places in other countries who could be invaluable to the FDN. But the FDN said no dice. They wanted nothing to do with any high-profile, powerful Cubans.

This was just one example of the strange contradictions in the methods and policies of FDN leaders. The line being fed to the Cubans in Miami was that when Nicaragua fell to the FDN, all arms would be taken from the Sandinistas and given to the Cubans, along with territory, to train, prepare and launch an invasion against Cuba from Nicaraguan soil. The promises made to Cubans were endless, as long as money and materiel flowed from their community, which it did at an astonishing rate. But the promises were empty.

Colonel Flaco Takes Off

Departure day finally rolled around and I was more than ready to leave New Orleans and the United States. I had spent the previous few days gathering all the equipment I had purchased and packing in my motel room. I had put on a uniform in the privacy of my room and stood in front of the mirror, looking at myself and feeling my confidence surge and my ego boosted because I was falling into the role like a pro. I had a couple of seabags to put all the gear into and looked like a Marine going off on a long overseas tour with all the equipment and clothing.

One thing made clear to me was that you didn't go into the country in uniform. Rather, tourist garb was the preferred method of dress and the confused tourist look was the preferred method of facial expression. When you passed Honduran customs you were to have your passport stamped as a tourist and nothing else.

Mario arrived at the Contempra to pick me up quite early because the plane was due to leave at 10 a.m. and he wanted to make sure I had all the information I needed when I met the FDN people awaiting our arrival. Mario said he had called ahead to the base in Tegucigalpa, known as La Quinta, and arranged for FDN officials to be at the airport. He also said the FDN had advised the Honduran secret police that Americans were entering the country on their behalf. This allowed those with an FDN sanction to virtually walk off the plane into a waiting vehicle without as much as a glance from anyone, except the other passengers, who wondered who you knew.

As the time for departure neared, Cisco had not yet showed. I told Mario that I had talked to Cisco the night before and was told he had car trouble in Birmingham and was returning to Huntsville. Cisco was supposed to have called me at 6 a.m., but I had not heard a word from him. I finally started making telephone calls trying to locate him and found him at his grandmother's. I asked him what the problem was. He beat around the bush, groping for excuses, and it was then I could sense in his voice that he had lost his balls and was afraid to go.

I put things in perspective for him when I told him what could happen if he failed to be on the plane when it left. Mario was close to shutting down the operation at that point, and I was getting a bit panicky, so I promised Cisco that I would prepay his ticket from

Huntsville to New Orleans if he would just get his ass in gear. He promised he would be there and we took him at his word.

Mario and I had breakfast and went to the airport to meet Cisco's flight. Time was running out and when Cisco arrived on the flight from Huntsville he sauntered off the plane like we had all week. Mario was furious and let Cisco know it. Mario tore into his ass in proper English and Spanish obscenities all the way to the international gate. He told Cisco how irresponsible he was and about how this was his last trip to Honduras for the FDN. It was as angry as I have ever seen Mario. Cisco had a way of bringing that out in people, but he looked like a man who couldn't hear and didn't care. He had heard all this before and was totally unfazed by Mario's tirade. To help calm Mario, I tried to reassure him that Cisco would do better now that he was finally headed south.

This pacified Mario long enough for us to get away from him and on the TACA Airlines plane. Mario literally walked us on board, still berating Cisco, as Customs officers eyed us closely. I was holding my breath until the plane was pushed back from the gate. Cisco was already fast asleep, like it was just another trip.

As we waited at the end of the runway for clearance to take off, my hands gripped the armrests on my seat like vises. My head was down and I was staring at the floor. I still wasn't sure Cisco and I wouldn't be yanked off the plane. When the pilot finally released the brake and throttled up on the engines of the BAC-111, filling the cabin with a conversation-stopping roar as the plane moved forward and slipped into the sky, I pressed my head against the back of my seat with my eyes closed and said to myself: "Yes, yes, goddammit, yes."

I was so thrilled that I was freed from the self-imposed bonds of an old stale life and with the fatal beauty of this genesis, this bold adventure, that I knew it would never ebb from my mind. The release of the plane's wheels from the asphalt was like cutting a taught rope that bound my very being to a reality that I could no longer live. This flash of pleasure in the midst of an insane belief that I would actually do what I imagined lifted me to a state much like an out-of-body experience. Oh, how sweet is the narcotic of fantasy.

The flight was shorter than I had expected. I thought it was a direct flight to Tegucigalpa, but it seemed we were airborne for less than an hour when the plane began to descend over the Gulf waters. I asked a flight attendant if we were in Honduras already. She smiled and told me we were landing at an intermediate stopover in Belize. I peered out the window as the plane glided over an area that looked like a military base. In fact, it was.

The airport in Belize City serves as a base for British troops and Harrier jump jets stationed in this tiny country to protect it from neighboring Guatemala. For the first time, I was able to get a close look at anti-aircraft missile batteries, revetted jet fighters and strange helicopters bunkered around this facility bristling with military hardware.

Our stopover in Belize City also gave me my first introduction to the slow, laid-back pace of life in Central America. It was the most uncontrolled airport I had ever seen, and here it was sitting right in the middle of a military base. The only uniformed people I saw were the taxi drivers. The airline itself, TACA, was more like a sky taxi servicing the small countries on a daily basis. Maybe that's why many people who flew the national airline of El Salvador called it Take A Chance Airlines.

We waited on the ground for several hours while other passengers wandered on and off the plane. I stayed in my seat, sweating and getting more and more impatient to reach Honduras. Cisco continued to sleep, blissfully unaware.

Dusk was approaching as we finally left, but within a few minutes the plane was descending again, bobbing and weaving through steep mountains as turbulence from isolated thunderstorms buffeted us. When we landed, I discovered that we still weren't in Honduras. We were in El Salvador, a stop I never even knew we would be making.

One thing about Salvador — the government probably spent more money on its airport than most of rest of the country. It was large and well-maintained, the most opulent by far in Central America. I scanned the field to see if it was also a military base. At first glance, it didn't seem like Belize. But it also did not look like what I had expected of Salvador. There weren't the bombed-out ruins or any other evidence of conflict in this strife-torn country.

As we approached the terminal, the Salvadoran passengers jumped out of their seats and began hauling down luggage and an assortment of personal items that included everything but live pigs and chickens. I noticed another TACA plane being pushed back from the gate, but did not realize at the time I was watching our connecting flight to Honduras depart.

I roused Cisco to a semi-consciousness state and told him that we had to deplane. I was expecting an American-style system, like most dumb tourists, but was stunned to see that the interior of this palatial terminal was crawling with soldiers. This most certainly was not New Orleans. Or anywhere else in the United States.

A ticket agent was advising those of us who missed the connecting flight to Honduras to stand in a certain area. She said it in Spanish of course, and neither Cisco nor I understood her, so I thought I was free to roam about. The agent got my attention fast when she rushed up and let me know, in broken English, that we must stay with the group. The granite-faced soldier behind her said it much more forcefully with his eyes.

I had wanted to see the Central American military, but I didn't think it would walk up to me in the airport. The Salvadoran soldiers had the airport blanketed. They were everywhere. And every one of them was dressed to the hilt. They wore olive drab uniforms with black leather belts with large, gleaming brass buckles that I would have given anything for.

Salvadoran soldiers never seem to smile when they're on duty. Their weapons are locked and loaded. They stare out from under their shiny black helmets, but it is hard to see their eyes because of a shadow on their faces from the front edge of the helmet. They were as impressive and as menacing a group of soldiers as I saw during my time in Central America. I saw no hesitation, no uncertainty in their faces, and certainly no one would have challenged them unless they were prepared to die, or were unusually stupid.

I was glad to get out of there and head for the Sheraton Hotel in downtown San Salvador, where the airline would put us up for the night. The small group that had missed the flight was hustled onto a bus without luggage or any personal effects not already in our possession. Although it was dark by the time we departed, occasional lightning strikes from sporadic storms revealed trucks, tanks and barrier after barrier manned by soldiers surrounding the airport. I was concerned that the contraband I was carrying would be discovered by curious TACA baggage handlers. I could see myself picking bananas here for the rest of my life. This was just the first of a long series of worries that dogged me throughout my ventures in Central America.

As the commander of this two-man force, I also was concerned we were in the wrong place for all the wrong reasons. I knew people would be waiting for us in Tegucigalpa and if we didn't show up, there might been some misunderstanding. I knew I had to communicate with Mario in some fashion and let him know what had happened. I was also assuming that our stay here would only be overnight.

Everything that I assumed turned out to be wrong. I was getting a quick education and all my errors would become object lessons for the novice adventurer running around banana republics disguised as a military adviser. I found I had to pick things up fast and use them as if

I had had the knowledge all my life. I could not afford to make many mistakes, because the system is not the least bit tolerant of ignorance.

Our small group consisted of four people — me, Cisco and two Honduran women returning from the U.S. One of the women was quite average looking and a bit chunky. The other, in her late twenties, was slender and strikingly beautiful. They stayed a healthy distance from Cisco and me and looked at us with suspicion. Cisco would make any female suspicious, though, because he looked at all of them like medium-rare steaks. His eyes gave him away in an instant and his intentions were obvious to everyone.

The beauty, I was to learn, was a Pan American Airlines supervisor from Tegucigalpa. Her name was Lourdes Graciela Garcia. I came to know her simply as Grace and over the next few weeks she became my friend, lover, courier and confidential interpreter. She also was my gun moll in Tegucigalpa and had events not transpired as they did, I would have married her.

But my thoughts were not on women as we were deposited at the entrance of the Sheraton and given meal chits and registration information. This hotel could have been right out of a Hollywood set with all the bright lights, mystique and shady characters milling around the lobby. You didn't have to be a rocket scientist to know that the tall men who wore sunglasses at night and had strange bulges in their coats were undercover police, even though they tried unsuccessfully to look like average guests. The only people they may have fooled were themselves. It was a very unusual sight for me, but I came to learn that this was the comedic norm in Central America.

The Hacienda police, as they were known in El Salvador, covered the Sheraton like a blanket. They were among the vast array of security people evident in front of houses, restaurants, stores throughout the city.

Every male, it seemed, carried a small leather purse that contained some type of handgun. These purses, or *bolsas*, as they were called, were the equivalent of a holster. I told Cisco that there were so many men carrying these bolsas in public that if someone yelled "draw" there would have been one helluva shootout.

Salvador was a Jekyll and Hyde country. During daylight hours the country was peaceful, lush and beautiful. It made me wonder why it wasn't covered with camera-toting tourists taking in the scenery of thousands of multi-colored flowers, exotic birds and elegantly architectured villas. Nightfall brought the answer. The city erupted with gunfire and explosions. Flashes from distant shell detonations illuminated the night sky with kaleidoscopic bursts of color. A death pallor seemed cast onto the city, filling it with fear I could almost grasp in the still humid air. Death was everywhere and even if I didn't personally see it, I knew it was close at hand and always there.

Anyone seeing and feeling this for the first time had to have mixed emotions. I wondered how on earth these people could exist in this hell in darkness, but I learned that with the rising of the sun, it faded away like the vanquishing of some evil spirit dying in the sunlight and the people would continue their daily lives as if it were only a mirage in the night.

What guts these people must have, I thought, cohabitating with death and fear, but outwardly displaying quiet resolve. I felt a sense of pride for these peasants caught in a vicious war similar to the one that I was now attempting to advance. I suppose I was hypocritical for feeling anything, because people like me were perpetuating the problem. But I was beginning to feel for these people and their lives. El Salvador had a lasting and profound impression on me. It was a place I knew that I wanted to get out of quickly and never come back.

But getting out of Salvador proved to be far more troublesome than I expected. One minute we thought we would leave for the airport and the next we were told "not today."

Ah, the beginning of Latino manna, the ever-present creeping delay syndrome that comes with the turf. It would have been a mercy killing if I had, at this point, taken my watch off my wrist and stomped it to pieces, for time meant nothing to these people.

I placed a call to Mario in the belief that he could do something about our plight. I did not want to stick around this place long and for some odd reason thought we were important enough, and that the FDN was powerful enough, to arrange for a military plane fly to El Salvador to fetch us. How naive. Mario must have thought I was bullshitting him when I asked about a special plane. He told me that he would notify everyone in Tegucigalpa about what had happened and for Cisco and I to keep a low profile. He told me to notify him as soon as I found out our actual flight schedule.

Mario wasn't fazed by any of this, but I was getting the hives, along with a case of Montezuma's revenge. As soon as I arrived in this country I was stricken with the problem and hadn't done a thing to piss off Montezuma. It did, however, drain me of all energy and ambition to go out and take in the sights or even make a half-hearted attempt to get laid. Grace was burning a hole in my brain because I felt a dramatic attraction to her. She later told me she felt the same way, but couldn't understand why I was acting so strange when we were around each other. What she didn't know was that I was doing a Jesse Owens to the john every five minutes and was embarrassed to strike up a conversation that might last longer than that. My brain had the urges, but the bod would not go along.

My only trip away from the hotel came the night we arrived. Since I had been so brilliant and packed my toilet articles in the seabags, I didn't have a toothbrush or a razor. Cisco and I talked a taxi driver into taking us a few blocks from the hotel to try to locate a drug store that might still be open. Not understanding the ground rules at night, I questioned why the taxi driver was so hesitant to make the trip. What I didn't know at the time was that we had two strikes on us when we left, being American and being out after dark.

We found a small market area and were attempting to communicate with some locals through the car window about directions when an M-16 rifle barrel was poked through the lowered back window and came to rest under Cisco's right eye.

The soldier holding this weapon didn't speak English and wasn't amused by our stupidity in venturing out after a curfew we knew nothing about. We were quickly told, in rapid-fire Spanish, to get our asses off the street and back into the hotel. We did, but the experience gave us incentive to learn more Spanish words, like "*pronto*" and "*adios motherfucker.*"

Knowing the local ground rules in any of these countries is the first cardinal rule. Acting a fool isn't a good idea, so I decided to get serious real quick. Cisco, however, was continuing to act a fool. He decided to buy Valium from the local *farmacia*, to take back to the U.S. and sell to cover his expenses for the trip and pay me back. It was his own version of creative financing. I repeatedly warned him not to do it, but he never took my good advice. It later proved to be a major mistake for him.

After four days of literal hell as a result of my physical condition, the nightly gunplay, Cisco's antics and the agonizing delays by TACA, we were told that there was a flight available to Honduras. By this time I had gotten better acquainted with Grace, but was at the end of my patience with Cisco. In just a few days, he had demonstrated his true self to me. He was a sneak thief, an unintelligent redneck who did nothing that wasn't aimed at his own self-gratification. He was useless and I now knew this, but it was far too late to stop what was underway. I just put the bit in my teeth about Cisco and trudged on.

When word came that a flight was available, there was a mad scramble by the several dozen people who had been piling up daily in the Sheraton as a result of bad scheduling and overbooking. People were hailing taxis, buses, private cars, anything that would roll away from the hotel and toward the airport.

The dash to the airport to be the first in line for the few seats available was like something out of the Keystone Kops. Taxis were cutting one another off, frequently swerving onto the shoulder of the road to keep from being overtaken. I paid our driver twenty bucks to beat everyone at any risk because I was ready to do anything to get out of Salvador. All the way to the airport we had a running battle with a family that had hired a pink Volkswagen to get them there ahead of us.

The race was a waste of time because the plane had more than enough seats to take all the stranded passengers with whom we had been incarcerated at the hotel.

The trip to Tegucigalpa took less than 40 minutes. I couldn't believe we were that close all the time. If I had known that I would have tried to walk to Honduras. I had imagined a flight of hours and the brevity of this trip after such a long delay in El Salvador was maddening. My experiences were putting me through a boot camp of patience that I would need to survive the things that everyone else felt were normal in Central America. Every event seemed like another in a long string of abortions or exercises in futility when I attempted to do anything. I was either wrong, scared shitless or dumbfounded by a lack of understanding of the language and people.

Even something as minor as landing in Tegucigalpa became an experience in terror. The runway there is only about 4,500 feet long and when you are approaching it with the plane standing on one wing, flying between the mountains that surround the airfield at nearly 200 miles per hour, you begin to make a real quick self-examination of your faculties, attempting to determine what the fuck you are doing in this place at this time.

Of course, the payoff comes when the plane touches down and the pilot jumps on the brakes with both feet and your face makes an immediate impression on the back of the seat in front of you that lasts for months. What a trip!

The plane door was opened onto a portable staircase that had been pushed to the side of the craft. I gathered my knees together, put my stomach and my heart back in their proper places and strolled out, trying to act like I had done this a hundred times before. Earthbound at last. Thank God.

Toncontin airport was a combination civilian facility and military base. The planes were parked away from the terminal and it was a good walk to the gate. As we exited the plane, it was like stepping into a scene from the movie "Missing."

Cisco and I moved into the long line of passengers waiting to be cleared through Customs. I intently watched the baggage being off-loaded from the belly of the plane and could not recognize anything that remotely resembled my seabags. The needle on my worry index began to rise. First the delay and now no equipment.

I stood behind a makeshift wooden barrier erected to separate Honduran citizens from visitors, straining to keep my eyes on the baggage. I wasn't paying much attention to Cisco when he grabbed my arm and asked me to look straight ahead. Standing there was a short, frail man, wearing Ray Ban sunglasses and an oversized black leather jacket. His mustache and somber expression reminded me of a Frito Bandito carica-ture. When Cisco saw him he shouted, "Lukey!"

Captain Leonel Lukey of the Honduran Secret Police was a powerful player in the back channel operations of the airport. He could make just about anything happen when he wanted it to happen. I came to know him as "you little shit," an endearment he thought absolutely hilarious.

Lukey motioned for us to step forward and I felt a little funny jumping line in front of the people who lived here. The Customs gate was opened and Cisco practically ran up to Lukey to shake his hand. I was intro-duced as Major Flaco, which caused Lukey to grimace slightly, as if someone had screwed up and hadn't told him someone important was coming.

Lukey was to become a good friend, but I sometimes wondered what made him tick. I told him, on a couple of occasions, that I wasn't a real major from the U.S. military, but that this was my nom de guerre. I don't think he ever truly believed me. He seemed frightened of me or what he perceived I could do, especially when I invoked the name of his superior Colonel Hector Applicano, the all-powerful head of the Secret Police.

I had been given Applicano's name and bona fides by Mario as a man who could be bought, but also trusted. I never attempted to explain to Lukey my real relationship with his boss, because I only invoked Applicano's name only when I really wanted to break some rules and knew that Lukey could facilitate it, which was rare. Lukey was a good soldier and tried his best. He used his authority well.

Our passports were stamped and returned without the Customs agent even looking up at our faces. We walked into the small baggage area, but our bags weren't on the carousel. I asked Lukey what could be done about this, in a manner as to suggest that the bags were "hot," and he calmly told me not to worry, that they would probably arrive tomorrow and he would see that they were delivered. I was afraid to ask if they would be inspected.

Two doors that served as exits from the passenger arrival area swung open repeatedly as people got their bags and departed. Each time the doors opened I could see several young men standing at a guardrail waving at arriving passengers. I figured they were merely greeting relatives, but Cisco kept waving back. Then he began to shout names and make gestures. Then I figured they were the FDN people sent to meet us. They blended right in with the crowd, but made no secret they had come to meet us. There was nothing secret about it. The only secrecy around this place was in my mind. Everyone seemed to know what was going on except me. I thought things would be more clandestine, more covert. But everything here was open and in full view of the airport officials.

A smiling, curly-haired man finally jumped the railing and entered the area without a challenge from any of the armed guards. He greeted Lukey first with a short burst of Spanish, then turned and gave Cisco a big hug. Cisco put his arm around the man and the two walked over to me. I held out my hand as they approached.

"This is Pulmon," Cisco said.

"*Buendía, Señor*," the man said, running the greeting together into one word and smiling broadly.

Pulmon was Donald Castillo. His nom de guerre means "one lung" in Spanish. He was Nicaraguan but had lived in Los Angeles for many years. He was one of many Americanized Nicaraguans who, for their own reasons, had volunteered to fight the Sandinistas.

Pulmon was intelligent and friendly, but he was also deceptive because, among other things, he was the No. 2 man in a nasty group of Contra urban commandos known as the RIC, or "Internal Command." He had been trained by the CIA as a demolitions expert and was well-versed in all forms and phases of war. The glint in his eyes told me he was for real. The boyish exterior was just a front.

The name Pulmon was given him because of an incident that occurred when he was a lieutenant in Somoza's Guardia Nacionale some years earlier. During the final battle for Managua, he was shot in the chest by an Uzi-wielding Sandinista soldier and left to die in the streets. A fellow officer rescued him from the streets and a slow death. A bullet had penetrated one of his lungs and treatment was so delayed that the lung could not be saved. This was no impediment to him, however. He could best most men with two good lungs in any physical endeavor. He rose early each day to run and exercise so that his handicap did not interfere with his ability to fight. He just had to be careful about catching colds or the flu.

La Quinta: Base of Despair

When we exited the terminal, we were quickly ushered into a waiting car with blacked out windows. We were instructed not to roll down the windows for any reason. Now the secrecy I had expected was beginning to be ratcheted up a few notches. The other men in the group, all well-armed, split themselves among our car and a chase car that stayed right on our bumper from the time we left the airport and headed for the FDN base camp in Tegucigalpa, La Quinta.

We headed northwest from the airport for just a few minutes before turning onto a road that took us through a large Honduran military base that housed a tank battalion. The asphalt soon ended, but we drove on. It seemed like we had driven at least seven or eight miles when we came to a stop in front of a barbed wire gate that resembled a cattle gate. It was dark by then and with the blacked out windows, it was damn near impossible to tell what was going on outside.

Suddenly, a series of flood lights illuminated the area and three poorly dressed but heavily armed men walked to the gate. They spoke briefly with the driver of our car and the gate swung open to reveal a steep driveway up a hill into what looked like a ranch complex. The driveway was little more than ruts and holes filled with chunks of rock. The car lumbered up the grade, the engine straining.

Once we reached the top, we could still make out only a portion of the complex because the lighting was very poor. We stopped in front of a ranch-style building made of adobe, and our escorts jumped out quickly to open the car doors for us. A small greeting party was waiting for us.

I was at somewhat of a disadvantage since I knew none of these people. Cisco had met some of them on prior trips, so I stood quietly in the background as he greeted them. The first to be introduced to me was the logistics chief for La Quinta, Romano. Then came an old man named Piyou, who was a propagandist for the radio station based here. After him came Toro, a hulking brute and commander of the RIC. These people seldom introduced themselves with their real names and prying into their business, I quickly learned, could be an unhealthy thing to do. They needed anonymity because many were wanted by various governments in Central America.

Everyone seemed pleased that Americans had returned to the fold after the deaths of Parker and Powell. We were treated with respect and kindness.

What I saw of the base took me aback. The reality of it could not have been further from what I had imagined. I had pictured a complex with whitewashed rocks in a neat circle around a flag pole and rows of barracks along the main paths of the base. I expected to see a helicopter pad and military vehicles.

There was none of that. There were a few old buildings, a concrete water tower and an open area with several men sitting in front of a black and white television. It looked like an abandoned ranch, not a base camp for a large guerrilla army.

After the brief introductions, we were led into a makeshift dining area to be fed. What I did not realize was that we were served the best of their food that night, depriving soldiers of food the following day. The meal was simple, consisting of two fried eggs, rice, red beans and a small slab of fried goat cheese. Had I ever sampled feces, it would probably have been a match for the fried goat cheese. It was absolutely terrible, but I felt obligated to eat it and act like it was delicious because I knew this was coming from some poor campesino's mouth. I wasn't really hungry, but wolfed it down to show them my macho gusto.

After the meal, Pulmon walked us outside to go over the house rules. Never, ever drink tap water, he said. Drinkable water was stored in a large military water bag hanging from a tree. Never flush a toilet more than once a day, since water was as scarce as it was tainted. And never take a shower that lasted longer than three minutes. Some resort, I thought.

That wasn't as bad as the sleeping area, though, which had at least five men in each small room. I was fortunate because Cisco and I shared a room with Piyou, Castillo and Romano. The other rooms were far more crowded. We even had a shower room, if it could be called that.

Cisco had been here before and watched with amusement as the "big shot" was brought down a few notches by the grim reality of living in a Contra camp. I could see now why anybody would be hesitant to return to this model of counterrevolutionary subsistence.

The emotions and stress of the past several days had taken a toll on me. I was tired, and dirty, and wanted nothing more than a shower and sleep. Pulmon had mentioned that we might hear some noise from Honduran military exercises that were conducted nightly in the area. I wasn't paying much attention to his warning because I had a bead on the shower and some sleep. Despite the smell and filthy condition of the shower stall, I took a long shower, consuming not only my share of water, but everyone else's in camp, I didn't care. It felt so good after not being clean or able to change my clothes for so long.

I got into the cot assigned to me and shuffled the dirty sheets around to find a clean spot to lie on. I had just slid into a deep sleep when an explosion went off that sounded like a mortar shell hit the toilet. I sat straight up in bed, eyes as big as silver dollars. If someone had cut my throat right then I would not have bled a drop. I was so white with fright that if they had put me on top of clean sheets they never would have seen me. I was scared out of my wits.

"What the hell was that?" I shouted at Cisco.

He said nothing and rolled over, quickly resuming his bellowing snore. The chatter of automatic weapons fire and a series of grenade simulator explosions quickly reminded me of Pulmon's warnings about the night exercises. I felt slightly embarrassed because of my reaction, but the soldiers in the exercise were so close it seemed as though they were running through the bedroom. I slumped back under the blankets and spent the rest of the night in a half-guarded state of alert.

Dawn came so quickly that my body felt like I had not slept at all. Pulmon was already up, tapping me and Cisco on the shoulder trying to get us out of bed. Days began early here and being VIPs made no difference in the scheme of things. I grudgingly left the security of my bed and got dressed.

I looked out at the portion of the base I could see through our one half-painted window. There were low, rolling hills at the far edge of a patch of land where cattle were nibbling the grass around several large military GP tents. I could see no evidence that any kind of military exercise had been conducted here last night because there were no shell casings, rundown shrubbery or residue from the rather loud explosions.

I washed my face and brushed my teeth, all the while cursing the fact that my bags had yet to catch up with me. I needed fresh clothes and had the urge to dress in a uniform of some type before making my appearance at chow. That was another in my growing list of misconceptions. The inhabitants of La Quinta dressed in civvies. No uniforms of any kind were allowed because this base was not here, as far as the Hondurans were concerned. The town of La Quinta was actually on the edge of the huge Honduran military base, but the base was invisible to the Honduran eye. It did not exist.

As I walked into the chow hall, everyone rose to greet me. I was treated like a celebrity, but was at a loss to know why. Pulmon asked me to sit next to him so he could translate. The same cast of characters that had been at dinner the night before was at breakfast, but others began arriving from town.

I was introduced to Oscar Montez, the code name for Orlando Montelegre, the head bookkeeper for the FDN and close friend of Mario's. He was well-dressed and spoke fluent English. He had arrived with a rotund man named Frank Arana, the head of the clandestine radio station and chief writer of propaganda broadcasts. Everyone in the FDN hierarchy in Honduras knew of our pending arrival and wanted to get a look at the person Mario had built up in a fashion that gave me more importance than I thought necessary. I don't know what Mario told them, but people were showing up at La Quinta just to look at me. One by one, others drove up in late model cars or bulletproof Toyota Land Cruisers.

I wasn't hungry for more fried goat cheese, which seemed to be the most abundant item at every meal, so I downed a couple of cups of coffee and said I was eager to get outside and get a good look at the base, which had quickly become a major disappointment to me.

Pulmon led me and Cisco on a brief tour of the base. He took us first to the concrete water tower, where he pointed out his "shop." Cases of dynamite, TNT, C-3, prima cord and C-4 plastic explosives were arranged to make a small working area for him. I was afraid to breathe hard for fear the whole thing would blow up.

Pulmon demonstrated how he manufactured charges of C-4 in five-, ten- and twenty-pound bundles to be smuggled into Nicaragua for use in sabotage activities. He wanted to show off his skills in measurements, types of detonation devices and various fusing techniques. But the guard with us was casually smoking a cigarette and splashing the ashes all over the place so I told Pulmon I would take his word about his expertise because I wanted to get out of there.

Pulmon then took us to the adjoining structure, which contained rows and rows of rifles. Most were U.S-made M-14s, which Pulmon claimed could not be used due to the weapon's inability to eject shell casings after the rifle fired. Pulmon was stunned when Cisco and I inspected the gas ports on the rifles and told him they were stopped up with cosmoline, a preservative and rust inhibitor used to seal new weapons for shipment. That's what was preventing the rifles from ejecting the spent cartridges.

Cisco took the toothpick from his mouth and punched a hole through the cosmoline, opening the gas port. Pulmon loaded the weapon and walked out to fire a few rounds, and the rifle worked to specifications. He acted like white voodoo chiefs had just freed the guns from a trance of malfunction. All of these perfectly good rifles had been taken out of service because the Contras, in their ignorance about weapons, did not understand the functioning of a gas-operated bolt. This little demonstration further ingratiated us with them. We were people who could help the cause with our expertise.

I noticed a row of 122mm mortars, which are large, relatively immobile weapons, sitting in a row out in the open. I asked Pulmon why they were not being used at the front. He explained that when the shipment was received from Israel the Honduran Army felt threatened by the mortars being in the Contras' possession. So, the Hondurans politely confiscated the sights and ammo, rendering them useless. At this stage I was still under the impression that if the Contras had these mortars they would use them. But, as I later learned, this wasn't the case. Using them would have meant taking the fight to the Sandinistas and that wasn't the goal here.

The most glaring example of what La Quinta and the Contras were all about filled me with a sense of shame. Most, if not all, of the field soldiers at this base were casualties of one type or another. These men, their bodies torn by gunshots and explosions, wandered about the base doing menial work by day. At night, they ate, watched television and slept on a concrete slab protected from the elements only by an old, leaking roof.

Out in the field, away from the main buildings, these wounded Contras got physical therapy by sorting loose ammunition and loading clips to be sent to the base camps in southern Honduras.

But the true purpose of these men was to be show pieces for the many outside contributors who came to see what was being done to the poor peasant fighters of this war. Their eyes were deep and dark, without life, without promise. It was as if someone had reached into their bodies and pulled out their souls. There was nothing left of them, except the damaged frame.

This disgusting display affected my overzealous craving to join this crowd of flesh purveyors who would stoop so low as to financially and politically benefit from the carnage of battle. What was even more surprising was that most of the men had not been wounded in battle. Most had self-inflicted wounds, sometimes accidental and sometimes intentional. The lack of training caused a large number of Contra deaths and injuries because the men frequently shot one another while walking around bases with guns loaded and off safety. Or they blew themselves up playing with hand grenades.

The Contra leadership vehemently denied that these wounds had been self-inflicted or accidental and claimed the men were fearless freedom fighters who had taken the brunt of many a Sandinista encounter and had been sent to La Quinta to receive prosthetics. Only a woeful lack of funds, the leaders claimed, prevented these wounded warriors from getting the artificial arms and legs they needed. What they did not say was that monies destined for prosthetic devices went to the local casino at the Honduran Maya Hotel each night in the pocket of the commandantes.

This horrifying spectacle of maimed Contras, hobbling around camp on crutches and being mistreated by their leaders, produced the first crack in my icy, mercenary veneer.

Las Vegas, Ho!

We spent three days at La Quinta waiting for transportation to the front. I was getting quite restless because we were not allowed to leave the base or even be seen walking around it in daylight. Everyone in camp was on edge about us and something else that was going on that they kept from us. Finally, late one afternoon, Toro came into the mess hall where we were drinking coffee and announced that we should prepare to leave for the front at 3 a.m. the following day.

Activity throughout the camp increased as preparations were made for vehicles to leave in different directions to confuse any Sandinista infiltrators who might be watching. A decoy truck laden with vegetables and hidden explosives was prepared to head for the Pan American highway in southwest Honduras and enter Nicaragua as relief food. Simultaneously, our vehicle would depart for the border to the southeast.

Pulmon brought Cisco and me each an Uzi sub-machine gun, three clips of extra ammo and a carrying case. The weapons were brand new. Things were becoming serious. The laughter died down and men stopped smiling. It was show time.

At 2:15 the next morning I was jostled awake by Pulmon. He spoke in whispers as those making the trip rose and slipped silently into the mess hall for breakfast and final instructions. Pulmon explained that we had to be extra careful and not get stopped because armed Americans traveling at this hour could quickly bring trouble. We were told that if we were approached by Honduran military or police that we should sit quietly and let the Nicaraguans handle everything.

A small Soviet-made truck, a Niva, pulled up to the front door and we got in. There was a passenger already on board. He was Flores, the communications officer for Las Vegas, the main Contra base. Flores was spooky. He never said a word. What I learned about him later fit the mold. I was told that he was an "asset" for the CIA and could not be trusted.

This morning, the atmosphere was not as relaxed as when we arrived. There was a sense that something was not quite right as we drove through Tegucigalpa on our way south. It felt bad. My senses were working overtime. Tanks filled the streets and blocked intersections. Troops jogged in formation in every direction. Checkpoints abounded and there were virtually no civilians anywhere.

Pulmon was very uneasy about all this. When he saw the display of military hardware in the streets he murmured under his breath, "Oh shit." Pulmon was not a man who normally displayed fear, but he was quite nervous about what we were seeing this morning.

Our truck darted around corners, up alleys and down back streets. Toro was not about to stay on any main thoroughfare where the military activity was concentrated. After about thirty minutes of driving, we stopped in front of a small row of houses near the southern edge of Tegucigalpa. We sat silently in the dark for about 20 minutes, wondering what was going on. English explanations had become extremely rare inside the truck.

Suddenly, a tall slender man walked briskly from the shadows and came to the truck. He opened the door and slid in next to Flores. This was Commandante 26, logistics chief for Las Vegas, who was returning to camp after a two-week vacation in the city. He spoke to Toro in rapid Spanish in what I believed was a recounting of the events that led to this high alert in the Honduran army.

A day earlier the FBI had arrested eight people in the United States and charged them with plotting to assassinate Honduran President Roberto Suazo Cordova and take over the government.[2]

The plot, which included General Jose A. Bueso-Rosa, the military attaché at the Honduran embassy in Chile and a favorite of American military officials, was to have been financed by $10 million worth of cocaine. That was the wholesale price. Retail it could have brought as much as $40 million. The 760 pounds of coke in 15 duffel bags was confiscated by the feds at a small airport in Keenansville, Florida, on October 28, shortly before the arrests were made in Miami.

Among those charged in the conspiracy were Faiz J. Sikaffy, a Honduran businessman who operated a seafood business in Miami, and

Gerard Latchinian, a Honduran also living in Miami who dabbled in the arms business. Sikaffy was upset with the Honduran government because he had lost $7 million when the government nationalized his cement business.

Implicated in the plot by Sikaffy and Latchinian, but never charged, were retired Army Colonel "Charging" Charlie Beckwith of Delta Force fame and Desert One infamy, and U.S. Army Major Charles Odorizzi. Sikaffy and Latchinian charged that the CIA, through Beckwith and Odorizzi, were interested in getting rid of Suazo because of what were perceived as his "Communist leanings."[3]

The conspirators planned to have Suazo killed sometime in the next few weeks and take over the government in the ensuing unrest.[4]

Latchinian laid out the plan for me from his jail cell in Florida several years later. He told of pressure being put on Suazo's government to cooperate with U.S. plans to expand its role in the country. Since there had been a growing disenchantment among the public and some politicians with both the U.S. and Contra presence in Honduras, Cordova threatened to oust the U.S. military unless hundreds of millions of dollars were paid.

U.S. officials, through the CIA, put together contingency plans for a coup attempt against Suazo and let it be known in certain circles so it would get back to him. A last-minute deal was cut for nearly $150 million dollars in aid to Honduras, thus scuttling the overthrow plan. According to Latchinian, cocaine was planted on the yacht that was being used by the conspirators and the DEA was tipped off.[5]

Suazo was not exactly the most stable of the Central American leaders. But he was certainly pliable, especially from external pressures from the U.S. Department of State and the CIA. That made him the perfect leader for those interests.

Suazo frequently was referred to by his opponents as *la vaca*, the cow, in part because of his prodigious girth but also because of the bovine banality of his personality and policies.

Suazo was easily led and even more easily influenced by money. A story making the rounds at that time concerned a statue that occupied a prominent place in the Catholic church in Suazo's hometown of La Paz, Honduras.

The town fared well during his presidency and was the beneficiary of much new construction. But the statue, known as *La Virgen del Socorro Perpetuo*, the Virgin of Perpetual Aid, said even more about Suazo's willingness to accept money from any source.

The statue was more commonly referred to as *La Virgen del Pasaporte*, the Virgin of the Passport. It seems a Spanish businessman accused in his own country of bilking millions from investors was given a Honduran passport in return for the statue. The ambassador who authorized the passport was fired, but the statue ended up in Suazo's church.

In this atmosphere of corruption and foreign intervention, it was not unusual for coups to be hatched.

Latchinian and Sikaffy later were convicted of their part in the conspiracy to assassinate Suazo and sentenced to lengthy prison terms. Bueso-Rosa pleaded guilty to three of the nine counts against him and was sentenced to five years in prison, but not before throwing his weight around and, not surprisingly, getting a lot of support from the Pentagon. Another of Bueso-Rosa's allies just happened to be a U.S. Marine lieutenant colonel named Oliver North.

By the time of Bueso-Rosa's sentencing North had become an incredibly powerful figure in the White House, possibly the first four-star lieutenant colonel in history. According to his notes, he was concerned that the Honduran might start "singing songs nobody wants to hear" if he went to prison.

Eventually, efforts to get Bueso-Rosa's sentence reduced involved the likes of Admiral John Poindexter, head of the NSC; Elliott Abrams, assistant secretary of state for inter-American affairs; Dewey Clarridge of the CIA; Nestor Sanchez, deputy assistant secretary of defense; and several U.S. Army generals.[6]

The capper on the whole Bueso-Rosa affair came in the spring of 1986. Two days before he was to plead guilty to charges that he conspired to assassinate the duly elected president of his country, Bueso-Rosa was slated to be the guest of honor at a lunch sponsored by the Defense Intelligence Agency in the Pentagon's executive dining room. After several lengthy meetings among senior officials from the CIA, the DIA, the Department of Justice and the State Department, DIA finally was convinced that the lunch wasn't such a good idea after all.[7]

The aborted coup explained why the Honduran countryside was crawling with troops that morning and why our FDN hosts had been jumpy for the past few days.

We quickly left Tegucigalpa and headed south. As the miles clicked off, the truck got smaller and smaller. The Uzis, which were supposed to be used for protection, were becoming painful excess baggage and kidney busters. Dawn began to break about 40 miles outside the city, just about the time the asphalt road turned to dirt. The potholes were numerous and deep. We stopped only to relieve ourselves a few times, then pressed on for the border.

Cisco and I tried to doze as the others yammered incessantly in annoying, staccato Spanish that neither of us understood. Cisco had earlier described the trip as "a short distance." It was anything but.

We had been on the road for nearly six hours when we entered Los Trojes, a small village in the middle of nowhere, but the midway point between Tegucigalpa and the big Contra base at Las Vegas. I lifted myself slowly from the car. Every muscle in my body ached. As my feet hit the ground, a cloud of dust dropped off me. I took off my sunglasses and looked in one of the side mirrors on the truck. I looked like someone had hit me in the face with a bag of dirt, leaving two white circles around my eyes. I felt so bad that nothing mattered now except eating, drinking something cold and walking the circulation back into my legs.

This little village was a hotbed of activity for the rebels. It had a print shop used for forging travel documents and a small factory to make uniforms. And all of this was going on right under the noses of the Hondurans, if not with their cooperation. It was obvious something was different here because the inhabitants walked by us as if we were invisible. It's a reasonable assumption that armed Americans would attract some attention in most parts of the world. But not here. It was as if we were part of the landscape.

I felt a bit better after we ate and reconciled myself to the fact that the trip was not going to get any smoother. I thought we would depart as soon as we had finished eating, but there was an unexpected delay while we waited for a vehicle coming from Las Vegas.

After waiting for nearly 2 1/2 hours, a red Toyota sped into the village from the opposite direction from which we had come. When it stopped, men began to pile out carrying suitcases and burlap bags. These were men from Las Vegas on their way to Tegucigalpa for a few days of rest. The burlap bags contained several AK-47 assault rifles being sent for repair.

When we finally left Los Trojes, we headed southeast. As I expected, the road got worse.

Near dusk, the truck slowed as we approached the first real military position I had seen since leaving Tegucigalpa. Foxholes and sandbags ringed a small hillside emplacement where Honduran soldiers were posted. A captain came to the passenger side of the truck and gave everyone in the vehicle a cursory glance. He paused only briefly when he saw Cisco and me. In spite of our Uzis, he acted like we were just another couple of Latin passengers.

Commandante 26 pulled his wallet out and flashed an ID card. Pulmon whispered that 26 carried the ID of the Honduran Secret Police. The captain backed off and waved to the sentry to open the wooden barrier blocking the road. We quickly drove on as Pulmon said something in Spanish about the Hondurans to 26. Then he told us that the soldier was stupid and anyone could get past him. It was becoming obvious the Nicaraguans thought as much of their hosts as their hosts thought of them.

The closer we got to the border, the more obvious the tension became among the occupants of the truck. Cisco and I were just tourists along for the ride, but our Contra escorts had become quite vigilant, scanning the skies and the steep mountains around us. Pulmon mentioned we were about to pass the spot where the road got the closest to Nicaragua, a place known as the "three-kilometer marker."

This area had been the scene of another helicopter shootdown only a few months earlier. An American soldier had been killed when the helicopter he was in was shot down by Sandinista fire from the Nicaraguan side of the border.

For the first time I began to see war damage. The spot where the chopper went down was behind a hill to our left and could not be seen from the road. But a row of peasant houses and small businesses were gutted from what appeared to be mortar rounds. The shattered remnants of a small village, now deserted, was spread on both sides of the road. There were no soldiers, no animals, no traffic except the bright red target in which we were riding.

It was hard for the driver to speed up because of road conditions, but in the midst of the tension and evident danger, Pulmon looked at me with a big smile and said, "The roads, they are good. No?"

They got even worse. As we neared the border, we were asked several times to get out when the truck crossed over some shaky bridges that were constructed from logs cut to cover huge gaps in the side of the mountains where there had been washouts. We had gone from flat, dusty farmland to heavily canopied mountain forests and the light was fading.

Base? Las Vegas? Military camp? Where was any of it? The short trip was now approaching thirteen hours of torture and my nerves were on edge. I began to act like a fidgety kid in the back seat, repeatedly asking how much longer the trip would take. Pulmon would only reply with a smile and talk about another point of interest, like I really cared at this juncture.

We rounded a curve and finally I saw my first live Contra in uniform. A large green bulldozer was parked to the side of the road and a half dozen very young men stood around it like they were guarding it from something. Their equipment seemed very sparse. A couple carried AK-47s, the others an assortment of vintage World War II rifles. They had no more than three grenades and two canteens between them. I continued to look them over as we passed, as much out of curiosity as anything else. Their odd-colored uniforms and lack of basic equipment puzzled me.

I had a feeling that we were finally getting close to the base. Darkness was closing in fast as we topped a small rise in the road and I spotted a small shack to our left with a Contra sentry sitting in it. We stopped and the driver spoke briefly with the guard. Pulmon explained that we had finally reached Las Vegas. I looked around and thought to myself that it must be well-hidden because the only thing I could see was the shack.

We began to move again, going down one hill, then up another. As we did, the base suddenly spread out before me. Las Vegas seemed to pop out of nowhere. There was a huge, open expanse of land dotted with numerous buildings and makeshift tents. The Contras used a light green plastic sheeting for most of the housing. Perhaps it was practical and cheap, but my first reaction was that the bright green tents would serve as a homing beacon for enemy aircraft looking for this supposedly clandestine base.

Our entrance into camp didn't draw much attention because the men were accustomed to trucks coming and going. We drove through throngs of literally thousands of people, all of them armed. It was an incredible sight and I was appropriately awed by this so-called secret army. I figured that if this was just one of several bases, then the army must have 30,000 or 40,000 troops. I didn't know how wrong I was.

Our truck stopped in front of a two-strand barbed wire fence that was used to divide the officers from the rest of the camp. The small wooden prefab houses sitting on the officers' side of the wire were the main operations buildings for the base. Several heavily armed guards were posted at a gate leading through the fence. These men looked like gorillas. Most of the Contras I had seen seemed short and dark, nothing like the group guarding the gate. These men were the hand-picked entourage and bodyguards of the camp commander, Commandante 380, chief of staff for the FDN, Colonel Enrique Bermudez Varela. I had at last arrived.

3

The Place That Time Forgot: The Cobra

It was obvious from the moment I uncoiled my aching body from the back seat of the truck and stepped onto this piece of Honduran dirt that these Nicaraguan *desplazados* had claimed for their insurgency that one man was in charge here—Colonel Enrique Bermudez, Commandante 380. He stood on the other side of the barbed wire fence surrounded by his bodyguards, lord of all he surveyed in this jungle encampment.

Bermudez was a short, dark man with curly hair and features that spoke more of his Indian heritage than his Spanish blood. He was aloof to most Americans with whom he dealt and condescending to the Nicaraguans who were around him. Except when he was drunk, which was often, his dark eyes were constantly moving, unable or unwilling to focus on whomever or whatever he was dealing with at the time. It was almost as if he were both suspicious and frightened at the same time.

While Bermudez wielded a great deal of power, he was also a terribly insecure man who frequently ranted and raved about how he had been deprived of his birthright in Nicaragua and now was forced to live in the jungle with campesinos he neither liked nor trusted while his wife lived in Miami and worked as a hairdresser.

Although Bermudez did not suffer these privations happily, he did so willingly because he was the absolute ruler of this no-man's land and knew that the absence of a leader in the field would have meant the end of the insurgency. That also would have meant the end of his chance to assume power in a new government in Nicaragua. As long as he controlled the soldiers, he knew he would have power unlike any of the FDN directorate once he returned to Managua.

Like most of the Contra commandantes, Bermudez was inept and corrupt. His military knowledge was minimal. His desire to actually wage war on the Sandinistas was held in check by political considerations over which he had no control. His army was largely an army in hiding in Honduras, feeding off the CIA and the American taxpayers. Except for a few military commanders in the field, the Contra army was largely a show army, designed to do little more than draw the U.S. military into the conflict.

I was in awe of the man and his power when I first met him. Just a few weeks earlier I had been an unknown to these people. Now, I was shaking hands with the leader of the largest guerrilla army in Central America and being led on a personal tour of the base. It was obvious from his demeanor that he thought I was far more important than I actually was. Mario's letter must have provided him with just enough information to inflame his imagination about my true purpose for being there.

Trailed by a gaggle of heavily armed aides and bodyguards, Bermudez chattered happily as we strolled around the compound through the approaching dusk. He pointed out the areas of which he was most proud — a large hospital with an air-conditioned surgery ward and pharmacy, an arms depot, a tortilla kitchen and, finally, on a small hill near the officers' quarters, Enrique's personal pride and joy — the Special Operations Company, known as COE.

The soldiers who served in this unit were the best the FDN could muster. They had the best training, the best equipment, the best food and the best housing. Unlike the common campesino fighters, these men received monthly salaries. Most were former Guardia Nacionale soldiers who enjoyed other perks, like a daily change of uniforms and a woman, if they so chose.

But, as good as these COE soldiers were, they had little exposure to combat. They were a showpiece for visitors, a highly trained and quite capable piece of propaganda. Only if the Sandinistas threatened this base were they to be used in combat.

My tour that first evening included a stop at one wooden building where Bermudez pointed to the side door of a helicopter and a stack of 2.75-inch air-to-ground rockets. This was all that remained of the Hughes 500D that carried Parker, Powell and Pozo to their deaths two months earlier. Bermudez said the day the ill-fated helicopter left Las Vegas he had ordered the removal of nearly half the rockets because the aircraft was overloaded.

He complained bitterly about the loss of the helicopter, but not about the deaths of the three men. He callously told me that without the helicopter he was now forced to travel to other Contra camps by road. There was no sympathy for the dead or remorse for what had befallen them. He was not in favor of the mission, he said, although he never explained who was responsible for ordering it. He said it had been nothing more than a waste of good equipment. Bermudez was one cold son-of-a-bitch.

Of all the Contra leaders I came to know, Enrique was the most devious and the most dangerous. Within a few minutes of meeting him I realized he was a cobra in a pit of snakes that didn't realize how dangerous he was. He was dangerous because of his ambition, and the people most at risk of his venom were the FDN leaders.

In spite of all my perceived misgivings about Bermudez, I came to have a strange respect for the man. I knew that he could provide me with the means to accomplish my goals. If he favored you, there was nothing he would not do for you, and you glowed in the dark.

The relationship I developed with Bermudez over the next few weeks was strange. There was a constant battle of wills. I knew the reality of his power, but kept him guessing about mine. Ours was a coalition based on each one feeding off the other's power. In his case, he was feeding off his perception of my power, while I knew that his dipstick went mighty deep.

Bermudez was further confused about my real role when Adolfo Calero showed up at Las Vegas several days after my arrival and had several private conversations with me, something he never did with the other Americans who came here. After that, Bermudez was afraid to say anything negative to me or about me because he thought I was the blue-eyed devil from Langley.

I became like his pet. Whenever he got bored he would tell his aides: "Go get Flaco."

When he learned I liked Pepsi, he ordered Commandante 26 to bring in cases of them. From then on, whenever I hit the door to Bermudez's hutch, I could hear the tops popping on the Pepsis they were opening for me. No one could touch those Pepsis without my permission.

Most of the higher ranking commandantes, rather than the typical nom de guerre used a numerical code name. The numbers were an abbreviation of the serial numbers assigned Guardia Nacionale soldiers in the Somoza regime. Each Contra commandante selected that part of his number he wished to use for code purposes. There was no logic to the use of the numbers, so they provided an outsider with no clue as to who among the numbered commandantes was more senior.

Bermudez even assigned Pulmon to be my bodyguard. Pulmon became my shadow while I was in Las Vegas because Bermudez was so fearful that something would happen to me. Pulmon knew where I was at all times. If I went to the john, Pulmon was there with the toilet paper. It mystified the hell out of Pulmon because he had not seen any other Americans treated like I was and no one told him who I was or what I was doing there.

I also respected Bermudez because he knew how to control the evils within his domain when no one else could or would. I also liked him personally because he was a lot like me.

Militarily, Bermudez had no idea what he was doing. At night he would sit in his house drinking and watching movies on his VCR instead of planning the campaign or working with his soldiers.

Politically, Bermudez was biding his time. He had no respect for the political leaders of the FDN, particularly Adolfo Calero, who was regularly being feted at the White House and praised by Ronald Reagan as one of the "founding fathers" of his country. Bermudez disliked Adolfo, but knew he needed him long enough to handle the political intrigues in Washington until he could get his ragtag army into Managua. He tolerated his superiors because he felt that in the end the soldiers would follow him rather than the political figureheads who seldom showed their faces in Las Vegas. Bermudez had his designs on power once the Sandinistas had been run off, and he saw his relationship with the CIA as the way to get that power. He did whatever the agency wanted.

Bermudez was lucky to have his current position. He just happened to be in the right place at the right time in the tumultuous months following the Sandinista takeover of Nicaragua in 1979.

Although a colonel in Somoza's Guardia Nacionale, Bermudez had spent most of the war years in Washington as a military attache and did not have the same smell as some of the other commandantes. In late 1979, Bermudez had latched onto a small contingent of former guardsmen in Guatemala that called itself Detachment 101. It was later reconstituted as the September 15 Legion.[1]

Over the next two years, Bermudez and other Nicaraguans who had fled the Sandinista takeover worked to build up the rebel movement with the assistance of sympathetic Argentine and Honduran military leaders. It was the Argentines, the scourge of Latin America with their death squads and wanton killing, who provided the first equipment and training for the fledgling Contra army.

Bermudez became the driving force in the Contra movement in the jungle, but in ways that go against all that is sane and civilized. Using the power of his military position, Bermudez could have leaped to the head of the movement at any time. But when I arrived in Honduras in late 1984, he was still biding his time, waiting for the right moment. He was an impressive man with all his grandiose talk and Latin swagger, but his self-aggrandizing ambitions would prove to be his Achilles' heel.

The Camp and its Characters

Las Vegas was a huge piece of land about 20 kilometers from the Nicaraguan border that had been "leased" from a Honduran farmer. The camp itself was on the floor of a valley between two high mountain ridges. The ridge to the south was quite steep and covered with thick growths of virgin timber. The only discernable feature was the path that zig-zagged up to the anti-aircraft emplacements. The ridge to the north was not quite as high or as imposing and had only one anti-aircraft position. The land sloped down gently from the north ridge until it ran into the south ridge, the gateway to Nicaragua.

I can think of no rational military strategy that would have allowed for how Las Vegas was laid out. Every person and every piece of equipment was vulnerable to attack.

While the camp was well-protected north and south, the east and west approaches were wide open. The theory behind placing the base on this particular piece of land was that the southern mountain ridge would serve as a natural barrier against any land assault by the Sandinistas. It worked, but only because the Sandinistas were not interested in making any incursion in force that deep into Honduras.

The Contras thought they were well out of range of Sandinista mortars and artillery, but they still occasionally found themselves the targets of Katyusha rockets lobbed across the border. The Sandinistas weren't much better at long-range warfare than the Contras because the rockets generally fell far to the north and rarely hit anything of significance.

The grounds within the camp were divided into unit areas. The most striking thing about this was that each battalion took its own piece of dirt and staked it out with borders of rocks that had been painted white. In fact, each battalion spelled out the initials of its unit with these rocks.

Since the dirt on the base was a bright orange clay, these white rocks and the light green tents stood out against it like glaring neon lights during the day. I was amazed that the Sandinistas hadn't taken the opportunity to launch bombing runs against the base because from the air Las Vegas must surely have looked like a billboard that read: "Bomb me! Bomb me!"

The largest section of the base was the parade ground, which doubled as a baseball diamond. Periodically, this field also served as the corridor for .50-caliber machine gun practice. Not infrequently, the two were held simultaneously, resulting in some rather strange games and some injuries baseball's inventors certainly never envisioned.

A small creek flowed from north to south through the base along which hundreds of soldiers and their families made camp. They bathed in the creek, washed dishes in it and drew their drinking water from it. Usually, the drinking water was drawn downstream while other men bathed upstream.

Fires burned all over the camp at night, despite the fact that this was supposed to be a clandestine base under threat of attack. There was no light discipline and no noise discipline at Las Vegas at night. The glow from hundreds of fires must have been visible for miles. This was an indication to me that there was really no fear of a Sandinista attack on Las Vegas.

The motor pool was on the north side of the two-strand barbed wire fence and all vehicles clustered in that one spot. The ammunition dump was south of the fence, buried under just enough dirt to cover its contents but not enough to protect it from shell fragments. The armory was directly across the road from the ammo dump.

Eight anti-aircraft emplacements had been placed in a way that made them useless if the base were attacked from either the east or west. In addition, each gun had been placed in a large hole dug in the bright orange clay with loose dirt thrown in a circle around it, providing a perfect bullseye. Even Stevie Wonder could have bombed this base into oblivion.

If an attack had been launched against Las Vegas, a smart and determined enemy could have destroyed everything of consequence with the accurate placement of no more than three bombs. It was a military target the likes of which I had never seen.

But for the inhabitants of Las Vegas, it was more like a POW camp than a military encampment.

When I arrived in Las Vegas and stopped at the two-strand barbed wire fence, I never imagined that it was anything more than a security barrier. But this fence served as the demarcation line between classes in the camp. The bodyguards were placed at the gate to keep out those who lived below the line. The commandantes could cross the line whenever they wanted, which was infrequently. The campesinos risked death if they came across the line uninvited.

I lived on the privileged side of the line. I was one of the elite. But I felt incredibly uncomfortable. I had been an underdog all of my life, living on the wrong side of the line. Now I was on the other side and I didn't like it. I went to Honduras championing American idealism, but here was a system of class separation that was worse than anything I had seen in Alabama as a boy.

One morning I invited a campesino to have breakfast with me above the line in the little hut where the commandantes ate. When the commandantes walked in and saw themselves in the presence of a lowly peasant farmer, it was like I had unleashed a social disease. Bermudez was incensed. The firestorm over that little incident lasted for days.

The commandantes feared the masses because of the potential power they had. When you start giving the campesinos a voice, when you tell them that what they have to say is important, you raise the specter that they may begin to think they are as good as the commandantes. You raise the specter of equality. To Bermudez and the other commandantes, that was totally unacceptable.

The best of the commandantes, the real fighters like Mike Lima, Tigrillo and Kaliman, didn't live above the line. They lived with the troops because they were campesino commandantes and couldn't relate to the Somocista way of doing things. Had they become part of the elite, they would have lost the respect and love of their troops.

The fear these people had of the Somocista commandantes became evident on my strolls around camp. In the mornings I often would get up early and go below the line to a small store run by a Honduran merchant. I'd buy Pepsis for myself and sit around talking with the campesinos. I tried to get a feel of what it was like to be one of them, but never felt like they were comfortable with me around. Finally it dawned on me that they were merely patronizing me out of fear. I was white. I represented power. They thought I represented the United States military. I was everything that worked against them and controlled their lives.

Below the line was like being in prison. I could identify with the feeling those people had. They were prisoners in their own army in a foreign land. The Hondurans feared them just as their commandantes feared them. Still, I felt more comfortable below the line than above it.

I was witnessing a Latin feudal system in the modern age. My naivete about Central America became painfully obvious because I did not know that such practices were a day-to-day reality here. The class separation and the differences between the haves and the have-nots being perpetuated in this remote jungle camp were astounding.

Some nights the commandantes would roast a pig over an open fire. In the flickering firelight I could see the gaunt faces of the campesinos pressing close to the fence just to get a smell of the roasting pig. They were desperate, dark, demanding faces that stared at us with a barely concealed contempt for what we had and what they did not. We were eating garden-fresh salads with Thousand Islands dressing and roast pork out in the middle of nowhere and the campesinos were starving.

During our many long talks, Enrique tried with some success to convince me that Nicaraguans were better than any other people in Central America. According to his version of Central American history, before the Sandinistas took over, Nicaragua had been among the leaders in the region in economic growth and culture. The Nicaraguans descended from their Spanish forebears were taller, fairer and more intelligent than the Indians they had conquered. The campesino was a short, dark ancestor of the Indians whom the Latinos believed were destined to be the providers to society's upper class. He explained that one was born into his station in life and ascending from the lower levels of society was virtually impossible.

He cited the Sandinistas as examples of low-class farmers who took the law and the country in their own hands and made a mess of it.

Bermudez should have been the ambassador for the elite of Nicaragua. He treated "his people" with a tolerant condescension that must have been much as slave owners treated their "property." He liked to say, but rarely convinced anyone, that his quarters were as spartan as those of his troops. His refrigerator, his stores of canned food, his liquor cabinet, his inner-spring mattress and his mahogany paneled office gave him away.

And when Bermudez walked among "his people," he had well-armed bodyguards accompanying him. Any of the campesinos foolish enough to try to get too close to him risked a swift death. The men respected him and wanted to believe what he told them was true. Bermudez saw the campesinos as a means to an end, objects to be tolerated until he had achieved his political goals.

Of the thousands of people in this camp, I never knew how many came of their own volition and how many were forcibly conscripted. The faces of the volunteers and the conscripts blended together in a sea of hungry, homeless people acting out the role of soldiers in a war whose goals were little more than indistinct mirages.

Camp propaganda was the only ration not in short supply. Too much information was given to these uneducated men, confusing them and driving ideological wedges between them and the Sandinistas and the policy makers in Washington. I came to believe that if most of these people had been given the true picture of what was happening to their country and why the U.S. had cut off aid, it would have been a far different war.

I could see in the faces of the young soldiers that most were here only because they hoped they could get food and medical care without having to pay for it. Political ideology meant nothing to them. Their desperate need for food, clothing and housing made it difficult to tell which were hard-core fighters who had some sense of direction and which were part of this rebel army simply because it provided some temporary shelter from the storm of oppression in their homeland.

The campesinos' lack of education served the masters well because they could feed off the superstitions, myths and beliefs of poor rural farmers who made up the bulk of the force. The religious beliefs of the people were constantly abused because the Contra leadership convinced them that the Sandinistas were atheists. To outsiders, the commandantes portrayed the soldiers as "Christian commandos" and each soldier was issued a small cross to pin on his cap as an insignia. Catholicism was the predominant religion of this army, but no priests were allowed in camp and only on special holidays was one permitted to minister to the troops.

My quarters at Las Vegas were elegant compared to the wood and plastic hovels of the soldiers. I had a small room in a wooden building next to Bermudez's office. The building contained maps pinpointing all the troop movements of the Contras and the Sandinistas near the border. The maps had been provided by the U.S. Army and CIA.

My hutch had wooden planks up to a level of about four feet and screen from there to the roof. Wooden drop shutters attached to the roof could be lowered for privacy, shade and protection from the frequent rain showers. I had a standard army-issue cot, a table and a lamp. An ordinary Contra fighter would have killed for quarters like these.

From my hut, a dirt path that served as the main artery in the housing area went up the hillside. On one side of the path was a house that served as the office and sleeping quarters of Roberto, commander of the artillery division. Nearby were two other huts. One belonged to Commandante 26 while the other, obviously the communications center, bristled with antennas. The whine of the generator and the constant radio chatter became a part of the background noise at Las Vegas.

A few feet in back of my room was a small tent with a hammock strung across the inside. These were the quarters of Cheppie, son of FDN Secretary of the Directorate Aristides Sanchez. Cheppie was the camp paymaster and handled all currency sent here for purchases. But his real job was to serve as a token symbol of solidarity from the upper class. As the son of Aristides, Cheppie was demonstrating his father's loyalty to the cause. Aristides was magnanimously allowing his son to be at the front while the sons of other FDN directors were safe in the United States.

But Cheppie, who was in his mid-20s and spoke English fluently, was too well-educated to be at the real front. Educated Nicaraguans were hard to find in this campaign and when someone with real education came along he was placed in an administrative position, not in a combat role. There were always plenty of ignorant campesinos for use as cannon fodder.

Cheppie was friendly, curious and eager to give up his dull administrative job and get into combat. But he knew that would never happen unless the FDN directorate saw a political need for an upper-class martyr to further its cause. Cheppie was also extremely loyal to Bermudez, a fact I learned when bits of information I confided to him about Pegasus got back to Bermudez.

Cheppie was like a kid in the wrong school yard at recess, very much out of place in the jungle and not quite sure what to do with himself. More typical of the Contras who had dedicated themselves to this cause was an intense and dangerous Nicaraguan who went by the nom de guerre Pecos Bill.

Pecos was about 5-foot-5, but his size belied his strength. He was incredibly strong, with muscular legs developed from years of walking in the mountains. His calves were larger than my thighs. He had an impressive black handlebar mustache and thick black eyebrows. When I first met him at Las Vegas he was dressed in camouflage BDU pants, an olive drab T-shirt and a well-worn bush hat with jump wings pinned on the front.

Pecos loved Americans and confided in me shortly after I met him that if he could be granted one wish in life it would be to become an American. Pecos thought all Americans were 10 feet tall and unequaled in bravery and intelligence. He tried to act like an American and talk like an American. He was particularly fond of American slang and threw it around in conversation simply because he liked the sound of the strange words and phrases. His favorite American word was "motherfucker." When Pecos talked about people, no matter what their rank or affiliation, they were usually referred to as "motherfucking sons-a-bitches."

Pecos was a delight to have around and I took an immediate liking to him, especially when I learned he was the man who had saved Pulmon from sure death in the streets of Managua years earlier.

Despite his easy-going personality, Pecos had a separate, dark side. He was a one-man war, loyal to the Contra cause for the time being, but loyal to himself above all else.

Pecos was with the Contras because he had no place else to go. A former Somoza Guardia Nacionale lieutenant, he was well-trained in communications, demolitions and guerrilla warfare. He was also well-schooled in murder.

His primary goal in life when I met him was to get revenge against the Sandinistas. According to the story Pecos related to me, he had lived on a 78,000-acre ranch in Nicaragua with his father, a colonel in the Guardia Nacionale. Shortly after the Sandinistas began their guerrilla war, a raiding party came to the ranch while he and his father were away. He claims that the Sandinistas raped and murdered his only sister, then took control of the ranch and turned it into a training base. His father later died of a heart attack and Pecos believed that the Sandinistas were responsible for robbing him of everything that meant anything to him.

After leaving Nicaragua, Pecos drifted to El Salvador, where he became a hit man in the right-wing death squads of Roberto D'-Aubuisson. But when Jose Napoleon Duarte ascended to the presidency, Pecos was forced to flee to Costa Rica. He didn't fare much better there. He was arrested for possession of explosives and given the choice of prison or deportation. He took the latter and came to Honduras, his quest for revenge never satisfied, his thirst for the blood of those he felt responsible for his losses in life unquenched.

Pecos drifted into the FDN as much for simple subsistence as for revenge. He had no passport or identification papers and had become a prisoner of the cause he was supporting. When Pecos took what the FDN offered, he could not leave the country or the FDN unless he went back to Nicaragua.

His only handicap was a love of booze. If Pecos drank, he got into trouble. That was one reason he was almost as feared by the Hondurans as he was by the Sandinistas, the Costa Ricans and the Salvadorans.

On one occasion, Pecos was given the job of leading a group of Contras to a Honduran military base to pick up ammunition. Pecos decided to have a few *cervezas* along the way, since he figured the commandantes wouldn't find out. But, with Pecos, there was no social drinking. He was either sober or he drank until he got roaring drunk. Pecos got so drunk that day that when the Contras arrived at the base the Honduran sentries would not allow them in. Pecos became incensed and ordered the Contras to aim their weapons at the Honduran soldiers. Within minutes the Contras had captured the entire base, setting off a flurry of heated exchanges between the FDN leadership and their Honduran hosts.

The idea of a group of rag-tag guerrillas taking over a military base in a country in which their very existence was denied was a bit much for the Honduran government. It was also more than a little embarrassing for the Honduran military.

The government of Honduras was wary of Bermudez and the intent of the Contra forces massed on its border. The Hondurans feared this threat more than the much-publicized threat from the Sandinistas. The Honduran army had only 17,000 men while the Contras, if pressed, could amass nearly 20,000.

Although the Contras lacked the training of the Honduran soldiers, the tactics used by the two forces were quite different. The Contras had more experience in terrorism and would not hesitate to employ those tactics when their existence was threatened. Although the bulk of the Contra army did not engage in such methods, the hard-core Somocista-led factions could be extremely brutal and occasionally demonstrated this on Honduran civilians.

The Contras often appropriated livestock and provisions from villages and farms. They simply took what they wanted. This practice, although never publicized to a great degree, was an ongoing problem for the Honduran people living near the Nicaraguan border.

Bermudez understood his position in Honduras. The Honduran government had literally given the Contras a portion of their land on the border with Nicaragua. A huge chunk of Honduras disappeared from the map. It was now Contraland.

The military checkpoint that Cisco and I went through on our trip to Las Vegas was actually the last place Honduran troops patrolled. It was the new border. The responsibility for that stretch of border not controlled by Honduras was given to the Contras and all civilians within this area lived under martial law imposed by Bermudez.

The U.S. encouraged this quid pro quo arrangement through aid packages and strong-arm tactics. It was a cozy deal for all parties because it provided a hiding place for the CIA's guerrilla army that was publicly disavowed by both the U.S. and Honduras. Las Vegas became the invisible little country within a country.

Whenever the rebels stepped outside their bounds, it put the Hondurans on edge because they feared some day the Contras might march on Tegucigalpa instead of Managua. So, when Pecos Bill made his little foray into the Honduran military base, it set off all sorts of alarm bells.

The FDN eventually apologized profusely for the incident and promised to keep Pecos Bill on a short leash in the no-man's land between the Honduran troops and the border, unless he was actually in Nicaragua.

Pecos was very valuable to the FDN in spite of all his shortcomings and was often assigned menial duties to keep him busy and out of trouble until his skills as a killer were needed. He never had to endure the harsh punishment meted out to others who broke the rules. I knew I could make good use of Pecos's ability to kill without remorse in Pegasus and asked Bermudez to have him permanently assigned to me. Bermudez reminded me of all Pecos's bad habits and said he was hesitant to approve my request. Pecos was a drunk and could not be controlled, he said.

For Bermudez to call someone an unreliable drunk after all the boozing I had seen him do seemed a bit strange, but I argued I could put Pecos Bill on the straight and narrow if I was given a few days to work with him. I struck a deal with Bermudez. I told him I would guarantee the sobriety and good conduct of Pecos if he were assigned to me. Enrique hesitated, but finally relented.

I knew I had to made an impression on Pecos somehow, so after telling him that he was now under my command, I asked to accompany me on a tour of the perimeter of the base to look over possible sites for building a training facility for Pegasus. We walked across the parade ground and through a wooded area onto a path that led to the village Espanol just south of Las Vegas.

Pecos was pleased with his new assignment and chattered away as we walked, wisecracking about all the "motherfucking sons-a-bitches" FDN commandantes who should not be trusted. He was walking directly in front of me and leading the way down the path when I asked him to stop for a moment. He did so without turning around. I quickly slipped my pistol from its holster and pressed the barrel into the soft skin at the base of his skull.

He flinched slightly when he felt the cold steel against his skin, then was dead still, realizing I had a gun pointed at his brain.

"What's going on?" he asked, his voice strangely calm, considering the circumstances.

"Do you believe I would kill you where you stand?" I said.

"Yes."

"Do you believe I would kill you where you stand?" I repeated, this time more forcefully.

"What have I done to deserve this kind of treatment?" he responded. "Has Commandante 380 ordered my death?"

"I'm acting on my own," I said. "I have to know a few things about you. But if you think I'm joking, just try something because it will be the last thing you ever try."

I told him to turn around and face me. I kept the gun leveled at his head as he turned.

"The one thing I expect out of any man is loyalty and honesty," I told him. "I must have people with me who I know will die before they turn against me. I hardly know you and you certainly don't know me, but I want to assure you I'm not kidding.

"I know about your drinking problem, but there's going to be no drinking on this mission. Business and booze don't mix. I lost my best friend because he couldn't control his drinking and I'm not going to lose anyone else because of it. If you like, I'll kill you now and save you the problem of killing yourself on the installment plan with booze."

Pecos Bill's face turned white as I talked. He knew I was serious.

He promised he would not touch another drop of liquor. I lowered my pistol and we shook hands. We had struck a bond.

When I told Bermudez I would take full responsibility for Pecos Bill, he shook his head and looked at me as if I were crazy.

"You've been warned," he said.

Despite the warning and Pecos Bill's unsavory past, he never caused me any problems after that day.

Las Vegas usually had all manner of strange characters filtering in and out. There were Cubans intent on getting involved in the war, but who had little success. There were Americans in civilian clothes who avoided everyone in camp and obviously were Agency types, despite the prohibition against them. And there were occasional journalists who found favor with the FDN and were permitted access to the camp.

Las Vegas also served as a secret safe house for high-profile Contras who participated in assassination activities throughout the region. Although their presence was publicly denied, murderers and death squad members frequently sought refuge in the camp. One in particular, Colonel Ricardo Lau, better known as Chino, was a favorite breakfast guest of Bermudez. Lau was the chief engineer and trigger man in the assassination of Salvadoran Archbishop Oscar Arnulfo Romero in 1980. Officials in Washington knew of Lau's presence in Contra camps, but vehemently denied repeated accusations that he was being given sanctuary.

Much of the activity involving these people — except for the reclusive Agency personnel — took place on the north side of the barbed wire fence in the officers' "lounge."

Dirt had been gouged out of the hillside on the north side of Bermudez's house and lined with mahogany planks. Ornate designs had been carved in the planks and plants sat along the base of the wall. Wooden benches and a table with a beach umbrella sticking out of it provided a rather incongruous addition to the otherwise military atmosphere of the camp. A colorful parrot in a cage and a baby coatimundi on a leash added to the strangeness of the scene.

This was the "lounge" and dining area for high-ranking officers. Lesser officers and guests ate farther up the hill, where a long wooden table with benches sat under a sheet of light green plastic.

The kitchen was the center of camp activity. It was a rather dilapidated affair, thrown together from scrap lumber. Smoke continuously billowed from under the eave of the roof because there was no chimney, but I later came to see this as advantage because the thick smoke helped keep away bugs. The kitchen operated around-the-clock and meals were considered the social highlight of each day. The Nicaraguan women who worked there usually pulled 12-hour shifts pounding dough into tortillas, ladling out beans and rice and slaughtering animals. It was easy to tell what the meat of the day would be by the screams of the dying pigs or cows at 3 a.m.

The constant pat-pat-pat of hands shaping tortillas became one of those sounds that was so much a part of Las Vegas that when the noise stopped, people jumped and looked around like something was wrong.

Eating was done in shifts. The food was bland and each meal was a carbon copy of the others. You either ate what was served or did without. There were no snacks, no between-meal treats. We were fortunate on the privileged side of the wire because we were fed three times a day. The rest of the camp frequently ate only twice, usually a handful of beans and rice and a tortilla, if that.

Although I had begun to get some sense of the problems with the war and this rebel movement the United States government was backing, I was still a gung-ho adventurer willing to overlook what I considered minor shortcomings in the system for my own shot at combat. It was not until I met Charles Bonnet that I began to get some real sense of what was going on here.

Bonnet was a veteran journalist working for *Time-Life* out of El Salvador. He had been inside Nicaragua with a company-size force of Contras for several weeks and had just returned. His hollow cheeks and sunken eyes told me he was telling the truth. Although he was a bit old for this type of warfare, he told me the only way to tell the true story was to experience the fears and privations of the troops firsthand.

He had been waiting two weeks to return to El Salvador, but the trip had repeatedly been postponed. When he learned about the Americans in camp on a special mission, he said he was not as eager to leave. I agreed to talk with him if he agreed not to photograph me or to pry into the true nature of our mission. I told him when the time came to go public, he would be the first to get the story. He would have fact, not rumor.

Bonnet was a tall, distinguished looking man in his sixties who carried himself with a self-assurance that told me he knew more about the war and the FDN than anyone else I had met. He had covered wars in Vietnam, Korea and El Salvador. He had interviewed both Ho Chi Minh and the legendary General Vo Nguyen Giap, architect of the French defeat at Dien Bien Phu in Vietnam some years earlier. What Bonnet saw in Las Vegas did not particularly impress him.

"Is crazy," he told me in his thick French accent.

"They plan and prepare and march, but they don't fight. Is crazy."

Bonnet complained about the system at Las Vegas and was extremely critical of the Contra movement. I wanted to share some of my observations of La Quinta, but feared critical evaluations of the war would get me sent home. So I held my tongue.

After our few talks in Las Vegas, Bonnet drifted out of my life and disappeared. I later heard he died in El Salvador. But in the short time I knew him, Charles helped open my eyes about the Contras. He knew my beliefs were misguided and tried to push me in the direction of truth about what was going on here.

Although I was generally suspicious of the press, I wanted to tell Bonnet what we were doing because I was proud of it and felt that a little press would help our effort. Some positive publicity would go a long way to build the image of CMA back in the States. But, as I was to learn, the FDN was extremely jealous of news from the front and maintained tight control over information. The FDN made every effort it could to influence the coverage and opinions of journalists given access to its jungle domain.

The FDN would stage events for the media, showing loyal campesinos cheering on their leaders, knowing those events would be seen and heard back in the States. For the most part, this was a misconception perpetrated knowingly by both the Contras and some major news organizations. Positive publicity was valuable propaganda for the FDN because of its frequent budget battles with Congress. I came to expect that of the FDN hierarchy.

What infuriated me about the process was the blatant collusion of some network reporters.

Making News, Contra-Style

Several days after my arrival in Las Vegas, an NBC news crew showed up with Adolfo Calero in tow. Correspondent Fred Francis led the team that consisted of cameraman Manny Alvarez, sound man Juan Caldera and a female producer.

I was busy with the COE troops when they arrived and ignored them until a soldier informed me Enrique wanted to see me in his office. He asked me if I wanted the news people to know about my presence here.

"That wouldn't be a good idea," I said. "But if we're spotted, don't tell them our names or anything about our mission."

Bermudez agreed and at dinner that night, I told Cisco, Pulmon and Pecos to stay away from the cameras and so our cover would remain intact. The Cubans in camp listened closely and also decided to stay out of sight in their tents.

Cisco and I returned to our hutch, turned the lights out and watched through the screens as Bermudez uncorked his private stock of liquor and beer for his guests while the obligatory barbecue was prepared.

Before long, Bermudez walked out of his house and came to where Cisco and I were watching the party. He said Adolfo wanted us to talk to Francis and his crew.

I was astounded. I told him I still didn't think it was a good idea. Bermudez understood what I was trying to say, but I could tell he didn't want to carry the news back to Adolfo. Bermudez turned and left the hut and I thought the matter settled until just a few minutes later, when Adolfo came to the door.

I had never seen the man before, but was immediately impressed by his size. He was about 6-foot-6 and 250 pounds. He had thinning white hair combed straight back from his receding hairline. He had a big smile on his face and I thought if he had a beard, he would have looked a little like Santa Claus with his big nose and red cheeks. I was surprised when I first saw him because he didn't look a bit like his brother, Mario. Adolfo was as neat and as dignified as Mario was slovenly.

Adolfo held out his right hand and patted me on the back with his left.

He said he was glad to meet me after hearing so much about me and tried to impress on me the importance of talking with the news crew. The smell of alcohol on his breath nearly knocked me over. I was immediately irritated. I was here on business, not to party. But Adolfo was the boss and there wasn't much I could do about it.

I told him that if he insisted, I would attend the meeting, but I would not reveal our identities or discuss our mission.

"Of course, of course, that is your choice," he said.

I repeated that under no circumstances did I want to be photographed. I frequently made it clear to FDN leaders that it wasn't because I was camera shy. I was protecting my identity. This unyielding refusal to be photographed added to my image as a mercenary and enhanced the aura of secrecy with which I surrounded myself. The more secretive I became, the more the FDN leadership believed I had been sent to them on a special mission from the U.S. government.

The party was well in progress when Cisco and I got to Bermudez's house and sullenly took our seats at one end of the rough, wooden table. The much-prized canned food had been broken out and there were bottles of beer and liquor all over the table. Francis and his crew sat to our right, Bermudez and Adolfo to the left.

"What are your names?" Francis said, his balding head glistening with sweat.

"I'd rather not say," I replied.

"What are you doing here?" he asked.

"We're here on a humanitarian mission, to see how we can help these people."

You would have thought I had insulted his mother. He was upset by my answer, but the female producer with him wanted to cut through the preliminaries and get right to the heart of the matter.

"We know you are with CMA and we know that you are here for something other than humanitarian reasons," she said accusingly. "If you want to talk, we'll work with you."

I lit a cigarette and looked at her as she leaned forward in anticipation of an answer. But instead of answering, I tried to steer the conversation to the presidential election in the United States. When she saw she was not going to get anything out of me or Cisco, she gave up and sat back in her chair.

Adolfo stepped in and began bragging to Francis about the progress of the Contras' military campaign. With proper funding from Congress, he promised, the Contras would be in Managua in a few months.

What neither I nor Francis knew at the time was that the Contra military campaign was going nowhere. The prohibitions imposed by the Boland Amendment and the FDN's lack of initiative were seeing to that.

Cisco and I took advantage of this unpleasant situation by eating as much canned food as we could hold. The steady diet of beans, rice and tortillas had gotten old rather quickly. As the party got more raucous, we excused ourselves and returned to our hut. We sat in lawn chairs and watched from a distance as the party, complete with guitar-strumming campesinos singing about victory over the dreaded *pericuacos*, the hated Sandinista "mad dogs," moved outside around the barbecue pit.

Like many political and military leaders unsure of themselves or their cause, these members of the FDN directorate found bravery in a bottle. The more they drank the braver they became and the larger their army grew.

It was getting rather late when Adolfo came to our quarters again and asked if I wanted to talk to him. I did because he was the only person who could authorize purchase of the equipment we needed.

He said we should give him a list and he would make sure we got everything on it.

In spite of his apparent drunkenness, Adolfo made it a point to tell me that I should not be in any rush with the "project" because election day was approaching and this could mean renewed aid for the Contras. Adolfo wanted no slip-ups now.

"I would like to hold your operation in reserve in case we don't get that aid," he said.

If that congressional aid was not forthcoming, Adolfo said he had decided to use extreme measures to get the attention of Americans. He planned to use CIA-recommended "spectaculars" to put the war in full view of the international community. He said if the U.S. was unwilling to continue funding the Contras, "the government of Red China will step in with all we need."

Adolfo began to talk in rhymes, often about subjects not related to the war or our participation in it. I assumed everyone was supposed to know what he was talking about, but I certainly didn't.

I quickly wrote out a list of equipment I wanted and handed it to Adolfo. He read it and I saw no surprise in his face, despite the size of my request. I asked for 250 Uzi sub-machine guns, 50,000 rounds of 9mm parabellum ammunition, 2,000 pounds of C-4 plastic explosives and assorted detonation accessories.

"Two ships from Israel are due in port within 30 days and I will personally see that you get your supplies from that shipment," he said.

Adolfo returned to the party, which went on into the night, long after Cisco and I fell asleep.

The camp was unusually quiet the next morning as Adolfo, Bermudez and the NBC crew nursed their hangovers. As I walked out my door, I saw Adolfo heading for the shower. He glanced back at me with a look on his face like he had never seen me before.

Francis soon followed Adolfo to the shower, but I intercepted him to try to smooth over any ill feelings he might have from our meeting the night before.

"I understand," he said. "I know there is a good story down here concerning Americans like you involved with the conflict."

"I can't tell you exactly what's planned," I said. "But someday soon I may release information that will curl your hair."

"When that happens let me know and I'll see that Tom Brokaw comes down to do the story personally."

He gave me two telephone numbers to call when I was ready to talk and we shook hands.

Adolfo and Bermudez were scheduled to give speeches to the troops that morning and after breakfast thousands of Contras began moving toward the parade ground. The road was lined with soldiers and their families, most of whom had been awakened an hour or more before dawn to get to the site on time. None seemed particularly enthused about getting up that early to listen to propaganda speeches, but it broke the monotony of sitting in camp waiting for something to happen.

That explained why the camp had been so quiet. All of the troops were moving south, out of the base toward an assembly area several miles away.

Our trucks, their horns blaring, pushed through the column of soldiers trudging towards the staging area. The soldiers carried all their battle gear. Many of them had antiquated weapons. Some of those on the road were walking wounded and others were being carried to increase the numbers in attendance for the speeches.

I had not seen the entire complement of troops in Las Vegas, so I had no real sense of their numbers. Not until our truck began moving down the road past a seemingly endless line of green-clad soldiers streaming south out of the base did I have some appreciation for the size of this army.

At one point, I decided to walk with the troops, but I soon cut this short because I was not prepared for the difficult terrain. I was still getting acclimated to the environment and food and I had little energy for any strenuous hiking. Within minutes of my decision to walk, I jumped back on the truck carrying Cheppie as he chronicled the trip with his camera.

Our truck convoy turned off the road into a large field that could have held three football stadiums. It was surrounded by tall weeds and at the southern edge was a tall mountain. It took over an hour to get all the troops into the area and once they were in place the trucks carrying the camp prima donnas, the COE, arrived. The COE troops were to be highlighted for this event and they were brought to the front of the huge crowd of soldiers to give the impression that the army was much better dressed and much better armed than it actually was.

The truck with the NBC camera was placed at the southeast edge of the field and Cisco and I hopped onto it so we would be behind the camera. That way we could be sure we would not show up on any of the tapes.

When the scene was finally set, Enrique began his speech to the troops. He spoke with a great deal of emotion. He waved his hands in the air and clenched his fists. Every so often the soldiers would raise their weapons above their heads and yell approval. Pecos Bill sat near me and tried to translate some of the speech, but he did little more than mumble because he was afraid Enrique would overhear him and chew his ass for talking during the speech.

The scene was almost religious. Between oratorical tirades by Bermudez, there was dead quiet, except an occasional rattle of equipment. I could see that Enrique had the attention of the soldiers. His words seemed to mean something to these men because their eyes lit up when he unleashed his passionate rhetoric. He finished his speech in a thunderous roll of applause that echoed off the hills and swallowed us in a wall of sound.

Adolfo had been standing expressionless with Fred Francis while Bermudez spoke. When it was Adolfo's turn to speak, he strode to the front of the men. The sun had come up in all its tropical glory and the temperature was going up with it. The men seemed to be getting restless.

I felt sorry for Adolfo as he began to speak. The uniform he was wearing obviously was not his own. The pants legs were rolled up above his shoes, his shirt was too tight and the cap too small for his large head. He had arrived in civilian clothing, but wanted to look like a soldier for this moment of staged glory before his troops so had borrowed a uniform that did not fit.

Adolfo began to bellow at the crowd in much the same fashion as Bermudez, but there was a striking difference in reception. The men looked at Adolfo like they had been ordered to do so. When he paused for applause, there was an awkward hesitation before the men held their weapons above their head and gave a desultory cheer, as if they had been given the wrong cue.

If Bermudez had asked the men to march on Managua that moment, they would have done so. If Adolfo had asked that, they would have looked to Burmudez for his orders.

Adolfo seemed to sense that he was losing ground and frequently turned to Francis and asked for re-takes of the shots. Francis wasn't pleased with the way things were going, either, because he came to the camera truck and talked with Manny Alverez about how this looked on camera. Alverez told him the crowd looked thin and in order for it to appear that thousands of angry Contras had gathered here, something had to be done.

Francis shouted across the field to Adolfo to have the men bunched closed together and to respond with much more vigor to the speech. The shot would show Calero shaking his fists at the crowd denouncing the Sandinistas and what they had done to Nicaragua.

I didn't know much about journalism, but I thought this was tampering with the truth.

"Isn't that what you folks might call 'staging?' " I asked Francis.

"What they don't know in New York won't hurt them," he said curtly.

I merely shrugged my shoulders.

"Maybe they do things differently down here," I thought to myself.

I didn't realize how differently. But it was all part of building the legend of the army designed for other purposes.

4

Begin the Beguine: Mercenary Intentions*

A voice was jabbering urgently in my ear in Spanish and a hand was nudging me on the shoulder. I crawled slowly out of a deep sleep and opened my eyes to see the frantic face of one of Bermudez's bodyguards looming out of the darkness over me. There was barely a hint of dawn in the sky.

When I did not respond to the bodyguard's Spanish, he went and woke Pecos Bill to translate.

"Enrique needs to see you, now," said Pecos.

I dressed quickly and walked down the hill to Bermudez's office. The huge camp was beginning to stir to life. Roosters were crowing and I could smell the smoke from hundreds of cooking fires. Bermudez was outside waiting for me, pacing nervously in the dirt, a grim look on his face.

"We just picked up radio traffic that the Sandinistas are going to launch an air raid against Las Vegas," he said. "They've never done this before. I think they know Adolfo is here."

I looked at the sky. It was heavy with low clouds that pressed down on the ridges north and south of the camp. There was no way any pilot was going to get through that soup and it would be at least mid-morning before the tropical sun burned it off.

Bermudez didn't buy that, though.

"Do you have field glasses?" he said.

"Yes."

"Take them up on COE hill and keep watch."

---

* The Beguine is a South American dance.

Too sleepy to argue, I retrieved my binoculars and trudged up COE hill to watch for Sandinista aircraft. The anti-aircraft batteries had been placed on alert and I found two very young, very nervous soldiers sitting behind a decrepit Chinese heavy machine gun in the middle of a circle of orange dirt. Neither looked like he had ever fired the gun before, yet this was virtually the last line of defense against any air attack.

The gunners looked to me for advice or consolation. I had neither. I considered my own stupidity briefly for standing so close to this bull's eye emblazoned on top of the ridge. The entire camp was an inviting target, but these anti-aircraft emplacements with their bright orange circles of dirt were the most obvious targets. I slowly edged away from the young gunners, leaving them to think what they would about me.

The cloud mass slowly settled into the valleys, making the camp invisible from the air. I was above the clouds. The peaks of the mountains and small hills protruded through the clouds and I considered this a blessing because I knew hundreds of people would die if Sandinista aircraft attacked.

I strained to hear the sound of jet engines or the familiar popping of helicopter blades. There was nothing. The silence was eerie. Not even the birds were flying this morning.

I did my duty and stayed on the hill for nearly two hours until the clouds began to burn away and it became apparent there would be no air raid.

Adolfo was long gone by the time I reported back to Bermudez. As soon as Adolfo had heard of a possible air raid, he hopped into his car and scooted back to Tegucigalpa. Not only had his speech to the troops gone badly, he had been chased out of his jungle sanctuary by phantom aircraft.

"Either your intelligence reporting system is flawed or they got some bad information," I told Bermudez. "Was your intelligence from Contra sources or U.S. sources?"

"I don't know where it came from," he said. "But I have no choice but to take everything as a serious threat."

I got the impression that this could have been nothing more than Bermudez's way of chasing Adolfo out of camp. It was difficult to tell when Bermudez was up to something, but I realized that I had to learn to read him better if I hoped to achieve what I wanted to do here. Getting on his bad side was the worst thing I could do, because he was the ultimate authority in this camp.

I did not argue with him about his decision to alert the camp because of faulty intelligence. But the more I thought about it, the less plausible an air raid or any military action against Las Vegas seemed.

The Sandinistas were not foolish enough to risk flying deep into Honduran territory to attempt to take out the FDN leadership. Honduran and U.S. radar along the border was impenetrable and any unauthorized crossing from the south would have brought an immediate response from the powerful Honduran air force units based at Tegucigalpa and San Pedro Sula.

Catching the Sandinistas in an overt air attack could have been the spark that ignited this guerrilla war into a major conflict involving U.S. forces. The Sandinistas knew that and were not about to initiate any military action that would play right into the hands of those who wished for such an incident. But explaining this to Bermudez was like trying to explain advanced calculus to a kindergarten class. It just didn't register. He wasn't bright enough militarily to grasp the concept.

Still, I saw this as an opportunity to try to convince him that changes were needed in the air defenses and layout of the entire camp. He seemed irritated by my suggestion and dismissed me by saying I should talk with Commandante 26 about restructuring the base. This was his way of putting off something he did not want to deal with.

It would have been easy to sit in judgment of Bermudez, Las Vegas and all the problems I had seen with the Contras during my first few days in camp. But, in many ways, I was no better than him or any of his commandante stooges. I was here to take advantage of the situation and put together a group with one mission — to kill people in the name of a cause that I was rapidly losing faith in.

In order to fulfill my mission I would have to overlook the misfeasance and malfeasance I was witnessing on a daily basis. I would have to hold hands with the devil himself. I had become a true mercenary.

I was intent on implementing Pegasus as soon as possible and got an appointment with Bermudez to discuss the operational aspects of it. Bermudez generally had a line of commandantes waiting to see him during the day, but he quickly dismissed them to talk with Cisco and me. Pulmon reluctantly accompanied us to translate.

As I explained my vision of Pegasus, Bermudez nervously rubbed his hands across his face and hair. He was trying to understand what I was laying out before him, but was having problems understanding not only the concept of it, but our English explanations.

Bermudez was embarrassed by his ignorance of English. He refused to admit that he didn't understand it because such an admission would have detracted from his image.

It was also obvious Bermudez lacked experience as a field commander. He tried to make up for his lack of expertise by bragging about his military training. He was particularly proud of having attended the School of the Americas at Fort Benning, Georgia, a training ground for future dictators whose alumni included the likes of Panama's Manuel Noriega.

Bermudez tried to convince Cisco and me that the Guardia Nacionale was misunderstood and was the victim of bad press. The unit had been a staunch ally of the United States in Central America, he said. But I could not help remembering news footage I had seen several years earlier of one of these "misunderstood" allies executing an American journalist.

Bermudez began to squirm as I related the plan to train the special Pegasus force at Las Vegas. He said he was opposed to such an operation because this camp was supposed to be secret. He did not want the ordinary soldiers to witness any of the training that would involve innovative tactics and special equipment. He wanted the Pegasus unit trained on a small Contra ranch near the village of San Marcos de Colon, nearly 80 miles from Las Vegas.

I objected.

I argued training Pegasus troops at Las Vegas would give other soldiers confidence to know that this unit was preparing to enter Nicaragua to deal a fatal blow to the Sandinista infrastructure. Although Bermudez didn't like the idea of the Pegasus unit training at his base, he liked the idea of getting credit for the operation. I was willing to let him believe anything as long as we could remain at Las Vegas. He told us he would pass on the plan to the FDN directorate before making a final decision.

As Cisco and I were about to leave the meeting, Bermudez asked us to wait for a few minutes. He walked to the door and spoke in Spanish to one of his bodyguards. The guard quickly scampered up the hill to the COE encampment and within minutes came back down, followed by two camouflage-clad soldiers.

The two warily entered Bermudez's office, took off their caps and sat down. They were introduced as the commanders of COE. First in command was a short, muscular soldier named Gustavo. Second in command was Aesop, a tall, light-skinned man who looked strangely out of place because of his Arab features.

I thought this was just a general introduction, but Bermudez had other ideas. Without fanfare he announced to Gustavo that command of COE was being turned over to me. I was shocked. Gustavo didn't blink an eye. He rose and saluted me, then turned and walked out the door with Aesop.

Pulmon seemed more stunned than I. He immediately started talking to Bermudez in Spanish about the decision. Bermudez said he felt COE troops were the only ones advanced enough to qualify for Pegasus. He also wanted them to receive more training. The decision would stand.

When we left the meeting, Cisco and Pulmon expressed concern that I had come on too strong with Bermudez. Neither had ever heard a gringo speak to Commandante 380 as I just had. But I told them if we were to implement Pegasus, Bermudez would have to understand this was not some average cross-border raid. This was a plan that would have major international ramifications.

"You're on your own on this," Cisco said. "I got you to Las Vegas, but that's as far as I go."

Cisco knew Pegasus would be a virtual suicide mission and wanted nothing to do with it. I had been candid with everyone about potential casualty rates. I predicted that chances for survival were 80-20 against because of the nature of the mission.

My plan called for a strike force of 240 Nicaraguans and 50 Americans. We would be airlifted from Ilopango military air base in El Salvador and inserted by parachute into Managua. After we destroyed our primary target — the dam north of Managua — and assassinated key Sandinista leaders, including Daniel Ortega, Roman Catholic Bishop Miguel Obando y Bravo and Interior Minister Tomas Borge, we would hit targets of opportunity in our retreat to the western coast. What troops were left would be extracted by small boats.

On a mission of this magnitude and obvious daring, I felt that the 80-20 odds were acceptable. No one disagreed.

A Chance for Change

It was eight days before my baggage finally caught up with me. The Contra uniform I wore detracted from my image because I looked like everyone else. Command presence is as much mental as it is physical and without my gear, I could not present the proper appearance for the troops.

The CIA had decided to put the Contras in uniforms because it wanted them to stand out from other guerrilla groups. These were democracy's guerrillas, and had to be well-dressed to differentiate them from Communist guerrillas. But the uniforms had to be cheap and easy to manufacture locally.

Most armies wore different shades of camouflage, olive drab or black Battle Dress Utility uniforms. The thinking was to find a color for the Contra uniforms somewhere between Honduran olive drab and Sandinista tiger-stripes. That would make identification in the field easier.

Unfortunately, the color chosen was the exact shade of green used in the uniforms worn by repair technicians at Sears-Roebuck. This odd green uniform was very distinctive, but brought the Contras the unwelcomed nickname "The Sears-Roebuck Army."

The numerous seabags I had shipped south were stuffed with gear I knew could not be obtained here. I had purchased special 7.62 x 59 cartridges for sniper weapons, field glasses, compasses and canned food. Tom Posey had given me a tripod and spare barrel for an M-60 machine gun. I had enough equipment and clothing for three men.

As I was sorting through the seabags, the truck driver who brought them into camp handed me a green metal box. I didn't remember this being part of my gear. The box held a AN/PVS-1 night vision rifle scope.

I was surprised. I was told it had been brought to Honduras by the Parker-Powell group and was being held in Las Vegas because the men did not know how to operate it, had no batteries for it and could not obtain the proper mounts to place it on an M-16 rifle.

I had purchased several boxes of rank insignia in New Orleans and was eager to issue it to those troops who would participate in Pegasus. It was customary among the Contras to avoid ranks. There were commandantes and there were troops. Class differences did not permit anything in between. But I was intent on starting a new tradition to create some incentive for the troops in my command.

I gave myself the gold oak leaf of a major. I gave Pecos Bill and Pulmon captain's bars because they were to be my squad leaders.

Pecos immediately put his rank insignia on his old Guardia Nacionale beret and walked into the main compound so that everyone could see he was now an officer in an elite unit. He wanted all the commandantes who had given him a hard time in the past to see him.

Pulmon was a little hesitant to display his rank, but finally pinned it on his cap and looked at himself in the mirror. He seemed to take great delight in this simple gift. He put on a clean uniform, spit-shined his paratrooper boots that he usually wore only on special occasions and strutted out of his hut like he owned the world.

Posey had sent along some old Marine insignias and I immediately began handing them out to my COE troops. The men were reluctant to wear them at first, fearing their commandantes might object.

When Pulmon told them I was their new commander, they accepted the gifts. It was like Christmas for them. There was a symbolism in these small gifts that gave the soldiers confidence in their own abilities they never realized they had. The more patches and insignias on their uniforms, the braver they became. That most of the men were lowly privates did not matter to them. A little piece of brass on their collars meant they were something more than they had been the day before.

Gustavo and Aesop ignored the insignias. I made them captains, but they rarely wore the bars. It was their way of letting me know that it meant nothing to them. They had been in the jungle too long and had been under the thumb of the commandantes too long to believe there was any way some skinny, blue-eyed gringo was going to change everything in one day with a few pieces of brass.

But for the ordinary soldier, this was a demonstration that there were differences. The rank insignias made each of them different and special. They had never known any military individualism because there had always been just the commandantes and those who served them.

As small as the gesture was, many of the soldiers would never again view the system as they had before.

Time began to freeze after Adolfo left and I began to rethink my plan of action. I had assumed that I would be able to immediately implement training for Pegasus. But other than being installed as the figurehead commander of COE, I was not permitted to do anything. I was told by Bermudez not to train any troops until Pegasus began to receive equipment from Mario. It was apparent that Mario was sitting on his hands because neither equipment nor information was coming in from him or Posey. I went through the motions each day of dressing, eating and walking through the camp, but I yearned to do much more.

The training regimen of the Contra commanders was the only thing that sparked any interest in me. I tried to discuss training methods with the instructors, but all of them had specific notions about how troops should be trained and most of those notions were quite strange.

Loud explosions could be heard throughout the day from the direction of the baseball field at the base of a hill where Tigrillo's Tiger Battalion was bivouacked. This particular training routine consisted of groups of soldiers gathering on the field and trainers standing atop the hill and throwing grenade simulators into their midst. The trainers would tell the men that this was what it was like in an artillery attack.

Hand grenade simulators contain about one-quarter pound of TNT and can be just as lethal as the real thing. Many frightened young soldiers were wounded unnecessarily in this manner, but the trainers seemed to get a big kick out of watching them scurrying about trying to get away from the bombardment.

I raised the question of the necessity of this type training with Commandante 26. He merely shrugged his shoulders and said it was necessary to demonstrate the shock of combat to the men. I told him that this method was more likely to frighten and injure the troops than to prepare them for combat, but my pleas fell on deaf ears.

The Contras' training methods for urban guerrilla training warfare were much the same. The only difference was that the troops frequently were trapped inside the small dwellings used for the exercise when the grenade simulators were thrown in. The concussion of these blasts out in the open could render a man senseless. In a confined space, they sometimes proved fatal. These losses were deemed "acceptable" by the commandantes. They truly believed this method of training served some purpose other than mere entertainment to break up the long, dull days.

I saw the waste and uselessness of this training. But I felt that raising questions about it would alienate me from the power structure. I knew I had to overlook this pointless abuse of people and military resources for the opportunity to put together the Pegasus team. But my patience was wearing thin as I envisioned myself doing nothing more over the next few months than watching war games and getting a good tan while all the planning of Pegasus fell apart and CMA's role diminished.

Cisco had been giving me a difficult time about remaining in Las Vegas. The air raid had spooked him. He wanted nothing to do with a Sandinista raid on the camp so I told him to pack his gear and return to the U.S. with a letter for Mario and Posey instructing them to get their asses in gear.

Before leaving New Orleans I had given Mario half the $10,000 Fortier had sent. I told him to hold it until we needed specific supplies or until I needed more money. My letter instructed Mario to take $3,500 and give it to Posey to purchase supplies. I was reluctant to trust Cisco with the letter, but felt I had no other choice. I was taking a big chance, but I had to do something to get this operation moving.

In the letter I also told Mario our trip had been a success. I told him I had established a good relationship with Bermudez and had gained his confidence. I said the mission, now known as Pegaso, was seen by Adolfo and Bermudez as the centerpiece of all future Contra operations.

I praised the commandantes and spoke eloquently about Las Vegas. I was particularly careful to avoid relating any of the misgivings I had about the shortcomings here because I knew they would get back to the FDN leadership. I also appealed to Mario's ego. He had never been in combat and I strongly suggested that he was the de facto leader of Pegaso. I thought perhaps that might stir him into action.

If left to their own devices, Mario and Posey would do nothing about Pegaso except talk it to death. Their concern was raising money and propagandizing the war, not implementing specific programs.

That was the way the FDN-CMA relationship worked in the States, though. Posey was a socks toter for Mario. CMA members got their rocks off going to New Orleans to load the planes with supplies and try to top each other with mythical war stories. Only Parker and Powell had played for keeps, and they were dead.

Enrique, Adolfo and the FDN loved the American volunteers, but only because of the sophisticated equipment, clothing and battle gear they brought to the frontier. The relationship worked as long as none of the warmongering volunteers showed up at the airport in Tegucigalpa ready to lend their expertise, not money or equipment, to the cause. Those who did were quickly ushered onto another plane bound for the U.S.

Election Day Blues

The uncertainty of the 1984 presidential election in the United States hung over Las Vegas like a cloud. Despite Reagan's overwhelming lead in the polls and the ineptitude displayed on the campaign trail by Democratic challenger Walter Mondale, the people in this jungle city were worried. They knew their very existence hung in the balance.

With Reagan, they were assured four more years.

With Mondale, their futures were in doubt.

No one in Las Vegas was more concerned about the election than Bermudez. Not only was his job at stake, but so were his dreams for power.

Bermudez believed this election would change the face of the war because Reagan and the FDN were irrevocably linked. They fed off one another. Reagan's entire political philosophy in Latin America was based on his support of the Contras. The FDN saw Reagan as its linchpin to recovering Nicaragua.

The campesinos looked at Reagan as if he were some sort of god who could and would singlehandedly deliver them from the Sandinistas and return them to Managua after the election. Somehow they had gotten it into their minds that if Reagan won, the 82nd Airborne Division would parachute into camp the next day and lead them into Nicaragua.

The night of the election, Bermudez invited Cisco, who was still waiting for transportation back to Tegucigalpa, Pulmon, Pecos and me to listen to the election results being broadcast over Voice of America. Bermudez had begun drinking early in the day, and I knew he wanted to elicit my assurances that Reagan would win.

Bermudez's insecurities and fantasies bubbled to the surface whenever he drank. The more he drank the more he talked and the more he revealed of himself.

Nightfall had brought an eerie silence to the camp. Fires dotted the hillsides and small groups of soldiers could be seen clustered around the few radios below the fence. Their weary faces were worried, yet hopeful.

Despite any misgivings he might have had, Bermudez ordered a pig roasted for what he hoped would be a victory party. A large pile of timber had been placed on the parade ground for the bonfire that would be the center of activity for the troops when festivities began. Guitar players were brought above the fence and as the ballot results began coming in, the excitement grew. The camp vibrated with expectation as states piled up behind Reagan's campaign juggernaut.

The network projections had Reagan the big winner early, but Bermudez was not about to celebrate until it was official. As we waited, he drank rum and stuffed canned ham and crackers into his mouth. And as he drank, he gathered strength from the booze and the emotions that flowed from the thousands of hopeful troops.

"Adolfo's a clown and a lackey for the CIA," Bermudez said.

"How do you mean?" I asked innocently.

Bermudez explained through his interpreter that Adolfo had convinced himself that he ran the army, when in fact he had absolutely no control over these men. Bermudez wanted it known that he was in charge here, not Adolfo, not the FDN directorate.

Yet it was evident he was a man torn between the reality of the situation and his own drunken fantasies. He wanted to believe he was in control of the big picture, when in fact his every action was controlled by the ultimate puppeteer, Uncle Sam.

"You don't know yet, Flaco? You haven't figured it out?" Bermudez said.

"Figured what out?"

"Our mission here is not to go into Nicaragua and take territory. We're not here to invade Nicaragua. We're here to create an environment that will allow your soldiers, your Marines, to enter this war."

I was stunned. I thought the whole object was to take dirt. This explained why plans for Pegaso had been stalled. This explained why so many of the Contras sat in Honduras. This explained why no provisional government had been set up in northern Nicaragua.

"There's no need for that, Flaco," said Bermudez. "That's not our mission."

"You mean all those soldiers out there will never get back to Nicaragua?"

"Sure, we'll get back. But we don't invade. We ambush here, we ambush there, then we come back and rest. Sooner or later the Sandinistas will slip up. Some day they'll do something to invite the Marines down for an invasion."

Bermudez walked into the back room of his hut where he kept his file cabinets and maps and motioned me to follow.

"Let me show you something, Flaco."

He opened one end of a large cardboard tube and took out three maps of Nicaragua. They were three separate plans for invasion using U.S. troops, he said. The plans were more than a year old, delivered by the CIA.

"This is what will happen when the time is right," he said. "It probably will start after a border attack by the Sandinistas. Maybe real, maybe not. We both know there is no real border around here."

Bermudez rambled on about the invasion, but I heard little of it. Finally I understood the millions of dollars being spent on this army. It was merely to provide the means of sparking a border confrontation that would allow for introduction of American troops.

Despite these invasion plans and the restrictions placed on him by his U.S. controllers, Bermudez was not content to sit in Las Vegas. He was getting restless and wanted to do something spectacular to stir up everyone. He wanted to march across the border and take the town of Santa Clara, where he would set up a provisional government. He knew it would be easy to take the town because troop strength there was cut following the Parker-Powell incident in September.

Holding the town was another matter. I told him we would need heavy artillery and a number of anti-aircraft weapons. The 122mm mortars sitting at La Quinta would be the key to the defense.

Bermudez wanted Santa Clara not so much for the military advantage it would bring him as for the political power. He wanted some control and had none in this government in exile. The army was a paper tiger in Honduras, always threatening but never striking.

Bermudez told me many times when he was drinking that if he had his way, he would have emptied Las Vegas and marched into Nicaragua, sacrificing every one of those soldiers to be the first into Managua. To him, it was a matter of raw, brute force. The political subtleties escaped him.

But Bermudez knew neither the FDN directorate nor its CIA handlers would permit such a bold and unexpected move. This made Santa Clara all that much more inviting to him, because he wanted to believe he needed the permission of no one to pull off such an operation.

It was the booze talking as much as anything. I always thought if the U.S. government really wanted the Contras to take Nicaragua, all it would have had to do was get the commandantes tanked up. They would have marched right into the teeth of the Sandinista defense. Liquor was the ticket to Fantasyland for these has-been warriors. When they drank, they relived the glory days under the protection of the dictator Somoza.

Many believed those glory days would return if Reagan was sent back to the White House.

Each time electoral votes were added to Reagan's rapidly increasing total, Bermudez proposed a toast. Except for Commandante 26, Pecos Bill and me, the crowd around the table got louder, more boisterous and drunker with each announcement.

I stuck to Pepsi, while 26 and Pecos abstained in deference to me.

It was apparent Reagan would win by landslide, but Bermudez wanted to hear the votes cast from the state that would put him over the top and into the White House for four more years before officially beginning the celebration. It finally happened about 11 p.m.

When the announcement that Reagan had won came over the radio, it was like an electrical charge surged through the camp. The news could not have spread any faster if everyone had his own radio. Bermudez was smiling broadly, offering more toasts and shaking hands all around.

Cisco left the party briefly and returned with his Uzi. Outside Bermudez's hutch, he pointed the weapon to the sky and shot off the entire magazine in celebration.

It was like pulling the cork out of a bottle of champagne.

Suddenly, the sky lit up as thousands of Contras fired their weapons into the air. Tracer rounds made graceful red and orange arcs through the night sky. The ground rumbled with explosions. Rifle grenades, hand grenades and grenade simulators were unleashed in a celebratory orgy of firepower.

I walked to the door with Bermudez to witness a spectacle unlike anything I had ever seen or would ever see again. Thousands of rounds were being fired skyward, creating a pyrotechnic display that could never be reproduced. I felt a surge of excitement for these people as they celebrated what they truly believed would be their emancipation, their freedom.

Although Bermudez was quite pickled by this time, he began to realize the celebration was needlessly burning up valuable ammunition. He began shouting to the commandantes to order a cease fire. His voice could hardly be heard over the steady automatic rifle fire and the jangling of spent shell casings hitting the ground all around us.

Finally, he grabbed Commandante 26 and pushed him toward the fence, ordering him to stop the firing and this waste of ammo. 26 had no more luck than Bermudez and had no real desire to stop the troops, who by then had lit the bonfire and were dancing around it chanting slogans about killing the hated *pericuacos*.

26 decided to join the celebration and pulled a parachute flare from the vast store of gadgets he kept in his hutch. He popped the flare directly above the troops on the parade ground, lighting up the area like it was day. The bright orange flare slowly drifted back to earth to the cheers of the men.

The cheers inspired 26 to continue his fireworks show. Everyone in camp referred to 26 as "Dirty Harry" because of the huge .44 magnum pistol he carried in a camouflaged shoulder holster, similar to the Clint Eastwood character. He wore a different uniform on each day and wanted us to believe that he carried a great deal of weight in camp, but he was terrified of Bermudez.

On this night, despite Bermudez's anger over the waste of ammunition, 26 was caught up in the celebration. Shielding himself from Bermudez, 26 popped another flare. Only this one wasn't aimed properly and it careened off a gun emplacement and fell into the COE barracks. A fire broke out almost instantly and soldiers could be seen scampering out of the trench that surrounded the barracks like rats from a burning ship.

Bermudez jumped in his truck and headed for the bonfire to try to put some limits on the celebration. 26 didn't notice Bermudez was gone and popped another flare in the direction of the baseball field. This one skittered across the ground and nearly hit the truck.

26 was mortified. He looked like a man facing sure execution. Had the flare hit Bermudez, there would have been no place in Las Vegas, or Honduras, for 26 to hide. 26 jogged back to his hut, telling us he would return with more flares. We didn't see him for nearly two days.

The Sandinistas down on the border must have been absolutely terrified to see this spontaneous display of firepower. They must have thought 50,000 soldiers were on their way across the border.

I felt a strange mixture of pride and amusement over that night. I wondered if the stuffed shirts in the Republican party would ever know that the biggest celebration of Reagan's reelection was staged by his non-voting campesino constituents living in hovels on the Honduran border.

I went to bed late but couldn't sleep. Something nagged at me. I tossed and turned until dawn.

Mornings in Las Vegas generally were cool, the camp covered by a light tropical mist that didn't burn off until after 7 o'clock. Usually I would walk down to the fence to try to catch a glimpse of soldiers returning from missions in Nicaragua. The number of casualties being carried to the hospital compound gave me some sense of how the campaign was going. Other mornings I would watch the soldiers foraging for small amounts of wood for their cook fires.

Something was different this morning. The entire camp was still. I thought perhaps the celebration had taken a toll on everyone.

Pecos joined me as I walked down into the camp.

"What's wrong with everybody this morning?" I asked him.

"These bastards are just a bunch of lazy sons-a-bitches," he said.

But the faces of the soldiers told me something else was wrong. They looked like kids who had waited up all night for a lost puppy to return home. The puppy didn't come home.

An election hangover was affecting the entire camp. These people actually expected to see U.S. troops falling out of the sky over the base when they rolled out of their bunks and jungle hammocks that morning. They believed all the political rhetoric they had been hearing about the war.

These unfortunate Nicaraguans living in wretched poverty were holding out false expectations about our political system. They had no idea what the election meant in real terms. They didn't know Reagan would be severely limited in his efforts to help the Contras by a reluctant Congress.

The soldiers in Las Vegas had no conception of genuine democracy. They believed if a president was reelected it was the same as giving a dictator free rein.

It was the beginning of the end for the Contras, and I think many of them realized it. They lost their faith in the United States that day. They were left without hope to face uncertainty and poverty alone. There was a sense of abandonment evident in their faces. There was no will, no spirit evident in the camp that morning. I felt sad for them, because after that nothing would be same.

A strange mental paralysis set in as they realized they would be there for the duration of the war, no matter how long it lasted. It could be many more miserable years before they went home, if they went at all.

5

Amazing Grace:
Another False Start

Cisco left the day after the election. I had instructed him to get to Posey as soon as possible to begin arranging the equipment and recruits for Pegaso. I told him to stay in close touch with me so that I would not be left here wondering what was happening in the States. Time hung heavy on me as each dismal day became a prelude to another dismal day. My time was spent walking about the camp watching soldiers mill around having as little to do as I. Some days were punctuated by meetings with Enrique to listen to his propaganda about border skirmishes and Contra victories taking place throughout Nicaragua. All I wanted was action and I was getting very tired of this waiting.

I was totally unaware of the fact that there was no telephonic communication between Las Vegas and La Quinta. Administrative staff people often spoke of talking with personnel at La Quinta, but they left out the part about the conversations being held over single-side band radio. I pestered Enrique each day about whether he had received a message from Mario or Cisco. Every day the same reply, "No."

My irritation with this stall in events overtook me and I finally went to Bermudez to tell him that I wished to be taken to La Quinta immediately. He advised that I should stay in Vegas for a while longer because I couldn't push the operation any faster from La Quinta. I begged to disagree. I insisted that I had to return and apprise the Directorate of the advanced equipment CMA planned to bring into the country. This whetted Enrique's appetite. He couldn't wait to get his hands on more gadgets. He relented and told me that Romano, the FDN's version of a mailman, was leaving early the next day for La Quinta and that I should accompany him, along with Pulmon, because he wanted me to travel only with those he trusted and knew were capable of defending me.

I called Pulmon and Pecos to my quarters to advise them that I was about to leave camp. I instructed Pecos to sleep in my room while I was away so he could protect my personal belongings and the equipment that I would leave behind. I stressed that Enrique would be watching him closely looking for any reason to bust him while I was not present. Pecos lamented that he wished he could travel with me, but understood his duty and would try his best.

Our travel back to La Quinta started around three o'clock in the morning. The trip would be a duplication in agony much like the first ride to Vegas. The only difference was that I drove part of the way back to Tegus because Romano was beat from making a non-stop round trip and Pulmon did not know how to drive this vehicle. Driving provided a small distraction from the grueling ride, but the end result was identical to the first. We arrived fifteen hours later at La Quinta dead tired. I sought out the musty bed I first slept in and dropped like a rock into a deep sleep.

I awakened after ten hours of rest and was greeted by the usual stench and filthiness of La Quinta. My hunger was so intense that I took a very brief shower and almost ran to the kitchen for some of that good ole goat cheese. I was surprised how good the cheese was beginning to taste, especially since my diet had been altered to meals of beans and rice, then rice and beans.

Pulmon had risen much earlier and was out getting his daily exercise. He walked into the mess hall to inquire how I felt. I told him that I had to get better food and better quarters than La Quinta offered. I told him that I wanted to leave the base and go into Tegucigalpa to a hotel, for this place just wasn't going to cut it for me. He acted a little shocked about my plan, but stated that he to had planned to go off base for a while to visit one of his girlfriends. I told him that I had to telephone Mario and for him to advise camp Commandante Cirro that I was leaving and have Romano put the call through to New Orleans.

HonduTel, the telephone company of Honduras, was not the most reliable carrier in the region, but far better than the majority of Central American countries. I was never sure who listened in on international calls because Honduras was riddled with various "spook" types who reported on each other's movements via phone. My call got through to Mario, who told me that Cisco had been arrested in Houston for possession of drugs, the Valium he had smuggled out of El Salvador. I could guess what had happened, but declined to comment further over the telephone until Mario stated that Cisco had told him that the drugs were mine. Then I went ballistic. The sorry son of a bitch had lied to cover his tracks and talked Mario into giving him my money under the pretext of legal expenses instead of the implicit instruction sent in the letter from me.

I told Mario that I would fill him in about all details on my visit to Las Vegas when I returned, but first I would have to arrange for a plane ticket. I told him that I was not going to stay at La Quinta any longer because the living conditions were terrible. At first Mario felt that I might experience trouble re-entering the country, but his curiosity was greater than his judgment about my returning. I told Mario that Enrique was on board with operation Pegasus and I had obtained information necessary to put our plans into action. This was very good news to Mario. He then began urging me to return to New Orleans even if I had to disembark at another port of entry. I told him that I would try to call him back with a flight schedule when I obtained one, but I had to first locate a Tan Sasha Airline office to exchange my TACA return ticket.

Pulmon waited for me to finish my conversation and told me that he was ready to depart. He handed me my passport, which had been taken by Captain Lukey as soon as we entered the country. Captain Lukey took the passports and had them stamped with dates that did not correspond to your actual entry date in case problems arose during your stay. Problems like being killed. This provided the Honduran authorities a credible explanation and they could claim ignorance about any Americans reported assisting the nonexistent Contras.

I asked Pulmon if there was transportation for us and he said that there were no cars at La Quinta, that they were all at the FDN headquarters in the former Brazilian embassy downtown. I thought how quaint, the big guys have their own embassy building to operate from. Well, we would do our thing in Tegus because the FDN would not have to worry about footing the bill and besides, I felt that if I was to be commander of a strike force that was greatly anticipated by the FDN, then they had better not lean on me about being off base.

When Pulmon and I approached the exit gate at La Quinta the guards were afraid to let us out. The practice of not allowing Americans to leave without armed escort was about to be challenged. A young FDN officer, Marcel, was alerted about our attempt to exit. He came to me and asked that I not go, but I told him that I had to make certain arrangements for a trip back to the U.S. that, as far as I was concerned, was classified. Marcel studied my words for a moment and must have figured that a retreat from this no-win situation would be in his best interest. He motioned for the guards to open the gate and bid us farewell and good luck. Pulmon was armed with a .45 caliber automatic, but I was clean as a whistle and held a valid tourist visa in my passport.

We waited for about twenty minutes until an elaborately decorated bus stopped to pick us up. I enjoyed the ride along the route that was not visible to me when I first came to La Quinta. Pulmon and I assumed the roles of simple tourists out to see the city. We arrived in the heart of Tegus after an hour's ride. The bright green Holiday Inn sign caught my attention quickly and I told Pulmon that this was where we would stay. I entered the lobby and asked about a vacancy. The desk clerk looked at both of us closely because we had the appearance of a couple of drifters. I thought I looked fairly clean, but our clothes were wrinkled, dirty and smelled from lack of washing.

The clerk first told me that he would have to check on a room, then changed his mind once I pulled a roll of U.S. greenbacks from my pocket. The ticket in Honduras, like many Third World countries, is the dollar. It buys you anything you can imagine. I offered to pay in advance and told the clerk that I wanted a two-room suite and a room service menu. He wrote out a receipt and called for bell boys to assist us to our room.

The Sheraton in San Salvador was a dump compared to this place, which at best would be considered a low-rent roach coach anywhere in the States. Compared to La Quinta, this hotel was a palace. When Pulmon and I entered the room, all I could think of was hot water. I told Pulmon to warm a chair while I took a bath. The soap cut away enough grime from me that it felt like I had new skin when I finished. Pulmon was next in the shower and probably put a stain in the tub that took weeks to clean because he personified the word dirty. Despite being squeaky clean, our clothes were still garbage, so I sent Pulmon out to buy both of us new clothing. While Pulmon shopped, I retrieved the telephone numbers given to me in El Salvador by Graciela Garcia and called her.

Grace was very surprised to hear from me. She had given me two numbers, one for her office at Pan Am and the other at her home. The home number was answered by a woman who did not speak a word of English so I decided to try the number at her office. I told her that I had just returned from a business trip in southern Honduras and was trying to make arrangements to convert my airline ticket from TACA to Tan Sasha airlines for my return trip to the States. I told her that I wanted to see her before I left and perhaps she could assist me with the exchange of the TACA ticket. She agreed to meet me in the hotel lobby in the afternoon to accompany me to the airline ticket office. Pulmon returned with our new clothes and we dressed to go out into the city for a brief look-see.

Pulmon and I ventured into the crowded streets in front of the Holiday Inn. We were rushed by several small children with out-stretched hands begging for money. Their faces were thin and dirty, but their smiles were bright. Pulmon spoke harshly to the kids in Spanish and motioned them away from us, but they persisted in following us in an attempt to obtain money from the tall white American.

One very brave little boy tugged at my leg and felt my pockets for change even as I displayed gestures with my hands that I had no money. They seemed very street smart and didn't buy my act. Finally I took the small amount of loose coins from my pocket and tossed them onto the street ahead of us so we could turn onto another avenue without being pursued. The children fought over the money, but soon came up sear-ching for us thinking I had more to give. This was a sorry sight to me because the Hondurans on the street made no attempts to discourage the behavior of the street kids. They were treated with much less compassion by their fellow countrymen than foreigners. I was to learn that these children were the throw-aways of society in Tegucigalpa.

Touring the city was almost a hardship. I was either begged for money or hustled by street vendors trying to sell handicraft, souvenirs or art work. Tegus seemed over populated. The streets were choked with people making their way along the plaza-style shopping areas that displayed many imported items that were very high in price. I had been told that Honduras was the poorest country in North America and I could see it was true.

The city was surrounded by hills filled with sharp contrasts in hous-ing. Expensive chalet-style houses dotted the eastern hills, while shanty towns covered the southern and western slopes. Smoke rose into the air from wood being burned for cooking, and most of the timber surround-ing the city had been cut away over the years. The Hondurans were literally cutting and burning their country to the ground.

The currency in Honduras is the *lempira* and at that time exchanged with the U.S. dollar at the rate of 2.3 to 1 dollar. This was the official exchange rate, but a large underground black market of moneychangers existed. The airport was generally the focal point of the black market operations because incoming foreigners gladly changed money for a better rate. The black market exchange rate was up to 2.9 to 1. This didn't seemed to be a great difference, but the country's pricing structure made the rate very attractive. If you were not approached at the airport, taxicab drivers were the next best currency vendors.

I was a bit relieved when we returned to the hotel. Grace was waiting for me in the lounge area. She looked entirely different than when I first met her in El Salvador. She wore a bright colored dress that fit like a glove and her long silky black hair was braided on top of her head. She was absolutely beautiful. I must have had a smile on my face that encircled my head. We approached each other with an almost childlike shyness. Grace was certainly tentative because women in Honduras are not supposed to meet men, especially in a public place like a hotel lounge, unless you want to be viewed as a whore. The Spanish traditions in Honduras are very strong and in my ignorance I was causing Grace to become involved in painful new situations that she had to balance between culture and her feelings for me. She began explaining the cultural differences to me with this encounter.

Grace was as intelligent as she was beautiful. Her humor and her class stood out above all else. She would confide in me, almost apologetically, that she was from a poor family, but had worked very hard to educate herself and land a job with Pan American Airlines. She worked for Pan Am for seven years and was promoted to supervisor status, in part because she spoke several languages. When we first met in Salvador, she was returning from a training class in Guatemala. She had traveled to Italy and the U.S., advancing her skills for the job. Any Honduran female that could move up the corporate ladder had to be outstanding because males dominated the scarce employment opportunities in Tegucigalpa. The very fact that Grace had reached the level where she now worked spoke well of her tenacious attitude and her business skills.

I thought how lucky I was meeting a gem of a woman in the midst of such a chaotic country while being on such an insane mission. I felt from the first she suspected that I was up to something that was extraordinary and not at all like the person I tried to portray to her. I told her that I was a tourist and businessman in her country, but the sight of Pulmon by my side immediately told her senses that I was lying. She saw through me and in many ways I was glad that she did. I did not want to play hide and seek with anyone outside the sphere of my covert activities, and Grace could play a vital role in helping me surmount problems that I was unwilling to share with people affiliated with the FDN.

Grace would become my much loved and adored counterpart. I was sure that she felt as I did about the honesty of our relationship. I brought her into a web of secret operations that could get her jailed or worse when she did not need it. Her warmth and her love would comfort me in times of loneliness and despair when my evolving attitude about the Contras beat me down with bouts of depression. Grace brought light into a troubled soul and risked everything she had earned to stay at my side during this transitional period. I trusted her more than anyone in Central America and sought her wise advice about aspects of a culture I hardly understood. She was frank and honest in her talks with me, but stood back in the shadows while I played this gray war game. I felt deep in my heart that I would most likely be with this gracious woman until the end.

Grace led Pulmon and me through the crowded streets to the Tan Sasha office. We entered just as they were about to close for the day. The counter attendant was eager to leave and appeared agitated when Grace inquired about a ticket change. We were advised that it would take a full day to convert the ticket and we would have to return tomorrow when the office first opened to be helped. This didn't sit well with me, but I was beginning to accept some of the *manna* practices and figured that pushing the attendant would only amount to swimming upstream. I told Grace that we would return the following day and submit the ticket for change. There was nothing else that we could do to rush the process; besides, I would have more time to get to know my newfound love.

Pulmon was anxious to see his girlfriend and asked me if I would give him permission to leave the hotel for his visit. He was concerned about his responsibility to me and my protection, but I didn't take this issue as seriously as he did. I readily agreed because I was to meet Grace later for dinner. Pulmon left and I dressed for my date.

Grace met me just outside the hotel lobby and we walked to a nearby restaurant to sample the local cuisine. Grace knew this area of town well because her office was adjacent to the hotel district.

She inquired if I had eaten Honduran-prepared dishes and, not wanting to give away where I had been eating lately, I replied, "A few." I told her that I had eaten in hotels, but had preferred Western meals. She opened the menu and translated line for line all the available entrees. I asked her to pick something that was real Honduran, yet not too spicy because my stomach couldn't handle pepper. She laughed and explained that most Americans harbored old notions about hot food in Spanish countries. She selected for me a chicken dish, *pollo el grande,* that was anything but hot. The saucy chicken was very rich in flavor and to my surprise I found that Honduran food set well on my finicky stomach.

Grace and I talked well into the night. I felt comfortable with her because she possessed a charm and wit that kept me edging toward a need to get much closer to this very attractive person. It mattered little that we both shared the same inner feelings about one another because her society dictated that a period of platonic relations must proceed any involvement. I was determined to abide by her standards as she had been knocked a little off balance by Cisco and I sensed that she may have thought I was just looking for a quick one-night stand.

I wanted to assure Grace that I was returning to Honduras shortly and that I wanted to continue seeing her when I wasn't busy with my job. At this point I felt it served no purpose to tell her exactly what I was doing, so I danced around my real objective in Honduras. She scoffed when I tried convincing her that I was not U.S. military, as she thought.

We finished eating and I walked her to the bus stop where it could be very dangerous for a lone woman at night. She lived in an area known as Camayaguela, which is south of Tegus, and we had to be careful not to miss the only night bus that could take her home. I got to where I could spot her bus among the dozens of ornately painted shuttles that traveled this route each night. I always waited until her bus disappeared down the dark street before I would leave the bus stop. I worried about her safety because some Hondurans did not like their women taking up with gringos.

The next day my ticket was exchanged and I was ready to get out of Honduras. I wanted to get back to New Orleans to try to get the attention of Mario and Tom in a way that might open their eyes to the possibilities that lay ahead for Pegaso. I felt the green light had been given by Adolfo and Enrique, and this was not the time for the timid. I felt that CMA had reached a crossroad in its relationship with the FDN and if it chose to pass up a direct combat opportunity, then the membership would be relegated to supply mules for the duration.

The FDN would never completely cut ties with CMA because of the donations being channeled through it. To ensure that certain leaders within the CMA movement never lost their appetites for war, "show and tell" trips were arranged so that these members could accompany supply flights to Honduras. This offered CMA members a chance to get ever so close to the so-called conflict and provided new material for them to broadcast to others upon returning from Central America. When any member returned from the theater in Honduras, he would redouble his efforts to help obtain goods for the FDN and, as a bonus, spread tales of high adventure to would-be warriors, thus recruiting more followers and contributors.

I called Grace, late on the eve of my departure, and told her my ticket was exchanged and that I would leave for Houston immeditately. I assured her that I would return in two weeks and I would call her. She sounded a little sad and probably didn't believe me, but I had to do what I had to do. I knew I would return somehow and Grace would play a part in my activities.

Pulmon had spent the night with friends and had not yet returned to the hotel. I needed to get the show on the road and elected to go ahead to the airport without his assistance. I ordered a taxi from the bell captain and left for the airport alone. I arrived at the terminal to find a large crowd of people in front unloading luggage and lining up for flights out of Honduras. This crowd seemed to be larger than usual. It seemed as though some Hondurans had planned long stays outside their country by the stacks of baggage accompanying them. I thought that perhaps the scare of seeing tanks and troops in the streets a few weeks previous may have sparked an exodus of upper middle-class citizens who feared a coup, which would affect them more directly than ordinary Hondurans.

I entered one of the long lines waiting on the flight to Houston. I was a bit apprehensive about departing in this fashion. I was fearful that I may be stopped or questioned about my stay and I was not accompanied by Captain Lukey or anyone from the FDN. I tried to act very nonchalant as though I had been through this process many times.

Pulmon entered the terminal without my noticing his presence. He approached and apologized for his delay, telling me that he had been to the hotel searching for me and when the desk clerk told him I had checked out, assumed that this was where I could be found. He looked around for anyone who might assist in getting me bumped up in the line to assure me a seat on this flight. Pulmon knew most of the security people at the airport and spotted a uniformed customs official. He walked over to him and chatted for a moment before bringing him over to meet me. He introduced the man as Captain Flores of the Department of Customs.

Flores was a cheerful Honduran and was very gracious to me upon learning that I was some kind of mysterious American needing a little extra assistance. Flores asked me to step out of the line and requested my passport. I looked at Pulmon, having a little reservation about giving up my documents, but was instantly reassured that it was all right. Flores took my passport to the immigrations counter and instructed the officer to place a departure seal on the page. This was done without hesitation and Flores returned smiling broadly. This kind of extra treatment generally required a big tip, but in this case Flores wanted to demonstrate to me that he held power at the airport. I knew he would be added to my mental list of those with whom I should cultivate a relationship for future needs.

Flores invited Pulmon and me to sit and have coffee until the plane was ready for boarding. I sat and listened to the Spanish conversation between the two of them and would flash a smile periodically to give Flores the impression that I knew what they were talking about. The bulk of my Spanish at this point consisted of a sentence that deflected questions and got me off the language hook. If asked if I *habla español* I replied *muy poquito*. This meant that I spoke very little Spanish, but the few words often amused the Hondurans and brought about fake laughs of surprise. This was all part of the game. Acting like a dumb tourist broke down suspicion of the host Hondurans, and at the same time, language of secrecy blunted further delving into your business.

6

Men at War: The Right-Wing Lunatic Fringe and Other Foreign Policy Experts

I left Honduras and returned to the United States with many un-answered questions about the war and my role in it.

I had begun to acquire a sense of self-importance that was all out of proportion to what I knew to be true. I was beginning to believe I was actually the shadowy, secretive operative other people thought I was. Their perception of me was becoming my reality. Separating the fantasy of Colonel Flaco from the reality of Jack Terrell was becoming increasingly difficult.

In a few weeks and without any real background, I had ascended to a relatively high position in that gray area between factions controlling the war. The CIA, DIA, NSC and U.S. military establishment provided the true backbone of the operation and pulled all the strings of their FDN puppets. I was sandwiched between them and the Contras with a small group of operatives who could easily affect the direction of either. By affecting the handlers and their puppets, we were in a position to exert a major influence on the Reagan administration's foreign policy in the region, a role none of us was qualified to handle.

At the time, though, I felt America's honor was at stake and would do anything necessary to defend that honor. It didn't matter to me whether I was on the payroll of a mysterious benefactor who went by the name Donald Fortier and who appeared to have direct government connections, or whether I was, as others saw me, an off-the-books loose cannon allowed to coordinate "volunteer" assistance.

I knew I was being protected and allowed to operate by someone or something that was opening all the right doors for me. I was dealing in an area not governed by any written policy. What I was doing could either enhance or extinguish possibilities for advancing a conflict that was a priority for Reagan and his administration, but that was being treated like radioactive waste in Congress.

I had taken on this false identity with the assistance of others and their fertile imaginations. But I was no hologram following computer-generated impulses. I was a flesh-and-blood being acting out this role that had placed me in a significantly powerful position. From my little corner of the war, I could lead other Americans in acts of war against Nicaragua that could result in devastating economic consequences for the region and major international political consequences in the United States.

That I had the power to lead other Americans to their deaths in this undeclared war seemed of little concern to those who were establishing the policy and allowing me to operate.

This image of me as the warrior-statesman-defender of American honor had become entrenched in my ego and was governing my personality, my actions and my thought processes. Still, I thought it extraordinarily odd that a person could step from virtual obscurity into a position of such importance in a covert operation of this magnitude without any real background or credentials.

I was torn between what I perceived as my patriotic desire to forcibly act upon a Nicaraguan political system I despised and the knowledge that any such act would be a capitulation of my principles. I realized that by going to war against Nicaragua, I would be aiding a group of elitist, power-hungry bastards who would toast their conquest on the corpses of those poor campesinos who died without representation in a class-segregated military.

The FDN leaders were not fighting for the return of democracy to Nicaragua. They were fighting for a return to the feudal system they knew and loved and they were using the lives of the campesinos to accomplish it.

I saw that and knew that, yet decided to stuff that awareness of human rights abuses into an unlit corner of my mind so I could go forward with my own plans to change the course of this war. My conscience was troubled, but I put on the airs of a hawk. I was like a man in love with love. I was doing it not so much for the rightness of it, but for the mere thrill of doing it.

My first stop in the United States before going to New Orleans was Houston. I checked into the Shamrock Hilton and took advantage of the good food, clean clothing and a soft bed to reorient myself to the real world and sort out the troubles with CMA and Pegaso.

Cisco's arrest for drug possession had the potential of becoming another public relations nightmare that CMA could not afford. To make matters worse, the $3,000 I had given Cisco in Honduras disappeared. Tom Posey and Mario Calero denied receiving any of it or the instructions for purchase of equipment. I called Posey and told him Cisco had to be permanently excluded from all CMA operations.

Cisco retreated into the background. He was given a minor role assisting Posey in gathering supplies, but to my knowledge was never again allowed to travel to Central America. At the time, I thought Cisco was the exception among CMA members. Unfortunately, he turned out to be the rule.

Posey was responsible for recruiting personnel, screening them and shipping to me only those who met certain standards. But Posey's standards weren't my standards. I needed men. Posey sent me a collection of derelicts, corner commandos and Vietnam has-beens who wanted the thrill of combat without any of its dangers or any of its responsibilities.

Posey had assured me that he would run background checks on each of the prospective CMA members through his buddies at the 20th Special Forces in Huntsville. Bill Courtney, one of the original CMA members who had been in Honduras when Parker and Powell were killed, was to do a computer check of each applicant. Those who met the qualifications would be passed on to me. Those who didn't would be told to hit the road.

It quickly became obvious that this was another of Posey's numerous fantasies. If he actually had access to government background checks through the 20th Special Forces, he would have learned I was not who I claimed to be. Posey and CMA knew nothing about me I did not tell them. It was logical to assume they knew nothing more about other CMA members than what was on their membership applications.

It was not unusual for Posey to oversell the abilities of CMA not only to its members, but to the media and anyone else who would listen. But there were other external forces at work, forces Posey knew nothing about, that managed him and manipulated him in a way to give far more credibility to the organization than it actually had.

CMA was more a propaganda organ for interests within the government than the cadre of freedom fighters Posey portrayed it as. It was that latter image that Posey sold to prospective members, though.

Posey had agreed to go through the CMA membership list and begin lining up potential recruits for Pegaso. The requirements were simple: Each man had to be available to go to Honduras on two weeks notice and stay a minimum of three months. I thought it would be difficult to find enough qualified people to agree to this, but Posey insisted he could do it.

Each man would be told to bring two sets of equipment, one for himself and one for a Contra soldier at the front, the latter to serve as payment for transportation to Honduras.

The staging area for Pegaso in the United States was the Contempra Inn in Kenner, Louisiana, an inexpensive little motel not far from the airport and Mario's house. It was inexpensive and relatively secured, which served our purposes well. Before I knew it, I had half a motel full of would-be warriors who had quit their jobs and left their families to venture into a war they knew little about. The motel staff could hardly perform their daily duties because of the number of men running around acting like CIA agents and trying to impress the chambermaids.

I had the foresight to talk to one of the desk clerks, a strange little man named Henry, and convince him we were on a secret mission for the government. My closely cropped hair, khaki pants, olive drab T-shirt and military jargon helped me pull off the ruse.

Henry was excited by the prospect of getting caught up in a secret operation and getting extra business that would make him look good in management's eyes. He was the night manager, but frequently worked double shifts and saw to it that this strange character named Flaco was taken care of.

Henry gave us special room rates, made sure all CMA members had adjoining rooms, screened telephone calls, took cryptic messages and explained away our strange behavior to anyone who came around asking questions. Henry even instructed the employees that we were secret government agents and if they talked about our presence they would lose their jobs.

As a result, no one at the Contempra questioned military gear being stored in the rooms or asked about the men in uniform walking in and out of the motel at all hours of the day and night.

Mario was becoming more and more enamored of Pegaso and the possibilities it held out for his advancement within the FDN. I purposely played to his ego and implied it was quite possible the command structure of Pegaso would need to include a high-ranking Nicaraguan, a high-ranking Nicaraguan named Mario.

In some ways Mario already felt like a military commander because Posey often referred to him as General Calero. Mario wanted the position, but needed someone else to convince Adolfo that he could better serve the FDN in Honduras than in New Orleans.

The Doctor Has Arrived

Doc Zorro was a man on a mission. Whether it was a mission from God, or Ronald Reagan or someone else, I never figured out. But it was clear from the first day I met him in New Orleans that he was on a mission that involved Nicaragua, the Sandinistas and the Contras.

Doc Zorro was the nom de guerre of Lanny Duyck, a former Special Forces combat paramedic and Vietnam veteran from Texas who thought he was a combination Dr. Kildare and Indiana Jones. I knew he wasn't Indiana Jones, but he had me convinced for a while that he actually was an orthopedic surgeon.

In late November Doc came to New Orleans from Dallas with several boxes of intravenous fluid and some scuba gear for the FDN. Mario asked me to take Zorro to the Behring warehouse and unload the supplies. As soon as I got into Doc's pickup truck I could sense the paranoia. There were guns everywhere. Doc carried a 9mm Beretta semi-automatic pistol and glowered at me from behind his black, heavy beard as if to say: "I'll use it if I have to."

Zorro wore a leather jacket, blue jeans, cowboy boots and an Indiana Jones fedora. On his right ring finger he wore a handmade ring engraved with the symbol of international mercenaries, the Phoenix of the French Foreign Legion. Despite his outward appearance, he was soft-spoken and talked as though he were well-educated. He seemed a far cry from the other troops being recruited by Posey, and I thought he was someone we could use in Pegaso.

Zorro further piqued my interest when he told me worked for a Texas oil millionaire named Maco Stewart and had access to large amounts of money. He said he was under instructions from Stewart that if he found a worthwhile project, all he had to do was pick up a telephone, call Stewart's money man in Houston, where the home office of Stewart Petroleum was located, and the money would be sent without any questions asked.

To substantiate this, Doc drove me to a marine equipment company to buy several outboard motors and a portable air compressor to be included with the scuba gear going south. The total price was about $8,000. He whipped out a wad of cash thicker than anything I had ever seen and began peeling off hundred dollar bills. Then he asked me to sign the receipt and give a phony corporation name. No problem, I thought. Any man with access to that much money could be a big help to me and Pegaso.

I began dropping hints to him about Pegaso like a fly fisherman casting about in unfamiliar waters. It didn't take long for him to rise to the lure and open his mouth wide. He was fascinated by the prospect and wanted to know how he could be a part of it. I told him I would welcome him aboard if he could swing some financing for supplies through his Texas oil baron.

We needed a quick infusion of cash because the original $10,000 from my Washington benefactor was running low. I told Doc we needed $50,000 for high-powered sniper rifles, night-vision scopes, silencers, black uniforms, 9mm pistols and a variety of other combat gear.

He didn't blink an eye. He simply picked up the telephone, called Houston and told Maco Stewart's money man to make arrangements to get the money to New Orleans.

Mario and I began spending the money even before we saw the first dollar. The troops needed poncho liners, hammocks and bush hats and Mario said if I gave him the money for these items out of Pegaso funds, he would ship our equipment south for free. At least, it would be as free as things were with the FDN. Anything passing through their hands had a hefty surcharge tacked onto it either in goods or money.

When I got Doc alone, I warned him to keep a close watch on the money or the FDN would spend it before we had a chance to buy anything. I was beginning to understand how the FDN worked. My lack of trust was beginning to show through the veneer of dedication to the cause.

Mario had a nifty way of making money disappear, especially if it belonged to someone else. And he had no compunctions about working any scheme that would bring in more money or more supplies for the cause. Of course, it was difficult to tell whether that cause was the FDN or the "Make Mario Calero Filthy Rich" campaign.

Mario frequently solicited donations of military goods from small companies throughout the South, playing on the anti-Communist and anti-Sandinista sympathies of their usually conservative owners. Mario would then take the supplies, ship some to the Contras and sell the rest, pocketing the cash.

But he would bill the government through the FDN for the total cost of the shipment and someone somewhere in the government would gladly cut checks for supplies that never got to the Contras. Mario was able to profit twice on the same set of goods, while the fighters in the field got virtually nothing.

Meanwhile, those patriotic company heads wrote off the donations on their income tax returns, meaning taxpayers often got dunned twice on Contra supplies.

None of the amounts with which Mario dealt were particularly small. He did $343,000 worth of business through Oct. 25, 1985, with a small company in Salisbury, N.C., called M&S Supply. He did $445,000 worth of business through a Chicago company called Front Line as of Sept. 26, 1985.

Those are just two of the dozens of companies he worked with whose sales figures I was able to verify.

Mario eventually asked company heads to write and notarize letters assuring anyone who read them that he had taken no kickbacks, bribes or commissions from any of the businesses.

Why did he go to those lengths to convince people of his innocence at a time when no one had yet accused him of any wrongdoing?

It was a nice little insurance policy.

Zorro's Tale

Doc Zorro walked with a noticeable limp and when I asked him about it he told me rather matter-of-factly that he was carrying two slugs from an AK-47 in his leg.

He said he had been wounded in a firefight with Sandinista soldiers in a small village on Nicaragua's Atlantic coast. I didn't know much about that region of the country or the people who lived there, except what I had read in some *Soldier of Fortune*-type magazines. Doc was well-acquainted with the region, though, and gave me an introductory lesson into the people and the politics of southeastern Honduras, a region that would prove to be not only my undoing, but the undoing of the Reagan administration's secret little war against Nicaragua.

According to Zorro's story, he had served for a while as the chief military adviser to a confederation of Indians known as the MISURA, an acronym for the Miskito, Suma and Rama tribes that live in northeastern Nicaragua and southeastern Honduras.

In 1981, Argentine military trainers, at the behest of the CIA, went to Honduras to arm and train the fledgling anti-Sandinista movement that became known as the Contras. In south-central Honduras they worked with remnants of Somoza's Guardia Nacionale and campesinos who had fled Nicaragua. In southeastern Honduras they worked with the Indians and developed them into a special forces unit that became known as the Tropas Especiales del Atlantico, or TEA (pronounced TAY-ah).

The Argentines found the Indians to be fast learners and far more eager for combat than the old Guardia Nacionale. So it was relatively easy to convince the TEA to participate in a raid on Puerto Cabeza on Nicaragua's eastern coast, the primary point of entry for Warsaw Pact and Cuban ships bringing in military supplies for the Sandinistas.

According to Zorro, the Indians' intelligence had terribly underestimated the strength of the Sandinista defenders and TEA troops got pinned down on the beach. They could not be extracted because of heavy Sandinista fire from bunkers and gun batteries. Doc said he was summoned during the night and told he was to be the field medic on a special rescue mission.

For the next 36 hours he walked through the jungle to the coast. There, he was told that Americans were among the attackers pinned down on the beach at Puerto Cabeza and that he had to help get them out before they fell into the hands of the Sandinistas.

When darkness fell, he was put into an Avon boat and paddled out to sea from the Honduran coast. The boat turned south and then west again toward Nicaragua. As they approached the beach, they began taking a massive amount of fire from 20mm cannons and machine guns.

Zorro and the other men in the boat scrambled up the beach and took cover under some abandoned trucks.

Suddenly, from out to sea, Zorro said he heard the sound of helicopters. When he glanced back, the whole sky lit up with tracer and rocket fire from two unmarked, black Hughes 500D Defender helicopters outfitted with rocket pods and machine guns. They were attacking Sandinista positions on a peninsula on the other side of a small bay.

The Sandinistas increased the intensity of their fire and rounds started hitting all around Zorro. He said he heard someone scream for a medic. He saw two men lying on a sand dune and crawled out through the fire to get to them.

He dragged the first man under the truck then immediately went back for the second. As he was inching his way back to the truck, he felt like someone stomped on his right leg. He said he didn't pay too much attention to it at the time because he was so frightened and just wanted to get back under cover.

When he began checking the two men he had pulled to safety, he discovered they were Americans he had seen around camp earlier. Both were dead. He couldn't figure out what they were doing here because Americans were not supposed to be involved in this war.

Zorro said he wanted to notify a TEA commander when a sharp pain shot up through his right thigh. He reached down and felt his leg. He was bleeding badly. He quickly cut through his pants leg and saw two bullet holes about three inches apart on his upper thigh. He felt the back of his leg, but there were no exit wounds. The rounds apparently had been fired from a great distance and had lost much of their velocity when they hit him.

As Zorro tended his wound, the firing began to let up and TEA survivors began retrieving their dead and wounded and dumping them in the Avon boats. One of the TEA commanders came to him and asked him to help. He said he was wounded and that there were two dead Americans under the truck with him.

At that point, he said, the TEA commander became frantic. He screamed for more men to help him get the Americans out from under the truck and onto the boats.

Zorro said he got separated from the bodies and was taken onto a boat that moved up the beach away from the fire. The helicopters made another run at the Sandinistas and the intensity of the fire picked up again. Zorro said the pain in his leg was getting worse and his medical bag had disappeared in the confusion.

Through a haze of pain he remembered several Indians and some Americans carrying him on a crude stretcher inland to a camp site seven or eight miles north of the battle. They stopped briefly to tend to wounds.

Zorro said he was developing a fever, but he remembered a TEA commander telling him what happened. The troops were being shot up on the beach and the commander had called for assistance from a CIA mother ship stationed offshore as a backup. The helicopters were needed to suppress the Sandinista fire and allow the TEA to withdraw.

Zorro said he asked about the dead Americans and was told they had been buried near this place and their grave sites noted for future retrieval of the bodies. He was told that under no circumstances was he to tell anyone about this battle because public knowledge of its failure could jeopardize the entire Contra effort.

Zorro was taken back to the camp in Honduras and treated for his wounds. The camp doctors did not want to operate on his leg and the bullets were left where they were. He was told to wait until he returned to the United States to have them removed. But Zorro knew if he walked into a hospital and asked to have two AK-47 rounds taken out of his leg, he would have to face a lot of questions for which he did not have answers.

When he showed me the wounds, there were two recently healed puncture marks on his upper thigh, which was still swollen. He said the leg bothered him only when it rained or was cold, but he was constantly taking pain pills.

In the months to come I tried to get independent corroboration of Zorro's story, but had little luck. Those who could back up his story either avoided the subject or claimed that such knowledge was a sure ticket to trouble.

Zorro used the wounds to enhance his reputation among his peers, but I was never completely convinced they were made by AK-47 rounds. Nor was I ever convinced of his story of TEA and his role in the ill-fated attack on Puerto Cabeza. But those were the sorts of stories I would hear again and again as the men who would be warriors filtered into the Contempra Inn, ready to go to war against the Sandinistas.

Legends in Their Minds

The pace began to quicken and Pegaso began to take shape. Mario was happily ordering all sorts of equipment for the FDN and viewed the Maco Stewart money as a separate account to plunder in the name of our project. Posey was en route to New Orleans with a contingent of the Memphis chapter of CMA and said many more volunteers were in the pipeline.

The first of Posey's recruits to arrive at the Contempra was a strange little Oklahoman named Richard Thompson. Posey had described him as "a quartermaster genius" and sent him down early to help with the supplies. But as soon as I saw Thompson I knew something was wrong.

Thompson was about 40 years old and had a just-out-of-the-asylum look on his face. I actually thought he was a retard. He was nervous and smelled like he had not bathed in days. He told me that he had left his elderly mother at home in Oklahoma and hitchhiked four days to get here.

He presented me with the two seabags of equipment Posey instructed him to bring, one supposedly for his own use and the other for a Contra. But when I opened the seabags, one was full of nothing but ear plugs used for industrial safety purposes and the other had assorted heavy woodland camouflage clothing used by the military in Alaska.

It was obvious Thompson's elevator didn't go all the way to the top.

When I asked about his military experience he said he had worked briefly in supply while in the Army, but was primarily a field grunt. Some "quartermaster genius" Posey had come up with.

Thompson was so broke he said he would have to stay at the nearest YMCA, but would stay in contact by telephone. He asked for directions to the YMCA and took off in that direction, a sad little man shuffling along the shoulder of the interstate highway toward downtown New Orleans.

I shook my head in disgust, not so much at Thompson, but at Posey. He was filling the motel and the ranks of Pegaso with characters who would have fared better in a zoo than in a combat zone. This mission was beginning to have a bad feel about it.

The next set of CMA "volunteers" showed up at Mario's house. They weren't much better than Thompson. They came from Memphis and had been recruited by Sailor, the Memphis arms dealer whose real name was Jim Turney.

In addition to Sailor, there were Doc Ohrman, whom I had met earlier, and a man named J.B. Smalley. A fourth recruit, Bob "Traveler" Bradford, was to arrive later that day.

My nervous system went into spasms when I looked at this motley group of "volunteers." It bore absolutely no resemblance to the image I was given of Posey's vaunted CMA storm troopers.

The Memphis group had something none of the others did, though — its own press entourage. Accompanying the group was Bill Thomas, a reporter with the *Memphis Commercial-Appeal*, and photographer Jim Gardner.

Sailor said he brought them along to provide some positive publicity and counter what some Catholic nuns were saying about CMA. I was insistent that there would be no coverage without my permission and Thomas and Gardner eventually flew to Honduras separately.

Posey said he had brought a trailer full of supplies with him to make up for those that would have been purchased with the money Cisco had misappropriated. But Posey's "supplies" consisted of little more than moth-eaten ponchos, four aging field telephones, CMA T-shirts and other non-usable military odds and ends. I knew this junk came from Posey's personal stash, but I was having trouble believing Posey was trying to cover for his buddy, Cisco. Only later did I learn that Posey shared the money with Cisco and dumped his military garbage on me in a thinly disguised attempt to cover his tracks.

My beliefs about the Contra war had been shaken and my emotions confused after my trip to Las Vegas. Now, Posey was giving me even more reasons to question the role of CMA. It seemed as if everyone was looking for a handout or trying to get into the pockets of others.

The quality of values people were bringing to this war disturbed me. I saw little personal loyalty or true dedication to the cause. This sorry group of volunteers was out for self-gratification. Posey privately sought financial enrichment while presenting a high-profile image of a staunch anti-Communist assisting the forces of good against the red menace in Nicaragua.

My problem was that I began to see through the farce, all the way from the players on the lower levels to the misguided policy that was being shoved down the throats of the American public with a nice red, white and blue wrapping.

The ultimate act of stupidity on my part was that I had the choice of walking away but chose to remain. My ego would not let me walk away. I was enamored of the power I felt was within my grasp. I was convinced I could accomplish something worthwhile, even with the sparse human and financial resources at my disposal. I began making excuses for my involvement in the war and convinced myself I had been given a mission I had to carry out. But the mission was clouded because I had had no communication with my original contact. And my sense of rightness and fairness was not buying into what was fast becoming an Alice-in-Wonderland adventure.

I decided if Pegaso was going to work and CMA was to be an integral part of the war, I would have to wrest control of the operation from Posey. He was director of CMA, but his skill and knowledge about how to conduct such an operation were even more limited than mine. Unlike me, however, he had no desire to learn what it would take to pull this off.

Besides making a few bucks from his involvement with the FDN, Posey had a burning desire to become the first American to have a street in Managua named after him, provided the Contras did the naming. He saw his role in the war as that of a good samaritan helping less fortunate people. I saw him as an out-of-control wrangler rounding up people with diminished abilities from the productive pastures of the ultra-right wing and herding them to New Orleans for me to lead to the slaughter in Nicaragua. He had no real concept of what he was asking these poor souls to do. I did and it was frightening.

Despite my misgivings about this group, I appointed Sailor as my first sergeant and second in command of the Americans. This role suited him well because he was adept at getting through to hard-headed individuals in his own special way. Sailor at least demonstrated he had some experience as a leader. He had a good heart, but would kick your ass if you disobeyed his orders or failed to perform a duty assigned by me.

We began making final preparations to depart for Honduras. Posey was given instructions on what equipment to buy and was told to make sure we had another 30 to 50 men ready to go to Honduras. Mario would be responsible for working out transportation details.

I drew up a disclaimer for the men to sign. No one would be allowed to make the trip without signing it because I knew what we were doing was illegal and I didn't want retribution from some grieving family member if something happened to one of the men. The disclaimer was designed to absolve the FDN and CMA of any responsibility for each man's actions. It also stated that the individual was not recruited by CMA or any agencies of the U.S. government and that he was not armed with a weapon other than that which he registered with U.S. Customs before departing.

In addition to the disclaimer, I told each man to make out a will that specified what would be done with his remains if he was killed. If a man was killed in Nicaragua, the disposition of his body would be left up to me.

Several days before we left New Orleans, I pulled each man aside for a personal interview on why he wanted to go fight a war he knew nothing about. Two more men had joined our sad little group, bringing the total to seven. One of the new arrivals was John "Big John" Cannon from Shreveport, Louisiana. I talked to him on the telephone several times, but knew little about him. The other was Bob "Traveler" Bradford.

Bradford was a former U.S. Army lieutenant who seemed out of place in this group. He was short and thin with light brown hair and an engaging, sincere personality. When I asked him why he wanted to fight he told me he had not had been in combat while he was in the Army and this was his best chance.

At least I got an honest answer from somebody. And finally I had someone with real military credentials.

No two of the men had the same reason for getting involved. Some thought there was money to be had, although Posey repeatedly assured me he was not promising them payment for their services. Others said it was the lure of combat. Others said it was to defend democracy. As I talked to the men, I saw no sense of fear or concern for what might happen to them in this war in which they had no real stake.

Doc Ohrman was a good case in point. He was static electricity in a camouflage uniform. He could neither sit still nor shut up. He irritated me so much that I frequently had Sailor physically restrain him. Doc had served in terrible combat conditions in Vietnam as a dust-off medic and I was at a loss to understand why he wanted more.

The night before our departure, I had Sailor police the men for weapons and instructed them what not to wear. I didn't want any problems from the Hondurans, who didn't take kindly to people coming into the country wearing any military-type apparel. I wanted this arrival in Tegucigalpa to be as smooth as possible.

The dropouts started the next morning. J.B. Smalley sent word he wanted to talk privately. When I went to his room I found him with John Cannon. J.B. said John wasn't feeling well enough to travel, but that the two of them would follow tomorrow.

"It's now or never, J.B.," I said.

"I guess it will be never," he said.

I stormed out of the room. Already our intrepid band of mercenaries had suffered nearly 30 percent casualties and we hadn't even left New Orleans. Their reasons for not going had nothing to do with illness, I learned. It had to do with money. There wasn't any money in this deal and that made their patriotism and anti-Communist zeal shrivel up and die in a hurry.

Mario was incensed. The tickets had been purchased and we already were in the process of loading gear into Posey's U-Haul for the trip to the airport. We must have looked like a contingent of National Guard troops preparing for weekend maneuvers. We had more than 20 seabags and 40 large fiberglass coffee bean sacks, all stuffed with miscellaneous military gear.

At the airport I collected all the passports and made one last head count. Traveler stopped me and said he had forgotten to pack his commando knife. It was still in his carry-on luggage. I told him to give the knife to Mario. Mario casually slipped the knife into the waist of his pants as he haggled with the ticket clerk over excess baggage charges.

These little foul-ups were an omen I failed to heed, much to my dismay.

Ready or Not, Here We Come

We flew south on Tan Sasha, rather than TACA. I wanted nothing to do with El Salvador after my first experience there. The flight went through Belize and San Pedro Sula, Honduras, before landing in Tegucigalpa. Everything went smoothly until we arrived at the airport.

I was expecting the usual welcoming committee at the terminal, but was surprised to learn the FDN had not been notified of our arrival. I scanned the customs area to see if I recognized any of the officers, but saw no familiar faces. Captain Lukey was departing the passenger area and I failed to get his attention. I began to suspect we were in for big trouble.

We were cleared through immigration without a question, but there was still the problem of getting through customs with all that military gear. I gathered the men near the baggage carrousel and told them to collect the gear and wait for me. This was the first international trip for most of the men and they were understandably nervous. The terminal was closing for the night and I had no idea what to do. I was playing it strictly by ear.

Finally, I spotted a sleepy-looking Honduran skycap, pulled out a wad of dollars and asked him to help us get the baggage out of the airport. He spoke little English, but asked if we were U.S. military. I nodded my head and he grabbed his hand truck, roused a dozing female customs official and began loading the bags while she stamped them cleared without ever looking inside.

For all she knew, we could have been carrying nuclear devices in those bags. Or cocaine. It didn't seem to matter to the Hondurans as long as they thought we were American military.

I commandeered two station wagons and had them loaded with our gear. Doc, Traveler and Thompson got into one taxi and Sailor and I got into the other. I thought I could find La Quinta, even in the dark. I gave instructions for the other taxi to keep us in sight at all times and we took off as I used hand signals to direct the driver.

We hadn't gone far when Sailor told me the second taxi was no longer behind us.

"*Alto!*" I yelled at the driver. At least I knew one good Spanish word.

We retraced our route until we came to the first road junction. We took this road and found the second taxi parked outside a Honduran military base with Doc Ohrman trying to give the guard his passport. He thought he was at La Quinta. The guard was even more confused than the taxi drivers.

I could just see myself sitting in a Honduran jail trying to explain to some State Department gray suiter why we were here and what we were doing with so much military gear. And I could see the headlines back in the States: "American Mercs Busted in Honduras," and "Hondurans Roust Would-Be Rambos."

"Shut your mouth and follow us," I yelled at Doc.

He jumped back into his taxi and our caravan set off again in search of La Quinta, leaving behind a rather dumbfounded guard.

It took some searching, but we finally came to the two white columns that marked the gate to La Quinta. After coming so close to creating an international incident, the columns looked like the gates to heaven.

But my relief at finding La Quinta quickly turned to anger over being abandoned by the FDN. We waited at the gate while the guards summoned someone in charge from up the hill. After a few minutes, two men approached. One was Marcel, the young communications officer who ran La Quinta when the staff was away for week end holidays.

"Flaco," he said with surprise, "what are you doing here?"

"Mario was supposed to call ahead and have us picked up," I answered.

"That's news to me," he said.

I was beyond angry now. I told Marcel I wanted to talk to Mario to find out who screwed up. And I wanted to talk to him now. If this was the way things were going to be handled, the other CMA volunteers coming in had an even greater chance of running afoul of the Honduran authorities.

The taxi drivers remained in their cars wide-eyed with amazement over what they had just been through. They refused to accept payment for the ride. They just wanted to get the hell away from the strange gringos that brought them to this mysterious place. After I insisted they take the money, they did so and left in a cloud of dust.

When I finally got Mario on the phone I let loose all my frustrations. It was not his fault, he claimed. He said he had called Frank Arana, public relations boss for the FDN, to tell him we were coming. That explained it all.

Fat Frank, as I called him, was a 300-pound mound of greasy black hair and bad table manners. He was a gambler and a boozer and preferred the luxuries of the Hotel Maya to the food shortages and lack of comfort in La Quinta. Fat Frank had a large, round face with a black goatee. He was a walking caricature. His lone saving grace was that he spoke excellent English.

When I finally saw Fat Frank the next day and questioned him about being abandoned, he brushed it off as a simple error that would not happen again. I told him we had been delayed long enough and needed to get these men to Las Vegas as soon as possible. But he said it would be several days because he could not get a truck.

"Flaco," he said, grabbing my hand and smiling that insincere smile of his, "you need not fear, we'll take good care of all of you."

That's exactly what I was afraid of.

Doc Ohrman presented me with my first command problem. He was causing problems with Thompson. Everybody liked to pick on Thompson, but it was like kicking a sick dog. I had to establish my authority over this group, so I told Doc to meet me in the mess hall.

I told him we were on a secret mission and not even the Contras were fully aware of what we up to. I told him all of us had to stick together and that he could be an asset to the group. But if he continued giving me problems or if I heard another complaint with his name attached to it, I would personally take him out and shoot him.

"I want to set an example for the men anyway, and you could be my example," I told him. "This mission is under martial law and I am the judge and jury here."

His face went white and he walked back to his quarters like a man who had just been hit over the head with a big club.

My tactics may have seemed a bit drastic, but I felt I had to instill some fear in all the men. There would come a time when that fear would keep everyone together.

The overriding concern of every member of the group was when would I allow them to carry weapons. These guys all thought that just because they were in Honduras, they were at the front. They all wanted weapons, not so much to use, but to carry. It was something that had to do with their perception of one another. The guy with the biggest gun was the toughest.

Their attitude about guns was identical to every other CMA member who came to Honduras. They had to carry a weapon to prove their manhood, if not to their buddies, then to themselves. The fact that they were in a camp of heavily armed counterrevolutionaries who were surrounded by the Honduran military that was even more heavily armed and suspicious about their motives never entered into their thoughts.

They had to have guns and they had to have them now.

When the time came for us to head to the border, I broke out two shotguns I had brought with me. There would be no issue of Uzis as there was the last time. But I wanted to allay fears the men had about being ambushed near the border by Sandinistas.

The men complained all the way to Las Vegas about the harshness of the trip. Every time one asked how much farther, I replied: "Welcome to the war."

Bill Thomas and Jim Gardner were waiting for us when we arrived. But some things had changed in my absence. Pecos Bill was nowhere to be seen. I had left him in charge of my gear, but I found a new lock on the door. Cheppie explained that Pecos had lost another bout with the bottle and Bermudez had banished him to the hospital.

To get Pecos back, I gave Bermudez a leather holster for a .45 pistol that U.S. military officers once were issued. I found the holster in New Orleans and had polished it and tied a leather cord to the bottom so Bermudez could strap it to his leg like a gunfighter.

When I handed him the holster his face changed completely. He smiled and invited me into his office for a *cerveza*. He wanted to know all about my trip back to the States. He wanted to know all about Pegaso and the gear we were bringing in.

It was almost as if this small gift opened the door for me to get inside Bermudez's head. After I gave him the holster, I was given access to him at any time I wanted. He now listened to my plans with more interest than ever before. I thought that if the gift of a holster meant that much to him, what if I had brought a Rolex?

No sooner did we show the men where they would be bunking than they began changing out of their civilian clothes and into their combat gear. Thompson was the first to emerge in full combat regalia. He had a jungle camouflage uniform with long sleeves that he had buttoned at the neck and the wrists, even though it was 90 degrees in the shade. He had a fatigue cap pulled down over his eyes and looked like he was about to launch a raid on someone. There was a bulge under his jacket from a pistol he had tucked into the pants as if he had to hide it from the authorities.

He was ready to go kill some Commies.

Another American had entered Las Vegas independent of us. Doc Ohrman saw him first and described him as a tired, haggard man who was resting in the hospital after a lengthy mission inside Nicaragua. That didn't begin to describe his poor physical shape.

When I saw the man, he was hobbling barefoot up the road to the fence that separated the haves from the have-nots. I met him at the gate and he asked if I had a spare pair of boots. I felt sorry for the man and told him I could probably scare up a pair for him.

He said his name was Robert Thompson but that he went by the nom de guerre of Pantera. He was a retired Florida Highway Patrol officer who had left his home in southern Mexico and come to Honduras to fight the Communists. He spoke Spanish, which instantly gave him a better chance to get involved here than most other Americans.

He told me he had just come back from a nine-month mission in Nicaragua with the campesino commandante Tigrillo and his men. Tigrillo and his band of 5,000 campesino guerrillas were a legend among the Contras. They fought the Sandinistas independently for several years, but eventually were forced to ally with the FDN because they lacked food, ammunition and medicine to continue to fight alone.

They had come to Las Vegas because Tigrillo had been shot in the leg and his wound required special surgery and a certain period of rehabilitation. His men would sit in Las Vegas waiting for him to recover. Pantera said many of Tigrillo's men felt if anything happened to their leader they would abandon their fight and return to their homes. They would not join forces with the FDN.

This caused a great deal of consternation among FDN commandantes because they knew these men would follow only Tigrillo. Losing these men would be a great loss of veteran fighters.

As we talked, Pantera remained on the other side of the fence. I asked him why and he said Bermudez had ordered him confined to Tigrillo's camp because of some statements he had made about the quality of the Contra fighting force. He could not come on our side of the fence.

Pantera claimed he had a mild case of gangrene in his feet and had been carried on a litter for nearly two weeks before he got to the hospital. Now he wanted to get back to Tegucigalpa to recuperate and regain the weight he had lost. He also wanted to join the other Americans in their tent. Bermudez wouldn't allow him to do either. Pantera asked if I would intercede in his behalf and I agreed to do so. If Bermudez didn't like you, you might as well be dead, but I would give it a shot.

Shortly after my return to Las Vegas, I turned my attention to implementing Pegaso. My first objective was to construct a Vietnam-style firebase. But none of the Americans wanted to do manual labor — they thought that was the name of the president of Mexico. And I had no real control of the COE troops, despite being placed in command by Bermudez. The COE's previous commander, Gustavo, resisted my every move and the men still followed him.

Lumber shortages also slowed the construction of the firebase. The resources of the sawmill had been diverted to cut lumber for Bermudez's new war room, which was being done in mahogany. Each day Bermudez strolled to the construction site like a king going to his castle. He knew when it was completed it would be the most impressive structure in camp, if not in all of southern Honduras. He wanted nothing to interfere with his construction schedule, not even the war.

The obstacles to getting anything done at Las Vegas were numerous. This was a five-day-a-week war. No one did any work on the weekends. Saturdays and Sundays were reserved for baseball.

The Contra soldiers, like most Nicaraguans, loved baseball and often played with only the remnant of a ball that had been taped many times to keep it together. They had no baseball shoes so they usually played in their combat boots. The more they played the more quickly the boots wore out and the less dependable they would be in combat. When I brought this up to Bermudez he brushed it off and went out and pitched a few innings.

In the following days, more Americans arrived. A second group of volunteers was stranded in El Salvador because they took TACA.

Zorro came in with two other men sent by Posey, Fred Henning from Tallahassee, Florida, and Gary Bennett from Texas. I knew nothing about either of them but figured they had to be better than Richard Thompson. Besides, we were starting to suffer some non-combat related injuries and would need replacements. Traveler refractured an old break in a bone in his foot when he stepped on a rock while walking across the parade ground and was laid up for a while. It was that kind of group.

I asked Zorro about the supplies we desperately needed to implement Pegaso. He said Mario had obtained the $30,000 in traveler's checks from Maco Stewart and had purchased some equipment. Zorro said he had seen bags and boxes of equipment marked for Pegaso in a warehouse at La Quinta, but had been told there wasn't enough transportation to get it to the field.

These delays were an indication to me Adolfo wanted Pegaso slowed. I was moving too quickly for him. He feared I was too militant and might prematurely launch our mission into Nicaragua. He still had political cards to play in Washington and Miami. I was also getting the distinct impression the FDN was using us to obtain cash and goods while placating the American "volunteers" with a taste of the action.

But the FDN was grossly underestimating my resolve to get the Americans more deeply involved.

Bill Thomas, the *Commercial-Appeal* reporter, was surprised to see the sudden influx of Americans into Vegas. To get him out of my hair and give me an opportunity to find some direction for my group of misfits and braggarts, I arranged a five-day trip for Thomas and Gardner to the Contra base Banco Grande across the Coco River.

My days were spent sorting out other people's problems. For hours on end I would sit listening to complaints and trying to figure out what to do about them. It was like holding office in a big corporation that produced nothing. Pegaso was a hamster on an exercise wheel, running like mad but going nowhere.

I found it hard to keep up with the activities of each man and our lack of training opportunities made the boredom that much more depressing for them. The tropical heat and stagnant air in the valley added to the dilemma. Tempers were short and flared over the slightest provocation.

My two Docs, Ohrman and Zorro, each had jobs that interested them and entertained them. Doc Ohrman dispensed drugs from the small camp pharmacy. Doc Zorro had appointed himself camp physician. It took me a while to figure out why they were so entertained and amused.

Then I found Doc Ohrman had a knack for maintaining unusually high energy levels, even in the withering afternoon heat when most of the men sought out shade. The energy, I learned, came from a bottle of Dexedrine he had taken from the pharmacy. Sailor had known about his habit but said nothing to me.

It seemed as if every member of this ragtag band was trying to do things in Honduras he could not get away with in the States. Doc Zorro was among the worst offenders.

One day I saw Doc Zorro walking up the dirt road in the center of camp wearing a surgeon's gown and mask. He was holding an X-ray up to the sunlight to view the image like a true MASH physician. The gown was stained with blood, almost as if he had dipped his hands in it and smeared it down the front.

He walked up to me, held up the X-ray for my inspection, and said: "Pretty good job, wasn't it? I've already done six operations this morning."

My jaw must have hit the ground. I was stunned.

The stupid son of a bitch was down there in the hospital doing surgery on those poor campesinos. Here was an ex-Special Forces grunt hacking away at bullet wounds, putting casts on broken bones, removing shrapnel and God knows what else, perhaps even delivering babies.

Zorro was quite composed about the entire affair and continued to practice medicine on these people. I didn't protest too strongly because Bermudez seemed impressed by the actions of one of these woeful American specimens who hadn't demonstrated they could find their asses with a road map. No telling what happened to the good doctor's patients, though.

The other Americans had no outlets like my pair of docs, and what I feared would happen did one steamy night.

It started with shouts from the GP tent where the men had their bunks. I looked up to see Richard Thompson picking up his clothing from the dirt road in front of the tent. Sailor was inside tossing clothes outside and cursing the cringing Thompson with every breath.

I rushed to the tent and Sailor snapped to attention. His face was purple with anger.

"What the hell's going on here?" I demanded.

"Thompson said he won't work on the base, sir," Sailor said.

"Why won't he work on the base?"

"He said he quit."

"He quit?"

"He said he quit, but I told him he couldn't quit because it wasn't a job."

"What did he say then?"

Before Sailor could answer, Thompson chimed in.

"I'm quitting the war and want to go home," Thompson said.

This brought a hoot of derision from the other men in the tent. They called Thompson a gutless wonder and said they didn't want him in the tent any more. If I hadn't been so frustrated with all of them, I probably would have laughed. They were like a bunch of kids who couldn't get along.

A number of Contras had gathered to witness this fallout among the men they were supposed to use as role models and I knew we would suffer as a result.

Thompson demanded I return his passport and give him a return ticket to the United States.

"I'm not running a tour business here," I said. But I told him at the appropriate time I would send him home.

"Let me take him in the jungle and kill him," Sailor said, brandishing an AK-47. "He doesn't deserve to live."

Sailor had a nasty temper and I knew he would have no compunctions about doing in Thompson. I told him this was a bit drastic, not to mention being against Honduran law. Had we been in Nicaragua, I would have let Sailor do it, because Thompson was a definite liability. But not in Honduras.

I ordered Thompson to sleep in the mess hall for his own protection and I confiscated his gun. Thompson cut himself off from the rest of the

Americans and wandered alone through the camp each day, waiting for the supply truck to take him out of Las Vegas.

When it finally arrived, it had several more Americans on it. But it was pretty much a case of garbage in and garbage out.

The new arrivals were from a so-called mercenary training school in Dolomite, Alabama, that went by the name Recondo. It was run by Frank Camper, a Vietnam veteran, military deserter and Defense Intelligence Agency snitch.

Recondo was not so much a mercenary training school as it was a money-making scheme and source of information for Camper. He preyed on the insecurities and the wallets of those who believed being a mercenary was a worthwhile occupation. The little training that candidates received only enhanced their chances of getting killed in a conflict like this.

A few of the Recondo people were exceptions and became valuable troops. But there was a deep rivalry between Posey and Camper that would lead to factionalization of a recruiting movement already in disarray.

The leader of this group was Donald "Ramos" Rossi. Ramos was skilled in escape and evasion techniques, was unusually disciplined and followed orders well.

The remainder of his group consisted of men using *nombres* de guerre of Mycroft, Thom, Coach, Frenchy, Pablo and Pappy.

Mycroft was a native of Chicago and a true product of the Camper school of bullshit and bluster. He kept a large wad of chewing tobacco in his mouth 24 hours a day. Mycroft was a suicide looking to happen.

Robert "Thom" Palmer was a heavyset Kansan who possessed few skills we could use in Pegaso. But, unlike most of the others, he was quiet and didn't get on my nerves.

Coach was from Texas and saw himself as a goodwill ambassador from the United States, not a worker or a fighter.

Claude "Frenchy" Chaffard was a former French paratrooper who spoke little English. He had been recruited and sent to CMA by a wealthy Boston businessman and former OSS officer named James Keyes. Frenchy was a "mole" for Keyes who in turn passed on information to Lieutenant Colonel Oliver North on the National Security Council. Frenchy was a waste of Keyes money, because he lacked jungle warfare skills and had problems speaking either English or Spanish. He would have fared much better as a comedian.

Paul "Pablo" Johnson, Camper's assistant at Recondo, was the worst of the lot. I had requested Posey find a sniper instructor and Johnson was picked. He had been in Lebanon working for the Druze militia until he ran out of money and was forced to pawn his passport with the State Department for passage home. Camper paid his bills and recommended him to Posey.

Pappy was a muskrat skinner from Maryland. That was the lone skill he brought to Pegaso. What an asset.

The remaining gem in my star-studded assault force was a reporter for *Eagle* magazine named James Adair. Adair came to Las Vegas to get the true story of the FDN for his magazine. He figured he could sell articles about the war to finance his adventures in Honduras.

Adair had a wicked sense of humor, especially about the Contras, but none of it found its way into print. He had a different perspective about these people, stating that the FDN army lacked everything but hunger, but his accurate insights played a key role in Pegaso over the next several months.

Being a patriot did not automatically qualify someone to go to war. Not one of these people was qualified to go into combat, and Bermudez knew it. I had long talks with Bermudez, attempting to put the best possible face on this group of misfits. But he was buying none of it.

He and the other FDN leaders were wary of putting Americans such as these in a position to kill or be killed. The political fallout would be horrendous if that happened and might mean the end of the Contras. So, we sat and waited for something to happen while the men strutted around camp with their weapons, never once thinking they might have to use them to defend their lives and the lives of other Americans.

7

A Call to Arms

Bermudez had become quite talkative since I had given him the holster. I was his gringo ear. He told me things about the war few Americans had ever heard, and he taught me things about how the war was being prosecuted that undoubtedly were classified information somewhere in the CIA headquarters at Langley and the Pentagon.

One of Bermudez's favorite topics was the Sandinista regime, what it had done to Nicaragua and how to rectify the mess it had made of the country. He believed any Nicaraguan who did not actively work against the Communists was one of them and deserved to be punished.

In Contra raids against economic targets in northern Nicaragua, particularly coffee plantations and farming cooperatives, any resistance brought immediate and brutal retribution. Even if the resistance came from civil militia or regular troops, civilians in the co-ops would die because the Contras and Bermudez considered them Sandinista sympathizers.

Commandantes in the field were given the authority to randomly select those who were to die. That was a field-expedient object lesson that told other civilians not to go along with Sandinista programs. Troops coming from Nicaragua often bragged how they ambushed targets of little value and killed people at roadblocks whose only crime was possessing travel documents approved by the Sandinistas.

The Contras gave themselves broad police powers within about 30 miles of the border and no one who lived there was spared.

Ammunition supposedly was in short supply, so Bermudez ordered prisoners to have their throats cut rather than waste a bullet on them. Bermudez also ordered that prisoners not be brought back to Honduras because of the food shortages. There wasn't enough food or housing for the Contras, so why waste any on prisoners? Only those young enough and pliable enough to become potential converts to the Contra cause were brought back.

On several occasions I had seen lines of young men and women marching barefoot through the camp under the watchful eye of instructors who carried long bamboo staffs. If one of these people got out of step or failed to respond to a command quickly enough, they were beaten by the instructors.

I first thought this was how the Contras ran their boot camp. But Pecos Bill informed me these young people were conscripts dragged out of Nicaragua. They were being bullied and beaten into submission and compliance with the Contra doctrine. Any attempt at escape meant instant death.

The female conscripts often suffered the most. Some were forced to toil in 12- and 14-hour shifts in the tortilla kitchen, where the heat and smoke were almost unbearable. Bermudez said this was an example of the dedication of Nicaraguan women in their fight against oppression.

The story about the shortage of ammunition also gave Bermudez an excuse to limit the speed with which Pegaso was put together. Without ammunition we couldn't conduct live-fire training exercises necessary to familiarize the men with their weapons. We were relegated to classroom instruction in military tactics, an exercise that quickly bored my gung-ho recruits. They constantly yammered for action.

The only times we were permitted to do anything that remotely resembled the type of military activity I had signed on for was when Bermudez needed to get us out of camp. That occurred when he had some special visitors coming to Las Vegas. Usually, those visitors were from the CIA.

Bermudez was intent on shielding us from the CIA and vice versa. Whenever he learned a CIA visit was imminent, the Americans were loaded onto trucks and taken on a phony patrol near the village of Aurenalis on the Honduran side of the border. We went through the motions a few times until one day we decided we had had enough of the charade. We simply lay down and napped until the radio call came to return to base.

Bermudez was in frequent contact with the CIA through a mobile communications center in a new Chevrolet truck that was parked near his hutch and provided the power for his VCR. The truck had an enclosed body in the rear that looked like a refrigeration compartment. Flores, the communications chief, was the only person I ever saw getting into that rear compartment.

When I asked Bermudez about it, he said the CIA had given him the truck, which contained a 1,000-watt Harris low-band radio with encoding and decoding equipment. There was one other truck like this in the country, he said, at the CIA's secret base at Aguacate.

"You want to talk to Langley?" he asked.

I declined. But neither I nor any other outsider ever saw the inside of that truck.

My patience with Bermudez and the FDN was wearing thin. I had been promised the moon but was getting nothing but beans and rice. I felt like I was on a slow ride to nowhere.

Bermudez may have sensed my frustration with the situation and my disgust with the FDN. One night, while he was entertaining some prospective Venezuelan contributors to the FDN at one of his lavish parties, he approached me all glassy-eyed and wobbly.

He said a battalion of Contras had been surrounded by Sandinista troops at a place called Wiwali near the Nicaraguan village of Rosario. He claimed the Sandinistas were trying to shut down the infiltration routes out of Honduras and he could not let that happen.

Pulling me close, Bermudez looked at me and said: "Would the Americans like to go with a counterattack force in the morning? You can observe or you can participate."

"We will participate," I said.

Finally, I thought, our time had come. I left the party and went to the GP tent to talk to the men.

"All of you told me you wanted to fight," I said. "Now you're going to have the opportunity. Be prepared to stand for inspection at 4 a.m. and be prepared to go into combat at dawn."

The men came alive instantly, almost as if I had given each a handful of amphetamines. They began scurrying around their cots, collecting gear. I knew none of them would sleep that night and it was useless for me to try to control their elation after they had endured so much boredom.

I returned to my room and began preparing my own gear. I could not decide whether to use a shotgun or an M-16. I had a bandolier that held 50 shotgun shells that could be comfortably worn over all my web gear. The M-16 magazines were bulky and heavy. I decided to go with the shotgun because it would be more effective in close-in jungle fighting.

I had six fragmentation grenades and one Belgium B-40 I kept on a neck chain. I would wear that in the event I was captured. The B-40 was small, little more than an inch in diameter, but it packed a powerful punch. When you pulled the pin on that thing, you would never know when it went off. Several men carried these tiny grenades for the express purpose of committing suicide if captured. But all of them said they would pull the pin and then hug a Sandinista.

When the initial excitement about imminent combat wore off and the men began to think about what might be in store for them, they began to get nervous. Doc Zorro was particularly edgy. I could see it in his eyes. He had never fully recovered from his combat experiences in Vietnam and now seemed to be coming unravelled. He had smeared his face with camouflage greasepaint and put on all his gear to help others who had no knowledge of what to carry or how to carry it. But Zorro was acting like a man whose mind was 8,000 miles away, in another jungle from which he never completely returned.

Sailor was like a mother hen attending to the needs of each of the soldiers. He checked their gear, tightened their straps and snapped their snaps. He made sure they carried everything they needed for the mission. The various weapons were checked and loaded, packs were filled and secured. Headbands were put on in the style of Vietnamese night crawlers. They actually began to look like real commandos. They could have convinced a lot of people they were seasoned veterans preparing for another mission.

The Cubans in camp had been invited to go along but were unimpressed by all the chatter and commotion. They knew these Americans were totally unprepared and ill-equipped to fight the Sandinistas. Many of these Cubans had been training for years in the Everglades for this moment and knew military inexperience when they saw it. They were openly smirking at the Americans as they prepared for their first taste of combat.

One thing these Americans did well, though, was scrounge. They came up with some badly needed grenades, some claymore mines and some LAAW (light anti-armor weapon) rockets from Contras who supposedly had no ammunition. The secret, according to Sailor, was to find the right commandante who could profit from the barter system, usually using American cigarettes.

Around midnight, when everyone began to calm down a bit, Doc Zorro came to my hutch and asked to talk. He expressed concern about the Pegaso supplies back at La Quinta and said he felt we needed this gear before sending anyone into combat. He said it was his responsibility to check on these supplies and it was important to do it now.

His eyes were wide with fright and his whole body was quivering as he talked. He insisted I go to Bermudez to get his permission to return to La Quinta. He wanted Bermudez to believe his leaving now was not a sign of cowardice. It was important for Zorro to have Bermudez's stamp of approval to get the heat off himself and the other Americans.

But he was scared. All his boasting about his Special Forces exploits were for nothing. He couldn't, or wouldn't, back up all that talk.

Zorro obtained a pass indicating he was a doctor to get him through the Honduran checkpoints. An ammunition truck was his ride out of camp. Dressed in blue jeans and a T-shirt, he rode out of camp the next morning on top of the truck, his face still painted green and brown. Despite his pass, he was stopped by Honduran troops and nearly arrested as he tried boarding a bus at Danli with a knife. He must have had even more trouble explaining the strange makeup.

The ammunition trucks that came into camp at dawn clearly established the link between the FDN and the U.S. military. There were tons of munitions that seemed to have come from nowhere. Bermudez had told me there was plenty of ammo being stored in dumps near the big American air base at Palmerola.

Bermudez's complaints about a lack of resources appeared to be little more than a smoke screen. He had all the right connections to get whatever he needed from the CIA and the U.S. military.

The boxes of munitions on the trucks were stenciled with information about their contents and lot numbers. They also had "CIA-Brazil" stamped on them. I asked Commandante 26 if this was old ammunition purchased with original covert funding from the U.S. "No," he replied, "this is new." The original materiel had been exhausted months earlier.

So much for the restrictions of the Boland Amendment.

Defense of Wiwili

The first light of dawn revealed thousands of Contras lined up near the fence waiting to be issued weapons and ammunition. Each unit took extra weapons, including M-60 machineguns, 60mm mortars and LAAW rockets. The weapons were literally being thrown out of the arms depot at the men. Heavy base plates and shells for the mortars were being strapped onto the backs of soldiers who would have to walk nearly 15 miles with their loads.

I was surprised by the amount of weaponry I was seeing. The picture I had been given of ill-equipped and poorly armed soldiers was a fraud. There were U.S. and Soviet weapons. Much of the U.S. equipment was new and was preferred by the troops. The Soviet materiel was older, especially the ammunition, and it eventually was set aside.

After the COE troops had formed up near the arms depot to wait for Bermudez, I spotted their commander, Gustavo, near the fence and asked him if he had any details on the situation. He said about 5,000 Sandinista troops had surrounded a 500-man FDN battalion at Wiwili, about 20 klicks from the border. The FDN troops were in danger of being annihilated.

I could sense the urgency of this mission because unlike other operations, the soldiers ran out of the base towards the infiltration point, not dragging ass as they did most other times.

Bermudez was fashionably late in making his appearance before the troops. But when he did, he was a portrait of military splendor.

He wore camouflaged BDUs and brightly shined black boots, as if he were going on parade. He was armed with a MAC-10 sub-machine gun and a .45 in the leather holster I had given him. As he walked toward his staff truck, I caught up with him and told him my men were ready.

"No participation," he said, waving his hand as if he were chasing away a pesky fly.

I stood there slightly dazed. Just like that he had called off our operation. I knew I would have a difficult time explaining this to the men. They were chomping at the bit to get into action.

Jim Adair, the *Eagle* magazine reporter, reacted more quickly than I.

"I'm not going to miss this," he said. "Besides, I'm not here to fight."

Adair rushed to Bermudez's truck and asked permission to go along. Bermudez nodded his consent. I tried to recover my composure and made one last attempt to figure out what was going on.

"Why aren't we being allowed to go?" I asked Bermudez.

"I cannot allow you to participate," he said. "I will explain my reasons when I return in a few days."

Then he was off to the war, leaving me standing there with my finger up my ass trying to come up with some way to tell the Americans.

The excitement and fear I had seen in the faces of the Americans quickly turned to shock and then to anger. Sailor was furious. He threw his AK-47 on the ground and began to shout curses at Bermudez. The men descended on me en masse, shouting questions and demanding I do something. Many of them wanted to take matters into their own hands and follow the column into Nicaragua. I decided against that. It would have been too risky, politically and militarily, to go free-lancing with this group.

I retreated to a table in the officers' mess to try to find some answers. I found none.

I made several more efforts that day to get the Americans involved, but to no avail. I even told Commandante 26, who was left in charge of the camp, that all the Americans were returning to La Quinta as soon as we found transportation. He spent most of the day sending radio messages to Bermudez about our intentions.

I felt this would either get us into the fight or thrown out of Honduras. If the latter happened, what the hell? We were being wasted anyway. Darkness came without any word from Bermudez.

Las Vegas was virtually deserted. Bermudez had thrown nearly every able-bodied soldier, except for the Americans and the artillery units, into this battle. Militarily, it was an incredibly stupid move. If the Sandinistas found out, they would have a field day chewing up Contra troops with their helicopter gunships.

Whatever hopes the American volunteers still had about getting involved in the battle faded the next morning when several trucks came roaring up the hill into the hospital compound. In the back were wounded troops, including several COE soldiers. Most had leg wounds.

One of the litter bearers told me a major battle was going on near Rosario. He said four COE soldiers had been killed. This puzzled me because COE was usually held in reserve and often was used for Bermudez's personal protection. But all morning the radios chattered with information about the Contras being engaged with three battalions of *pericuaco* regulars since dawn.

That day there was a continuous stream of dead and wounded Contras coming back from the battle. I don't doubt that the Americans who saw them were relieved they had not been allowed to participate.

Bermudez returned to camp two days later. He went directly to his hutch and refused to see anyone except runners bringing radio messages from the front. I could see him, sitting at his table, his head propped between hands, reading the stack of battlefield reports, looking like a man who had the weight of the world on his shoulders.

The dead and wounded continued to flow back to Las Vegas. COE troops arrived looking tired and dirty, but, for the most part, seemed to be intact. Jim Adair came back half-starved and nearly ran over people trying to find something to eat.

As he wolfed down beans and rice, Adair filled us in on what had happened over the last few days.

He said when he arrived at the front, he could hear sporadic gunfire in the distance, but no major battle was in progress. Some of the Contra troops had gone on ahead of him and his group remained on the edge of a steep hill along with Bermudez and the command post, which was nothing more than a tent guarded by a .50-caliber machine gun and a few sentries.

Not until he got to the front did Adair realize he left in such a hurry he forgot all his gear but his camera, film and a weapon. Nights in the mountains can get quite cool and Adair had no blanket or sleeping bag. The only thing he could find was a fiberglass sack used to store coffee beans. From then on he was known as Sacko.

As Adair ate and talked around mouthfuls of food, the Americans crowded around to learn what they had missed. What he described was a slapstick scene worthy of a Woody Allen movie.

Neither the Contras nor the Sandinistas attempted to conceal their presence or positions from the other in the valley floor below the command post. Campfires were started on both sides of the valley and there was an undeclared ceasefire while the troops cooked their evening meals. After dark, the two sides shouted curses at each other, but there was no shooting. This was a 9-to-5 war.

Adair said from his vantage point in the seam between the hills, he could see most of the maneuvering that began about 4 o'clock the next morning when the Contras set out their version of an ambush. The ambush consisted of Bermudez walking out of his tent, signalling his troops to start fighting, and walking back into the tent.

The fire from both sides was intense as the soldiers stood virtually face to face in British-style picket lines. The trees and underbrush, originally thick with foliage, began to melt away as thousands of rounds zipped through them. As the firing continued, trees no longer provided cover and casualties began to mount on both sides.

Bermudez stood at the edge of the hill watching the battle while sipping a cup of coffee. The .50-caliber machine gun in front of the command post poured fire into the valley, but Adair said he couldn't tell which side was getting the worst of it because the soldiers could not control the recoil of the weapon and sighting was bad, at best.

The battle went on for nearly eight hours, until dusk, when the Sandinistas began pulling out. Instead of taking advantage of the situation and inflicting maximum damage on the retreating enemy, the Contras allowed the Sandinistas to retreat in peace. Bermudez declared the ambush a success and returned to Las Vegas.

There was a saying down there that "the last side to finish the breakfast dishes loses the battle." In most cases, that was true. The Sandinistas and the Contras employed crude and outdated tactics. Soldiers refused to fight from foxholes because they believed if they dug in, they would be buried there. Instead, they often stood in the open, upright and flat-footed, firing at the enemy until one of them dropped.

Adair said Bermudez had denied him permission to go down into the valley after the battle for pictures. Adair wanted to find out how badly the Contras had suffered, but that was strictly forbidden for journalists. Bermudez was quite protective of the image of the fighting ability of the Contras and if anyone found out how bad they actually were, there was little chance Congress would allocate money for them.

As we listened to Adair, Bermudez came to the table to give us a brief after-action report. He proudly reported the Contras captured 30 AK-47 assault rifles, 4 soldiers and 26 entrenching tools. We all looked at one another as if to say: "Is this man for real?" After committing nearly every soul on the base to battle, after leaving the camp unprotected, after wasting the lives of many young men, he had the balls to brag about 30 rifles, four soldiers and 26 entrenching tools.

Bermudez also informed us that Sandinista radio traffic indicated at least half the attacking force had been lost. I found this statistic rather amazing because that would have meant the Sandinistas suffered more than 1,000 casualties.

The numbers game as played by the Contras was so out of whack that if anybody had bothered to add up the alleged casualty figures they would have found the entire population of the country had been killed several times over during the course of the war.

Adios, Las Vegas

Shortly after Bermudez returned from the battle at Rosario, he began doing damage control with me. He said it had been a mistake to ask the Americans to participate. He said if one of us had been killed or wounded, Adolfo would cancel Pegaso. Adolfo had left strict orders that implementation of Pegaso had to wait until after the congressional vote on funding.

Bermudez said he would try to work out the problem with the Americans and indicated some might be allowed to go on future combat patrols. That mollified me temporarily. I had other problems, though. I couldn't figure out why Pegaso supplies were not being forwarded to the front and American volunteers were drifting into Las Vegas without any control.

Posey had to have some answers, but he was nowhere to be found. I decided to go back to La Quinta to track him down. I left Sailor in charge of the Americans and took off for La Quinta aboard Romano's mail truck.

We hadn't traveled more than five miles from Las Vegas when Romano slowed the truck to allow another truck approaching us from the opposite direction to pass. As it did, I saw Posey sitting among several men in the back. I ordered Romano to stop and jumped out.

Posey was his usual apologetic self, full of excuses about why he had not been in touch. He said he had been at a small Contra base called La Ladosa with Bill Curtis, a CBS news correspondent. The Contras had had some problems with CBS over several of its stories and Curtis was sent south to patch up things. Curtis was being given the royal tour of Contra bases and Posey was one of the tour guides.

Posey seemed surprised that the Pegaso supplies were not getting to us. I told him either we got organized, or we backed out of the war. He agreed to accompany me back to Tegus.

On the ride back he told me about an article that Bill Thomas had written in the *Memphis Commercial-Appeal.* It portrayed CMA in a positive light, but accompanying the story was a map that showed Las Vegas was in Honduran territory. In December 1984 the Hondurans and the FDN were still denying they were using foreign territory to prosecute the war. The Hondurans were not at all happy about the article and were demanding answers from the FDN. Despite the possible political fallout, Posey saw the article as a recruiting tool for CMA.

Posey and I had significantly different opinions about publicity. This article could mean more support for CMA, which meant more publicity for Posey. He liked being the center of attention. But the article could also mean the end of CMA involvement in the region. In addition to the map, the article contained a photo of Sailor, Traveler and Doc Zorro brandishing weapons.

Posey wanted nothing more than to be the recruiter and conduit for volunteers going to Honduras. He wanted nothing to do with them once they reached their destination. He would handle that and publicity, but little else. He was blissfully ignorant of the fact that at this point, logistics were more important than the publicity he was trying to generate.

Posey was obsessed with the deeply rooted anti-Communist beliefs that controlled his behavior. But he had no real knowledge of the ideology he so despised. He based his beliefs on traditional Southern values taught in the fifties and sixties during the height of the Cold War.

I was content to let Posey have the press recognition if our Pegaso operation was successful. But I told him he must consider placing someone in charge of logistics for the group. He agreed. He always agreed. But I knew he had to be pushed to agree.

I could not help but like Posey because he was friendly and eager to please. He just happened to get caught up in the glare of national attention while he was trying to prove something to himself. In doing that he became caught up in his own anti-Communist holy war. He felt trapped after the Powell-Parker incident and was trying to make amends by aiding CMA volunteers in their quest to enter the war.

All the grandiose notions I had of being a mercenary were being beaten down by the reality of the situation. There was no glory here. There was no honor. Had there been a strong, charismatic leader who could devise tactics and implement strategy, it might have worked. But I had surrounded myself with dreamers who were trying to get involved in a war that neither needed nor wanted them. That someone with the limited abilities of Posey could be in such a position spelled disaster for the naive volunteers he was recruiting and for the foreign policy the United States government wanted them to carry out.

The Bill Thomas story was stirring up more of a fuss than I realized. The Hondurans were up in arms. The FDN was up in arms. The State Department was up in arms. Even Mario was pissed. He wanted to know who had leaked the information. He said he would have to do a lot of talking to explain this to the FDN directorate in Miami.

Because of the heat being generated by the story, I decided it would be safer for Posey and I to leave Tegucigalpa and hide out in La Quinta. That would also give me an opportunity to check out Doc Zorro's story of the Pegaso supplies being warehoused there.

There was a large warehouse near the water tower at La Quinta, but it was off-limits to foreigners. I was always curious about its contents and was determined to find out what it contained. I had to enlist the help of Frank Arana, the FDN publicity chief, to get inside. Despite Fat Frank's considerable girth, he did not want to challenge me. There was a rumor floating around the Contra bases about how cold-blooded I could be. I didn't do anything to dispel that rumor because it helped open doors, just as it did at the warehouse.

When the warehouse guards reluctantly let us inside, my concerns about the Pegaso supplies were confirmed. I saw several seabags piled near a wall with the word "Pegaso" stenciled on them and asked when they had arrived. No one seemed to know. But I did not see any of the equipment that was to be purchased with the $30,000 from Maco Stewart.

Posey said he just hadn't had the time. I was furious and told Posey CMA had to be restructured if Pegaso was to work. He agreed with me, as he always did, but I wasn't sure anything would be done.

The warehouse also had long rows of shelves stacked with canned goods. The Cubans at Las Vegas told me tons of food were being shipped to La Quinta from Miami by the Cuban exile community, but none of it was getting to the front.

Bermudez told me the campesinos could not eat canned food because it made them sick. He also said he didn't want empty cans lying around in the field because the Sandinistas could use them to trail Contra soldiers to their camps. So, the donated food was stored at this facility for the sole purpose of supplying FDN officials and their families. This was the FDN Kroger.

While I was at La Quinta, word reached me that a strange American had been looking for me. I knew a lot of strange people, but no one strange enough to come down here looking for me. I was puzzled, but not particularly concerned.

One afternoon, Posey, Pulmon and I were sitting near the main office at La Quinta when we saw a short, muscular American approaching. The man had a mustache and goatee and wore a sleeveless shirt that exposed the massive arms of a weight lifter. On his upper left arm was a large USMC tattoo. He had a no-nonsense look on his face that told me he was no tourist looking for a little excitement.

"Are you Flaco?" he asked.

"Yes," I replied.

"Adolfo told me to look you up. I'm glad I found you because I've got a pocket full of plane tickets and I've travelled all over Central America looking for guys like you. You just don't know how many bars I've been hanging around in trying to hook up with some mercs."

"Where do you know Adolfo from?" I asked.

"My girlfriend is a friend of Adolfo's daughter and I got this job doing security at the safe house," he explained.

He explained that he was installing an alarm system at the FDN safe house in Tegucigalpa and training bodyguards for members of the FDN directorate. All of them feared assassination and thought trained bodyguards were a necessity for the cause.

He told us his code name was Tirador, or "Shooter." He claimed to be the current Pan American pistol champion and had instructed at various shooting ranges in Miami for several years. He also claimed to own several parcels of real estate and a gym, all of which he placed into escrow while he ran around Central America playing mercenary.

His real name was Joe Sam Adams. He was a former Marine from St. Louis looking for some action. He said if we allowed him into the organization he could donate a great deal of special equipment.

I took an immediate liking to Joe because there was no foreplay with him. Everything was right to the point. He demonstrated his bona fides by field-stripping an Uzi and then showing us how to convert our semi-automatic weapons to full automatic.

Joe knew weapons but, as I discovered much later, not much else. Nevertheless, I felt I could trust Joe. He was someone who could do my bidding while I was ironing out the millions of details that seemed to be a part of getting Pegaso up and running.

Despite the adverse publicity about American involvement in Central America as a result of the Bill Thomas story, I decided to take a chance and return to Tegucigalpa. I had to get away from the FDN for a while, away from the war. I had to find someone outside this realm of would-be warriors to talk to. I had to find some female companionship. I called Grace and made a date for dinner. She seemed happy to hear from me.

My loneliness must have been evident to her. She smiled and was quiet as I told her how beautiful she was, how sexy she was. When I invited her to my room, I was surprised that she did not protest. She walked straight to the elevator like she lived there.

When we got into the room I found myself fumbling for words like an awkward school boy on his first date. I didn't know what to say or do. She finally took the initiative and put her arms around me, kissing me deeply and passionately. I slipped my hands under her dress and caressed her warm, smooth body.

Grace had soft, dark skin covered with a velvet-like layer of fine, black hair. She had large, firm breasts, a small waist, and long, silky legs. Her body aroused me like nothing else I had ever experienced. When our bodies came together for the first time, she whispered in my ear, "Go slow."

I did, and from that night on we were inseparable.

Grace committed her career, her heart and her soul to me and my quest. She became a full-fledged member of the group and assisted us through her position as a supervisor at Pan Am by furnishing intelligence on the movement of FDN officials or anyone else we needed to keep track of. She stashed suitcases containing civilian clothing at her house when we went to the border. At times she held money, guns and passports at her residence so that these items could be readily available when we came back to Tegus. She was a far better soldier than most men I met in Honduras.

I stayed at the hotel for two days until Fat Frank Arana showed up and announced the Honduran government had ordered all American advisers to leave the country because of the fallout from the Bill Thomas article. Frank said he needed to have a confidential meeting with me to work out a slight problem FDN was encountering.

The problem had to do with the FDN's concern over my reaction to the expulsion order and the Americans at Las Vegas. FDN leaders were concerned I might make a fuss about it and create more problems for them. They were convinced I had some connection with the U.S. government in Washington and could cause them major problems. I sensed their fear and played off it.

The meeting was something more than I expected. Frank brought two men with him. One was Aristides Sanchez, Secretary to the directorate of the FDN. The problems must have been serious for him to show up.

The other man was a gringo. He wore a suit and looked right through me when he entered the room. He didn't offer an introduction and Frank and Aristides didn't offer one. The man never said a word the whole time he was there. He sat and listened while the two FDN officials relayed their problems to me.

I knew enough by now not to question the gringo about who he was or what he represented. He had Agency written all over him. But there was something more, something I couldn't quite pin down, something that said he was more than Agency by the way he seemed to intuitively understand what was going on here. That something told me he was from Donald Fortier and the group he claimed to represent.

Frank and Aristides said only I could solve their problems. The Americans at Las Vegas were refusing to leave unless they received a direct order from me. The Americans feared something had happened to me and were not about to budge until they found out what was going on. I was impressed by their loyalty to me, considering how badly I thought of them. Sailor was doggedly obeying my orders and I knew if anyone tried to force him out without my say-so, there would be gunplay.

I wrote out an order for Frank to pass on to the troops at Las Vegas so they would leave without resistance. I told them I knew they were proud Americans and that they had acted in good faith, but the time had come to temporarily abandon the mission. I advised them not to carry any weapons back to the United States because of the problems they might cause.

There was one another problem. The FDN thought I was too valuable to lose. Frank and Aristides said they couldn't let me go back to the

States. They believed the controversy would eventually blow over and they wanted me to continue forming the special unit for a strike into Nicaragua. The FDN would pay for me to go into hiding somewhere, but I had to decide where and let them know.

After Frank and Aristides left, I called Mario. He was aware of the fragile political situation involving the Americans and knew the FDN wanted me to stay in the vicinity. He suggested I go to Roitan Island in the Bay Island chain off the eastern coast of Honduras. I could take some time off and relax.

I still thought it best to return to the States to do damage control with the American volunteers, but Mario would not even consider that. I had to get out of Honduras to let things cool off, but I had to be close by so the FDN could bring me back quickly as soon as the tensions eased.

The FDN gave me 1,000 lempiras, about $500, for my stay on Roitan Island. It wasn't much, considering how valuable Frank and Aristides said I was to the cause. But it was enough to keep me in hiding for a while. I called Tirador and told him I was disappearing for a while. I didn't know when, but I said I would be back in touch.

When I left for Roitan Island, I was convinced I was not in need of rest or relaxation. But I did not realize how much my health had been affected by all the running back and forth among the U.S., Honduras, Las Vegas and La Quinta, eating bad food, not sleeping enough and being worried to distraction by the motley crew of Americans foisted on me.

I had lost weight I couldn't afford to lose and was experiencing problems with my lungs. The stress had depleted my energy resources and as I began to wind down from Pegaso, I felt worse and worse. I began questioning my ability to physically survive this.

My sense of fatalism convinced me to leave a record in case something happened to me. I knew when I finally got the chance to gather my thoughts, I had to write down as much of what I had gone through as I could remember and ship it back to the States. These chronicles would serve as an explanation of what really happened in the event someone tried to devise a cover story to hide my participation in the war.

8

Yesterday Once More:
The Shadow of Doubt

Roitan Island off the east coast of Honduras is a scuba diver's dream and a honeymooner's paradise. Its gin-clear waters, white sandy beaches and remote bungalows without television or telephone offer the ultimate in privacy and isolation for newlyweds and those who just want to get away from it all.

It was a perfect hiding place for me. But I was an oddity on the island. I was there alone. And I was not there to snorkel or scuba dive. The young American woman who managed the resort at Anthony's Key, near the little town of Cockson's Hole, noticed I was without a bride or diving gear and asked what I was there to do.

"I just came to rest up from a job in Honduras," I told her.

"Are you with the military?" she asked, staring at my closely cropped hair.

"Not exactly."

She didn't press the issue. The islanders, most of whom are black and closer to Jamaican heritage than Honduran, were trying to build the tourist trade and if a stranger showed up who didn't want to answer questions, so be it. The atmosphere here was built on service, solitude and serenity. Here, there was none of the overbearing officiousness I had encountered on the mainland.

My bungalow was on a small island in the middle of a lagoon that had the most incredibly blue water I had ever seen. A water taxi operated 18 hours a day and if I needed to go into town, all I had to do to call the taxi was pound on the empty scuba tank that hung near the end of the pier with a wrench.

From the sun deck on my bungalow I could look out over the lagoon and the island's white beaches. There were no concerns about the Contras, the FDN or the CMA here. It should have been the perfect place for me to relax and escape the war and the foreign policy blunders that had brought it to this phase, when those who ran the war were spending more time fighting Congress than the Sandinistas.

But, for me, Roitan Island was no island paradise. I could not enjoy the beach or the surf. Telephones are my lifeline to the world and without one I felt lost, alone and confused. The only phone on the island was in a house on the highest hill in Cockson's Hole and I was sure it was monitored. I wanted to stay in contact with Mario, Posey and Joe Adams, but was reluctant to use the phone because of the feeling someone was watching me. My paranoia was getting the best of me.

There were too many questions spinning around in my head.

Why had the FDN put me on this island and none of the other CMA members?

And why had I not heard from my mysterious benefactor in Washington who had identified himself as Donald Fortier?

It had been more than two months since my last telephone conversation with him. If he and the group he claimed to represent were so intent on getting information about CMA, why had no one contacted me for the information I had gathered?

I was also troubled by the war, the people who were fighting it, how it was being fought and my involvement in it. The Boland Amendment had turned what was supposed to be a major foreign policy initiative into an ad hoc operation financed through private donations.

The lines between civilians and the military had been blurred. Civilians were being recruited to act in a military fashion while active-duty military personnel were participating as civilians to get around congressional restrictions and to avoid creating political problems in Honduras.

There was no congressional oversight and no executive control of the operation. Ineptitude, corruption and criminal activity were endemic. The foreign policy goals of the United States were of secondary concern to many of those involved. The Contra war had become a money-making scheme designed to pad the pockets of a few individuals. Americans paid with their tax dollars while the Nicaraguan campesinos paid with their lives. In some instances, pecuniary interests took precedence over patriotism. There was a lot of money to be made in this war.

None of it made any sense. Yet I had to make some sense of it or go crazy trying.

I felt I needed an insurance policy that told the true story of what was happening here and how I had gotten involved in it. I decided to put on paper everything I had seen or learned. I began writing letters to myself and sending them to Teri Cassil, a friend in the States who was handling my affairs there while I was gone. I knew Teri would come to my defense if my body showed up without a reasonable explanation of how I had died or why.

I was reluctant to leave a paper trail about my involvement in the war. But, for this operation, in order to protect myself I had taken the precaution of hanging on to certain documents I knew could be valuable. The most important was the letter of introduction Mario wrote to Enrique Bermudez for me. I had steamed open the letter on my first trip, copied it and retained the copy. I knew that letter would be irrefutable evidence of my involvement with the FDN in case its commandantes developed a sudden case of brain paralysis.

I would not be silenced, in life or in death.

Each day during my stay on Roitan Island I sat at the table on my sun deck writing down every detail of my involvement I could recall. My writing allowed me to access memories that, standing alone, meant little. Tied together, they presented a clear pattern.

I saw myself getting deeper and deeper into the foundation of the FDN and gaining power and credibility as I did. I was being told secrets and shown things that no other American had seen or heard.

I was fascinated by the fact that I had been elevated without appropriate background checks into the upper levels of this organization that for many years had been run by the CIA. The CIA seemed to have lost control of the operation, or its sense of what it was trying to do here. Its agents in the region were running around like so many loose cannons on the gun deck, while I had moved into a position to provide some stability to the operations.

I certainly didn't see myself as a leader, but I had enough power, through acquired knowledge, to give valuable input that could affect the course of the war. I knew I was treading on dangerous turf here because if I decided to use this knowledge the wrong way, it could be my epitaph.

I was on the threshold of getting so deeply involved with the FDN that I would never be able to get out. Yet I was frustrated by the FDN leaders and their reluctance to allow CMA any leeway due to concern over the vote on congressional funding. Adolfo was easily influenced by political pressure from Washington and I knew that meant we may never get to attain our original goals.

I also knew that if I continued to ascend in the FDN hierarchy I would either self-destruct or be done away with because I knew too much for my own good.

I began thinking of alternative routes to take in the event Adolfo decided against implementing Pegaso. The Miskitia, where the MISURA Indian confederation was in dire need of help, seemed a viable option and I seriously began considering it, based on what Doc Zorro told me several weeks earlier.

Despite the pleasant climate on the island and good food, my health continued to deteriorate. I was losing weight, had no energy and constantly took antibiotics, hoping I would get better. Nothing worked.

I walked the beaches when I could no longer sit still and began to feel like a caged animal. I wanted to get back into action. I wanted to discuss some of the things I was thinking with another human being. In this world I had created for myself I was like an actor, daily donning a mask and playing a role created for me. I needed someone to relate to the real me, the Jack Terrell whose emotions were much more changeable than the cold and calculating Colonel Flaco.

Still, I liked my new self and had convinced myself that the new me could quite possibly alter history in some fashion. I wrote in one of my letters that I had found my destiny after a life of searching and fumbling through the charade of materialism that had dominated my life for many years. I revelled in the power and potential of changing history and only occasionally felt the fear of knowing that one day I would probably take a terrible fall from the pedestal I had constructed for myself.

I went into this operation with the knowledge I might not survive it. In doing so, I got a look at a side of life only the suicidal see. I was calm in stressful situations that might make ordinary people throw up their hands in despair. I had gotten to the point where in combat I felt virtually bulletproof. My behavior was not normal by any acceptable social standards. But this was not normal society. I was creating the rules and shaping my society as I went along.

On Roitan Island, I had to face the beast that is within all of us. I either had to accept it or totally reject it. If I blinked or backed away, the opportunity I had to make history could be forever lost. I had to make the decision which side to come down on and then forever bear the consequences of my decision.

I was seriously questioning my own beliefs and principles during those long, tortured sessions with pen and paper. I knew the disadvantages of continued attachment to the base and corrupt organization that the FDN had proved itself to be. And I knew the disadvantages of following my principles that told me to run away from the FDN.

There was a constant mental tug of war between what I felt was the right and decent thing to do and the guilt I felt about everything I had seen in Las Vegas with the Contras. I was becoming self-righteous and indignant about human rights abuses. I feared far worse acts were being committed in the name of freedom. This was totally unacceptable to me.

I began questioning my own sanity because I was trying to justify how I could judge the actions of the Contras while being available to kill people under their banner. The hypocrisy ate at me. I felt I was losing sight of my values. But I also felt I had to continue to try to change the direction of this war. I always thought there was some honor in war, but I was contributing to the conditions that aided those who acted without honor.

I was beginning to question my own credibility as a human being. What was it that had brought me to this point in my life? Where had I come from and why? The past unfolded before me like a macabre parade of characters and events as I sat there on Anthony's Key, staring out over the blue lagoon straight into yesterday.

No More Cavaliers

Growing up in Birmingham, Alabama, in the late forties and early fifties had imbued me with the proper doses of patriotism, conservatism and anti-Communism that seemed necessary to become part of the war in Central America. These inbred beliefs were part of the family, part of being Southern.

My sense of adventure came from elsewhere. It came from my relationship, or lack of one, with my parents. They were not equipped with adequate knowledge to deal with a son with an IQ of 182 Beta. It was easier to ignore the problems I created than recognize my needs in trying to cope with thought processes far beyond my years. My intelligence was given no useful direction and it manifested itself in rude, spiteful behavior that eventually turned criminal.

I was the oldest of three sons in my family born after two girls. As the firstborn male, my father saw himself in me. The problem was, I never saw myself in him.

Billy Reynolds Terrell was a scion of the upper-middle class white community in Birmingham. He went to work at Southern Railroad on the night shift and I hardly ever saw him, except sleeping during the day. He rarely spent time with the family because he saw his role as sole support and would never shirk that responsibility.

My father wanted me to be a carbon copy of him and go to work on the railroad, a tradition on his side of the family. Five generations of the Terrell family had worked on the railroad, and I was expected to be the sixth. Even before I reached my teens I had a job lined up as a yardmaster as soon as I got out of college or high school.

But I didn't care one bit about trains. All I remember of my younger years is riding trains. My father had rail passes that let us go anywhere. Whenever we went somewhere, it was on a train. By the time I was 12 and my precocious and devilish nature had made itself known to everyone, I let him know I didn't care one bit for railroads and had no intention of following him into the business.

My mother, Vivian, performed the duties of both mother and father in the family. She suffered from chronic back problems that caused her to be irritable most of the time. She was a strict disciplinarian and once provoked, could dish out beatings that kept us fearful of her wrath. Under trying circumstances, she did the best she could raising five children.

I was stubbornly independent and never gave in to my father's demands or expectations. The more he wanted me to be like him, the more I resisted. I wanted him to recognize that I was different. To get that recognition, I did everything he didn't want me to do.

At 13, I started running away from home. I knew there were great undiscovered regions to be explored and the lure of the unknown tugged at my imagination. I ran with people my parents knew little about, people I found exciting because they wanted to live on the edge of life and lawlessness. I was continually bored without mental challenges and each new escapade away from home was like a dare that fired my imagination. I had intelligence and energy to burn. But I was a kid who loved destruction and performed all manner of cruelties against people and animals. My childhood was anything but normal.

It was a strange time for me. I always did exactly the opposite of those around me. When I did not get my way, I generally took it out either on some poor animals or one of my sisters or brothers. I sometimes felt singled out for punishment and this gave me an excuse to commit additional acts of terror in the neighborhood.

I did poorly in school despite my potential. I just wasn't interested in learning and hated the control teachers had over me. I thought I was smarter than they and acted out comedic roles for my classmates to deflect attention from my low grades. I wanted to be the class clown to gain attention that I didn't get at home. But even my friends and classmates grew tired of my act and moved on.

This isolated me even further from normal behavior because it became a test to me to demonstrate that I was somehow as good as those who shunned me. I needed to conduct myself in such a way at school and home to make damn sure I did not go unnoticed.

I refused to read books. Reading was boring. What few books I read offered no challenge. I was able to figure out the ending before I got more than a few chapters into them. I could not understand the value of a schoolhouse education or realize how it would be more beneficial than what I was able to teach myself. I was a little person with a large brain out of place in the world. I could communicate with those much my senior, but could not actually live as they did. I was caught between stages of life, too smart to be young, too young to be an adult. I fit nowhere.

The lack of a true education became an obstacle I kept running into. It was like an invisible wall in front of me all my life. I couldn't understand why I wasn't advancing past it. The more frustrated I became, the more disinterested I was in learning.

I was my own greatest enemy. My refusal to accept education enabled me to make the quantum leap from a kid with limitless potential to a dumb, uneducated adult.

Everything I learned in life was through self-taught assimilation that evolved from my instinct for survival. I never wanted people to see me for what I truly was — an unenlightened person who never knew the joys of literature. I squandered my intelligence in the search for personal fulfillment.

Although I found books to be a waste of my time, it was a book that more than anything or anyone else determined my course in life.

By the age of 15, I was spending much of my time at the Alabama Boys Industrial School (ABIS), a reform school for recalcitrants and malcontents such as myself. We referred to the school as "Air Base In Spain," trying to fool ourselves into thinking it was something other than what it was — a reform school for snotty-nosed brats. We were tough guys, or so we thought. But we were actually a bunch of frightened kids in search of some direction in life.

One winter day when I was bored, I crawled under a large wooden table in the recreation room in my dormitory to find some warmth. For company, I pulled a book in with me. It was a nondescript volume titled *J.E.B. Stuart: The Last Cavalier*, by Burke Davis.

At first I found the book to be dry and dull, a lifeless commentary on the life of this Confederate general. I had thoughts of putting it down and looking for something else more entertaining. But as I read on, the book reached out and grabbed me as no other book ever had.

Here was the true story of a man who possessed great wisdom and intelligence. The pages were filled with poetic, inspiring letters to his wife recounting his battles, his fears and his hopes for a better world when the war was over. His words cast a spell over me. Here was the man I wished I could be.

I felt a kinship with Stuart. I identified with him and I respected him like I had never respected anyone. I could not put the book down and read it cover to cover. That was a first for me. It was also a last. Never again would I be enthralled by words as I was that day.

This book and Stuart's life became the model by which I was determined to live the rest of my life. His principles, humanity, love and compassion gave me another view of what I thought I could be and what I felt others should be. Coupled with the remnants of my Southern upbringing, a mold was cast that day into which I poured myself. I combined what I was and who he was. The mixture fit like a glove. Now I felt some sense of belonging to something, not a person and not an idea, but something with deep meaning that permitted me to take on self-discipline and regimented thought.

The book made such an impression on me that I even acted out the role of this cavalier in real life a few weeks later. It was an event that would scar me and mark me forever.

Two friends and I decided to escape from ABIS. We stole a 1949 Ford and began a short-lived criminal career through northern Alabama. I had acquired a gray Confederate officer's hat with a yellow Ostrich plume in it and rode shotgun, literally, a .12-gauge in my lap, as we drove through the piney woods in search of adventure and trouble.

We found what we were looking for at several gas stations. We stole gas and food and at one point the owner of one of the stations came creeping out of the back room in his night shirt, a revolver in his hand. I stood by the window, the .12 gauge leveled at him.

I motioned to one of my companions.

"Is someone coming?" he said in a whisper.

I nodded my head.

"He's dead," I whispered back.

"No!" came the frantic reply. "Let's get the hell out of here."

I lowered the gun and we hopped in the car. We roared away as the owner began blasting away at us, hitting the car four or five times. One of the rounds ripped the headliner, ricocheted around the car and dropped to the floor, where we found it the next day.

I thought I was Jeb Stuart reborn. I had evolved from a truant in a reform school to a joyriding adventurer acting out life much like a play. I had graduated from a runny-nosed imp to a fearless, skinny little shit with a self-styled persona from the past bound to commit some terrible act if placed in the right circumstances.

I was carrying things to the extreme in my newfound identity. I possessed the capabilities of becoming a murderer, or worse, because my imagination had totally run away with me. I could not separate the fantasy in my head from the illegality of what I was doing. I was breaking the law, yet had no sense of what I was doing. It all seemed perfectly right to me and never dawned on me that this venture was a crime.

I was feeling as immortal as the man I had taken my identity from, but could not see the waste I was making of my life.

My arrest brought everything into focus. The judge showed me no mercy and I was jailed for playing a role in which I was unable to understand the difference between life in one's head and life in the real world. It didn't matter then which character I chose to serve the time as — fantasy rebel or juvenile delinquent.

The charges were auto theft, grand larceny and burglary, the combined sentences 18 years and two days to be served in federal reform schools and state prisons. In another era I probably would have gotten little more than a slap on the wrist. But Southern justice being what it was in those days, the judge decided to make an object lesson of us.

At the age of 15, I was staring down a dark tunnel. I was about to spend my most impressionable years behind bars in the company of others who had done things far more horrible than I and were far more worldly than I.

I was not just being sentenced to prison, I was being sentenced to become a completely different person. Entering prison, I was a kid with the street smarts of a career criminal and the naivete of a teenager on the edge of manhood. I had become a person not even my family recognized.

Prison was the catalyst for development of all my strengths and weaknesses. In prison I found I could act out any role I chose because most of my peers lacked the basic knowledge and common sense to see through me. The mind games I played were needed to survive in a hostile environment of thieves, thugs and killers.

In prison I could be all the things that I could never be on the streets. I could be a lawyer, a doctor, an adviser or a tactician devising appeals for empty-minded petty thieves who could hardly figure out how to break into a refrigerator, much less work their way through the court system.

I relished this role because it gave me a sense of superiority that I needed as much as a drug addict needs a fix. The more superior I felt, the greater the rush.

The reality was that I was simply a smarter ant in a hill of ants. I was a misguided kid with untapped resources and undefined goals continuing to be the smart-assed person I had always been, but learning things I could never learn on the outside. I was in a place of great danger living with people who fed off one another like animals, but I never felt any sense of danger or fear. I believed I was in a world totally separate from them, living with them yet apart from them. I never considered myself one of them.

In prison I found the attention I craved. Not because I was young and vulnerable, but because I was smarter than just about everybody else around me. I used my brains where they used their brawn. I learned early I could manipulate less intelligent and weaker minds. I found I could talk myself into and out of situations with ease. I could avoid trouble and potentially dangerous situations simply through the art of bullshit. I became a manipulator, a con man, somebody who could get things done when other inmates couldn't. It was a skill that later became invaluable.

Not only did I get the attention I desired, but I found a sense of family in prison that I had never known on the outside. I was much closer to the guys inside than I had been to any member of my family, except perhaps my mother. There was a feeling among those in prison that we were all society's discards, unwanted, unloved and unneeded. We thrived on our rejection from society.

The one thing I did not expect to find in prison was a man who would become the father to me my own father had never been. John C. Watkins, the warden at Alabama's Draper Correctional Center, was the youngest prison warden in the United States. I came to his attention one day in 1961 at the age of 20, when I acquired the combination of the safe in the office of the chief clerk and stole $50.

Rather than punish me, John thought anybody with enough moxie to pull off a robbery inside a prison deserved some special attention. He took me under his wing and gave me the opportunity to become one of a select group of men that got his undivided attention.

John was an innovator in dealing with criminal behavior. He introduced methods of rehabilitation at Draper that at the time were considered reckless. He designed a program for inmates who demonstrated the intelligence, personality and will to become something other than a lifer in prison. Good behavior was rewarded by astonishing liberties and bad behavior was treated harshly. He gave love and respect to the men with the same ease with which he doled out solitary confinement. He never gave up on anyone and always seemed to be the first person to toss out lifelines to those who most needed help.

I became John's secretary. The job carried a great deal of responsibility and enabled me to exercise an unusual amount of personal power. I had access to John any time of the day or night and was granted passage through all the gates of the institution, a rare privilege for an inmate.

I had so much freedom I could have simply walked out the gate and kept going. But I felt allegiance to this man, not from fear or from his position. We had an unspoken bond between us, much as that bond between a father and son. This was strangely different, though, because it was based on respect and special attention to needs that only John could understand.

Prison had its own code of ethics that few people on the outside could ever understand. We were stereotyped by the public, but the image was deceiving, especially among the men I became a part of at Draper. Just because we were behind bars did not mean we were all necessarily evil people. We adopted our own rules and regulations to govern ourselves. Everyone was held accountable to these standards. We served time, lived and died, but we lived by principles of a higher standard than those expected of most "normal" people. John instilled this in every man who came in contact with him.

John and I became quite close during the years I was at Draper from 1960 to 1965. We often referred to ourselves as Martians because each considered the other to be so specially gifted that we could not be of this earth. I once told John, years after my release, that I had become what he made me.

I used prison to learn about things that I couldn't learn on the outside. I learned about people and their vulnerabilities. I learned about the legal system and its shortcomings. I even learned about the military.

One day while wandering through the prison I stumbled on a Civil Defense shelter in the maintenance tunnel beneath the cellblocks. The shelter was crammed with canned food, medicine and military manuals in the event of a nuclear war.

I devoured the military manuals, learning about weapons, learning how to build bombs, learning how to organize military units. I learned how to field strip an M-1 rifle and a .45 pistol through the pages of the manuals, but without any hands-on experience. I learned theory, but no practical application. The knowledge I acquired in those many hours I sat reading through the manuals served me well much later, though.

Not all my time in prison was spent behind bars. Early in my sentence, I was given a look at the real world outside Alabama. It was an initiation into the strange world of Washington politics and the network of foreign and domestic intelligence agents who inhabit it.

In 1958 I was serving my first sentence at the National Training School for Boys in Washington. I was 17 at the time, untutored about everything but prison life. One day I was called to the office and told I had been selected, sight unseen, by a Washington businessman and former Naval underwater demolition team (UDT) officer who would be my "sponsor." It was part of a school program to provide male role models for the boys and to give us an opportunity and an incentive to see what life was like on the outside.

Milton G. Nottingham became my first mentor. He also gave me my first glimpse of Washington political life, introducing me to a world unknown and a life so foreign to an Alabama boy that I was dazzled by it.

Milt had connections to the Central Intelligence Agency and was the business partner of Tongsun Park, the alleged Korean CIA agent. Milt and Park shared ownership in the Georgetown Club, a place where congressmen and senators often gathered to let down their hair and their secrets.

Milt's relationship with Park caused him great anxiety for a time when controversy swirled around allegations that Park was buying favoritism for Korea through bribes to members of Congress. Park eventually was deported, while Milt escaped being tarnished by the scandal. There were detractors in Washington, though, who felt Milt never came clean about his involvement in the affair.

Milt was quite wealthy and headed a well-respected shipping agency. He once told me he earned more money than the president of the United States, a remark that surprised and shocked me. I couldn't conceive of anyone making more money than the president. He had also been president of the Merchant Marine Academy Alumni Association, which gave him access to businessmen who shared a long tradition in maritime service.

I was privy to many of the secrets Milt had about his dealings with the Navy, the Korean government and the CIA. I asked him early on if he would use his influence to get me into the CIA, but he told me it was not a place where I would want to work. Besides, I was too young.

After I returned to Alabama to finish out my sentence in a state prison, Milt corresponded with me frequently and made it clear he eventually wanted me to come live with him. Through Milt I had developed a desire for money and a fascination with power. I was determined when I got out of prison to do things no other ex-felon had ever done, to break barriers no one had ever broken, to be someone I had never been before.

When I left Draper prison in 1965 at the age of 24, it was like leaving my family. It had been my home for most of the eight years I served and I felt closer to the people inside than I did to anyone outside.

I had spent my formative years behind bars and my emotional development was anything but normal. My sexual beliefs and experiences were based on an all male sub-culture that, given the fact that I was practically a virgin, provided me with no real information about how I should handle women in or out of bed.

I wasn't ready for the social changes that had taken place while I was stagnating in prison. I was raised to believe living with someone outside marriage was not permissible. I didn't know that the social and moral fabric of the country was changing. I didn't know that the same values I had grown up with were no longer relevant. So, I married the first woman I felt could help me make the transformation from felon to useful member of society.

Love wasn't the primary incentive for getting married. I saw marriage as little more than a steady piece of ass and my ticket back into society. I didn't fully grasp the responsibility of such things as a job, bills and children. Another social failure was at hand.

My first marriage produced two daughters, one of whom died within a few months of her birth after being involved in an automobile accident, plenty of grief and, eventually, a divorce. The other was adopted by the man who married my ex-wife and I lost touch with her for over sixteen years.

By the late sixties I had opened a ambulance service in Montgomery, Alabama, with the financial backing of my brother, who was also my partner. We had a ton of creative ideas and the business became a minor success. I eventually broke with him and went in another direction, ending up with Peggy, the woman who became my business partner and second wife.

Unlike my first wife, I was truly in love with Peggy. Our thoughts and dreams meshed perfectly. When I left my brother and went to work for the State of Alabama as the first ex-felon to be hired as a correctional officer, Peggy was right by my side. With her support and encouragement, I graduated first in my class from the federally sponsored Law Enforcement Planning Administration academy in Alabama. Peggy was my equal in intelligence and desire and our collective pool of ideas never seemed to run dry.

We were rarely out of each other's sight and we became a world unto ourselves. We made money easily, but Peggy never spent much for herself. She allowed me to have anything I wanted, and more. Peggy and I enjoyed even more success as we branched out into a hearse and ambulance sales company that covered several states.

My marriage to Peggy produced my only son, William Randolph, and more of a unique opportunity to me to forge a strong emotional bond with another human being. I loved and trusted Peggy. I thought I would be with her forever.

Then, at one point in our marriage, as we worked long and demanding hours, Peggy was tempted to stray. She rejected the opportunity, but neither my ego and nor my antiquated value system could handle the slight. I walked out of her life to sulk and seek revenge over a transgression that never occurred. My emotional immaturity had caught up with me.

Despite a successful business and what would seem to be a successful marriage, I abandoned both in 1974 and moved to Mississippi to start all over again. It seemed the harder I worked and the more I succeeded, the more quickly I looked to move on to something that provided greater challenges.

In Mississippi I was re-introduced to the strange and mysterious world of intelligence operatives and mercenaries. Unlike the times I spent in Washington with Milt Nottingham learning how the policy makers developed these schemes, in Mississippi I became acquainted with those who carried out the schemes.

J.D. Hill, a 13-year veteran of the Army Special Forces, became a close and trusted friend during this time. On weekends J.D. invited me to training sessions with his Army Special Forces Reserve group, even though I was a civilian. I learned quickly and loved every bit of it. I became Special Forces without the paperwork. I was already a pilot, a scuba diver and a parachutist, and now I was able to combine all these things and devise a different identity for myself, if only in my own mind.

I went into the ambulance business again, got married and got divorced for a third time, all within a few years. My personal life was a shambles as I went through marriages like someone trying to make up for eight years of lost time.

But business had never been better. I had money. I had aircraft. I had my own ammunition assembly facilities. I had weapons galore and a large ranch where I could hone my shooting skills. I invited cops, military people and anyone else who wished to belong to my inner circle of bizarre acquaintances to join my shooting matches and be treated to certain perks in exchange for knowledge they possessed or goods, guns or explosives.

It was a social club for me and a free ride for the participants. It all worked to my advantage, though. My skills in covert operations and low-intensity conflicts grew by leaps and bounds.

Some weekends, J.D. Hill and I would go to the Northeast Mississippi Parachute Club in Batesville to practice jumping. It was a local hot spot for an assortment of strange characters, some of whom would bounce back into my life in later years.

One was Barry Seal, a pilot so good people used to say he could fly a refrigerator if it had wings. Seal later became an informant for the Drug Enforcement Administration and was gunned down on orders from Colombian drug lords after the White House leaked photos he had taken showing them working with top Nicaraguan officials on a drug deal.

Another of these characters was a former Republic Airlines pilot and parachute jumpmaster named Cliff Albright. Only a few years after Albright signed off on my last static line parachute jump at the Northeast Mississippi Parachute Club, he re-emerged as a participant in the Contra war as a member of Civilian Military Assistance. He was among those CMA members in Honduras when Parker and Powell were killed.

The more I talked to people like J.D. Hill and his buddies in Special Forces, and the more they filled my head with tales of international intrigue, adventure and excitement, the more I wanted to be part of it. J.D. and I talked frequently of traveling the world and fighting wars for profit. We even considered going to Nicaragua when the Sandinistas were trying to overthrow dictator Anastasio Somoza in the late seventies.

My time with J.D. was like going to military school. All his friends were vets and many craved the same action as I. Often, we would take stolen explosives to remote areas and blow things up to just to get a better understanding of how particular explosives work and how much damage certain size charges caused.

I learned the jargon of the spooks, the operatives and the rogues. I was brought into the "bubble," which meant becoming a part of the tapestry of people available for covert operations.

Over the next few years I built my ambulance service in Mississippi into a multimillion-dollar business. But the more successful I became, the more restless I got. There was a wanderlust inside me that I fought against because it was distracting, something for dreamers that I believed would lead to my destruction.

All my big talk of adventure with J.D. came to an end one night when his wife put five rounds from a .357 Magnum right in the middle of his chest. He drank too much and they argued about it frequently. This night she decided she had had enough of him and his drinking.

Not long after J.D.'s death, my mother died. These were two people I had allowed myself to get very close to, and with them gone I was lost and alone. Once again I abandoned a successful business. Only this time instead of starting a new one, I spent several years drifting around the country, looking for something to spark my interest.

I was so devastated by the loss of my mother and J.D. that all I could do was drive and talk into a tape recorder about the life I had lived and the pain I was feeling from a world in which I did not fit.

I was searching for the something that stayed steps ahead of me. I was chasing a dream of the future and trying to outrun the ghosts of the past.

I never could quite outrun those ghosts. I was ashamed I had been in prison and had difficulty dealing with it. In business, my past became the weapon competitors used against me. My capabilities were measured not by what I could do, but what I had done as a reckless teenager. As much as I wanted to let those ghosts die, others refused to allow it to happen. They kept the ghosts alive to torment me.

My prison record became the only rock detractors could throw at my credibility. The record has been used over and over in attempts to bring me down. I walked away from society when I broke the law, and I have learned I will never be completely able to re-enter it because of that indelible stain.

A Time for Returning

The longer I remained on Roitan Island and the more I relived my past, the more depressed I became. I had to gather enough strength to get out of this pool of depression and get CMA and Pegaso back on track.

I knew I had only two choices. I could either follow my heart, which told me that what I and the Contras were doing was morally indefensible. But that would entail going back to my dead end life. Or, I could make a pact with my darker side and remain with the Contras and try to convince myself I could change the system from the inside.

I chose the latter. I chose to stay with the Contras because they were the only ball game in town and I wanted to be a player.

I had been cloistered on this island for two weeks and decided to go into town and attempt to make a telephone call to the States. There were several people waiting to enter the house that held the island's only telephones and switchboard. A young woman sat in front of an Edison vintage switchboard. She wore a headset with a old carbon microphone attached. She screamed into the mike because of bad connections as she pushed plugs into the board. There were just two phones and making connections to the States sometimes was an all-day affair.

I gave the operator Tom Posey's number and waited 45 minutes before the number rang through to his Decatur produce warehouse.

He told me the other CMA members made it safely back to the States after being ordered out of Honduras. I told Tom to tell Zorro and Tirador to meet us at the Contempra Inn in three days. I had important business about CMA to talk over with them. It was time to restructure the organization.

Tom was hyper about the publicity that had been generated on CMA's behalf by the Bill Thomas article. He said he was receiving dozens of telephone calls from potential volunteers. I told him not to accept any more men for the project until we held the meeting and could establish some standards within the organization to prevent another fiasco such as the one that had recently occurred at Las Vegas.

I told Posey not to tell Mario I was leaving Roitan. I didn't want the FDN pulling any strings that might keep me from getting out of the country. I wanted to get off the island and be on a plane bound for the United States before anyone in the organization knew where I was or what I was doing.

When I arrived back in New Orleans, none of the meeting participants was there.

Zorro was still in Houston, meeting with Maco Stewart about the $30,000 he had given Mario several weeks earlier. Maco was upset because the FDN could not explain what happened to that money. He wanted Zorro to get an itemized account from Mario because he knew Pegaso had received neither money nor equipment.

Tirador was in Miami. He was planning to drive back to St. Louis before coming to New Orleans. He said he had talked to a Swedish gunsmith in St. Louis about manufacturing silencers for our Uzis and was talking with a company about producing the black web gear for the Pegaso unit.

Posey was still in Decatur, pushing produce and CMA donations.

Since it would be several days before everyone would assemble for the meeting, I called Mario. He was surprised I was back in town and wanted to know what I was planning. He got quite agitated when I told him Maco Stewart wanted to know what had become of his money. He said he still had $27,000 of it but that Maco could come and get the balance anytime he wanted. He was offended that his honor and integrity were being challenged.

I also tried to impress on him the importance of pushing on with plans for Pegaso.

"If Adolfo is going to use CMA the way he said he would if the vote in Congress goes the wrong way, we're going to have to go back to Las Vegas and start serious training," I said.

"Adolfo has to personally approve anyone going to Honduras," Mario replied.

"Fine," I said. "I'll go directly to Adolfo in Miami."

Mario wasn't pleased that I would go over his head, but he knew better than to challenge me.

When Posey showed up the next day, I immediately began restructuring the organization. I told him he could best serve CMA by acting as the administrative head, not as the field commander. He had no real desire for combat anyway, but he did not want to lose his grip on the organization that had brought him so much notoriety. He liked the limelight, but didn't want to risk his life for it.

When Tirador arrived, he had his girlfriend in tow and immediately checked into the Sheraton instead of the Contempra. He was trying to demonstrate that he was a high roller who didn't want to stay in a place that didn't have room service.

Tirador talked freely about what he claimed was unlimited access to weapons and gear through connections he had made while working as a bodyguard for various Colombian drug dealers. He said he also worked at the notorious Tamiami Gun Shop in Miami where all manner of strange customers came to practice shooting under his tutelage. He said most of his students were Latino and that he had gained a great deal of knowledge about Spanish mentality that he could contribute to the group.

I saw early on that Tirador was doing much the same thing as I. He was trying to talk his way into the organization through bluff and bluster, all the while knowing he had little combat experience. I felt we could overcome this deficiency and told him I needed an executive officer, someone who would be second in command of military operations.

Tirador liked the offer, until I told him this was a "pay your own way" war. He said he would do what he could to help us gain necessary weapons and equipment, but that his primary role in Honduras was the arrangement he had worked out with Adolfo for security.

When Zorro finally slithered in from Houston, dressed to the hilt in his Indiana Jones garb, the quorum was complete. We gathered in my room at the Contempra and I laid out my plan. I told them my first experience with CMA in Honduras had been a total abortion. It was incumbent on us to reorganize the group so we could present a solid front. Otherwise, CMA would be shut out of the war.

I said each of us had to take a specific role to get us moving in the right direction. Zorro would be the financial officer because of his connections with Maco Stewart. Tirador would be in charge of internal security, which would include checking out potential members before they were allowed to join. Tom would be the director of the group and make arrangements to purchase all the equipment we needed. I would be the military commander. No CMA member would participate in any combat operations unless I personally approved. I would remain outside the country and set up bases while handling distribution of men being sent into Honduras, placing them where I felt they could be the most effective.

I also suggested we go as a unified group to Miami to meet Adolfo and demand action and show him we were willing to put our butts on the line for the FDN. This suggestion didn't make Tom happy because he thought it might destroy the relationship between the FDN and CMA. I told Tom that it made little difference because the FDN was going to continue using CMA until it got what it wanted from Congress or the American public. When that happened, the FDN would drop CMA before anyone knew what happened.

To forestall that, we had to get in Adolfo's face and confront him. We had to forcefully convince him to include CMA in the FDN's plans. And we had to do it before he knew we were coming. We didn't want him to leave town before we got there. We made arrangements to fly to Miami the next day.

9

The Casting Call: Backstage with the Manipulators

The South Miami park was cool and dark and smelled of cigar smoke. On the sidewalk, partially hidden by a line of cars parked along the street, a phalanx of bodyguards armed with handguns, shotguns and Uzi submachine guns stood watch.

Ten old men, their faces hidden in shadows cast by their wide-brimmed Panama hats, sat around a cement picnic table in the middle of the park whispering to one another in Spanish.

It would have been easier to break into a Mafia meeting than this late-night gathering of the leaders of Brigade 2506, one of the old-line, hard-line anti-Castro Cuban groups in Miami. These men represented the unofficial governing body of the city's Little Havana. If they approved of you and what you represented, you were assured safe conduct and well-being. If you went against them, you were likely to be banished or fed to the alligators in the Everglades.

Tom Posey and I were brought to this meeting in December 1984 by Jose "Joe" Coutin, CMA's representative in Miami and the leader of a group known as the Cuban Legion.

Coutin's group was among several anti-Castro groups in Miami that included Brigade 2506, Alpha 66, Omega 7 and CORU. Some were militant, others political. The stated goal of all of them, though, was the ouster of Castro, even though many who fled the country in the early '60s were too old and too comfortable in the United States to be dabbling in revolutions.

The only real connection many of the aging exiles had with Cuba was a few distant family members who remained behind following the mass exodus when Castro wrested power from Fulgencio Batista. The fiery spirit of the early '60s was gone. The community of exiles was slowly coming to grips with the realization that each succeeding presidential administration had absolutely no intention of sponsoring another revolution in Cuba, and each succeeding generation of Cuba-less Cubans looked on the United States as home.

Many of the children of these exiles had no heart for a fight in a country they had never seen. They knew nothing about toiling in the sugar cane fields of Cuba. They didn't know, and in many instances didn't care, about Cuba. They had become Americanized and viewed Brigade 2506 and its members as relics of a distant past, a curious antique handed down by their parents and brought out for display a few times a year for parades and speeches.

Brigade 2506 drew much of its support from the residual of intelligence assets and operatives left behind in southern Florida after the massive CIA operation to retake Cuba in the early '60s, known as JM Wave. The CIA had created a vast pool of dedicated Cuban assets ready to spring on any Latin American country where there was the slightest hint that Communists were making inroads into the government.

These assets, many of whom developed into killers and criminals who were in many ways worse than the mafioso with which they had dealt during Batista's reign of terror and corruption, had been handled by CIA station chief Theodore Shackley. Many remained in close contact with their former boss, the famed "Blond Ghost."

The U.S. government kept many of these Cuban assets on leashes and used them when political brush fires flared up around the world. The government knew it could depend on the Cubans because the Cubans were ruthless and would do whatever they thought necessary to further the aims of the United States, even if it involved criminal activities such as gun-running, drug smuggling and political assassinations.

Some of these Cubans helped run the secret war in Laos. Some became "plumbers" in the Watergate scandal. Men such as Felix Rodriguez, also known as Max Gomez during the Iran-Contra affair, was an adviser to George Bush, and his national security assistant, Donald Gregg, now the ambassador to South Korea, oozed up out of this seamy residual.

Groups such as the Cuban Legion attempted to muscle in on the older outfits, but found themselves unwelcome. They had to bring something of value to the cause before they would be accepted by the old-line anti-Castroites. Coutin wanted to use CMA, me and my plans for Pegaso to win favor with the Cuban godfathers of Brigade 2506. Which was why he took us to the meeting in the park. We were to be his ticket to respectability and power in Little Havana.

Coutin was a rather nondescript Cuban of average height and build who would have easily disappeared into any crowd of Cubans. He and his wife, Hilda, a striking, dark-haired woman who talked constantly about how wonderful her life had been in Cuba before Castro, ran a store called the Broadway Boutique.

The Broadway Boutique was the most unique store I had ever seen. It was a one-stop shopping mart for romantic terrorists. It was a combination gun store, military surplus warehouse and lingerie shop. Here you could shop for an Uzi at the same time you shopped for a negligee for your wife or girlfriend. When you entered Broadway, you had to pass through the lacy bras and panties before you got to the showcases with the guns.

Joe Coutin's real claim to fame came much later, when he allegedly sold the machine guns to the Colombian hit squad that murdered DEA informant Adler Berriman "Barry" Seal in Baton Rouge in 1985. Joe allegedly made a good deal on those guns. Word on the street was that he received a kilo of cocaine for them. Joe and Hilda eventually were busted on the coke charge.

Joe and Hilda were typical of many of the Cubans I met in Miami. They were waiting for something to jump-start them and get them into action. When I met Coutin in Miami, he was convinced I was the ticket to get his Cuban Legion involved in the war in Nicaragua and thus win approval of Brigade 2506.

But when Coutin introduced me to the group's leaders that night in Miami, not one of them looked me in the eye. They stared down at the table as I began my spiel about the war and how we intended to get the Cubans directly involved. It was almost as if they had already made up their mind about Coutin, me and Pegaso. I was a gringo outsider, and the old-timers didn't like to work with gringo outsiders.

My plan was to integrate the Cubans into the Pegaso group. They would be used as interpreters, liaison with the Spanish-speaking troops and fighters. But Americans would be in charge. The Cubans didn't like the idea of anyone being in charge of them. I had learned that several weeks earlier in discussions I had with some of the Cubans I ran into in Las Vegas.

One of those Las Vegas Cubans, a tall, stately man with graying hair, called himself Felix. He said he had spent 16 years in one of Castro's prisons and would do anything he could to bring about Castro's downfall. He and five other Cubans had been brought to Las Vegas by their commander, Hubert Matos, to evaluate the possibility of bringing more Cubans to Las Vegas to train and fight with the FDN.

Felix told me his group had gone on a five-day reconnaissance mission inside Nicaragua. Although disappointed at not engaging the Sandinistas, they had high expectations of setting up a Cuban battalion at Las Vegas as their means of atoning for the Bay of Pigs fiasco.

Felix wasn't sure of the motives of the FDN because the organization seemed in no hurry to allow anyone but Nicaraguans to get involved in this war. When he learned what I was trying to do with CMA and Pegaso, he was even more miffed because he felt this fight belonged to the Latinos, not the gringos. The gringos had let them down once before at the Bay of Pigs.

What those Cubans didn't know, nor did any of the Cubans in Miami, was that the FDN had no intention of allowing them to be a part of "their" war. The FDN and its leaders didn't like the Cubans, didn't want them involved and certainly weren't about to let them use their real estate — at least the real estate they hoped some day to come into possession of — to get back at Castro, despite many promises to the contrary.

The FDN simply wanted the Cubans' money.

Adolfo Calero repeatedly told the Cubans that in return for their financial support they would be allowed to set up a base inside Nicaragua from which they could launch an attack on the island. Adolfo was playing the Cuban card in Miami as adeptly as Mario was in New Orleans and other areas throughout the South. In return for bundles of cash, food, clothing and the goodwill of the Cuban community, both of the Caleros made promises they either couldn't keep or had no intention of keeping. It was all an FDN propaganda ploy. But the Cubans were so willing to believe anyone who said he would give them an opportunity to get back at Castro they believed even Adolfo's nonsense.

There was no love lost between the Cubans and the Nicaraguans in Miami. The Cubans believed they were superior to the lowly Nicaraguans, whom they regarded as little more than illiterate coffee bean pickers. And the Nicaraguans thought the Cubans were little more than boat people, and often derisively referred to them as "Marielistas."

The FDN had a ticket to the war, while the Cubans could only sit back and watch, hoping eventually to be invited. Adolfo kept teasing them, but had no real intentions of allowing them to grab any of his glory. The Cubans were being conned, and I felt sorry for them. But I could not say anything without jeopardizing my own efforts. I had to play along, all the while knowing that the aspirations of the Cubans should have been directed toward creation of a separate front they could finance and control. They would have no chance of success attaching themselves to this cancerous bunch of would-be warriors that was the FDN.

During my presentation to Brigade 2506 members, none of them said a word. Five minutes into the meeting I could tell it was a lost cause. When I finished they told us they would get back with us. They never did.

My main purpose in going to Miami was to meet with Adolfo Calero and press for money and equipment for Pegaso. But I found myself caught up in this Cuban connection and could not break away from it. There were Cubans everywhere demanding some of my time, encouraged by Posey and Coutin. The days became a blur, meeting upon meeting stacked one on top of another so that I had no time to catch my breath, much less sleep or eat.

Every time I turned around there were a dozen telephone messages for me at the front desk of the Howard Johnson motel where we stayed near the airport, or someone was knocking on my door wanting to meet with me. I thought I might have to hire a secretary to handle the appointments. I was the sounding board and focal point for every Cuban with a grievance against Castro.

Posey kept stressing the importance of getting the Cubans involved in the war and, for a while, it made some sense. Castro was supplying weapons and trainers to the Sandinistas. Why shouldn't we bring in anti-Castro Cubans to fight against that? The Miami Cubans were huge contributors of both materiel and money. Posey said that if we helped the Cubans enter the war, we could expect backing from all the Miami-based exile organizations, but we had to agree to take some of their men to Honduras with CMA.

Getting the Cubans to agree to that was another matter. Getting them to agree to anything was another matter. Every Cuban I met had his own ideas about how the war should be fought. None of the leaders of the exile organizations wanted his troops to be subordinate to another. I could tell early on that the Cuban connection was not going to work. Let them sit back in Miami, send supplies and talk about the war. Bringing them and their factionalized petty politics into the war would be a disaster.

Joe "Tirador" Adams called Adolfo and tried to set up an appointment since he knew him better than the rest of us. Adolfo told Joe he was surprised we were in Miami and expressed a great deal of reluctance to meet with us. But, he told Tirador, if we wanted to take a chance, he might be able to squeeze in a few minutes for us.

I was offended by Adolfo's attitude toward us, but decided to press on with the meeting. We might not get another chance.

That meeting proved quite instructive, not so much for what Adolfo had to say, for he said virtually nothing, but for the opportunity we had to see the manner in which he lived.

I was still laboring under the naive and mistaken impression that Adolfo was a dedicated revolutionary living in impoverished exile, suffering for the cause and the people to whom he had dedicated himself. I should have known better.

As we drove towards Adolfo's house in southwest Miami the housing developments got larger, the homes more expensive. When we finally turned off the main road I thought Tirador was lost and had taken a wrong turn. No revolutionary could afford to live in this place of huge, perfectly manicured lawns and luxurious houses of stucco, stone and glass.

Adolfo lived in a large, well-kept Spanish-style ranch house on a cul-de-sac near the back of the development. A small, white foreign sports car was parked in the driveway and a late-model Chrysler was in the garage.

Adolfo answered the door and it was obvious he was in a foul mood. He seemed annoyed by our presence and didn't let us past the foyer. We were treated with all the courtesy of an insurance man making an unexpected house call.

I told Adolfo we urgently needed to talk to him about operational problems and that Zorro had a message for him from Maco Stewart about money.

"If you can do it in 30 minutes, go ahead," Adolfo said curtly. "But if it's going to take more time than that, come back tomorrow. I didn't expect you to show up on my doorstep. I've got other business to attend to."

Through the sliding glass doors to the patio I could see two Latino men sitting at a wrought-iron table. Adolfo clearly had something going on with them he didn't want us to hear. I knew it would be impossible to get anything done with Adolfo in this mood and told Posey we'd try again tomorrow.

We left and headed back to the hotel.

The Cubans in Miami weren't the only people interested in getting involved in the war. All manner of con men, thieves and smugglers interested in making a quick buck approached Posey with a variety of strange schemes to raise money for CMA. Posey always thought people who approached him with an idea for a fund-raising scheme had the best interests of the Contras in mind, when in fact they wanted to do nothing more than make money for themselves.

Outsiders generally thought CMA was connected with the Honduran military and had a free pass to any area of the country. Drug smugglers and gun runners wanted to use CMA as conduit for safe passage of their merchandise, and Tom would have let all of them operate if someone wasn't there to tell him otherwise.

One outlandish scheme Posey considered involved trapping rare birds in Honduras, flying them out of the country illegally and selling them at inflated prices in the United States. Two men Posey and I met who proposed this scheme said if we helped them, they would give us free transport for our goods. Posey naturally liked the idea, but I shut it down in a hurry, I didn't want to get involved with any smuggling ventures outside what we needed to implement Pegaso.

During this time in Miami I got an unexpected promotion. From the time Mario Calero gave me my nom de guerre, "Flaco," I was Major Flaco. But in Miami, Posey began introducing me as Colonel Flaco. People immediately assumed since I was a colonel, I knew what was going on. I was treated with the utmost respect and courtesy, frequently called sir and occasionally saluted by some of the real hard-line, military Cubans. Many of the people we met thought I had connections to the U.S. military and acted accordingly around me.

When we finally set up the meeting with Adolfo, I decided to put on my pin-striped suit so I would look like a man on business and not a buddy who had stopped by for a cup of coffee and a chat.

We drove out to Adolfo's house in Tirador's car again, past the manicured lawns and swimming pools. I was still amazed that a revolution so in need of money could afford to spend this much on a house for its leader.

Adolfo answered the door, a portable telephone to his ear, and motioned us to enter. He continued talking on the phone as he led us into the sunken living room. The place was immaculate, appointed in expensive white furniture and glass-top tables.

Adolfo was in a completely different mood than the day before. When he finished his call he was all smiles and handshakes.

"Flaco, you look so elegant," he said as he shook my hand.

"We need to discuss the problems we had with arms, supplies and communications while we were in Honduras," I told him. "What about the arms from Israel you promised us?"

"There is going to be a two-month delay," he said. "Just concentrate on training the men and learn to be patient. Flaco, you are too go-go. Your impatience could lead to trouble for us."

"Adolfo, I'll give you my personal guarantee that no American will get involved in combat if you see to if that we have enough equipment to train. I want to get as many Americans as possible into the bases down there to help the Contras."

"How many men are you talking about?"

"Fifty."

I thought he was going to swallow his tongue.

"Fifty!" Adolfo replied incredulously. "That is far too many Americans. I would prefer a more clandestine unit until the congressional vote. If the vote is not in our favor, then you can bring in a thousand if you want."

When the conversation again turned to the equipment, Zorro asked Adolfo what had happened to the $30,000 Maco Stewart had donated.

"That's just a drop in the bucket," Adolfo said, his temper flaring. "If you want the money back, I'll write you a check for it right now."

Zorro said he didn't want to create any problems, but Adolfo got up, went into a bedroom, and came back with a checkbook. He quickly wrote out a check on his personal account for $25,000. But when he handed the check over to Zorro, I could see it wasn't made out to him or Maco Stewart. It was made out to Mario Calero.

Not only did Mario have Maco's original $30,000, now he had an additional $25,000.

As we were pondering the check, the doorbell rang and Adolfo ushered in the two men I had seen sitting on the patio the day before. One was Felipe Vidal Santiago. The other was known simply as Jesus.

Vidal, who was also known as Morgan, was a short, thin CIA asset and one of the most heinous little Latin bastards I've ever run across. He was a member of Alpha 66, CORU and Omega 7. He liked to brag about the fact that he had participated in murders, gun-running, drug-trafficking and any other dirty little deed that came his way without a second thought about its legality or morality.

Vidal's reasoning behind commitment without conscience was that his family had been murdered in Cuba by Castro's military. But it seemed to me that he simply enjoyed being evil.

Adolfo said Vidal and Jesus were from Costa Rica and he asked them to join us because he wanted to get their input on a plan to get FDN trainers into that country. Until then, Costa Rica had been the exclusive province of Eden Pastora, the former Sandinista commandante who became disenchanted with the new government and set about to overthrow it again with his group known as ARDE (Democratic Revolutionary Alliance).

Pastora initially had been adopted by the CIA, which gave him money and weapons, including helicopters. But Pastora wouldn't cooperate with the FDN. He referred to its leaders as "homicidal Somocista sons of bitches," which didn't set too well with the homicidal Somocista sons of bitches.

When the CIA threw its support to the FDN, it tried to starve Pastora out of Costa Rica and the anti-Sandinista revolution. That didn't work. Then it tried to harass him out. That didn't work either. Pastora was being dangerously stubborn and something had to be done about it.

The answer was for the FDN to open a southern front operating out of Costa Rica, much as it was doing in the north out of Honduras. Pastora would be forced to cooperate or give up the fight.

"ARDE is out," said Adolfo. "The United Nicaraguan Opposition, UNO, will be the main group on the southern front and will be fully supported by the FDN."

UNO would be made up of Alfonso Robelo and his 150-man unit on the northeast frontier while Fernando "El Negro" Chamorro would have a smaller group of fighters in the northwest. But Adolfo said he wasn't happy with the way Chamorro was handling his side of the campaign.

"He's an old drunk," said Adolfo.

And Robelo, according to Adolfo, was planning to get out of the fighting business and into the political business.

"All our efforts on the southern front could be destroyed," he said.

"CMA can handle the southern front," I piped up.

Adolfo turned and looked at me, a thin smile creeping across his face. Posey, Tirador and Zorro seemed shocked. All their thinking had been directed toward operating out of Honduras. Now, all of a sudden I had shifted gears on them and they weren't prepared.

"We're being frozen out in Honduras by politics," I explained. "Since we can't train men in Las Vegas, why not let us put together an operation in the south? It would require far less time and we wouldn't have the same political problems. We could squeeze the Sandinistas between us."

Adolfo's grin had become a broad smile. He liked the idea.

"If you mount a credible force, I will see to it that you get all the arms and ammunition you need," Adolfo said. "I have a contact in Costa Rica who has the facilities for a base for you. He will handle all the supplies and government contacts. He would be happy to help."

"Who is he?"

"His name is John Hull."

According to Adolfo, Hull was an Indiana farmer who had moved to Costa Rica some years ago and bought land along the border with Nicaragua.

Hull was far more than just another rancher, though.

Hull was a naturalized citizen of Costa Rica who left Evansville, Indiana, in 1968 to open a large citrus and cattle farm in northern Costa Rica. By late 1984, with the Sandinistas well-entrenched in Managua and the Contras beginning to flex what few muscles they had, Hull had become a key player in the CIA's plans to open a southern front for the FDN because of the location of his ranch.

The ranch was large enough and remote enough to train large numbers of troops without too much interference from the Costa Rican police. Hull also was well connected in the government of Costa Rica and knew how to work the system.

"I want you to meet him before you do anything," said Adolfo, pulling out his personal telephone directory and writing down several numbers. "Here are his numbers for Costa Rica and here is a number for him in Denver, where he is visiting relatives. Call him there."

For the first time since I had gotten involved with CMA and the FDN, Adolfo was encouraging us to get out in front of the operation instead of taking a back seat.

"I've talked with Langley about the operation and they're going along with my decisions on it," said Adolfo.

I thought it rather strange that the CIA was directly involved in this while the Boland Amendment was still in place, but Adolfo bragged he talked with the CIA as many as four times a day to give and receive advice.

Vidal wasn't too enthralled by the turn of events. He said he had worked with John Hull for quite some time and that there were Cubans already working out of Costa Rica. When Adolfo left the room to answer another of the innumerable telephone calls he received, Vidal said he did not trust the FDN because of previous unfulfilled promises. He said that arms promised to them many times never reached men in the field and some of the men returned home out of frustration.

Vidal's complaints about the FDN's unkept promises later were confirmed by Joe Coutin when I told him about the possibility of CMA's involvement in the southern front. Past Cuban experiences down there were exercises in frustration, he said.

Coutin said a Cuban named Rene "Ho Chi Minh" Corvo was operating out of the Hull ranch along with Felipe Vidal. He said Corvo was disliked by the Cuban community because he was believed to be involved in running drugs and guns. If CMA worked with Corvo, said Coutin, we could forget the support of the prominent Cuban groups. I told Posey to check out Corvo and let me know later what he had learned.

After the meeting with Adolfo I wanted nothing more than to grab a bite to eat and get some sleep. My physical condition was continuing to deteriorate, but I had no time to stop or consult a doctor since I was being swept along by a pace of events that was out of my power to control. I was running strictly on adrenaline at that point. As I picked up the phone to call room service there was a knock on the door.

I was in no mood for another unscheduled meeting with another Cuban with a scheme to get involved in the war. But my visitor turned out to be a blessing. He was a Cuban intent on aiding the war effort, but more importantly for me, he was a doctor.

Dr. Manuel Alzugarey was a thin, dour-looking man with graying hair and the no-nonsense manner of a man with a mission in life. That he had agreed to make a house call on me at the request of Joe Coutin spoke not only of his devotion to the anti-Castro cause, but of my importance in the hierarchy of this covert endeavor.

Dr. Alzugarey told me he had been supporting the FDN, ARDE and MISURA by sending medicine and doctors to their camps. He said he personally accompanied the last shipment and was nearly arrested by the Honduran military at San Pedro Sula when he refused to allow them to take their usual tariff. Only when he threatened to alert the press about the illegal tariffs did the military relent and allow him to continue to Tegucigalpa.

He said Joe Coutin had told him my story of the Cuban-donated goods being stored at La Quinta and wanted to know more. As I related the entire episode to him I could see the anger in his eyes.

"The son of bitches will pay for screwing Cubans," he said angrily. "The FDN likes the milk, but they don't like the cow it comes from."

Dr. Alzugarey told me to come to his clinic the next day and he would examine me. He also promised to do what he could to assist CMA independent of FDN. He had had enough of Adolfo Calero's lies.

When I finally was able to break away from all the Cuban meetings and get a few minutes to myself, I went to Posey's room to call John Hull. He seemed to be the key man at the moment, the pivotal contact in Costa Rica for CMA's involvement in the war. I dialed the number in Denver and a pleasant-sounding man answered the phone.

"I've been expecting your call," Hull said when I introduced myself.

"I don't want to get into a lengthy conversation now," he continued, "because I'm visiting my daughter and I have another appointment."

"I'm planning to be in Houston in a few days," I said. "Could you meet me there?"

"That will be fine," he said.

We made arrangements when and where to meet and rang off. No sooner had I hung up the phone with Hull than Posey came into the room with another of his fantastic schemes.

He said he had just talked to a man from Tennessee named John Cattle about aid for CMA. Cattle told him he had been advising the Miskito Indians in southeast Honduras for several months, working closely with Steadman Fagoth, leader of MISURA.

During that time, Cattle said he had stumbled on a stash of weapons that included anti-aircraft missiles. He wanted to sell the weapons to the FDN and had the approval of Fagoth to go ahead with the deal.

Most of the weapons had been furnished to the Indians by the CIA early in the war. They included AK-47 assault rifles, RPG-7 rocket propelled grenades, M-1 carbines and Ruger Mini-14 rifles. Cattle claimed that among these weapons were four French Sabre anti-aircraft missiles with launchers.

The FDN was always eager to buy weapons, especially high-tech stuff that could give them some edge over the Sandinistas' air superiority. The anti-aircraft missile would be jewels if they could be recovered. Posey said the sale price for the entire stash was $150,000.

"How do you propose to get those missiles away from the MISURA?" I asked him.

"Cattle said he would deliver the weapons to a designated spot where we could pick them up with an airplane and fly them out," Posey replied.

Posey wanted to offer Cattle $80,000 for the package, charge the FDN the full amount and keep the $70,000 balance for CMA. Posey wanted me to go to Adolfo and try to sell the deal to him. I was reluctant, because the whole thing reeked. If the government wanted to set up Posey and CMA on weapons charges or Neutrality Act violations, this might be the method.

Posey had a bad habit of believing anything anybody who claimed to be anti-Communist told him and this guy Cattle, if that was his real name, seemed to be offering too much too quickly.

If the deal were real, though, it could significantly help my sagging finances. I hadn't received any money from my Washington benefactor in quite some time and had gotten into the habit of keeping $1,000 in wallet for emergencies. I also knew if times really got tough I could abandon CMA, return to Las Vegas and live with the Contras there for as long as I liked.

Cattle showed up at the hotel the next morning and I agreed to have breakfast with him before visiting Dr. Alzugarey for my medical exam. I was immediately put off by Cattle's appearance. He was short and stocky with gray hair and several days stubble on his face. He wore blue jeans and a wrinkled flannel shirt. He looked like he had been sleeping under a viaduct for some time.

Despite his slovenly appearance, Cattle was quite the salesman. He spun an intriguing tale about his work with the Indians in the Miskitia, as that region of southeastern Honduras was known. It was the second time I had heard of the place and was just as fascinated by Cattle's description of it as I had been with Zorro's tale of derring-do some weeks earlier.

Cattle claimed Fagoth's fighters had captured 10,000 new AK-47 rifles in a raid on an FDN convoy on the Rama Road and did not report it either to the FDN or CIA. Fagoth was using the weapons to bargain with because the Indians were weapons rich but cash poor. Cattle said the weapons were buried near a river and if we could make a deal with the FDN, he would fly down and make arrangements for their recovery.

I was leery of the deal and of Cattle. It just didn't sound right. But I told Posey that we would proceed cautiously, in case there was something to it. I suggested we set up a meeting with Adolfo. Cautiously meant that any serious discussions about weapons purchases and any final transactions would have to take place outside the continental United States, just in case Cattle was a government informant.

We left the weapons deal at that and I went to see Dr. Alzugarey. He checked me over, X-rayed my lungs and recommended I go see another doctor, a specialist in internal medicine. The other doctor, also an anti-Castro Cuban, saw me immediately. He told me I had some type of bacterial infection and possible liver damage. He gave me a gamma globulin shot to ward off hepatitis and some vitamins and suggested I get a few weeks' rest.

"That's impossible under the circumstances," I said.

"I can only suggest what's best for you. I can't enforce it," he said. "But if you continue going like you are, you're heading in a dangerous direction."

The examination, the medicine and the advice were free because of who they were and who they perceived me to be. The doctor's advice stayed with me. I knew I had to slow down for a while. I had to stop taking appointments. I had to stop seeing people and let my brain and my body rest.

But there was a stack of phone messages waiting for me when I returned to the hotel.

Tirador had called confirming an appointment with Adolfo to discuss Cattle's weapons deal. Zorro had called and said he was trying to make an appointment with Maco Stewart in Houston about the same time I was to meet with John Hull.

If we had fought the war with the same intensity as we held meetings and made telephone calls in Miami, the Contras would have been drinking champagne in the streets of Managua and dancing on Danny Ortega's grave within months. But the FDN talked a lot better than it fought.

Despite my reservations about Cattle's arms deal, Adolfo seemed interested. But he said the price was too high. He could get weapons cheaper from his buyer in the Dominican Republic.

He was interested in the Sabre surface-to-air missiles though, because he wanted the world and the Sandinistas to know that the FDN possessed such weapons. That would reduce the probability of an air strike on Las Vegas. But before proceeding on the deal, he wanted to make sure it was not a scam being run by Fagoth and the Miskitos. He wanted verification that the weapons existed.

"Tirador and I will go to the Miskitia to confirm it," I said. "We'll get Cattle to come with us in case of any slip-ups."

"I'll pay $100,000 for the lot if it's for real, because the missiles alone are worth that much to us," said Adolfo. He said if the deal went through, he would have a plane fly from the CIA base at Aguacate to pick up the weapons in the Miskitia. He would pay Cattle in cash, taking the money out of one account in Panama and transferring it to another in Miami.

"We need those weapons in the Neuva Segovia area and the Indians aren't doing anything in the war now," Adolfo said. "Besides, the Indians are too stupid to know how to use those missiles."

When we returned to the hotel, I told Cattle that Adolfo offered $75,000 for the lot. Cattle thought for a moment, then agreed to the price. I planned to skim $25,000 off the top and use it for CMA and Pegaso. It didn't matter if Adolfo or Cattle found out. It was all part of doing a deal like this. Everybody expected a cut somewhere along the line, and I wanted mine if the deal went through.

I told Cattle we would meet him in Honduras in three days. We exchanged telephone numbers and he returned to Tennessee.

I still had a feeling that we might be rushing into something with a man about whom we knew absolutely nothing. There was a good chance Cattle was working for the Bureau of Alcohol, Tobacco and Firearms and had been sent to nail us.

"We might spend the war in Leavenworth," I told Posey and Tirador.

"But if I find he is working for BATF, I'll kill him and leave his body in Nicaragua."

Maco-Mania

Shortly after wrapping up the meeting with Cattle, Zorro called and said I had to fly to Houston that night. Maco Stewart, our potential money man, had arrived and would be in town for only one day. I made arrangements to meet Tirador and Posey at the Honduran Maya Hotel in three days for the Cattle deal and went immediately to the airport to catch the next flight to Houston.

Zorro had rented a suite at the Warwick Hotel near Rice University and was waiting for me when I arrived. Over a room service meal, I probed Zorro for information about this mysterious oil man.

"You have to understand he's a little nuts," Zorro said. "He's also an alcoholic. If he's been drinking, we may not get anything done."

As Zorro talked about Maco, a picture of a strange, demented man emerged. Maco was interested in getting into the war against the Sandinistas for only one reason — money. He repeatedly came up with offbeat schemes to raise money for the Contras, schemes that would also contribute to his own considerable financial portfolio.

One of his strange ideas involved using ultra-light aircraft to fly into Nicaragua to recover wounded soldiers. He had ordered two and planned to fly one himself. They wouldn't have been much of a match for the Sandinistas' helicopter gunships and anti-aircraft artillery.

Maco's next plan was to raise money through a trade agreement with the FDN. Maco promised to convince his millionaire friends to buy war bonds. The bonds would have a face value of $50,000 each and could raise millions. The money would be given to Adolfo in exchange for the rights to an island off the eastern coast of Nicaragua in the Miskito Cays. Maco had his attorneys working on the legalities with the Securities and Exchange Commission in Washington.

Adolfo had agreed to let the buyers have the island if they could take it and hold it until the war was over. Then, the occupants of the island would create friction with the new government of Nicaragua and a petition would be drafted and presented to the United Nations requesting recognition as an independent nation. The Nicaraguan government, controlled by the FDN, would not fight the request.

If the United Nations approved of the separation, the island would become a haven for United States businessmen seeking offshore tax dodges. The possibilities for making money through this were endless.

It was late and I was tired, but Zorro said Maco wanted to meet with me as soon as he closed an oil deal in another room in the hotel. He suggested we go to the restaurant on the top floor to wait.

When we arrived the restaurant was completely deserted except for the waiters and bartenders.

"What's going on?" I asked Zorro.

"Maco's rented the restaurant for your meeting," he said.

"The whole restaurant?"

Zorro nodded his head in affirmation as we sat down.

I was impressed.

We picked a table near a large window that overlooked the city. The staff stood bunched near the kitchen door, eyeing us curiously. I ordered a margarita and sipped it slowly as Zorro and I made small talk waiting for Maco to show up.

After about 30 minutes, the elevator doors opened and a tall, heavyset man emerged. He was about 6-foot-3 and nearly that big around. His eyes were steel blue and his curly brown hair was tinged with gray. He bore an amazing resemblance to Orson Wells. He appeared quite nervous as he shook my hand and introduced himself.

The first of several straight vodkas was on the way as soon as Maco sat down. I glanced at Zorro and he gave me an "I told you so look" with his eyes.

"What's your role in the war and how do you think I could be of help?" Maco asked quickly. He seemed to be all business.

I gave him an overview of Pegaso and my dealings with the FDN. He seemed totally disinterested about the war or who was fighting it. He told me he had spent some time in the Miskitia and hoped to open a cocoa bean processing operation there using the Indians as cheap labor. He said he had given tens of thousands of dollars to a Miskito Indian named Roger Herman to get the business going, but little had been done. He figured he would aid the Indians by giving them jobs while making huge profits by selling the processed cocoa in the States.

He also asked how much I knew about the seafood business along the eastern coast of Nicaragua. I told him the Sandinistas controlled the fishing and shrimping in the area and there was little chance any outsiders would be able to make any money working there.

The more Maco drank, the more he loosened up. Every time he brought up a new scheme, he prefaced it by saying: "If I waved a magic wand," could this or that be made to happen?

"My concerns are strictly military," I said. "If you want to capture business from the Sandinistas, you're in for a big investment."

"If I could wave a magic wand, could you take and hold a small island in the Miskito Cays?"

"Yes."

"How much will it cost?"

"How long do you want it held?"

"Until other plans can be instituted."

I explained that such a venture would require several hundred men. It would also require high-speed patrol craft armed with heavy machine guns and 40mm cannon to secure the waters around the island and sophisticated anti-aircraft weapons to hold off the Soviet-built Mi-24 Hind-D helicopters that would be sent to dislodge them.

"That's your problem," Maco said. "All I want to know is how much will it cost?"

I looked down at the table and thought for a moment.

"At least $1.5 million."

"I'll give you $1 million cash for the job," he shot back.

"Frankly, I don't think you could do it for that. The international political ramifications would make it difficult to hold the island."

Maco quickly jumped to another subject.

"How much will you charge to sink a French battleship in Puerta Cabeza?"

I was at a loss. I knew of an old battleship used by the Sandinistas, but it was just a coastal patrol vessel used around San Juan del Norte. Nothing I knew of operated out of Puerta Cabeza.

"There's an old French ship that travels between two ports," Maco said. "I want it either sunk or captured in one piece. I sent eight sets of scuba gear to be used on the assault originally planned by Zorro."

Now I knew the reason for the scuba gear sent from New Orleans when I first met Zorro.

Zorro had told Maco he had eight specially trained former members of the Navy's elite SEAL team members in his group who could go in and take the ship. I knew then that Zorro was bullshitting Maco. Zorro had found a sugar daddy and was getting rich off his fantasies and fears. Maco wanted in on the action, but Zorro had convinced him he had to buy his way in through him. Like everybody else I had run into in this war, Zorro was scamming Maco just as Maco was scamming Adolfo just as I was scamming everybody I came in contact with.

Zorro told Maco whatever he wanted to hear, which ensured the money kept flowing. I told Maco the truth about his plans, especially the one to capture the ship, and he didn't like it one bit.

"How much would it cost to sink the ship in Puerta Cabeza?" he asked.

"I can get that ship sunk for $185,000," I said. "That will be for men and equipment. If you want the ship captured, the price will be much higher."

"What about double the $185,000?"

"No way. It will cost much more. We're talking about major logistical nightmares here to capture the ship and hold it."

It was obvious Maco was willing to throw his money away on foolish ventures. And I knew that if I didn't take it, someone else would. I told him we needed to settle on one plan and that Pegaso was my priority.

"I can't support the FDN because I have no control in the decision-making process," he said. Maco wanted a position in the war from which he could call his own shots. He was so used to working for himself that he found being subordinate to someone else totally unacceptable.

"The bastards want my money, but they're not willing to play my game," he said bitterly.

"The Miskitia was the place to be," he said. The Miskito Indians would view him as their savior and he would have control of their economy. He would set up his cocoa processing plant, give them jobs, buy their red beans and rice crops and sell their citrus fruit and seafood.

To help ingratiate himself with them, he said he planned to take several American Indians into the Miskitia to meet with their Central American brethren. He asked how much I would charge to lead them.

"Twenty-five thousand," I said. "That includes room, board and travel inside Honduras. But if I agree to do it, I will be totally in charge. I'll have the final say on everything, including what the Indians should wear and the equipment they can bring into Honduras."

"That's reasonable. We'll work out the details when we get to Honduras."

"How soon do you want to make the trip?"

"In about a week. Let me notify the Indians and get them to Houston."

The Full-Court Press

My meeting with Hull concerning the southern front was planned for the morning after my session with Maco Stewart. I made arrangements for Zorro to take notes of the Hull meeting and then we waited. And we waited. And we waited. The morning passed slowly into afternoon and I began to wonder whether Hull would show up. Finally, about 2 p.m., there was a knock on the door.

Zorro answered the door and I heard someone ask: "Is this the room of Colonel Flaco?"

Zorro ushered two men into the room. One of the men was about 50 years old and had thinning white hair. He wore a short-sleeve white shirt and khaki trousers. I assumed this was Hull. The other man was tall and thin and appeared to be in his thirties. He wore a blue blazer, khaki trousers, a blue shirt and oxblood loafers. He looked like a refugee from a college fraternity.

"I'm Robert Owen," he said.

The name meant nothing to me.

Hull explained that Owen, a former aide to then Indiana Senator Dan Quayle, was a liaison officer for a government agency that had a vested interest in this meeting. That government agency, I later learned, was the National Security Council and Lieutenant Colonel Oliver North.

Owen was a bag man for North. He regularly carried $10,000 a month in cash from North to Hull to keep the Contra operation in Costa Rica alive. Owen was North's plausibly deniable contact with the FDN, a private citizen hired to do the administration's dirty work. Owen was known by the code name TC, "The Courier," and believed Ollie was the next conservative messiah.

"What's your background?" Hull asked me.

"I don't discuss my true identity or my role with the organization with outsiders," I replied. "The FDN Directorate knows who I am and will vouch for me."

"Adolfo tells me that we're to put together a plan to train troops in Costa Rica."

"That's my understanding."

Hull said he had come to the United States with his daughter because of increasing tension along the border. But his security concerns had nothing to do with the Sandinistas. He brought his daughter to the States to prevent her from being kidnapped by drug dealers. Hull's ranch was the key refueling point for U.S.-bound drug planes from Colombia and the smugglers got upset when Hull began charging exorbitant landing and refueling fees. He feared for his daughter's safety, but now that she was safe, he could concentrate on the southern front.

"How do you feel about Eden Pastora?" Hull asked. "Are you connected with him in any fashion?"

"No," I replied. "I thought you worked with him."

"Well, what do you think of him?" Hull continued.

"All I know about him is what I've read in newspapers and magazines."

"Let me tell you about him," said Hull, visibly upset. "He's a Communist son of a bitch. He flies a Sandinista flag in his camp. We used to do business with him but he was so careless that the Costa Rican government started putting heat on us."

Hull said he had seen Pastora's people selling and trading ammunition with the Sandinistas and that some of the weapons sent to ARDE that had been stored on Hull's ranch ended up being sold on the streets of San Jose by Pastora's people.

"This is the kind of guy we've got to get rid of," said Hull. "He's got to go. ARDE is not coming into this deal. We don't want them in this deal at all."

"Do you want to kill him?"

"Yeah, we want to kill him," Hull said.

When I began discussing details about training in Costa Rica, Hull said we could use his ranch, but that all activities would have to be extremely clandestine because of the Costa Rican government's aversion to getting involved with the Contras.

He said men coming from the United States would have to arrive in groups of no more than four at a time, wear civilian clothes at all times and keep their personal weapons hidden until they went across the border into Nicaragua. They were to travel under the guise of ranch security, not as Contra trainers. They would have to train with .22-caliber rifles to avoid arousing the curiosity of the Costa Ricans. But when we crossed the border, we would have any weapon we needed.

Owen said little as Hull and I discussed specifics of getting CMA trainers into the country. It was not until I mentioned that I wanted 240 men on the operation that Owen reacted. He jumped to his feet, said he had to make a telephone call and left the room.

When he returned, Owen told Hull that he didn't think that CMA could be used in this operation.

"Why?" I said.

"Two hundred and forty Americans is far too many," Owen said.

"You misunderstood me," I said. "I meant the combined force of Nicaraguan and Americans would be 240. Only about 30 Americans will be involved."

This seemed to placate Owen, but he said it was absolutely imperative that no one outside the organization be told we were planning to send CMA members into Costa Rica to train the Contras. Unlike Honduras, he said, where the government looked more favorably on our actions, the government of Costa Rica was sensitive about anyone using its territory to aid the Contras.

Hull and Owen expressed concern about a *Life* magazine article coming out soon about a friend of Hull's, Bruce Jones, who was openly aiding the Contras from his ranch in Costa Rica. Jones, Hull said, would probably be deported and the Costa Ricans would be keeping a closer watch on military activities in the northern part of the country. The publicity could cause problems for them and the Contras. Owen said Jones got carried away in his quest for publicity and was afraid CMA might do the same thing.

Owen's condescending manner irritated me. He must have taken holier-than-thou lessons from North. I decided to leave the room for a while. Excusing myself, I said I had to meet someone in the lobby. Instead, I went to the nearest pay phone and called Adolfo Calero in Miami.

Adolfo was livid when he came on the line.

"What the hell are you doing trying to put together an operation with 240 Americans?" he demanded.

"Did you just get a call from Rob Owen?" I asked him.

"Yes."

"Well, Mr. Owen didn't stick around long enough to get an explanation of the breakdown. We're talking about 153 men from Robelo, 70 from Chamorro and about 30 Americans."

"Oh, that sounds more like it. You better get up there and explain that to them."

"I already explained it to Hull," I said. "But why is Owen coming down here and reporting to you?"

"That's his job," Adolfo said. "He is supposed to give me information about what's going on."

"Well, what he told you was premature because we barely got started when he made his phone call," I said.

"It is important that Owen know exactly what our plans are because he will convey them straight to Washington," Adolfo said.

Adolfo made it clear that the shots for development of the southern front were being called in Washington. Both Hull and Owen were working for the United States government. Not only was the NSC and the White House involved in this, so was the CIA. Had I known in advance I would be talking to Company people, I would have used different tactics. Here I was trying to impress what I thought was a farmer and some college kid with CMA's potential when in fact I was looking down a gun barrel pointed at me from Washington.

When I got back to the room, I was still hot that Owen had run off half-cocked.

"Look," I told him, "you don't have to leave the room to make telephone calls to Calero and tell him what's going on. You didn't bother to wait for the breakdown on the troops before you called him."

From that moment on, Owen and I didn't get along. He thought I was too confrontational and too militant. But all I had done was show Hull what an incompetent fool he was.

I told Hull CMA would carry out the mission under whatever conditions he and his people set. He saw that I was backing down somewhat from my previous position and smiled, saying we should all get together again in two days in Miami at Adolfo's house for a special meeting.

I left Houston the following morning for Miami. Tirador met me at the airport and said a movie producer was in town trying to get in touch with Tom and me. He was interested in doing a movie about CMA and the Parker-Powell shootdown.

Loher H. "Larry" Spivey was a caricature of a fast-talking, money-spending, flashy-dressing, back-pounding, womanizing Hollywood producer. He claimed to represent Orion Pictures, although we never knew for sure whether he actually represented anyone in Hollywood. His primary connections were in Washington.

Spivey and I took an immediate dislike to one another and I gave up on his so-called film project before it even got started. I found it curious that all sorts of strange characters like Cattle and Spivey were suddenly showing up out of nowhere trying to help CMA.

My suspicions were confirmed much later when I learned Spivey was an FBI informant sent to Miami to keep tabs on Posey and this mysterious Colonel Flaco whose name kept popping up in various communiques. Spivey also had direct contact with Oliver North, who was becoming concerned about the militant attitude demonstrated by some CMA members.

To the people in Washington, fighting wasn't the way to win this war; politics was. The only battles that counted were those that were fought and won in Congress and the media. Those of us willing to actually prosecute the war on the ground were liabilities to the administration's no-combat stance.

Spivey said he would pay Posey's way to Washington to promote CMA with various congressional leaders. Spivey's intent, though, was not to give Posey more credibility. It was to cut him away from a group that had become dangerously militant to the administration.

The high-profile and extremely gullible Posey would be easier to manipulate than someone like me. Posey was viewed in Washington as the weak link to our operation and with him out of the chain, the organization would fall apart.

I told Tom I had no problems with him going to Washington, if that's what he wanted. I had more important things to attend to. The meeting at Adolfo's house to discuss the southern front was scheduled for the next day.

At the time, I had no way of knowing how many lives that December 20, 1984, meeting would affect. Nor did I know of the role it would play in the downfall of Oliver North's secret Contra aid network.

10

A Declaration of Independents: The Courier, the Farmer and the Assassin

By December 1984, Miami was a city of intrigues. Everybody had an agenda that was attached to the war in Nicaragua but was not really concerned with the final goal of overthrowing the Sandinistas.

The Colombians were pouring cocaine into the States through Miami using pilots and aircraft that on the return trip ferried weapons to the Contras.

The Cubans were using the war as an excuse to once again try to drum up interest in the overthrow of Castro in Cuba and Communism in Latin America.

The U.S. military and Reagan administration policy makers were using the war to complete construction of their aircraft carriers in Central America — the U.S.S. Honduras and the U.S.S. Costa Rica — and strengthen their stranglehold on the region.

And all manner of strange and slimy creatures oozed out from under rocks and slithered into Miami in search of guns, gold and glory. Among the saddest of these spectacles was Tom Posey, the Alabama farm boy and produce salesman who suddenly found himself playing with the big boys in a game of international intrigue.

Posey had this dream of being a CIA agent, so when he found himself dealing with people who actually had ties to the Agency, he became star-struck. Posey was willing to work with anyone who claimed to be an anti-Communist zealot or who had connections with an intelligence agency. At times, Posey snitched for the CIA, the DIA, the FBI and the NSC, providing information on people who once had been his friends.

In Miami, Posey was transformed from a poor old country boy into a scheming, finagling liar who would have turned in his wife if it meant advancing his own personal agenda. I was among those he was willing to abandon to the authorities.

I had returned to Miami in search of quality manpower, money and supplies to get Pegaso positioned for a real strike against the Sandinistas. But the harder I worked, the more barriers I found in my path. The goal of ousting the Sandinistas through direct military action seemed not to be the true purpose of this so-called "war." The Contras were merely a bluff, as were all the U.S. military preparations in Costa Rica and Honduras.

Whenever anyone such as me put together plans that had some military value, we were declared "too militant" and were excised from the flock. The true goal of the Reagan administration was destabilization of the Sandinistas to the extent that the government of Nicaragua would eventually disintegrate without resorting to direct military intervention.

But the destabilization efforts needed outside help, and the imposition of the Boland Amendment meant the administration had to privatize the pressure on the Sandinistas. That privatization — which was a violation of the spirit of Boland, if not the letter of it — meant a lot of people turned their heads to immoral and illegal activities that were taking place in the name of democracy and support of the freedom fighters.

I was as deeply involved as any of them. I had my own deals going. There was CMA and the southern front, which each day seemed to lose some of its viability for me and what I wanted to do. There was Maco Stewart and his plans for the Indians, which promised a much-needed infusion of cash. There was the John Cattle arms deal, which seemed somewhat of a long shot.

My problem was I didn't know which of these groups or individuals would give me the pipeline for money and supplies I needed once I got to Costa Rica or Honduras. I had never received anything from any of them. Not the FDN, not CMA, not the Cubans. Their promises all came up empty. They were more intent on pushing their own personal agendas than actually fighting a war and bringing democracy to Nicaragua.

The only deal which seemed to be working for me at the moment involved Maco Stewart and his plan to take American Indians into the

Miskitia. His bookkeeper had wired me a $5,000 advance on my $25,000 fee and I began purchasing some equipment and paying off hotel bills.

I still had some hopes for CMA on the southern front, and on the morning of December 16, 1984, Tirador, Posey and one of Joe Coutin's men, Marcelino "Pedrico" Rodriguez, drove out to Adolfo Calero's house to discuss the plan.

I had not been told who would be attending the meeting and was surprised to see Enrique Bermudez sitting in Adolfo's living room when we arrived. He greeted me with a big smile and a warm handshake.

"I'm surprised to see you," I said. "I thought you'd still be in Las Vegas."

"I came for the meeting," he said. "I also want to spend some time with my wife."

It was no secret that Bermudez's wife, a Miami based hairdresser, didn't think much of her husband playing the role of the diligent revolutionary in the jungle. She wanted him back in Miami with her and frequently threatened to leave him if he did not see her more often.

Adolfo's living room quickly filled with the high level players in the FDN and their connections to Washington.

John Hull, the Costa Rican farmer, and Rob Owen, Oliver North's courier, were there. So were Aristides Sanchez, the general secretary of the FDN Directorate, Felipe Vidal, a Costa Rican attorney named Donald Lacey and the man known only to me as Jesus.

Two other men sat outside on the patio at the wrought-iron table, looking in through the glass doors. The hair of one of the men had a strange orangish tint to it as if it had just been badly dyed. I probably would not have noticed him had it not been for his hair. I was curious as to why this man who was not introduced to any of us had dyed his hair. The more I looked at him the less Latin and the more Arabic he looked.

More than a year later, while looking through photographs at the Ministerio de Justicia in San Jose, Costa Rica, I saw a picture of the man with the dyed hair. Only in the photo his hair was black. Costa Rican police said his real name was Amac Galil, a Libyan being sought in connection with the attempted assassination of Eden Pastora at his camp at La Penca, Nicaragua, on May 30, 1984.

The would-be assassin with a homemade bomb, apparently posing as a journalist, bungled the job that day. Pastora was only slightly wounded in the explosion during a press conference, but eight innocent people were killed, including an American journalist.

With so many high rollers in the FDN present I felt I had somehow missed the boat on this gathering. This wasn't going to be just a meeting to discuss contingency plans about the southern front. Something else was up.

Adolfo opened the meeting by saying he had discussed the Houston meeting two days earlier with Hull and Owen.

"I have decided to send Posey to Costa Rica first instead of you, Flaco, to determine the needs for a southern front," Adolfo said. "This is no reflection on you, but you would be too visible and too impatient. I have gone over everything with John Hull and it is very crucial that the person selected for the first trip be as close to a tourist as possible."

I was shocked. Posey had neither the background nor the intelligence to pull off this kind of job. He didn't know the military situation or what we would need to support us in the field.

"I should be the one to make the trip because it will be my responsibility to set up the operation," I argued weakly.

I could see that Adolfo's mind was made up. I was being cut from the mission and what appeared to be CMA's last best chance of getting involved in the war. I figured Owen was behind the decision. My frankness with him during the Houston meeting apparently had created in his mind the image of someone spoiling for a fight. My militancy scared him and the White House.

"What about Pastora?" I said, hoping to retain some viability in the south.

The mere mention of Pastora's name had the same effect of jamming a red-hot poker up Adolfo's ass. He jumped up, his face blood red under his neatly combed white hair.

"Pastora! Pastora!" he shouted. "I don't want to hear any more about Pastora! He calls us 'homicidal Somocista sons of bitches.' He's got to go! He's got to go!"

Adolfo was looking directly at me as he said it. It was as if he were giving me a direct order to get rid of his most hated and most feared enemy. Adolfo seemed more concerned about Pastora and his affect on the FDN than he did about the Sandinistas.

The tirade went on for several minutes until Adolfo calmed briefly and lit a cigarette. He took a deep drag, leaned back against the wall and said quietly: "Are there any suggestions?"

"We discussed this in Houston," I said. "Are you looking for a scenario?"

Adolfo said nothing as he looked around the room, glaring at us.

"We screwed up the first time when we put the bomb under him," Felipe Vidal broke in. "The timing was wrong and the guy who was supposed to carry it off didn't do things the way he was supposed to."

At this time I knew nothing of La Penca, and I looked around trying to figure out what was going on. Hull and Owen and everyone but the CMA members nodded their heads in agreement, as if they knew exactly what Vidal was talking about.

Adolfo again asked for suggestions about how to handle Pastora.

I had no compunctions about killing Pastora. Based on what Hull had told me in Houston, I figured he was a collaborator. Hull said he flew the Sandinista flag in his camp. That was enough for me. Pastora deserved to die. So, I outlined a plan for the Pastora's assassination that would make it appear as if the Sandinistas had done it.

Pastora would be lured into a small village near the Costa Rican border on the pretext of holding secret peace talks with FDN officials. Adolfo would fly to Costa Rica to make it appear legitimate, but would be out of the country before anything happened, thus keeping the FDN clean.

When Pastora arrived for the meeting, a company of FDN soldiers would get rid of his bodyguards, change into Sandinista uniforms and take him across the border into Nicaragua.

The next morning, Pastora would be dragged into the village of El Castillo, where he was well-known and maximum exposure would be guaranteed. There, he would be hanged. The Contras dressed in Sandinista uniforms would accuse the villagers of collaborating with the Contras and give them enough trouble to lend some authenticity to the event. American advisers accompanying the group would observe from a distance.

The assassination group would be trained on Hull's ranch in Costa Rica, but segregated from the other Contra forces. This group would be carefully selected and trained by no more than five Americans, including me.

If the mission were successful, the Contra soldiers would be flown to Las Vegas and integrated into separate FDN units.

Following the death of Pastora, the FDN would renounce the Sandinistas for treachery and name Alfonso Robelo as head of a new organization, UNO, to coordinate the Contra efforts from Costa Rica. All former ARDE members would be absorbed into UNO or dispersed among other Contra units. Pastora's assets would be transferred to Honduras and the FDN would be in full control of the war against the Sandinistas.

I looked around the room when I finished. No one blinked. No one protested. Everyone had been down this road before and was unconcerned about the conspiracy of criminality involved in an assassination plot.

I was not concerned either. There was a certain justification involved in this, a justification of advancing the cause. I guess I shouldn't have expected anything more from the room full of seedy characters. In my view, the op had been sanctioned by the U.S. government because of the presence of Hull and Owen, who had close ties to the CIA and the White House.

This was the flip side of politics and government policy as I knew it. It neither surprised me nor frightened me to know that our government operated in such a fashion. I felt our group was being tested and offered a way into the inner circle. This plan was the test of our loyalty.

When the meeting broke briefly for coffee, I pulled Posey and Tirador aside to ask them about the assassination plan. Posey knew CMA could not survive another bad publicity hit if the plan went awry, but was not about to argue with Hull, Owen and a roomful of conspirators. Tirador liked the plan, but wondered what would become of us if we failed.

"If we fail, we're dead men," I told him. "Maybe we're dead men just for being involved. We're going to have to go along on blind trust."

As we stood talking, I could see Adolfo looking at me from across the room and smiling. As I looked around the room, it seemed as if everyone else was doing the same thing. Then it dawned on me: We were lambs being led to the slaughter. We were being used by the FDN.

The Shell Game

Nothing could be done in Costa Rica until Posey did his reconnaissance, so Tirador and I flew out of Miami to Honduras to try to put together the arms deal with the mysterious John Cattle.

I realized my knowledge about the depth of corruption and the intrigues within the FDN had reached a point that it could prove to be my undoing if I didn't watch myself. The FDN would not hesitate to waste anyone, not even an American, who threatened their power structure. Whacking Pastora, while internationally significant, was small change compared to future events that could assure the FDN power in Nicaragua.

Adolfo felt he had everything going his way at this point. He had the absolute backing of the Reagan administration, including the CIA at a time when it was illegal for the Agency to be involved. But in this war, it was illegal only if you got caught.

We breezed through customs in Tegus because every airport employee thought we were U.S. military personnel attached to Task Force 160. Our short haircuts and OD seabags were better than a diplomatic passport. We checked into the Honduran Maya under assumed names. Tirador and I had so much confidence in ourselves at that point we thought we ruled the world and could do virtually anything we wanted.

We stayed at the Maya for several reasons. The primary one was the view. The hotel sat on the side of a hill in the center of town and I always requested a room on the fifth floor facing southeast because from there I could see everything from the parking lot below to the American Embassy compound just up the street.

From my room we could watch the U.S. military traffic at the Maya. The embassy had a number of white vans with dark windows that shuttled military personnel around Tegus. I often saw men in full combat dress, camouflage face paint and loaded M-16s exiting vans in the hotel parking late at night. The parking lot guards were so used to the loading and unloading that it was considered normal for heavily armed Americans to enter the hotel at odd hours.

I could also see the FDN safe house across from the Argentine embassy, which gave me good intelligence on anyone entering or leaving it. I could even see the air traffic lanes used by military aircraft when they departed Tegus.

The Maya was a hangout for news people, foreign intelligence operatives and military personnel who sat around the coffee shop blurting out what undoubtedly was classified information about their comings and goings.

Tirador and I learned about Task Force 160 at the Maya coffee shop from an Army captain from Texas. He thought Tirador and I were part of a highly secret military group and talked freely to us about activities going on at the border. We knew night missions were being flown into Nicaragua and that some of the helicopters had been shot down. We even made jokes about cover stories being used by the U.S. government to keep the public from knowing Americans were being killed on missions inside Nicaragua.

I was surprised how openly American servicemen talked about their assignments in a public restaurant in Honduras. Most apparently thought they were in Vietnam or some place where everybody was a good guy. But if Tirador and I had been Soviet agents, we would have been highly decorated for all the information we picked up sitting around the Maya coffee shop.

Cattle didn't show up for his scheduled meeting at the Maya and couldn't be found at any of the numbers he gave me. Posey, who was still back in the States, had no explanation. Another one of his great deals had fallen through. I told Posey to find out what the hell happened to him. He said he would get Jim Turney in Memphis to run down the elusive John Cattle.

I waited for two days. Finally, Posey called, sounding like a whipped dog.

"John Cattle doesn't exist," he said.

"What?"

"Cattle's real name is John Fairburn. He's just been released from federal prison."

"What about the deal?"

"He probably knows Steadman Fagoth," Posey said, "but not enough to get the weapons away from the MISURA."

I knew CMA now was in deep shit with the FDN. Our credibility was on the line. If we didn't produce something out of this, Adolfo would make sure we did nothing but tote socks for the rest of the war. Our only choice was to go into the Miskitia on our own and try to work the deal without any point of contact. It was risky, but worth the chance. Besides, we needed to obtain permission to get the Maco Stewart group into the area and this was an opportunity to press that issue.

But how to get there?

A taxi driver we met earlier named Caesar Recondo suggested a charter airline called SETCO. Caesar was our black market money changer, our guide to the Tegucigalpan underground and our fixer. He was, like most taxi drivers, intimately familiar with the city, but he was smarter than most and spoke enough English for us to communicate with him.

Caesar's choice of SETCO was not by accident. SETCO was owned by a major Honduran drug lord named Juan Matta Ballesteros and was the airline of choice of the FDN and various drug dealers transporting their wares in and out of Honduras. SETCO, or Air Contra, also became my primary airline. The people who worked there thought I belonged to the CIA and wrote receipts for my trips that read: "Received from CIA, 4,300 lempiras."

After making arrangements for a trip the next morning, Tirador and I went back to the hotel, where Grace joined us in my room for dinner.

As we were eating, the pilot of the plane scheduled to fly us into the Miskitia called to say he was in the lobby. We invited him up.

Miguel Cruz was short, dark and friendly. He spoke no English so Grace did the translating.

She explained we wanted to make a trip to the Miskito Indian village of Rus Rus, located in the southeast region of Mocoron, and needed to know the regulations. He evidently thought we were military because of the amount of military gear strewn about my room and the pistols on the bed and said he needed to point out several features on our route.

As he traced a line on my map from Tegucigalpa to the Miskitia, he pointed out the CIA base at Aguacote and a line of high mountains close to the border that we would have to avoid because it was restricted air space. He said SETCO did all the flying of personnel and supplies for the CIA when the Contra war first began, but, since the aid ban, that had ended.

The only limitation on the trip was that it had to be made in one day. We would leave at daybreak but had to be back in Tegus before sundown.

I told Miguel we would pay extra for his silence and intended to use SETCO often in the near future. I wasn't sure if we would be able to do anything outside the Stewart trip, but hoped for more once we met the Indians that would be independent of the FDN.

I was reluctant to tell anyone in the FDN what we were doing because I had no doubt efforts would be made to stop us. An American acting alone in this war was automatically in trouble because the FDN was extremely jealous of its territory and would report anyone not conforming to its demands to the Hondurans and the U.S. Embassy. Deportation was the next step.

If there was another incident involving Americans that reflected badly on the Hondurans, the FDN could be in for some serious difficulty in its home away from home.

Still, the FDN leaders knew they had to allow some American participation because they needed the publicity and the money from the States. Although the FDN was closely linked to the Reagan administration, it knew it also had to appeal to the Democrats in Congress to win the funding vote. That meant caving in to the liberal Democrats on the issue of Americans in combat, so the FDN bowed to pressure and said no more Americans would be allowed across the border.

When I learned the FDN was playing both sides of the fence, I became more determined to break away from it and its political games. I was not about to allow the FDN to subvert me and use me as its leaders saw fit.

I had no intentions of playing politics. I wanted to go to war.

Kinsmen in the Wilderness

Miguel set the Cessna 182 down on the dirt and grass strip and taxied to a stop near a small hut where three Honduran soldiers eyed us curiously. Americans visitors to the Miskitia were not uncommon. Various missionary groups tried to work their magic on the Indians over the years and the Honduran guards were used to seeing white faces. Only Tirador and I didn't look much like Gospel preachers with our short hair and military bearing.

On the way in we had buzzed a village several miles south of the runway to let people know a plane was in. But it was more than an hour before we heard the noisy engine of a truck approaching the field, and it came from the opposite direction. It was the local bus service from Puerta Lempira. Tirador, Miguel and I jumped onto the running boards and hung on as the truck took off for the village.

We drove south into an area that was much more tropical than the pine-studded grasslands where we landed. The road was bad and twice we had to get off and walk across poorly maintained bridges while the truck followed slowly. At one point we crossed a river on a hand-pulled ferry and waited while the truck crept to the top of a steep, muddy ridge on the south side of the river.

At the top of the ridge the truck got back on a dryer road and we reboarded for the trip into the village where a number of new huts were being built for Indian refugees from Nicaragua who were coming in daily.

Women sat in circles weaving palm strips into 10-foot square sections that would be used as roofing. The floors of the huts were made from bamboo that had been cut in half and woven into planks. The walls were a mixture of wooden planks and bamboo poles cut to a length of three to four feet.

The people in this village were different than other Hondurans I had seen. They were darker and shorter and their high cheekbones and black hair told me they were of Indian descent.

Children, many of them naked, ran beside the truck chattering and laughing as they pointed up at Tirador and me.

The truck stopped near a small general store in the center of the village and disgorged its passengers into the 19th century. I had stepped back in time to another era, one without modern conveniences, one without communications, one without hope beyond the next meal.

A Caterpillar diesel generator sat rusting next to the store. There must have been electricity in this village at one time, before lack of parts or mechanics or initiative deprived the Indians of that luxury. Old junk trucks were strewn about corroding away and serving as roosts for the village chickens.

The store itself had little to offer, and the woman who ran it had even less. She seemed unconcerned about white people being in town but when I asked her if she could direct us to the second in command of the MISURA military, I got no response.

I then invoked the name Steadman Fagoth, the MISURA leader whose well-constructed house sat at the end of a nearby private airstrip. Still no response. I told Tirador that we should go to Fagoth's house to see if anyone there could help us.

Although there were Honduran soldiers all around, they ignored us as we walked up to the house and stood next to a wooden fence. Miguel said something in Spanish to a young boy on the porch and he immediately got up and walked to a cluster of houses next to a small creek.

An older woman in a cotton dress and a camouflage bush hat emerged from one of the houses and followed the boy back up the path to where we were standing.

"I'm Edna Fagoth Mueller, Steadman Fagoth's mother," the woman said in surprisingly good English.

She invited us to follow her down the path and across the creek to a house that literally looked more like a pig sty. Pigs lay snorting and grunting in mud puddles around the yard, and chickens pecked the dry portions of ground for seeds and insects. The placed smelled like a barnyard and, in a sense, I guess it was.

I explained to Edna we had come in search of the man in command of the MISURA since her son was in the States and was not allowed to return to the Miskitia. He had made some threats over an open microphone during a radio broadcast about executing Sandinista prisoners. The Hondurans and his American benefactors in the CIA had hustled him out of the country and into Miami to keep him out of trouble with the Sandinistas.

Edna said she knew nothing about any military presence in the Rus and wanted nothing more than to tell Americans the Miskitos were badly in need of food and medicine. It was obvious people were malnourished and many of them were in need of medical treatment.

I told her I sympathized and wanted to take pictures of this crisis to show to organizations in the States that might help.

"Everyone who comes here takes pictures, then leaves and we never hear from them again," she said.

"A group of American Indians wants to come here to see firsthand the misery their brothers are suffering," I said. "American Indians have suffered much the same fate as the Central American Indian and these people want to help."

Edna seemed interested in this idea and agreed to take me on a tour of the village while Tirador and Miguel went in search of a radio transmitter. She tried her best to hide the fact that the MISURA military were headquartered in this area, but occasionally I saw soldiers in the distinctive Sears-Roebuck green uniforms of the Contras walking around.

The suffering in this village was unlike anything I had ever seen anywhere, even in the worst slums in Tegucigalpa. It was even worse than photographs I had seen of starving Ethiopians. There was no sanitation and human waste was everywhere, attracting swarms of flies. Many of the children had no clothing. Meals consisted of beans and rice three times a day, occasionally spiced with a bit of pork or chicken.

Edna said there were about 300 Nicaraguan refugees in this area, but that there were many more camps to the east with a total population of 40,000. I couldn't understand how these people survived.

Here was a small-scale Ethiopia right in our back yard and nobody in Washington seemed to care. Little more than 750 miles from New Orleans, an entire race of people was facing extinction by starvation and Washington turned its back.

I was deeply touched by what I saw that day. I could feel the eyes of the children staring at me in fear and hunger and hope. My own troubles seemed so insignificant that I took a vow I would not let this go unnoticed. I would find a way to get the message to the right people, whether it be north of the border or south of it.

Politics had no role here, although these people were victims of a political policy gone mad. The displacement of thousands of starving people was lunacy, if not outright genocide. I was sick that my own country would let this happen and angry that the FDN was a part of it.

I told Edna I had a plan to help these people if they gave me a chance. I knew they had been promised heaven and earth before, so I wasn't going to give the impression that I could create a miracle. But I said if I returned to the area, I would bring about change if I had to do it through force.

As Edna and I talked, I heard a vehicle coming from the south at high speed. When it topped a rise in the road I saw Tirador riding on the back of a dark green Toyota truck with several men carrying automatic weapons.

"These men are from the general staff of the MISURA," Tirador said as he jumped off the truck.

A tall, dark Miskito Indian approached me and introduced himself as Alejo Theofilo Barberra, G-4 logistics chief for the MISURA. He spoke fluent English and told me that they had seen the plane, but thought we were from Friends of America, one of the American missionary groups that worked in the area, and did not bother to come to the airstrip.

The group consisted of Hilton Fagoth, G-2 in charge of intelligence and the brother of Steadman; Raoul Tobias, G-1 head of the military wing of the MISURA; Selso Wiggins, first secretary to Steadman; Archibald Theofilo, a member of the political wing and a black Spanish Creole; and Chang, a military commander known for his daring exploits and tactical knowledge.

I introduced myself as Colonel Flaco and my assistant as Tirador. The general staff must have figured we brought good news about something because their faces reflected eager anticipation.

When I spoke, Alejo translated first into Spanish and then into Miskito so that everyone knew what was being discussed. I was afraid to say too much about Steadman Fagoth because I didn't know who among them owed allegiance to him or whether his expulsion changed the chain of command.

Raoul was younger than most of the other men and wore a beard, which was unusual among the Indians. His skin was much lighter than the others and he was soft-spoken. But he had a good sense about the war and his role in it.

Raoul said Steadman was gone and it was up to the rest of the people to try to continue their fight against the Sandinistas.

I told him Tirador and I represented a group in America called CMA and that our primary mission was to provide assistance to Contra groups in the form of medicine and supplies. We also provided trainers and advisers when appropriate.

This piqued their interest. I told them we planned to escort a group of American Indians to the Miskitia so that they could get a better look at what was happening to their brothers and see if they could help them in some way. My primary mission, though, was to return after the Indian visit with many American advisers and much equipment to wage war against the Sandinistas with the MISURA. This drew an even better response.

"Do you represent the American military?" one of the men asked me.

"Not necessarily," I replied.

I was jockeying for position and needed to gauge the commitment of these men and their troops before I told them exactly who I was and what I represented. I had to know if they approved of several outsiders coming in and possibly becoming commanders. I told them that this was an extremely secret mission and not even the Honduran regional commander could be told of our presence.

We would be operating outside the FDN, I told them. This news produced knowing smiles among the group. Alejo said the FDN had been using them and depriving them of their rightful share of aid being sent to Honduras. There was no love between the two groups. The MISURA had been promised up to 30,000 lempiras a month, about $15,000, by the FDN for expenses. But the FDN had reneged on the agreement and was furnishing money to the Indians on an "as needed" basis, which meant very little cash got to the Miskitia.

The FDN considered the MISURA a waste of time and money. But the FDN did not want the Indians to get too powerful because they feared the MISURA wanted their independence more than they wanted to fight Communism. That much was true.

The Indians hated Communists for crimes they committed after they took over as much as they hated Somoza for the oppression they suffered for decades at his hand. The Indians saw the FDN as little more than surrogates of the old Somoza regime. There would be little difference in their treatment whether the Contras or the Sandinistas won the war. For the Indians, the only peace was total independence from all sides.

The staff told me every time a war broke out in Nicaragua the Indians were asked to help fight and overthrow the sitting government. But when the fighting was over, they had no voice in the new government. The Indians were truly Nicaragua's blacks. They gave their lives for their country and got nothing in return.

Political buzzwords like Communism and democracy meant nothing to these people. They were totally apolitical. They understood they were living decades behind the times, but they were happy in that life and simply wanted to be left alone.

When I heard this message it was as if a lightning bolt shot through my brain. The circumstances here were unique. These people needed someone to counsel them and assist them. This was the place to fight the war. These were the people to fight it with. While I was achieving my own goals, I would be helping them build their own homeland.

I felt as if I found my destiny. If I was to do anything good or lasting in this war, this would be the place I could pull it off. But I knew I would have to do it mostly on guts and gambles. And I knew I would have to do it independent of the FDN.

1. *Jack Terrell in 1979 as president of his successful emergency medical service company in Columbus, Mississippi.*

2. Tom Posey displaying ammunition and military items he stored at his home in Decatur, Alabama.

3. Mass gathering of FDN Contras during a seldom-held religious holiday at Las Vegas, Honduras. Notice the large white letters and bright blue shelters virtually inviting an air strike.

4. *John Hull, an Indiana farmer who resettled in Costa Rica, allowed his ranch on the Nicaragua border to be used by the CIA as a training camp for Contra troops.*

5. *Formation of MISURA soldiers and American advisers on the first day after arrival at TEA base.*

6. The command hutch of Colonel Flaco at TEA.

7. Donald Castillo, also known as Pulmon, posing for intelligence photo prior to Sin Sin Bridge raid.

8. MISURA *weapons placed on a hand-made rack to prevent the* Indians *from carrying loaded guns in camp.*

9. *Jack Terrell and Jim Adair teaching MISURA troops how to use* det-cord *and M1 fuse ignitors at TEA.*

10. *Jack Terrell accompanying American Indian chief on the trip to San Carlos in Nicaragua.*

11. *Miskito Indian refugees gathered to greet American Indians.*

12. MISURA military general staff entering TEA base for a conference.

13. Remains of Miskito Indians allegedly murdered in a Sandinista raid at San Carlos, Nicaragua in 1982.

14. All-female company of Mon National Liberation Army at Three Pagoda Pass in Burma.

15. Jack Terrell examining weapons inventory of the Mon National Liberation Army.

11

The Disengagement

The FDN, by choosing Posey to go to Costa Rica ahead of me, had unwittingly given me a choice of fronts in the war against the Sandinistas in which to get involved.

First and foremost was the front in the Miskitia. The possibilities there were limitless. The Indians had not given me the same baptism of bullshit as did the FDN, and I sensed they had become estranged from the war primarily because they lacked supplies necessary to sustain operations deep inside Nicaragua.

There was still the possibility of reaching the southern front, either through the FDN or Eden Pastora and his ARDE group. Whacking Pastora would be no easy task, and if I went into Costa Rica under the auspices of the FDN, I would not have the same freedom I had now. But if things with the FDN got too bad, I could always go to Pastora and tell him what his friends up north were planning.

The longest shot was staying with the FDN and working out of Las Vegas. But it appeared Adolfo Calero and the FDN directorate didn't want me involved with them because of my militant attitude. Like a scorned lover, they were determined not to let anybody else have me, primarily because of the knowledge I possessed about the way they did business.

Too much knowledge can be a liability, but fear of that knowledge can be an asset. I had enough on the FDN and its Washington pipeline to wreak havoc throughout Honduras and Costa Rica if I was shut out of both countries. They knew it and feared the knowledge I had.

The way to use this to my advantage was to appeal to the FDN's greed. I had to find something the FDN needed from the Indians and barter it for access to them and the region while maintaining a semblance of a relationship with the FDN. That would seemingly get me out of the FDN's hair and into an area where the FDN thought I could do little harm.

I would let Posey have his way in Costa Rica as long as he provided men and equipment for my efforts in the Miskitia. I would give Posey the impression I was still on board with CMA, even using the organization as a front in Miskitia. But I finally came to the realization that I had to go my own way if I was to get anything done.

The Advent of Misadventure

With the personal blessing and a signed note from Edna Fagoth, I returned to Tegus to make preparations to bring in the American Indians.

I called Dave Robbins, Maco Stewart's money man in Houston, and told him to put the Indians on the plane. We would be ready for them in two days. I also gave him specific instructions on what they should and should not wear. I strictly forbade anything resembling military dress. No camouflage. No tiger stripes. No olive drab. No military green.

The Indians were to bring sleeping bags, mess kits, medical kits, back packs and enough extra clothing for five days. But none of the equipment or clothing was to be military. The Hondurans didn't have much tolerance for foreigners showing up at the airport in military clothing and carrying military gear unless they had the FDN's stamp of approval. These guys didn't have that stamp.

I also told Robbins there was to be no booze.

"And make sure Maco brings the cash," I said.

I reserved a suite for Maco on the ninth floor of the Honduran Maya. It was no secret I was trying to impress him. I needed his money and how he perceived me and our operation would be the basis on which he judged decisions for future funding.

I also reserved seven rooms at the hotel under my storefront operation, Delphi Company. Delphi was nothing more than me, but I had business cards printed with the company's name and a telephone number in Miami that was answered by Tirador's girlfriend, Sue Driscoll. On the face of the card were the words "International Contingencies" to lend a certain air of mystery to the business. People who saw the cards thought I came straight from the Agency.

Sue would only take messages at the Miami number and would never talk to anyone at length. She doubled as a secretary and cargo handler and was excellent at it. When she sent packages to Honduras with the name Delphi written on them, Customs people thought they were exempt from examination.

The situation at Toncontin International Airport in Tegus was so lacking in command and control that I often found by merely walking around and dropping names I could get things done. I was banking on my perpetual powers of bullshit to get the Maco group in. But this was one time when it nearly let me down.

When the flight from Houston landed and Maco's party of Indians got off the plane, my heart fell into my stomach. Every damn one of those Indians was wearing something camouflage. Jackets, vests, hats, pants. The Honduran military guards rushed the plane as soon as they spotted them. I didn't know whether to run and leave them to the Honduran dogs or jump in and get chewed up with them.

The Honduran troops escorted the group to the terminal and confiscated their passports. I looked frantically for Captain Lukey, my secret police contact who was at the airport just minutes earlier. Lukey had vanished. I walked downstairs to the exit door and looked for a familiar face. I found a Customs official I knew and tried to convince him the Indians were hunters.

But as I tried to explain this, other Customs officials were pulling all sorts of military gear out of the Indians's luggage. To compound the problem, the Indians had been drinking on the plane and began getting surly with the guards.

This had all the makings of a disaster. Not only could the Indians wind up in jail, but my hoped-for source of funding would disappear because I was not able to do any of the things I promised. Maco was getting extremely impatient and said he thought he might cancel the trip because the immigration people told him the group would have to stay at the airport overnight and be on the first plane back to the States in the morning. I couldn't let this happen because we needed the money.

Captain Lukey finally returned to the airport and I was able to convince him the Indians didn't know any better about the camouflage clothing. I promised it wouldn't happen again. He let the Indians pass.

At the hotel, I passed out room registration cards and told each Indian to write a false name and passport number. I didn't want Immigration checking on our movements.

As I was doing this, Maco lifted his pants legs and pulled an envelope from each sock. Each envelope contained $9,900. Then he reached into his pocket and pulled out two $100 bills. The $20,000 was the balance of my fee. Maco told me he did it this way to keep the IRS from asking him about two $10,000 transactions to this strange Delphi Company.

That night, we gathered in Maco's suite so the Indians could learn who they were dealing with and I could get some idea what I was faced with. Tirador had returned to Honduras to assist me, as did an employee of Joe Coutin, a man named Masareno Rodriguez, who went by the nom de guerre Pedrico.

Pedrico was a rabid anti-Communist and one of the few Miami Cubans I could trust. He looked military, he acted military and he was intent on dying in the war against Communism, wherever that might be. He left his wife and family in Miami and vowed not to return until he was dead or Communism was run out of the hemisphere. He agreed to serve as our interpreter.

As the Indians introduced themselves, I asked them if they wanted to carry firearms. Only one said he did. The others said they were not there to fight, but to establish solidarity with their Central American brothers and see what they could do to help them.

I warned the group that a form of martial law was being imposed on this trip and I would personally deal with security breaches and misconduct in the strictest manner. I told them I would be harsh with them because I wanted to make sure they survived. None appeared enthusiastic about my overly dramatic speech and all of them appeared uncertain about continuing on.

A Visit with the Spirits

When we landed in the Miskitia the following morning, Alejo and Raoul came to the airstrip to meet us in a single truck. Since there was not enough room for all of us and the luggage, I sent Tirador and the group ahead to get settled in while Pedrico and I remained behind with the gear.

I had brought my own radio communications on this trip and told Tirador to find out how far we could communicate in this terrain. Most of the radios being used here operated on low frequencies and mine were VHF, making them practically monitor proof. I intended to use them on missions inside Nicaragua.

As Pedrico and I waited for the group to return, I lay down in the grass next to the pile of luggage and looked up at the sky. The breeze across the airfield was warm and pleasant. There was a feeling of security here, a feeling of being home. It was not unlike the feeling I had many years before when I would lie in a hammock outside my house in Birmingham on summer afternoons, drifting in and out of sleep with the wind gently blowing across my body and rustling the grass.

After the madness and the mania of Miami, I told Pedrico, the tranquility and serenity of this place was like heaven to me. I knew I could stay here forever. My life had been one of constant movement and constant mental fatigue, worrying how I could survive on what few real skills I possessed and having to maintain images I had created in a world I didn't fit into.

Here in the Miskitia all my concerns melted into the quiet winds. The feeling of being needed and respected overtook me. An inner peace settled over me like a warm blanket and I wished I could hold onto that feeling forever.

I was totally detached from the inanity of the Cubans and the FDN. I felt I had finally escaped the ghosts of my past.

For the first time in my life my mind was totally clear. It felt as if I had just walked into the arms of the family I had never known. There was a sense of freedom and a sense of belonging because I could identify with these people. They were like me, prisoners and outcasts in their own country.

"Tirador to Flaco. Tirador to Flaco. Come in," Tirador's voice crackled over the radio.

"Tirador to Flaco. Tirador to Flaco. Can you read me?"

"Where are you?" I replied.

"At the hospital in Rus. The truck is on its way back to pick you up."

One thing I learned quickly about the Miskitos was their sense of scheduling. They never kept one. If they said they were going to meet you somewhere, you could add at least an hour to the arrival time. To them, it wasn't important when you arrived. You arrived when you arrived.

There was not enough room at the hospital in Rus to keep the entire group, so Raoul decided to move all of us deeper into the Miskitia. No sooner had I rejoined the group at the hospital than we reboarded the trucks for a drive to an isolated place near a MISURA camp known as Cym, southeast of the airstrip.

We drove past Cym for several more miles until the trucks reached the crest of a hill and stopped. A young Indian soldier armed with an AK-47 stood near a stack of sandbags that was covered with a poncho. The guard saluted Raoul and opened a gate that consisted of nothing more than a piece of wood lying across the road.

Barbed wire was strung along the entrance road to what appeared to be a large, abandoned base. It dawned on that this was the training based set up by the Argentineans for the famed MISURA special force known as the Tropas Especiale del Atlantico, the TEA of which Doc Zorro had spoken some weeks earlier.

The trucks stopped in front of three huts that appeared to have been command posts and we got out.

It was like stepping onto sacred ground. The hairs on the back of my neck stood on end and chills ran down my spine. I wasn't the only one who could feel the spirits of the long-dead Indians who had trained there, those who had been sacrificed for a cause without reason, a war without honor. The American Indians talked about how they too felt the spirits of the dead.

This was like a holy place and I knew this was where we would create the center for everything we wanted to contribute to the Miskitos. I and my American trainers would come back and rekindle that spirit among the Indian warriors once known only to the TEA. We would attract Indians from all parts of the Miskitia to fight the Sandinistas and make them forget the tragedy that had befallen the TEA.

The camp was well laid out and the jungle had not yet reclaimed it four years after it had been abandoned. It wouldn't take much work to get it back into fighting shape.

There were still a few ramshackle structures standing. I could see where tents had been set up, where there had been a parade ground and the remains of a jump tower. The roads were still lined with neatly cut pine logs.

Bunkers were dug along the perimeter every 20 feet and protected in front by thick logs. It appeared the base's previous inhabitants were expecting a Sandinista attack.

There were spent shell casings scattered everywhere and ammo boxes lay rotting in the open air. The buildings contained parachutes, outboard motors, chain saws and thousands of rounds of belted 7.62 x 59 ammunition, all of it covered with rust.

Much of this materiel could be salvaged and used for training.

I demonstrated how the rusting ammunition could be made usable by dousing it in a combination of old crankcase oil and diesel fuel. It made an excellent gun lubricant and instead of throwing away rusted ammunition, as the Indians frequently did, all the old ammo could be saved.

This was like magic to them. Although they could live off the jungle, the Indians had problems dealing with machinery and modern conveniences. I put everyone to work immediately salvaging materiel for our new training base.

As Tirador and I explored the base, we found a shooting range still intact with numbered target posts lining the rear of the parade ground like a picket fence. In the tall grass near the range was a mock up of an airplane with a metal arch that was once used to teach rudimentary parachute skills.

The layout of this base was definitely more sophisticated than I thought possible in this part of the world. It had U.S. military written all over it.

The Miskitos wasted no time arranging trips to the border area. The first day was a tour of a refugee camp called Karasanka. The trip took all day by truck and on foot. The disease and malnutrition in Karasanka were identical to what I had seen in the Rus. Even the American Indians who came from some of the most impoverished communities in the United States were affected by what they saw.

Maco was getting jittery. He wanted me to produce Roger Herman for an explanation about the money he had invested in cocoa beans, but which apparently had disappeared. I began to see the side of Maco that Zorro told me about. Maco was arrogant, demanding and flaunted his wealth. He complained that most people conspired against him and lied to him all his life.

I chalked his ramblings up to a lack of liquor and pacified him as best I could. He spent most of his time in his hut, reading or brooding.

The Miskitos watched us everywhere we went, even though we were some distance from the border. They watched us bathe, watched us eat and made bed checks on us several times a night. Most of our guards were combat veterans and took their jobs seriously. We had no reason to be nervous or edgy when we went to bed.

But our first morning in the TEA camp I was awakened by the strange sound of singing. I thought at first it was a dream. It was pitch black and when I looked at my watch it said 4 a.m. I couldn't figure out what was going on.

Through the door of my hut I could see a large group of Miskitos gathered around a fire on the far side of the compound. They were singing Gospel hymns in their native language, songs like "The Old Rugged Cross" and "Rock of Ages" that I had heard in church as a boy. It gave me chills to hear their deep, melodic voices echoing through the jungle darkness, their AK-47s slung across their backs, the firelight throwing shadows across their dark, devout faces.

The Miskitos were Moravian Baptists, Christianized and baptized some years before by German missionaries who came into the region, some of whom stayed and intermarried. There was nothing phony about the Miskitos and their religion, not like the so-called "Christian commandos" of the FDN.

The Miskitos did not advertise their faith. They simply lived it. Their faith carried over into everything in their lives. War, food and family came second to their religion. I found several commanders who were preachers and had been educated by missionaries.

I quickly developed a deep respect for their beliefs and never uttered a word of protest when they felt it necessary to pray even when combat was imminent.

The primary purpose of this trip was the spiritual communion of the Indians. The American Indians and Miskitos talked for several days about a commonality of suffering and oppression and it became obvious even to me there was a bond here no non-Indian could understand or be part of. I was making a lot of money for this excursion, but felt duty-bound to make sure each side got what it wanted from the trip.

The Council of Elders, second only to the Assembly of Chiefs in the MISURA power structure, met with us while we were in the TEA camp and requested we visit the village of San Carlos inside Nicaragua. We were told that in 1981 the Sandinistas massacred 284 civilians there.

Alejo told us it had been a difficult time when the Sandinistas occupied all the Indian villages along the Coco River, forcing villagers to relocate to re-education camps. He said that in those days the MISURA had no weapons to fight helicopter gunships except .22-caliber rifles.

According to Alejo, during one assault by helicopter gunships, a young Indian took his rifle and began shooting at the aircraft, striking the pilot in the head. The helicopter crashed. This demonstrated to the people that although they were outgunned, they could still fight back and achieve some success. The Assembly of Chiefs pulled together more than 300 tribes and declared war on the Sandinistas. They vowed to arm themselves from the bodies of dead enemy soldiers. The war effort that began with machetes, .22- caliber rifles and courage developed into a full-blown revolution.

When Argentine Special Forces came to train them, the MISURA resented the intrusion. Alejo said the Argentineans had no respect for them or their culture, often ridiculing them and comparing them with the FDN. The MISURA eventually threw the foreigners out and vowed not to be subservient to anyone again.

I asked Alejo how he felt about American trainers. He said now that the MISURA army had scaled down its operations, most of the soldiers had returned to their homes. They could no longer fight without food or medicine.

But, he said, if we got involved and opened a supply line from the States, the general staff would start returning previously trained soldiers to form units that they would allow us to direct. They even agreed to allow Americans into combat in Nicaragua. He said they would be proud to serve with brave men who came to die for them.

Dying for them meant earning the eternal respect of the MISURA, especially for those who volunteered to do it and were not ordered to fight some larger military command. If the U.S. Army dropped into the country and died fighting, it wasn't the same to them as someone volunteering to assist them.

I told Alejo it was time the MISURA received the recognition they deserved. It was time the world noticed the MISURA and their pleas for independence. I told him it was time for Americans to put their lives on the line for the MISURA.

I could see this kind of talk inspired him. I was lighting fires of independence within the MISURA leadership. I was carefully weaning them from the dictatorial control of Steadman Fagoth, the one man among the MISURA who concerned me. If he knew a gringo was attempting to oust him from power, there could be big problems. I had to try to win over Fagoth's faithful while rendering him incapable of governing the Indians from Miami.

Once I did that, these people would be ready to follow my lead.

The trip to San Carlos was risky. We would have to take trucks to the village of Auasbila three hours from the TEA camp by bad roads. At Auasbila we would get into a boat for a run down the river to San Carlos.

Ausabila was a Honduran village inhabited by Miskitos. There was a small Honduran military outpost in the village that served as a listening post to monitor Sandinista activity across the river. The river itself was a free-fire zone. You played in the middle of the river, you took your chances.

One long dugout canoe would be used for the trip. A single 35-horsepower engine would be attached to the rear to be used more for guidance than power. I knew it was going to be a tough trip when the motor fell off before we got started and had to be fished out of the muddy water. Then it had to be cleaned and reattached to the boat. I wondered how the boat would stay afloat, as narrow and shallow as it was. But this was normal transportation to the Miskitos.

We crammed 23 people into that boat, plus a radio operator and an oarsman. I told Pedrico to sit near the bow, Tirador at the stern and I would sit in the middle in case we began taking fire from the Nicaraguan side of the river. Our return fire would be more evenly spread that way.

Hilton Fagoth acted as the navigator. The length of the boat combined with the number of people crammed into it made it impossible for the boatman to see where he was going. Hilton stood in the bow dipping a 12-foot pole into the water and shouting out depth and direction. Alejo had warned that no one could stand except Hilton and that if anyone moved suddenly the boat could capsize. I thought we would all eventually take a bath, but Hilton and the boatman handled the craft with ease.

The trip was slow because our weight made the boat sit low in the water. We sat with our butts in the water that collected in the bottom of the boat, trying to will it to move faster. We were concerned about Sandinista patrols that were known to pop up on the south side of the river. The farther we traveled, the smaller the boat got but the more inviting a target we seemed sitting in the middle of the river.

We constantly scanned the brush on the southern bank for movement. The Honduran side was devoid of vegetation. The banks on the north side looked like they had been grazed to the dirt by cattle, but we were told people removed the vegetation for food. The Nicaraguan side was green, rich and thick, but people were afraid to cross the river to harvest anything.

A few villages and an occasional lone hut stood along the Honduran side and as we passed them children would wave and shout loudly because they thought we were a MISURA raiding party. The American Indians in the boat became dead quiet when we passed the Rio Waspuk, an imaginary line that indicated real enemy territory. Raoul locked and loaded his weapon and the rest of us did likewise.

I whispered to the Indian sitting in front of me to pass along the word that if we began taking fire, everyone was to get as low as possible, but should not stand up or jump overboard. If the fire was from heavy weapons like mortars, they were to fall back into the water on the northern side of the boat and swim for it.

After five hours the boat reached a steep clay embankment where a single aging MISURA soldier stood guard. The boatman drove the nose of the canoe into the bank to secure it and we finally climbed out and up the bank into a tangle of vines and tropical foliage. After a short walk we came to the village of San Carlos, or what remained of it.

The burned out hulks of houses, huts and stores were still visible. Alejo said the place had been left as it was found years earlier after the Sandinistas swept through it, killing, burning and looting. It was a strange and eerie place. Pieces of furniture were still intact but the buildings around them had burned down. Rusted pots, pans and eating utensils were strewn about the ground in the thick grass.

The American Indians had stopped and gathered around something and I decided to investigate. At their feet was a pile of human skulls, neatly arranged at the foot of what once was the porch of a house. They were visibly shaken by the sight.

The old Miskito soldier standing guard served as the caretaker of this village of the dead. It was his duty to preserve the site and tell those who visited what had happened here. He said the Sandinistas had come to San Carlos years earlier and told the more than 800 villagers they had to leave. It was part of a relocation program aimed at getting the Indians out of the border areas. The Sandinistas claimed it was being done to protect them from their enemies in Honduras. They were told they would be allowed to return to their homes as soon as it was safe.

But the people did not trust the Sandinistas. They began questioning the need to move. They said they had not seen any enemy troops trying to cross the river. They questioned why anyone wanted to come to San Carlos. They were poor people and had nothing to offer anyone except a share of their food.

The leader of the Sandinista company was described as a Cuban officer. The Miskito soldier said he wore a dark green uniform with red and gold epaulets. He said several other Cubans assisted the soldiers, who began searching the huts for those they described as "gangsters and murderers" in hiding. The troops were searching for young men and weapons.

The village elders gathered the people together and told them not to go because this was their home and their land and the Sandinistas had no right to force them to leave. When one of the soldiers shot and killed one of the elders, it was the signal for all the troops to open fire on the villagers.

It seemed strangely reminiscent of the American Indian massacre at Wounded Knee in the 1890s, when U.S. soldiers opened fire on peaceful Indians for no real reason.

When the gunfire started, the young men of San Carlos retrieved hidden weapons and fired back, but they were seriously outnumbered and out-gunned. The Sandinistas chased down villagers in the jungle and shot others as they tried to swim the river to Honduras.

The old Miskito said 284 villagers died in the massacre that day. Livestock was shot, the church, houses and huts were set afire, and the bodies of the dead were thrown into the fires.

The American Indians were visibly moved. One pulled a feather from his pocket and inserted it into his headband. Others were crying. One of the Indians had brought along sacred ceremonial tobacco to be used on special occasions. He got out the tobacco and rolled a cigarette, since no pipe was available. Then two of the Indians knelt by the skulls and another sang an ancient death song while the remaining tobacco was sprinkled around the skulls.

The cigarette was lit and passed around the group as the Indians prayed that the spirits of the dead would be released from the constraints, the pain and the suffering of earth.

Despite my initial problems with these American Indians, I found myself caught up in their ceremony and their sense of brotherhood. They were demonstrating to me that the plight of Indians is much the same everywhere. My view of them was changing and I was beginning to get some insight into the Miskitos and why they felt as they did about the Sandinistas, the Hondurans and the FDN.

We left San Carlos saddened by the fact that so few people knew what happened here. Although the media were fond of reporting on Contra atrocities, Sandinista massacres seemed to be conveniently overlooked. And San Carlos wasn't the only village where this had happened.

The Chameleon Effect

The MISURA were on the dole from the FDN, a situation the Indians did not like. The FDN picked up plane fares for the political arm, but provided few other necessities. Suspicious chiefs among the MISURA were beginning to question why Steadman Fagoth spent so little time among his people and why his mission to obtain relief supplies in Miami was showing so little progress. Steadman was living high and handsome in Miami but he was not putting food in their mouths or boots on the feet of the soldiers.

Raoul did not want to speak badly about Fagoth because he was afraid, as most Miskitos were, that he would find a way to return to the Miskitia and launch reprisals against those who challenged his leadership. They believed his exile was temporary.

Steadman Fagoth had strong support in many sectors of the Miskitia and had held a death grip on the Assembly for years, but it was beginning to wane because of his absence and lack of productivity. I sensed his power could be taken away but now wasn't the time to talk about coups. I had to work at it slowly.

I told Raoul he must take a firmer stance and become more of a voice in the decision-making process. I told him that the position of the MISURA should be independence and nothing else. No politics. No game playing.

I saw I could manipulate Raoul and through him the general staff. They could be slowly weaned from Steadman Fagoth's leadership. I told Raoul the general staff should begin holding regular meetings to discuss direction of the war efforts.

Raoul always thought I was an Agency man and that when he talked to me the message was going straight to Washington. He wanted to gain stature with Americans because he needed a passport and wanted to know if I could arrange it for him. The entire general staff was without passports because the FDN had confiscated their documents to keep them in line. A few political people had been issued passports through the FDN, but only those who could be controlled.

I simply told Raoul if he would give me free rein, I would soon have him at the head of a large army. He rose to the bait and soon began telling me the most guarded of MISURA secrets. I was shown maps, charts and locations of arms, ammunition and powerful radio communications stations. I became the first white man to share these secrets, which had been sought by the FDN, Argentineans and the CIA.

Pedrico had been translating my conversations with Raoul and the look in his eyes told me he understood I was brokering power and setting the stage for not only myself, but for other Americans and Cubans to fight with the MISURA.

I was convinced I could pull off an end run with this organization and totally upset U.S. policy in the region because the FDN continued to sit in Honduras and do nothing. I was eager to get rid of my tour group and get on with my plan. The Miskitia would be my base of operations. I no longer even considered working with the FDN, either in Honduras or Costa Rica.

Tirador didn't really comprehend the complexities of what I was doing. Physically, he was strong. He was also loyal. But he was a slow learner and I knew if I was to allow him to run things in my absence I would have to teach him slowly exactly what it was I was trying to do.

When I told him we could move into this place and form whatever kind of force we wanted, using the CMA as recruiters, there was a blank look on his face, as if he really didn't understand what I was talking about. We would have the decision-making power, I told him, and the MISURA would back us up. We would use the CMA and FDN for our purposes, but in reality would be acting independently of them.

I did not want to project myself as leader, dictator or ruler of the MISURA, but I wanted to point them in the right direction to win back the self-respect and dignity someone had stolen from them.

In order to do that I had to come up with a plan that would allow me to utilize the FDN and CMA to benefit the Indians without either organization realizing it. We would use the FDN for transportation and acquiring needed supplies. And we would use CMA to recruit trainers.

But neither organization would be an ally. They would be business partners and nothing more. We would fulfill our military desires and the Indians would get their independence. I thought it was a fair bargain for both sides.

The disorder within the MISURA was being used against them. If they could be truly united, they would become a fighting force more powerful than the Contras and a political force that Washington would have to recognize. It had become obvious to me Washington was backing the wrong people in this war.

Maco's venture was coming to an end, but he had done little to win over the MISURA. No one liked him and his demanding, whining ways, no matter how much wealth he possessed. He constantly tried to get Alejo to find Roger Herman for him to find out what happened to his cocoa bean money. He asked for a meeting of the general staff to complain about being swindled over his cocoa project and then tried to purchase the entire harvest of beans and rice.

Maco thought buying their food would give the people something to work for, but I thought this was kind of backwards. Thousands of people were starving and he was trying to buy what little food they had. It didn't make any sense.

Maco tried to wheel and deal with the MISURA, but found no takers for his grandiose financial quick fixes. The MISURA saw that his only motive in dealing with them was profit, and they had no desire to cooperate with him. He was dealing with them as all whites have dealt with Indians over the years — from a position of power. They didn't need and didn't want another white man coming in getting rich off their labors while taking no risks himself.

The Miskitos had had enough of Maco, and Maco had had enough of the Miskitia, as had the American Indians. For American Indians, the trip had been too much like stepping into their own past. Everybody wanted to get home.

Before we departed, I convinced Pedrico to remain behind at the TEA base. He was to guard our equipment and recruit Indian soldiers. He was also to be a tangible sign of my personal pledge to return with American trainers and additional supplies.

In the plane on the way back to Tegus, I told Tirador that as soon as we arrived he was to contact Oscar Montez, the FDN's money man in Honduras, and drop hints about a deal offering weapons in exchange for food, medicine and clothing. If Montez could crack the MISURA arms supply network, he would gain stature in the FDN. We would have what we needed for the Indians and Montez would be indebted to me. Montez was to be informed we were bringing back plenty of U.S. dollars, which was sufficient incentive for him to begin gathering supplies at Aquacate for later shipment into the Miskitia.

All the messages relayed to Montez were part of my elaborate plan to use the FDN for the benefit of the Indians. The FDN would become unwitting accomplices, but they would be getting something of value in return. They needed weapons and we need transportation and supplies.

Maco hit the bar at the Maya even before he checked into his room and cleaned up. He started with several large tumblers full of straight vodka and chased them with scotch. When the alcohol kicked in, he became a totally different person. He asked Tirador and me to join him and began running through all his elaborate schemes that he seemed to have forgotten during his five sober days in the Miskitia.

Maco said he wanted us to return to the Miskitia and install a leader in the MISURA who would respond to what he wanted done. He wanted something done to Roger Herman if his money was not returned or the cocoa plant did not materialize. He wanted to know how much money I would need to get his ultralight aircraft into Honduras and how much to begin preparing to sink the ship in Puerta Cabeza.

We listened, but said little, allowing Maco to drink himself into a stupor. We had no intentions of assisting him in any of his wild schemes, but did not want to offend him too much because we needed his money.

I made some calls to the States to find Posey, who had disappeared; to re-establish our Cuban connection in Miami through Joe Coutin, which appeared a lost cause; and to keep Mario Calero in eager anticipation of his role in Pegaso. I needed Mario in a position where I could get help from him without giving him secrets he would pass on to his brother.

Mario had become confused and concerned about us because he could see we were working ourselves into the war independent of the FDN. But he did not want to make too many waves because he thought there was still a possibility I would bring him south to become a field commander. He had no desire to spend the war in New Orleans, but had even less desire to confront Adolfo. Mario expected me to act as a go-between and continued to assist me and seek my advice even though he was not quite sure what we were doing.

Mario had become convinced I was somehow connected with the U.S. government. I did nothing to change his perception. It would work to my advantage not only with Mario, but with everyone else with whom I dealt in Honduras, particularly Oscar Montez.

This faulty perception of me and nearly everyone connected with Pegaso opened more doors than I could have imagined. As I rolled along I seemed to pick up credibility more by accident than on purpose. It made me wonder about the real people working on behalf of the U.S. They must have been real losers for someone like me to walk in off the street and pick up the stature I did.

But there was also the possibility that my secretive contact in Washington, Donald Fortier, helped open some of these doors. I had not heard from him in several months, but wherever I went, things seemed to get done almost as if by magic and I wondered how much of a role he played in all that happened to me.

I began to feel a rush of power and I liked it. I told Tirador that in order to continue with what we were doing, we had to become adept at what I referred to as "the chameleon effect."

I told him we must develop the ability to change and blend into each and every environment in which we found ourselves. If we were thrown on a brown tree, we must turn brown. If we were hidden in green forests, we must turn green.

Regardless of which camp or side or political faction we were among, we must appear to become part of that group. If we were in the midst of the FDN, we were FDN. If we were in the Miskitia, then we were MISURA. We needed to become chameleons in order to survive in what was becoming an increasingly hostile environment.

12

Out of the Bubble:
The End Run

Miami was a madhouse of schemes and scams and slick salesmen trying to swing deals to get involved in the war by the time Tirador and I returned in late January 1985. The primary purpose of all this activity was not the ouster of the Sandinistas, but the making of money. Schemes were disguised in anti-Sandinista rhetoric because as long as these manipulators had the appearance of being for democracy and against Communism, they got the green light from the Reagan administration to do just about anything they wanted.

What Richard Secord, Albert Hakim and John Singlaub were doing on a grand scale through their Washington contacts — making tons of money by selling arms at grossly inflated prices to the Contras — the Miami-based organizations were doing on a more limited basis.

Politics and principles had no place in this war. It was all about money. Ousting the Sandinistas was secondary to making money.

Adolfo Calero was the appointed leader of the FDN, but his troops did little fighting. They sat in Honduras sucking tax dollars out of American citizens while Adolfo sat in Miami getting fat and rich.

Steadman Fagoth was the director of the MISURA, but he had little real regard for his own people. He collected money for the cause, but the cause turned out to be Steadman Fagoth and his family.

John Hull was the CIA's man in Costa Rica, but he dabbled in every illegal scheme from assassination to gunrunning to drug smuggling because of the money it brought him.

Brigade 2506 was nothing more than a collection of Cuban godfathers who lived on dreams of an era that had long since passed and could never be brought back.

Eden Pastora, the ARDE leader, was a victim of his own beliefs and principles. He didn't like gringos. He didn't like the FDN. He didn't like the Sandinistas. He was a maverick who was closer to being a true patriot than all those I had dealt with to date. But his own fierce independence was about to eliminate him from any significant role in the war because of Washington's tight control of it.

Tom Posey by this time was dancing to the tunes played by John Hull and Robert Owen. Posey was enthralled by Hull's ties to the CIA and Owen's ties to the White House through Oliver North. He saw them as being far more important in the scheme of things than I and allowed himself to be pulled down into the cesspool of illegal activities they had going in Costa Rica.

When Hull and Owen spoke, Posey jumped. So when Hull asked for five members of CMA to come to Costa Rica, Posey put together a team consisting of two of the original Las Vegas team — Donald "Ramos" Rossi and Paul "Pablo" Johnson — and three other men I did not know.

They were to go to Costa Rica wearing lapel pins that said: "Alabama Tourists" so they could be identified. They would then be taken to Hull's ranch to do his bidding.

Purely by accident, Tirador and I intercepted the team at the Miami airport when we arrived from Honduras. I immediately took control of the situation, ordered the men not to board the plane and sent them to a hotel in the Miami area to await further orders.

It was clear Posey was making an end run on me and I didn't like it. He was nervous when I finally tracked him down by phone at his home in Decatur.

"I took those people off the plane," I said. "They had no business going down there without my approval. We had an agreement on how things like that would be handled."

"Hull said he needed the men," Posey replied. "Now I'll have to call him and tell him what happened."

"That's your problem. We've got to get together to iron some things out."

Posey said that during his recent trip to Costa Rica, Hull told him that he wanted the five men to serve as trainers for Alfonso Robelo's troops and a faction of Contras once headed by Bruce Jones, the American citrus farmer whose picture in *Life* magazine had gotten him tossed out of the country.

"I came up with that plan at Adolfo's house," I told Posey, "and now I'm being cut out. Why?"

"Hull and Owen said you were too militant and in too much of a rush to get things done. They want a different approach," he said.

Adolfo agreed with Hull and told Posey to get men who would be less aggressive than I was.

Posey said he had been given a plane ride over the border region and saw recently constructed secret airstrips designed for regular U.S. Army forces that would be used in the invasion of Nicaragua. The airstrips and surrounding land were to be used as a staging area for men and equipment sent in from Panama and El Salvador.

According to Posey, part of CMA's mission in Costa Rica would be to train Nicaraguans to serve as guards for these airstrips.

It was clear Posey and I were working in opposite directions. His entire focus was on Costa Rica. Mine was on the Miskitia. He thought CMA could handle both fronts simultaneously, but I knew it was sheer lunacy. We would have enough problems keeping organized on one front.

Posey had no enthusiasm for my plans for the Miskitia. I told him we had a better chance of doing what we wanted there and with more control than we would have in Costa Rica. But he was enamored of what Hull and Owen were telling him and saw the war in the south as his way of gaining stature with the CIA and the White House.

When I learned Posey had been keeping 12 volunteers in a Tallahassee motel for the past month, I rented a van and sent Donald "Ramo" Rossi to pick them up and bring them to Miami. At least a few of them might be what I needed for the trainers I promised to take back to the Miskitia.

My primary purpose in coming back to Miami this time was to gather this team of trainers and pick up some supplies before heading back to the peace of the Miskitia. But, as usual, as soon as I hit town it was as if an announcement had been broadcast on all the radio stations. My phone rang constantly with calls from people who wanted to see me about one scheme or another. Those who didn't call showed up at the motel demanding an immediate appointment.

I dreaded the prospect of not getting enough sleep and having to eat sandwiches through long, useless meetings with people who sought nothing more than personal financial gain in the war.

One of the few visitors who proved worth my time was an intense, dedicated Cuban named Carlos Cassell, a former intelligence agent for both Fulgencio Batista and Fidel Castro who saw me on the advice of Joe Coutin.

Cassell fled Marxist Cuba and came to the U.S. to track the movements of all pro-Castro Cubans here. His reputation among the Miami Cubans was good. He said he would share with me his 18 years worth of information on Cubans known to be operatives, agents or combatants in the many conflicts in Latin America because of his desire to obtain financing to have his information computerized. He probably had more raw intelligence on pro-Castro Cubans in the States than the CIA.

"What do you know about Felipe Vidal, Rene Corvo and John Hull?" I asked.

"Plenty," he replied eagerly. "Did you know that Posey is cooperating with Hull and Robert Owen on the Costa Rican plan, independent of you or other CMA people?"

"Any ideas why?"

"Posey sees you as a threat to his leadership. He thinks you're going to take over the whole operation."

I laughed. That was the last thing I needed.

"What about Corvo?"

"He's been working Posey hard to head the Costa Rican operation because he already has some Cubans in southern Nicaragua that Posey could never get to."

"How many men?"

"About a dozen. But they're not soldiers. They're up to their eyeballs in drugs, guns and all sorts of other illegal things. You may have stumbled onto a big business operation here that is more interested in the war for the money they can make."

"Who's involved?"

"Hull, Vidal, Bruce Jones, and some Costa Rican government ministers. The southern front is just that, a front for drugs. I would advise you not to get involved unless you are into that sort of thing."

Cassell said Hull had approached Posey about bringing men into Costa Rica for various projects because Hull did not want me. He felt I would not be as easily swayed as Posey if I found out some of the things going on at his ranch.

"Things like what?" I asked.

"Like drugs," said Cassell.

Drugs, Guns and the American Way

Hull, Owen and Felipe Vidal had come to Miami with Bruce Jones. Jones was now persona non grata in Costa Rica because of advance copies of the *Life* magazine article featuring him as "A C.I.A. Man in

Nicaragua" making the rounds. He had become as infamous as he had become famous for his support of the Contras and his admitted ties to the CIA.[1]

Now, Jones couldn't go back to his adopted home near the Nicaraguan border and was at loose ends trying to come up with some scheme to cut his losses. He called me to set up a meeting about a business proposition. He said he knew a Cuban who was interested in exporting seafood from Costa Rica and wanted me to help the deal go through.

Jones had talked with Posey about my connection to Maco Stewart and Jones felt I could convince Stewart to invest in his scheme. I agreed to meet Jones and his partner at the restaurant in the Howard Johnson's motel on LeJeune Boulevard near the airport.

That Howard Johnson's was drug central in Miami, although I didn't know it at the time. It was also CMA's unofficial Miami headquarters. Drug deals were being done at the motel at the same time we were discussing the overthrow of the Sandinistas. The night manager was feeding information on CMA to the FBI with one hand and running drugs with the other. It was a great setup for him, but it inextricably linked us with the drug mafia that infested South Florida like a new species of cockroaches.

When I showed up for the meeting with Jones, Posey and a Cuban named Francisco "Paco" Chanes were waiting with him. Posey introduced the two and said they wanted to discuss importing flash-frozen lobster into the U.S. from Puerta Limon, Costa Rica. If CMA could arrange to sell the lobster here, the organization would get a share of the profits.

Posey said he thought I could talk to Maco about helping with buyers and getting the containers of seafood in through the port at Houston. It all seemed so simple to Posey. As usual, he left all the hard work and details to someone else. After his preliminary spiel, Posey excused himself by saying he had to meet with John Hull and patch up CMA's relationship with him after my decision to pull the five men off the plane.

Jones was a frail, balding man with sallow skin and a weak chin. An unknown expatriate until recently, the *Life* article had made him an international celebrity for a few minutes and he was reveling in the glory. Although he had lost his farm and his resident visa, he felt the recognition would earn him money and lasting fame.

But Jones had miscalculated. By going public he had alienated himself from the underground privatization of the war being carried out by

Hull, Owen and their Washington colleagues, most specifically Oliver North.

Jones was in need of money to support his family and survive in the States because his assets were frozen by the Costa Rican government. He and Chanes had gotten together on the seafood deal, or what they said was a seafood deal.

Chanes was a salesman of the first order. He was smooth, but persistent. He was short and stocky with dark hair. He wore an expensive silk shirt open at the neck to show off several gold chains. He also had several heavy gold bracelets on his wrist.

Chanes said he was a partner in a Miami company called Ocean Hunter Seafood. Ocean Hunter bought seafood from a company in Limon known as Frigorificos de Puntarenas. According to Chanes, one of his partners, Luis Rodriguez, operated the business in Costa Rica where they were trying to develop a frozen shrimp patty for use in fast-food restaurants like McDonald's. They had visions of developing a McShrimp burger, or something of the sort.

According to Chanes, their shrimp boats often caught lobster that could not be returned to the sea. He said the company had facilities to flash freeze these lobsters for shipment to the States, where they would bring top dollar.

If I could arrange for Maco Stewart to buy the lobsters, he would see that CMA got a nice chunk of the money simply for acting as the middleman.

"We're in the war business, not the seafood business," I told Chanes. I was not impressed by the deal and had no interest in getting involved.

Chanes then offered to pay my way to Limon to look at the plant. He felt once I saw the operation I would be convinced this was a good business deal and a potential major source of money for CMA.

"Why don't you take this up with Posey?" I asked. "He's the director of CMA and the main fund-raiser."

"There are certain realities about the business Posey doesn't understand," Chanes said. "And he doesn't have the right connections to get the product into the States. Even as we speak there is a ship at the port of Miami with a container of lobsters that could go to waste in a matter of days if a buyer is not located. Miami is not the best place to do this. It's much too competitive. We're looking for a new port of entry."

I was getting the feeling I was being pressured to handle this transaction for a hidden reason. Every time I found an objection to his pitch, Chanes would counter with a benefit that was supposed to sway my thinking.

I told Chanes I was simply too busy with the war effort to consider a business venture that I knew absolutely nothing about. I started to leave the table when he asked Jones to excuse himself so that he might talk to me privately about extra benefits of his proposal. Jones evidently knew what was going on because he smiled and excused himself.

When Jones was gone, Chanes leaned over the table and said softly: "If you help get the lobster into the States, I can arrange for special compensation."

My curiosity was piqued.

"What kind of special compensation?"

Chanes reached down and lifted a briefcase onto the table between us. He smiled and tapped the top of it with his hand.

"I can give you a million good reasons to help us find a port of entry."

I didn't need Chanes to paint a picture. This was a drug deal, a cocaine deal. It wasn't the lobsters they were interested in getting into the States. It was what was in the lobsters.

He was offering me a million dollars if I helped get cocaine into the States hidden in the frozen lobsters. Drug-sniffing dogs had trouble smelling cocaine through the iodine in the seafood and if Customs thawed out the lobsters looking for drugs and there were none, the government would have to compensate Ocean Hunter for the loss.

It would have been very easy for me to get rich. All I had to do was keep my mouth shut, play their game and do business with Frigorifico de Puntarenas. If I did that, I could be living in a mansion in Brazil, or wherever I wanted.

I'll run guns, but I draw the line at drugs. The idea that someone was using this war to run drugs into the United States infuriated me. I knew I was being self-righteous about this, but there are certain things I do not condone and will not justify. Drug running is never justifiable, no matter what political cause its profits may advance. I may put a gun to someone's head and pull the trigger, but I won't put a hypodermic needle in his hands.

Those principles made me a liability within the FDN and a liability to myself. I was ruthless in one sense and morally rigid in another. I would only go so far in what I would allow myself to be involved in. Political assassinations and war, yes. Drugs, no.

If we had gotten involved in the cocaine business, we would have had the one thing we needed most — money. But I knew we were not going to fight one evil with another evil.

When the deal to bring in cocaine fell through, Frigorificos de Puntarenas became a prime launderer of drug money.[2] Later investigations by the Miami police and the FBI indicated Ocean Hunter was using "narcotics transactions" to fund the Contras.

Posey later asked me if I struck a deal with Chanes.

"I'm not interested," I said.

I never broached the subject of drugs with Posey again. But I always wondered if he knew what Chanes was doing. If he didn't, I couldn't understand how. He was either incredibly stupid or incredibly naive not to have not found out about all the drug runners who were infiltrating the Contra movement and giving it a bad smell.

Another End Run

I knew before I returned to the Miskitia that I had to meet with Steadman Fagoth, the MISURA leader now living in comfortable exile in Miami. I wanted Fagoth to think we would be working in his best interests by taking American trainers into the Miskitia, thus making it easier to accomplish the job without an open break in the leadership of the MISURA.

Since Fagoth was in exile, he would be dealing from weakness. I wanted to position him so that he would believe we were his only link to his people and by him remaining out of the Miskitia and raising funds for our effort he could become a more powerful leader. I didn't believe this for one minute and didn't know if he would fall for it either. But I knew I would have to isolate him from his people in order to pull off our rebuilding project.

Fagoth was a virtual dictator. He demanded full and unquestioning loyalty. It was his way or death. He remained leader of the MISURA through fear. But now that he was gone, the people realized they could operate without him. I got the sense that Fagoth saw his power ebbing and was desperate to return. I was dealing from a position of strength.

Fagoth wasn't exactly what I had pictured. He was thin, dark complected and had a beard to rival Castro's. He spoke fairly good English, but when he wanted to talk politics, he spoke in Spanish.

He expected people to call him commandante and seemed to be cut from the Castro mold. He espoused socialism, not democracy or Communism, as the cure for Third World ills. For the MISURA, only autonomy from Nicaragua would end their suffering.

Fagoth was a disappointment to me. I had expected much more. He was caught up in his own power, even though his only power base now was with his people in the States. He was trying to portray himself as a powerful and important man, even in exile. All I saw was another salesman trying to peddle a scheme and make money off the war.

The purpose of my meeting with Fagoth was to iron out any troubles before they happened. I didn't need him coming back to the Miskitia and kicking us out once we got our operation entrenched.

He said he had no problems with our project. Anybody who killed Communists was a friend of his, he said. But if we could help him get back to Honduras, it would make things better.

This was a two-edged sword because getting him back into the country would give me a strong hand in decision making. I would have restored him to power. On the other hand, if I could block him from getting back and build an effective fighting force, I could keep him and his way of thinking out.

I met with Fagoth once more before I returned to the Miskitia. He and Wycliffe Diego, his right-hand man and political expert in the States, showed up unexpectedly one day at the Howard Johnson's. Both seemed unusually nervous. They said they had some official papers for me to take back to Alejo for distribution among the MISURA.

"I've talked to several people about the situation," Fagoth said. "I'm happy you're going to fight against the Sandinistas. I want you to help my people and try to get more Americans involved in our struggle."

At this point he brought out a briefcase full of papers and letters. Each of the letters had a $100 bill stapled to it. He gave me instructions about where to deliver each letter. One was to his mother, Edna. One was to a brother. One was to a nephew. He had a number of letters to relatives and friends, all with money attached. I was to personally deliver each one.

When the personal business had been completed, I told Fagoth I wanted a letter of introduction from him to the general staff. The letter was to state he had talked to me and approved of my actions. This would be the end of his reign, as far as the general staff was concerned. They would have no fear of reprisals now. Fagoth happily wrote the letter I requested on MISURA stationery and gave it to me.

I thanked him and told him I would tell his people he was with them in spirit. Fagoth seemed to buy my bullshit and I figured unless I did something horribly wrong, even if he came back to the Miskitia, I wouldn't have any problem with him.

Rebels With a Cause

Posey was in a big hurry to get back to Alabama. He seemed uncomfortable around me now that he had thrown in with Hull and Owen and I had turned down the coke deal. Before he departed, we were to meet with Hull, Owen and Vidal at another Howard Johnson's north of where we were staying.

Joe Coutin had given Posey a .380 caliber automatic to carry for personal protection while he was in Miami. But Posey didn't like carrying the weapon with him when he went to meetings in hotels. Before we left the room we shared, Posey said he wanted to leave his gun behind. It was lying on the table between the beds.

I picked up the gun and tossed it into one of the two black, soft side bags on one of the beds. Posey and I carried the same type luggage and I thought I had tossed the gun into my bag. We went to the meeting and didn't give the gun another thought.

We met with Hull and Owen, but only briefly. It was obvious they did not want me around. They had made the decision to cut me out of all planning sessions and discussions about the southern front. I told Owen he was making a big mistake letting Posey handle something he wasn't equipped to handle, but Owen had already made up his mind.

Owen tried to impress me with the fact he had Washington muscle behind him. He threw Ollie North's name around and invoked the power of the National Security Council as if he ran it. He bragged about the $10,000 he ferried to Hull from North each month and generally tried to convince us, but to no avail, of his importance in the war effort.

I finally told Posey he could do what he wanted with the southern front. My plans for the MISURA would proceed with or without his help.

We left the meeting and headed back to the motel. Posey was in a rush to catch his flight back to Decatur and grabbed one of the black bags as he rushed out the door. I was tired and immediately went to bed.

I had just dozed off when the telephone rang. It was Joe Coutin. He was in a panic.

"Posey's in Dade County jail," he said.

"For what? I said, trying to shake the sleep out of my head.

"For trying to carry a weapon onto the airplane."

That woke me up in a hurry. Posey didn't matter as much as the public relations hit CMA could take from this.

"Hold the line," I told Coutin. "Let me check my bag."

I rummaged through the other black bag and discovered I had mistakenly tossed the pistol into Posey's bag. He hadn't bothered to check the bag before he got on the plane. It was an innocent mistake by both of us. Stupid, but innocent. I told Coutin I would go to the jail and try to get Posey out on bond since it was my mistake that got him in there.

When I arrived at the jail, Coutin was waiting. Instead of being angry or embarrassed by his arrest, Posey found he was something of a celebrity among the guards, some of whom were anti-Castro Cubans. One in particular, Jesus Garcia, was ecstatic that the famous freedom fighter had come to his jail. Garcia joined CMA that night.

Garcia later became the catalyst for a series of events that shed a great deal of light on illegal activities on the southern front in which the Contras and CMA were involved.

We paid Posey's bail and took him back to the hotel. I tried to explain to him that it had been a simple error, but he didn't want to hear any explanations. He later accused me of setting him up.

That was the beginning of the end of whatever tenuous relationship Posey and I had up to that point. A barrier had been placed between us. He never trusted me again and actively began working against me.

But by then, plans were already in motion to move into the Miskitia in force. Ramos had returned from Tallahassee with seven of the 12 men Posey had stockpiled there. I had no idea what I would have in this group. My previous experience in Las Vegas left me with a bad feeling about Posey's gung-ho recruits.

I had left strict instructions that the new men were not to leave the hotel, not to make telephone calls, and not to do anything that would call undue attention to them. To see if they were following instructions, I paid a surprise visit at the fleabag motel where we were keeping them. When I arrived, I noticed most of the men sitting around the swimming pool. Nothing seemed out of the ordinary. I greeted each of the men and went from room to room, looking at the equipment they brought. I was impressed. Most were far better prepared than the first crew that had come to Las Vegas months earlier.

Five of the men — Traveller, Mycroft, Pablo, Thom and Pappy — had been among the first crew of CMA volunteers in Las Vegas. The other two, Caballo and Chico, were new.

I talked with each of the men in an effort to determine if they were mentally prepared to institute a training regimen for the MISURA, participate in combat strikes inside Nicaragua or perhaps become saboteurs.

I was trying to separate good intentions from the reality of combat and killing. This was a guerrilla war, and I would make demands on them no regular military would. I wanted them to accept the burden of personal responsibility and make them understand I wasn't putting a gun to their heads and forcing them to make this trip into the unknown.

I desperately wanted this mission to be a success. So much so that I once again overlooked the warning signs from these men that should have told me they were no more qualified or ready for this kind of stress than a child. Everyone was acting out his own fantasies, including me. It was contagious.

Some, like Mycroft, were extremely intense and projected the air of confidence that you might expect from a real soldier. Others, like Chico, were intimidated and followed what appeared to be peer pressure from classmates of Frank Camper's Recondo School. All had good reasons, from their point of view, why they wanted to go.

All said they would follow any order and would fully commit themselves to the cause of the MISURA, no matter what happened to them.

I had the men. I had the equipment. All I needed now was money.

For a counterrevolution that was literally rolling in money from the CIA and NSC and various private benefactors, I was having a hell of a time coming up with enough cash for our plane tickets to Honduras. I hadn't seen any money from my Washington contact for some time and thought he had given up on me.

To get the tickets we finally resorted to what all enterprising Americans do when they are short of cash — we used a credit card. A dozen one-way tickets to Tegucigalpa, please. And charge it.

If it wasn't so serious it would have been absolutely hysterical.

I was depending on the Cubans and their long-promised radio marathon to provide long-term funds for our operation. Without it and some logistical support back in the States, our butts would be hung out to dry in Honduras. We might die of starvation before the Sandinistas got to us.

But I also realized that this time there was a far greater chance that this would be a lone-way trip for some of the men. As I did in New Orleans, I had them draw up wills and leave all their photographs, letters, notes and identification papers except for their passports behind.

Two days before we left I called them all together.

"Don't be embarrassed if you want to back out or you have reconsidered the situation and decided not to go," I told them.

"Make sure this is what you want to do because when you go into the country you're going in for a three month minimum, the conditions will be very, very bad, the food will be bad, at best, and I cannot promise anything except hard work, action and the possibility of injury or death.

"I'll come back tomorrow and I want an answer from each of you."

I looked around the room and tried to gauge what each man was thinking. It was like looking at a blank wall. Each had made up his mind about what he was facing and wasn't about to be dissuaded by anything I had to say.

The next day I repeated my message.

"This is your last opportunity to tell me if you have any doubt in your mind as to what we're doing and as to my intentions and the intentions of this mission," I said.

"We will be involved in a situation that will mean the taking of life; we will be involved in a situation that means we will be representatives, in an odd fashion, of the people of the United States, even though we are acting independently, on our own and without the direct permission of the State Department or any other agency."

Once again I got the same blank look from all of them.

There wasn't much more I could do. I had to go with what I had, whatever my misgivings about them. I ordered them to begin packing.

We made the usual preparations. No weapons, no camouflage clothing or military clothing of any sort, including combat boots, would be allowed in the airport or on the plane.

When I started packing, I was amazed at the amount of equipment we had accumulated. We had ammunition, pistols, uniforms, food and threaded barrels to be used for silenced weapons. We had a Manlicher SSG .308 sniper rifle. We had several high-powered scopes, a 175-pound pull crossbow and aluminum crossbow shafts.

When we put it all together, we had more than 50 seabags stuffed with equipment, food and gear. We had enough to equip a small army.

The night before we left, I lay in bed running through a checklist of things we had packed and trying to sort through the factions that were trying to take a role in the war.

I felt we had a green light from Adolfo, even though we were moving away from the FDN. I had met with him several days earlier and he said he would be allowed to go south when the political temperature was right. Our relationship with the MISURA would help the FDN much more if I could find their secret arms hideouts and pass the information on.

Adolfo was now in a position to have influence in two separate areas without direct intervention by Contra forces under his command. Hull would handle the southern front assisted by CMA and we would aid the MISURA in Honduras.

But all future plans of any consequence — including the assassination of Pastora — were on hold until Congress voted on whether to restore aid to the Contras. The FDN was prepared to break with the U.S. if it did not receive the support it felt necessary to win. Should Congress go against the FDN, its leaders were ready to launch attacks against Nicaragua that could cost many American lives and stir public opinion against the Congress.

I realized we could become the sacrificial lambs for the overall Contra program if the vote went against the FDN. Even if that happened, I had no doubts there would be a flood of men heading south from the States to avenge us and defend democracy, just as we had done following the deaths of Parker or Powell, just as we were doing now.

13

Indian Wars:
Hit the Dirt Running

Someone was watching me. I didn't know who. I didn't know how. But someone knew my every move. He knew what hotels I stayed in. He even knew my alias, Frank Winchester, the name I used when traveling. It was all I could do to keep from looking over my shoulder when I walked down the street to see if someone was following me. In meetings where there were people I didn't know, I looked around and tried to determine if one of them came from Donald Fortier and his insiders on the National Security Council.

I had not had contact with Fortier or anyone who claimed to represent him since the $10,000 was passed to me in the motel parking lot in New Orleans back in October. But that didn't mean my movements and whereabouts weren't known to those who had an interest in me and what I was doing.

That was brought home to me rather forcefully after landing in Honduras on February 6, 1985 with my patchwork army of would-be warriors and drugstore commandos in tow. Tirador and I dispatched the men to a rundown hotel called the Istmania in the northern part of Tegus to keep them away from the military and media traffic at the Honduran Maya. Tirador and I went to the Maya, our normal base of operations. As I was checking in under the alias Frank Winchester, a smiling desk clerk looked at me and said: "Would you like to get your belongings out of the safety deposit box, Mr. Winchester?"

"What safety deposit box?" I said.

"This one," he replied, handing me a claim check for a safety deposit box in the name of Frank Winchester. I was temporarily rendered speechless. I had not rented the box. Nevertheless, I took the claim check, retrieved the box and opened it. In the bottom was a bulky hotel envelope. On the back of the enveope, near the bottom, someone had scrawled: "Good luck."

Inside the envelope was $15,000 in crisp, new $100 bills.

A few minutes earlier I was broke, living on credit cards and bullshit. Now, I had $15,000 of somebody else's money to continue my version of the war. My Washington benefactor had come through again.

I stuffed the money in my pocket and finished checking in.

My first order of business in Tegus was to contact Oscar Montez, the FDN's money man, to set up the arms-for-food swap. He had to be drawn into the deal as a willing participant in order for it to work for both sides.

Archibald Theofilo, the MISURA representative, had met us at the airport and on the way into town asked me again to press Montez on why the Indians weren't receiving their fair share of the money going to the FDN from Washington. The MISURA had been promised 30,000 lempiras a month, about $15,000, but were getting virtually nothing.

Archibald's request was a clear indication the MISURA had decided to allow me, an American, to deal for them with the FDN because their efforts to date had been fruitless.

I sent Tirador to the FDN safe house to arrange a meeting with Montez. To make Montez more receptive, I sent along $3,000 of my newly found money to be exchanged for lempiras. The FDN regularly laundered dollars at premium rates. The published exchange rate was two lempiras for each U.S. dollar. The black market rate fluctuated from 2.4- to 2.5-1. The FDN paid even better rates, anywhere from 2.6 lemps to 2.8 to the dollar.

The FDN hoarded U.S. dollars because they were as good as gold in the region. This sudden and unexpected infusion of cash would make Montez look good in the eyes of the FDN directorate and increase his stature. By helping him, I was helping myself.

When Montez arrived at the Maya later that afternoon for our meeting, he greeted me warmly, as if I were a long-lost friend. I knew Montez was frightened of me because he thought I came straight from the Agency, but he didn't show any fear.

I had choreographed the meeting in my head as best I could because I needed the upper hand. I needed to deal from a position of strength and to put Montez in a position where he would be obligated to deal with me. I decided to put him at an immediate disadvantage. No sooner did Montez sit down than I pulled a Smith & Wesson 9mm automatic pistol out of my bag and handed it to him.

He seemed stunned for a moment.

"Is this mine?" he asked in disbelief.

"Yes," I said. "Is there someone else in the room?"

I thought Montez would break down in tears.

"Everyone has a personal pistol except me. I could never afford a weapon like this," he said.

That gun sold for about $550 in the States. Down here, it was worth three to four times that much.

"It's a gesture on my part to demonstrate our friendship, despite our political differences," I said.

I don't think a Cadillac would have made him any happier. Montez's reaction to the pistol was much the same as was Enrique Bermudez's to the holster I had presented him several months earlier. Small gifts meant a lot to the Nicaraguans. It told them you thought of them outside the realm of normal business. Now, Montez was beholden to me.

As Montez sat fondling the pistol, I presented my plan to trade weapons for supplies. I told him the MISURA had an abundance of weapons but lacked food, boots and uniforms. I was willing to send the FDN 30 RPG-7 rocket-propelled grenades, three M-60 machine guns, two cases of 40mm ammunition for their M-79s, six cases of AK-47 ammunition and two 24-pound anti-tank mines.

In return, I wanted 500 pairs of boots, 500 uniforms, several thousand pounds of beans, rice, sugar and incidentals such as car batteries.

Montez said the FDN had a plentiful supply of RPG launchers but were desperate for projectiles and propellant. On my initial visit with the MISURA I noticed several boxes of propellant lying around deteriorating and I felt confident the Indians would have no objection if I traded these.

Montez said he had certain reservations about the deal because no one in the FDN had been able to successfully work with the MISURA. They were suspicious, demanding and infuriatingly independent. The existence of large stocks of weapons in the Miskitia was well-known, but neither the FDN nor the U.S. government had been able to discover their whereabouts.

"Let me worry about that," I said. "But it all boils down to this: No supplies, no weapons."

Montez made one telephone call before agreeing to the deal. It was to Mario Calero in New Orleans, who seemed dumbfounded that we had returned to Honduras without his assistance. Mario was enthusiastic about the deal, though. He and Montez were close and Mario knew if Montez gained power in the FDN, he gained power. They were trying to rid the FDN of Aristides Sanchez, and this plan that called for a workable alliance with the Indians, something no one had been able to pull off before, might just be their ticket to increased stature within the organization.

The deal was a gamble for all of us. I still had to convince the MISURA it was in their best interests. If it fell through, the FDN could make life even more miserable for them. But if the deal was successful, life could get much easier for the Indians. The FDN was the only counterrevolutionary group in the region with access to air transport through SETCO. The MISURA could not afford the 4,300-lempira charge per trip for SETCO to deliver supplies and evacuate wounded. Through the FDN the MISURA could utilize SETCO and the CIA base at Aquacate without having to pay high rates.

A successful deal would also give me the leverage I needed to get Americans involved in combat in Nicaragua through the MISURA.

I was seen as an apolitical broker for both sides. Although I was looking out for my own interests, I had won the respect of both sides for dealing fairly. The FDN felt it could not deal with Steadman Fagoth. He was a radical and the FDN thought the only way to bring him into line was to cut off aid and starve his people.

I told Montez I would contact him when I had the weapons ready for shipment and requested he begin stockpiling the supplies for the Indians. I also asked that all equipment belonging to the Pegaso project being stored at La Quinta be sent to the Miskitia.

After meeting with Montez, I took a taxi to the Istmania to meet with the men. I found a bunch of unhappy troops as we assembled in the dining room for one last good meal before going into the bush and a steady diet of beans, rice and tortillas.

I had ordered the men to stay in the hotel to avoid any problems with the increasingly suspicious Honduran police. They wanted to get out. They wanted to go sightseeing. They wanted to buy souvenirs. They thought they were tourists.

"You better get geared up for the worst, because where you are now is Hollywood compared to where you're going," I said.

I allowed them two beers each with their meal, knowing it would be their last alcohol for at least three months. There would be no drugs and no alcohol in camp.

"If I catch you drinking or fucking around with any wacky weed, your ass is dead, and I mean dead," I told them.

I ate sparingly and later returned to the Maya, where I had dinner with Grace. I knew this could be the last time we would see one another for a long time and she sensed it. Despite the numerous separations during all my scrambling back and forth between Honduras and Miami, Grace and I had become unusually close.

Whenever I saw her it was as if a cloud of doubt and uncertainty was lifted. My thoughts turned from war to her. She made the madness of all this somehow tolerable. And she was a loyal soldier, taking our civilian clothes and personal papers to her house for safekeeping. She was running unusual risks for me, but seemed not to mind.

The Die Is Cast

My return to the Miskitia was cause for great joy and celebration.

The Indians were happy to see us because I had kept my promise and returned with American trainers and equipment.

Pedrico was particularly happy to see me because he thought we had abandoned him in the jungle. He was disappointed that his Cuban friends in Miami had sent him neither supplies nor money. He had been a faithful member of the Cuban Legion for years, going out into the swamps around Miami and practicing several weekends a month for years in preparation for an invasion of Cuba. Now that he had actually gotten involved in a war against the Communists, he had been abandoned by his own people.

To lift his sagging spirits I gave him a new pair of boots and a few other goodies to let him know that even if his Cuban friends had forgotten him, I hadn't. Of course, I needed Pedrico at that moment more than the Miami Cubans did. He was the one interpreter I could trust. He had also established a good rapport with the Indians during our absence and had become an invaluable asset to the operation.

We immediately took the men to TEA base, where other MISURA soldiers had been brought in to begin re-training in my system. The Indians inspected us with as much curiosity as we inspected them.

Raoul, Alejo and Hilton stood back and watched with obvious enthusiasm as the Americans moved into camp. There hadn't been this kind of activity under Steadman Fagoth. They didn't have trainers. They weren't getting supplies. Now that he was out and the general staff was in charge, Americans were coming in and bringing supplies, sophisticated equipment and a new enthusiasm to the cause.

The Americans I brought with me were not exactly the pick of the litter. The Indians were expecting the A-Team. They were getting the Z-Team, thanks to Posey's recruiting methods. But I had to make do with what I had.

Our current group included eight people, counting myself, who had been in Las Vegas several months earlier. It included Bob "Traveler" Bradford, the former Army lieutenant; Robert "Thom" Palmer, the quiet, heavyset Kansan; Donald "Ramos" Rossi, a graduate of Frank Camper's Recondo School; Mycroft, the tobacco chewer from Chicago; Paul "Pablo" Johnson, Camper's No. 2 and so-called sniper expert; Pappy, the Maryland muskrat skinner; and Jim Adair, the *Eagle* magazine journalist.

I called Adair from Miami the night before we left and asked if he wanted to join us. If we did something remarkable or noteworthy, I wanted the world to know about it and Adair had so oversold his credentials I thought he was the person to do it. He jumped at the chance to get back into the war and met us in Tegucigalpa.

The remainder of our group consisted of Tirador, Pedrico and five others whose real names I never learned: Pen, a skinny American about whom I knew little; Caballo; Chico, the first black American volunteer and a graduate of Camper's school; Perez, an undocumented Marielista traveling on Joe Coutin's passport; and Lobo, an overweight Cuban opera singer.

It was a real menagerie. Once we got organized, the true personalities of some of these would-be warriors emerged.

Shortly after Pappy arrived, he killed a possum, skinned it and made a hand puppet out of the pelt and skull. Pappy called the puppet Daniel Ortega. He did puppet shows for us in which the evil Daniel Ortega was pitted against the right and might of the United States. Mycroft was the voice of Ortega. Danny was always made to look the fool in the puppet shows and lost his epic struggles with the U.S.

Lobo was one of the strangest. He would walk around camp singing the aria from the "Barber of Seville" so loudly that it made the trees shake. That and his snoring were so bad we banished him to his own tent on the other side of camp. We could still hear him, singing or snoring at all hours of the day and night.

Lobo also didn't take well to the cuisine of beans and rice. He got so desperate for food at one point he tried to order pizza from Miami through the mail. Much to his dismay, Pizza Hut didn't deliver that far south.

Once my Z-Team had dressed out, I could see I was in for a wild ride. They wore a strange assortment of uniforms that included camouflage fatigues, jauntily cocked berets and shoulder holsters. This was military Fantasyland for these guys.

We divided the men into two squads, with Pablo and Ramos as squad leaders. Not the best of choices, but they had to do for the time being. They would report to Tirador, who reported to me. Pedrico, because he was my interpreter, was outside the normal chain of command and reported directly to me.

Putting Pablo in charge of anything was a mistake. He was moody and withdrawn and had absolutely no leadership abilities. He was also an alcoholic, something unknown to me until we found him in his tent one day unable to work because he was in the initial stages of the DTs.

The afternoon we arrived at TEA base I called the men together for my grand speech. They lined up in front of me at attention, a pack of wannabe Rambos armed to the teeth even though we were at least 20 miles from the Nicaraguan border.

"I have fulfilled my promise," I told them. "You're in the border area. You're now in the war. But the rules of the game are going to change. You are now under martial law. I set the rules and regulations here. Violation of certain rules will result in immediate execution."

I paused to allow the words to sink in. Their eyes slowly widened to the size of silver dollars as they realized what I was saying.

"This is what you wanted," I continued. "This is a very, very serious business. You're in a combat zone. We are here as independents. Some people might say we're breaking the law. But we will carry our mission out in a professional manner following a military chain of command.

"Tomorrow, you will start cleaning up the camp, scavenging the area for military items that can be used or recycled to work to our benefit and generally presenting a picture to the MISURAs that we have our shit together.

"We must set an example for the Indians. They will learn from us by observing us. Set up a challenge for them. If we do things in a certain manner, they will mimic us. Stay clean. Stay orderly. Present yourselves at all times in a military manner."

I warned them against getting involved with the local women or wandering off from camp looking for beer.

"Don't do anything to disgrace us," I told them. "We have to be the leaders. We must set the example so when the time comes to do something, they will know we are willing to do it with them.

"I am a very uncompromising person. If you do what I tell you to do, you will have a very smooth three months here. If you try to buck me, if you try to go against my rules, I will make your life so miserable you will either do them in confinement or you will be dead."

It may have been a bit melodramatic, but the speech had the desired effect. They knew now they were not operating under U.S. law, Honduran law or Nicaraguan law. They were operating under Colonel Flaco's law and my law was the only law here.

We had plenty of work to do. We had to secure the base, clean it up, rearrange and rebuild portions of it so that it would become a viable military training base. It would take a lot of hard work. It was not going to be all guns and glory.

Every work detail had an equal number of Americans and Indians assigned to it. If we told two Indians to dig a latrine, two Americans dug alongside them. If two Americans scoured the grounds for old ammunition, two Indians went right along with them. The MISURA had a tendency to throw away anything that was either too heavy to carry or they didn't know how to operate. I had to break them from that thinking.

The more I saw of the base, the more impressed I was. It obviously had been designed by professionals. And the supplies that had reached here, the remnants of which were strewn all over the ground, indicated they had come from the U.S., Israel and the Soviet Union, among other places. Some of it obviously had been captured. Some had been donated.

I hoped eventually to have at least 500 Indians in camp and set about repairing and rebuilding the dormitories for these men. The Indians were quite comfortable stringing their hammocks between two pine trees and sleeping there. Often I would see them just before nightfall, their hammocks strung four deep between two trees like four large, green cocoons. But I wanted to modernize their living conditions while they were training.

I brought two Honda generators from Miami and enough extension cords so we could crank up the generators and have electric lights at night. In time, we would wire the entire camp and each of the tents for lights and also lit the roadway.

It was important to keep the men busy. The more jobs they had to do, the more tired they were at night and the less chance they would start roaming around and getting into trouble. I also wanted them to stay occupied as much as possible so they wouldn't start thinking about the legal and political ramifications of what we were doing here. Not that this bunch would do too much deep thinking anyway.

I also considered it imperative to keep them out of the planning loop. Tirador, Pedrico and I would be the only ones who would actually know what was going on in the sessions we had with the MISURA general staff and the FDN. I didn't want all these American cowboys running around with our plans in their heads because of the likelihood if they were captured they would spill their guts the first chance. The men would know only what was necessary to accomplish a certain mission and no more.

The Indians wasted no time in letting us know what they wanted out of our participation in the war. About an hour after sundown our first night in camp, a convoy of trucks carrying the entire general staff and more Indians who were to be integrated into the training unit arrived at TEA base.

We rigged one of the huts so we could have an electric light in there and the entire general staff filed in, quiet and unsmiling. The single, naked bulb cast harsh shadows on the faces of the Indians as they sat on one side of the table. Tirador, Pedrico and I sat on the other side.

"I am glad to be back among the MISURA," I said to open the meeting.

"On our first visit we promised we would bring trainers and equipment to start laying the groundwork to advance your cause. We have done that. Now, our intentions are to fight with your people for that cause. Our blood is the same color as your blood, our cause is your cause. We will fight together, and if necessary, die together."

As I spoke, my message was translated first into Spanish and then into the language of the Miskitos. During the pauses for translations I looked around the table to gauge the reaction of the general staff. Their faces showed no emotions, but their eyes seemed to say they were pleased with what they were hearing.

I told them we wanted to reactivate TEA, that we wanted to get some men in and start training them, that we wanted to get a hard-core group of at least 500 first-rate soldiers prepared to go into Nicaragua to fight with methods they had never used. We wanted to run night missions using unconventional weapons, including silencer-equipped weapons and crossbows. We wanted to run intelligence and psychological operations and long-range reconnaissance patrols. We wanted to do as much as possible as quickly as possible.

I even alluded to the possibility that if things went well in Miami and we were able to obtain enough money, we may get into riverine operations, airborne operations and other activities that the general staff never considered.

I didn't want to promise we would actually do any specific exotic operation because I knew if I gave my word on something, I would have to do it. I wasn't going to go out on a limb and make promises I couldn't keep. That would mean an instant loss of credibility and I couldn't afford that at this early stage of our involvement.

I was trying to be upbeat yet cautious because the shadow of Steadman Fagoth and his power still loomed over me.

The general staff seemed totally unimpressed by Fagoth's letter of introduction. Members indicated through Alejo, who became their voice, that the fact I had kept my promise to them when so many others had not cemented the bond between us. They trusted me and didn't need a letter of introduction to validate that trust.

When it came time for the Indians to speak, Alejo did the translating. One of the general staff would speak and Alejo would begin, "Colonel, we wish to . . ."

Alejo was extremely polite, but also extremely direct. He was a former Moravian Baptist minister who knew the nuances of all the languages in which we were dealing. He was a good negotiator and an excellent spokesman.

He said the MISURA were happy that we had arrived. Now, their men could be trained to fight much better than they had been trained before.

"We are willing to follow you in any direction you want to go or do whatever you think is necessary," said Alejo.

The message from the Indians was loud and clear: There was nothing we could ask them that would not be granted. If we wanted to take 1,000 men into Nicaragua, so be it. If we wanted to send 100 Americans into Nicaragua to fight, so be it. We were given virtual carte blanche.

But, said Alejo, while the Indians were willing to fight and had the weapons to fight, they had no boots, no clothing, no food and no medical supplies to carry out these missions.

"How are you going to get the food and supplies we need to accomplish what you are proposing?" Alejo asked.

"I have had discussions with certain people and certain groups about getting those supplies you need," I said, "but I am still working out the details. It may take a little time."

I didn't want to get into the arms-for-food deal I had discussed with Oscar Montez of the FDN at this meeting. I wanted to make sure I knew the Indians and the general staff well enough before I proposed something they had been resisting for years.

Alejo said the boot shortage was so critical that small patrols going into Nicaragua through the village of San Jeronimo had to stop on the Honduras side of the Coco River and wait for another patrol to come out so they could get their boots.

Most of the Indians owned no more clothes than they wore. A few wore the distinctive Sears – Roebuck green of the Contras. But most of the others had a hodgepodge of camouflage, olive drab or Sandinista uniforms taken from the bodies of dead soldiers.

We were starting from scratch here. It would be a slow, laborious process to bring the Indians up to speed on food, clothing and training. Two things they had that the Contras did not were weapons and desire. The former could always be obtained in this war. The latter was something that could neither be drilled nor ordered into a man no matter what we did.

If the desire to fight for your country is not there, no amount of prodding by outsiders could produce it. The Indians had the desire. All they needed was the means.

The Indians were so eager to get started that at that first meeting they began discussing their list of military priorities. High on the list was destruction of the bridge network that provided access from Managua and the interior of Nicaragua to the Atlantic coast. Destroy a series of bridges and the Atlantic coast would be cut off and at the mercy of the Indians.

Two bridges in particular were critical. One was at Sin Sin, about 85 miles inside Nicaragua across the Rio Likus. The other was at Yulu, on the Rio Tuapi about 20 miles farther along the road to Puerto Cabezas.

The Indians wanted the bridges destroyed before the rainy season hit in April. The bridges at Sin Sin and Yulu were key on the Sandinista road network used to supply their northern bases in Bullkamp, Trankara, Waspan, Leimus and Bilwaskarma on the Coco River. Destroying the bridges also would effectively cut off the large Sandinista garrison at Puerto Cabezas from outside supplies and reinforcements.

The rains and low clouds would severely limit the Sandinistas' air superiority and give the Indians some parity in ground attacks.

The strategy was excellent.

"But it's a bit premature to talk about going on interior raids, especially of this magnitude," I said.

I offered to begin preliminary preparations by holding demolitions classes and teaching their men how to rig charges and where to place them to get the maximum benefit. They seemed pleased by this and went on to other business.

That other business was money.

The Indians were incredibly sincere in their religious beliefs and their desire for autonomy. But they were also great con artists, a skill developed over many years of dealing with gullible white missionaries who could never say no.

The Indians told me about the thousands of refugees they had. They told me about how poor they were. They told me about all the repairs that needed to be made to their trucks and how they had to buy food for this camp and that camp.

"Colonel," Alejo said, "do you have any money you can give us because we have these bills to pay and we have these repairs to make and we have this much food to buy?"

He rambled on about who they owed and pulled out a fistful of bills from stores in Puerto Lempira where they bought on credit. They owed one store 28,000 lempiras, about $14,000 at the official exchange rate. Alejo said they feared their credit would be cut off in Puerto Lempira unless they paid some of the bills.

I had about 10,000 lemps on me, but I didn't want them to know I was carrying this kind of cash.

"I can give you a little money," I said, "but I can't come up with all of it."

I normally limited my donations to 1,500 lemps per session.

I figured I would try to pry loose from the FDN some of the 30,000 lemps a month the Indians were owed the next time I met with Oscar Montez in Tegucigalpa.

This was a key step for me and for them. In essence, I was being asked to run their business. They had the bills, they had the needs and they saw me as the person who could solve all their problems. Whether I talked to the FDN or the U.S. government, they would listen to me because I was an American, not an Indian.

The meeting broke up with general good feelings on both sides and Tirador and I returned to our hutch, dead-tired but pleased with our first day in the Miskitia.

I told Tirador it was obvious we were going to have quickly present them with the plan to trade weapons for food because there was no way we could support 50,000 Indians living in poverty along the border.

As we lay on our bunks talking ourselves to sleep, Tirador turned to me and said: "Do you see something on the roof that looks like a hand doing push-ups?"

I looked up at the thatched roof and saw the biggest, ugliest spider I had ever seen. Its body was larger than my hand.

"I'll take care of this," I said and pulled out my 9mm Browning.

I squeezed off one round and drilled the spider dead center, splattering it against the dried thatch. But before its remains hit the ground, dozens more huge spiders came tumbling out of the thatch right on top of us.

Our feet never hit dirt. We were outside that hut so fast you would have thought the whole Sandinista army was chasing us. There were spiders all over us.

As we stood there in our underwear brushing off the spiders, the Indians came rushing up to us to find out the reason for the gunshot. When we told them about the spiders, they started laughing so hard I thought some were going to die.

"They eat your mosquitoes," the Indians told us.

"Let them eat somewhere else," I grumbled and walked back inside to clean out the hut. I didn't sleep well that night.

The hymn singing woke me again before dawn, the deep voices resonating among the trees and making the camp sound like a great cathedral. It was eerie, yet moving.

A truck carrying Alejo, Hilton and Raoul arrived before first light. They wanted to get an early start and asked me to accompany them on the rounds of several other camps. I took Pedrico with me to interpret and let Tirador behind to begin camp cleanup.

It became standard procedure when I traveled anywhere with the MISURA for me to sit in the cab of the trucks rather than in the back because I was treated like a commander and commanders just didn't tough it. This also allowed them to segregate me from everyone else so we could hold private conversations about subjects the general staff didn't want others to hear.

As we left the camp that morning, Alejo started talking to me about my role here. It was obvious he was trying to determine whether I was serving in any official capacity for the U.S. government. He told me many times people had come to the MISURA with great promises that were never kept. Only after much debate among the general staff and the Council of Elders was it agreed that one last time would they trust an outsider.

The problem with most outsiders, Alejo said, was that they did not understand the Indians. Outsiders saw the Indians as merely an extension of the Contras, not as a separate people with separate needs and different political goals.

The Indians didn't really care about the differences between Communism and democracy. The way they had been treated, one was just as bad as the other. Their primary goal was autonomy for all the Indians of the region, not incorporation into some other political framework that would subjugate them, terrorize them, and starve them out of existence as the current political factions were doing.

Now that the Sandinistas were in power in Nicaragua, Alejo said, it was the duty of all Indians to fight them, not so much because of the ideology, but to gain enough power to press for autonomy.

The Sandinistas were wary of the Indians in Zelaya Province because they knew the Indians were fighting for their lives and not for a political ideology. They knew if they attacked the Indians, the Indians would throw everything they had back at them. Firefights against the Indians weren't like firefights against the Contras. Indian firefights were small-scale, vicious wars. Because of that, the Sandinistas placed a tremendous amount of military firepower in Zelaya Province that included Soviet tanks and helicopter gunships around Bullkamp and Trankara.

I assured Alejo that the Americans I brought with me had committed themselves to the Indians. Whatever cause the Indians fought for, we would fight for. Whatever the Indians died for, we would die for.

It was obvious Alejo was still wary of me and had been instructed by the general staff to feel me out. Although they had agreed in principle to my plans, I was still on probation. I still had to prove myself.

But I had won a certain measure of trust because Alejo said I would be allowed to view the entire stockpile of weapons. I had heard numerous rumors of the Indians' weapons caches, but no one I knew had seen them. The CIA tried to find them and couldn't. The FDN tried to find them and couldn't. Now I was to be given access to the one thing of value the Indians possessed.

The truck bounced and creaked along the rough dirt roads that crisscrossed the Miskitia between the Rus Rus River and the Coco River basin. The closer we got to the border and the Coco, the more jungle-like the land became.

The first of the Indian camps we came to was Crem Crem. It was little more than a group of wooden huts with thatched palm roofs on the side of a creek bank. It had been raining several days and was quite muddy, yet the village was neat, almost as if it had been cleaned up for inspection. In a sense, it had, for when I stepped from the truck I found the military contingent from the village waiting for me in formation.

The "soldiers" ranged in age from a boy who looked to be no more than six years old to a toothless, wrinkled old Indian whose age could have been anywhere from 50 to 100. There were about 50 men, and they were trying as hard as they could to look military and impress the gringo who had come to help them.

Alejo introduced me as the commander of an American military detachment and asked me to say a few words.

"My name is Colonel Flaco," I said, as Pedrico translated.

"I have come from the United States with several other Americans. We are here to aid the MISURAs and to train them to better fight your enemies. We are proud to be a part of the MISURA movement."

When I finished, I walked down the line of men, pausing briefly about every third one, patting him on the shoulder and saying a few words about how we were pleased to be part of their struggle.

It was difficult to tell what they were thinking, but I got the distinct impression from their eyes and their faces they thought the U.S. Marines had landed. Here was a well-dressed, well-fed, well-armed American assuring them their cause was his cause. What else could they believe?

After my brief speech, Aljeo and several of the camp officials led me down a muddy path to two large buildings made of heavy bamboo. They stopped in front of one, unlocked a heavy padlock and motioned me inside.

The smell of gun oil and gunpowder hit me immediately when I walked in. As my eyes adjusted to the dim light, I was shocked to see literally thousands of weapons stored inside.

The ceiling rafters were lined with rifle after rifle after rifle. There were M-1 carbines of World War II vintage that looked as if they had just been taken out of the shipping crates. Under them were rows of Ruger mini-14s. There were cases and cases of 60mm mortar, AK-47, .30-caliber, .50-caliber and 7.62x59 ammunition stacked as high as 12 feet.

In another section of the same building, I found hundreds of new M-60 machine guns, 60mm mortars, 12.7mm Soviet heavy machine guns, .50- caliber machine guns, boxes of American-made anti-tank mines, hand grenades and just about every other weapon that could be utilized in a guerrilla insurgency.

No wonder the Indians had been so secretive about this stuff. It was worth a fortune. But it was just sitting here, not doing them or their cause any good.

"Take as many as you need," Alejo said. "Take them all, if you like. Our arsenal is at your disposal."

Never in my wildest dreams could I have imagined having access to this much firepower.

But that wasn't all. There was more. Adjacent to this building was another stocked with similar amounts of weapons. There were artillery shells, Soviet 82mm mortars, mortar shells, 75mm recoilless rifles, LAAW rockets, Soviet and Chinese RPG-7 rocket-propelled grenades, Claymore mines, cases of C-4 plastic explosives and Soviet "bouncing Betty" mines.

Many of the American-made weapons had come from the CIA after the Argentinians had been brought in as trainers. But the Indians had captured thousands of additional weapons and tons of ammunition from the Sandinistas, including 10,000 brand-new AK-47s during an ambush of a convoy on the Rama Road. With these weapons the Indians could wreak havoc on the Sandinistas in Zelaya Province.

I was trying to mentally keep a running inventory of what I was seeing but was experiencing sensory overload. And I was just scratching the surface. We went to two other locations — a cave and a cemetery — where equal amounts of arms and ammunition were stored.

In yet another building I found ALICE packs, stacks of pistol belts, suspenders and other non-lethal goods that made me wonder why they had so much and were still complaining about shortages.

"At one time we had nearly 4,000 men in the field," Alejo said, "but we ran out of food and ways to resupply them. Once we trained a man, we would bring him back, take his equipment and his weapon, put them in storage and then let the man go into the refugee community as a reservist.

"When the right time came and we had enough food and medicine, we would call up the men to launch an attack."

"If we need a few men how many can I get on a couple of days notice?" I asked.

"Oh, I can probably get you two thousand."

"Two thousand?" I said. "That's way too many at one time. All I want to know is whether I come up with about 500 really hard-core people on short notice."

"That's no problem," he said. "Men are not the problem. Arms are not the problem. Food, medicine, boots and uniforms are the problem."

Alejo was ensuring that these needs would be indelibly stamped on my brain before the day was over.

The main operation base for the MISURA, their Las Vegas, was known as Sym Sym. It was just a few meters from the border and the Coco River, built on two sides of a large creek. One side housed the officers' quarters, a communications shack, a meeting shed, a storage shelter and a sewing room. The men and their families lived on the other side of the creek.

In Sym Sym I found more weapons, except here they were scattered about in the houses like so much bric-a-brac.

Loose 60mm mortar shells without safety pins in the nose lay on the floor in some houses. In other houses I found LAAW rockets leaning up against the walls, many with the end covers missing. I would rummage through different boxes and find a jumbled mixture of Claymore mines, plastic explosives, hand grenades and belted ammunition.

These people could do some serious damage if these weapons were used in the right fashion.

The biggest surprise of all was in the communication shack. A 1,000-watt Harris radio, the type used exclusively by the CIA and supposedly classified, was sitting on a table, dusty and unused. It had encoders and decoders with lockout coding switches. The last time I saw a transmitter like this was in the FDN camps where the Contra commandantes used them to communicate with other countries, the U.S. military and their CIA handlers.

"Why isn't this radio being used?" I asked Alejo.

"We don't know how to operate it," he said, almost apologetically. "And our electricity source is not very good."

"I want this radio moved to TEA so can start communicating with Tegus and who knows who else," I told him.

"We will bring it to TEA tommorrow," Alejo promised.

With that radio we could contact the FDN in Tegucigalpa, Aguacate, Las Vegas and even the States.

I also found a number of portable PRC-77 radios in the communications shack.

"What's wrong with these radios?" I asked.

Alejo shrugged his shoulders and talked with several of the camp leaders. From what I could gather, they had problems getting the batteries recharged so they just abandoned them.

There was no question the operation here had to be centralized. Most of the equipment and weapons had to be transferred to TEA. The number of refugee camps had to be reduced to cut down on the traveling time.

We had all but a few of the ingredients here to bake us one hell of a military force. We had the men, the weapons, the communications equipment and the desire to do it. We were in the right place to do it. All we needed was a steady stream of food, medicine and clothing to build a military for the MISURA that would make the numerically superior FDN look pitiful.

Once we plugged the gaps, we could create a force the Sandinistas would have to deal with, a force that would draw attention on an international level, a force that would actually go into Nicaragua to fight rather than sit back in a safe haven in Honduras waiting for the United States military to intervene.

We would carry the fight to the Sandinistas. We would hit them during the night and during the day. We would hit them in their strong spots and we would hit them in their weak spots. We would make them shift emphasis from the Rio Segovia into Zelaya Province, forcing the Sandinistas to shift firepower now arrayed against the FDN. We would change the balance and the focus of the war. We would make a difference.

My mind was spinning with possibilities as we left Sym Sym for the return to TEA base.

That night, after dark, we held the second in a never-ending series of nightly meetings between myself, Tirador, Pedrico and the Indian leaders.

There were some new faces in this second meeting. They belonged to the Council of Elders, according to Alejo. This was a five-man body elected from what is known as the General Assembly. The 500-plus General Assembly was made up of chiefs and sub-chiefs from the Suma, Rama and Miskito tribes from throughout Nicaragua and southeastern Honduras.

The Council of Elders was elected by the General Assembly and spoke for it in matters of state. It also appointed the five members of the political arm and the five members of the general staff.

Now, the Council of Elders had come to listen to the gringo and his plan for Indian autonomy.

The elders were very religious men. Most were ministers. They were trying to cope with an unmanageable refugee problem at the same time they dealt with a difficult military situation. The strain of these two problems showed on their faces.

In a way, I was trying to take some of the burden off them. My mere presence here was telling them I would help them deal with both edges of this sword.

When the meeting began, the elders immediately brought up the Sin Sin Bridge raid. They wanted to know what I intended to do, how I intended to do it and how many men it would take.

"I don't want to rush things," I told them. "We've only been here a couple of days and we're still trying to get our feet on the ground. but we will carry out these missions. We've got nothing but time because there is not really any progress being made in this war. I don't want to do things so quickly it will endanger the lives of any of our people."

Why my words were translated, they nodded their heads soberly.

"Do you have any recent intelligence on the bridge?" I asked.

"Yes," one man replied, "from about three months ago."

"That's not recent intelligence," I said.

They said they could send some men in to observe the bridge again, but they didn't have strong enough binoculars to observe it from a distance.

I turned to Tirador and told him to get the 30mm telescope I had brought with me. When he returned, I gave the telescope to Alejo.

"Give this to your men. Have them go in, observe the bridge, give me an accurate drawing of what they see and get a head count of soldiers. How long do you think this will take?"

"Probably 10 to 12 days," Alejo replied.

Inwardly, I breathed a sigh of relief. I needed to buy some time to get the Americans and the Indians ready. The elders and the general staff were intent on destroying the bridge as quickly as possible and apparently were under the impression the Americans had to expertise to do it now. Two previous attacks on the bridge were failures and resulted in numerous casualties because they had no expertise in night operations.

When the subject of food and medicine was brought up, I glanced at Tirador as if to say: "Here goes nothing."

There was an almost imperceptible shrug of his shoulders and he settled back to listen to what would be our make-or-break pitch to the Indians on the weapons-for-food deal.

"I have discussed your problem with Oscar Montez and members of the FDN Directorate," I began. "They are aware of the situation. But in order for us to open channels with them again, we must trade weapons for food."

The Indians looked at one another in shock and surprise. Their faces told me what they were thinking: "What the hell is this guy talking about us giving up some of our guns to the Somocista sons of bitches? No way."

"You've got to remember this," I continued. "Your struggle is a struggle against a double-barreled situation. Your struggle is against the Sandinistas, but it's also against the FDN because you are fighting for independence and autonomy. You are not fighting as a second front against the Sandinistas, even though the Sandinistas occupy your territory. Several battalions of FDN soldiers also occupy parts of Zelaya Province."

About 4,500 men under command of Contra Commandante Tigrillo were sitting just north of the La Rosita, La Constancia and La Bonanza area, the gold mining district of Zelaya Province. Everyone was interested in the province's mineral wealth — the FDN, the Sandinistas, the White House, the CIA, the missionary groups and the Indians.

Whoever controlled those mines controlled a sizable portion of the economic base of Nicaragua. If the Indians got control of the mines it would mean that any government in Managua would have little chance of surviving without their approval and assistance. And if the Indians declared autonomy, it would mean the FDN would have to open that second front to ensure some economic stability once it took power, if it ever did.

"You must know this," I said. "In order to do what you want to do, in order to achieve your independence, you must use the FDN to accomplish the things that you cannot do for yourself, that the United States government will not do for you and that we cannot provide for you.

"By trading a few weapons of the many thousands you have you can get the food and uniforms and boots that you need. You will come out on top in this tradeoff because you will be giving up a little to get a lot. You can also start turning the tables and using the FDN as they have used you for years."

Finally, the gringo made some sense to them. They had been obstinate and had been bucking the system for years. Now, I was telling them how to use this same system to their advantage.

I gave them a list of weapons the FDN needed. I made it clear I would not trade away anything that would create a shortage among the Indians or could possibly be used against them in the future.

"We will give them just a taste. We will give them exactly what I told them we would give them and if they bring in what they have promised, then we will go into future negotiations. But if they don't fulfill their end of the deal, we don't fulfill our end of the deal."

When the translation had been made, the Indians nodded in agreement. We were going to set up a barter system. They would get boots, uniforms, some food and accessories while the FDN got weapons and ammunition.

In just a few days I had worked my way into the inner circle of the MISURA. I had been baptized by them and was now working for them. It was time to implement my plan to take the war to the Sandinistas.

14

Exodus: Indio Delta Alpha

The more I talked to people about Steadman Fagoth, the more evident it became they had no love for him or his methods. I was operating under the assumption Fagoth could return at any time and put an end to the American involvement here. I was also concerned that members of the general staff or the Council of Elders were Fagoth backers and might at any time cut us out of the loop if we did or said something they didn't like.

I was treading gingerly on the question of Fagoth and what loyalty to him remained among the MISURA leaders. I rarely said anything specifically negative about him, but let it be known that he was not the answer to their problems.

Alejo began making it a habit after the nightly meetings with the general staff to come to my hutch for a cup of instant coffee. We talked about life in general and mostly avoided subjects that would best be discussed at the meetings. But as I gained Alejo's trust, he began revealing the darker side of Fagoth and how he ruthlessly ran the MISURA for his own benefit and that of his family.

The MISURA knew Fagoth sold weapons to different groups and to the Hondurans. But they were afraid to object because of his reign of terror.

I suggested to Alejo it might be in the best interests of the MISURA for the general staff to take control away from Fagoth and run the war the way they saw fit. Fagoth was in exile in Miami and was in no position to listen to or understand the day-to-day problems here. And when he was in the Miskitia, his methods were so high-handed and self-centered that people were afraid to say anything to him.

Since we were shifting the campaign's emphasis from fighting the Sandinistas and defeating Communism to fighting the Sandinistas and gaining autonomy, an entirely new approach to leadership had to be taken.

Eventually, Raoul, Hilton and Selso would join Alejo in our little gab fests. They sat and listened as we talked. Neither Raoul nor Hilton understood English, so Alejo would tell them what he thought they needed to know. My messages about Fagoth went directly through Alejo to members of the general staff and it was not long before I could see their loyalty shifting to me.

Acquisition of the Harris radio proved a major coup. It arrived at TEA base the morning after my visit to Sym Sym along with an Indian named Leonard, who had been assigned as its keeper. Leonard began erecting the antenna as soon as he arrived and I went into the hut we designated the communications shack to see what we had found.

The Harris radio was about three feet square and about three feet deep in a black case. Leonard was pretty sharp about radios, but he didn't understand the principle of using scramblers, encoders and decoders. In order to talk with the CIA or people who had CIA-equipped radios, you had to have daily codes or weekly codes that you would put into the encode and decode boxes in order to match the codes of other radios. If you didn't have the right codes, you couldn't send or receive to a particular radio.

I decided to disconnect the coding assembly boxes from the main transmitter and receiver and use the radio primarily as a high-powered transmitter. That way we would be able to keep in touch with our units in the field and with Tegucigalpa.

The FDN safe house in Tegus had two communications channels. Channel A was 41.36.3 and Channel B was 62.10.4 in low band. If you wanted to talk to someone in the FDN you had use the code words "Tango Indio Oscar."

If you called a MISURA radio you used the code words "Indio Whiskey Charley."

I assigned a code name to our unit to be used when we were in the field or if anyone wanted to get in touch with the Americans. Only the code words "Indio Delta Alpha" would bring us to the radio.

After Leonard finished with the antenna we powered up the radio. On our first test we just keyed in a particular frequency and called out on it. We immediately got an answer from someone in Guatemala. We didn't know whether they were military or not because we broke the conversation off real fast when the receiver started talking in Miskito. It was highly unusual for someone in Guatemala to be transmitting in Miskito.

Leonard and I looked at the radio like it was black magic or something.

I told Leonard evidently we had contacted a key radio center that had people fluent in the language of the Miskitos. This was a bad sign. It told me we had keyed into either a CIA listening post or a high-echelon Guatemala listening post that was monitoring radio traffic from the Miskitia.

I told Leonard that instead of scanning channels and listening to traffic, we would go into specific transmission and receiving time slots. We would communicate with Sym Sym at 6 a.m., noon and 5 p.m. every day. We would also set up a routine radio check with field units inside Nicaragua.

The procedure was that if we were in the field and our time to call in was 8 p.m., we would come on the radio with "Indio Delta Alpha to Indio Whiskey Charley" and Indio Whiskey Charley would acknowledge by saying "Indio Whiskey Charley to Indio Delta Alpha." We would end radio contact at that point, which was our code for saying: "We're OK, everything is going according to schedule."

The Indians had a bad habit of getting on the radio and talking about their in-laws and their out-laws and two or three generations of relatives, which gave the Sandinistas the opportunity to home in on them. I ordered radio traffic cut to transmissions and acknowledgements. If someone made any transmission in excess of his call letters, we knew he needed help.

This type organization was completely new to the the Indians and Leonard thought it incredibly fascinating. He sat down and immediately began drawing up a schedule to communicate with units in the field based on the intelligence maps we had brought from Sym Sym and put on the wall.

We knew where each MISURA unit was operating inside Nicaragua all the way down to Bluefields and what their activities were supposed to be that day. At this point there were eleven radios inside Nicaragua with groups ranging in size from small patrols to main bodies of forces operating under people like Eduardo Pantin.

Fortification

I had a plan to fortify each of the bases in the Miskitia and we began with TEA, since it would be the primary training base. We re-established the perimeter, put mines around it, dug bunkers and machine gun emplacements and laid out fields of fire.

I had Chico and Pen working on the armaments, Traveler and Caballo cleaning ammunition, Lobo and Perez conducting M-16 classes and Thom giving classes on the M-60 machine gun that included everything from changing barrels to proper use of an assistant gunner. Small training sessions and cleanup details were going on all over the base.

I instructed Jim Adair to select eight men for what I described only as "a special demolitions job." It was the Sin Sin Bridge raid, but I didn't want him or his pupils to know exactly what they were training for. The men had to have previous combat experience. They were to learn how to put C-4 charges together, how to use M-1 fuse igniters and the differences among det cord, military waterproof fuse and commercial fuse.

Ramos and Pen returned from Crem Crem with a large assortment of weapons, 400 pounds of C-4, some Claymore mines, firing caps and igniters of different types. I instructed the men how to attach a fuse igniter to a fuse and not put it on det cord. I showed them how to insert blasting caps and taught them how many pounds of explosives would do how much damage. I didn't want to get into the technical end of explosives and things like foot pounds of pressure per square inch, but we had to let them know just how powerful the explosives were.

To demonstrate I took a piece of det cord about 18 inches long and wrapped it around a pine tree about six inches thick. Then I ignited it. The resulting explosion cut the tree clean through and echoed for miles.

The blast brought one of the general staff members rushing into camp demanding to know what had happened.

"We just had a demonstration of what det cord can do and how lethal it is," I told him.

He was nervous and angry.

"If any explosives are set off or any firing is conducted, I have to give the colonel of the Honduran military in the Mocoron 48 hours notice and get his permission," he said. "This is so the refugees will not be upset and think an invasion is taking place and so the Honduran military won't go on alert."

I told him I was sorry, but I hadn't been informed of the stringent rules. I told him it wouldn't happen again.

We had an incredible amount of activity going on right under the noses of the Honduran military and they didn't know it. There was no reason to alert them with foolish demonstrations of firepower. The longer we could keep the affairs at the base a secret from the Hondurans, the better for us. The Hondurans assumed TEA had been closed permanently and I didn't want to do anything to change that belief. They would find out soon enough what we were doing, but we would deal with that when the time came.

The Indians were instructed in use of various firearms without actually firing them. If they knew how to use an M-60 or an AK-47, we would put them into an M-16 or M-79 school. We would find out what they didn't know and teach it to them.

For the Sin Sin Bridge raid, I wanted at least four good M-60 teams and six M-79 gunners.

Each night Tirador and I would meet with the general staff, and each night more and more responsibility was placed on me. They asked me how many men should be placed where, how the food should be distributed, who would be allowed in the hospital and who wouldn't, how I could get badly wounded men to Tegucigalpa, how to evacuate people from the field and any number of other things.

It seemed as if I was getting bogged down with administrative minutiae for the entire population of the Miskitia, not just TEA base, the Americans and the MISURA. I was putting in 18 hours a day on administrative chores alone. I felt I had the ability to do it, but I wanted to make sure my judgment was right and that what I was telling them would benefit them because that would boost their confidence in me.

When I finally received a radio message from the FDN that Oscar Montez wanted to meet with me in Tegus to finalize the weapons exchange, Tirador and I flew back and checked into the Maya. Montez refused to come into the Miskitia because he feared for his life and insisted he would meet me only in the city, where he felt safe.

"How are things going?" Montez asked as he settled himself into a chair in my room.

"Couldn't be better," I said. "We've been working for the FDN in the Miskitia, and with us as the liaison we have the MISURA right where we want them."

Now came the other half of the equation. I had to convince Montez I was working on the MISURA in the best interests of the FDN, just as I had convinced the MISURA I was working on the FDN in their best interests. If the deal was to work, neither side could realize what I was doing. If they did, I was finished. I had to keep a wall of secrecy between the two organizations so they could not be able to compare notes. Not that MISURA would ever sit down with the FDN, but the FDN might get suspicious if they learned I was building a strong military that could present a challenge to it.

Montez told me had 500 pairs of boots, 500 uniforms and the accessories we wanted, but he would have to ship them in two different loads because it was too much for one plane. He wanted to know if he could get the arms on the first plane, before the second shipment of supplies arrived.

"We'll have to work on trust," I said.

I agreed to his proposition, feeling reasonably certain he wouldn't try to screw us.

"When this deal is complete we will talk about other needs and other deals," I said.

We set a date for delivery, exchanged radio frequencies and shook hands on the deal. I needed to exchange some dollars for lempiras and told Oscar I would come to his office after I made a few telephone calls.

Oscar was eager to show me around the new safe house. It was a large, expensive house with heavy security. With the FDN supposedly broke, I wondered how it could afford such a fabulous house.

Montez had a small office with several filing cabinets behind his desk. I handed him $1,000 in U.S. currency and he turned to one of the legal-size file cabinets and opened a drawer that was filled almost to the top with $100 bills.

My mouth dropped open as I watched him stack my money on top of what had to be at least $1 million. When he finished that, he opened another drawer. This was filled with Honduran lempiras. Another drawer had Nicaraguan cordobas — though they were virtually worthless at the time — another had Salvadoran colones and still another had stacks and stacks of traveler's checks, the preferred currency of the FDN Directorate.

I was so stunned by the sight of all this money in a luxurious safe house belonging to a supposedly broke organization that I don't even remember the exchange rate Montez gave me, or if I thanked him.

I walked out of the office in a daze and said to Tirador: "I can't believe this. All I've heard from these people is how they're so broke and they can hardly make ends meet and if the U.S. doesn't give them some type of aid they're going down the tubes.

"I just saw a drawer full of money that you wouldn't believe. These people are in the money business, not the war business."

I didn't know then how true that was.

Upon my return to the Miskitia, I had a meeting with the general staff and told them the deal had been approved by the FDN. If we were to hold up our end of the deal we had to get the weapons together and marked because the plane would arrive to pick them up in two days.

We had the arms shipped in from Crem and got them boxed up for shipment. I made it a special point to write in big letters on each box:

"Oscar Montez" so everyone would know this was his deal. He would be able to use it to his advantage within the FDN.

Shortly after I returned from Tegucigalpa, Ramos came to me and told me the men were hungry.

"What do you mean?" I said.

"While you've been gone we didn't eat but one meal," he replied, almost embarrassed to admit it.

"What are you talking about you didn't eat but one meal?"

"Alejo said we were out of food."

"Well, I'll get in touch with Alejo tonight at the general staff meeting and find out what the hell is going on. Is there anything to eat down there now?"

"They said they thought they were going to fix bread and coffee for supper."

"I'll get to the bottom of this," I promised.

That night at the general staff meeting I was angry and confrontational. I took charge of the meeting from the beginning and let them know I was not happy with the way they were treating the Americans.

"Alejo," I said, "I've given you money, money and more money, and there is no excuse for our people being without food."

One of Alejo's favorite sayings was "them boys." He would say: "Well, them boys at 50 Base and them boys at San Geronimo and them boys at Karasanka just don't have food and we've been trying to equally divide it."

"But Alejo, we cannot feed this entire nation on what little bit of money and food we have," I said. "We have to concentrate our food in an area where we are going to have people going into combat because these are the men who need the nourishment. The other people, I sympathize with the fact that they've got to eat, but we just can't support them."

Alejo agreed with me, but was reluctant to do anything because he was the G-4 and the Indians looked at him as being responsible for food, whether they were active military or refugees.

He would come up with bizarre excuses and tell me he could not find food in Puerto Lempira just to avoid having to face his people and say: "The Americans are sitting at TEA eating like kings while the rest of you are starving to death."

"I'm going to give you some more money," I said to Alejo. "I want you to go to Puerto Lempira and pick up every canned good, especially meats and sardines, you can find for the Sin Sin Bridge mission. The men going into Nicaragua are going to have to eat.

"This is a mission that you want, that you consider very critical, so if you consider it that critical then you're going to have to back up the needs of the troops."

I learned later the general staff purposely diverted food from TEA to extort money from me. They were creating a synthetic shortage in our camp and diverting food to other camps to keep getting money from me. They felt I had a lot more money than I actually had.

The money situation was getting desperate, though. I didn't have many lempiras left. I had exchanged $10,000 of the $15,000 I received in the mysterious envelope with Frank Winchester's name on it and all of it had gone directly to the MISURA for food and incidentals. I had been free with the money because I felt it would solidify our position. But the MISURA were using it because I was their only source of funds.

The responsibilities on me kept increasing. I had run from responsibility all my life. But here I felt it was my duty to take on whatever they asked me to do, whether it was negotiating with the FDN, the United States government or the Sandinistas.

At first I was reluctant.

But the general staff would say: "There's something you've got to do. You've got to talk to the FDN. You've got to find more money. Here's a list of truck parts we need. Here's a list of food we need."

"Look," I told them, "I haven't got the authority, I'm here as an independent. We've got no political connections."

Raoul looked at me and smiled.

"If you were given the official authorization by the MISURA people to negotiate for us," he said, "to handle our affairs in Washington and with the FDN in Tegucigalpa, would you then do it?"

I immediately realized the implications of what he was telling me.

"Do you realize what you're doing?" I said. "That's transferring power to a U.S. citizen that would virtually make me responsible for the entire MISURA nation."

The general staff looked at me, nodding their heads in approval.

"Sure," said Alejo. "You've demonstrated your loyalty. You've demonstrated that you have the ability to do the things that we cannot. We're uneducated. We don't have the expertise and the knowledge that you have, so therefore we're appointing you as our head."

The statement didn't shock me as much as it should have. It seemed like the natural order of things.

"The only way I can accept this," I said, "is if you have the authority of the Council of Elders and the general staff, in a written document, where if challenged either by a U.S. official or the FDN, I will have credentials stating that I am indeed the sole spokesman for the MISURA."

They agreed and the next day came to camp with the document. It was a letter authorizing me to do all the things they wanted me to do. Colonel Flaco had become chief spokesman and agent for the MISURA, the first time the Indians had allowed an outsider to speak on their behalf. (See Appendix 1).

The only formality lacking was for the document to receive approval of the assembly of chiefs. A meeting of the General Assembly was scheduled March 21, 1985, and the Indians had already begun slowly making their way to the border area from throughout Nicaragua and Honduras.

I had a copy of this historic document made and sent to Oscar Montez. He seemed pleased to finally be able to deal with someone he had dealt with before, someone he didn't fear as much as he feared the Indians.

"Since you're the spokesman and you're the one who's been appointed leader, then I won't have to do business with anyone else," Montez told me in a radio conversation. "I can cut off Archibald Theofilo, Ardan Artolla, Steadman Fagoth and anybody else who wants money. Unless they ask your permission, or you give me permission, then I won't do it."

I told Oscar that was fine, but the FDN owed the MISURA 25,000 lemps for the month and I expected it. He told me he would send the money on the first plane down.

When the radio message came that the plane had left Aguacate, we drove to the airstrip and waited. And we waited. And we waited. Finally, after about two hours, an old C-47 came limping in.

Much to my surprise, Pulmon, my old bodyguard from Las Vegas was the first man out of the plane. He was followed by several armed FDN commandos and Commandante Cirro. It appeared the FDN didn't trust us.

They sent half the boots, half the uniforms, a few car batteries, a little medicine and a complement of commandos to ensure we didn't steal the supplies and the airplane.

The Honduran airport guards were their usual curious selves and came to investigate the loading and unloading. There was a great deal of jabbering back and forth in Spanish and I could tell things were not going smoothly. Suddenly, Pulmon rushed over in front of me and started pushing against me.

"What the hell are you doing?"

"I'm protecting you, Colonel Flaco. I'm protecting you."

Tirador was off to the side taking pictures because I wanted to document it for use in our intelligence files to show the FDN had shipped us goods and we had in turn given them arms. When he saw Pulmon's strange antics, he laughed and said: "This man don't need protection. We got plenty of protection standing around here."

I grabbed Pulmon by the shoulders, pushed him aside and told him: "Just stand here and we'll get this resolved."

Raoul and Alejo got the Honduran guards aside and told them to close their eyes, that the Indians were guarding this part of the border and what was going on here might save their lives.

The Hondurans shrugged their shoulders and retreated to a safe distance.

As the unloading continued I turned to Cirro, who appeared to be in charge, and asked: "Where's the money?"

"What money are you talking about?"

"Oscar was supposed to send some lemps to us."

"Well, Oscar was going to come down, but he couldn't make it. He'll be on the next flight."

"When is the next flight coming in?"

"In about two days. I want you to sign these requisitions and receipts saying you received the goods."

After Selso counted what we had received, I signed the requisitions and the FDN party got back on the plane and left, except for two men. Pulmon stayed because of his loyalty to me. He told me he had volunteered to come here when he heard I was in the Miskitia. Another man named Papillon stayed behind also. Papillon was a Pecos Bill type. He rarely spoke and gave the impression he was all business.

I thought Pulmon and Papillon had been sent here by the FDN to monitor my activities but eventually dismissed the idea. Pulmon was a close friend and I had no doubt he would stop a bullet for me if it came to that. The Americans became fiercely jealous of Pulmon because he was close to me and took charge when they failed to show any leadership. He also spoke Spanish and was highly trained, which made him an asset among this motley crew.

This was a big day for everyone. The MISURA saw I could deliver what I had promised, even though we did have to give up a few arms. They had received some of the uniforms and boots they needed and it appeared a supply pipeline to the FDN had opened.

Alejo was overyoyed.

"This is the first time anybody has come and really done anything they said they would," he told me.

I promised we would do even better in the future.

I went back to TEA base and got on the radio to Oscar Montez. I thanked him for the supplies, but wanted to make sure he knew the deal was not complete until the other plane arrived.

"Where's the money?" I said.

"Well, I didn't have time to get it to Aguacate because we were rushing, trying to get some of the supplies from Tegus to send to you, but you will get the money," he promised.

We had made great strides in just a few weeks. The only barrier now was getting the Americans into Nicaragua to blow the Sin Sin bridge.

The Sin Sin Bridge Raid

I had run out of excuses. The assault team had been training, we had gotten TEA base cleaned up, we had the camp running in an orderly fashion and the FDN deal had been consummated. Now the Indians wanted a combat operation to show we were indeed what we had billed ourselves to be.

I called the Americans in and asked them if they were ready to go on a combat mission. Most were eager to get on with it. This is why they had come here.

"The only drawback," I said, "is if we go, all Americans go. No one will be left behind. Everyone will have to be present on the mission. If we divide the group and something happens to those inside Nicaragua, the American press and the State Department will jump on the rest wanting to know what's going on.

"If we stay together, we eliminate the chance of misinformation getting out about what we're doing here. The only time we will divide and go in different directions is if we are inside Nicaragua and we are running a two- or three-pronged attack. If you don't feel like you can hack it, I want to know now. You've been down here long enough to get acclimated, to see what it's like, to see what the food's like. I want a show of hands of the people who want to go and will agree to these terms."

Every hand went up. But I could see some of the men raised their hands reluctantly. They were afraid if they said no or tried to stay behind I would have them detained, or worse.

I told them once we received updated intelligence on the bridge, we would build a mockup for practice. It would be a night raid, conducted quickly and efficiently.

Adair would head the demo squad with Mycroft as his assistant. Ramos would be in charge of the six-man M-79 team. Thom and Pappy would share responsibility for the M-60 crews. The M-60 and M-79 teams would throw fire into the Sandinista compound and engage it while the demo team was working.

Tirador would lead an eight-man team to support the demolitions squad while it was placing the charges. Tirador's men would either lay down suppressive fire or provide a covering barrage while the demo team withdrew.

We would be more than 80 miles inside Nicaragua and would have to walk in fully loaded for battle at the bridge and on our way out. The march in would be five-plus days through some of the worst terrain they had ever seen. If we got hit either coming or going we had to have the ability to fight our way out or to fight long enough for a rescue column to reach us.

"You'll be taking up to 300 rounds of ammunition each. The M-79 gunners will be taking a minimum of a dozen extra rounds above the normal load of twenty," I said.

We had brought MREs and C-rations from the old Pegaso operation in Las Vegas. Ramos was to divide them equally among the Americans and see that everybody had enough to eat for at least seven days, which was about as far as the stock would go. We would have to improvise on the rest.

"All of this will fall into place," I said. "It's going to take several days and the mission is at least a week away, so this is going to give you plenty of time to prepare, to get your shit together, to get your weapons together."

About 30 men, including the Americans, would leave from TEA base. The remainder of the 85-man assault force would come from 50 Base, another MISURA encampment near the Coco River.

The plan was workable. But I knew the five-day hump in would be treacherous for me and the men. I could tell none of them was looking forward to that. I know I wasn't.

Things progressed rapidly over the next week. We had gotten a drawing of the bridge and the fortifications around it. (See Appendix 2.) We had assigned a code name to the raid. It would be "Indio Delta Alpha," the same as our radio call sign. I asked the general staff for another unit to be sent into Nicaragua ahead of us as a diversion. The staff agreed to have Eduardo Pantin move from his base inside Nicaragua to the village of Suhi.

Everything seemed to be as ready as it was going to be and the go signal was given.

The day before we departed, I called for an inspection of the Americans in full battle gear.

I saw immediately that this was going to be more difficult than I thought. Some of the men looked like airborne Rangers and were outfitted properly. Others looked like they belonged in the Salvation Army.

Equipment quality varied greatly. The Recondos from Frank Camper's school appeared to be better equipped for a long trip. The Cubans, Lobo, Perez and Pedrico, were woefully underprepared and lacked many necessary items. Lobo wore a backpack that was literally tied to him with parachute cord. Perez had borrowed equipment from the Indians and looked pitiful.

I walked among the men suggesting changes when I spotted deficiencies in their gear. Some had so many it was impossible to fix all of them.

I told each man to draw his entire allotment of ammunition and place it on him to demonstrate how it would be carried. The weight of their loads would be tremendous, considering the distance we had to travel and the poor physical condition of most of them. Once fully loaded with ammo, rations, weapons and extra clothing, each man carried nearly 100 pounds in extra weight.

I asked each man if he felt he could carry this much equipment and ammo, and each said without reservation he would have no problem. It might not have been a problem for short distances on flat ground. But we would be humping for days through muddy savanah's and mountains.

Adair carried the heaviest load. In addition to the explosives, he was doubling as the medic. The combined weight of the loads equalled twice what the other men would be carrying, but he insisted he could handle it.

We tightened straps, muffled loose equipment and broke out the camouflage face paint to hide our white faces once we went across the border. I tried to take every precaution I felt would help the men survive the hardship that lay ahead.

The infiltration route was many miles from TEA and trucks were brought in to transport the troops. The trucks arrived late in the afternoon because daylight travel was more likely to attract Sandinista ambushes.

Our plan was to cover the distance between TEA and 50 Base overnight, rest, then begin practice maneuvers the next day.

I boarded the first truck with Alejo and most of the Americans. I told them to keep their gear and weapons out of sight as much as possible and not draw attention to themselves as we passed through villages.

The convoy left TEA and headed east towards Leimus at a rapid clip. Alejo feared being spotted by Sandinista mine-laying crews that did their work at night. As we drove I could see headlights in the distance. They were Soviet trucks and the mine crews slowly making their rounds. Occasionally, whenever we got close to the border, the headlights on our trucks were turned off.

The "short" trip to the border turned out to be nearly 11 hours. It was a brutal ride of deep potholes, creaky bridges and clouds of dust. The Americans in the back complained loudly about the length of the trip and their discomfort, but we drove on out of the hills and into a region of grassy savannahs that looked almost like a rice paddy in the truck headlights.

Finally, we came to an area where several large trees that appeared to be cypress sprouted out of the savannah. Strung between the trees, high off the ground, were several large green cocoon-like objects. When the headlights of the truck hit them, Indian heads swathed in stocking caps popped out of the cocoons. They looked like Smurfs hanging from the trees.

This small contingent of men was to serve as our guides to 50 Base.

"It's just a few meters across the savannah to the base," Raoul assured me.

As usual, I believed him. But, like everything else in the Miskitia, nothing is what it appears to be.

I ordered the men off the trucks and into single file behind the guides. We set off along a small, muddy footpath through the savannah in darkness so complete we couldn't see anything in front of us, much less our feet or the path.

Because of the amount of equipment each man was carrying, we had problems staying on the narrow path. I took my flashlight and attempted to find my way along the path, but stepped off only to find I was nearly waist deep in water. Despite the warmth of the night, the water was extremely cold and left me in shivers. Raoul walked past me without a light, strolling on as if he radar. The Indians were amazing when it came to navigation in the elements.

All I heard from the Americans was: "Squish, squish, squish, splat. Goddamn it!"

Finally we came to a creek about 25 feet wide. The only way across was a large tree fallen tree. Doing it during the day would have been bad enough. But the log was slippery and we had to do it at night. Beneath the makeshift bridge was a drop of at least 30 feet.

The Indians went across it like it was nothing.

I was the first American across, trying to show some leadership, and nearly fell several times before I got to the other side. Traveler was next. He made it about 10 feet before he disappeared into the creek with a scream and a splash. After we rescued him, the rest of the Amerians shinnied across on their butts.

"Welcome to 50 Base," Alejo said when we reached the far side.

People thought 50 Base was an actual base but it was nothing but a patch of weeds out in the middle of nowhere. We were in an area behind a village where the Indians didn't want us seen because they thought we would scare their families.

We unrolled our ponchos and hammocks if we had them and tried to get some sleep. Sleep didn't come easily, though. They had some real guerrilla mosquitos down there. They weren't afraid of anything. You'd have to wear gloves and mosquito netting to keep them off you until about 10 a.m. when the sun came out.

We tried everything to keep the mosquitos off — Jungle Juice, Off, whatever. We started calling the Off "Pissed Off" because that's all it did to the mosquitos. You put a little of that on you and you became a big target. If you used aftershave you were an even bigger target because you didn't smell like everyone else.

The Indians had no problems with the mosquitoes, but our sweet white meat seemed to be a delicacy.

Ramos and the Recondos had built some small grass huts surrounded with mosquito netting. They also cut small pieces of the netting and draped it over their bush hats to stop the mosquito assault. Everyone wore long sleeved BDUs, but the constant harassment from the insects made me miserable.

After a night of terrible restlessness from the long trip and fighting the millions of mosquitoes biting me through the cloth of the hammock, I rose with the usual morning hymns from the Indians. A fire had been started near the river where the Indians sang and where a breakfast of beans and flower dumplings was being prepared. Heavy fog covered the ground.

It was painfully clear that living on bases like Las Vegas and TEA was heaven compared to the reality of the bush. This is what every American had sought, including me, and now it was show time. Superman's cape was showing some wear and tear that morning. The Indians acted as if this was just another day on the job, and in a sense, it was, while the Americans were hobbling around that morning like old men.

Alejo, who had spent the night in the village, came into our camp and told me Pantin would leave for the border late that afternoon to begin the diversion.

Pantin was unusual among the Indian commanders. He was a well-educated, fair-skinned Indian who wore wire-rimmed glasses and a red beret with a *Soldier of Fortune* pin on it. He was articulate, eager to fight and had a good sense of what the war was all about.

I spoke with Pantin for over an hour. He said our presence would definitely boost morale, but he had numerous reservations about our ability to cope with the harsh conditions in the Miskitia. He said it would take time for us to get acclimated and he would help if he could, but he preferred to remain inside Nicaragua because of the intense political infighting among the confederation members. He said the dangers of combat were a breeze compared to playing commander in the refugee camps.

We selected the additional men for the raid from 50 base, bringing the assault force to 73 Indians and 12 Americans. I began running men through a series of practice assaults to familiarize each with his mission. The actual raid was to begin before dawn, when the vigilance of the guards was its lowest. Each maneuver in a series of maneuvers would be started by a signal sequence from my red-lensed flashlight. All squad leaders were to use light communication to move men around the objective.

The six M-60 teams would be arrayed in a semi-circle on the outer edges of the perimeter of the mine field guarding the bridge. A LAAW team would be dispatched to a spot near the Sandinista communications hutch and fire on it as the first element of our ambush.

Every move was time-specific and certain redundancies were built in to maintain the effect of surprise and what would appear to be over-whelming firepower, even though we most likely would be outgunned in a straight fight. I hoped to both frighten the Sandinistas and prevent reinforcements from the garrisons near Santa Marta and Maniwatla from reaching Sin Sin before the bridge was blown.

Based on all available intelligence, I believed the plan was sound. The drawing provided by the Indian recon team showed a mine field inside rows of fencing around the entire bridge. The Santa Marta road ran right through the fortifications and the river bed was open, allowing access for the demo team.

We had brought four 24-pound anti-tank mines that were to be buried a mile from the perimeter of the bridge on the Santa Marta road to slow any reinforcements.

Hitting the camp and blowing the bridge was no problem, but extracting our men was another matter. I had no doubts that if the Sandinistas were able to call for assistance that helicopter gunships would be dispatched to find our force. I had exchanged several M-16s and their 5.56mm rounds for FN-FAL rifles, which fired a high-velocity 7.62x59 round, to serve as our anti-aircraft defense. It wasn't much, but it was all we had.

If the Sandinistas sent Mi-8 helicopters, we had a chance of dropping them. But the Mi-24 HIND-D flying tanks could not be brought down with small arms. We would have to run and hide if those things started chasing us.

The morning we left 50 Base we divided into groups of six and boarded small boats that took us through a swamp and deposited us deep in the tropical forest near the Coco River. From there we had what the Indians described as a 4 1/2-hour hike to the village of Suhi, our jumpoff point into Nicaragua.

The trip may have been 4 1/2 hours for the Indians, but not for the Americans.

We hadn't gone far when the column began to string out as the overburdened Americans lagged farther and farther behind. In addition to the packs, each American carried a bulletproof vest Tom Posey had obtained in the States and given to me in Miami. The vests proved to be nothing more than heat traps and several of the men who wore them began suffering from dehydration and heat stress.

I walked ahead of the group with Selso Wiggins and the radio man. The more we walked, the more weight the men lost, most of it in the form of abandoned ammunition. They'd toss away their ammo, but not their food. Everyone was bitching. Everyone was tired. The war had lost its brilliant luster for these Americans.

Selso and I made it to Suhi at dusk, although I was damn near dead with fatigue. Pedrico had kept pace with us, but eventually dropped back to assist those who were having problems keeping up. The column stretched for miles and by darkness only a few of the men had made it to camp.

I ate a meal of eggs and beans, hung up my clothes to dry and fell into a deep, fatigued sleep in a hammock. I was completely drained.

The next morning I was awakened by the crowing of roosters and the bitching of the last of the stragglers just coming in to camp. Ramos,

Tirador, Pen, Pappy, Thom, Pulmon, Papillon, Adair, Pedrico and Mycroft had made it. They told me they had spent the night on the trail.

Pablo, Lobo and Chico quit and Perez had nearly died from drinking a bottle of IV fluid he thought was water. They were escorted back to 50 Base and were being held in custody by Alejo, who had remained there.

The men who made it to Suhi were covered with mud, but no worse for the wear. They began complaining that the Indians moved too fast and they needed time to get in shape. I advised them that they had had plenty of time for that and now were paying for it. I had problems keeping up too, but my pride wouldn't let me stop or drop out.

Selso arranged for the late arrivals to grab a bite to eat but we had to press on because Pantin had moved his blocking force into position.

The Americans continued to complain about the speed at which the Indians moved. The Indians were light and fast. The Americans couldn't keep up with them. The gringo Supermen were being walked into the ground by these uneducated peasants. Our image as saviors was suffering.

After the meal, I assembled the men for final instructions. I had everyone check their packs and ammo supplies. I ordered the bulletproof vests left in Suhi. They were more of a hindrance than a help at that point.

Just as we prepared to depart, the radio chattered to life. Pantin had engaged the Sandinistas. We smiled at one another, knowing the raid had started. Then came a message for me. Alejo wanted to talk to me. It was urgent.

"What's the problem?" I asked Alejo.

"You must return to 50 Base," he said, his voice frantic. "There is a terrible problem here only you can handle."

"I've got to move out," I replied. "Pantin is in jeopardy."

"You must return now. You must."

Alejo was begging me to come back for reasons I could not fathom. He sounded desperate. After agonizing over whether to stay with the men or return to 50 Base, I decided to leave the men in Suhi, walk back to 50 Base, take care of the problem and return for the raid. I had spent so much time planning it I wanted to be in on it. Besides, I doubted that these men could carry it off by themselves.

Selso said it was not possible to wait for my return because Pantin and his men could be lost if we delayed. But I told him I could not approve what amounted to a suicide mission and the men would have to wait for my return. The men argued with me as I collected my gear for the return trip. I continued to refuse.

They finally became so insistent about continuing with the mission I called Tirador and Ramos aside and asked them if they were sure they could complete the mission after seeing the number of casualties incurred on just the first day.

They promised they would be succssful. Against my better judgment, I gave in.

I emptied the food from my pack and distributed it among the others. As I finished, a young Indian woman took my pack from me, slung it on her back and began walking north to 50 Base. The Indians assigned the woman to carry my ALICE pack as a gesture of respect. It felt bad and it looked bad. The last image some of these men had of the great Colonel Flaco was a woman carrying his pack off into the bush while I followed meekly behind.

Later, after we had gone our separate ways, the men would claim I had abandoned them and left camp with a woman carrying my pack.

I hurried back to 50 Base, concerned about Alejo's frantic appeals for my return. The woman carrying my pack said nothing and set a rapid pace along the muddy jungle trail. I was back by early afternoon, dripping with sweat and exhausted.

Alejo greeted me with a smile, a handshake and the news he had locked the four dropouts in a storeroom. He was much calmer now than he had been on the radio just a few hours earlier. I wanted to take care of the problem and rejoin the raiding party.

"What's the problem?" I asked.

"The people are on the brink of starvation. You must go to Tegucigalpa for food."

"What about the second load of supplies from the FDN?"

"It never came."

I knew the FDN was a bunch of thieves, but I thought at least Oscar Montez would deal fairly with me. If the situation was as desperate as Alejo said, I would have to work fast. I reluctantly decided to abandon the Sin Sin Bridge raid and return to Tegucigalpa.

I collected the four chastened Americans from detention and began the long drive back to TEA base. During the drive, Alejo apologized profusely for pulling me off the raid. But, he explained, the general staff had decided no commander should accompany his men on such a high-risk mission.

I learned later the general staff had assigned Selso to accompany us knowing they would pull me off the mission. They thought I was too valuable a commodity to risk. The MISURA hierarchy agreed that I would not be allowed to go in harm's way. They knew if something happened to me there would be no more money and no more connections.

I told Alejo I would go to Tegus and Washington if necessary to get the food and supplies, but I would not leave until I knew what had happened on the raid.

I left specific instructions with the raiding party to report in each day at 6 a.m. and 6 p.m. using our code system. I spent four days in TEA listening to the radio. The check-in times began to vary on the first day and on one occasion the code system was completely abandoned, indicating something was terribly wrong on the mission. There was no indication if the bridge had been blown, or even if an effort had been made. Meanwhile, Alejo kept pressing me that the food situation was becoming more critical by the hour.

I decided to fly to Tegus and scrounge up what I could for the Indians before there was a major disaster.

Oscar Montez was no help. In fact, he displayed an unusual disdain for me that I had not seen before. It seemed he knew something that might not bode well for me or the Indians. Something was going on that I was not privy to. I decided to fly on to Houston to enlist Maco Stewart's aid.

There was a sense of urgency in my mission now. The Indians were starving, the Americans were at great risk inside Nicaragua, and the FDN was stonewalling me. Things didn't add up, and I didn't know why.

When I arrived in Houston on March 5, 1985, I called Maco's office. He wasn't in. I told his secretary to leave a message that I needed $10,000 to save the Indians from starvation. She said she would would pass on the message. Later that afternoon, she came to my hotel with a check for $5,000. She said it was all Maco was willing to give.

I was getting desperate now. My last hope was Washington, but I didn't know anyone there who could help. Then I thought of Sen. Jeremiah Denton of Alabama, my senator, the highly decorated former Vietnam prisoner of war who had voted for every Contra aid bill in Congress. He was an outspoken supporter of the Contras. He had publicly expressed sympathy for the Contra cause. Even if he couldn't help me, he might know someone who would.

I called Denton's office and was directed to Meg Hunt, one of his aides who handled Central American affairs. I gave her a quick rundown of the situation in the Miskitia and told her the Indians were on the verge of starvation and desperately needed food. She seemed rather indifferent about me and the Indians until I said the magic word — drugs.

When I had first arrived in the Miskitia, the general staff told me about a problem they had with drugs. The Miskitos did not have a drug culture or a drug problem. But some of the intelligence missions run by the Indians had uncovered evidence of cocaine laboratories run by Colombians in Zelaya Province. In some instances the Indians were being used as mules to transport the processed cocaine across the Nicaraguan border into either Honduras or Costa Rica for shipment to the United States.

They couldn't run the stuff directly out of Nicaragua because anything coming off the coast there was being stopped. So they got the Indians to carry it across the border and from there they were home free. It was a perfect cover, not only because of the logistics, but because the Indians had no idea what they were doing. All they knew was that someone had given them more money than they could earn in a year to carry a package of powder a few miles through the jungle. They were paid 100 lempiras each for the trip, which was like a fortune to them.

The Indians said the Sandinistas were running the labs, but all they really knew was that they were Spanish people. They didn't know if they were Nicaraguan, Colombian or Cuban.

Although the cocaine labs were in Nicaragua, there was no evidence the Sandinistas were actually in the drug business. I suspect the labs were run like a franchise operation, with the Sandinistas collecting rent on the land and the facilities that were controlled by others.

I marked the locations of the labs on my map and brought it with me to the States. One of the labs was just southwest of Bluefields on the Caribbean coast. A second lab was south of that, on a tributary of the Rio Kukra. A third was a few miles northwest of the coastal city of Barra del Rio Maiz. All were in extremely remote areas.

When I told Meg Hunt I had the map showing the locations of the drug labs, she immediately perked up.

"I was supposed to go to North Carolina for the weekend, but since you have so much knowledge about the Indians, why don't you come to Washington and I'll meet with you when you get here?"

I agreed to take the next plane to Washington. At last, I thought, I have found someone who understands the situation.

Little did I know I was setting myself up for the biggest fall of my life.

Persona Non Grata

When I got to Denton's office in Washington, I was ushered into a conference room by Meg Hunt, where she introduced me to another aide, a man named Joel Lisker. They knew me only as Colonel Flaco, not as Jack Terrell.

I tried to explain about the food and medical shortages in the Miskitia but every time I paused, Lisker brought up the issue of the drug labs. It was obvious they were more interested in that than they were about the Indians.

At the time, Denton was on a Senate subcommittee dealing with the drug problem. His political fortunes were waning back in Alabama as a result of his occasionally erratic voting record and lack of production. He was living off his reputation as a POW and needed something newsworthy to increase his stock.

My information could do just that, but I wasn't about to trade away the only hole card I had without tangible evidence the MISURA would receive help.

We went back and forth on the issue for a while until I mentioned seven Americans were on a combat mission inside Nicaragua with the Indians. It was like somebody hit a scramble button at a Strategic Air Command base. They jumped up from their chairs and started running around the room, making telephone calls, throwing their hands in the air and generally acting as if the fate of the western world was at stake.

I sat there watching them, somewhat amused but also angry that we were not addressing the key issue here.

It was always my understanding the mission was to take dirt, to take the fight to the Sandinistas and recapture Nicaragua. But Hunt and Lisker were so concerned about Americans getting involved in the war that it confirmed my long-held suspicions that the government had no intention of taking any Nicaraguan dirt. Attacks on strategic targets were not what they wanted. It went against their entire policy.

"I need to talk to North about this," Lisker said as he picked up a secure telephone and dialed a local number.

I heard only one side of the conversation, but Lisker let me know he was talking to Oliver North at the White House. North did not want to talk directly to me, Lisker said, because then he could deny the conversation ever took place. Lisker became the mouthpiece through which North tried to swing a deal with me about the drug labs.

I wanted a trade. I would tell North and Denton's people where the labs were if they would send down C-130s loaded with food and medicine for the Indians.

North was more interested in the publicity value of showing the Sandinistas as drug runners than he was in helping the Indians. But I had to play what cards I had.

"I will give you that map when that first C-130 loaded with food and medicine hits the dirt," I told Lisker. He relayed the message to North.

I knew if I told them exactly what they wanted to know, the Indians would never get the food and I might never be allowed to leave the country and get back into the Miskitia.

Hunt and Lisker pleaded with me to give them the information before they would promise the food. They said they needed some time to obtain satellite photos to verify the existence of the labs. If the labs were there, I would get everything I wanted. I felt they were stalling for time.

They asked me to make a list of the supplies we needed and I wrote down a lengthy list of food, medicine and non-lethal accessories that would not violate the Boland Amendment. This was a resuce operation, not a military mission.

Hunt wanted to know if I could recall the Americans from inside Nicaragua and I told her I could, but I wouldn't. Lisker threatened to use his power to keep me from going back to Honduras. I've never liked threats. People I deal with usually don't make threats. They just do what they have to do. But Lisker had that typical sanctimonious Washington personality that comes with the territory. When he started threatening, I stopped cooperating.

I told Lisker and Hunt I had to think about their offer and could be reached at my hotel.

I went back to my room, discouraged and depressed over the turn of events. My naivete about how the system operated in Washington was showing. In that town, no one ever does anything out of the goodness of their hearts. If they can't gain politically or financially from something, they won't do it. Helping the Indians was not a priority here. Screwing the Sandinistas was.

The time had come for one last desperate measure — call in the press. I saw it as a way of protecting myself and ensuring that I would be able to get the story out even if I was prevented from returning to Honduras.

Tom Posey had given me the nmber of an ABC-TV correspondent named Brian Barger. Brian had contacted Posey about going into Nicaragua with an American team and filming them in action. I called and arranged a meeting at my hotel.

Brian was a likable, easygoing guy as journalists go. He knew a great deal about Central America, including the key people in the Contras, and spoke Spanish. His father was a career diplomat and Brian had lived all over the world as a child. He was still seeking combat footage of Americans when I contacted him.

At that first meeting, I was evasive, secretive and told him only that I was in Washington seeking help for the MISURA. I gave him a brief outline of my conversation with Meg Hunt and Joel Lisker and how Lisker had threatened to keep me from leaving the States. I told him if I was accompanied by someone from the press, Lisker might back off.

Brian was eager to make the trip and said all he had to do was get the crew together and pack some clothes. I told him if he would come directly to the Miskitia, I would get him inside Nicaragua with the Americans. We struck a deal and I told him to be ready to go in a few days.

I had decided Washington wasn't the place for me to get the help I needed. I called Meg Hunt and told her I was leaving. She asked me to wait until she could speak with me one more time and came to the hotel. We met in the lobby and talked, while Brian Barger watched, just out of hearing.

Hunt told me it was my "patriotic duty as an American" to give them the coordinates to the drug labs. The patriotic appeal had lost its edge by then. It just didn't ring true. It wasn't a matter of patriotism for them. It was policy. It was politics. They didn't care that people were starving down there. They were concerned about their political agenda.

I told her again that as soon as the first C-130 touched the ground in Mocoron, I would give them all the information they wanted.

We were at an impasse. Upset over my refusal to deal with her, Hunt left the hotel.

Later, when reporters tried to verify my visits to Denton's office, the staff would only say they remembered a strange, thin, gray-haired man who came to the office and asked to see Denton. They called me Flacko Whacko.

My refusal to play Washington's political game cost me dearly and began what would be a two-year war with Oliver North.

I had never seen the man, never talked with him and wasn't even quite sure who he was or what he did. His name had come up in the Houston meeting with Hull and Owen the previous December when I asked Owen who he was working for.

"The NSC," Owen replied.

Fortier had referred to the NSC in my conversations with him but I still wasn't sure what it was.

"What is the NSC?" I asked Owen.

"You know," he said, "the National Security Council. Ollie North."

North's name came up again in the January 5 meeting at Adolfo Calero's house during the discussion of the assassination plot against Eden Pastora and my name showed up in North's notebook that day.

But North was still just a name. He wasn't a face or the malevolent presence he would later become. I didn't learn how powerful he was until long after we had gone to war with one another.

North saw me as a threat to his private empire and this clandestine little war he was running out of the White House. If the Indians became fully involved in the war, it would have been a disaster for his program. And since I was the chief spokesman for the Indians, I had to go.

White House concern about my involvement with the Indians is evident in a memo written to North by Rob Owen on January 31, 1985, and released during the Iran-Contra hearings. In it, I am referred to only by my code name, Colonel Flaco. (See Appendix 3 for full memo).

"Would seem a good idea to deal with Flacko [sic] as soon as possible," Owen wrote. "Probably will not be scared off as he believes he has done nothing to violate the neutrality act. If he is held [he] probably will still move forward after he is let out, unless he can be locked up for a good long time. Best bet might be to dry up his funds, have someone talk to him about National Security and put the word out that he is not to be touched. But, if possible it might be wise to do this in someway that it doesn't ruin whatever pr potential CMA has for the good of the cause.

"Posey has been doing the best he can to either sit on Flacko or deal him out, but that is not possible because right now Flacko knows too much and it would do no one any good if he went to the press. He has got to be finessed out."

Instead of being the NSC's man in Central America, I had become a threat to what Oliver North and CIA Director William Casey were trying to do. My independence and initiative were frightening to them. I had gone from supporter of their cause to a threat to it.

North told the State Department to get rid of me, to get me out of Honduras and away from the Indians, and to do it immediately.

Miami

I left Washington and flew to Miami. I wanted to make a dash for Honduras but needed to purchase extra equipment for our continued survival. I bought another generator and chain saw. I picked up various small items that could not be purchased in Honduras and booked the first plane out.

I had not received any word about the success or failure of the Sin Sin Bridge raid and was getting quite worried. The National Security Council and the White House had knowledge of our activities now through Denton's office, but I dismissed the possibility of trouble and pressed on.

When I checked in at MISURA headquarters in Tegus, I found a rather frantic Archibald Theofilo. He told me that I must return to the Miskitia immediately because there was trouble in the camp. I couldn't imagine what trouble he was talking about, but left as quickly as I could.

The plane was met by Alejo as soon as it touched down in the Rus Rus. He rushed up to my door and virtually yanked me out of my seat.

"The mission was a complete failure," he said. "Now the Americans are threatening to kill Indians."

We hurried to TEA base. The moment I arrived I could tell something was very wrong. Most of the Americans were standing in fixed defensive positions, heavily armed and wearing bulletproof vests. Tirador rushed up to me when I got out of the truck. His eyes were glazed from lack of sleep and fear. He had lost weight and appeared nervous.

"What's going on here?" I asked him.

"Get out! Get out! Get the fuck out!" Tirador screamed at Alejo.

Alejo retreated a safe distance and Tirador launched into a long, rambling story of what had happened in my absence.

The bridge raid had indeed been a disaster. The food had run out early and at one point Mycroft had nearly shot an Indian over some food. The men were shooting deer with M-79 grenade launchers and lighting fires at night. They threw away ammunition. They buried the C-4 on the trail. They lagged far behind the Indians, who walked them into the ground.

He said that once they reached the Sin Sin Bridge they found three times as many troops as Indian intelligence told them were present.

"Did anyone actually approach the bridge?" I asked Tirador.

"No," he said. "We had to stay back because there was no tree cover. We sent out a patrol and they came back and said it was too fortified to attack."

Tirador said he felt the Indians had sold them out and led them into a trap.

No one would listen to his orders, he claimed, so he had Pulmon, Papillon and Pedrico locked up at Sym Sym for insubordination and treason.

Tirador was babbling. He had evidently lost control in Nicaragua. He had assumed command but was unable to command. Mentally, he couldn't handle leadership. He had always been a follower and would always be that. When he was put in a leadership position, he fell apart.

He had even gone to the local Honduran military commander and informed him of our presence. The night before, a contingent of Honduran soldiers came to TEA base and told the Americans they had to leave.

Things were falling apart in a hurry. All my plans for the MISURA were evaporating. The NSC knew we were here. The Honduran military knew we were here. It was only a matter of time before we had to make a decision on how to handle the outside pressures that would be brought to bear on us.

But the first thing I had to do was some damage control.

I spent the rest of the day getting the Americans calmed down and disarmed. Our relationship with the Indians had suffered because of the conduct of the Americans on the mission, but I was not sure how much. I planned to find out the next day. I never got a chance to do it.

The next morning, March 13, 1985, Major Morales from the G-2 office in Tegucigalpla walked into camp backed by two companies of Pumas. He asked to speak to me privately and we walked to one of the makeshift classrooms that was covered with a parachute.

"You're leaving," he told me. He was polite, but forceful.

"What do you mean we're leaving?" I said. "Who ordered this?"

"This is not the will of the Honduran military. We think much of what you have done is for the better. It has reduced our problems with the Indians. They seem to have a sense of order about them. But you have to remember who's leash we're on. These orders come from your State Department. We have been ordered to get you out one way or another. You can go quietly. But if you resist, you are surrounded."

He and his troops meant business. We were leaving. It didn't matter much to them if we were breathing or not when we got on the plane.

He gave us a day to get our gear together.

The Assembly of Chiefs was planned for March 21. I had designed a flag for the new Indian nation that I planned to unveil at the meeting in which I would be firmly placed at the head of the confederation of tribes. That would put thousands of soldiers at my disposal, and with the proper training they would be able to wreak havoc in Zelaya Province if we did not first sign a peace treaty with the Sandinistas.

The Assembly of Chiefs was shaping up to be a major foreign policy disaster for the Reagan administration and a major coup for me. But it appeared I would never get to that meeting.

The general staff and Council of Elders were unusually somber the night before we were to leave the Miskitia.

"Stay with us," the elders pleaded.

They said they would defy the Honduran military. They said they would take us into Nicaragua and set us up at a base they had been building near Awasbila. They said they would protect us at the risk of their own lives.

My first reaction was to do it, to plunge deeper into the jungle where neither the State Department nor the Hondurans could touch us.

Had I taken the bit in my teeth and refused to leave Honduras, I could have taken one-third of Nicaragua out of the war by having the Indians declare autonomy and sign a peace treaty with the Sandinistas, something both sides were willing to do it at that point.

But I knew my continued presence among the Indians would only bring them more misery. If I stayed, we would be totally isolated from both sides. What little assistance we were getting through Honduras would be cut off.

I decided to leave, thinking perhaps I could return after the political situation cooled down. The Indians knew that wouldn't happen, though.

The next morning there was an Israeli cargo plane waiting for us at the airstrip. As we loaded the plane for the flight back to Tegucigalpa under the watchful eyes of the Honduran military, the Indians came to say their goodbyes and plead with me one last time. Grown Indian men who rarely showed emotion were standing there crying like babies because we were leaving.

"Come back," they begged me. "Please come back. We'll give you land. We'll give you a house. We'll give you a wife."

It was a sad moment for me. The Indians thought a lot of me. They wanted me to stay, along with Pedrico, Pulmon and Papillon. They didn't care about the others. Raoul was furious over the conduct of the other Americans and asked me: "Is this all your country has to offer us?"

I couldn't apologize enough for the actions of the men I had thrust upon them, but the damage had been done.

By this time, the Americans had virtually mutinied against me. Ramos informed me that Tirador was now in charge and that the group would no longer take orders from me. That was fine with me. That absolved me of any responsibility for this band of misfit lunatics.

I had risked all on this mission and these men who turned out to be losers. I spent thousands of dollars in an attempt to get Americans involved in the war where they could make a difference. In a sense, the blame was as much mine as theirs because I ignored signs that told me they were incapable of doing anything in a professional manner. I so desperately wanted this to succeed, I convinced myself of the lie that they could handle it.

When we arrived in Tegucigalpa the plane taxied over to the military side of the airport. As we were opening the doors to get out, a Honduran soldier with a sub-machine gun walked up, pointed it in the door and made it very clear that we were to stay in the airplane.

That was about 11 a.m. We sat there in the airplane on the tarmac until nearly 8 p.m. Caballo had a bad case of dysentery but there were no toilets on the plane and the Hondurans wouldn't let him out. He relieved himself in the cockpit. It was a bad scene.

About 8 p.m. two white vans with smoked glass windows showed up. They had armed guards inside. We were loaded in the vans and taken to the U.S. Embassy. They told us we were being tossed out of the country and took our passports hostage. Stamped in the front of my passport was a large "VOID." Underneath it were the words: "This passport is only valid for return travel to the United States on or before Mar(ch) 18, 1985." It was signed by Lincoln V. Benedicto, consul general.

We spent the night in a cheap hotel downtown, still under guard. I told the Americans not to bring any weapons or ammunition back into the U.S. because I was sure we would be checked closely. They ignored me and spent the night stuffing rifles, ammunition and C-4 plastic explosives into their seabags.

I separated all my military gear from the civilian gear and later that night called the FDN. I spoke to Oscar Montez and told him I had some things I wanted him to keep: my pistol, the SSG sniper rifle, all my uniforms and some expensive handheld radios. We sneaked out through the hotel's side door and took the gear to Oscar's office.

The next morning the vans took us to the airport. Grace came to see me off. We talked quietly while the Rambo wannabes held a press conference. They had called some local media, told them they were being thrown out of the country and posed for pictures while telling stories of battles that never happened. They were myth makers, story tellers and hypocritical patriots to the every end.

The press conference over, the embassy guards walked us through Customs and put us on a plane to Miami.

The Honduran adventure was over.

On the flight to Miami I sat alone, pondering my future. I felt as if I had let down the Indians. In my zeal to help them, I had brought them nothing but more misery. They had believed Americans were a people of great kindness and many skills. I left them with the impression that we were rude, obnoxious, cared only about ourselves and were unable to perform even the most simple of tasks without assistance.

The Miskitia had become home to me and I felt as though something died in me that day I left. The inner peace I found among the Indians could never be replaced.

I also felt I had been sold out by my own country. I had tried to do what Reagan and his conservative minions wanted us to do: overthrow the Sandinistas. But now I was being punished for doing just that. I no longer had any connection with the beliefs with which I had lived my entire life.

I was a man without a country.

15

Down and Out on Bourbon Street

I thought I would die in the Miskitia. In a lot of ways I looked forward to it. For me, dying there would have been the most peaceful way to go in a violent setting.

There was no money in what I did there, no fame. I had just disappeared into the jungle with people who accepted me for what I was and among whom I felt totally at home.

I felt I had grabbed the only brass ring that would ever come along in my life. Now, not only was my own government going to take that ring from me, they were going to beat me over the head with it.

I knew I had run afoul of the U.S. government, but wasn't sure to what extent until we arrived in Miami. I was walking through the airport when two men came out of the crowd and started walking beside me. They wore suits, the nondescript bureaucratic FBI or CIA type. Their faces said they worked for the government.

They walked next to me for a few minutes before one of them spoke.

"We just want to advise you to keep your mouth shut and keep a low profile," he said.

Then they were gone, peeling off like planes out of a formation. Anyone watching from a distance never would have known that a conversation had taken place. But from that moment on I knew I was marked by my own government.

I returned to the States bitter, disillusioned and angry that my own government had betrayed me and taken from me the one thing I had ever really cared about, the only thing I had ever believed in.

I didn't care about the war anymore. I didn't care about the government I once believed in. I didn't care about myself. I didn't care about anything. My spirit had died.

From the time we left the Miskitia until we arrived in Miami we were under guard, either by the Hondurans or by U.S. embassy personnel. But when we got to Miami the Customs people thought we were military and didn't check one of our bags. Some of the deported Americans against my advice brought back weapons, explosives and other illegal equipment. There's no telling what happened to it because, except for Tirador, my association with them ended at the airport. I never saw them again. The adventure, the war, was over for us.

A small contingent of press was waiting for us at the airport because of the interviews given in Tegus by Adair and Tirador. Adair again played the role of the aggrieved freedom fighter, trying to convince the reporters that a grave injustice had been done to brave Americans freedom fighters by kicking them out of the war.

I was amazed by the arrogance of my fellow deportees. Most acted as if they had just arrived from a monumental victory in Nicaragua. The more they talked, the greater their exploits became. The truth about their total collapse on the Sin Sin Bridge raid would be lost in a flurry of self-congratulation and self-adulation over their Central American service.

I again avoided the cameras, sneering at Adair as he made a fool out of himself, then turning away, disgusted by the senselessness of a war where this could be allowed to happen.

Joe Coutin met me at the airport and offered to take me into Miami along with a few stragglers from the group. I declined and went to a nearby Sheraton hotel. I wanted to be alone. I needed a bath, a shave and a decent meal. I also needed to sort out in my head the events of the past 72 hours and try to find some direction. I needed to get away from Miami and everything it represented.

I was desperate to get back to the Miskitia, alone this time, and thought Maco Stewart might help. I called him and he encouraged me to come to Houston to talk. I had no idea what I would do if Maco failed to come through for me.

Houston and Maco proved to be dead ends. He was no longer interested in pouring good money after bad in the Miskitia. His interest in the war had waned. I tried to talk him into hiring me for security work, but had no luck. Maco was gracious enough to pick up my expenses in Houston and gave me a few days work repossessing a pickup truck from Lanny "Doc Zorro" Duyck.

Over the years, Zorro had convinced Maco that the CIA was targeting him because of his wealth and involvement with the Contras. Zorro was getting $5,000 a month to "sweep" Maco's offices for nonexistent listening devices. Zorro played on Maco's paranoia until Maco got tired of him and his wild schemes and stopped paying.

The two were also arguing about the $30,000 Maco had given the FDN for Pegaso. Maco accused Zorro of swindling some of that money that actually went to Mario Calero. I never saw any supplies or equipment purchased by the illusive $30,000. The money was talked about frequently and I had seen Adolfo transferring $25,000 of it to Mario, but no one seemed to know what happened to the money. The intended recipient, Pegaso, never saw a dime.

Zorro had moved to Dallas and set up a small fencing company. I talked to him a few times trying to convince him to give up the truck. He said he needed it for his work and he was suspicious of me. He thought I had been sent by Maco to whack him because of their falling out. He was also bitter about CMA, claiming the organization had sold him out.

I finally had to hire two private detectives in Dallas to repossess the truck, since I wasn't licensed to do it, and got it back to Houston. Maco said he didn't have any other work for me but said I could use the truck and he would pay my expenses as long as I stayed in the Houston area. But living in a Houston hotel with nothing to do was little better than living in an expensive jail cell.

I was trying to deal with my depression over the events in the Miskitia and searching for a way to get back there.

I called Grace and asked her to join me in Houston. I was lonely and feared for her safety now that I could no longer get back to Honduras. She had provided help and information and by doing so placed herself and her family at risk. She took two weeks of vacation and flew to Houston. Her upbeat spirit kept me going and I felt there might be life after the Contras. I even began thinking about marriage again, if I could find steady employment.

I wasn't going to find it in Houston, though. Jobs were scarce and my skills were limited. I needed a city where I could live in anonymity and try to work my way back into society, although by then I felt like a total outcast. Grace sensed my despair and disillusionment and said she would stay with me until I righted myself.

I didn't want to return to Gulf Shores or Mobile because of all the bridges I had burned there with family and friends. New Orleans, even though it remained the hub of Contra resupply, seemed an ideal place to get lost while I dealt with emotions that were pulling me in a dozen different directions

The Contra war was beginning to bite almost everyone connected with CMA or Tom Posey. The group's name had been changed to Civilian Materiel Assistance to eliminate the military connections and Posey had come down on the side of the hard-core players. But while he was doing that, he was also passing information about the group and its members to anyone who claimed to have a government connection. He was a snitch for the FBI, the DIA and the CIA. Anyone who dealt with Posey concerning the Contras or CMA eventually had his named passed on to one of those agencies by the produce dealer who desperately wanted to be a spook.

Posey wasn't the only CMA snitch. Paul "Pablo" Johnson was the eyes and ears for Frank Camper, head of Recondo, who was a long-time CIA and DIA informant. Camper even tried to take credit for Pegaso.[1]

And Claude "Frenchy" Chaffard was passing information to his Boston contact, James Keyes, who passed it to Ollie North and the CIA. Just who was informing on whom will never be totally known, but a lot of people were doing a lot of talking and I figured that at least half the CMA volunteers were snitching on the other half.

With all the snitching going on, it's no wonder we didn't get much done.

I was supposed to be snitching for Donald Fortier and the NSC, but I had not heard from him or anyone connected with him in months. The only clues that they were still in contact were the envelopes filled with cash.

Posey's efforts to circumvent me and get CMA involved in Costa Rica through John Hull had ended disastrously. The five-man team he had sent south was arrested on April 24, 1985, by Costa Rican officials and charged with Neutrality Act violations. The only two I knew were Robert "Pantera" Thompson, the former Florida Highway Patrol officer, and Chaffard. The others were Peter Glibbery, a British mercenary; John Davies, a former member of the elite British Special Air Service (SAS) unit, now working as a mercenary; and Steven Carr, a young American adventurer who wanted to try his hand in the war.

I was extremely curious how Posey came up with such a diverse team when he claimed he was unable to get qualified people for Pegaso and sent me nothing but crap. The five were languishing in a Costa Rican jail as summer of 1985 began.

I tried to put CMA, Posey, the war and the Indians behind me as I moved to New Orleans. I decided to live in the French Quarter because

I wouldn't look out of place with the assortment of fruits and nuts there. I found a room at a small apartment complex called the Beauregard House. The complex was being renovated at the time and I got a top-floor apartment without air conditioning for half price.

To help pay the rent, I agreed to do maintenance around the complex and assist the contractors with the renovations. Within a few weeks, I was given the job as manager, paid a small salary and given a free apartment.

The job couldn't have come at a better time because I was broke. I threw myself into the job of maintaining and promoting the complex over the summer, as much to keep busy as to keep my mind off the events that had transpired in Honduras.

Grace had joined me in New Orleans and got a temporary job as a cashier. We had a place to live, steady jobs and money coming in and seemed well on the way to becoming useful members of society.

But something gnawed at me throughout that summer. There was a lingering bitterness and anger over what had happened to me and the Indians in the Miskitia. And there was an overwhelming sense of guilt and depression that I had let the Indians down.

My mind had become a blank slate, wiped clean by the experiences down south. I had no focus to my life or my political ideologies. Once a confirmed conservative, I now stood with neither side. I despised my own government for what it was doing to the Indians and how it had allowed the war to become corrupted by corrupt people. I also found no solace in the whining of the Sandinista supporters.

I was questioning everything about myself, my beliefs and my country. I tried to figure out who I was and what I believed in. It was like sinking into a black hole.

My politics had been wrapped up in my emotions when I first went to Central America. But with the Indians, it wasn't a matter of politics. With them I discovered feeling without politics.

Once I left the Indians, the myth that was Colonel Flaco died. But I could not go back to being Jack Terrell again, back to being what I was and who I was before I went to Central America because I had been changed by the experience.

I didn't understand what was happening to me, but thought it might help if I put it down on paper. I wanted to look at it, or at least get it out of my head. I bought an old Royal manual typewriter and began writing in minute detail about what had happened to me over the past year. For days on end I sat in the loft of my apartment on Bourbon Street pounding out page after page of experiences with the FDN and the Indians.

That typewriter became my rope to reality. That typewriter held me on the earth for a month and kept me from blowing my brains out. I wasn't writing a book. But I felt it was necessary to get my feelings out so I could be rid of them. I felt that once I had expunged my soul of this anguish I was feeling, I could go on with whatever life had in store for me.

The first volume was 450 pages. The second brought the total to more than 1,000 pages and still I wasn't finished. Neither was I satisfied or consoled. Later, in a fit of depression, I burned the second volume.

On into August the depression continued and the feelings of guilt worsened. I kept in contact with the Indians and with members of the FDN and CMA, trying in some way to get back into the game. But there were no opportunities for someone who had been targeted by the government.

I was angry, but there was no focus for my anger. I still didn't know who had wronged me. I also didn't know why. The confusion over where to strike or who to strike made me dangerous. I was ready to be a terrorist. I didn't care who I hit or who I hurt.

I had not felt this kind of hatred since a run-in years earlier with the bureaucracy of the Alabama prison system. After my release from prison I was intent on breaking barriers and erasing the stigma of being a convicted felon. I went to work for the Department of Corrections as a dog warden and in 1973 was the first ex-felon in the state's history chosen to attend the Federal Law Enforcement Academy at Bay Minette, Alabama.

I graduated first in my class and came back to show my boss, Commissioner of Corrections L.B. Sullivan, my diploma. I had never been prouder of myself and thought I had finally cleared the last barrier to becoming a productive part of society, untainted by the conviction for which I had won a pardon two years earlier.

But no sooner did I step in Sullivan's office than he fixed me with unsympathetic stare and said: "Resign or be fired."

Sullivan was a political antagonist of John C. Watkins, the warden at Alabama's Draper Correctional Center who had befriended me years earlier. I was caught in the middle of their feud and became a victim of the prison bureaucracy and its political infighting.

If I had had a gun that day, I would have killed everyone in the room, including myself. The pride I felt in my accomplishments was shattered with those four unfeeling words from Sullivan. I had convinced myself

I had become a free man despite my prison record and had worked my way back into society. In an instant, Sullivan devastated me.

I never felt hatred like that again until I was kicked out of Honduras and prevented from helping the Indians. The system had wronged me again. Only this time I didn't know where to direct the anger I felt. All I knew was that in some fashion the U.S. government was responsible.

Press reports hinting of a White House-orchestrated private aid network to assist the Contras had been appearing since June 1985. But it was not until August that names were attached to the scheme.

The first name belonged to Marine Lieutenant Colonel Oliver North. On August 8, 1985, the *New York Times* published a front-page article in which it was revealed that a top NSC staffer was responsible for the scheme to aid the Contras. Although the staffer was not named, it was widely known in Washington that the staffer was North.[2]

The following day I was sitting in my apartment at the Beauregard House when the telephone rang.

"It is Friday, August 9, 1985. Is this Jack Reynolds Terrell?" a voice asked.

I was a bit taken aback. The call was eerily reminiscent of the one I had received 10 months earlier from Donald Fortier of the National Security Council, the call that had started me on this strange odyssey.

"I can tell you who I am by referring to the fact that I worked with Don," the caller continued.

"Who is this?" I asked.

"Just call me Mr. Smith."

"What do you want?"

"How would you like to get some revenge?"

It was as if somebody threw a rope into the pits of hell and yanked me out.

That call played right into a mind that was ready to explode on someone, if not myself. "Mr. Smith" was giving me an opportunity to get some direction and focus in my life again. He was rescuing me from myself by giving me the opportunity to get back at whoever had stopped me from doing what I thought my country wanted me to do. I was determined to inflict as much pain as had been inflicted on me. It was payback time.

I was leery of Mr. Smith at first, but was able to glean enough information from him to assure myself that he probably had worked with Donald Fortier in some capacity. He certainly knew what I had been doing. Besides, it didn't really matter to me if he wasn't who he said he was. I would have worked for the devil just for a chance to get back at those who I felt had wronged me.

Mr. Smith never appealed to my patriotism, as had Meg Hunt from Jeremiah Denton's office. He never offered me an ideological excuse for what I would be doing. Perhaps he knew that appeals to whatever patriotism I retained would have been useless. I was beyond politics. All he offered was simple revenge and I jumped at the chance. It was as if a leash had been taken off a mad dog.

In that one short telephone call I became a dangerous person, ready to strike in any direction because of what I felt was an injustice done to me and the Indians. My agenda became one of treachery. They were wrong in using the system to back thugs and I wanted to show them they were wrong.

The only time I felt I belonged anywhere was in the Miskitia. In those few brief weeks with the Indians I had been given a glimpse of something I thought was right. It was a gift from the Indians, but it had been taken away from me by my own government because what I was doing didn't fit the agenda of those running foreign policy.

Over the next few months I received numerous phone calls from Mr. Smith. He often was a different person, but he was always "Mr. Smith."

Sometimes Mr. Smith was casual and chatty. Sometimes he was all business. Sometimes he had a faint Southern accent. Other times he came from the Midwest or the Northeast.

Whichever Mr. Smith called knew of my rage and my willingness to get back at the system. But Mr. Smith would not allow me to strike out blindly. There had to be a focus to what I did. There had to be targets, not necessarily specific individuals, but institutions within the government that were responsible for the mess in Central America.

During these conversations we plotted strategy on how I could best use the information I had obtained during my time with the FDN, CMA and the Indians, in addition to the information I would be fed by Mr. Smith.

The more I learned about how the system operated to create policy and problems in Central America, the angrier and more antagonistic I became.

Of course, I did not know the forces at work against me at the time. I didn't know that North, Owen, John Hull and others intent on preserving their private enterprise were trying to kill Colonel Flaco, if not physically, then surely figuratively through character assassination.

In an April 1, 1985, memo from Owen to North, updated on April 9, my name was again brought up as a potential source of trouble to the enterprise and that something should be done about me.

"Flako [sic] is back in business," Owen wrote. "He has established himself in New Orleans and is working on some new scams. He is staying at the Providence Hotel. It is time someone paid him a visit and told him to go back to the hole he comes from."[3]

In time, North became the focal point of my anger and resentment toward the government. North was the wrong that had been done to me, the man who had assaulted my self-worth and dignity, the man who had taken from me the one thing I wanted most in life — to be left alone with the Indians.

Mr. Smith often talked not so much about North and the NSC as he did about the CIA. He frequently bemoaned the fact that in recent years established procedures at the Agency were being bypassed and anyone who disagreed with the policies of CIA Director William Casey often found himself stationed in some God-forsaken place such as the north African country of Chad.

All the proper protocol within the Agency had been eliminated under Casey's reign of terror, and there was a sense of instability and fear among the veterans, Mr. Smith complained. The Agency had become compartmentalized and the chain of command was being ignored more and more frequently.

More worrisome to some of those veterans was that things were being done without appropriate authorization, things that were outside the scope of what the Agency could and should be doing.

The breaking point came when Casey authorized the bombing of a hotel in Beirut, Lebanon, on March 8, 1985, in an effort to kill Hezbollah leader Mohammed Hussein Fadlallah. The car bomb missed the mullah, but killed 82 innocent people.[4]

That got the attention of a lot of folks in the Agency. Here they were, accusing terrorists like the Irish Republican Army of torching folks, and yet the director of Central Intelligence was authorizing a bombing of this magnitude that failed to hit the intended target.

People were saying something was wrong with the way the Agency was being run. They decided the Agency was out of control. Something had to be done to bring it and the NSC, which essentially was being run by the CIA, back into line.

The people with whom I was dealing let me know there was a group of people, some apparently within the CIA and others within the NSC, who decided to right the wrongs they felt were being done in the name of democracy. Because I was dealing with several different people on the telephone who claimed to be Mr. Smith, I knew this operation was something more than one rogue agent. This was an organization, however loosely knit, that decided to take matters into its own hands and work outside normal channels.

I was chosen to do the dirty work and take the risks for two reasons: I had done what Fortier asked me to do without complaining; and I was expendable, a disposable patriot.

When I asked Mr. Smith one day what I should call this group, he thought for a moment and replied: "Call it Internal Command and Control, InComCon."

It was my belief that InComCon was not made up of super-patriots. It probably consisted of a group of people intent on preserving their jobs and pensions and shifting the focus of the Contra fiasco away from them and onto North and Casey.

But they provided me an outlet for my anger and desire for revenge. They wanted to use me as much as I wanted to use them. I was an opportunist looking for a means to get back at the government, and InComCon, or whatever its name was, provided that means.

I didn't care if they had a problem with the CIA. My only concern was that they were providing the means with which I could hit back at someone. My feud was personal, not political. No one ever understood that except me. I would use either the right or the left to achieve my goals.

In the end, both sides used me.

InComCon wanted me to go to Washington, where my information would have a better audience. I was lost in New Orleans, a voice shouting in the wilderness. But in order to have some credibility and the credentials that would ensure I was listened to in Washington, it was decided that I should first attract the attention of federal law enforcement agencies in New Orleans.

Throughout the fall of 1985, Mr. Smith and I worked out plans to attract the media and federal agents. I had to be believable, yet retain this sense of mystery and the icy persona of Colonel Flaco that would generate interest and fear among those with whom I was dealing.

Mr. Smith was of little help to me in learning to deal with the media. He was totally out of his league. He didn't know how they operated, didn't know what they wanted, didn't know how to use the information at our disposal. It was left to me to find a way to work with some of the Washington-based public policy groups that might have some interest in my information. That would provide me with a base of support and credibility.

Despite my break with CMA and FDN, I maintained some contacts with past associates.

Bruce Jones called me from his new home in Arizona and suggested I get in touch with John Hull about a job as a security guard on his ranch. I knew that was a one-way ticket to a shallow grave and passed on it.

Hull was having credibility problems with his CIA contacts at the U.S. Embassy in Costa Rica because of prison interviews given by Glibbery and Carr the previous July that detailed Hull's involvement with gun running and the NSC. Hull was on the defensive, but his CIA contacts were keeping him operational and free from Costa Rican investigators because his ranch was crucial to the new Contra resupply effort beginning in earnest at Ilopango military air base in El Salvador.

I was also in touch with Tom Posey and Mario Calero and an assortment of journalists. A lot of people were finding me because I wasn't really in hiding. The only people who couldn't find me was the FBI.

Cables had been sent from the Miami FBI office seeking information about Colonel Flaco for an investigation that was taking place there concerning Jesus Garcia, the prison guard who had befriended Tom Posey, on a charge of illegally possessing a machine gun.

I was living on Bourbon Street with a listed telephone number but still I was invisible to the FBI.

Not until I picked up the telephone in January 1986, called the FBI office in New Orleans and asked to talk to someone about Central America did the Bureau find me.

They wouldn't come to me, so InComCon and I agreed to go to them with my information.

Charlie Calhoon, an agent with counter-intelligence, and his partner came to my apartment to talk to me shortly after that call. They were nervous and unsure of me or my motives. They gave me the impression they thought I was just another right-wing nut until I showed them information on the private aid network. When they returned to their office they learned a nationwide alert had been issued for me and soon were back at my apartment for more information.

Charlie began sending cables to FBI headquarters in Washington about our conversations. Copies of those cables and many documents I gave him were later forwarded to the CIA. The result was that while the FBI had its hooks into me, I now had a direct pipeline for getting information to InComCon. The information went from me to the FBI in

New Orleans to the FBI in Washington and then to the CIA, where Mr. Smith and InComCon had access to it.

Through this channel, InComCon was able to fine-tune our strategy based on what I already knew about the extra-governmental operations in Central America.

Charlie Calhoon was in way over his head with me. He had no idea what he was getting involved in when he agreed to talk to me. He and his partner were virgins on the issue and didn't realize the significance of the information I was giving them. After a while, they began to lose interest.

To keep them interested, I concocted a story that I had become so disenchanted with the whole mess I planned to defect to Nicaragua. I told them I wanted to live in Managua and hoped eventually to go to Cuba to become a terrorist.

The plan was totally bogus, but it ensured interest would remain high and the cables to Washington would continue to flow uninterrupted.

The bogus defection plan was so involved I arranged a meeting with a representative of the Sandinista government through a journalist. In Nashville I met with Manuel Cordero, an official at the Nicaraguan embassy in Washington, who was giving a speech at Vanderbilt. We talked briefly about what the Nicaraguans would do if I came down, but Cordero was noncommittal and I had no real intention of defecting.

I also talked with DEA agents about the drug labs in Nicaragua. They were so interested that a DEA official was dispatched from Washington with 12 questions for me. Ten questions were drug related and two were military related. I never answered the questions or met the official because I told my DEA contact, Nicklous T. Cooper, I would not become a confidential informant.

I had seen enough snitches in prison and far too many in Central America and knew I didn't want to be one of them.

My credibility was much in question in late 1985 and early 1986 because I was being given information by Mr. Smith and InComCon that was valuable only in a broader context of the Contra war and Washington's political intrigues to which I was not privy. In many instances, my information had little impact because it was ahead of its time. No formal investigation was going on and the media were just beginning to scratch the surface of this monumental scandal.

I began passing on information to a journalist I met while trying to contact a CBS reporter, Ike Pappas. Instead of sending Pappas to do the story, CBS sent researcher Carroll Dogherty. Dogherty and I met at the

Marriott Hotel in New Orleans one day in the fall of 1985 and I gave him some photos and documents I had relating to the Contras in Honduras. Dogherty had just returned to work after cancer surgery and was still in pain. My strange tale did nothing to ease his discomfort. He asked to make copies of the documents, but instead of copying all of them, he took selected portions of my field notes and passed them on to two journalists in Costa Rica, Martha Honey and Tony Avirgan.

This husband-wife team was continuing an investigation of the May 30, 1984, assassination attempt on Eden Pastora in the village of La Penca. Avirgan was one of the journalists badly wounded by the explosion and Honey was intent on tracking down the people responsible for wounding her man.

Honey and Avirgan printed a portion of my notes in the first Spanish-language version of what would become known generically as the "La Penca Report."[5]

The excerpts of my notes used in the report related to the December 1984 meeting in Miami in which the assassination of Eden Pastora was discussed.

"The termination of Zero [Pastora] discussed with Adolpho [sic], Aristias, John Hull, Donald Lacy and a man not identified but told [he is with] 'Company' [during] meeting at A.C. house [in] Miami," I wrote. "Many people involved. Some look like Cubans, some Nicaraguans, some Argentinean. A.C. very upset with statements made by Pastore [sic]. Says he is Sandinista. Must die. Big problem.

"Asks me to put it together and not tell them how it will be done, just do it. Will have complete cooperation of all Costa Rican officials. Have several safe houses in C.R. under control of John Hull and Bruce Jones. Seems Rob Owens [sic] in on most of this. His role not clear. Am told he is private consultant and liaison man for U.S. [Company].

"Must make hit outside U.S. Protection being given in country by FBI and others for Zero. Must appear that Sandinistas did it. Discussion on capturing Zero and having men dress in captured uniforms. I am told this must be very visible hit and people must believe the Sandinistas did it. Am told to let Hull know when ready to move. . . A.C. open to anything. He desperately wants and needs southern front."[6]

Release of that information in Costa Rica, where John Hull and Rob Owen could get their hands on it, virtually signed my death warrant with the administration. I had exposed its disinformation and assassination campaigns and would not be allowed to forget it.

I was so incensed by the unauthorized use of my notes in the La Penca Report that I called Martha Honey and demanded to know why she had placed me at risk. She made no apologies about using my notes, but seemed surprised and pleased to hear from me.

"We've been searching everywhere for you," she said, "especially after reading your notes."

The legend of Colonel Flaco had drifted into Costa Rica, even though I had never been there, and Honey and Avirgan saw me as a key to their investigation. We talked frequently over the next few months and in February 1986, they paid my way to Costa Rica to meet with them.

Despite the obvious danger to me from Hull, Owen and their Cuban cohorts in Costa Rica, I flew to San Jose on February 25, 1986 and spent three days with Honey and Avirgan going over my papers and notes.

Their focus was on La Penca: who was involved, who was responsible and how I was involved. I wasn't much help to them because all I knew of it was what I had been told at the meeting at Adolfo Calero's house in December 1984.

While in Costa Rica I also contacted mercenaries arrested the previous April on John Hull's ranch to see if they could shed light on how Hull and Posey had gotten things screwed up so badly.

Honey and Avirgan obtained a fake press pass and letter of introduction for me from UPI Television Network in London. The letter said I was on assignment for the network in Central America for February and March. It was signed by "James P. Jones, Assignment Editor," a figment of the imagination of Avirgan and Honey (Appendix 4).

La Reforma Prison in San Jose was a medieval place, hot, smelly and full of noise and flies. I met Peter Glibbery, one of the two Brits, and Steve Carr, the American adventurer, in a small visitors' room that was devoid of any decorations or furniture except a small table and the chairs on which we sat.

Carr and Glibbery had been in prison for more than 10 months and it was obvious they were suffering from bad food, terrible living conditions and a lack of outside support. In Costa Rica it helped to have a benefactor in the country who ensured that you received food, clothing and toilet articles on a regular basis. Glibbery and Carr and, to my knowledge, the other three, had been abandoned by their sponsors in the States — Tom Posey and Frank Camper — and by John Hull in Costa Rica.

Glibbery had never heard of Colonel Flaco, but Carr knew the name, if not the face. Both men were wary of me at first because they feared a possible setup. They knew I had worked with CMA and, by extension, the FDN, the CIA and John Hull. They thought I was a Hull informant sent to test them.

But after talking with them for a while I was able to break down their defenses. They were alone, miserable and without hope of seeing freedom anytime soon. They had been lured into what seemed to be a great adventure, only to be lied to and abandoned after being arrested.

Glibbery explained how the five-man team had come to Costa Rica on promises Hull never kept. The team wasn't permitted to stay anywhere near Hull's elegant home. Their mission was ill-defined and they spent all of their time fighting boredom, none of it fighting the Sandinistas.

According to Glibbery, strange events occurred regularly on Hull's ranch.

A number of Americans of some apparent importance arrived at various intervals, met with Hull for a while, then departed. One of them, according to Glibbery, was Andy Messing, a high-profile Contra supporter in Washington and director of the National Defense Council. But Messing's business card indicated he was something else. "Andy Messing, Arms Dealer" was on the card he gave Glibbery.

Carr said that on March 6 the previous year, he and Robert "Pantera" Thompson were flown from the Fort Lauderdale-Hollywood airport in south Florida aboard a CV-440 cargo plane owned by Florida Aircraft Leasing Corp. and leased by American Flyers, a secretive air cargo company in south Florida.

American Flyers was owned by Daniel Vasquez III, who had been convicted of illegally running guns to Cuba in the 1950s and again in the 1960s.[7] The air cargo manifest for the trip listed "50 cartons medical supplies" and "30 cartons clothing." It was, according to the manifest, "a relief shipment to the refugees of San Salvador."[8]

Some relief shipment.

Aboard the plane, according to Carr, were a 14-foot 20mm cannon with 150 rounds, 30 G-3 automatic rifles, a box of M-16 rifles, some 60mm mortars and a .50-caliber machine gun with 250 rounds of ammunition. All of the weapons came from the home of Rene Corvo and Frank Chanes of Ocean Hunter. Carr's claims were later backed up by FBI documents.[9]

According to Carr, the plane flew from Fort Lauderdale to Ilopango in El Salvador, the arms were transferred to an Islander cargo plane belonging to the Salvadoran Air Force and they were then flown to Hull's ranch.

More troubling than the arms shipments were claims by Carr and Glibbery that much of the activity around Hull's ranch involved the transshipment of cocaine to the United States.

Carr said he had personally witnessed cocaine being loaded on aircraft that regularly landed at Hull's ranch. Before they were allowed to take off, the pilots were charged exorbitant fees for landing rights and refueling.

Glibbery said at one point he overheard a call Hull received from someone in Washington expressing concern about the drugs. Washington wanted to "clean up" Hull, according to Glibbery.

Carr and Glibbery confirmed my earlier suspicious about the real reason for the southern front. It was a drug front. The information provided by Carlos Cassell and the offer from Paco Chanes only reinforced what I was hearing from these two. There remained little doubt in my mind that the U.S. government had knowledge about the drug trade being advanced under the protection of its war against the Sandinistas.

John Davies, the other British mercenary, refused to talk to me. But Pantera, the former Florida highway patrolman, was happy to see me because I represented the first semi-friendly face he had seen in a while. He had lost at least 50 pounds since the last time I saw him because of the meager prison food that was being restricted due to Hull's influence.

Pantera was disoriented and talked in riddles most of the time, but he told me enough about the drug trafficking schemes on Hull's ranch to support Glibbery and Carr.

Human mules were humping 10 to 12 kilos of cocaine each from the labs around Bluefields and taking it across the Rio San Juan onto Hull's ranch before being flown to the States.

The drugs were being processed in labs in Nicaragua because at that time the Colombians were having problems getting ether they needed for the final step in processing coca paste into cocaine. They'd ship the paste from Colombia into Nicaragua, where they could get plenty of ether, process the paste into cocaine there, and then take the cocaine out through Costa Rica and Honduras.

Hull's ranch was the most convenient transshipment point. But the drug shipments also provided a good source of funds for the Contras. They supposedly were going to do this only until Congress reestablished funding for the Contras. It was short-term, creative financing in the incredibly lucrative commodity of cocaine.

The five mercenaries knew the ins and outs of the scheme and that knowledge made their lives virtually worthless as long as they stayed in Costa Rica. Glibbery, Carr and Pantera were wide-eyed with fear when I talked to them. Hull had a lot of influence in Costa Rica and could just as easily have them killed as he could ensure they spent many years in prison.

The fact that Carr and Glibbery had given a press conference the previous July talking about the arms shipments, Hull's connections to North and the NSC made their lives absolutely worthless. That press conference helped initiate a FBI investigation into the Contras out of the Miami field office, but that only further complicated other inquiries being made at the time.

According to the three men, Hull was using his influence to have food and mail withheld from them until they retracted their statements to the press. I knew about American prisons, but didn't realize that in Costa Rica the prisoners depended not on the prison system for their well-being, but on family and friends outside.

The five mercenaries had neither family nor friends to help them. They were, it seems, surrounded by enemies who wanted them dead.

Although Posey had sent the men south, he now refused to acknowledge they were alive and threw in his lot with Hull. Posey didn't want to take a chance of getting tossed out of the inner circle of Contra supporters by doing the right thing for these men he had recruited.

I took as many notes as I could, including registration numbers of planes, descriptions and locations of arms, explosives and mines and names of people involved. I promised the men I would do what I could to help them and returned to New Orleans on February 28.

The day I got home I received a telephone call from John Mattes, an assistant federal public defender in Miami.

"I represent Jesus Garcia," Mattes said.

"I know," I replied coldly.

Garcia was the Dade County Correctional officer I met while getting Posey out of jail the previous year. He had been arrested with a machine gun but claimed he was working for the government at the time. He also claimed to have knowledge about CMA's role in an alleged plot to bomb the U.S. Embassy in Costa Rica and kill Ambassador Lewis Tambs, making it appear as if Colombian hit men had done it.

Mattes was trying to dig up information about CMA's role in the Contra war and their connections to the FDN.

I was not very communicative or receptive to Mattes's call. He said he was looking into CMA in an effort to help his client. He said he had been hearing the name Colonel Flaco since he got involved in the case nearly a year earlier but had been unable to track me down until now.

Mattes told me he wanted to meet with me and pass on my name and my information to people in Washington who were interested. Those people were investigators in the office of Senator John Kerry, the Massachusetts Democrat whose staffers had started nibbling around the edges of the Contra mess.

I agreed to meet with Mattes, although I was suspicious of him and his motives.

On March 14, 1986, Mattes came to New Orleans with a whole entourage. He had his own investigator, Ralph Maestri, plus Dick McCall from Senator Kerry's office, and Stephen Kurkjian, a reporter for the *Boston Globe*.

They were nervous as cats and expressed surprise not only that was I still alive, but that I was still talking. I pulled out my 450-page mea culpa, slammed it down on the table and said: "Do you know what you're getting into?"

At that point, they didn't. They were all wide-eyed innocents stepping into something that forever changed their lives. But if they wanted to do it, I was more than willing to help them. At last someone with some power was listening to me.

Mattes was an intense, direct questioner who didn't back down, even from me. Although he didn't know all the details of what was going on around him in regards to the secret war, he had enough street smarts to know he was onto something much bigger than a Cuban named Jesus Garcia toting a machine gun.

We talked in the apartment for a while, then went out and walked around the French Quarter while I regaled them with detail upon detail of what I knew, who did what and when, and who was involved. Like everybody else, they didn't believe me at first. It was a matter of sensory overload. They couldn't absorb all I was telling them.

Ten days later, Bob Parry and Brian Barger of the Associated Press came to New Orleans to talk to me. Barger was the ABC correspondent I met in Washington and who followed me to Honduras, only to see me get thrown out of the country. He went to work for the Associated Press and teamed up with Parry to dig up information about the illegalities of the war down south.

I gave Barger and Parry details of the Central America fiasco from my perspective. I also provided them with copies of documents, photos and other pertinent information they felt might add to the growing story of White House involvement in the private aid network.

As we were sitting there talking, the telephone rang. It was Charlie Calhoon from the FBI. Charlie wanted to know if I would be available that day to talk to Jeffrey Feldman, an assistant U.S. attorney from

Miami who was investigating CMA and the Contras. All of a sudden my world was swimming with Contra/CMA investigators.

"Sure," I said, "I don't have anything else to do. But I'm tied up right now. Call me back in an hour."

He called back in an hour but I told him I was still busy and that I was talking to a couple of congressional staffers. Calhoon seemed surprised.

"Don't talk to anyone from Congress," he said. I thought it rather strange that the FBI would be warning me against communicating with someone from Congress, but I shrugged my shoulders and hung up.

A while later, Calhoon called back and said he was taking Feldman and FBI special agent George Kiszynski to a hotel and that they would be in touch the next day.

On the morning of March 26, 1986, Calhoon came to my apartment, picked me up and drove me down to the federal courthouse, where Feldman and Kiszynski were waiting.

Kiszynski was the FBI agent who had questioned Tom Posey and the so-called film producer Larry Spivey in Miami back on January 8, 1985. And it was from Kiszynski's office that Spivey made a telephone call that day to the White House, apparently to Oliver North.

Feldman and Kiszynski wanted me to run through the whole gory story again. It was the third time in 10 days I had told the story. This time I was questioned for 16 hours. Like everyone else who heard the story, Feldman and Kiszynski were overwhelmed by the amount of information I had and staggered out of the office like drunks, their eyes glazed, their heads spinning.

Feldman returned to Miami, confused and unsure what to do. He met with U.S. attorney Leon Kellner and expressed his concern about the "thousands of allegations" regarding the Contras, CMA, drugs, mercenaries, arms shipments and assassination plots.[10]

Kellner told him to go to Costa Rica to try to sort it out. Feldman found only more problems there.

While meeting with Tambs, Feldman produced a chart showing Oliver North at the head of a resupply pipeline that included Rob Owen and John Hull. Tambs face went white and he called for the CIA station chief in Costa Rica, Joe Fernandez who went by the name Tomas Castillo.[11]

Castillo went ballistic when he saw the chart and told Feldman that Hull was a CIA asset. He said he should be notified before any action was taken against Hull. Then he bragged that it was Oliver North who introduced him to Ronald Reagan the previous week.[12]

Feldman's off-hand remark to Tambs that he was looking at the "big picture" that included not only possible violations of the Neutrality Act but also possible unauthorized use of government funds produced a flurry of activity among the directors of the illegal network.

On April 7, 1986, Owen wrote North a memo providing details of the Feldman-Tambs-Fernandez meeting and of concerns about what the five mercenaries in La Reforma Prison might say.

"Feldman looks to be wanting to build a career on this case," Owen wrote.[13]

Later in the memo he tells North he will not cooperate with the FBI investigation.

"If and when I am contacted by the FBI I will not answer any questions without an attorney present. Even then, I will not answer any questions. It is the only way I can see to stem the tide."

"Perhaps it is time I retire from this line of work and focus on another part of the world and against another group of Godless communists."[14]

Justice Department officials later tried to deny they were aware that Feldman's investigation involved allegations of drug smuggling, assassination plots and gun running. But everyone who even came close to this investigation knew narcotics were among its key ingredients.

If Justice didn't know what was going on, it was the only government agency that didn't.

My information was finally beginning to have some effect. On April 10, Barger and Parry wrote a piece for The Associated Press detailing the FBI inquiry of alleged drug smuggling, gun running and assassinations by the Contras and their U.S. supporters. I was among the sources Barger and Parry referred to in the story.

That same day, Kerry issued a press release saying his staff was investigating CMA and Contra gun-running.

When the Barger-Parry story hit the papers the next day, along with news of Kerry's probe, North and other members of the Reagan administration hit the roof. Not only were they fighting the war down south, now they had to do full-time damage control at home.

But I had returned fire for the first time since getting kicked out of Honduras and it felt good. Now it was time to get fully engaged in my private war against the administration's public policy.

By late March 1986 I was becoming a real nuisance to North. He had gotten me out of Honduras and away from the Indians, but he hadn't gotten rid of me or been able to shut me up. To make his life even more miserable, I began working closely with Senator Kerry's office.

The information I provided became the genesis of the Senate Foreign Relations subcommittee on Narcotics, Terrorism and International Operations headed by Kerry. That subcommittee spent two years investigating drug smuggling and gun-running in Central America and later branched out to include money laundering in Panama — which indirectly resulted in the invasion of Panama by the U.S. military, the capture of Panamanian strongman General Manuel Noriega and the unraveling of the international scandal involving the Bank of Credit and Commerce International.

Kerry's investigators took my information and ran with it. They compiled an initial document called "Genesis of an Investigation" that was based largely on information I gave them. Without me, they would have had a tough time taking their first step. But once they took that step, they were off and running. They knew how to get things shaken up in Washington and they did just that.

Kerry's people feared I might suddenly have an unexplained accident because of my new open-mouth policy. They wanted me to come to Washington where they felt it was safer and get hooked up with an organization to help me disseminate my information. I thought I would wind up at the Washington Office on Latin America because it had an intense interest in Nicaragua. But I didn't care where I went, as long as the information got out. I simply placed my fate in the hands of Kerry and his people and let them lead me where they would.

InComCon at this point was not really sure how to use me, other than to give me information that at times I didn't fully understand. It was not within their purview to either place me or assist me in Washington. They basically blueprinted my strategy but could not control where I waged my campaign of revenge.

I had no idea if my stay in Washington would last a week, a month, a year or longer. It was like walking into a dark alley with strangers. But this was the opening I had been looking for and I wasn't about to turn down the invitation down, no matter what the cost.

Grace sensed I was about to embark on something that was dark and evil. I refused to listen to her. Revenge blinded me. Just as I had thrown aside everything and everyone to get into the war, now I was about to throw aside Grace and everything that was precious to me.

Before leaving for Washington I tried to convince Grace I wasn't worth her time or love. I had neglected her in my quest for personal justice and was about to do so again. She had fallen into the background of my life. I was torn between trying to keep her and deal with the desire for revenge that burned within me and would consume me if I didn't act.

She had felt the neglect when I sat alone for hours in front of the old Royal typewriter, painfully reconstructing my misadventures. She had given up her family, her dignity and her job because of me. If she returned home alone and unmarried, she would be disgraced.

She was dedicated to me as no one had ever been. I could trust her as I trusted no one else. My decision to go to Washington was the end of our relationship, but not our love.

I saw her only once more, when I went to Costa Rica several months later. We met briefly, talked for a while, but I could tell she was sad and disappointed that I had rejected her in favor of my own need for vengeance. Then she was gone.

I later heard rumors she had been killed, execution style, shortly after her return to Honduras because of her relationship with me. I cannot now, nor will I ever, be able to reconcile trading her life for the folly of engaging in what would prove to be a hopeless war against the Washington power elite.

When I first embarked on this odyssey, I was politically naive and idealistic to the point that I actually believed that what I told investigators and the press mattered. Kerry's people had convinced me that what I had to say was important and would receive its proper hearing only in Washington. I told myself I was going to Washington to pull some of the pilings out from under the government's pier.

On April 4, 1986, I flew to Washington accompanied by Ron Rosenblith, Senator Kerry's administrative assistant, to become a high-profile whistleblower. It was a decision that I came to regret within days of my arrival.

16

Shoot The Messenger: Ready on the Right, Ready on the Left, Ready on the Firing Line

The paranoia and suspicion settling over Washington and those probing the Contra mess were evident as soon as Ron Rosenblith and I landed at National Airport on April 4, 1986.

We were met by Dick McCall and Jonathan Winer of Senator John Kerry's office; Scott Armstrong, a former *Washington Post* reporter who now ran an organization called the National Security Archive; and Michael Fonte, a former Catholic priest who was to serve as my bodyguard.

I felt relatively relaxed, but my welcoming committee was edgy and concerned for its safety as well as mine. They thought some mysterious assassin was going to pop out of the crowd and whack me before I got out of the airport, so they hustled me into a waiting car, nervously scanning the crowd for would-be hit men.

I was put into the back seat of an older Buick while McCall drove and Winer rode up front on the passenger side. Armstrong got into a van in front of the Buick while Fonte drove a third car behind us.

We left the airport and turned south towards Alexandria, our car hemmed in by the two other vehicles. We had gone only a few miles when McCall goosed the Buick, passed Armstrong and abruptly wheeled the car back to the north while the other two vehicles continued on south.

I smiled when I realized I was part of a vehicle shell game. The efforts to protect me were well-intentioned, but amateurish. What, or who, they were protecting me from, I could not understand and did not ask. I certainly didn't feel any danger here. After spending so much time in Miami and Honduras, I was used to life-threatening environments.

Washington might have been life-threatening, but they don't kill you with guns and knives there. They do it with innuendo and rumors. They do it by ruining your credibility.

McCall and Winer seemed to relax as we crossed the Maryland state line and Armstrong and Fonte rejoined our caravan. I settled back to enjoy the ride and look at the scenery. Washington was beginning to stir from its usual winter torpor even though it was still quite cold. The trees were beginning to show some green, the cherry blossoms were unfolding in a blizzard of white and there was a sense of renewal and revival in the air.

We drove north for a while before turning east and driving for more than an hour, leaving the main highway and turning onto a narrow, paved road shortly after passing Annapolis. We drove along that road for little more than a mile before turning into a driveway that took us to a large, modern house sitting on the edge of what appeared to be an inlet from the Severn River or the Chesapeake Bay.

Mike Fonte stayed outside the house to serve as a lookout while the owner, a man named Jack Blum, greeted us at the door and ushered us inside.

Blum was a short, squat, smiling Washington attorney with graying hair and horned rimmed glasses. He had a private practice but also served as the counsel for a liberal public policy think tank called the International Center for Development Policy. Blum was also being courted by Senator Kerry's office to serve as the lead counsel on what Kerry hoped would be a formal Senate investigation of the Contras and illegalities by them and their supporters.

Blum led us into the dining room and we took seats around a large table. Blum was still something of a virgin on the issue and he asked me to lead him through my involvement with the Contras. He explained that the group also wanted to see how valid my information was and whether I could stand up to the kind of intense, politically oriented questioning I would be likely to face if I testified before a congressional committee on the subject.

I was extraordinarily defensive with these people. I didn't know who they were or exactly what they wanted from me. I was not eager to get involved with a group that would wring information out of me until I was dry then cast me aside. I wanted to make sure what I had to say would get heard by the right people in the right places.

Blum was the patient counselor, leading me through my story step-by-step, episode by episode, trying to make me feel at ease. But he made it clear he wanted more than I had to offer at that point. I had only a few pieces of the puzzle to show. He wanted the whole puzzle.

Scott Armstrong was not as patient or as understanding as Blum. He played the devil's advocate, dissecting pieces of my story, putting new shades of meaning on them, trying to catch me in lies or half-truths.

With Armstrong and me, it was dislike at first sight. He was fat and sloppy with dirty blonde hair, blue eyes and a chipmunk-like face that belied what appeared to be in internal anger that had nothing to do with me, the Contras or this meeting.

Armstrong acted like a man who was bitter at the world. He had done research for the *Washington Post* on the Tongsun Park scandal but had not been able to wrap up a few loose ends that still frustrated him. He also was a researcher and reporter on the Watergate scandal that brought down Richard Nixon. But Bob Woodward and Carl Bernstein of the *Washington Post* got all the credit and all the glory. They had even had a movie made about them. Armstrong was left to seethe unnoticed in the background.

In the Contra scandal, Armstrong saw his chance for redemption, revenge and the recognition he craved in Washington. And at the moment, I was the soul source of information about what had actually transpired inside the Contras from the fall of 1984 through the spring of 1985. Armstrong saw me as his ticket to Washington fame and fortune, both of which he desperately desired and thought he deserved. His thinly disguised internal bitterness kept oozing to the surface as he questioned me.

Armstrong had a copy of the voluminous notes I had typed out in New Orleans and kept referring to it as he assumed command of the questioning. He was much more hostile and direct than Blum and I became even more defensive.

"Don't believe everything you read in there," I said, referring to the notes. "That thing is seeded with misdirection and misinformation. It's a road map for me. It's something to spark things in my mind. It won't spark anything in your mind."

Armstrong was intent on discovering the identity of my source in Washington. I wasn't about to tell him about InComCon and Donald Fortier because he never would have believed that. But after careful reading of my notes, he believed the source was Milt Nottingham, the Washington businessman who had befriended me nearly 25 years earlier when I was in reform school.

Armstrong, during his research on the Tongsun Park affair, had tried to connect Nottingham with criminal wrongdoing. He had been unable to do so and was still frustrated by that.

"That's got to be Milton Nottingham," Armstrong said of my source.

"The description in my notes may lead you to believe that, but it also may be a red herring I threw in there to confuse people," I said.

"Do you know Milton Nottingham?" Armstrong demanded.

"Yes, I do."

"What can you tell me about him?"

"Nothing beyond what I've already told you."

"How do you expect us to believe you if you won't be truthful with us?"

That caught me off guard. They asked me to come to Washington. They asked me to give them every bit of information I had about the Contras and their illegal activities. Now they were accusing me of being less than truthful with them about something that had nothing to do with the Contras.

Winer, a short, feisty attorney working for Kerry, sensed the meeting was about to degenerate into a verbal free-for-all between Armstrong and me. He stepped in and suggested we adjourn and try again another day.

"We're going to take you to a house in Virginia until we can determine your role in the investigation," Winer said.

We left Blum's house and got back in the vehicles. This time, Mike Fonte drove me as our little caravan went back through Washington and into Virginia. It was a much longer drive this time and darkness overtook us as we turned onto a dirt road that wound around hills and valleys deep in a heavily wooded area.

I had no idea where I was but could tell by the silhouette of the house that loomed out of the darkness that it was huge.

The house belonged to Maurice Rosenblatt, a wealthy Jewish lobbyist and supporter of various liberal causes in Washington. He had come to Washington in the 1940s to help pressure the U.S. government to support the new state of Israel and stayed to lobby on its behalf. He had agreed to allow his mansion to be used as a safe house for me.

Waiting for me at the house was a tall, thin man with glasses. He shook my hand, welcomed me to Washington and introduced himself as Lindsay Mattison, executive director of the International Center for Development Policy. I had no idea what that was, but Mattison had an easy smile and natural congeniality and did not seem threatening.

"I want to talk to you about your experiences," Mattison said. "But stay here until we need you and figure out what to do with you."

McCall and Winer returned to Washington while Fonte was left with me for security. I was told not to walk outside, not to use the telephone and not to sit in front of any windows. These guys thought there were people out there in the bushes waiting to pop me.

I was confined in a gilded gage and felt uncomfortable with nothing to do. I also felt very much out of place in the middle of all this opulence.

After several days of isolation, I told Mike to get on the telephone and tell whoever was responsible for me that I didn't come to Washington to be kept in hiding. He called Lindsay Mattison and told him I was getting edgy and might walk away. Mattison recognized the potential problem and had me driven into Washington, where he had reserved a room for me at the Capitol Hill Hotel. Once there, I felt much more relaxed and more in touch with my purpose.

The choice of hotels was not for my convenience, but for theirs, I discovered. From the hotel it was a short walk to the International Center for Development Policy, a think tank Mattison had created.

Mattison was quite a mover in Washington political circles. He had helped found the influential Center for Defense Information before moving on to the International Center, which was a bit less specific in its orientation in that it focused on what he referred to as "Third World conflict resolution."

The International Center's offices were in a renovated brick townhouse at 731 Eighth Street Southeast, directly across from the Marine Barracks and just up the street from the Washington Navy Yard.

Mattison served as its executive director. The president and show-piece was Robert White, the former ambassador to El Salvador who had been fired by the Reagan administration because of his criticism of its policies in Central America.

White was a fair and honest man who believed in what he was doing. Mattison was a salesman. He sold ideas and himself. To White, the International Center was a means to make a statement. To Lindsay, the International Center was a means of making money.

Virginia Foote, Mattison's wife, was an associate director of the Center, but her main job was handling the paperwork generated by the various sections of the operation. The center had people working on concerns about Central America, South Africa, Korea, Taiwan, the Philippines, Burma, congressional lobbying, a global project to save trees and a general fund-raising initiative.

Most of the center's employees were highly educated Americans, foreign nationals living here in exile or run-of-the-mill activists championing one liberal cause or another. The great thing about most activists, in Mattison's eyes, was that they worked cheaply because they believed the cause was more important than money. Political idealism was what made a lot of people in Washington like Mattison rich.

Mattison had gone to great lengths to dig up damaging information about Nicaragua. He had hired Edgar Chamorro, a former member of the FDN Directorate who turned against the organization and became a witness in the World Court trial on Nicaragua, which the U.S. refused to recognize. Chamorro was being used to present a different perspective on the Contras, a totally negative perspective.

Mattison didn't really care how he obtained information, as long as it appeared to be credible. His methods seemed strange at times, but I thought his intentions were honorable and that making a difference in Washington and the world meant something to him.

At least that's what I thought in 1986.

But I soon came to realize that Mattison was a quintessential liberal, ready to use any means to further his particular political agenda and his personal financial agenda. Like most liberals in Washington, he had a deep-seated distrust of anyone who didn't fit his particular political mold. Since I didn't fit anyone's mold, he not only distrusted me, he feared me.

But he recognized my marketability. I could be good for business and he figured he could put up with me long enough to bring in publicity and money that the center needed at that time.

Mattison had never spent much time in the real world. He was used to dealing with people inside the Washington Beltway and knew little of what went on outside it. He was a political animal, but was incredibly naive about the way the real world operated and totally ignorant of people like me.

The morning after my first night at the hotel, Mattison called and said arrangements had been made for me to work at the International Center. He said he would come by the hotel and walk with me so I could find my way.

That first day at the center was unlike anything I had ever experienced. When I stepped across the threshold it was like entering an ice box. The Center's employees stared at me with a thinly disguised mixture of fear and disdain on their faces. If was almost as if Lucifer incarnate had walked into the midst, took off his jacket and asked for a cup of coffee.

I represented everything they were working against. In their eyes, I was a right-wing mercenary killer, a tool of the Reagan administration. They were polite, but many treated me as if I were radioactive and avoided me altogether.

Mattison had made some arrangement with Kerry's office on funding an investigation of the Contras. Kerry did not have the budget to pursue the numerous allegations being brought to his office, so Mattison volunteered to finance the effort in return for being allowed to use information derived from the investigation in his fund-raising letters. It was a practical arrangement for both Kerry and Mattison because they were willing to take huge amounts of flak from the administration generated by information being fed to the press about the unfolding scandal.

I was a novelty at the time, since I was one of the few people who had been inside the Contras, the FDN and CMA, knew their dirty little secrets and was willing to talk about them. Mattison and Kerry were intent on getting as much out of me as they could. Mattison wanted publicity and the money it generated. Kerry and his people wanted some guidance on who to look for, what to look for and how to find both.

On April 8 I went to Kerry's office in the Russell building for another meeting with Jack Blum, John Winer, Ron Rosenblith, Dick McCall and Scott Armstrong. Armstrong had been retained to check out my story and immediately told me he had problems with my veracity.

But those problems had nothing to do with my charges against the Contras and their supporters. They had to do with Milt Nottingham. Once again Armstrong tried to get me to give up Nottingham. Once again I refused.

Armstrong seemed to be using this as a gauge of my credibility. He made it clear that if I was unwilling to reveal information about Milt and his association with Tongsun Park, then everything else I had to say about the Contras was bullshit.

Once again, the meeting went sour. Kerry's staff got little useful information about the true nature of their investigation, Armstrong got nothing about Milt Nottingham and I got a headache and a healthy dislike for Armstrong. He was petty and judgmental and seemed determined to tie up the decades-old Tongsun Park affair before moving on to anything else.

But I wouldn't play Armstrong's game. And because I wouldn't, I became a prime target for his wrath. Armstrong began a campaign in Washington to discredit everything I said. He advised other journalists not to deal with me. I was, he claimed, a liar out for personal gain.

Armstrong had acquired a copy of my criminal record, which I had never tried to hide, and used this against me. I was an ex-con and couldn't be trusted or believed, he told people. He was the left-wing equivalent of Tom Posey, a petty, spiteful man who had never gotten what he believed to be his just rewards in Washington.

Under other circumstances, I might have taken pity on Armstrong. But in Washington, I found myself out of my league dealing with professional purveyors of innuendo and half-truths such as Armstrong.

Mattison was upset when he learned that Armstrong was working at cross purposes. Armstrong's non-profit National Security Archive was to become a repository for information gathered from Freedom of Information Act requests and through individual investigations. This group was supposed to back efforts to expose illegal Contra activities, but began to withdraw its resources from certain think tanks, including the International Center, because of jealousy over who should control witnesses brought to Washington.

Since I was a prime witness at the time and Armstrong couldn't control me, Mattison's access to information at the National Security Archive was severely restricted.

These petty jealousies were a dividing force among the many organizations in Washington involved in the daily fights for scraps of information to use in their fund-raising appeals. Each organization had its own agenda and although the groups tried to present a semi-unified front in their opposition to government policies, the back-stabbing that went on as a matter of survival amazed me. They reminded me of jackals tearing up a wounded animal.

I knew Kerry's staff was in deep water on this issue and was looking for a few life preservers. The efforts by Kerry and his aides so far had been relatively unfocused. They had been unable to attract the attention or interest of other senators on the Foreign Relations Committee and get a formal investigation started. The Republicans were doing all they could to blunt the efforts of Kerry and fellow Democrats to bring this mess into public view.

I was impressed by Kerry. He was openly working on something that if it went sour could mean the end of his political career. The Republican attack dogs in Congress were already trying to take chunks out of his butt for his efforts to open an investigation.

But Kerry didn't see this as a political issue, as the Republicans were trying to make it. Nor did he see it as an issue he could exploit for personal aggrandizement.

As a Vietnam war veteran, Kerry had experienced firsthand the disastrous foreign policy decisions that resulted in the deaths of more than 58,000 Americans in Southeast Asia. On the issue of the Contras, he wanted to prevent a repeat of foreign policy run amok that would cost American lives.

Kerry was one of the few people in Congress with the courage to confront the Reagan administration and expose its failed Contra policy while partisan political vultures circled around him. He seemed unafraid to be the point man in the attacks on the policy and the furious counterattacks launched against liberals who the administration and its backers in Congress said were using lies to derail the Contra aid votes.

Kerry stood up to the sniping from within Congress and without because he and his aides sensed they were on to something that led directly into the White House and were they intent on following that trail, no matter where it led.

For several days I hung around the Center with little to do. I didn't hear from my friends. I didn't hear from my enemies. I didn't hear from the people who had encouraged me to go to Washington, InComCon.

I had no money coming in and would have starved had it not been for the room-service meals at the hotel and a hundred dollar bill Maurice Rosenblatt gave me. I was restless in Washington, because no one had told me yet what their plans were for me.

I knew that once I gave my information to the people in Washington, I had little future left. I was going after a presidential administration and its foreign policy and I knew that once I did that, my reputation would be worthless. Kerry's people told me they would see if I qualified for the witness protection program, but I knew I wouldn't. I was simply a whistleblower, and we were in a class by ourselves. No one wanted to help or protect whistleblowers and there were no provisions anywhere to aid those of us who operated outside the government once we were spent.

Mattison tried to take quick advantage of my publicity value by bringing journalists to the center to interview me. That way, he said, my story would get out to the public much more quickly than waiting for congressional hearings.

The first interview was a disaster. Mattison arranged for five reporters to interview me at the same time. Only three showed up. And only one of them, James Ridgeway of the *Village Voice*, wrote an article.

Ridgeway's article said congressional investigators who once viewed me as "the John Dean of a 'Contragate' have backed off and are taking a second look." My background was questioned. My credibility was question. The whole tone of the article was that I was a dubious source.[1]

I was appalled. I had dealt with the reporters on a good faith basis, but evidently lacked the skills necessary to put the correct spin on my story. Telling the truth was not an advantage in Washington. It seemed that reporters, investigators and the general public wanted to be told things they wanted to hear.

My dealings with the media had been minimal and produced mixed results in the past. William Thomas and Richard Gardner of the *Memphis Commercial-Appeal* had been given access to the Contra headquarters in Honduras in December 1985, then had violated confidences and allowed photos and a map to be published that compromised the Contras and put innocent people at risk.

Brian Barger and Bob Parry of the Associated Press were much more professional and much more open-minded in their stories about the Contras and their wrong-doing. They didn't have a political agenda.

I was offended whenever articles appeared that cast doubt on my credibility because I was on a crusade. My credibility became a real sticky issue in Washington. Many reporters found that while my information was good, they couldn't use my name in their stories because they feared their media colleagues would charge them with using "unreliable" sources.

Despite the problems with the first interview, Mattison pressed on and found that the more I talked, the more interesting I became to the media. He decided to take me on as a consultant, paying me $3,000 a month plus expenses. This had a two-fold purpose. First and foremost, it kept me on his leash and enabled him to manipulate me as a source of information for the media. The other was to provide me with enough money to sustain me and keep me from looking for work with other think tanks.

I had moved out of the Capitol Hill Hotel and was using a condominium owned by Mal Warwick, the owner of the mailing service that Mattison used in his fund-raising appeals.

In my role as a consultant, I was given access to a computer and a office on the top floor of the center. I wasn't sure what I was supposed to do except talk to people. And Mattison kept me busy doing that.

Carroll Dogherty, who had first talked to me in New Orleans in 1985, was based in Washington and said he wanted me to meet with the producers of a new CBS television magazine, "West 57th Street," about my allegations.

We arranged a meeting at the International Center. Dogherty brought three people with him: Jane Wallace, the reporter/talking head for the piece, and co-producers Leslie Cockburn and Ty West.

Leslie was not at all convinced CBS should do the piece involving me. In fact she was downright hostile. She challenged my information, my background and told me she didn't think I had anything worth saying on national television. She was openly suspicious of me because of my background and the fact that I had been involved militarily in the war.

I was still sensitive about people challenging my credibility. Where I came from, you took people at face value until they proved otherwise. I didn't realize it would be so difficult in Washington just getting my story out. People had a tendency to disbelieve me because of my background.

I didn't feel I had to convince Leslie of anything, though, and became more and more hostile toward her. If she felt I was fabricating my story, she could go talk to someone else.

After a long meeting, it was decided my story needed further scrutiny before CBS would air a piece. Most of the information I had could be corroborated only by those people I was accusing and CBS saw big problems with that approach.

Besides, I could not shed much light on Leslie's primary interest, drug-running. I could only provide information that in most instances would be considered hearsay in court.

During that initial meeting, Leslie treated me like a creature from outer space. She had never met anyone like me and couldn't understand anything about who I was or where I came from. She thought I was deceiving her about my background because she had been told I was a highly trained operative who could be a disinformation agent posing as a friend to the liberal cause while gathering information about Reagan administration detractors.

Like many of the other journalists who came to see me, the CBS crew left the first meeting disappointed that I hadn't given them a smoking gun. But I hadn't come to Washington with one, despite claims being made on my behalf by others.

I was a bit puzzled that InComCon had not contacted me. They had wanted me to come to Washington. They had wanted me to make a big splash. Now, it seemed, they had left me high and dry with no information to use other than my personal experiences.

Finally, in early May 1986, Mr. Smith called me at the Center. He said he had lost track of me. I was amazed I couldn't be found me because I was sitting right in their laps and half of official Washington seemed to know where I was.

Once the connection was re-established, InComCon's methods took a new direction. When Mr. Smith came on the line, the conversation began with the day and date of the call.

For example, Mr. Smith would call and begin the conversation: "This is Monday, May 15th, 1986. How are you?"

This was standard operating procedure on every call I received from InComCon for the next two years.

During this call from Mr. Smith, I was given a list of 40 names and a brief biography of each that told of their role with the Contras, with drug-smuggling or with gun-running. The list, Mr. Smith said, could be released to the press or anyone else who might have interest in it.

The list contained names of people I knew nothing about, but Mr. Smith assured me they were connected to the illegalities. When I added those names to a growing list of known operatives, drug- smugglers, gun-runners and government officials, it became known as the Summary of Contra Participants and eventually grew to grew to include more than 150 people.

I now had a project which required investigative skills to flesh out the brief bios.

While working on my list, I continued to give interviews. In the best traditions of Washington pack journalism, for every journalist who interviewed me and did a story, a dozen more beat a path to the center's door.

Not only were journalists interested in me, so too were anti-Contra forces that were growing in number in Washington. When they learned there was someone in town who had been inside the FDN and was willing to speak out against it, they began circling the International Center like vultures.

Just as the political right adopted me when I espoused the appropriate sentiments, now the left tried to adopt me and make me the object of their suffocating affections.

Among the most brazen of the left-wing Washington-based groups was the Christic Institute, a Jesuit-backed public policy think tank headed by a publicity seeking lawyer named Danny Sheehan.

Sheehan had previously worked on several high-profile lawsuits, including the Karen Silkwood/Kerr-McGee case; the Pentagon Papers; the Wounded Knee, South Dakota, shootings; and the Attica prison uprising. In the FDN and its supporters, Sheehan saw the ultimate conspiracy and the ultimate conspirators who had shaped the world and controlled U.S. government affairs since the end of World War II.

What began for Sheehan as a relatively low-key effort to aid Costa Rican-based American journalists Martha Honey and Tony Avirgan investigate the role played by the U.S. government in the assassination attempt on Eden Pastora the previous May at La Penca developed into a full-fledged and highly improbable conspiracy theory.

A civil lawsuit was being prepared charging a host of people with federal violations of the Racketeer-Influenced and Corrupt Organizations Act, usually referred to as RICO. Those people included CIA veterans Thomas Clines, Theodore Shackley, Rafael "Chi" Quintero, and John Hull; CMA members Tom Posey and Bruce Jones; military veterans Richard Secord and John Singlaub; and a host of others like Rob Owen, Frank Chanes, Albert Hakim and Adolfo Calero.

Sheehan was going after a lot of targets. But instead of singling out a few of the most vulnerable, he decided to try to hit all of them with a shotgun approach that was doomed to fail from the start.

The suit read like "Tom Clancy does the Wizard of Oz."

Virtually everything that happened in the world since the end of World War II, from the Cold War to John Kennedy's assassination to the current problems in Central America, could be attributed to a small cabal of military and political leaders who were using guns and drugs to fuel their own ambitions for power and feed their bank accounts, according to the suit.

It made great reading, if you believed in grandiose conspiracies.

Unfortunately, Sheehan saw me as one of the linchpins of that conspiracy and was determined to dig out of me every little bit of information I had that might bolster his delusions of grandeur.

Sheehan began a low-key campaign to enlist my help and information. He arranged a meeting with Mattison to discuss combining investigations of Contra wrongdoing. It would save money and resources, he claimed.

The meeting was held at the offices of the Stewart Mott Foundation on a patio that adjoined the building. Sheehan showed up with his wife, Sara, who served as the Christic Institute's executive director and the beauty to Sheehan's beast. We sat at a wrought iron table while Mattison and Sheehan talked about me as if I was invisible.

I was a ham being sliced to feed both organizations. The only question was who would pay the carver.

Their disinterest in my opinion of the matter was fine with me. Sara was quite attractive and I had more time to ogle her while my fate was being discussed.

Sheehan wanted me to work in his shop but have Mattison pay me and give the Christic Institute half of whatever funds I brought in. Sheehan felt his organization had a leg up with the staff and research it had done to make full use of me and my knowledge.

Mattison sat and listened politely, but rejected the offer. He had decided to put distance between himself and the Christic Institute because Sheehan's position was becoming too radical even for most of Washington's other radicals. Mattison still had to answer to the International Center's backers and wasn't sure he could explain the ramblings of this wild-eyed, curly-haired Harvard liberal who was running around the country like Chicken Little proclaiming the end of Western civilization was at hand.

I was a spectator to this political maneuvering within the liberal community. People like me, people with information, were treated very abstractly by these groups. We were something less than human beings to them, but the information we provided was the fuel that turned the wheels of their particular political machines. It was all very impersonal. Whistleblowers and witnesses were merely products used to feed cash cow operations.

I had gone from one set of pin-striped sharks, the Contra leaders, to another, those who operate the public policy think tanks and their financial backers. Just as I had been with the government, I was an expendable asset, a disposable patriot, with these liberals.

Mattison walked rather gingerly around me my first few days in Washington. His personality was such that he could joust with anyone, as long as it was verbal. I was different. I was someone out of his youthful past, someone with a potential for violence, someone he had not had to face since insulating and isolating himself in Washington. He would not be perfectly honest with me because of a fear that I might react with something other than words.

Mattison invited me to lunch a few days after my arrival at the center to discuss these concerns, although I didn't realize it at the time he extended the invitation.

We walked a few blocks to a small Italian restaurant near the Capitol, chatting along the way about my job and my background. He seemed cordial and relaxed.

But no sooner did we sit down than he started ordering martinis. One after the other. Bang. Bang. Bang. He seemed to be determined to destroy himself before mid-afternoon.

I am a virtual teetotaler and sat there in amazement watching him suck down those things like they were water. He must have knocked back five martinis before the food arrived. I started to wonder what was going on. Had I gotten myself mixed up with an alcoholic?

Finally, Mattison looked at me, his eyes glazed, and said: "I had to get drunk enough to tell you this. If you get mad at somebody down at the center, or somebody says the wrong thing to you, promise me you won't kill them."

I had to stifle a laugh.

"Lindsay," I said, "you didn't have to get drunk to tell me that."

It was like that wherever I went in Washington. To the lefties, I was a right-wing mercenary nut who would kill anybody who looked at me the wrong way.

To the righties, I was a traitor who had gone over to the other side and become a left-wing mercenary nut.

But I quickly learned that by playing one side against the other I could do what I set out to do by coming to Washington — inflict pain on those responsible for the grief and misery I still felt about the Indians. I used anything I could to hurt them.

I was not doing what I was doing for the liberals, as was frequently charged. Nor was I doing it for the conservatives or the International Center. I was doing this for myself. I would have chewed up a liberal as quickly as I would have a conservative.

Nobody in Washington ever understood that about me. Everyone thought I had a hidden political agenda. But they could never figure out what that agenda was.

A Stranger in Their Midst

Interest in the private aid network being run by Oliver North from the Executive Office Building next to the White House began to increase slowly as the news leaks became a steady torrent. Other disenchanted Contra supporters drifted into Washington with tales similar to mine. Many Washington insiders were skeptical of me because they were not sure who I was or what I wanted and rushed to these new sources.

But on May 5, 1986, National Public Radio ran a report on the Contras by Bill Buzenberg that featured me and my accusations. It started a whole new round of finger pointing and elevated my accusations to another level.

I told Buzenberg about the gun running. I told him about the drugs. I told him about Mario Calero skimming profits from aid shipments. I told him about human rights abuses and other Contra wrongdoing.

Buzenberg also interviewed Tom Posey for the piece. Posey's reaction was typical.

"It's all bull hockey," Posey told Buzenberg. "He has never had anything to do with that, because none of it was ever done in the first place. Now, what he has done, he has heard stories, read newspapers, and got articles, things like that, and put it in his words."[2]

Posey said I was a liar and questioned my credibility.

"Everything that Jack Terrell told us was a lie. He never was in the military. He even made emphasis that he was working for the CIA and that he had money from the CIA to help finance the war down there. Now we come to find out all this was nothing but lies. He himself said he served time in prison and that was about the only truth he told us."[3]

It was Posey's contention that anyone who had ever been in jail was automatically a liar. My prison record was practically the only stone my detractors could throw because they were timid about opening further debate that could be extremely damaging to them.

They couldn't challenge the quality of my information, only the quality of my life.

Buzenberg's piece fanned the flames a bit more and the two sides of the issue retreated a bit further into their respective corners. The White House trotted out its damage-control experts and picked up the pace of its efforts to silence critics through intimidation and smear tactics.

The existence of such a campaign was suspected in Washington at the time, but no one could ever pin it down. The Iran-Contra committee later uncovered the domestic spying, disinformation and dirty tricks operation run out of the White House that targeted Congress, the media and the public.[4]

A draft chapter of the Iran-Contra Committee report containing that damaging information was never released to the public. It was blocked by Republicans in the Senate and House.[5]

Run by top-level CIA veterans, this internal propaganda ministry had but one function: Sell the Contra war to the American public. It did it by concocting outright lies about the military effectiveness of the Contras and by attacking the credibility of whistleblowers, journalists deemed not in line with the administration and anyone else who disagreed with the Contra policy.

I was among those targeted, as was Senator Kerry. Oliver North actually met with FBI agents and asked them to investigate us because he believed we were connected with foreign agents.[6]

What North and this group did was vicious, venal and a total of corruption of the legal processes of government. Their scurrilous attacks on individuals scarred them for life, while the perpetrators of this outrage crawled back into the dark reaches of the White House basement. Not a one of them was ever held accountable for what they did.

On May 21, 1986, at the request of Martha Honey, I flew to Costa Rica to testify in a $500,000 lawsuit brought against her and Tony Avirgan by John Hull as a result of their report of the May 1984 La Penca bombing. In the September 1985 report and subsequent press conference to release it, Avirgan, who had been wounded in the explosion aimed at Eden Pastora, and Honey charged that Hull had been involved in the planning and execution of the assassination attempt.

Hull had responded by charging the couple in a Costa Rican court with "injuries, falsehood and defamation of character."

This was not a libel case. Hull had sued Honey and Avirgan as individuals, not as journalists. That meant the case would be heard by one judge in a lower court, not by three judges in the country's Supreme Court. That increased Hull's chances of influencing the judge into a favorable verdict in his favor.[7]

I flew to Costa Rica with John Mattes, an assistant federal public defender from Miami who had represented Jesus Garcia. Mattes was also scheduled to testify for Honey and Avirgan against Hull.

San Jose, Costa Rica, was brimming with people who were investigating the Contras for one reason or another that May and many of them seemed to congregate at Honey's and Avirgan's house.

John Winer from Kerry's office was there, as was Danny Sheehan from the Christic Institute and Leslie Cockburn from CBS News and several other people I didn't know.

Also in attendance was Peter Glibbery, the British mercenary who had just been released from La Reforma prison. Glibbery, Steve Carr and the other three mercenaries had been unexpectedly released a week earlier after more than a year behind bars.

John Davies and Claude "Frenchy" Chaffard had gone underground. Robert "Pantera" Thompson had taken up with Hull. Carr and Glibbery, despite pressure from Hull and his associates not to testify at the trial, agreed to be witnesses and stayed with Honey and Avirgan.

But by the time I arrived, only Glibbery was left. Carr walked out of the house one day and never came back. He later called Honey and

Avirgan and told them U.S. Embassy officials threatened he would be sent back to jail if he testified.[8]

Carr felt intimidated by Hull and wanted to get out of the country. Embassy officials, in violation of Costa Rican law, gave him a bus ticket to Panama and had a border guard help him get across the frontier without a passport.

"They [embassy officials] told me to get the hell out of Dodge and they helped me to do so," Carr told Honey.[9]

In Panama, Carr was assisted by U.S. and Panamanian authorities to get out of the country and into the States, where he was promptly arrested and thrown in jail in Naples, Fla., for parole violation.

Carr knew he was in danger, even in the States, because he continued to speak out about Hull's drug smuggling, which he claimed to have witnessed. He was marked for death and he knew it. He told me repeatedly he believed John Hull would have him killed.

He also wrote to his mother of those concerns. In one poignant letter he wrote:

September 10, 1985

Dear Ma,

Just found out today. I'm supposed to be shot on my return to Fla. It seems a guy names [sic] Morgan/Felipe who worked for the FDN and John Hull has been given orders to shot [sic] me and Pete [Glibbery] because we spoke out against John Hull.[10]

In another letter to his mother, Carr wrote:

I'm supposed to be eliminated very soon. One of John Hull's hired guns is in Miami awaiting my return.[11]

On December 12, 1986, Carr was found dead in Van Nuys, California. Police said he died of a drug overdose, that he had swallowed three bags of cocaine and had admitted it to the people with whom he was staying at the time.[12]

Although Carr was a former drug abuser, three autopsies were unanimous: there were no signs of drugs in Carr's body and no indications he had injected, ingested or imbibed anything containing drugs.[13]

No one was keeping much of a secret that it had been an inside job. In April 1987, Peter Glibbery called John Mattes and said Hull was pressuring him to recant his stories about the southern front. When Glibbery refused, Hull shouted at him: "The CIA killed Steve Carr and they can do the same to you."[14]

This level of intimidation by Hull and U.S. Embassy officials in Costa Rica was unprecedented. Glibbery was under a death threat, and many witnesses feared reprisal if they testified. Even Eden Pastora was reluctant to show his face in court. When he did, he was escorted by a large, heavily armed security force.

I had received several anonymous telephone calls prior to leaving the States telling me if I got off the plane in Costa Rica I would be shot. I didn't take these threats seriously, but no one was eager to stand too close to me in San Jose.

John Winer was getting his first taste of being part of my world and he was extremely uncomfortable with the thought that he could be caught in a hail of bullets aimed at me. I found most of the threats to be more humorous than intimidating, though, because the people I knew who would carry out a hit-for-hire wouldn't bother with the threats. They'd just do it and go have a beer to celebrate the end of another work day.

The night of May 21, Leslie Cockburn and I resolved our differences about the "West 57th Street" piece. She was seeing the process from the inside down here, not observing it from a distance through other people. Like many other journalists, once she came face-to-face with the beast that was the Contra war, she had a much better understanding of those of us who had lived with it for years.

The trial began the next morning, but I still wasn't sure I would be needed to testify, so I lingered over a late breakfast at the Holiday Inn in downtown San Jose. Leslie Cockburn came rushing into the restaurant, expressing concern about my safety and saying I would indeed be needed to testify. One crucial witness, Carr, had disappeared and they didn't want another to vanish at the last minute.

I was to replacing Carr on the witness stand for Avirgan and Honey. Robert "Pantera" Thompson, who had been one of our crew in Honduras and one of the five mercenaries in La Reforma, was there to testify for Hull. Glibbery and Mattes were also in the witness room.

Security was unusually heavy for a Costa Rican court. There were three checkpoints, including one with a metal detector. Guards with Uzi sub-machine guns lined the walls.

I remained sequestered until late afternoon. I was the last person called. When I entered the courtroom, television lights nearly blinded me. The courtroom was filled to capacity with press and curious onlookers. I was told to take the stand, which was nothing more than a single, hard-backed chair positioned against one wall just inches from Hull and his attorney, Alberto Rodriguez Baldi.

It was another not-so-subtle form of intimidation.

What should have taken minutes turned into over an hour on the stand because of translation difficulties. The Spanish interpreter had been provided by the U.S. Embassy and tried to inject certain interpretations of words that put different meanings on what I said. The judge at one point reminded the interpreter that she wasn't the only person in court who understood both languages.

I repeated my story about my encounters with Hull, the Pastora assassination plots and Hull's involvement in them, and Hull's CIA affiliation. My testimony became so strung out as a result of the translation problems that a recess was called. As I stood and stretched, Hull leaned over the table, his bald head glistening with sweat from the television lights, and said to me:

"You must be pretty pissed off at Posey to be down here cutting my throat."

"No, John," I replied calmly, "you cut your own throat."

When court reconvened, Hull sat there and stared at me. I was close enough to see his brain working and knew that if he had the opportunity, I would end up fertilizing the grass on his ranch from an unmarked grave.

The attorney representing Avirgan and Honey, Oto Castro Sanchez, surprised me when he asked what role Pantera had played with the FDN. I had been briefed on most of the questions I would be asked, but nothing was mentioned about Pantera.

Before the trial, Pantera tried to pass himself off as a freelance journalist involved with the FDN for a story. He was not, he claimed, a combatant. Hull had turned him or intimidated him and Pantera was staying at Hull's house. Hull even provided the sport coat and tie Pantera wore to court.

The questioning from Castro went like this:

Castro: "Do you know why Robert Thompson came to Costa Rica?"

Terrell: "Tom Posey was supposed to send Robert Thompson to Honduras. Nevertheless he came to Costa Rica as an instructor."

Castro: "What type of instructor?"

Terrell: "Military, to John Hull's house."

Castro: "Did Robert Thompson inform you if he had participated in the transportation of 42 kilos of cocaine to the northern sector of Costa Rica?"

Terrell: "When I met with Robert Thompson in La Reforma, he told me that Rene Corbo had gone into Nicaragua with a large quantity of money and had brought back 42 kilos of cocaine which they assigned him [Thompson] to guard within Costa Rica. He told me that they had not sent him to Costa Rica to guard drugs and that he had destroyed the cocaine before because this wasn't his function."

Pantera's face got redder and redder as I testified. It got so red I thought he would explode from the blood building up in his head.

When I finished my testimony and walked to the corridor outside the courtroom where Leslie Cockburn was waiting for me, Pantera rushed up and began shouting.

"You're a liar," he screamed. "They'll kill you for what you said."

"Fine," I replied. "Any time, anywhere you want to settle this, let me know. You have my telephone number."

Pantera stormed off. I saw him only one more time, the following day when he and Hull returned to court to hear that the suit had been rejected. Hull had lost.

After my noisy confrontation with Pantera, a man approached me, introduced himself as an official of the Costa Rican Organization of Judicial Investigation (OIJ by its Spanish initials), and handed me a piece of paper. It was a subpoena. The OIJ wanted to talk to me about the La Penca bombing.

The following morning, May 23, I arrived at the OIJ offices shortly before 8 a.m. The offices were upstairs from the courtroom where I had testified the previous day. I was led to a desk and offered a seat in front of a man with an old manual typewriter that had a half-dozen sheets of typing paper and carbon paper stuffed into it.

An interpreter was brought into the room. He explained that Costa Rican investigators had been told I was one of the few people who had claimed to have seen the alleged La Penca bomber, Amac Galil. They wanted a statement from me about what I knew about him and wanted me to look at some photographs.

From 8 a.m. until 3:15 p.m., I sat and answered questions from three investigators, essentially repeating what I testified to in court. The process was even slower than my testimony because the typist made repeated mistakes and had to sift through each copy to correct the error before we could move on.

Near the end of the session, the investigators hauled out a board that contained more than 100 photographs. I was asked if I saw anyone I recognized. I picked out one I had been shown during my testimony. It was identified as a photo of Amac Galil, the alleged La Penca bomber.

But that photo was blurred and the man's features were hard to distinguish. Finally, I spotted another face I recognized. It was the man I had seen sitting on the patio at Adolfo's house in January 1985, the man with the orangish hair, the man with the Arab features.

The investigators took both photos off the board and turned them over. On the back was the same name: "Galil."

I told them I did not recognize another face on the board.

I spent another two days in San Jose, sightseeing and spending a last precious few minutes with Grace before returning to Atlanta on May 26.

When I got there I received an urgent call from Lindsay Mattison. The Christic Institute suit had been filed and I was needed in Washington immediately to begin preparing my testimony and to continue my interviews. The media attention was greater than ever.

What I did not realize on my return to Washington was that my testimony against Hull in Costa Rica had triggered an all-out counterattack on me and my credibility. Hull, his right-wing backers in the Heritage Foundation in Washington, and their mouthpiece, the *Washington Times*, saw me as a turncoat and a threat to the administration's private enterprise aiding the FDN.

The Heritage Foundation was one of the key players in the administration's war efforts during this time. In addition to aiding the Contras, it backed anti-Communist factions in Vietnam and the Mujahadeen in Afghanistan.

One of its organizations was called the Committee for a Free Afghanistan. It was run by a woman named Karen McKay, who also was a major in the Army reserves who spent a lot of time at the Joint Special Operations Command at Fort Bragg, North Carolina.

McKay tried to recruit me to work with the Mujahadeen at one point, and we were close to making a deal when she happened to mention my name in a conversation with her next-door neighbor, a man she called Larry.

Larry was Oliver Laurence North.

From then on, I was persona non grata at the Heritage Foundation and among Washington's conservative establishment.

As hard as they tried, neither the conservatives nor the liberals were ever able to get a handle on me. The liberals were wary of fully embracing me and bringing me into their fold because they weren't sure what to make of me.

That was evident in the manner in which Sheehan and the Christic Institute dealt with me. It was almost as if they knew they needed me, but didn't really want to have anything to do with me because of my background.

Sheehan had been telling people for weeks that I would be the star witness in his massive conspiracy suit once it was filed. It was Sheehan's public posturing about me shortly after my arrival in Washington that originally brought me to the attention of retired Air Force General Richard Secord, one of North's closest associates in the private aid network.

Secord wanted to know just how much I figured in the Christic Institute suit in which he was named as a co-conspirator and what I was telling federal investigators and Congress about his role. Secord stood to gain a great deal financially from the schemes to aid the Contras through private contractors. Anyone who disrupted those efforts was a threat.

Secord hired Glenn Robinette, a former CIA agent, in March 1986 to investigate me and find out what I knew about the affairs of the United States government in Central America and how much of it I was going to tell Danny Sheehan and the Christic Institute.[15]

I could have saved them a lot of time and money. I had no plans to cooperate with Sheehan and the Christic Institute. When the time came to be deposed for the Christic's civil suit, I took the Fifth Amendment more than 100 times.

What Secord, Robinette and North didn't know was that I wanted as little to do with the opportunists on the left as those on the right.

But I wanted to see North and his buddies sweat. I wanted to see them worry. I wanted to know that every morning they woke up they had to think about Jack Terrell because they weren't sure how much I knew about them and their operations.

I had created a character with an attitude that made them afraid of taking a chance that I might have enough information to get them. It was an attitude that said: "Fuck with me and see how much I know."

They couldn't afford to take the chance that I didn't know anything, that I was merely a spectator. They had to come after me to find out. Then, when they discovered I knew more than they originally thought, they tried to silence me. When that didn't work, they tried to buy me out. When that didn't work, they would try to kill me.

In the summer of 1986, I became the prime source for news leaks on the Contra war. I was like a switchboard. Every few days, Mr. Smith called with some new information and I passed it on to journalists who by then were in a feeding frenzy.

Because of the accuracy and timeliness of my information, I was frequently accused by those who ran the International Center of being a CIA plant. But they didn't want to get rid of me, no matter what my affiliation, because I was good for business. I was attracting media attention, which attracted donors. The International Center's fund-raising campaigns that had been drawing a few thousand dollars a year suddenly began attracting hundreds of thousands of dollars.

The scandal began in earnest with the news that Carl "Spitz" Channell had been indicted for his fund-raising efforts on behalf of the Contras. Channell was a high-profile money sucker who had set up an arrangement with North to fleece old ladies out of their money in the name of helping the freedom fighters.

North acted as the primer by schmoozing with certain well-heeled contributors, giving them inside information and updates about the Communist menace. Channell was the closer.

The most recognized name among the many funders was Ellen Garwood, who contributed $1 million to Channell and was rewarded by having a military surplus helicopter named after her. The Huey was supposed to be used for medical evacuation purposes in Honduras, but I never knew of a single mission that the much-publicized showpiece helicopter flew.

Although Channell's staff, which was known as "The Gay Gestapo" because of the lifestyle and tactics of its members, generally handled the stroking of the funders, Channell got hefty kickbacks. He was the first to cut a deal and cop a plea to avoid prison. But his fall opened the door to more controversy about the private aid network.

I thought my relationship with the FBI ended when I left New Orleans, but I learned that just the opposite was true. Ellen Glasser and David Beisner, special agents from the Washington field office, contacted me and asked for a meeting somewhere away from the International Center. I met them for lunch at a small hamburger joint on Eighth Street.

Glasser was reserved and strait-laced in the manner of all female FBI agents. The only thing I learned about her was her husband was an FBI agent in North Carolina.

Beisner, dressed in the usual conservative FBI blue suit, did most of the talking. He told me my case had been handed off to him by the New Orleans office. He had become my case officer. The primary focus of his questions that day was why I chose to work at the International Center. The FBI knew little about the place, he said. But I didn't know much more than them.

Beisner was particularly interested in foreign connections that were maintained by the center. I knew of a few of the causes it supported, but little else. Beisner told me to learn as much as I could about my hosts and he would check with me again.

I told Beisner I wasn't happy in Washington because people were writing me off as a liar or a nut. I felt as though I were swimming upstream alone. Despite the help from InComCon, Kerry's people and the International Center, I felt my information was slipping through the cracks unnoticed.

Beisner told me he had friends who might be able to get me a job doing some type intelligence work overseas, but he would have to check it out and call me later.

About a week later, Beisner called and invited me for a drink at a small pub near the Capitol. When I arrived, he was sitting alone and had already had a couple of drinks. I declined his offer of a drink and he launched right into the purpose for the meeting.

He wanted information about supporters of the International Center and how records about them were kept. I told him that all the information on supporters was kept on computer disks. He asked me if I knew whether the center received money from foreign sources, especially Communist countries. I told him that I wasn't aware of this, but I knew that some employees had direct access to Cuban and Nicaraguan officials. I didn't see any problem with this because those connections were no more than any other left-wing organization in town had.

Finally, after another drink, Beisner got to the meat of the matter. He wanted copies of the disks or computer printouts on everyone who contributed money to the International Center. He wanted to have them checked out to determine their political affiliation. He thought everyone on the center's mailing lists was Communist, socialist, or had left-wing leanings.

In exchange for this information, he would get me connected to a friend of his working at the U.S. Embassy in Manila who might help me get into civilian military intelligence work. Might.

It was a big risk for me to take and the entire thing smacked of a setup. It didn't sound like the FBI I knew. I was familiar with CoIntelPro, the FBI counterintelligence operation of the 1960s and 1970s dealing with domestic spying. But I thought things had changed after Watergate.

Apparently the FBI in the Reagan administration was carrying on in the grand tradition of Richard Nixon.

Here was an FBI agent asking me to commit a crime, or a least become a co-conspirator in a criminal act, with him. He did not tell me if his plan was sanctioned by the Bureau, but I had to believe that he wasn't working alone. I refused his offer and we parted company.

In June 1986, the Contra affair really became energized. June is normally the time when everyone in Washington looks forward to summer vacations, long weekends on the Maryland shore and trips into western Virginia. But this year, the smell of scandal hung in the air over the capital like the odor of a landfill. People were holding their breath because the stench was so bad.

The two sides were taking up battle positions on the issue as Republicans and conservative Democrats continued to defend the policies of the Reagan administration, while liberal Democrats continued to chip away at the administration's armor. No one was sure how far they should go, because bucking a popular administration meant political death in Washington. But it was clear that the scandal was growing larger and the criticism increasing to a point where something had to be done.

On June 25, John Kerry charged in a closed-door session of the Senate Foreign Relations Committee that "some American officials decided to circumvent the clear prohibitions of the Boland Amendment, as a result of that it appears that the contras and the infrastructure set up to support them determined that they had a license in a sense, to violate laws."[16]

At the end of the session, Senator Richard Lugar ordered a "staff inquiry" to look into charges that the Contras and Sandinistas were involved in drug smuggling.[17]

The Press, the Pimp and the Police

Lindsay Mattison had a strange sense about the ebb and flow of media and politicians in Washington. He knew there was growing interest in the developing scandal in the media and Congress, despite efforts by White House damage control experts to limit or distort information.

But he was frustrated that the major media agenda-setters, the *New York Times* and the *Washington Post*, were virtually ignoring the story. Mattison, like so many others in Washington, believed that a story wasn't news and wouldn't be taken seriously until it was carried in either of those two papers.

The Associated Press and smaller newspapers outside the Beltway were doing most of the dirty detective work on the issue, and their reporters appeared far more eager to uncover the scandal than reporters from either the *Post* or the *Times*. But the effect of stories from these papers was similar to small artillery trying to hit targets at a great distance.

I cooperated with any reporter who came looking for information, but often felt I was doing little more than providing background information instead of front-page material.

I was depressed because all my good intentions and all my hard work trying to get my story out were being turned back against me by a powerful force that was waging an effective campaign to ruin my credibility. Everything I said became twisted and distorted by the spin doctors sanctioned by the White House and by reporters who were after bigger fish that I could not give them.

I didn't understand the time lag between news stories and action taken by Congress. I expected immediate results and was frustrated when I didn't get them. I overestimated both the pace at which Congress works and my own impact in Washington.

Mr. Smith called frequently, but often sought opinions from me about progress I thought we were making. I had few answers for him. I needed ammunition if I was going to do any damage to those I had in my sights.

The information he gave me often was vague and appeared to go in no particular direction. I remember one conversation I had with Mr. Smith that made little sense at the time, but appears to have some meaning in the larger context of what was going on in Washington.

"Have you talked to anyone about Oliver North lately?" Mr. Smith asked.

"I've mentioned him a few times," I said.

"You might want to talk about him some more," Mr. Smith replied.

"In what capacity?"

"Just mention his name."

There was nothing specific. Just a hint to reporters to go snooping around Oliver North, to shine some light into a few dark corners and see how many rats and cockroaches scurried away.

Mr. Smith and InComCon assumed I had a better understanding of events and information than I did. I just played along with their game.

On June 25, 1986, I appeared on "West 57th Street" to air my charges on national television about the administration's private aid network. I focused on the NSC's involvement with the Contras and how Oliver North through Rob Owen had made it clear that no matter what restrictions Congress placed on the aid, he was going to find a way around them.

"There is a cancer on the presidency and it's growing," I said.

I called it Contragate.

After that program aired, Secord and North set into motion plans to silence me. I became a prime target for their wrath. I was going around Washington shaking trees and waiting for people to fall out of them. Now North came shaking my tree.

On July 10, 1986, North wrote in his schedule book: "Robinette, 9:30 meeting [with Terrell]", "Secord payment to Robinette [for investigating Terrell]."[18]

The following day, North's schedule book indicates that Robinette and I met at 1711 Massachusetts Ave. On July 12, the book reflects still another meeting with Robinette.[19]

I was introduced to Robinette in late spring 1986 by the head of an independent news organization, the Washington News Network, headed by Walter Gold. Gold was an ardent supporter of the Contras and the Reagan administration and part of the covert White House propaganda ministry.

Gold lured me to his office with a promise that I would be able to view a video no other news outfit had. The real reason for getting me there was to introduce me to Robinette, who played the role of unconcerned visitor while Gold showed me the tape.

The video was of footage shot at Ilopango Air Base in El Salvador. It showed Salvadoran military officers watching a C-130 taking off. As the camera panned across a section of the airfield, it showed several cargo planes sitting on the tarmac.

One of them, a C-123 painted in camouflage colors, had the Star of David, the emblem of the Israeli Air Force, on its nose. The footage, Gold said, was shot in 1985 and provided evidence of international collusion by U.S. allies in supplying military equipment to the Contras at a time it was illegal. The Israelis continually denied any participation in the Contra war, but this video would have provided evidence to refute that.

I asked Gold if he could get me a copy of this tape because I wanted to get it to CBS for possible use on one of their news programs. He was quite agreeable to my request, but shifted my attention to Robinette.

Robinette had introduced himself as an attorney representing what he referred to as "an investors group out of Pennsylvania and New York who want to do a movie on you and a book on you."

He asked to see some of the information I had that could help his investors make a final determination about the feasibility of the project. I showed him several pages of a book proposal done by a freelance writer. He seemed interested and said we would meet later to discuss the proposal.

Although I didn't learn Robinette's true identity until more than a year later, when he testified before the Iran-Contra Committee, I didn't trust him enough to divulge the true source of my information. I wasn't about to let him know that someone inside the government was feeding me information.

Of course, there weren't many people in Washington I trusted during that time. I'm not sure I even trusted myself.

Robinette was fascinated with how I knew so much. In his later memos to North and Secord and in FBI interviews, he indicated there was something more to me than what I was letting on, but he just couldn't put his finger on it.

"There is more to Terrell than what meets the eye," Robinette told FBI agents Beisner and Glasser in an interview on July 24, 1986.[20]

"There is something about Terrell that is scary."[21]

Of course, I did nothing to try to make Robinette want to trust me. I maintained an icy, reserved demeanor that made people unsure whether to hate me or fear me.

With Robinette, there was more fear than anything else. Just how much fear was evident one Sunday while we were having lunch at a little cafe in Georgetown.

I accepted his invitation primarily because I was lost in Washington. I was staying in the condominium owned by Mal Warwick, which I often referred to as "the box," near the Brookings Institution. I was working six days a week, but Sundays I had nothing to do because the liberals didn't want to be around me too much on a social basis. They still saw me as a nasty right-wing mercenary who might kill them if I got upset. They used me politically, but tried to stay away from me socially.

I accepted Robinette's invitation for lunch just for something to do. We were sitting there talking casually when he leaned across the table and said: "What would you do if somebody ever betrayed you?"

I looked him right in the eye and said: "I'd probably blow their goddamned brains out."

He appeared startled.

"Let me put it on this basis," I continued. "Even if you were to do it, I would do the same to you."

His hand was on his coffee cup and the cup started rattling against the saucer. His face turned as white as his hair.

"You're serious aren't you?" he said with a shaky voice.

"You're goddamned right I'm serious," I said.

From then on Robinette was so leery of me that when we walked down the street he would be four feet from me. Since he was hiding his ties to Secord, he knew that if I ever found out who he was and what he was doing he would be in deep shit. He would have to spend the rest of his life looking over his shoulder to see if I was there.

That attitude made me doubly dangerous to North, Secord and their enterprise. Not only did I have the information they were frightened of, they knew I would use it regardless of the consequences.

It wasn't concerned at that point with what became of me. I didn't care if they killed me because to kill me would have given me credibility and made me believable. I have no doubts that option was considered more than once. I have no doubts that someone said: "We need to kill this fucker."

Several times Robinette called and asked me to "take a drive out into the countryside." I don't think he had the guts to pull the trigger, but Secord and North had enough thugs in their employ who would have done the job without batting an eye.

But, instead of coming at me head-on, they came at me from ambush. They tried to destroy my credibility because they couldn't dispute the information I was furnishing. The more of a threat I became to their enterprise, the more determined they were to silence me.

North couldn't target someone just because he was a nuisance and a stumbling block to his plans. That never would have flown, even in the anything-goes atmosphere of the White House at that time. North had to make me even more of a threat than I was.

So, I became a "terrorist threat" and a potential presidential assassin.

Where did the threat come from? It came from the heads of Oliver North and FBI Executive Assistant Director, Oliver "Buck" Revell. It was an incredible bit of fantasy woven from unrelated bits of information. (See Appendix 5.)

This new "threat" enabled North to unleash the enormous powers of the White House and the U.S. government against me. Just as I had targeted the U.S. government for revenge, now the government was targeting me.

On July 15, 1986, Robinette told North I was going to be the star witness for the Christic Institute suit. I was going to burn down their house, Robinette said. I was going to link Hull, Owen and Secord to drug smuggling and assassination plots against Pastora.[22]

That same day, information reached North through the FBI that a plot by Sandinista backers to assassinate Reagan might be in the works. That information, according to a deposition given later during the Iran-Contra hearings by Revell, came from a source familiar with "a mercenary who would avail himself to conduct assassinations."[23]

Two days later, the FBI decided I was that mercenary. The information was quickly passed to North through Revell.[24]

That was all North needed to classify me as a "terrorist threat." In doing so North was then able to bring to bear on me the same powers of the White House that he had used to force down the airliner carrying the terrorists responsible for the murder of American Leon Klinghofer aboard the "Achille Lauro."

North had been given unusual powers in a network of White House groups that sprang up in response to international terrorism between 1984 and 1986. The Terrorist Incident Working Group (TIWG) was created by North in 1984. Within that, an even more secretive unit known as the Operations Sub-Group (OSG) was established in early 1986.[25]

Working through these groups, North had access to an unprecedented amount of information obtained from intelligence agencies and military sources. He could call in, as he did in the "Achille Lauro" incident, whatever military or intelligence assets he needed to deal with the problem at hand.

These were the assets he decided to use against me. To North, an opponent of the administration's political programs and foreign policy apparently was the same thing as an international terrorist.

On the night of July 17, 1986, Robinette was preparing for a dinner party for 10 people at his house when North called.

"Hey, aren't you talking to a guy named Jack Terrell?" North asked Robinette.

"Yeah," Robinette replied.

"For General Secord?"

"Yeah."

"You've got to come down here right away," North ordered.

"Where?"

"The White House."

"I've got this dinner party. I can't . . . ."

"Come down."

"Christ, I got this dinner party . . . ."

"You come down and bring all your documents."[26]

It was an order, not a request.

When Robinette arrived, North told him the reason for the urgency. "The man's going to kill the president," North said.[27]

Robinette almost fell over. There was nothing I had told him that indicated I would cause physical harm to the president. All I was interested in doing was setting the record straight on the Contra wrongdoings. My revenge was not physical. Even Robinette had admitted as much to FBI agent Ellen Glasser earlier in the day.

"Robinette stated that he believed Terrell did not present a threat to President Ronald Reagan. Terrell appeared to have no loyalties to any outside government," Glasser wrote in her report of that July 17 interview.[28]

Robinette later reiterated it in other FBI interviews.[29]

And in a July 15 memo to North, Robinette said I did not want to align myself "with any political group or cause" except to expose the skimming of funds and aid the Miskito Indians.[30] (See Appendix 6.)

North was insistent. In his eyes I was a threat to the president. North urged Robinette to write another memo about me. This one repeated what Robinette had written two days earlier about me being the star witness in the Christic Institute suit and elaborated on what he perceived as the "dangers" I posed to their enterprise.

According to that July 17 Robinette memo, I "could be embarrassing to R[ichard] S[ecord]," and "could be dangerous to our objectives." In Robinette's words, I was a "serious threat to us."[31]

This memo confirmed efforts had been undertaken by "Project Democracy" to buy me off just so I would stop talking. At one point in my meetings with Robinette I was offered a chance to set up a helicopter service in Costa Rica.

"The 'investors' would require that he [Terrell] reduce or stop his 'political talking' as it would 'affect our investment,' "Robinette wrote to North of the offer. Through that buyout, "we would have [Terrell] in hand and somewhat in our control."[32] (See Appendix 7.)

North was satisfied.

"You've got to talk to the FBI," North told Robinette. "Do you know Buck Revell?"

"Nope," Robinette replied.

"Well, here's his number. Call him up."[33]

Robinette called Revell, who told him he was sending a car to North's office to pick him up.

Robinette protested. "Well, I can't . . . I've got this dinner part-."

"No, you've got to get down here right away," Revell broke in. "We'll send a car for you right away."[34]

North instructed Robinette to show Revell the memos and the pages from the book proposal relating to the FDN's involvement with drugs. Robinette met the FBI car and three unsmiling agents outside North's office on 17th Street just south of Pennsylvania Avenue and was whisked to the FBI offices. There, eight FBI and Secret Service agents confronted him and had him tell the story of his dealings with me once again.[35]

While Robinette was being grilled by the FBI and Secret Service, North went to work fabricating the extent of my threat to the president. The memo was addressed to his boss, National Security Adviser Admiral John Poindexter. Where I was a "dangerous threat" in Robinette's memo, I became a "terrorist threat" in North's memo to Poindexter:

SUBJECT: Terrorist Threat: Terrel [sic]

Several months ago, a U.S. citizen named Jack Terrel became an active participant in the disinformation/active measures campaign against the Nicaraguan Democratic Resistance. Terrel's testimony was used in the Avirgan/Honey suit in Costa Rica and has been entered in the Florida law suit against Richard Secord, et al.

Terrel has appeared on various television "documentaries" alleging corruption, human rights abuses, drug running, arms smuggling, and assassination attempts by the resistance and their supporters.

Terrel has also been working closely with various Congressional staffs in preparing for hearings and inquiries regarding the role of U.S. Government officials in illegally supporting the Nicaraguan resistance.

After the "West 57th" piece by CBS two weeks ago, Project Democracy officials decided to use its security apparatus to attempt to determine how much Terrel actually knows about their operations. One of the security officers for Project Democracy [Robinette] met several times with Terrel and evaluated him as "extremely dangerous" and possibly working for the security services of another country.

This afternoon, Associate FBI Director, Oliver Revell, called and asked for any information which we might have regarding Terrel in order to assist them in investigating his offer to assassinate the President of the United States [deletion] The FBI now believes that Terrel may well be a paid asset of the Nicaraguan Intelligence Service (DGSE) or another hostile security service.

Mr. Revell has asked to meet with the Project Democracy security officer who has been meeting with Terrel. A meeting has been arranged for this evening. The FBI has notified the Secret Service and is preparing a counterintelligence/counterterrorism operations plan for review by OSG-TIWG tomorrow.

It is interesting to note that Terrel has been a part of what appears to be a much larger operation being conducted against our support for the Nicaraguan resistance. We have not pursued this investigation — which includes threatening phone calls to the managing editor of the *Washington Post* — because of its political implications. It would now appear that [deleted] of Terrel's activities, this may well be much more than a political campaign. (See Appendix 8.)

Poindexter, the ultimate technocrat, knew he was in over his head on this and refused to discuss it with Reagan. Poindexter sent the memo back North and told him to rewrite it.

At the bottom, Poindexter scribbled a note to North: "Give me another memo, for the President this time including the results of OSG. What do you want me to tell AG (Attorney General)?"[36]

A second memo was somewhat more restrained. But it still listed me as a "terrorist threat" and included the nonsense that sprang from North's overactive imagination that I was an asset of a foreign security apparatus. Poindexter also rejected this one.[37] (See Appendix 9.)

Finally, on the third try, Ollie got it right.

Dated July 28, 1986, this third memo lists as its subject: "Terrorist Threat: Terrell."

No first name. No identifying characteristics. Just "Terrell." At least North spelled my name right this time.

According to this version of the memo, I was a threat because I "became an active participant in the disinformation/active measures campaign against the Nicaraguan Democratic Resistance."

The memo went on to say "It is important to note that Terrell has been a principal witness against supporters of the Nicaraguan resistance both in and outside the U.S. Government."[38] (See Appendix 10.)

Ronald Reagan looked at it, initialed it and went back to sleep.

Only days earlier, I was considered by the FBI to be a cooperating witness in an ongoing investigation into drug-smuggling, gun-running and possible violations of the Neutrality Act. Now, I was the focus of the investigation.

I was followed everywhere I went. My telephones were tapped. During a late July trip to Miami, FBI agents surreptitiously entered my room and went through my trash looking for incriminating evidence.

According to the July 28, 1986 report from the FBI dumpster divers:

> In addition to the various gum wrappers, cigarette butts (and) cigarette packages deposited in the trash container, a copy of the *Miami Herald*, morning extra copy, Thursday, July 24, 1986, was found in the trash container. A cursory research of the newspaper indicated that an article had been torn from page 16A of the main section of the newspaper. Another copy of the same edition of this newspaper was obtained and this other copy indicated the torn newspaper article dealt with an opinion by Admiral John Poindexter in which he stated that the relationship between the Nicaraguan Contras and Colonel Oliver North did not violate a congressional prohibition on United States involvement with the rebels.
>
> Two Marriott note pads were observed on a table in the room and appeared to have indented writing upon them. This indented writing appeared illegible to the naked eye. In addition to the two note pads, four pages of Marriott stationery [were] also obtained and, to the naked eye, appeared to have no indented writing.[39]

What great detective work. I wonder how long those guys had to go to school to learn to do that.

While I was in Miami, more than a dozen FBI agents were assigned to monitor me and my movements and investigate my alleged threats against the president.

The issue of those threats finally came to a head the last few days of July.

David Beisner called me at the International Center on July 28 and asked if I would meet with the FBI at 10 a.m. the next day. His voice was calm and did not provide any clue as to what the meeting was about. He said I would be picked up in front of the center by agents, but that the session wouldn't take long.

The next morning, a plain, dark blue car driven by a lone agent stopped on Eighth Street in front of the center. I walked out and got into the car. The agent didn't offer his name, but was friendly and we chatted amiably on the short drive down the street to the Washington Navy Yard and the FBI office. It was so polite and low-key it wasn't funny. I've gotten worse treatment from traffic cops than I got from the FBI that morning.

After clearing security and being patted down in the lobby, I was led up to the fourth floor and a large conference room.

I could see I was expected. A dozen people were sitting around a large table. I knew some of them, including Ellen Glasser and David Beisner. But the majority of the people in the room were strangers. All of them looked official and all of them wore identification cards clipped to the breast pockets of their suits. But most had turned the cards over so I could not read their names. They must have thought I was one dangerous character.

On the left side of the table were FBI agents. On the right were Secret Service agents. I was asked to sit at one end of the long table. At the other end, facing me, was a well-dressed older man who said little but obviously was in charge of this tribunal.

After a few polite exchanges, one of the Secret Service agents looked directly at me and said seriously: "We've gotten information that you intend to try to assassinate the president of the United States."

At first I thought I didn't hear the question right. When the full impact of what he said hit me, I nearly fell out of my chair.

"You're joking," I replied.

"This isn't a joking matter," the agent barked. "We want an answer."

"Who told you that?" I asked, my anger rising.

"Our sources and methods are classified," the agent said curtly.

"I know I've done some crazy things in my life and I may not agree with the position of my government," I said, "but I would never think about killing my president, regardless of how I felt about his policies."

"Would you be willing to take a polygraph test to back up what you just said?"

"You're goddamned right I will! When can I take it?" I angrily retorted.

The agent looked around at the other agents and said: "How about right now?"

"Let's go," I told them and rose to leave.

I was placed in a Secret Service car, which sped away from the Navy Yard followed by two other cars filled with agents. We drove to the center of the city and turned into a parking deck that took the convoy three stories underground. I was led from the parking area to a small room equipped with a polygraph machine and a see-through mirror that ran the length of one wall on my left.

Two Secret Service agents prepared me for the test, while a third read me my rights.

"You are entitled to have an attorney present," the agent told me.

"Fuck an attorney," I said. "Let's do it now. Let's get it on."

As the agents prepared me for the test, I was asked to intentionally lie on certain preliminary questions to get a reading of my emotional reflexes to determine when I told the truth and when I lied.

One agent said they got strong readings from the preliminary test questions and that it would be an easy test to administer. My blood pressure was so high at that I'm surprised the needle on the machine didn't rip right through the paper.

I asked only one favor from the examiners. I wanted them to at least give me the courtesy of telling me whether or not I passed the test once it was complete. Both agents were young and probably would be placing their asses on the line by telling me, but one of them winked to let me know he would give me a post-test indication if I passed or failed.

Almost from the beginning it was clear that this inquisition had nothing to do with Oliver North's fantasy about my threat to the president. This was a political matter, not a criminal investigation.

Virtually every question was political.

Among them: "Do you agree with the president's policy in Central America?"

"Have you ever been in the Nicaraguan embassy?"

"Do you know Martin Vega?"

Martin Vega was the chief of security for the Nicaraguan embassy in Washington, but at that time I had no idea who he was.

In two days of polygraphing I was never asked "Are you going to kill the President of the United States?"

The only question that approached that subject was: "Have you ever threatened a government official?"

But who hasn't? Especially if you've ever dealt with the IRS.

Here were government agencies, supposedly non-partisan and non-political, being used for a political investigation. It was the same sort of thing we used to accuse the KGB of doing. But here it was going on in Washington, D.C., under the noses of high-ranking Reagan administration officials, if not at their direction.

The testing went on for two days. At the end of the second day, as I was unstrapped from the machine, two FBI agents and several Secret Service agents were standing by the door. One of the Secret Service agents walked up to me, offered his hand and said: "We just wanted to know where you stood."

I had this funny feeling I had just been fucked but hadn't gotten kissed.

I was angry and bitter, but I felt fortunate I was able to walk out of that room. A message had been delivered to me and I received it loud and clear. That message said: "Stop fucking around in political matters."

The next morning I called Bob Parry of the Associated Press and told him about the polygraph session. He exploded in anger. He wanted to do a story about it, but I talked him out of it.

"These people have made it clear what they could do to me," I told him.

According to later testimony by Revell, the polygraph "eliminated [Terrell] as being a threat to the President. . . . That particular portion of our involvement vis-a-vis him ceased at that point."[40]

I tried to rebound, but found I had little luck making any headway against the administration's concerted disinformation campaign. The covert operations to aid the Contras continued unchecked.

Then, on October 5, 1986, a lone Sandinista soldier standing in the jungle lifted a 20-pound SA-7 Grail surface-to-air missile to his shoulder, sighted in on a low-flying C-123 and pulled the trigger.

It was the beginning of the end for Oliver North and the Enterprise.

17

Government for Sale: A Heavy Price to Pay

InComCon's "Mr. Smith" called frequently between August 1985 and August 1986, but I never heard from Donald Fortier again. And I never really knew anything about the man who recruited me until I learned much later he had taken ill with stomach cancer in May 1986 and died Saturday, August 23, in Georgetown University Hospital at the age of 39.

A brief obituary on page 6 of the second section of the *New York Times* that Monday was headlined simply, "Fortier, Aide to Reagan, Dies."[1]

In the story, Reagan called Fortier's death "a great loss to my administration and the United States."[2]

It may have been more of a loss than Reagan ever realized.

Fortier was one of those faceless bureaucrats who come to Washington from middle America all bright-eyed and eager to make a difference before sinking into the political morass on the banks of the Potomac.

He came from Ohio, which is about as middle America as you can get, and worked for the Rand Corporation in Los Angeles before moving to Washington in 1975 and taking a job as a staffer with the House Foreign Affairs Committee. In 1981 he went to work at the State Department and became deputy director of policy planning. Within a year, Fortier had worked his way into the White House and a job as director of European Affairs for the National Security Council.

By 1983, when the Reagan administration's covert policies were in full swing, Fortier had become the deputy national security adviser, No. 3 man on the NSC. Ahead of him in access to the president were only Robert McFarlane, the national security adviser, and Admiral John

Poindexter. When McFarlane resigned, Fortier moved up to No. 2. But he was a virtual unknown to anyone outside the White House.

Fortier played a key role in the NSC. He helped develop the Office of Political-Military Affairs, which had control over a wide range of security issues that had political-military implications.[3]

Fortier, by some accounts, was also responsible for helping develop the concept of the arms-for-hostages deal and overseeing the Swiss bank account into which money from the arms sales destined for resistance movements in Afghanistan and Nicaragua was deposited.[4]

And, according to McFarlane's testimony before the Iran-Contra Committee, Fortier had responsibility for Latin American military affairs and was given the job of selling Congress on Contra aid packages.[5]

Fortier's assistant was Marine Lieutenant Colonel Oliver North. When Fortier became ill, North took over the job. And when Poindexter became swamped with paperwork without Fortier as the gatekeeper, North became his own boss and promptly ran amok.

Over the years, I have had a great deal of difficulty understanding my role in the Contra affair. I know how bizarre my tenuous connection with a member of the National Security Council must appear.

Was it actually Donald Fortier who called me that Sunday night in September 1984, and asked me to go to Central America to keep an eye on some Alabama cowboys?

Quite possibly it was not.

There is a chance the caller was not Fortier and was actually someone else using his name. The caller could have been someone who disliked Fortier and used him name so that he would be discredited if I ever got caught or talked about him. Fortier, it would appear, had too much power and prestige to lose by getting personally involved in such a deal.

By the same token, the call to me came at a crucial juncture. The NSC/CIA was feuding with the Defense Intelligence Agency and the Pentagon over their roles down south and had no eyes or ears in those camps. I offered myself at just the right time.

But does it matter whether the caller was actually Fortier?

Not really.

There was someone, later several someones, inside the government who used me to expose certain aspects of the government's operation, for whatever reason. And Fortier was certainly in a position to know everything about me and much about what was going on in Honduras and Nicaragua.

Fortier's death did not mean the end of InComCon. It carried on, using me to furnish information about the private aid network to the news media until North's "Enterprise" finally crashed and burned in October 1986.

The who, or what, of InComCon was never revealed to me. Neither did Mr. Smith provide many clues about his location or the organization for which he really worked. On one occasion though, shortly after I moved into an apartment in Rosslyn, Virginia, across the Key Bridge from Georgetown, Mr. Smith called to welcome me to the neighborhood.

"I see you've got a pad," said Mr. Smith. "I see you've moved over here with us."

The CIA has some of its personnel and business offices in Rosslyn just a few blocks from my apartment. And its headquarters are just up the Potomac in Langley.

I came to believe that InComCon was composed of a group of people, not just one person, and Mr. Smith was a composite, much as Woodward's "Deep Throat" had to be a composite.

I came to believe that "Deep Throat," or what was described as "Deep Throat," was one of the original versions of InComCon. In both instances it served as a system of checks and balances to an administration that was dangerously out of control by leaking selected information that brought that administration to its knees.

It was just far more dramatic and far better publicized in the Watergate case than in mine.

InComCon's primary purpose in dealing with me seemed to be leaking information for reasons greater than any I could understand. I had many questions that went unanswered during my time as a whistleblower. In some cases, the information I received was leaked before it could do the most damage, thus adding to my confusion about what direction I was being led by this shadowy group of individuals.

A thousand times I asked myself: "Why me?"

The Reagan administration was particularly paranoid about leaks and came down hard on those doing the leaking. In the wake of several news leaks in 1983 about Reagan's plan to bomb Libya, he talked about forcing his Cabinet members to submit to polygraph tests. Secretary of State George Shultz hit the ceiling over that one.

"The minute in this government that I'm told I'm not trusted is the day that I leave," Shultz said.[6]

In 1984 Reagan signed, but never implemented, National Security Decision Directive 84, which called for all administration personnel who had access to top secret information to sign an agreement that would have permitted any of their speeches or writings to be censored for the rest of their lives. It was the ultimate in government censorship and bureaucratic paranoia.

In retrospect, it's also my belief that a "bureaucratic leaking battle," as it has been described, got me the entree to CMA and Central America.

I approached CMA at a time of heightened friction between government agencies over who was doing what down south. Following the Parker-Powell shootdown, someone within the administration leaked a story to the *New York Times* about Operation Elephant Herd, in which the CIA collected low-cost weapons for the Contras. These included the military version of the Cessna Skymaster aircraft that accompanied the Parker-Powell chopper.

But the chopper had been borrowed from the U.S. military, or the DIA, and they were not happy that it was in the CIA's control when it got shot down.[7]

The DIA and CIA began checking on one another and leaking selective bits of information that would embarrass the other agency. I walked into CMA just when the NSC/CIA types needed some friendly eyes down south to keep track of what the other guys were doing.

The collective Mr. Smith had an agenda with his leaks, although I was never told what it was and was never able to determine it. At the height of my involvement with onInComCon, I asked Mr. Smith why his information seemed only to prompt debate between the media and the White House while making my life a living hell. Since I was the source of the information, I was the person being called a liar. I was the person being monitored by government agencies. And I was the person doomed to a future of public uncertainty about my veracity.

It would have been foolhardy to attempt to convince an already skeptical press I was not acting alone, that there was someone inside the government feeding me information. The media were leery enough of me. To tell them I had a secret source would have only increased their doubts about me.

Mr. Smith assured me there was a purpose to the madness, that I was being used for purposes he could not reveal. But it was difficult for me to stand back from my personal motives and view the bigger picture as Mr. Smith wanted me to.

Impeachment of Reagan may have been InComCon's true goal. But I came to believe those in control of InComCon were willing to settle for a public lynching of high administration officials in a congressional hearing. In September 1986 there were rumors in Washington about a formal inquiry into the mess, but it had not yet reached the level of a Watergate.

Reagan and his staff had learned well the lessons of Watergate. Nixon had tried to protect the people loyal to him during the cover-up and ended up being forced out of office. The Reagan administration was willing to cut every infected part from its body to remain in power and avoid impeachment.

"Save the old man at all costs," was the watchword of the administration as summer slipped into fall of 1986.

Time hung heavy on my hands because I seemed to be a squirrel on a wheel, switchboarding and providing background information on Contra participants that largely fell on deaf ears of reporters I classified as computer potatoes. They wanted me to do all the work for them.

The vast majority of journalists I dealt with had a shallow view of the Contra war and who was responsible for it. Many were afraid to report certain aspects of the story because the Reagan administration had no compunctions about using its disinformation/dirty tricks office within the NSC to pressure reporters, editors and publishers not to print stories about White House-sanctioned arms, drugs and violations of the Boland Amendment.

With few exceptions, reporters steered clear of those subjects.

Each day I went to work at the International Center, I felt I was standing at the bottom of a tall mountain, knowing I would have to try to climb it before the day was out.

It would have been easier for me to have dictated a cassette tape of what I had to say and simply hand reporters a copy when I was interviewed. I was doing little more than repeating my story over and over again. They were fascinated by my life as a mercenary. They got their thrills vicariously through me.

The investigation of the Contras had slowed to a crawl in September 1986 and even I began to lose interest in it and look in other directions.

Lindsay Mattison and the International Center were supporting the efforts of various dissident groups throughout the world to return to their homelands and create opposition parties or factions within those parties that would challenge the incumbent governments, usually governments that were aligned with the United States.

Shinbom Lee, a Korean dissident, and George Chang, a member of the Taiwanese opposition, requested Mattison's help in setting up a clandestine radio station that would broadcast left-wing propaganda into their respective countries. Mattison asked me to assist them in obtaining information about radios and antenna equipment that could send a low frequency signal several thousand miles.

The station was to be built somewhere in the Philippines, utilizing contacts in the "people power" revolution of Corazon Aquino and with the backing of the International Center's former president, Raul Manglapus, a longtime foe of recently ousted Filipino strongman Ferdinand Marcos. Mattison assured Lee and Chang the station would be allowed to operate.

Chang, whose group would finance the operation, wanted to visit Manila to talk with officials of the Aquino administration to be sure this project could be launched without too many delays. I was asked to go along to ascertain the security needs for the facility.

On September 8, 1986, I left for Manila with Lee and Chang. It was a great relief to be out from under the pressure of Washington. I needed a break from the endless bullshit and this seemed to be the perfect working vacation.

I fell in love with Manila and the Philippines at first sight. Manila, for all practical purposes, was just another American city with a Spanish accent and lower prices. Manila had all the usual fast-food joints, but its night life was far livelier than anything in the U.S.

We settled into the Silahis Hotel on advice of our escort and former Marcos opponent Bonifacio Gillego. Bonnie had lived in exile in the U.S. for years because he would not be a part of the dictatorial Marcos government. He was a former military man and returned home only after Aquino took power. Bonnie was then seeking elected office as a congressman from his home district of Sorsogon. This was the province in which we planned to build the radio station.

I enjoyed the country and its people and saw the Philippines as an alternative to living in the States, where I had become a marked man. George Chang held out the possibility that if the station was built, I could manage it and organize the security because I had the necessary backgrounds in both fields.

When we returned to the States, I was thinking more about the Philippines and how quickly I could return than about Contragate. But my daydreams were soon shattered and my plans for the radio station abandoned. History took another strange turn and I was caught up in it.

On October 5, 1986, a C-123 transport plane carrying 10,000 pounds of ammunition for the Contras left Ilopango military air base in El Salvador. It flew over southern Nicaragua to avoid the heavy Sandinista anti-aircraft artillery in the north.[8]

Bill Cooper, a former Air America employee, was the pilot. Wallace Blaine "Buzz" Sawyer, a part-time Southern Air Transport employee, was the co-pilot. Eugene Hasenfus, a former Marine who had also worked for Air America in Southeast Asia, was the loadmaster or "cargo kicker." A 17-year-old FDN soldier served as assistant kicker and handled the radio.

The Contra resupply flights had become routine for the crew. So routine, in fact, that in late September after one resupply mission Cooper wrote in a letter: "Ho-Hum, just another day at the office."[9]

But on October 5, a Sandinista army patrol near the village of El Tule about 90 miles southwest of Nicaragua spotted the C-123. Among the patrol was a soldier whose job earned him the nickname, *El Flechador*, the archer. He had been trained to use the SA-7 Grail anti-aircraft missiles supplied by Cuba and the Soviet Union. Despite the poor track record of the SA-7 against large aircraft, *El Flechador* was on target with his arrow this day.

The 4 1/2-foot missile hit the C-123 in its right engine and wing. The explosion blew part of the wing off and started a fire. Hasenfus, who was wearing a parachute, jumped immediately before the plane could go into a full spin that would have pinned him inside.[10]

Hasenfus was the only survivor. The other three men were unable to bail out and died in the crash. Hasenfus was captured by the Sandinistas and paraded before the international media as evidence of U.S. government involvement in the war against them. This time, they had a solid case.

Despite denials from the State Department, the White House, the Pentagon and various private aid organizations of responsibility for the downed plane, a clandestine U.S. military search operation was launched with assistance from Costa Rican authorities.

Felix Rodriguez, the Bay of Pigs veteran and CIA contract agent who was running the Contra resupply efforts out of Ilopango under the name "Max Gomez," called Donald Gregg, Vice President George Bush's deputy national security adviser, to tell him the plane was missing.[11]

Gregg later denied ever discussing Contra aid with Rodriguez. But telephone records unearthed from a safe in Rodriguez's house in San Salvador forced Bush's office to revise its script. Gregg had indeed discussed Contra aid with Rodriguez, Bush's office said, but the call about the downed plane had gone to Gregg's deputy, Colonel Samuel Watson.[12]

The crash site was a treasure trove of incriminating documents that dragged the U.S. government right into the war.

Found on the bodies of the dead crew members were identification cards from Southern Air Transport Company, the major CIA proprietary airline in Central America. Hasenfus not only had a SATCO ID card, he had one from the Salvadoran military that showed he was an "adviser" in the "Grupo U.S.A." at Ilopango.[13]

The downed C-123 bearing the tail number N4410F had been a flying file cabinet and possessed a unique and somewhat shady history.

Once used as a drug-running aircraft by renowned smuggler Barry Seal, the C-123 was purchased by SATCO from Harry Doan, owner of Doan Air Services in Daytona Beach, Florida. The aging aircraft had been retro-fitted with high powered engines and special cameras at Rickenbacker Air Force Base near Columbus, Ohio, for the photo intelligence mission into Nicaragua that produced front-page pictures of Colombian drug lord Pablo Escobar and Sandinista official Frederico Vaughn loading cocaine onto the aircraft.[14]

The pictures were released by Oliver North to the *Washington Times* over the objections of the Drug Enforcement Administration and were reprinted in newspapers around the world. They were especially a big hit in Colombia. In North's zeal to paint the Sandinistas as drug runners, he signed Barry Seal's death warrant by releasing those photos.

On February 19, 1986, two men approached Seal's white Cadillac Fleetwood in Baton Rouge, Louisiana, pulled out sub-machine guns and opened fire. Seal was dead about the time he realized his former Colombian cronies had come gunning for him. The two gunmen and four other men were quickly arrested by the FBI. All were Colombians. Three were convicted and sentenced to life without parole.[15]

North, like many in the White House, was willing to spend any asset, contractor or individual involved in Nicaragua for propaganda purposes that would make the Sandinistas look like butchers, narco-terrorists or dupes of the international Communist conspiracy. Whatever it took, North was willing to do. It didn't matter to him who died in the process.

Drugs were the glamour issue at the time. All the blame for America's problems with cocaine was placed by the White House on the Colombians. And the Colombians, according to the White House, were receiving assistance from Communist regimes in Central America.

But what no one in the White House wanted to admit, and few of the media in Washington were willing to explore, was that the Contras and their supporters were dealing drugs to provide creative financing during those times when Congress cut off aid.

The cache of records recovered from the downed C-123, coupled with the insistent pleas from Hasenfus that he was working for the CIA, became the first silver bullet fired into the NSC's private effort to win a war that had no popular support.

On Wednesday, October 8, 1986, I was sitting in my office on the top floor at the International Center when the receptionist buzzed me and told me I had a telephone call.

"Mr. Smith is on line two," she said.

I picked up the receiver and punched the blinking button.

"Hello."

"This is Wednesday, October 8, 1986. How are you?" said Mr. Smith.

"Fine," I replied.

"Did you know or do you have any knowledge of Eugene Hasenfus, William John Cooper or Wallace Blaine Sawyer?"

"Hasenfus is all over TV."

"Go to the CAB [Civil Aeronautics Board] today. Request the monthly reports from Southern Air Transport. That is the only public record you are going to find on that airline."

"Then what?"

"Use your best judgment."

I hung up the telephone and walked uptown to the CAB. The Southern Air Transport logs were there, just as Mr. Smith said they would be. I was amazed by what I saw. There were sheets of unexplained flights to Bogota, Barranquilla, Havana, the Cayman Islands, Howard Air Force Base in Panama City and other strange ports of call in the Caribbean. There were frequent flights in and out of Ilopango military air base in El Salvador. There were unexplained cargo weights going down and coming back.

In addition to working in the Caribbean, Southern Air was heavily involved in flights from Portugal to both sides of the civil war being waged in Angola. The names of pilots, dates and routes clearly indicated this airline was anything but a standard cargo carrier.

Southern Air was an enigma in the air cargo industry. It had vaulted from a small cargo line grossing a few million dollars a year to a giant corporation that by 1985 was grossing over $100 million a year. The company had been purchased from the CIA in 1973 by a group that included SATCO Chief Operating Officer James Bastian and president William G. Langton, both of whom had previous ties to proprietary airlines during Air America's heyday in Southeast Asia. SATCO was awarded the purchase of the airline by CAB despite a $2 million dollar higher bid by another group.

The personal stationery of William Langton was found in the debris of the downed C-123 along with hand-written instructions for Bill

Cooper to check in with U.S. Embassy officials David Passage, deputy chief of mission, and Bill Hall, an embassy representative in El Salvador, at a time when U.S. government officials, including Reagan, were vigorously denying they knew anything about the illegal air operation.[16]

Another notable name in the plane's records was that of Rob Owen. He seemed to be everywhere during the war but remembered being nowhere much later when it came time for an accounting of who did what.

I copied the logs and began sending them all over town. Within a few days I was provided copies of papers that had been among the belongings of Cooper and Sawyer by Melinda Rorick, a Nicaraguan sympathizer who worked at the International Center and had high-level contacts in the government in Managua. The papers came to me before they were released to the press.

Many strange details about the role of the U.S. government and its private contractors came out of those CAB logs, in addition to other vital pieces of what appeared to be an incredibly elaborate puzzle. Names began floating to the surface of people involved in North's "Enterprise" who had previously remained anonymous.

Retired Air Force Major General Richard Secord was one of those people. During the same time he was coming after me through Glenn Robinette, for what he feared I would release to the Christic Institute, he was responsible for much of the airlift operation through his company, Stanford Technology Trading Group International.

At the time though, I had no idea Secord had targeted me because of what he feared I knew. I was acting simply on information developed through the paper trail in CAB and SATCO records.

Richard Secord was North's lead man in the private "Enterprise" created specifically to keep the Contra effort alive when the Boland Amendment cut off funds. CIA Director William Casey suggested to North that Secord was an excellent candidate for the job because he had expertise in covert operations in Southeast Asia.[17]

But Secord had little love for his former employer, the U.S. government. He was still bitter about his untimely departure from the Pentagon as a result of his involvement with Edwin Wilson, the rogue CIA agent who sold arms to Libya and Moammar Ghadaffi. The only way Secord would agree to get involved with the Contras was if he could make money out of it. Lots and lots and lots of money. Secord was determined to make up for being slighted by the government by stuffing his own bank account.

Secord's involvement with clandestine warfare dated to 1966, when he went to Udorn, Thailand, to handle the operations and logistics of the secret war in Laos. He had just completed more than 200 combat missions in South Vietnam but was still full of piss and vinegar when he went covert. Known as "the Fat Man" to his classmates at West Point, the pudgy Secord became known to the Lao as "The Buddha," an honorific that had as much to do with his power and wisdom as his shape.[18]

One of Secord's plans in Laos called for planes to dump loads of Calgonite dishwashing detergent on the Ho Chi Minh trail to make it too slippery for the North Vietnamese to travel on. That plan, like all others aimed at the trail, didn't work.[19]

Secord also had served as an Air Force adviser to the Shah of Iran from 1963-65, telling him what to buy and whom to buy it from. Secord returned to Iran in 1975 as head of the U.S. Air Force advisory group. In 1980 he was one of the chief planners for the ill-fated rescue attempt of American hostages in Iran and later was involved in a second rescue attempt that was never carried out.[20]

When Reagan came to power in 1981, Secord was appointed deputy assistant secretary of defense for international security affairs, a job that gave him enormous power within the Pentagon over military sales to more than 40 countries. In that position he was called on by the administration to lobby for the sale of Airborne Warning and Control System (AWACS) electronic surveillance planes to Saudi Arabia in 1981. It was in that capacity that he met North and Robert McFarlane.[21]

The following year, Secord was linked to Wilson and former CIA agents and secret war veterans Thomas Clines and Theodore Shackley through a $71 million contract with a company known as EATSCO, the Egyptian American Transport and Services Corporation. Wilson later charged that Secord had a 20 percent secret share in the company and was using his considerable influence in the Pentagon to get contracts for EATSCO. [22]

Secord hotly denied the allegations and the Justice Department refused to prosecute him. But Secord retired the following year, his reputation permanently smeared and took a job with Stanford Technology, a Vienna, Virginia, firm that specialized in electronics and security systems. Secord's partner was Albert Hakim, an Iranian who had been introduced to him by Ed Wilson years earlier.[23]

When Secord agreed to run North's "Enterprise," he and Hakim opened a Swiss bank account under the name Lake Resources. They dumped millions of dollars into that account from weapons sales, including money generated by the illegal sale of missiles to Iran.

Secord had numerous military and political contacts in Washington, in addition to tentacles spread throughout the world in back-channel operations, that enabled him to use the Contra war as a profitable business venture. So what if people were dying in the name of a bankrupt foreign policy? Where there's a war, there's money to be made and Secord thought nothing of profiting from someone else's suffering.

As payback for loyalty in the past, Secord brought on board the "Enterprise" many former military officers and intelligence associates.

One of them was Colonel Robert Dutton, a former Air Force buddy of Secord's who retired on May 1, 1986 and immediately assumed operational command of the "Enterprise," reporting directly to North.[24] The CIA's Felix Rodriguez, who was calling himself Max Gomez, was on the ground in El Salvador, but Dutton was the boss.

Another of Secord's cronies involved in the "Enterprise" was Air Force Lieutenant Colonel Richard Gadd.

Gadd retired from the Air Force in 1982 and took a job as a liaison between the Joint Special Operations Command at Fort Bragg, North Carolina, and the Joint Special Operations Agency, created by the Reagan administration to improve unified special operations efforts by the Army's Green Berets, Air Force commando units and Navy SEALs. This was the same structure that employed Major Karen McKay and Secord.

According to information obtained from InComCon, Gadd was a business partner of Secord's in a company known as International Service Corporation, which sold arms to the Contras. Gadd was also connected to Corporate Air Services, which served as paymaster for the resupply operatives at Ilopango. This particular corporation was run by a mysterious character, Edward de Garay of Lancaster, Pennsylvania. Among de Garay's employees was pilot William Cooper.

InComCon was particularly insistent about getting Gadd's name out in the press, but few people picked up on it. There was little interest in Gadd among the media I dealt with. I could do little more than throw his name onto the ever-growing pile accumulating on my desk.

Most of these names were given me by InComCon and were included in my list of Contra participants. But until the Hasenfus shootdown, I could not connect any of them with a particular operation. After Hasenfus, the picture InComCon was sketching for me began to take on some detail.

I was beginning to connect the dots.

In addition to the individuals involved, I found numerous storefront operations stacked one on top of another hiding their links to North and the NSC. All the people involved in this operation had one thing in common: Dutton, Secord, Gadd and Clarence Louis Stearns had all been members of the Air Force's secret 1st Special Operations Wing at Hurlburt Field in Fort Walton Beach, Florida.

It appeared a "good old boy" network of former military and intelligence types ran a separate, private intelligence and operations branch of the government. The trail was so obvious that most congressional investigators never even saw it when they stumbled across it. To them, such a thing was totally unbelievable, and the "Enterprise" came up on their radar screens as an aberration and not part of a larger problem. No one could comprehend the efforts the Reagan administration would go to keep the Contras together, body and soul.

Before the Hasenfus shootdown I was just throwing pebbles. After it, I started throwing boulders. Hasenfus was the incident that gave everybody the smoking gun and the paper trail that took the government's secret little war apart.

I became the prime source, for the *Miami News* for its stories on Southern Air Transport and the connections with Ilopango and El Salvador.[25] The *Miami News* rarely printed my name, nor did a lot of other papers who used me as a source. They knew if my name popped up as a source the stories would be far more controversial than they already were.

Within days of the C-123 shootdown and capture of Hasenfus, the true story of North's "Enterprise" started coming out of the shadows. Attention was diverted from me for the time being, but the government still wasn't through with me. Some people held grudges and blamed me for upsetting their little schemes.

Scooping Meese

Media interest in the shootdown of the C-123 began to wane by late October. Hasenfus was awaiting trial in Managua, and officials of SATCO and the Reagan administration were effectively stonewalling.

The stonewalling began within hours of the plane's crash. Tomas Castillo, the CIA's man in Costa Rica, sent a secret cable to Robert Dutton.

"Situation requires we do necessary damage control. Did this A/C [aircraft] have tail number? If so, is it the same one which refueled several times at ... Please advise ASAP. If so, we will have to try to cover quickly as record of tail number could lead to very serious implications."[26]

Elliott Abrams, assistant secretary of state for inter-American affairs, went before congressional committees three times between October 10 and October 15 and each time categorically denied the U.S. was involved in the Hasenfus flight.

An occasional article in an outside-the-Beltway newspaper made links between proprietary airlines and suspected shipments of arms overseas, but no new incriminating evidence pointed to the heart of the "Enterprise" at the NSC.

The story broke in another direction on November 3, 1986, when it was revealed that the United States had been selling missiles to Iran in violation of its own policies in an effort to gain the release of hostages in Lebanon. The news gave some members of Congress whiplash as their attention went suddenly from Central America to the Middle East. The Reagan administration appeared to be dabbling in covert activities all over the globe.

When the missiles-for-hostages story began to gain steam in the media, I was called by many reporters who wanted to know what I knew about this effort. I had no firsthand knowledge of the missile scam and had little interest in matters not directly related to the Contras.

The pace of the probes into the White House covert and possibly illegal activities began picking up again. Only this time, just as many conspiracy buffs as reporters were calling me for my take on the situation. Everybody seemed to have answers, but no proof.

Lindsay Mattison was reveling in it all. There was a major scandal in Washington, I was one of the major players and the International Center was profiting greatly from the publicity. Money was pouring into the center and during one board of directors meeting Mattison said: "You can all thank Jack Terrell for your salaries."

Several new staffers were brought on board during this time to augment my efforts. One was David MacMicheal, the former CIA analyst who left the Christic Institute and came to the International Center to write extensive reports for distribution to members of Congress opposed to Contra aid. David became a friend, but by doing so also became a subject of surveillance by the FBI.[27]

David had resigned from the CIA after he was asked to alter reports that would provide a more favorable political tinge, even though the alterations were not true. David is one of the most brilliant men I have ever met, but the only thing that rivals his intelligence is his stubbornness. Once he gets involved in an issue, he is there for the duration.

David helped me understand how the game was played in Washington and how best to fight the government. We were from different ideological corners, but our friendship transcended politics.

In addition to David's political tutelage, Robert White, the International Center's president, provided frequent private seminars about the subtle political undercurrents that flowed around every issue that made its way to Washington.

White's outspoken opposition to El Salvador's right-wing death squads while he was serving as ambassador to that country earned him the everlasting enmity of the Reagan administration and forced his resignation in 1981.

White was a true diplomat and handled subjects with equal measures of eloquence and knowledgeable candor. I called it diplo-ease.

But White detested violence. One thing that bothered him more than any other was hearing tales of violence committed in the name of political reform. White was uncomfortable around me, especially when I talked about some of the things I had done. He was non-violent to the extreme, but despite our differences in that regard I paid close attention to his opinions. He helped educate me about politicians and how to deal with them.

Bob's heart was in the right place and that was all that mattered to me.

Friday, November 21, 1986 began as all days began at the center. I had my usual cup of coffee and walked up to my glass-enclosed office for another day of switchboarding. The revelations about missile sales to Iran lingered in the press, but no one had come up with the key that might unlock the mystery of what had happened to the money.

Since it was Friday, all I could think about was the long, lonely weekend sitting in my small apartment in Rosslyn waiting for Monday.

My telephone rang and the receptionist told me Mr. Smith was on the line. I was so accustomed to his calls that I felt no particular anticipation. InComCon's calls had become little more than cheerleading sessions, trying to keep me pumped up so I could make discoveries for myself or provide enough information so journalists could do it themselves.

"It's Friday November 21, 1986," Mr. Smith said. "How are you?"

"I'm making it and that's about all," I replied casually.

"The money is going to the Contras," he said tersely.

I sat up and paid attention. The key had been handed to me.

"You're shitting me," I said.

"Not at all. Call your press people and see how this goes down."

"How? Who's in this thing?"

"Listen, just throw this out and let them figure out how and who."

"I need more than this," I said.

Mr. Smith's voice became even more terse.

"Use your contacts and go through the steps," he said. "It won't be as painful as you might suspect. This is important. Believe me, this is important. We'll talk again."

The phone went dead and I sat staring out the window trying to assimilate what I had just heard. I wondered how big a fool I was about to become by suggesting without any proof, without any documentation, that money from the missile sales to Iran had been diverted to aid the Contras.

Bob Parry of the Associated Press called while I was mulling this around in my head and I mentioned the possibility of the money being sent to the Contras. He surprised me and said he had been thinking the same thing. I told him I would see what else I could learn and call him back.

I walked out of my office and across the hall to Bob White's office. He was talking with his secretary and a few staff members when I interrupted and asked him what he thought about the possibility that the money from the missile sales went to the Contras.

It was possible, he said, but he had his doubts. I told him I was going to contact selected journalists and give them the story.

"I know it's true," I told White, "but I can't reveal my source and I don't have any paper to back me up."

White smiled and shrugged his shoulders as if to say: "Do what you have to do." He was used to my wild claims coming true.

I returned to my office and began going over my list of more than 200 reporters with whom I had dealt in the last few months. I wanted a small group of heavy hitters whose stories would have the biggest impact. But I also knew that these reporters would be the hardest to convince.

My first choice was Steve Engelberg of the *New York Times*. When I told him about the money being diverted to the Contras, he was quite skeptical. The more I talked, the more annoyed he became and I got the distinct impression I was pestering him. He told me he would look into it, but I felt it was just his way of politely getting rid of me.

Next I called Chris Drew at the *Chicago Tribune* and repeated what I told Engelberg. I got much the same response. I called Dan Grothaus of the *Houston Post*, Mary Martin of the *Miami News*, Mike Kelly of the *Baltimore Sun* and several other journalists trying to get one of them to listen. No one seemed interested in what I had to say. I was getting nowhere. All of them apparently thought this was a little too bizarre even from me to waste their time on.

I left the office late that night having met with nothing but rejection. I felt my news zinger needed more distribution. Since I wouldn't get an audience over the weekend, I decided to wait until Monday to see if anybody out there was interested. I had been badgered by reporters for months over trivial matters and now that I possessed the equivalent of a nuclear bomb, my information was getting lukewarm responses. My information was too incredible to believe.

Washington and the media are strange entities. In that city more than any other, there is a mentality of pack journalism. The media are like cattle in a pasture. They feed only in those areas known to all the other cows. Rarely do they venture into parts unknown.

Monday came and went with much the same response to my information. I checked in with reporters I had talked to the previous Friday and was told the information was being closely studied. That meant they may have made a few telephone calls, but there was nothing urgent about it.

InComCon didn't call and by Monday night I was starting to think that perhaps this was little more than a fishing expedition by Mr. Smith to see what sort of suckers he could reel in.

The next day, Tuesday, November 25, I was sitting at my computer attempting to write a narrative about the events I had covered during my time at the International Center when I heard a loud cheer from the first floor.

I looked down from my third floor window into the conference room below where several center staff members were huddled around a small television set. One of the group started shouting my name.

"Jack! Jack! Come see this!"

I passed Mattison's office on the way. He was smiling and clamoring for the telephone. He was trying desperately to contact someone at Senator Kerry's office. He told me that Attorney General Edwin Meese was on television announcing that profits from the arms sales to Iran had been sent to the Contras.

I paused for a moment, stunned. Mr. Smith and InComCon had really delivered a fast ball this time.

I walked into the conference room and listened as Meese did the administration's mea culpa. Oliver North had been fired. John Poindexter had resigned. There would be a full investigation.

Staff members kept shaking my hand and patting me on the back, asking how I knew four days earlier about the diversion of funds.

"It was simply a matter of deduction," I said. "All my evidence pointed to this conclusion."

It was total bullshit, but they bought it.

I could not believe Meese was holding this press conference. Why was he putting a straight razor to the throat of the Reagan administration when he didn't have to? There was no proof yet, no smoking gun, no paper trail. Why now?

This administration had proven time and time again it was incapable and unwilling to tell the truth about its involvement in the not-so-secret war in Central America. Now Meese was claiming it was going to right all the wrongs.

Something much larger than the accidental discovery of a document must have brought on this sudden admission of guilt after years of lying about it. There must have been pressure from within the White House of enough magnitude to push Meese in front of those television cameras and admit to an illegal activity that could bring down the president.

No clear explanation has ever been given to explain the reasons, but I have since concluded that perhaps the administration decided to launch a preemptive strike on the press once the White House learned journalists were asking questions about the politically dangerous secret of diversion of funds to the Contras.

Meese's revelation sparked a gold rush on the center. The telephone lit up like a Christmas tree as reporters from all over Washington began calling.

I returned to my office and called Steve Engelberg, thinking it would be virtually impossible to get to him. He answered immediately, his voice excited.

"Do you believe it now?" I said.

"If you told me the sun wasn't going to rise tomorrow, I would print it," he said.

He told me he had to get off the line and get to work on the story.

Now that Meese was admitting where the money went, people were eager to listen to me. Those reporters with whom I had shared the information the previous week must have been banging their heads against the wall for sitting on the story of the year. But they had done so because I was the source and my credibility was still in question.

There were many times during my stay in Washington I was given information by Mr. Smith and InComCon to dispense that I could not personally back up with documents. But no sooner had I disseminated that information than it mysteriously was given some credence by some source on Capitol Hill or within some other government agency.

People could never nail me down on my sources, which irritated the hell out of them. It also scared them because they couldn't put a handle on me. They couldn't tell if I was coming from the right or the left. Some days it appeared as if I was coming from both sides. Other days it appeared as if I was coming from neither side, that I had my own agenda. I was giving them information they didn't want to hear and they couldn't figure out where it was coming from.

Even today the people in Washington with whom I have dealt feel I have a larger agenda, that I am still working for some government agency. They can't quite figure me out.

I frightened people in Washington. That demeanor I had developed in prison of "Fuck with me and see what happens to you" kept people on edge. I dealt easily and frequently with journalists, but I became a pariah among congressional committees because of my background and my attitude.

The center became a hub of media activity after the Meese admission. The stairs to my office sagged and groaned under the weight of cameramen and reporters standing in line for interviews. CNN, ABC, CBS and foreign television media were there to hear what I had to say. The print media sent anyone who was breathing.

Almost overnight I became an oracle. I found it humorous because with the release of one piece of the puzzle I gained a measure of credibility that I had fought so hard to obtain over the previous 18 months. I didn't have that much more to offer the media, but now they might listen closer to the things I had been saying all along.

The new slant on wrongdoing in the name of the Contras got congressmen off their butts and into the fray. They wanted blood. And the best way to get blood was in a nationally televised hearing. Those kinds of hearings also are quite good for posturing to the electorate back home. With few exceptions, they didn't want to get involved until they could look good back home.

My time in Washington reinforced my lack of respect for the system that runs our country. Washington is where the policy makers weave the nation's moral and social fabric. But the process is shoddy, the quality control nonexistent. I had been deceived. The American public had been deceived.

The only difference between us and the Communists was that our terrorism is more democratic and we camouflage it in red, white and blue appeals to patriotism.

The Road to Rangoon

Meese's admission let loose the hounds of journalism on Contragate, which quickly became Iran-Contragate because of the missile sales. My job was finished.

But the Reagan administration wasn't finished with me.

Sometime over the weekend of November 29 and 30, the offices of the International Center were broken into. Someone climbed onto the roof of the building next door, threw a brick through a second-story window at the center and climbed in. Files were ransacked throughout the center, but the most damage was done in the offices of those people dealing with Central America.[28]

Computers, typewriters, television sets, radios and telephones were all in place. The only things missing were my files on Southern Air Transport that I had obtained the previous month from the Civil Aeronautics Board.[29]

I had no doubts the Reagan administration was continuing the fine work of its predecessors in the Nixon administration. It was Watergate plumbers redux. Only this time the plumbers were smart enough to not get caught.

It wasn't the last straw, but it was enough to convince me that my days were numbered and it was time to get out of Dodge for a while. I began entertaining other offers for work. I found more than I wanted through the International Center. My name had become well-known in the community of those seeking assistance for their extra-governmental activities.

Among them was Timmy Bevadra, a deposed prime minister from Fiji who wanted to stage a counter-coup and get back into power. Through his American attorney and a backer from the Pacific Forum, I was approached to form a strike team and was asked to prove U.S. government involvement in his ouster.

Another offer came from Tabo Imbeke, one of the leaders of the African National Congress. Imbeke interviewed me in Montreal, Canada, and asked if I would train ANC guerrillas to hit targets in predominantly white neighborhoods in Johannesburg, Pretoria and other major cities in South Africa. After our lengthy meeting, he gave me his ANC lapel pin to remember him, but we were never able to reach agreement.

The South African Defense Forces, clandestine division, also solicited me to assist them in forming "hit" teams to locate and dispose of ANC members living or visiting the States. The same SADF contacts mailed resumes of potential candidates for those hits hidden between two cardboard menus from a local pub in Dunnottar, Republic of South Africa.

The International Center was involved with many of these groups, especially those that leaned to the left. Publicly, Mattison's agenda was Third World conflict resolution. Privately, he provided a forum for revolutionary groups and their leaders who espoused the particular brand of socialism he felt should be imposed on downtrodden, ignorant masses of the Third World who were incapable of governing themselves. He felt the only way to save them was to enslave them in a bankrupt political system that has never proven it will work anywhere.

In many cases, the phone simply rang and I found myself talking to strangers who seemed to know a great deal about me and the reputation I had attained. In my business, events have a way of finding people and I was being found time and time again.

The most intriguing offer I received came from a group known as the Committee for the Restoration of Democracy in Burma. CRDB was an international organization of Burmese expatriates headquartered in Washington. It was run by Tin Maung Win, son of a former Burmese ambassador to the United Nations, and a pipe-smoking, gnome-like former guerrilla fighter named Ye Kyaw Thu (pronounced ye jaw thoo).

The group was struggling to attain recognition and backing in Washington, and the International Center provided some measure of encouragement. CRDB had little money and virtually no public or private support in its efforts to oust the socialist military government in Rangoon. It was the ultimate underdog and I identified with it.

Burma is a dizzying collection of ethnic groups and factions, none of which have any love for another. The CRDB was comprised mainly of Burmese ethnics, who make up the majority of the population. Through Win and Thu, who had strong contacts with the other ethnic movements, CRDB was trying to gain some power in what then was a fledgling umbrella organization of ethnics known as the National Democratic Front (NDF).

Some of the ethnic groups had been fighting for more than 20 years to gain a voice in the Rangoon government or achieve autonomy from it, but they had been doing it separately. The NDF provided an opportunity to unite military forces and resources for a push against the Rangoon government.

One of Thu's strongest contacts was with the Kachin ethnics from northern Burma and their leader, a former school teacher turned revolutionary named Brang Seng, who was referred to affectionately as "the chairman." The Kachins had been vital to the allied war effort against the Japanese in World War II and now controlled a large number of jade mines and opium fields to which the Rangoon government had no access. Federal troops could advance no farther north than Mandalay, where the Kachins were in control.

As a result of their jade and opium, the Kachins were the richest of the ethnic groups. They were also the most feared by the poorer, smaller ethnics in central and southern Burma because they were among the best guerrilla warfare and jungle fighters in the world, having honed their skills over the previous five decades of constant combat.

By the summer of 1987, I was working closely with Thu and Win and making plans for a trip to Burma. I made the decision that I could no longer tolerate Washington and moved to Manila. I was also indirectly urged by anonymous officials in the U.S. government to seek other employment and was often threatened over the telephone.

I wasn't about to roll over for anyone, but a future in the pit of vipers that Washington had become was not to my liking. Lindsay Mattison agreed to let me return to the Philippines to continue work on acquiring a license for the propaganda radio station, but from Manila I could easily travel to nearby countries where there were always job opportunities for someone with my expertise.

I was content to languish in the Philippines waiting for work and occasionally talking to reporters calling from the States. I had no desire to return to Washington because I had been excluded from testifying before any congressional committee. My information helped light the fuse that ultimately caused the explosion, but my credibility continued to be a touchy subject on Capitol Hill.

Despite my differences with Tirador from our Central American fiasco, I invited him to join me on the Burma initiative and he agreed. On December 2, 1987, we left my apartment in Manila bound for Bangkok and the start of what we hoped would be an operation that would make a difference in Burma.

Once again I had taken a nom de guerre. This time I was known as Colonel Green. Tirador was Colonel Blue. We decided on this mission that all foreign advisers would use colors for their code names.

The mission was to operate under a more professional infrastructure than CMA and we would be known as the Burma Liberation Expeditionary Force (BLEF). We designed shoulder patches and emblems that were manufactured for us by a tailor from India. This operation was to become everything the mistake-ridden Pegaso was not because I had learned well from its failure.

Arrangements for much of our initial trip were addressed at a meeting with Brang Seng and his top military aide, Colonel G. Zau Seng, in Tokyo in late September. I was corresponding with several members of the ethnic groups involved in the war in Burma and was kept up to date on their needs and desires for assistance. When I departed Manila, it was with full intentions to begin a long-term involvement in the war and put the Contras, Congress and the press behind me. I was tired of all of them.

I knew I could utilize my talents for a better purpose, one not orchestrated by the U.S. government, while assisting underdogs in a struggle where political considerations were minimal. I would return to the life of a so-called mercenary, but my return would be out of the need for financial survival, not ideology. I was leery of attaching myself to anyone's cause for any reason other than money.

No longer would I place myself in a position of responsibility for a starving minority. No longer would my beliefs be manipulated by an underlying secret political agenda. And no longer would I allow patriotic values to determine my destiny. This was a straight-up business deal, right or wrong.

The Kachins and one of the smaller ethnic groups, the Mons, wanted a better military, not political indoctrination on how to set up their new government with a blueprint from the White House. I was not there to impose democracy or any other form of government on these people. We simply wanted to train soldiers to kick ass.

Our activities while in Thailand were sanctioned and overseen by the Thai secret police. We were assigned the top commander for southern Thailand, Colonel Kong, a burly, smiling man with a crew cut and a long history of covert operations that dated back to the use of Thai mercenaries in Laos. Kong would open any door necessary for the successful completion of our mission.

Entering Thailand was much different from entering Honduras. We carried no lethal weapons and didn't waste time dealing with corrupt immigration officials. We entered the country cleanly, quickly and legally. We were sanitized.

I set up operations out of the Rex Hotel in the Sukhumvit area of Bangkok, a tourist area that featured high-rise luxury hotels as well as those that were more nondescript and had much lower prices. It was easy to get lost in the crowd at the Rex and along Sukumvit.

We held campaign strategy meetings at the hotel with Brang Seng and staff members from his military arm, the Kachin Independence Army (KIA), and his political arm, the Kachin Independence Organization (KIO). The political nature of the NDF was such that jealousies between the Kachins and the leaders of the largest ethnic minority, the Karens, had to be dealt with. We had to appear to be one part of the whole confederation, although we were trying to exert more than our fair share of influence.

General Bo Mya, a Jackie Gleason lookalike who headed the Karens, had once headed the NDF. But when Brang Seng arrived from the north, it was decided a more centrist and less powerful leader was needed to head the confederation so it would have more of a chance to remain intact. That job fell to Saw Maw Reh, leader of the Karenni National Progressive Party.

Saw Maw Reh was a kindly, graying, soft-spoken man who had seen more than 40 years of desultory guerrilla warfare and was prepared to carry on with another 40 years. He was well-respected by other members of the ethnic groups, but had little desire to prosecute the war at a faster pace. He was slow and deliberate and not given to taking chances.

Dealing directly with the NDF would have been a waste of my time.

Ye Kyaw Thu had used his personal influence as a legendary guerrilla fighter and the Washington-based influence of CRDB to get me in the front door with the Kachins, the most militant of the ethnics. Now it was up to me to convince Brang Seng I could put together a plan that would relieve pressure on his Kachin forces in the north and redirect the attention of the government forces to the southern peninsula.

My plan, which was to become known as the "Ye Offensive," called for the ethnic armies operating out of southeastern Burma in areas held by the Karen and Mon ethnics to sever rail and communication lines and take over that part of the country south of Moulmein on the Andaman Sea down to Victoria Point, the southernmost tip of Burma.

Once that was accomplished, the ethnic leaders under the NDF coalition were to set up a provisional government and establish diplomatic relations with other countries before striking out militarily against the government in Rangoon.

The plan called for a joint military and political front by the ethnics. If we could hold the fragile coalition together, the plan was workable. But I discovered the ethnic divisions to be far deeper than I had imagined. The powerful Karen ethnics never signed on to the plan because they were in the process of establishing an alliance with Khun Sa, the kingpin of Southeast Asian opium and heroin.

Khun Sa operated out of the Shan State to the east of the Karens, but was having trouble maintaining his smuggling routes through Thailand and China. The Karens had centuries-old smuggling routes through

Three Pagodas Pass in western Thailand and appeared willing to trade access to it for much-needed weapons Khun Sa could supply.

My "Ye Offensive" needed manpower, logistical support and political approval of the Karens. Without them, nothing could be done because the remaining ethnic groups simply didn't have the logistical network necessary to get the job done.

My first exposure to the fighting forces of the ethnics came near Three Pagodas Pass, where on December 10 and 11 Tirador and I met with Nai Non La, leader of a faction of the Mons known as the Mon National Liberation Army.

The military here was coeducational. They believed in equal opportunity at death. These people were all business. They were not equal in firepower to the Contras, but the fire in their eyes showed me they had a purpose and a willingness to fight. They were constrained in their efforts to unseat the dictator General Ne Win only by lack of equipment and support.

After dealing with the Contras for so long it was refreshing to see units of dedicated fighters with organization and direction.

The trip to the Mon enclave near Three Pagodas Pass went well and on our return to Bangkok we began preparing for a longer trip to the NDF headquarters at a jungle village called Manerplaw.

I made the trip to Manerplaw alone. Ye Kyaw Thu and his associate, Colonel U Thant Zinn, had gone on ahead and Tirador had to return to Manila to take care of some personal business that involved his Filipina girl friend, who just discovered she was pregnant.

Colonel Kong escorted me to the town of Tak, northwest of Bangkok, where I was turned over to a general of the Border Patrol Police. He would arrange safe passage through the village of Mae Sot to the Moei River, where I would board a long-tailed boat for the trip to Manerplaw.

The trip to the river resembled the drive to the Contra camp at Las Vegas in Honduras. It was long, rough, bumpy and dusty and several times came within gun range of the enemy. This time the Burmese, not the Sandinistas, were the enemy.

I arrived at Manerplaw on Sunday, December 20, just in time for the Karen New Year celebration. Manerplaw sat on a steep bluff on the west side of the Moei River near its confluence with the Salween River. It was the typical Thai-Burma village that had thatched roof huts with split bamboo walls and teak floors. But this village had electric lights provided by portable generators and, since it was the Karen New Year, there was dancing and music and fireworks throughout the night.

The huts of the ethnic groups were arrayed throughout camp not in order of strength or importance, but in order of security. The Karens occupied the most northern of the hutches, which were quite well-appointed by jungle standards. The Kachins were far to the south. But their huts were far more luxurious than any of the others. They had their own generator, a television, a VCR and refrigerator.

Although I came into camp as a guest of the Kachins, I was assigned sleeping quarters in the Karen guest house. I thought nothing of it, but Ye Kyaw Thu thought it strange and was offended by the gesture. Not until much later did we learn the reason I was placed there.

December 21 dawned cold and gray, with a trace of fog in the air. Although we were near the equator and the days were quite warm, winter nights in the tropical jungle can get quite cold.

The Karen guest house had a large veranda with a teak floor where I took my breakfast and coffee. As I sat there updating my journal the morning after my arrival, a tall, thin man with dark skin and Oriental features approached and asked who I was.

Not knowing who he was, I lied. When he asked what I was doing there, I told him I was a guest of CRDB and the Kachins. I told him I was a writer covering the civil war in Burma, but I suspect he knew better.

He introduced himself as Dr. Em Marta, a representative of the Karen Department of Foreign Affairs. He wore a cheap, ill-fitting suit and tried to convince me he knew everything that happened at Manerplaw.

He gave me a questionnaire to fill out and said it was required of all visitors to Manerplaw. I filled it out with as much wrong information as I could and handed it back to him.

Dr. Marta was particularly curious about why I did not want an appointment with Bo Mya. The fact that I expressed no real interest in the plight of the Karens made him even more suspicious.

It didn't take long to figure out NDF headquarters was useless for my purposes. My talks with various ethnic military leaders were brief and pointed. Every group wanted help, but none had any money, except for the Kachins. It was the same story throughout the world: People wanted help, but they didn't want to pay for it. They thought people like me should do things out of the goodness of our hearts.

Brang Seng was sitting on millions of dollars worth of raw translucent jadeite, but had no way to get it to market. I had suggested a helicopter be leased to fly several loads of the valuable mineral into Thailand, but the Chairman said we would not be allowed official flights from Thai airspace into Burma.

But, he said, if I could arrange secret flights in and out of his territory, he would cooperate fully and the Thai government would allow the sale of the jade once a small import duty was paid. This was a tantalizing offer because Brang Seng promised me a 50 percent share of the profits.

It was up to me to initiate the mission because the Kachins were unwilling or unable to advance funds for the expedition.

It was the same story in Burma as it had been in Central America: There was no money, no political backing and no way to get the job done without holding hands with the devil, which in this case meant either the U.S. government or the Soviet Union. It was the same dog and pony show, just different dirt.

Dealing with the Burmese entailed a lot of bowing and scraping. A snail's pace would have been fast for these people. They also had a way of dancing around issues, rather than meeting them head-on. they weren't big on confrontations. I was too direct for them and I don't doubt they were embarrassed by that directness on more than one occasion.

After several long, boring days and a few meetings with the Kachins and Brang Seng, I received word that the NDF had given tentative approval to my plan. I made preparations to return to Bangkok and put the plan into motion. I was scheduled to leave on the morning of December 24 with several other people.

While I was in Manerplaw I was particularly watchful of where I went, who I talked to and what I ate. It wasn't so much paranoia as it was prudence. In this line of work you never know who might come after you, or how, and in Burma I was dealing with people and political considerations that were unfamiliar to me.

The night of December 23 I let my guard down. No evening meal was prepared at the guest house and the steward who prepared food for me offered only two fresh oranges. He claimed that a delegation from Khun Sa's Shan United Army had arrived and he was busy preparing native dishes for them. I didn't think too much about the fruit, although I would have preferred a heavy meal because the trip back to Bangkok was long and arduous, with few opportunities to stop for food.

The next morning I awoke shaking and sweating. My insides were seething. I had severe abdominal pains and bouts of nausea. I could barely move. My senses told me I had to get out of that village, out of that jungle, and back to the anonymity and security of Bangkok.

I went down to the river to catch the boat scheduled to take me downriver, only to learn it had already departed. I had been left behind. I was told another boat would leave in two hours.

Colonel Zau Seng saw me standing by the river and when I told him of the mixup, he invited me to the KIA house for breakfast. I was so weak I could barely make it back up the bluff from the river. I was suffering severe stomach cramps. I originally thought it was a reaction to a traditional Burmese dinner from two days earlier, when everything we ate was spiced with hot chilis. By the time I sat down with Brang Seng, I was hurting so badly I didn't even want to look at food.

Brang Seng talked about a change in plans as I sat and suffered. He wanted me to move into Mon territory, where soldiers could be brought from various ethnic groups for training. He felt we had to train in a place where Bo Mya had no control over the people. Since Mons and Karens were traditional enemies, the Mon States seemed the perfect place to put together an army.

Brang Seng wrote a letter addressed to the leader of the New Mon States Party that he said provided his blessing for me to conduct military actions. The letter was to be opened and read only by Nai Shwe Kyin, the leader of the other Mon faction.

I was given several thousand Thai baht and told to meet Brang Seng at Three Pagodas Pass in a week. Neither I nor the letter ever got there. The letter remains sealed to this day.

During our conversation I lost track of what Brang Seng was saying because my temperature was steadily increasing and my stomach was twisted in knots. I was burning from the inside out. I was hot and then chilled. When I finished with Brang Seng, I stumbled to the boat landing and was escorted down river by a Karenni officer and several of his men.

When the boat reached the point where I was to be transferred to a truck to Tak, I could hardly move. My fever was blinding and I had a severe case of diarrhea. When I thought the cramps had passed, I moved into the front seat of the truck, covered by a heavy field coat. I was bone cold and sweating profusely in the jungle heat.

I hardly remember transferring from the truck to another vehicle, finally arriving in Bangkok late at night, half dead. I kept thinking it was no more than a case of the jungle trots and that it would eventually pass. But it got so bad I took a taxi to the nearest hospital. I barely made it to the emergency entrance where I collapsed and was carried into a room.

Over the next two days I alternated between periods of unconsciousness and dim reality as I lay on the cool hospital bed. An English-speaking doctor talked with me and drew blood in an attempt to find out what ailed me. When he received the results of the blood tests, he asked if I had been exposed to chemicals in recent days.

I could think of none, but he said he believed I had received a high dose of some sort of poison. I thought I had an acute attack of bacterial dysentery, but the doctor thought it was arsenic poisoning.

I started thinking back. What could it have been? The only thing I could think of was the oranges. It had to be the oranges. My own death sentence had been delivered to me in two oranges. Somehow, I had cheated it.

An investigation conducted by the KIO and CRDB indicated the plot to poison me had been the work of Dr. Em Marta. According to the investigation, he apparently had injected arsenic into the oranges and had them served to me.

I could never determine the reason I had been targeted for assassination. It could have been my relationship with Brang Seng. It could have been my role in the military situation with the Karen enemies in the Mon state. It could have had even more far-reaching implications. After all, I was now operating in the backyard of one of my stateside enemies, General Richard Secord.

After being released from the hospital I could do little more than lie in bed at the Rex Hotel. I had no energy for anything else. Ye Kyaw Thu and Colonel Zinn visited me often and Tirador returned from Manila.

But I could not regain my stamina fast enough to get the Mon State initiative underway and Brang Seng canceled the mission. We had fallen far behind schedule and he had to leave the country on business.

Tirador and I returned to Manila and after several weeks of proper eating and rest I regained my strength. But the "Ye Offensive" was put on indefinite hold and eventually canceled when I was barred from returning to Burma by a U.S. federal court magistrate, which ultimately closed the books on my participation in that conflict.

One night in late January 1988, after my return to the Philippines from Burma, I was sitting in my apartment in Manila when the telephone rang. It was Mr. Smith.

"You better get back to Washington," he said.

"Now what?"

"You know North trashed you real good, but no one knows exactly how bad," he went on.

"We have information about a document recovered from North's safe concerning you and it's going to be released on the Hill in a couple of days."

"What do you want me to do about it. I can't think of anything more they can do to me."

"This isn't about doing something to you. It's about doing something to them. Just get your reservations taken care of and make an appearance no later than January 21. It will become clear why I am making this request."

"Man, you people sure know how to make my life miserable," I lamented.

"It's up to you. Go or stay if you wish, but I wouldn't pass up this opportunity. Good luck."

The conversation was like many in the past — short and to the point. But this time I had absolutely no idea what the hell this was all about. I figured I better go to Washington, if for no other reason than to satisfy my curiosity about the document.

I arrived in Washington within two days and took a taxi directly to the International Center. Lindsay Mattison's glass-enclosed office looks out on the lobby and when I opened the front door, baggage in hand, he looked at me as if he had seen a ghost.

"What the hell are you doing here?" he said as he rushed up to me.

"I just decided to pay the center a visit. Why? What's up?"

"You know goddamned well why. How did you know the Robinette document found in North's safe was being released today?"

"I don't know what you're talking about," I said.

"This is more than a coincidence," Mattison said. "You're a goddamned CIA plant, aren't you?"

I laughed at his suggestion because I had heard it all before and walked up to my office. Everyone I met along the way seemed excited about the release of the document. My sudden and unexpected appearance, they believed, had been planned to coincide with the document's release.

John Winer in Senator Kerry's office thought the same thing. My arrival was just too timely, just too convenient. I asked Winer to have a courier send a copy of the document to my office.

The document was an assessment of me written by Glenn Robinette, who had been hired by Richard Secord to determine what I knew about his involvement in the "Enterprise." The most significant part of the document, though, had less to do with me than it did with the efforts North made to shut me down. I had been the object of a dirty tricks campaign orchestrated by North.[30] (See Chapters 16 and 18 and Appendix 5.)

No one seemed to know who had released the document, but it was clear to me that InComCon had delivered another swift kick to the butts of the Reagan administration.

After a few *Newsweek* articles and a piece on ABC about the document, I retreated to Manila in the hope that I had made a final curtain call in Washington.

But my enemies back in the States were not through with me. Many had long memories and strong grudges against me because of what I had done to their operations in Central America. My name kept popping up in the Contra drug-smuggling, gun-running investigation in South Florida.

I was going to be made to pay in some fashion for what I had done to wreck the U.S. government's plans for the Contras. Whether it would be with my life or with jail was the only question.

The Iran-Contra hearings were at their height during this time. But by then I had become a bit player in the unfolding drama. I had pretty much outlived my usefulness both for the media and the congressional committees.

Besides, there was no real interest at getting at the truth in those hearings. The very name was misleading. It should have been called the Iran Missiles Committee because of the lack of attention paid to the FDN, the Contras and what went on in Central America. By executive fiat, the committee restricted its investigation to the sale of missiles to Iran and the money derived from it.

There was no investigation of the numerous allegations of FDN drug involvement, no investigation of the corruption that plagued the FDN leaders, no investigation of the use of private citizens to further foreign policy, no investigation of how Lieutenant Colonel Oliver North personally redefined protocol at the NSC, no investigation of how Casey ran the CIA as his personal fiefdom.

Bill Casey sat in front of several congressional intelligence committees and spent Ollie North like a bad dollar bill. But just when Casey got to the point where he was talking about some of these issues in detail, he developed a fatal case of one-day brain cancer. Like a good soldier, he took most of his secrets to the grave.

The Iran-Contra Committee treated the Contra issue like it had rabies. Whenever Contra issues were raised, the hearings either went into executive session or turned into an ad campaign for Oliver North-style patriotism.

North became the great martyr for guns, drugs and the American way. He did everything but come to the hearings with bleeding hands and feet, dragging a cross behind him.

The hearings were like an audition for patriots. The general public didn't see anything more than a soap opera farce. The characters became greater than the evidence and the impact of the hearings was minimal. Had the American public been allowed to see and hear the truth of what actually went on in Central America, it would have been like slicing Uncle Sam in half live on national television.

Although the hearings were a farce, those who had helped make them possible by revealing sensitive information about illegal activities found themselves scorched. They got too near the fire. Everybody who touched the Iran-Contra issue in some fashion was burned by it. Journalists, prosecutors, long-time government employees, anybody who touched this mess was torched.

For those of us who got involved in the Iran-Contra affair, it was like taking a stroll through Chernobyl.

18

Selective Prosecution: Internal Affairs

I knew I would be made to pay in some fashion for what I had done to wreck the U.S. government's plans for the Contras. I had been too outspoken and — more devastating for the government — too honest in what I said for them to ignore me.

It would have been much easier to deal with an attempt on my life than jail. Those kinds of direct action I can understand and deal with. But the government chose once again to come at me from ambush as it did in Washington. This time it came at me through the courts and did so in such a fashion as to catch me totally off guard.

I had contributed a great deal of information to the South Florida investigation of the Contras and their connections to drugs and guns during my March 1986 interviews with Assistant U.S. Attorney Jeffrey Feldman. I was a cooperating witness for the government in what I thought was an honest attempt to dig out the roots of the corruption.

Jesus Garcia, the former Dade County corrections officer charged with possession of a machine gun, had gotten the ball rolling in 1985 when he told his attorney, assistant federal public defender John Mattes, about many of the illegal schemes the Contras and their supporters were involved in.

Garcia was convicted of possession of a machine gun and a silencer in December 1985, and Mattes was working on an appeal that would show there was a broader conspiracy at work here, one that had involved gun-running to Central America that the government had ignored. Garcia claimed he had been set up by Posey's Civilian Military Assistance because he refused to participate in the plot to assassinate Ambassador Lewis Tambs.

Had the government not been successful in prosecuting Garcia, there probably would have been no Contra investigation, no attempted federal coverup of it and no Iran-Contra hearings. But Mattes, who had gotten his law degree from the University of Miami just a year earlier, thought Garcia got a raw deal and began investigating what seemed to many to be rather ludicrous allegations concerning the Contras, drugs and guns.

Mattes has this blonde-haired, blue-eyed Joe College look about him, but he's a prosecutor's nightmare. When he gets his teeth into something, he won't let go, no matter what the consequences. That's what happened with the Jesus Garcia case.

In late 1985 and early 1986, Mattes was trying to flesh out the stories and charges he was hearing about CMA and its members. The more people he talked to, the more he was told the man with all the answers was a mysterious Colonel Flaco. And the more he dug, the more he found that the trail of characters involved in Contra illegalities led right into the White House.

One of those characters was a man who called himself Alan Saum. Saum was responsible for Garcia's arrest. Saum claimed to be a Marine Corps major and intelligence operative. He showed up in Miami one day, looked up Garcia and mentioned Tom Posey's name. Garcia figured Saum was another CMA member and invited him to spend some time at his home. After a few days, Saum went to the FBI and told agents about Garcia's machine gun.

Then Saum disappeared, leaving behind a pile of papers and documents that included the name of Vice President George Bush and a White House telephone number.

The Marine Corps didn't know much about Saum, except that he had been discharged before completing boot camp because he tended to cry uncontrollably and was afraid of his drill instructors.[1]

The only other things learned about him were that he was a neighbor of John Hull's in Evansville, Indiana, and that he had connections to the office of then-Senator Dan Quayle of Indiana.

Whoever he was and whatever his intentions, Saum served the government's purpose by getting Garcia out of the way. But by icing Garcia, Saum also set into motion a series of events that helped reveal the extent of the government's involvement in Central America.

By January 1986, Mattes was regularly sharing information about the Contras and their supporters with the FBI in Miami. The FBI launched its own investigation of Contra gun-running and drug-trafficking based on what Mattes was uncovering.

Mattes also was sharing his information with aides to Massachusetts Senator John Kerry, who had expressed interest in the illegal activities in Honduras and Costa Rica.

But Mattes was still trying to figure out how all this related to the White House. At the time, he knew he was walking down some very dark alleys, knocking on doors he shouldn't be knocking on. His investigator, Ralph Maestri, told him that he would know when he came to the right door because somebody would open it and kick him in the teeth.

That's exactly what happened when he finally tracked me down in New Orleans in March 1986. Rather than getting kicked in the teeth, it was more like the phantom of the opera taking off his mask. Mattes figured there was something ugly under that mask, but he didn't know just how ugly until it was removed.

I was the first person Mattes talked to who could corroborate Garcia's incredible claims of drug-smuggling, gun-running and assassination plots that were sanctioned by the White House. At the time, it seemed beyond the realm of possibility to him that the White House would involve itself in such a penny-ante operation.

As soon as Mattes talked to me, he knew he was in too deep. There was no way out. He figured his innocence would protect him and convinced himself that if he kept everything in front of him, nothing could creep up behind him.

But within days of returning from New Orleans, Maestri began picking up word on the street that he and Mattes had stepped over the boundary. They didn't know whose boundary, but they knew they were on the other side and there was no going back. For the first time in many years, Maestri began carrying a gun.

They knew they were being investigated as much as they were investigating. They just didn't know who or why.

In late March 1986, Mattes, Maestri, Ron Rosenblith of Senator John Kerry's office and Steve Kurkjian of the *Boston Globe* ignored warnings about their safety and went to Costa Rica to follow up on information I had given them.

In San Jose they bluffed their way into La Reforma Prison to talk to the five mercenaries who had been caught on John Hull's ranch in April 1985. They found much the same thing I had when I talked to them several months earlier. These were five paranoid, frightened men sitting in a hellhole of a prison, figuring somebody was going to whack them for what they knew about the government's illegal activities.

But they once again corroborated what I had been telling Mattes, right down to the $10,000 being delivered to Hull each month by Rob Owen.

The British mercenary, Peter Glibbery, knew about the money and the guy delivering it, but didn't know Owen's name.

"This guy kept coming down here, a preppy guy who looked a lot like you," Glibbery told Mattes.

"Wait a minute," said Rosenblith. "I know him. It's Rob Owen."

The mercenaries were able to describe Owen right down to his loafers.

They also told Mattes of the drug shipments from Hull's ranch and the arms shipments and weapons being stored for the planned assassination of Ambassador Lewis Tambs.

The pieces were starting to fall together. What began for Mattes as an investigation with a centralized focus on an assassination plot targeting a U.S. ambassador that was hatched in the coffee shop of a Howard Johnson's motel in Miami had widened into a broader probe. Now the focus was on the war in Central America, the U.S. government's involvement in it and various illegal activities sanctioned to support it.

The more Mattes investigated, the fuzzier the Tambs assassination plot became. It was just a small detail in the larger picture. But the broader picture of the war was becoming clearer and clearer.

Soon after returning from Costa Rica, Mattes met with FBI agents involved in the case. He was told to shut down his investigation. He was told to close the books and walk away from it. It had run its course, he was told, and there was nothing to it except a few out-of-control cowboys who wanted to get involved in the war.

Mattes was stunned. He knew there was something more here than just an investigation of a Cuban-American with an illegal machine gun and a few out-of-control cowboys. He protested. Then he protested louder, as only John Mattes can protest when he's angry.

The meeting quickly degenerated into a shouting, screaming match between Mattes and about a dozen FBI agents. This was no debate with the FBI debating team. There was nothing calm and rational about this. Had they not been wearing suits, and had the meeting not taken place in the FBI offices, I don't doubt that Mattes, as pugnacious as he is, would have taken on all of them in an old-fashioned brawl. He's that kind of fighter.

Mattes was told if he didn't get off the case there was a good chance he'd wind up testifying before a grand jury. And those were the nice threats.

That's when he knew he had really stepped into something he would never get out of. He smelled a conspiracy and coverup. He tasted it. He felt it rolling around him and over him. Justice was being impeded and the FBI in Miami was a party to it.

Two days later, Mattes was called to the office of Jeffrey Feldman, the assistant U.S. attorney in the southern district of Florida, to again discuss the investigation and his role in it.

At this meeting, Mattes was confronted by two FBI agents, an assistant U.S. attorney and Feldman, a large, dark-haired man who dressed in expensive suits and who was as abrasive as Mattes.

Again Mattes was told to shut down his investigation and go home. The feds said he was obstructing justice and impeding their investigation. Again it was not much of a discussion. It was another screaming, shouting barroom brawl without the beer and fisticuffs by five men in nice suits.

Within days of that meeting, Feldman went to Costa Rica and started probing into dark corners. While there he had the fear of Ronald Reagan and Attorney General Ed Meese put in him by CIA station chief Joe Fernandez (see Chapter 15) when he showed Tambs and Fernandez the organizational chart featuring Ollie North, John Hull and Rob Owen as the star players in the Contra resupply network.

Feldman returned to Miami like a whipped dog. He had no more interest in pursuing the case. His future and his pension were on the line. He knew the White House and the Justice Department in Washington were interested in the case and he was one of the cockroaches who would get stepped on when the lights were turned on if he didn't find a place to hide.

White House interest in the Feldman probe dated to early March. A 38-page memorandum written by FBI agent Kevin Currier, who had investigated the Garcia case and mentioned Garcia's charges of drug-smuggling, had been forwarded to Washington and Oliver "Buck" Revell, executive assistant director of the FBI. Revell sent a five-page summary of the report to Deputy Attorney General D. Lowell Jensen, who in turn met with Meese about the investigation.[2]

Why was the attorney general of the United States interested in a low-level criminal investigation in Miami? It doesn't take a rocket scientist to figure out that it had national security implications. Even a lowly assistant U.S. attorney could deduce that.

Interest in the Feldman investigation went even higher than Meese.

On March 24, 1986, the same day I met with Brian Barger and Bob Parry of the Associated Press in New Orleans, Lowell Jensen from Justice went to the White House to brief National Security Advisor Admiral John Poindexter on the investigation. It was the first time he had ever gone to the NSC to brief anyone on what seemed a relatively low-level criminal probe.[3]

It was about then that Justice decided to take the investigation out of the hands of the people actually doing the investigating.

An internal routing slip for a copy of the Revell memorandum shows it went from Steven Trott, an associate attorney general, to Mark Richard, a deputy assistant attorney general. On the routing slip Trott wrote:

"Please get on top of this. [Jensen] is giving a heads up to the NSC. He would like us to watch over it."

"Call Kellner, find out what is up, and advise him that decisions should be run by you."[4]

Despite the threats conveyed to Mattes in his March meetings with Feldman and the FBI agents, he didn't stop his own investigation of Garcia's allegations. The threats served only to make Mattes dig in his heels and probe deeper. Instead of turning around and running away, Mattes kept poking around in the government's business and knocking on doors. Only now he didn't share any of his information with the FBI or the U.S. attorney's office.

The threats directed at Mattes by Feldman and the FBI agents were, for the most part, subtle and indirect. There was nothing subtle about John Hull's threats. Of course, there was nothing subtle about John Hull. He was convinced he had the right and might of the U.S. government and the CIA behind him and felt he could get away with anything.

On May 22, 1986, Mattes testified in a Costa Rican court in Hull's libel case against Martha Honey and Tony Avirgan. (See Chapter 16) It was a tense, life-threatening time for all of us who testified against Hull.

But Mattes never backed down in his testimony. He laid out the whole scenario involving drug shipments and gun-running from Hull's ranch, Hull's ties to the CIA and his work with the FDN and various CMA mercenaries.[5]

That night, Mattes was having dinner with a number of people, including Danny Sheehan of the Christic Institute, Honey and Avirgan, when Hull walked up to their table and loudly announced: "You know, son, I'm never going to forget what you did today."[6]

Then he walked away while the diners were left open-mouthed with surprise. No one said a word to Hull. The man had balls the size of bowling balls.

When Mattes returned to the States, he was called into the office of public defender Theodore Sackowitz. Sackowitz read Mattes the riot act. Sackowitz's ass was on the line. Mattes's ass was on the line. Mattes was told once again to get out of the case, to leave it alone. His case load in the public defender's office went from 15 active cases to more than 40 virtually overnight. He was obviously being overburdened so he wouldn't have time to work on the Contra case.

But again Mattes refused to back down. He continued to assist Kerry's investigators in his spare time. The influence that the narco-terrorists were trying to exert over the most powerful law enforcement agency in the world was too horrifying to dismiss with a wave of the hand. Like a bad car wreck, Mattes found himself unable to walk away from the case.

He pressed on.

By this time, Feldman was well into a series of rewrites of a lengthy prosecution memo on the Contra case he had done at the request of his boss, U.S. attorney Leon Kellner. By May 14, Feldman, in agreement with FBI agent Currier, recommended in a 20-page rewrite that a grand jury be convened.

"Due to the political nature of this case, I am not sure such violations could be successfully prosecuted in South Florida," Feldman wrote.[7]

Kellner marked out that paragraph and wrote in: "I concur, we have sufficient evidence to institute a grand jury investigation into the activities described herein."[8]

But less than a week later, at the urging of Assistant U.S. Attorney Richard Gregorie, Kellner changed his mind about the grand jury and called for additional interviews by the FBI.

Why the sudden change?

Was it the persuasiveness of the bearded, brooding Gregorie?

Or was it some other factor, like influence from Washington?

More than likely, it was more of the latter than the former.

On June 2, Feldman was taken off the Contra/CMA case by Kellner and assigned to an obscure case involving heroin being smuggled from Thailand. The case called for Feldman to travel to Thailand and ensured that he would be out of the office or otherwise tied up through June and July 1986, two of the most critical months in the investigation because a vote on aid to the Contras was scheduled for August.[9]

That same day, Special Counsel Larry Scharf, on orders from Kellner, resubmitted Feldman's prosecution memo with a number of changes. The most significant of these changes was in the conclusion. Where Feldman indicated the case was ready to go to the grand jury, Scharf rewrote it to say: "a grand jury investigation at this point would represent a fishing expedition with little prospect that it would bear fruit."

Feldman was never shown the changes before the altered memo was sent to the Justice Department under his name.[10]

The investigation by the south Florida U.S. attorney's office of Contra drug-smuggling, gun-running and assassination plots was essentially, dead in the water.

The spring and summer of 1986 was a time of great aggravation for North and his cohorts. They were concerned about Kerry's investigation. They were concerned about the South Florida investigation. They were concerned about my allegations. They were concerned about continuing press reports regarding the role of North, the FDN and CMA in possible illegal activities. The brick walls started going up to obstruct the investigation and cover trails.

A massive coverup and disinformation campaign was started.

The rewritten Feldman memo was leaked to selected "friendly" journalists in an effort to cast doubt on Kerry's charges and to further chip away at my credibility, which was a key issue in Washington.

The *Washington Times*, North's personal propaganda tool, ran a story on June 3, 1986, headlined "Anti-Contra witness said to fabricate story." Using Tom Posey and Rick Messick as its only sources, a former Special Forces soldier planted in the Senate Foreign Relations Committee to pass on information to the administration, the story took me to task for my role in providing information on which the Christic Institute had based its conspiracy lawsuit, even though I never cooperated in that suit.

According to the story: "Sources [Posey and Messick] say Jack Terrell, who operated under the pseudonyms of 'Col. Flaco' and 'Frank Winchester,' made up much of the diary which claims that he and several defendants in the lawsuit plotted in December 1984 to assassinate Eden Pastora, commander of the Democratic Revolutionary Alliance, because Mr. Pastora refused to cooperate with a rival rebel faction."[11]

The story went on to say "He [Posey] said he witnessed Mr. Terrell writing his diary in Honduras and quoted him as saying, 'It makes good reading even if it isn't true. Who's to prove different?'"[12]

Just as North had used the *Washington Times* to get the Barry Seal photographs published that he thought would establish the link between the Sandinistas and Colombian drug lords — photographs that eventually got Seal murdered — now he was using the paper in a disinformation campaign against me at the same time Glenn Robinette was investigating me. (See Chapter 16.)

It was all incredibly perverse that the government would go to these lengths to justify its illegal activities. The coverup and disinformation campaign was massive. The FBI, CIA, State Department, Justice Department, members of Congress and some journalists in the Washington media were involved.

By comparison, Watergate was a tightly knit conspiracy of just a few people at the highest levels of the government.

Contragate reached into all levels and all departments of the government. There were so many people involved in the coverup they started tripping over one another during the summer of 1986. When I was being tailed by the FBI in Miami in July, there were tails for the tails. It was like an FBI convention following me around.

The coverup and disinformation campaign aimed at the Kerry probe and the information I was feeding Kerry's investigators became very Machiavellian. The primary source of much of this was Messick, an aide to Senator Richard Lugar on the Senate Foreign Relations Committee.

Messick had a prior conviction for possession of cocaine but was able to gain access to classified documents because of his White House connections. He was passing information about the progress of Kerry's investigation to the Justice Department and to North at the White House. Messick was a mole doing his utmost to keep North's enterprise from being discovered and to subvert the legal process in Washington. But to the Reagan-era White House, anything was justified to keep the boss in power and keep his pet programs alive.

What Messick did was a total subversion of the constitutional checks and balances built into the government. Through Messick, the White House was running a covert operation on Congress.

Messick actually began his own investigation of the Kerry-Mattes probe. But it was not so much to prove or disprove their contentions as it was to learn what Kerry's investigators and Mattes knew. No matter what Messick found, he was going to say he had investigated the issue and found nothing there.

It was a brilliant piece of disinformation strategy. You investigate the investigators and then claim they have nothing. That way you discredit not only the investigators, but the investigation itself.

It was absolutely Orwellian in its concept. But that was the Reagan White House of the mid-'80s.

Meanwhile, Feldman's recommendation that a grand jury be impaneled for the Contra/CMA drugs and guns case sat gathering dust on Kellner's desk. Kellner didn't want to touch this. It had the stink of politics, the stink of Washington, all over it.

The unusual interest in the case expressed by Ed Meese and the Justice Department made Kellner reluctant to push it in front of a grand jury because everyone knew that if people started telling the truth about this, it would have enormous political fallout.

Finally, on July 31, 1986, FBI agent Kevin Currier sent Feldman a 200-page prosecution memorandum outlining the suspects in the case and the evidence that had been obtained. Currier believed that the memorandum "would force their hand, that the United States Attorneys, upon seeing the [FBI reports] and the evidence we had, would have to make a decision, one way or the other, regarding the grand jury in this matter or taking it to prosecution."[13]

Kellner continued to sit on the investigation. Four weeks after Currier's prosecution memo and nearly six months after the investigation began uncovering solid evidence of criminal wrongdoing, Feldman confronted Kellner about why the case was in limbo.

"Politics are involved," Kellner said.

"Why are you telling me politics are involved when you told me [in April] politics aren't a factor to consider?" Feldman replied.

"Politics aren't a factor for you to consider, but they are a factor for me to consider," Kellner said.[14]

Kellner told Feldman to sit on the investigation.[15]

The investigation languished on through September and into October.

October 5, 1986, the day of the Hasenfus shootdown, was a landmark day not only for the Reagan administration (see Chapter 17), but for the U.S. attorney's office in the southern district of Florida.

It was the day Kellner's people suddenly discovered there was a war going on in Central America.

They had ignored several years of countless newspaper articles and television reports in south Florida in which journalists proudly proclaimed: "I trained with the Contras."

They ignored numerous public fund-raising efforts by pro-Contra groups and proclamations by local politicians supporting the Contras.

The war had been going on since 1983 and they chose not to pay any attention to it.

They were living right in the middle of a Latino culture that thrived on supporting anti-Communist factions throughout Central America with their money, their guns and their blood. It didn't matter that it was illegal. It was anti-Communist and that was all that mattered to the Latinos in south Florida.

The federal legal system in south Florida ignored the war out of moral cowardice despite the fact that they had been sued in 1983 in an effort to get them to close the Contra training camps in their jurisdiction. The suit failed to stir the federal prosecutors and they refused to do the right thing and buck their bosses in Washington.

But when Hasenfus was shot down, Kellner's assistants suddenly decided there needed to be a real investigation into the war they maintained didn't exist.

That day, the balding, bearded, assistant U.S. attorney, Richard Gregorie, decided to send Currier's prosecution memo back to Kellner recommending a grand jury be convened, which he did so the very next day.

My God! It was nothing short of a miracle!

Richard Gregorie had seen the light!

And when Gregorie saw the light, Leon Kellner saw the light. Kellner agreed with Gregorie: Call out the grand jury.

But they had a problem in Miami. There was a lengthy paper trail showing the U.S. attorney's office got caught with its pants down. Every single one of them. Now, they were trying to retrieve their trousers and catch up with the rest of the civilized world that knew all along about the war in Central America.

The Miami grand jury also had a problem. It couldn't really investigate anything because it was waiting to see what Congress would do. It was waiting to see what independent counsel Lawrence Walsh would do. It was waiting to see whether any of the assistant U.S. attorneys presenting evidence to the grand jury would be indicted for obstructing justice in the very case they were supposedly investigating.

The final sordid twist was that instead of using the information provided by me, Garcia and other whistleblowers against those responsible for the illegal activities, the grand jury used it to investigate us.

It was all part of the coverup. The grand jury was impaneled specifically to target those who had caused the Reagan administration so much trouble — namely me and a few others.

Throughout late spring and early summer of 1988, rumors kept reaching me about the grand jury and its intentions to come down hard on CMA members with its indictments. Feldman was calling my family and friends, asking questions about me and dropping broad hints about the indictments.

The grand jury loomed over me like a dark cloud as I bounced back and forth among the Philippines, Washington and Atlanta. I had no money, no job and no future and was trying to put together something to survive.

I had accepted from the beginning the inevitability that I would be indicted. But I had been there before facing tougher charges than any the government could bring against me. And who was I to fight the U.S. government?

I considered the Philippines to be my home. I felt out of place in Atlanta and was getting clear signals from Lindsay Mattison and the International Center that I had outlived my usefulness in Washington. Every time I tried to call Mattison it seemed he couldn't come to the telephone because he was in a meeting or on his way to the Soviet Union or otherwise tied up. The signals were clear. The International Center was through with me.

The International Center did provide me with a lawyer, former Washington, D.C. Assistant U.S. Attorney John Hume, to assist me when Sheehan and the Christic Institute came calling for their deposition. Hume was a no-nonsense attorney who was told by Lindsay he had a very small budget to work with in leading me through what promised to be a Christic Institute-planted minefield during the deposition. Our options were limited, Hume told me in a meeting at his office on February 11, 1988. We agreed that I would take the Fifth Amendment on anything that happened prior to 1986 during the deposition the next day.

Friday, February 12, 1988, dawned bright and cold in Washington. I arrived at the Mott House on Maryland Avenue shortly after 9 a.m.

Leslie Cockburn from CBS News was there with a copy of her new book, *Out of Control*. She pressed a copy into my hands and wished me good luck.

The Christic crowd was there too: David MacMichael, a former CIA analyst, Sheehan and two other attorneys, Andrew Love and George Shadoan. A Miami attorney, Joseph J. Portuondo, was there representing Adolfo Calero.

Shadoan did the questioning and began with general inquiries about my current residence and my job with the International Center. But within a few minutes, Shadoan began asking about my involvement with the Contras and I began invoking my Fifth Amendment privilege.

Throughout the morning the exchanges with Shadoan went something like this:

Q. "Did you travel to Costa Rica in May of 1986?"
A. "I invoke my Fifth Amendment privilege."
Q. "Have you ever met John Hull?"

A. "I invoke my Fifth Amendment privilege."

Q. "Have you ever met Martha Honey?"

A. "I invoke my Fifth Amendment privilege."

Q. "Have you ever met Tony Avirgan?"

A. "I invoke my Fifth Amendment privilege."[16]

Whenever Shadoan asked anything about my relationship with CMA, the FDN, the Contras or anything else that occurred before 1986 that could indirectly have a bearing on the Christic Institute lawsuit, I invoked my Fifth Amendment privilege.

Shadoan led me through every little detail that I had talked about to journalists, that I had testified to in Costa Rica. And to each question the answer was the same: "I invoke my Fifth Amendment privilege."

I had warned Sheehan and his backers that I would not cooperate with them because they had placed me in jeopardy by claiming I would be the star witness in their ill-fated lawsuit. Besides, Sheehan attached so many strings to his "help" that I would have become a professional testifier on his behalf before he gave me up to federal prosecutors.

Sheehan had done everything he could to wring testimony from me, but all he was getting were my Fifth Amendment answers. He was getting absolutely no information that would be of any good to him.

Sheehan grew increasingly frustrated throughout the morning as the non-answers piled up. On into the afternoon we trudged, Shadoan patiently leading me through question after question and me just as patiently not providing any answers.

Unbeknownst to Hume and me, Sheehan raced over to federal district court during the lunch break and filed a motion to keep my subpoena in force. Sheehan argued I was improperly invoking my Fifth Amendment privilege during the deposition and wanted more time to depose me.

Sheehan knew my testimony was vital to his case and would do anything to get it, even though he had no compunctions about allowing that testimony to be used against me later. He felt I should pay for whatever "crimes" I admitted to while generating vital information for his lawsuit.

Shortly after 4 p.m., Sheehan handed Hume an order to appear immediately before Judge Aubrey Robinson in federal court. Hume was furious. I was incensed that Sheehan would stoop so low.

Hume and I went over to the court, where Robinson promptly dismissed the motion.

"I will die and go to hell before I will ever help you," I angrily told Sheehan as we left the courthouse.

The federal grand jury in Miami pressed on and by late February and early March it had everyone running scared. Joe "Tirador" Adams kept calling, wanting to know what I was hearing. In one of the calls he said Tom Posey was particularly frightened about what might happen to him.

I broke one of my promises to myself about communicating with Posey and called him at his home on February 17. The fear was evident in his voice. He said the government had used him and abused him.

"The NSC, the FBI and Customs sold me out," he said.

He also confirmed that FBI agent George Kiszynski called North in January 1985 to tell North about me shortly after Posey became an informer for the FBI.

I was being squeezed from five different directions at the time and felt very uncomfortable. I needed some breathing room but couldn't find any, no matter where I went.

I was broke and just trying to find enough money to get by day by day.

The south Florida grand jury was bearing down on me like a runaway train.

The Burmese were still after me to follow through on plans to assist them.

The Christic Institute was pressuring me for a deposition on its civil litigation involving Honey and Avirgan.

And the International Center for Development Policy was doing a fast back-pedal because of the money it would cost to defend me. Hume estimated it would cost anywhere from $100,000 to $400,000 to put up a credible defense and Lindsay Mattison suggested I contact the American Civil Liberties Union in Miami to see if it might handle my case.

By early June it was apparent that it was only a matter of time before the grand jury unsealed its indictments. Joe Adams was getting panicky. He said he had been offered a good deal to cop a plea. I urged him to fight. But without me there to personally convince him it was in his best interests to fight, Joe was falling apart, just as he had done on the Sin Sin Bridge raid.

During this time I talked frequently with John Mattes by telephone. He was angry about how the grand jury system had been fixed to target me and other CMA members and said if I was indicted, he would take a leave of absence to defend me.

In late June, the Christic Institute lawsuit was dismissed. The news was welcome because Sheehan then had to devote his time to appealing that decision and not to getting me to testify on his behalf.

Word that I had been indicted reached me on July 8 while I was in the Philippines. The indictments were still sealed, so I wasn't sure what I was being charged with, but it was obvious it would be a political lynching. My telephone rang all day with angry callers sympathizing with me and my plight.

After talking with John Hume, I agreed to return to the States for the arraignment, even though I could have stayed in the Philippines for the rest of my life and escaped the charges because of a lack of an extradition treaty between the two countries.

The problem with that was that it would have made it appear as if I was running away. No matter what happened in the case, if I refused to return for trial it would have looked like an admission of guilt. I decided to fight. Besides, I knew I was right. The government was wrong and I was going to prove it.

I started a full-scale media blitz as soon as I hit the States. I talked to anyone and everyone who would listen about the injustice of the little guys getting indicted.

"I will subpoena government officials at the highest level," I told one reporter. "I will put the Contra policy on trial. I won't take the fall for Rob Owen, Ollie North or Ronald Reagan."[17]

"It's a case of very, very selective prosecution," I told another. "They're going to hang the soldiers and let the generals walk."[18]

I needed to spark some interest in my case because I needed a defense fund. Lindsay Mattison agreed to pay Hume to represent me at the arraignment and post my bond. After that, he said, I would have to find other counsel and suggested I talk again with Mattes and former Miami ACLU head Jim Mullins.

On Monday afternoon, July 12, Hume and I met with Assistant U.S. Attorney Jeffrey Feldman to discuss the arraignment. Feldman, ever his obnoxious self, claimed he had documents and witnesses to put me away for a long time.

"I know you better than you know yourself," he sneered.

He said there would be no deals for me. Nothing less than three years of jail time. I wasn't interested in deals anyway. I was prepared to fight.

Feldman also said if I tried to exploit the case in the media I would just make things worse for myself.

"And if you get John Mattes for your attorney, I'm going to flush you down the toilet," he said.

Big deal.

I wasn't at all impressed by Feldman's threats. They sounded more like they were coming from a man who had been backed into a corner and saw no way out. He was all bluster with nothing to back him up. On the scale of threats I had received over the last few years, these ranked near the bottom.

On Wednesday, July 13, 1988, the indictments were made public at the federal courthouse in Fort Lauderdale, Florida. Seven of us got hammered — myself, Joe "Tirador" Adams, Tom Posey, Mario Calero, Maco Stewart, Joe Coutin and Alex Martinez, a Miami stockbroker and anti-Castro Cuban who had gotten mixed up in this mess.

The indictments were laughable. The same investigation to which I had contributed significantly more than two years earlier suddenly wheeled and went after me. The U.S. attorney's office nabbed me, just as it set out to do.

It was preposterous that not one of the big players got indicted. John Hull escaped. So did Rob Owen, Ollie North and Adolfo Calero.

What was really strange about the indictments was the timing of their release. They were unsealed the day after Meese announced his retirement, effective later in the year.

Meese had been taking a lot of heat for his role in the coverup and he was beginning to unravel. I have no doubt the indictments were orchestrated by the White House as a preemptive strike to make it appear as if lame-duck Meese and the Justice Department were doing their jobs.

Tirador and I each were indicted on six counts. Two charged us with Neutrality Act violations and two with shipping and transporting a firearm while in violation of the Neutrality Act. Another charged us with conspiring to cause a false statement to be made in registration of a firearm. The final charge was for violating an incredibly obscure law: conspiring to cause someone to fail to put a luggage tag on a bag that contained a rifle. I wonder how long they had to dig through the law books to find that one.[19]

Bill Casey, Oliver North and John Poindexter sent missiles to terrorists and tens of thousands of guns to the Contras and never had the first weapons charge brought against them.

But I was being busted for taking one bolt-action rifle to Honduras allegedly to commit a crime of violence in a war the U.S. government sanctioned and ran.

Those who had created the war charged me with a crime of violence in prosecuting it.

But what was the mining of the harbors in Nicaragua, planned and directed by the CIA's Duane Clarridge?

What was the assassination manual, sponsored by the CIA?

What were the shipments of weapons to the Contras by North's secret "Enterprise?"

It was so incredibly bizarre that it was obvious this was nothing more than an attempt to get me for helping ruin the administration's plans in Central America.

Joe Adams and I both faced up to 33 years in jail and $33,000 in fines.

The indictments were beautifully crafted in their insidiousness and vindictiveness. The government was claiming the Boland Amendment had ended the war. Therefore, I was in violation of the Neutrality Act since all my alleged illegal actions had occurred while Boland was in place and there was no war.

Only two years earlier the Department of Justice said I was a liar and that there was no secret war in Central America. In 1988, Justice said not only was I not a liar, but I was the one who prosecuted the very same war it said didn't exist.

The indictments were the symbolic climax of a system used and abused by a few people for their own perverse ends. The U.S. attorney's office in Miami stood the law on end to get at me. And not one single person in that office, the FBI, the Justice Department or Congress, save Kerry's office, stood up and said: "Hey, this is wrong."

It was like a train bearing down on me. No one with any authority to stop it would take the risk. Only Mattes had the courage to step forward to help. Everyone else stood by and watched while justice was abused and the train rolled on.

The other five named in the indictments got off lightly. They were charged only with Neutrality Act violations, except for Coutin, who was charged with giving his passport to one of our volunteers, Perez the Marielista.

Perez was the only member of our expedition into Honduras who was jailed in Tegucigalpa for failing to have proper papers to get into the country. He languished in prison for months and may have remained there except for efforts by the Miami Cuban community to get him out.

I figured if I went down on these charges, I would go down swinging. I would bring everyone else down with me, from North to Poindexter to Meese to anybody else who had a hand in the war and the conspiracy to thwart the investigation of the White House's role in it.

I was a commodity whose usefulness had come to an end. I had been exploited in Central America. I had been exploited in Miami. I had been exploited in Washington. Now, it was time to do away with me.

What Goes Around Comes Around

Mattes had been eager to get involved with my case from the beginning because of his knowledge of it. After I was indicted, he decided he was going to represent me one way or another. He knew he probably wouldn't get the case as a public defender and the only other way to get the case was to take it. That meant going into private practice.

Eight days after the indictments and 12 days before I was due to be arraigned, Mattes walked into his boss's office and told him he was resigning to go into private practice. He didn't have any money. He didn't have an office. He didn't have a telephone. He was stepping off a cliff on principle.

Having Mattes as my attorney was like having an educated pit bull as a defender. Mattes is tough, demanding and backs down to no one. He'll stretch the limits of propriety. He'll rattle opposing attorneys by telling them they're so bad they need to go back to law school or that their mother wears combat boots. Anything to throw them off stride.

And that's when he's not personally involved in a case. He's even tougher and meaner when things get personal. In my case, it was personal. He and Feldman and other assistant U.S. attorneys had had several bitter arguments over the investigation and Mattes was still seething.

Arraignment on the federal charges was Monday, July 25, 1988, before U.S. Magistrate Lurana Snow in Fort Lauderdale. Feldman was prosecuting the case because the new U.S. attorney, Dexter Lehtinen, had recused himself.

Lehtinen, who was given the job when Kellner resigned under pressure, had been an ardent Contra backer and at one point had represented General John Singlaub, one of those named in the Christic Institute lawsuit.

My indictment was signed by the new acting first assistant U.S. Attorney, Mark Schnapp, who later went on to be the briefcase toter for defense attorney Roy Black, who represented William Kennedy Smith in his West Palm Beach rape trial.

When I stepped forward to be formally charged, Mattes was sitting near the back of the courtroom, lost in a sea of lawyer-like suits and faces.

When Snow asked, "Do you have an attorney?" Mattes stood and began walking toward the bench.

"I do," I said as Mattes stepped forward to join me.

I thought Feldman was going to die right there. His face turned white, then red, as he realized what was happening.

"I object, I object," he spluttered. "He can't do that. Judge, judge, he, he, he, I object. He can't do that. He can't take this case. He's got a conflict of interest."

Snow looked appropriately annoyed by Feldman's outburst. Feldman was literally screaming at Mattes and me. He had lost control. He knew if Mattes took the case, he was finished. Mattes knew more about it than Feldman.

And Feldman was not trying to win the case as much as he was trying to protect his ass and that of everyone else in the U.S. attorney's office who had contributed to the coverup.

Mattes had a personal score to settle on this case, though. Not only was he angry with Feldman, but he was angry with the entire U.S. attorney's office because of the way it had mishandled the case.

Shortly after the arraignment, Mattes confronted Feldman and told him: "You fucked me and I'm going to nail you to the wall."

Their relationship, never good to start with, went downhill from there.

When Snow asked Mattes about the conflict of interest charges, Mattes calmly replied he had resigned his job as assistant federal public defender the previous week and was now in private practice.

Snow shrugged her shoulders and moved on. She set my bond at $25,000, the same as four of the other defendants. Maco Stewart, who was then living in France, had his bond set at $5 million. But he could afford it.

The other member of this nefarious group of warmongers, Joe Adams, didn't bother showing up for the arraignment. Instead, his attorney had agreed the previous Friday that Joe would plead guilty on one count in return for a ridiculously light sentence.

In a ruling so swift it stunned all of us, Joe was given one day's probation and a $50 fine by Judge Norman Roettger, who was scheduled to hear the case.

Lehtinen, the U.S. attorney, called it a victory for his side.

"When a defendant pleads guilty, it's considered positive by our office," Lehtinen told reporters.[20]

But the light sentence was a clear message that tough times were ahead for the government. Roettger showed no inclination to bow to intense government pressure and be the executioner for those of us who had run afoul of the administration and were charged with its misdeeds.

After the arraignment, Mattes and I walked outside into the bright Florida sunshine and were confronted by a cluster of reporters.

"Take a walk and let me handle this," Mattes said.

I casually smoked a cigarette while he went to work on the media, displaying all the proper ingredients of moral outrage, indignation and anger and setting them and the courts up for what would be a prime theme in my defense.

"How can you indict someone for a government-sanctioned activity?" he asked. "How can you make the absurd claim that we're at peace with Nicaragua?"[21]

Jim Mullins found Mattes a tiny, second-floor office in a building in Little Havana that housed Garcia's Gun Shop, which had supplied some of the weapons for the disastrous Bay of Pigs invasion. There was a 15-foot long neon gun just outside the window looking out on the street. It was one-stop shopping mart where you could get legal help upstairs and an AK-47 downstairs. It was perfect for Miami.

The indictments were successful in doing one thing: chasing away my so-called supporters in Washington. When those indictments were unsealed, my backers ran for cover. Virtually every single person and group in Washington that had used me for their own benefit and had promised financial support for my legal bills went into hiding.

The International Center for Development Policy, which had put up $10,000 for attorneys' fees to prevent me from being deposed by the Christic Institute, suddenly "ran out of money."

Lindsay Mattison had personally promised me help with the defense fund, but backed away from contributing. The think tank for which I had worked for more than a year, attracting millions of dollars in donations because of the information I was passing on to the press, offered me neither financial nor moral support.

A year earlier I had been a hot commodity. Now I was too hot to handle. All my liberal "friends" and Washington "progressives" found other, more important causes to support.

Mattes and I were left to fend for ourselves. We quickly discovered the road to justice was paved with our own money, which didn't go very far.

Sometimes lawyers think too much. They get all involved with the technicalities of the law and the philosophy of justice and they fail to see the simplicity in some things. Simple things that can be easily explained by a child sometimes are too confusing for lawyers to handle.

Confronted with simple truths, their systems shut down. They are unable to handle them.

In my case, Mattes honed in on that simple truth he discovered sitting alone one night in a bar: The government couldn't charge me with violating the Neutrality Act since the government was not at peace with Nicaragua.

A six-year-old could articulate it, but not a lawyer. Because it was so straightforward, so direct and to the point, the lawyers in the U.S. attorney's office, especially Feldman, would be hard-pressed to figure out the logic of this argument.

But what Mattes was doing was challenging the government's right to prosecute me.

Little more than three weeks after my arraignment, on August 12, 1988, Mattes filed what became known as the "at peace motion."

In it he argued the simple truth that neither I, nor any of my co-defendants, could be charged with violating the Neutrality Act since the U.S., while not technically at war with Nicaragua, also was not at peace with it.

Mattes argued the government had sanctioned me, knew what I was doing and could have stopped me at any time, but didn't. He was trying to force government agencies involved in prosecuting the war — specifically the CIA, DIA and NSC — to talk about why they had not stopped me.

To support his contention, Mattes included documents ranging from Ronald Reagan's Presidential Finding of December 1, 1981, authorizing covert actions against Nicaragua to affidavits from participants in the Contra war to a letter from Senator Barry Goldwater to Bill Casey chastising him for the mining of the harbors in Nicaragua in early 1984 and failing to inform Congress.

"The Defendants seek intellectual consistency on the part of the Government," Mattes wrote. "By suggesting through an Indictment that we are 'at peace' with Nicaragua, the Government is asking this Court to ignore the millions of dollars spent on the Contra program and to ignore the thousands of deaths of combatants, including Americans. Such a position by the Government ignores the reality of the last eight years and the involvement of Congress and the President in those events."[22]

Our lack of financial support was depressing to both Mattes and me. John continued to plug away at the case, but I was becoming more and more depressed. On more than one occasion, I was on the verge of telling

Mattes to get the best deal he could and cop a plea. I just wanted to be finished with the case and get on with my life.

On Friday, September 2, 1988, I wrote in my diary: "John is upset about lack of financial support, as am I . . . . If no support is forthcoming, then he is prepared to plead me out when he returns [from vacation]. I told John to do it. This has worn me out, despite the fact I am innocent. The system has failed."[23]

Just when I was at one of my real low points and considered throwing in the towel, Mattes came up with the real clincher that turned the case in our favor and sent the government running for cover.

On October 7, 1988, Mattes filed a motion to dismiss on the grounds of selective prosecution.

The motion threw the U.S. attorney's office into a panic because it served notice Mattes was going to take the case right into that office and into the offices of the Department of Justice and the FBI in Washington. He would call FBI agents and the likes of Feldman, Kellner and 200 other assistant U.S. attorneys as witnesses.

It was unique, to say the least. A federal prosecutor as a witness against his own case.

Feldman was rattled. He knew he could take the fall for this thing if it went sour.

At that point, Mattes changed tactics. Instead of confronting Feldman, as he had so many times in the past, Mattes invited him out for a drink. They agreed not to swear at one another, not to shout at one another and not to walk out on one another, as was their custom. They met several times in dark, smelly Miami bars that only alcoholics could love to talk about the case and Feldman's role in it.

Mattes told Feldman that he was being exploited. Mattes said Feldman was the victim because he had been put on the investigation, then had his prosecution memo altered and used for political purposes. Feldman should have been the hero and Kellner the villain, Mattes said.

Mattes urged Feldman to save himself and become a witness against his own office and the Justice Department. It was a subtle, yet effective campaign of terror that Mattes waged. But nobody could have done it better.

Slowly, ever so slowly, Feldman began to see the light.

Mattes eventually set up meetings between Feldman and Kerry's investigators in September 1988. Feldman was secretly subpoenaed to be deposed in Washington. Feldman also talked to special prosecutor Lawrence Walsh about the coverup, all the while remaining an employee of the U.S. attorney's office in Miami.

Early in the fall of 1988, Feldman announced his resignation, effective later in the year. But in his lame-duck status, he became a valuable asset to my case, to the Kerry investigation and to Lawrence Walsh.

Feldman became the John Dean of the Justice Department's coverup. He still had access to documents in Kellner's safe that helped prove the extent of the coverup. He was a whistleblower extraordinaire. His self-righteous indignation of only a few months earlier had been turned on his own bosses instead of on me.

While Feldman was busily ferreting out documents, pre-trial hearings began that spanned a five-month period from the fall of 1988 until spring of 1989. Those hearings concerned whether the U.S. was at war with Nicaragua.

No one in the U.S. attorney's office in Miami wanted to take up where Feldman left off because my case was considered a career killer by every assistant U.S. attorney who survived the minefields of the Kellner administration. A new prosecutor was assigned the case. Eric Duvalier, a pragmatic attorney with little background knowledge of the Contra network, was called to carry the government's standard.

Duvalier was the attorney of record when the issue of my passport came up. I was forced to give it up when I surrendered to federal authorities in July and Feldman argued that if it was returned to me, I would "go to Burma and Thailand and start wars."

Mattes and I went back to court on October 12 to try to get my passport returned. Duvalier was totally lost on the Burma issue.

"If you promise me you won't go to Burma and Thailand and start a war, you can have your passport back," Judge Lurana Snow told me.

Feldman didn't show up in court, but Snow sent him a message about the passport.

"One small victory," I wrote in my diary.[24]

In December 1988, David MacMichael was called by Mattes to testify about the nature of the war against Nicaragua. MacMichael, a former CIA analyst with the highly secret National Intelligence Council, had provided an affidavit for the "at peace motion" supporting our contention that this was a war in Nicaragua, not peace.

During MacMichael's testimony, Duvalier found he could not cross-examine him because MacMichael was the repository for a great deal of classified information on the war.

Roettger warned Mattes that if he as much as lightly touched on matters of national security while questioning MacMichael, he would convene a grand jury to indict Mattes for disclosing classified information.

Duvalier felt he had greater latitude with his cross examination, but MacMichael turned the tables and refused to discuss sensitive matters relating to the war. Duvalier was stymied.

Roettger then asked Duvalier and Mattes to prepare briefs about U.S. Special Forces troops and Navy SEAL teams participating in operations inside Nicaragua during the period of the Boland Amendment. The judge wanted details of these operations and gave Duvalier and Mattes 10 days to produce them.

When time came to present the briefs, Mattes explained he had no access to the information that might shed light on U.S. involvement and therefore had nothing to submit to the court. Roettger turned to Duvalier, who had received briefings from various government sources.

"Judge," said Duvalier, "I can't tell you the answer to that question. Our answer is classified."

The answer was classified!

A federal prosecutor was telling a federal judge that he could not talk about activities of U.S. troops inside Nicaragua. He was saying without really saying it that U.S. troops, not just surrogates like me, had been used in the war against Nicaragua.

Roettger agreed to hear testimony about the use of U.S. troops in his chambers.

What he heard is still classified.

But whatever he heard was enough to convince him that whatever was going on in Nicaragua certainly was not peace.

In a ruling handed down the following July on the "at peace motion," Roettger wrote:

"The Court finds the evidence overwhelming that the United States was not 'at peace' with Nicaragua during the time charged in this indictment. Further, no evidence presented at the [closed)]hearing contradicts this finding."[25]

In our minds the ruling established once and for all that the U.S. military had troops carrying out missions inside Nicaragua. It was the first — and only — time that information had been made public. But the media passed over it as if it wasn't there.

The government was having other problems with its case.

In the spring of 1989, Mattes was reading a deposition Kellner had given to Kerry's subcommittee the previous fall when something that jumped off the page. Kellner said that in July 1986 he had gone to a federal judge seeking a "PEN register" on me to learn who I had been calling from my motel room in Miami.[26]

It was the first time we had received any concrete information that wiretaps were involved. But the information had passed right over the heads of Kerry's investigators. Nobody on the committee thought it important enough to contact Mattes or me about it.

Mattes went right to work and filed a series of motions requesting the PEN registers and sought a subpoena for Kellner to explain them. The government denied knowing anything about wiretaps on me. But it also could not find records of FBI interviews with me or my polygraph by the Secret Service in 1986.

The wiretaps were the heart of our case. We knew the wiretaps would probably show that the U.S. government was tapping not only my phones, but also the phones conversations of at least one U. S. senator — John Kerry — without the proper legal authorization. We wanted to find out what other phones it had connections on.

On July 11, 1989, Roettger ruled on the "at peace" motion. He dismissed all the Neutrality Act charges against all of us.

Only the two non-Neutrality Act firearms charges against me, and Coutin's passport charge, were left intact.

Roettger excoriated the government in his ruling. He made it clear that if the government was going to lure people such as me into its private wars, he wasn't going allow it to later come back and prosecute us.

He cited all the undeclared wars in the country's history to reject arguments that punishing people invited to these wars under a vague federal statute known as the Neutrality Act was nothing more than an attempt to use the judicial system to get back at those who became disenchanted with the program and blew the whistle on it.

"The facts of this case simply do not support the Government's argument that peace broke out between the United States and Nicaragua on October 12, 1984," Roettger wrote of the imposition of the Boland Amendment. "The facts, as laid out in bare-bones form in this Order, show that Boland II cut off Congressional funding to the Contras for a period of some ten (10) months, but did not stop the administration from seeking and coordinating aid for the Contras from other sources. . . . The mere fact that Congress refused to fund the Contra cause for a brief period of time is not equivalent to saying that the United States was 'at peace' with Nicaragua."[27]

Roettger could not dismiss all the counts against me because of technicalities, but Mattes pursued dismissal of the last two with renewed vigor.

After a ruling like that, the government would normally walk away from the case and drop the other two charges. Not in my case. The writing was on the wall for the government, but it refused to give up. It was going to prosecute me on something, no matter how minor the charge.

But Mattes had the government down and he wasn't about to let it up. He was like a pit bull on its ass. He wanted those wiretaps and he wanted them immediately.

The government refused to turn over the wiretap evidence, though. The prospect of this sensitive and damaging information coming out in open court so unnerved the government that it decided to quit rather than risk further damage. The prosecution threw in the towel in early 1990 when Mattes indicated we were ready to go to trial.

On February 17, 1990, while working in Hong Kong on legitimate business for a change, I received the following telex:

> CONGRATULATIONS Jack... We beat the government. Case
> is over. We Won. Regards,
> John C. Mattes

Just like that it was over. The years of worry and doubt had ended. I felt vindicated, but not satisfied. The ache was still there because of what had happened to the Miskitos. The anger was still there because of what had happened to me.

Instead of focusing my efforts on exposing government wrongdoing in Central America, I had been forced to spend the two previous years defending myself. I had gone after the government with a vengeance and it came back at me in kind. Only its resources were greater and it was able to do far more damage to me than I did to it.

The private supply operation ended, but everybody still got rich and nobody really suffered because of it. Secord and General John Singlaub made millions. Ollie North is making millions. William Casey is lying peacefully in his grave, all those secrets about who actually did what lying there with him.

The government never really said "uncle." It never really admitted defeat. It never said it was wrong for what it did to me. It simply gave up and walked away. Not a single soul from the government ever said he was sorry for the miscarriage of justice that had been carried out here.

Mattes and I had done little more than turn on the flashlight in a kitchen full of cockroaches. They went scrambling away when the light went on, and although we tried, we failed to squash any of them.

19

A Matter of Survival:
Cory's Hired Gun

Finding a refuge from Washington and its political infighting became a matter of prime importance in late 1988, not only for my mental well-being, but for my physical survival.

Mentally, I was drained by my four-year association with the Contra mess. My brain had been wrung out like a sponge and I had nothing else to offer those seeking answers to questions that had no answers. The Iran-Contra Committee decided I was of no use to it, and InComCon had disappeared from my life following the disclosure of the diversion of funds to the Contras from missile sales.

I was back to where I had been in September 1984 except I was four years older, a lot wiser and much poorer. Lindsay Mattison had given me my walking papers from the International Center in October and my funds had quickly disappeared. Normal employment was not visible anywhere on the horizon because of the high profile I had obtained and because I was the consummate jack of all trades and master of none.

I attempted to find a niche in the Philippines, but the people with whom I tried to do business were not eager to deal with an American.

Eventually, I landed a job with a Hong Kong-based company that dealt in aquaculture projects in China. I was appointed director of special projects and given the task of selling pond-raised prawns to the American market.

It felt strange to be in a legitimate business for a change. And while I weaned myself from many of the back-channel military contacts I had made through my association in the Contra war and the International Center for Development Policy in Washington, I maintained a few contacts in the event something went wrong with my job.

It did, when one of the deals I put together fell through because of an American buyer who refused to deal honestly with the Chinese. I was let go, but I was told to try to salvage the deal and could set up shop in any country I wished. My first thought was Manila because I maintained a small apartment there and had absolutely no desire to return to the States.

The Philippines were seething when I returned in early 1990. The people were desperately trying to adapt to the unsteady administration of President Corazon Aquino after years of psychologically numbing patriarchal rule by Ferdinand Marcos.

In December 1989, a coup attempt had been launched against Aquino by rebel military forces. The Reformed Armed Forces Movement (RAM), headed by Lieutenant Colonel Gregorio "Gringo" Honasan, had come close to toppling the government, and Aquino had asked for and received American military assistance to put down the threat.

U.S. Air Force F-4 Phantom jet fighters were sent from Clark Air Force Base to provide air cover and stop rebel planes from rocketing Malacanang Palace. Under the euphemistic code name "Persuasion Flights," the Phantoms streaked through the skies over Manila, preventing rebel planes from attacking while loyal Philippine Air Force pilots counterattacked the rebel air base at Sangley Point, destroying several planes and helicopters.

The U.S. air assistance turned the tide for Aquino and allowed forces loyal to her to retake captured military facilities. She was indebted to the U.S. government at a critical time: The treaty allowing U.S. military bases on Philippine soil was due to be renegotiated.

RAM forces withdrew into Makati, the business district of Manila, and dug in using tourists as unwitting shields against government offensives. Talks between RAM and loyal military leaders produced an uneasy cease-fire and rebel soldiers retreated to their barracks for what was described as a brief "time out" in the fighting.

I was in Hong Kong at the time, listening to reports on the radio and wishing I could be in Manila. But all flights into and out of the Philippines had been canceled.

When air service resumed, I returned to the Philippines and poverty, a geo-political businessman without a cause to champion, without a war to fight, without a job.

When I settled back into my apartment, I called Raulito Manglapus, son of Secretary of Foreign Affairs Raul Manglapus. I came to know Raulito through the Manglapus family business, Uni-Prawn, a modern prawn hatchery in Manila. I had tried to obtain mother prawns for export to China when my employer opened a new pond development, but the deal fell through because it is illegal to export breeder prawns from the Philippines.

I pursued the relationship with Raulito because he had many business contacts and I needed to get something going that could provide me with enough financial security to remain in Manila.

"Where do you stand?" I asked Raulito when I talked to him.

The Philippines had been factionalized by the recent coup attempt and the citizens were extremely paranoid as rumors of another coup circulated throughout the city.

"You should meet with my father," Raulito said. "He'd like to talk to you about the situation."

Raul Manglapus is as much a part of the history of the Philippines as was Marcos. A former unsuccessful presidential candidate, Manglapus was one of the few post-World War II politicians with the temerity to challenge Marcos. But that challenge cost him. He was forced into exile in Washington and for a while wrote books and dabbled in Third World conflict resolution.

Manglapus had once served as the president of the International Center and was very close to my former boss, Lindsay Mattison, and his wife, Virginia Foote.

In January 1990, the elder Manglapus invited me to his home in San Lorenzo Village to discuss two issues of much concern in the Philippines at that time: the continuing presence of U.S. military bases and frequent coup attempts against Aquino by right-wing factions in the military.

Manglapus is a gentle man and well-known in his country as a pacifist. He is also a staunch nationalist and leader of the anti-bases faction within the government. Although I was pro-bases, I tried to speak in theoretical terms.

During our conversation, Manglapus also expressed interest in my role in Nicaragua with the Contras. He seemed impressed with my brief explanation of what I did there.

After we had talked for a while, Manglapus said he wanted to put me on his payroll for 10,000 pesos a month, about $425 U.S. dollars, to be his intelligence officer.

I was somewhat surprised by his offer, since I had provided him with no great insight. What I had given him could have been obtained by reading a few magazine or newspaper articles about the issue.

We met a second time a few weeks later. Again we talked about the U.S. and the Philippines and again Manglapus wanted insight into the American mind. But this time he changed the direction of the conversation slightly. This time there was more emphasis on military coup plotters and what could be done to discourage or stop them.

"Gringo" Honasan was making repeated efforts to destabilize the government. He was young, handsome and daring and he was quickly gaining public support. Getting rid of him and the threat posed by RAM was a government priority.

Manglapus said he believed the death of Honasan could be a huge political victory for Aquino and that any measure should be used to ensure his demise.

Then he asked me something I never thought I would hear from the lips of such a devout pacifist. He asked me if it would be possible to bring in a team of Americans to do the job that the Philippine military was either unable or unwilling to do. He wanted to know if we could "take out Honasan."

At first I thought it was merely wishful thinking on his part, the fanciful musings of a politician under pressure seeking extraordinary solutions to extraordinary problems. I found it difficult to believe this gentle man was actually talking about assassination.

I told Manglapus anything was possible for the right amount of money.

He wanted to know what such an operation would cost and how payment should be made. I said the standard contract fee for something like this was 50 percent in advance and 50 percent on completion. If I got involved, my price would be $250,000.

I figured they could pay at least that much since a bounty of five million pesos had been offered for Honasan.

Manglapus, as usual, took detailed notes throughout the meeting. But, because of the nature of our discussion, I sensed the notes were not so much for his personal use as they were for use in briefing someone else. My instincts told me he had to report to someone above him and wanted a clear record of what we had discussed. Manglapus appeared to be nothing more than the point man in this plot.

It was strange, but ingenious: using a pacifist to solicit a hit. Who would have suspected it? And who would believe it if the information became public?

When I asked Manglapus if he knew the implications of what he was proposing, he indicated he did.

And when I bluntly asked if his boss, President Corazon Aquino, would know anything about this, he replied that she "would be aware of the project, but would not take any part in the operational aspects."

The international political fallout could be catastrophic for the Aquino administration if the plan backfired.

Before I left, Manglapus told me that he had to carry this information "upstairs" and that he would be in touch with me soon.

At a third meeting, Manglapus said his people were unwilling to pay 50 percent in advance. I wasn't sure whether they were concerned about getting their money's worth or that taking this much cash out of government accounts would be difficult to explain. Despite my misgivings, I had become intrigued by the plan and wanted to see where it led. I also needed the money.

I told Manglapus I would come up with a counter-offer.

Several days later, I called Manglapus and asked if his people could put up enough money to get the hit team into the Philippines. That would enable us to set up logistics for the operation while we worked out the remaining details.

"Would they be willing to put up 850,000 pesos?" I asked.

"I'll have to get back to you," he replied.

Assassinations done right are cold and calculating, a simple business deal. Those who get involved on both sides usually know the parameters and the protocol. Those who are seeking the assassination usually have the money ready when they start looking for someone to do the job. That wasn't the case here. This was a job being contracted by amateurs.

Manglapus soon called back and said the money was available. We scheduled another meeting at his home the following Sunday, the second week of July 1990.

I arrived on schedule. Only this time I took a micro-cassette recorder in the small bag in which I carry my .45 automatic. It's not unusual to carry a weapon in the Philippines. But carrying a tape recorder to a meeting like this could get me killed in a heartbeat.

I wanted some insurance in case things started to go wrong since it would be my word against that of Manglapus. I knew my word wouldn't carry much weight once they started dragging out my background.

I was having mixed emotions about this job because of how it was developing. I was dealing with an amateur who obviously was taking his orders from someone higher in the Philippine government.

We sat on the sofa with the recorder in my bag between us. I began taking notes just as Raul was doing.

As we talked, Manglapus began to elaborate on the other targets in this mission. In addition to Honasan, Lieutenant Billy Bibit, Colonel

Eduardo "Red" Kapunan, Colonel Alexander Noble and Captain Rex Robles, all members of the RAM infrastructure, were added to the list. All were fair game.

The ratchet was being cranked up. This project was becoming both ambitious and far-reaching in its political implications.

"How can we do something in order to back up an explanation that the NPA [the Communist New Peoples Army] did it? Is it possible to throw in an NPA corpse there or something?" Manglapus asked.

"What I'm saying is that it will look like an ambush," I replied.

"It will look like . . ."

"The intention," I broke in, "is we are going to kidnap certain people, with certain information, that we know that they have, and locations and information that is vital to breaking this infrastructure. Once . . . those bridges are broken then you can forget RAM and all the rest of it. They will become totally impotent."[1]

The plan dictated that certain security parameters be put in place to ensure that it would not be compromised. My main concern was that the identities of those taking out the contract might become known before the contract was completed. If that happened, they would never make it out of the Philippines alive.

I suggested that the code name "Jeremiah" be assigned to the project. There was no deep philosophical meaning behind the name. It just popped into my head. Manglapus accepted it and we agreed that all communications would be conducted under this name.

I was assured that my team and I would be paid the balance of our money, but nothing could be put into writing.

"You only have my word, I guess, because I can't put it down in writing," Manglapus said.

"I just told them it had to be a trust situation," I said.

"A trust situation. The fact that you're being given this [money] in advance, which originally there was reluctance about this, you know."

"Yes."[2]

The arrangement to pick up the money would be made through Raul's Chief of Staff, Maria Ferria, who lived just across the street from him.

As we finished the meeting Manglapus told me he would be making a speech before the United Nations General Assembly in September.

"I hope it happens before then," he said.[3]

He said he planned to go to Jakarta, Indonesia, for eight days, Singapore for two days and India for two days, but would be back in the

Philippines briefly before leaving for the U.S. if I needed anything more. He seemed pleased with this arrangement.

Driving away from Manglapus's house I took the recorder out of my bag and rewound the tape. The quality was not as good as I had hoped, but I had captured the bulk of the conversation. Raul's distinctive voice and my voice could be heard over the sound of the window air conditioner and the incessant baying of Raul's German shepherd.

As I listened to the conversation again, one thing jumped off the tape: the idea to make it appear the NPA was responsible for the hit on Honasan and other RAM members.

My insurance was far better than I had hoped.

Manglapus and I had agreed on a 90-day time limit for the mission. Since it was then late July 1990, I would have until around November 1 to do the job. But I decided to wait for the initial payment of money before swinging into action.

On the afternoon of July 23, 1990, I received a call at my apartment from Manglapus's Chief of Staff, Maria Ferria.

"Is this Jeremiah?" she said.

"Yes," I replied.

"The package is ready to be picked up."

I had told Raul I would not be the person who made the actual pickup. I decided to use my secretary, Melba Reymundo, for that. I trusted Melba.

Since I didn't own a car, the pickup had to be made by taxi. I had used one particular taxi, owned by the Melanie Taxi Company, many times and had a fee arrangement with the drivers.

One driver, Efrin Sistoso, had been on many unusual trips with me and was the main driver I used for the trips to San Lorenzo Village to meet with Manglapus. I hired Efrin, picked up Melba and headed for Manglapus's home. Since this was something that could get both Efrin and Melba in more trouble than they needed, I told them to forget everything they saw and heard on the trip.

It's easy to buy a bad memory in the Philippines with the right amount of money.

The pickup time was 8 p.m. The light would be fading and identification of people would be difficult. I still wasn't sure I wasn't being set up.

I told Efrin to pull the taxi up to the driveway of the house and stop. I told Melba to get out, walk directly to the front door and tell whoever answered she had been sent by Jeremiah.

Within seconds Melba was walking back to the taxi carrying a shopping bag with a large pasteboard box inside. I told Efrin to take me back to the Marbella, my apartment.

I didn't want to go into detail about the money while in the taxi because there was no telling what Efrin might do if he learned we had 850,000 pesos in the back seat. I told Melba it was a present for me and that I would explain it when we got back to my apartment.

When we got there, I pulled the heavy box from the bag and placed it on a glass dining table. Melba's mouth dropped open when pulled the lid back from the box. All she could see inside was money in stacks of 100- and 500-peso notes. There were 85 stacks, each with 10,000 pesos.

I told her to count the money and she dove into the box like a kid at Christmas. She knew she'd never see this much money in one place again in her lifetime.

As Melba was counting the money, I got out my camera to provide another piece of my insurance policy. I put a number of stacks of the money on the table along with a copy of that day's *Manila Bulletin* newspaper clearly showing the day and date. I took several photos of the money to validate its existence and the date it was photographed.

The sheer bulk of this much currency made it impossible to hide. I had to be in and out of the apartment from time to time and the worry of leaving this much money lying around was something I didn't want to deal with. I asked Melba if she knew a money changer on the black market who could change this into U.S. dollars. She did, but I decided to wait until the following day to make the exchange so it could be done during daylight hours. The exchange was made without any problems.

With the money in hand, I started putting out feelers to different Filipinos and to one American about participating in this gig. Joe "Tirador" Adams was my first selection.

But when I called him at his home in St. Louis, I got his answering machine. I simply left the message, "We got the job." I had been talking to Joe for some time about a possible job, and I figured he would understand what I meant. I never heard back from him.

It didn't matter, though, because things ground to a halt.

I was spending the money for personal living expenses and weapons that would be used on the hit. I moved to another section of Manila and it was not until late October 1990 that Raul got back in touch with me and requested an update.

We met again at his home. He wanted to know what I had done and how much progress had been made. He reminded me his backers had put up money and expected results. He also indicated they were ready for the big payoff, the death of Honasan.

I didn't want Raul and his backers to know what all I had done, so I started giving him a number of excuses. Among them was my concern about sweeps by government troops in Albay and Sorsogon provinces, areas known as hideouts for RAM personnel.

Raul didn't know and I didn't tell him I had recently gone to Legaspi, the capital of Albay province, and met with Captain Rex Robles. Robles didn't know I was a would-be assassin stalking him, or that I was acquiring information about him and RAM. Robles proved to be an extremely talkative man, but in the end gave little information beyond what I already knew about him and the organization.

As Raul and I continued to talk, he expressed concern about the general state of politics in the Philippines.

Then, he wandered into totally virgin territory.

"Could you drop a LAAWs rocket into Eddie's bedroom in Ayala Alabang Village?" he asked.

I was stunned into silence. Fidel "Eddie" Ramos was secretary of defense in the Aquino administration. All my previous discussions with Manglapus had been about the assassination of rebel military leaders. Now he was talking about having me fire an anti-tank rocket into the home of a high-ranking political figure.

The Aquino administration was concerned about the 1992 elections and the possibility Ramos would declare himself a presidential candidate. Although Aquino, by law, could not run for a second term, there were rumors that an effort would be made to abridge the constitution and keep her in power for a second term. The future of the Philippines was being put on Cory Aquino's shoulders and her opponents had become targets for assassination.

In addition to Ramos, possible presidential candidates included Ramon Mitra, the speaker of the house; Vice President Salvador Laurel; and Senator Juan Ponce Enrile, a RAM advocate.

Raul even wanted me to obtain information on an Aquino relative, Eduardo "Danding" Cojuangco, her estranged cousin. He wanted all of Danding's movements reported to him, especially if he traveled outside the country, because the administration planned to lock him out of the Philippines.

Raul made it quite clear that all these men were possible targets for assassination.

A civilian hit list wasn't something I had bargained for. Neither was it part of our original deal. The equation had swiftly changed. Who were the real targets? What was going on here? I couldn't figure out exactly what was happening, but I could feel the quicksand under my feet. It was time to bail out of this operation as quickly as possible.

I took the money and ran because the plan had gotten out of control. I could handle the assassination of rebel military leaders, but I never would have accepted the deal if I had known civilian political leaders were going to be added to the list.

I felt the assassination of political opposition candidates was better left to the people it might serve. If the Filipinos wanted them dead, then it would be up to them to do it. If I got involved in this, there was little chance of my getting out of it alive. And I'm not sure whose purpose my death would serve in this case.

The day before my departure from the Philippines I called an old friend, Jose Luis Alcuaz, the former commissioner of the Department of Transportation and Communication. Lingoy, as Alcuaz was better known, met me at the Manila Pavilion Hotel, where I was staying after moving out of my residence.

I played the tape for him of the meeting with Raul and showed him the pictures of the money. I also had the original envelopes with Raul's name and bank name on them, representing the monthly payoffs of 10,000 pesos.

Lingoy was shocked. I told him I might use this information at another time, but he should hold it in case I developed a serious case of Filipino lead poisoning. He agreed, because he was still bitter about having been fired by the Aquino administration. But he expressed fear that if this information ever was made public, all of us could die.

On December 7, 1990, I departed the Philippines and returned to the United States and an uncertain future.

People Like Us

I had few options available to me in the States. The assassination money had dwindled rapidly and I was quickly approaching financial insolvency. I decided to return to Atlanta because I could live with my sister until I found a job and a place of my own. My future seemed bleak and I felt terribly out of place in the States.

My employment record was not particularly good and I knew it would not be easy to find a job that would keep me interested enough to remain in the country. When I contacted friends in Washington for suggestions about how I might best fit into the job market, I found only a few who would talk to me, much less offer assistance.

It was as if curtains were falling around each segment of my life one by one. I was alone and of little use to any legitimate business. Since I was still viewed by those with particular political orientations as nothing more than a mercenary and someone who was untrustworthy, my opportunities for acquiring a lifestyle of normalcy and legitimacy were extremely limited.

As I was pondering my future, I received a telephone call from Lingoy Alcuaz in Manila. He told me he was leaving for the States in a few days and wanted to know if I could meet him in Los Angeles. I told him I was broke and was not able to travel.

His voice was tense and his cryptic manner of speaking told me he wanted to discuss something important with me. I guessed it was the Manglapus affair. I told him I would talk with him if he came to Atlanta, but this was the best I could do.

Lingoy and his wife, Baby, came to Atlanta in late January and checked into a Holiday Inn near Hartsfield International Airport. He called me after they arrived and I agreed to meet him in the motel coffee shop.

Lingoy is a large, round, unkempt man with a bad haircut who wears cheap, ill-fitting suits and seems to be constantly nervous. Despite his appearance, he has some stature in the Philippines as a prophet, where fortune telling is a national past-time and those who can predict the future are lionized.

Lingoy, by some strange quirk of fate, had accidentally, but accurately predicted the failed coup attempt against the Aquino administration in December 1989 in one of his newspaper columns.

That one prediction increased his stature in Manila immeasurably. Physically, he was already a big man. After the coup prediction, he had an ego to match.

Through the newspaper column, Lingoy possessed a forum to voice his opinions and concerns about the political atmosphere in the Philippines. But he also used it in his personal attempts to thwart any re-election bid by Aquino. He felt she was not the right person to govern.

The Philippine presidential election was scheduled for May 1992 and a large field of candidates was expected. Aquino remained popular among the masses, but her political image was of a weak and indecisive leader. The military resented her, mostly because she was a female trying to govern a male-dominated society. Her political party had come apart since her election and many people with political ambitions tried to distance themselves from her and her administration.

Lingoy was one of those people with political ambitions. But his aims were slightly lower. He merely wanted to be elected to the House or Senate. The information I had given him about Manglapus and the assassination plots could be a strong political weapon and he came to Atlanta expressly to explore a public release of it. His intent was personal publicity, not the exposure of plans by the Aquino administration to dispose of opposition.

Lingoy had a copy of the tape I had secretly recorded at the Manglapus residence, but he assured me no one had heard it. I gave him the copy to be released in the event I had some unexplained accident, but he did not have permission for its general release.

The tape, if released in the Philippines, could have devastating consequents for Aquino politically and could wreck sensitive negotiations underway for U.S. bases to remain on the islands.

Manglapus was the chief Philippine negotiator on the bases treaty and I was concerned release of the information could be viewed as a political dirty trick by the U.S. to discredit Aquino. This certainly was not the case because my intentions were to never make this public knowledge unless something happened to me.

I called Lindsay Mattison at the International Center to warn him his old friend Manglapus was up to his ass in an assassination plot, but he wasn't interested. His attention had turned to the Soviet Union and he had no time for me or Manglapus.

I asked Chris Isham, a producer for the investigative division of ABC News, to join Lingoy and me in our discussions. I had briefed Chris over a period of time about certain aspects of the plot without filling him in on the details.

My real concern with Lingoy was that for his personal political purposes he would release the tape to the Philippine press without my knowledge. I didn't want to be caught off guard.

Lingoy and I talked for most of the three days he spent in Atlanta about ramifications of the information I possessed.

Lingoy returned to the Philippines agreeing not to release the information unless I gave him the go-ahead. What I didn't realize was that he had already set into motion a plan that would enable him to benefit financially and politically from the tape.

No sooner was Lingoy back in the Philippines than I began getting word from friends in Manila that rumors were floating around town concerning a plot in which Manglapus was involved. Lingoy was marketing the tape and a typed transcript of it.

By September 1991, my sources in Manila said the story was about to break whether I wanted it to or not. I decided to go on the offensive.

I called Chris Isham at ABC and told him I was ready to go on camera exposing the plot. I wanted to make a preemptive strike in my words and under my conditions before the Philippine press got its hands on the story.

I placed certain conditions on my interview with ABC because I needed time to return to Manila to finish some personal business. Once the story broke, I would forever be barred from returning to the islands.

And ABC needed some time to test the tape to see if it was authentic before it further investigated the story.

Analysis of the tape was less than satisfactory. The tests showed the tape had not been spliced, but voice analysis could not conclusively prove the voice on the tape belonged to Manglapus. The noisy air conditioner in the background made it impossible to come up with a definite identification.

ABC pressed on with the story and in late September I flew to Paris to meet Bill Redeker, the network's Far East correspondent who would conduct the interviews. From there I proceeded to Manila to finish my business before the segment aired.

Lingoy was still being evasive about his plans for the tape and I advised him to wait until after the ABC piece ran before he did anything.

I had gone to the FBI in June 1991 and informed agents about the plot.[4] I wasn't sure about my culpability in this conspiracy and made a conscious decision to talk with the FBI about it. After briefing agents on all my information and providing them with duplicate copies of the evidence, I was advised that no crimes had taken place in the U.S., but extradition to the Philippines was another matter and they were not sure what the government there might do.

Manglapus and his controllers could not allow me to live in Manila possessing this kind of information. I was dead if I remained and I was dead if I talked. I had few alternatives.

If I waited for someone else to use the information, for their own particular political purposes, I was in a position of having to defend myself against accusations of being a right-wing mercenary thug. If I got out ahead of the story and explained it from the beginning, I would have to defend myself against charges I was fabricating the story and trying to profit off it.

I chose the latter course.

ABC was still concerned about the tape and as one last measure of proof about my story asked me to take a polygraph test. I agreed and flew to Miami on October 15 to meet Chris Isham at Slattery Associates for the test.

George B. Slattery, the examiner, has more than 30 years experience as a polygraphist and is considered one of the best in business. The questions he devised were designed to show if I was telling the truth about the assassination plot and the tape.

The questions were simple and direct and I felt totally at ease because I knew I was telling the truth.

Q. "Regarding Raul Manglapus allegedly agreeing to pay you to kill Gringo Honasan; do you intend to answer truthfully each question about that?"

A. "Yes."

Q. "Are you lying when saying that you and Raul Manglapus planned and agreed to have Gringo Honasan killed?"

A. "No."

Q. "Are you lying when saying that Raul Manglapus agreed to pay you the equivalent of 250,000 U.S. dollars?"

A. "No."

Q. "Are you lying when saying that you and Melba Raimundo (sic) picked up 850,000 pesos from the residence of Maria Feria [sic]?"

A. "No."[5]

The examiner's opinion about my veracity?

"Based upon a careful analysis of Jack Terrell's polygrams, it was the opinion of this examiner that there were no significant or consistent psycho-physiological reactions consistent with deception to the relevant questions and answers."[6]

I had passed the final hurdle. Now all I could do was wait for the piece to air and for the Philippine press to erupt.

On October 18, 1991, the piece finally aired on ABC's World News Tonight. Redeker had interviewed Manglapus in New York during his visit to the United Nations and ran the incriminating tape recording while the cameras rolled. Manglapus was visibly shaken.

When Redeker asked Manglapus why he would pay me $30,000, Manglapus replied: "Well, there might have been other reasons. This fellow was selling things to all kinds of people."

Manglapus later denied even paying the money.[7]

During the interview with Redeker, Manglapus called me a "provocateur," halted the taping and walked out of the room, a guilty man if ever I saw one.

It was all the Philippine press needed to go into a feeding frenzy. The standards in the press corps are not quite as exacting in the Philippines as they are in the U.S., and it's quite easy to slip a few pesos to a reporter here or an editor there to get the "proper" slant on a story. I knew when the story hit the papers, the pro-Manglapus forces would try to bury me, while the anti-Manglapus people would use their media resources to support my contentions.

It played out pretty much as I figured. Manglapus supporters used contacts in the United States to dig up information about my credibility and background and once again the same old tired charges of having a prison record, of being of dubious credibility, were dragged out.

Manglapus denied knowledge of the plot and Aquino stood by her man. The Philippine press hammered away at the story, but began taking ideological sides once a formal investigation was launched by Philippine Senator Ernesto Maceda, chairman of the Senate Foreign Affairs Committee.

I was portrayed as a "Rambo," a liar and a con-man. Some of the charges were so ludicrous they were funny. One paper said according to FBI records I had been arrested 13 times from 1959 to 1962 "for crimes such as auto thef [sic], burglary and robbery, including cases related to the Federal juvenile delinquent administration."[8]

The Federal juvenile delinquent administration?

Both that administration and my arrest record were figments of the imagination of Manglapus and his reporter for the *Philippine Star*, which has as its editorial slogan, "The Truth Shall Prevail."

I originally believed the story and the evidence would stand alone because it was as close to a smoking gun as anyone would get. Once again I was wrong as my detractors in the States cranked up their assaults on me and my credibility.

Foremost in the anti-Jack Terrell parade were the people for whom I had worked and whom I had trusted for more than two years — Lindsay Mattison and Virginia Foote at the International Center for Development Policy. They were venal, vile and vindictive in their condemnations of me.

"Jack Terrell is an absolute con-man," Virginia Foote told *Asiaweek*. "We were taken in by his initial bright, Southern-gentleman impression until we found him dishonest and got rid of him. He was nothing but trouble."[9]

This from a woman who wrote of me after my arraignment on the trumped up Neutrality Act charges in July 1988:

"Since leaving the war, he has been an eloquent voice in the struggle to expose U.S. government misdeeds in Central America."[10]

I was "an eloquent voice" when it served the International Center's political and financial purposes. I became "nothing but trouble" when it once again suited the center's political and financial purposes. Once more, I was an expendable asset, a disposable patriot used to advance the agendas of others.

I shouldn't have expected anything more from those people who have become mired in the cesspool that is Washington. But I did. I thought they would have some loyalty, some class, some honor.

The worst of the vitriol came from Lindsay Mattison, the one man I thought would stand with me in uncovering wrongdoing in Third World countries. Mattison proved his moral cowardice in a letter to Manglapus in which I was accused of doing everything but assassinating John F. Kennedy.

The letter was released at a press conference in Manila given by Manglapus and got wide play in the Philippine press.

Following are portions of the Mattison letter:

> If I had thought of it, I would have told you that Jack Terrell claimed to have worked for the CIA (a claim later proved false by official statements of the CIA). He also claimed to have been involved in plans to assassinate Eden Pastora by the Contra leadership (Calero and others). This claim also proved false, as it never came up throughout two years of Iran-Contra hearings, FBI investigations, or a long lawsuit by Christic Institute on the bombing of Eden Pastora.
>
> I would have told you that in my two years of knowing Jack Terrell, he constantly asserted inside knowledge of secret subjects including the October Surprise — that is, the charge that George Bush and other Republicans made a deal with Iran to hold US hostages until after the election. The House of Representatives now has a special task force — headed by Lee Hamilton — to investigate this, and has never even called Jack Terrell. Which is to say that nearly every journalist has refused to go further. They don't believe him, can't check out his stories, and think he is making things up to make himself important, sell his life story, and make a movie. I agree. After two years, I was never able to confirm the specifics of Jack's stories about Calero, Pastora, the CIA and the rest. My feeling is that he hangs around mercenaries, foreign agents and jour-

nalists and puts pieces together and then retells a plausible story of his own.

This from the man and the institution who paid me $36,000 a year to reveal information on plots and criminality in Central America. This from a man who in his own words wrote to me in June 1988:

Dear Jack,
I am no longer in a position to pay your salary.....Costs exceed income here . . . . bills exceed assets...and that is that. Wish I were magic! I'd send you to Burma, Manila and other exotic spots, but I can't.
Nain will give you a summary of severance due you by the Center . . . .to ease the transition. She can work out how to carry the insurance as well.
You and I have been through too much together to make this easy, but I am too far in the hole to continue our relationship. John Stockwell has a Speakers Bureau which produces income for him, and I'd be happy to help you pitch them. And, if books or movies seem a good idea, I'll be happy to back up your pitch for them."
But, the Center is broke. So let's stay friends, and in close touch on legal cases.[12]

He signed it "With affection."

What was fascinating about Mattison's alleged change of heart about me was his admission that he supposedly had been duped by me for more than two years. This great Washington mover and shaker, this big-time political player in Washington, was telling people that somebody without a high school education had conned him into believing something that now he knew was not true.

But what Lindsay did with that letter was also tell people that the International Center's work on Central America for two years was nothing but bullshit, a total fraud.

If that's the case, he ought to willingly give back the tens of thousands of dollars people donated to him during that time. It's the only right thing to do, if I was as much a fraud as he says I was.

I felt no malice towards Mattison or the International Center when I was let go. That was business. They had served me well and I had served them well during my employment. But the letter to Manglapus hurt me deeply. I found it difficult to understand how my champion could become my chief detractor almost overnight. I guess I still didn't understand Washington politics.

After Mattison sent the letter to Manglapus, he called me. Not to apologize, but to explain, he said.

"It's intramural," he said laughing. "You understand."

It's intramural. Just like the Mafia.

I responded in an angry letter dated November 1, 1991:

> I wanted to respond to your call yesterday. I feel that unlike your self-professed "cowardness," you had more balls than Adolf Hitler for calling me.
>
> Your projected "fence riding" facade strikes me as one of hypocrisy being put forth under the auspices of loyalty to Raul. I doubt that you know loyalty goes with other principles which you selectively chose to exercise. I expect you to be loyal to Raul, that is not the case in point. I simply point out that your system of loyalty applies only to those that are found worthy of your system. Certainly not the likes of a person such as I. I am simply a commodity to people like you and an informational prostitute to your organization. If funds can be generated at your expense, then loyalty doesn't enter the picture.
>
> I find it strange that you and everyone connected with the Center found it necessary to turn on me like a dog in the defense of another when you woefully lack sufficient knowledge about what transpired between myself and Raul. You have elected to take at face value his version of the incident and spend a "trouble maker," as I have been described, in the process. I may not possess the credentials of Raul, but I served the Center and its causes with no less fervor.
>
> I now find that my blind faith and trust in people like you and your Center was mislead. You have claimed to be taken in by my "initial bright, southern gentleman impression" and then branded me as "dishonest" and "got rid of him" pronouncement. I find this both loathsome and a prime example of what people like you can do to another when you espouse human rights, honesty and moral virtue. This is mere pandering to funders who may be taken in by your demagoguery. You are indeed the carny which you profess to be.

My only regret is that I truly believed in you and your philosophy of life. I thought you were a man of care and of dignity. Now I suggest that you take a close look at yourself and what you do to the 'refuse' you leave behind when you have spent people like those you accuse of spending. Ollie North could learn from you and I know you will take that as a compliment.

You claim that I "stuck a stick in Raul's eye." No, I didn't, he did it to himself. The incident happened and nothing you or anyone you have retained to "trash" me can do will ever change that fact. I do not know his motives, but I suspect who was his "puppeteers." That is his problem, not mine. I only sought to get out in front of the story which was coming out anyway. I tried to protect the information and I have publicly stated that I thought Raul was only a messenger in the affair.

Your tactics and your attempts to discredit me in the face of the stance both you and the Center took in my defense for two years will not bear fruit. You have only managed to give me the determination to dig my heels in and fight the fight with more zeal. This story will not soon fade and I will now go and testify to my firsthand knowledge of what actually happened. Had you had the good sense to look before you leaped, you may have found that there is more to this than you could have ever imagined.

I just wanted you to know my deep hurt and my loss of respect for you and everything you taught me about what now appears to be nothing but lies and false affections. People wonder what propels a person like myself, but when you are used, lied to, promoted and thrown away by so-called progressives and liberals, then never ask yourself why.

In my entire relationship with you and the Center or anyone connected with its activities, did I ever attack, discredit or do anything other than staunchly defend its goals and aspirations? There was a time in my life when I was proud to be aligned with the Center and all that take the same views. Now, with the exception of a few really "loyal" friends, I find myself once again questioning the process of ideology.

I hope that in the future, you can obtain the ability to look over your ego and your false sense of right and wrong, to look at true facts of what happens in situations which now proceed. I can at least respect Raul, even though he allowed himself to get trapped in the intrigues of others. Never take a stance when you have no evidence or knowledge of what happened in the first place. Telling you this will be like talking to a wall, but it is true.

I will close this by simply saying that once again in my life have I become intimate with betrayal for the sake of agenda. I wish I were so rich that I could afford to lose a friend.

The Manglapus affair played well in the Philippine press, whose tabloid-style journalism has no equal, not even in London's Fleet Street. As time wore on and the plot itself became old news, my background and my credibility became the objects of national speculation and derision. I was life imitating art, a flesh-and-blood Rambo ready to wreak havoc on the Philippines.

As I had expected, I was barred from going back to the Philippines. I was persona non grata.[13]

Senator Ernesto Maceda forged ahead with his investigation, but his motives were a product of personal politics, for he had little support from his colleagues. Maceda saw this inquiry as his path to free publicity for the forthcoming elections in which he planned to run for president.

My story was holding up, though. Efrin, Lingoy and my former maids testified before Maceda's committee and supported me. Manglapus refused to testify, issuing a statement through his lawyer that his testimony would "denigrate his position as a member of the Cabinet and cause serious embarrassment to the government before the diplomatic community."[14]

Maceda chose not to subpoena the testimony of Manglapus because he had been "my professor in college."[15]

Manglapus's refusal to testify did not bode well for the Aquino administration. Manglapus looked like he was hiding something. And Maceda's refusal to subpoena him made it appear as if Maceda was a part of the conspiracy.

Maceda wanted my testimony, but since I was barred from returning to Manila, he decided to come to me.

On November 11, 1991, I flew to Los Angeles to give a sworn deposition to Maceda that he would present to the Philippine Congress in lieu of my personal appearance. Maceda listened to my story for more than four hours and finally concluded: "My own feeling is that at least for most parts of his story, he [Terrell] looks very credible."[16]

He said he would have halted the investigation if he had found my testimony "preposterous" or "unbelievable."[17]

Lingoy accompanied Maceda to Los Angeles, and even though he had precipitated the untimely disclosure of the affair, I found it hard to be angry with him. He seemed to sincerely believe that justice would actually be served and I would eventually be allowed to return to Manila one day. I had lived in Manila too long to know that would never happen.

The great investigation into the plot dissolved shortly after Maceda returned to Manila. He was elevated to president of the Senate and this put a quick end to his search for truth and justice. He, like all other politicians, was a prisoner of his own game and his own lack of ethics. Truth was once again a casualty in the quest for power and position.

Politics in the Philippines smelled just as bad as it did in the United States.

Justice wasn't served, in my opinion, because the Philippine government went to extraordinary lengths to ensure that my revelations about the assassination plot worked against me. I had prevented a crime, not executed one, yet I was the one assailed for revealing the truth. Had I carried through with the assassinations, history would have been rewritten for this beleaguered country.

As it was, though, fate dealt the Philippines the cruelest blow.

The bases treaty was rejected, sentencing thousands of Filipinos who had depended on them for their livelihood to lives of abject poverty.

Mount Pinatubo erupted, destroying Clark Air Force Base and taking hundreds of lives.

Typhoons battered the islands, destroying crops, lives and the national will.

To compound the problems, Imelda Marcos returned from exile with her high-profile divisiveness that bodes ill for the islands for years to come.

Meanwhile, the people of the Philippines continue to suffer under a repressive feudal system that offers no hope for justice, no hope for change and no hope for a better life.

20

In The End: Lost In My Life

I've lived this life and it didn't count.

Several years ago, my sister said to me: "You're 45 years old and I don't know who the hell you are. I've known you all my life and I don't know who you are. You have lied to us, to your family. You have lived a lie."

That's exactly what Oliver North told the Iran-Contra Committee: Covert action is nothing but a lie.

Those of us who get involved in this business lead lives that are lies to those who know us, or think they know us.

My family learned about my life and what I did when they read it in a newspaper.

Those who work in covert operations become two, three, four or five people. They lose their identity. They don't know who they are anymore.

Sometimes my phone rings and somebody asks for Frank Winchester. Or they might ask for Colonel Green. Or it might be Colonel Flaco. Or Iceman, or Jackie or Pete.

By the name they use for me, I know immediately what part of my past they come from. That part of my life, that character that I created to live that life, comes back instantly because a traveler from that time has come to visit me.

Those who work in covert operations get to the point where they question their sanity because after a while they're not really sure who they are and what their life is all about. Many times I lost touch with the real me and became someone else. I created a myth and I became the myth.

To this day some people I have known for a long time tell me they don't believe that I'm Jack Terrell. They tell me they believe I'm someone they don't know, someone with a hidden agenda.

It's difficult to do a self-examination of a life I don't really understand. It's just here. It just happened. I didn't sit down and plan my life to come out like this.

My life of disarray and misdirection began when as a youngster I allowed myself to be molded into a person without real purpose. I robbed myself of a future through selfish desires to become something I could never be. I was a romantic, a cavalier adventurer born 100 years too late.

Unable to deal with the era into which I was born, I chose a path in life that took me into a world of high adventure, dark depression and isolation from everything considered normal. I treated life much like a buffet, only selecting those items that pleased me while I neglected those that would build character and a traditional lifestyle.

Looking back on the trash heap of my life, I don't feel proud of anything. I don't feel I've accomplished anything. After 50 years on the face of this earth, I don't feel that I've contributed to anything in a positive way. For me, the bad far outweighs the good.

Living with that past has become my earthbound purgatory, where I attempt to understand why my feet were placed on a path that has taken me in a direction that I may never have chosen under other circumstances. The future is some dreaded dimly lit point in time where I cannot determine my own usefulness to society.

Although my existence has been like most humans who march through time leaving nothing but a trace, an essence, of their trek from birth to death, I have never considered my life to be exceptional nor unusual, even though I participated in events that others thought unusual.

The residue of my passing will be noticed only by those who have an interest in scrutinizing an aberration of a man who demonstrated a lust for living outside the bounds of conformity.

Everyone stops, at some stage of their life, to take stock of the sum of their accomplishments or their failures. Some feel pride and rejoice in fulfillment of expected standards of behavior imposed on them by society. Others, however, are remorseful for having been scorned by society because they could not live within the restrictive confines of its standards.

I have come to believe that society is like a circle in the dirt. If one remained inside the circle, life is considered normal. But if ever a person steps outside the circle, they are labeled as different, banished from the circle and never permitted to return.

Those who break society's rules stepped outside the circle. Hard work and perseverance could win temporary re-entry, but the problem with this arrangement is that once one becomes a temporary, he remains a temporary forever. There can never be a washing away or cleansing of the action that resulted in dismissal from the circle. The permanents who dwell within the circle never forget and never forgive.

I became a temporary, but once back inside the circle, I showed the ultimate disdain for the permanents by becoming someone they feared and refused to trust. I followed few of their rules and became one of the forever unforgiven.

Setting myself apart from everyone who lives what is considered a normal life made me one of the eccentric minority. I had to settle for a life in which I shared a limited future with those who found themselves in the same situation.

I began my assault on life with determination and overambition, but found that stability had not been fostered in me. I reached goals, but was never satisfied. The goals were mere illusions in my quest for something I could never attain.

Once I achieved a particular goal, I would spiral back down into realms of the unknown, where I would again allow my self-indulgent need for unattainable challenges to take control of my life. Mystery beckoned me and ignorance fueled my desire to drift into the world of adventure, where I felt I would fit.

Gradually, I found what I sought. I aligned myself with those whose ideological bent convinced them the world needed a change through unconventional means. War was glorified and the death of any alien belief was of paramount importance.

This way of thinking, coupled with friendships with those who regularly practiced aggression, got me a first-class ticket into the world of spooks, assets, cutouts and covert operatives. There I found some solace because misery always loves company. We shared the same beliefs, the same traits and the same strange mental makeup.

For those of us who deal in covert operations, dealing with aspects of normal life is difficult, if not impossible.

Frequently, our personal lives are a shambles. I've been married five times, yet don't have anything that remotely resembles a home or a family as it is thought of by normal, average people.

The only family I ever had was when marital relationships briefly filled the gaps between reckless adventures. My children became estranged from me and grew up never really knowing me. Instead of clinging to my family, I clung to those people who were like myself.

Developing emotional attachments is a virtual impossibility for me because of the personality I constructed in prison to protect myself. The strange and sometimes violent nature of my business also distanced me from normal emotions.

Once one gets involved in this business, it's difficult to talk to normal people because we've got nothing in common with them. Talking to us is like talking to Martians. The only people we can talk to are others like ourselves.

Anybody who gets involved in covert action has to have some type of character defect. Many operatives are manic-depressive, high-intelligence people with bland backgrounds.

Most have photographic memories. At one time I had almost total recall. It was like having a Polaroid in my mind.

Most have strange methods of justifying what they do and why they do it.

And most people in my line of work have no careers, other than the one we're in. If we can't support ourselves through jobs in our chosen line of work, we're forced to take odd jobs, often menial jobs, because we never know when that next telephone call might come that will require us to pick up and leave everything behind, as I've done many times in the past.

It's the challenge of the unknown, and the lure of the exotic, that keeps us tied to this lifestyle. You don't quit the business, it quits you only when you are deemed unfit due to age or physical ability or are considered untrustworthy.

Sometimes I'm not even sure I was in "the business." Sometimes I'm not even sure what "the business" is.

My involvement in it was not what one expects. It happened by accident. I didn't go to college, get recruited, get checked out, get hired and go do covert operations while a green government check was automatically deposited to my account every month.

I got a phone call one night from a man I didn't know and had never heard of who offered me $50,000 to do a job for him.

Sound unbelievable? Of course it does.

Did it happen? Yes, it did.

Not a day goes by that I don't wonder how and why I was chosen for this assignment. I have been unable to come up with a plausible explanation. Neither have I been able to explain it to the satisfaction of anyone else to whom I have told the story.

People just can't accept the fact that it happened. But it happened. I know it happened, and that's all the explanation I can offer. It's impossible to explain the inexplicable.

No doubt my recruitment was handled in the manner it was because it would be so unbelievable, so it could never be traced back to the source. All I know is after those telephone calls I was given access to a network of people, events and money that were out of reach to the average, normal citizen.

When I accepted that job, I was drawn into an army of gray soldiers and disposable patriots.

We do the dirty work behind the scenes that enables politicians to take the credit for compromise frequently forced by our efforts. The services of men such as myself are sought by many nations and political groups trying to become nations. But we are accepted by none, not even by our own government until our special skills or deniability are needed.

Then, when we're no longer needed, we're disposed of.

In most cases we're simply ignored and allowed to pass peacefully into anonymity. But when we're perceived as a threat for what we know, we're targeted by the same government that employed us.

Was I targeted when I decided to go public with my knowledge of the Contras?

Without a doubt.

But why I was the object of such venality from Oliver North and his cohorts is as much a mystery today as it was when I first learned of it.

Why did North take time out from waging a war in Nicaragua and selling missiles to Iran to get into a pissing contest with me?

What did I know that was so dangerous to him?

Why did I become the lightning rod for the counterattack on those opposed to the administration's policy in Nicaragua?

The only answer I can come up with is drugs.

Once people figured out what was going on in the war, the focus turned to drugs and everyone connected with the administration went ballistic and cranked up the machinery for the counterattack.

Drugs were the most glamorous and most damaging of all the issues surrounding the Contras. When I announced my intentions to set foot in that arena, it was decided that I would not be allowed to do so without paying for it.

Where I had been a minor player in the tragedy, suddenly the highest levels of the White House were taking notice of me and trying to shut me down. Only something like that would cause the administration to risk it all by going after me.

It wasn't something that happened gradually. It happened in a two-month span between May and July 1986.

It began with John Hull's defamation of character suit against Honey and Avirgan in late May. Hull thought he had the judge and the trial bought and paid for. He intended to demonstrate in a court of law that Honey and Avirgan were liars.

It was all part of the CIA strategy to discredit those who opposed the Contras and publicly dispute their information. It was a balls-to-the-wall, in-your-face active measures campaign designed to elicit sympathy for the Contras and their supporters and give impetus to pro-Contra aid forces in Congress.

But the trial backfired. Hull lost when testimony painted him as a drug-dealing terrorist.

Then, in late June, the administration learned I was going on the CBS news magazine "West 57th Street" to air my drugs and guns charges on national television.

The same day that program aired, John Kerry went into a closed meeting of the Senate Foreign Relations Committee and said drugs would be the focus of his subcommittee's investigation.

Drugs were the only issue that scared the administration. North's notebooks have numerous references to drugs. It was unacceptable to the Reagan administration that anyone would be able to link the Contras to drug-smuggling.

North skirted the issue of my drug disclosures by labeling me a "terrorist threat" in the memo that went to Reagan.

Then, when I went to Miami in late July and showed a list of Contra drug connections to FBI agent George Kiszynski, a PEN register suddenly appeared on my telephone.

On my return to Washington I spent two days being polygraphed by the Secret Service.

The ongoing disinformation/active measures campaign was put into motion to either shut me up or discredit me to the extent that my charges of drug-running by the Contras and their supporters would not be taken seriously.

Seen in that context, the mystery of why I was targeted was not all that mysterious. To some degree, it goes with the turf.

There are numerous reasons people like me allow ourselves to be drawn into this line of work in which, in an instant, we can be perceived as an enemy by the same people for whom we worked. It's a little like playing with snakes. You play long enough and eventually the snake will turn around and bite you.

Other reasons have to do with patriotism, a blind belief that the United States should do anything in its power to extend its influence around the world.

I found that most people have purely mercenary intentions. For them, the money is the only thing that matters. Whoever has the money has the right politics.

Some are drawn into these affairs because of some need to live on the edge, to experience the adventure that their mundane civilian lives cannot provide.

The operations usually are put together in such a way that those doing the hiring get all the benefits and take few of the risks. The soldiers are "volunteers," just as Dana Parker, Jim Powell, Bill Cooper, Buzz Sawyer, Eugene Hasenfus, myself and others were volunteers in Central America.

Sometimes we fight the wars and sometimes we are used as advisers to the proxy armies built to fight the wars that larger nations do not want to fight.

The Mujahedeen were America's proxy army in Afghanistan for more than 10 years. The Mujahedeen were long on fighting skills, but seriously short on political skills necessary to turn a proxy army into a legitimate government entity. The factional in-fighting among the Mujahadeen will go on for years in Afghanistan, just as it had gone on for centuries before there was a United States government.

The Contras were just the opposite. They had plenty of political skills but none of the military skills necessary to become a real threat to the Sandinistas. Most of the Contras wallowed for years in the refugee camps along the Honduran border, waiting for the U.S. Marines to lead them back to Managua.

The Contra leaders also allowed themselves to partake of the corruption that is endemic to all covert actions. A corrupt revolution, or counterrevolution, will never produce a stable government working in the best interests of the people. Ronald Reagan's "freedom fighters" would have been no less corrupt than the Somoza regime out of which they sprang and would have been as inept at governing as the Sandinistas.

The world of covert operations and extra-governmental affairs is unknown to most Americans. It is a world where the lines between civilians and the military are blurred. Civilians are recruited to act in a military fashion, while active-duty military personnel are occasionally called on to participate as civilians to avoid creating political problems in the host country.

When as a participant in these covert operations you convince yourself that any act you do is legal, moral and justified because it is being done to protect your country from political threats, it's literally a license to kill.

But once you start questioning that absolute authority, that belief that what you're doing is good and what the other side is doing is bad, you have taken the first step to relegating yourself obsolete and of no further use to those who put together such operations.

Whether you start questioning yourself about a mission, you're no good on that mission. The true believer, the people who won't question orders, are those capable of doing the most horrible things.

And when you differ from the objective set for you or start openly questioning those for whom you work, they call you a traitor.

When you're a part of the inner circle, there are no political tags assigned to you. You're merely a businessman doing a job. But if you leave and start dissenting, they will find the most convenient tags and slap them on you to ruin your credibility. You become a liberal, or a leftist, or a nut.

During an operation, the gravity of what you are doing is obscured by the determination to do whatever it is you have been programmed to do. If you whack a bunch of people, blow up cars and hotels, murder children, it doesn't make any difference.

Something in your character sets you apart from normal people and once it's trained and propagandized to where you start believing what people are telling you, you lose your sense of right and wrong and in some cases, your sense of morality.

In the end, when the veil of perceived sanction is lifted and you no longer have the protection of that invisible barrier that justifies all your actions, then those unspeakable acts committed in the name of freedom and democracy come back in a more objective retrospective. Finally, you understand the impact. You say to yourself: "Did I do that?" Usually, you did.

That's when your conscience kicks in and you begin to feel the guilt for what you have done. Where you were detached from reality while you were doing it, when the veil is taken off you are able to see reality again. When that reality is viewed in conjunction with history, the effects on one's mind can be devastating.

Every former intelligence agent who was involved in anything unusual feels a detachment from society because he is something of a non-person. But he also often feels extreme guilt for what he has done. Many must have an outlet that allows them to escape, or temporarily suppress, the reality of what they've done.

Nobody in this business is religious. You don't grab on to religion except as a last resort because the guilt runs so deep not even religion can mitigate it. The guilt becomes a very personal thing that you carry with you every waking minute. Even though you perceived what you did as a mission, you carried out the act. You bombed the building and killed innocent people. You blew up the car and several kids with it. You planned the ambush and caught unsuspecting civilians in the crossfire.

No policy did it. No intelligence finding did it. No politician did it. You did it.

At any point in the process you could have said no, but very few ever say no. The perceived peer pressure to complete the mission, no matter how distasteful, is incredible.

You can't talk to normal people because they don't understand what you're talking about. If you walked up to some guy in the park and started talking about why you killed 13 civilians to save your country and protect the national interest, he'd look at you like you were insane. And maybe you were at the time.

The only people you can talk to are the people who lived what you lived. But by the time you get around to talking to them, they're as screwed up as you are.

Everybody who has been in this business is scarred. We're all mental cripples, trying to figure out why we feel the way we do. The centrifuge spins you around and around and when it spins you out, the effect is unreal. It's like a satellite thrown out into deep space. You're lost and can never come back. Never again can you be part of the world you came from.

If your mind is strong enough, you keep the lid on the Pandora's box in your head. If you open that box and let some of the demons out, you can never get them back in. They whirl around in your brain and torment you forever.

I operated totally on instinct. That's why I trust maybe one out of every 200 million people. I have never, ever trusted people to let them inside my head, because that's a mental capitulation that leaves you totally exposed and vulnerable to that person. No sane person wants to get inside my head, anyway. It's a scary place.

I cannot count the enemies I have made and I often wonder how I have survived as long as I have. Sometimes I think I'm immune to danger. Or bulletproof. Every morning I wake up I'm the most surprised person in the world that I'm still here. Still alive.

I have had only a few friends in my life, and all of them are dead now. I envy them. I envy the dead. Their worries are over. Being alive and being a survivor is the hard part.

One of my few best friends was my mother. When I was growing up, I despised her. But when I got to the point where I stopped looking at her as a mother, as an authority figure, I got to know her as a person and we became quite close. After that, I didn't see her as a mother. I considered her a friend.

She was the only human being in this world who knew everything about me and to whom I could talk openly. She was the only person I came close to trusting 100 percent, even though I never trust anyone 100 percent. When my mother died it almost destroyed me because she carried a lot of me with her.

Maybe my kids will grow up to be something. If they do, it won't be because of me. I once wrote my son that he should never want to be like me. He should try to be everything I wasn't. I want him to look at my life and say: "I'm glad I didn't turn out like him."

He should feel lucky that he didn't live around me and take on any of my traits. That may be my only contribution to this planet, that I didn't influence anyone else to be like me.

I feel a terrible sense of disgrace, shame, dishonor and guilt about the way I've lived. Some of the things I have done are totally unpardonable, unforgivable. I have killed in the name of causes, some of which I believed in, some of which I didn't.

Some people tell me God will forgive me. But I don't care about God forgiving me. I don't have to live with God. I have to live with me. I feel that before I can be forgiven, I have to forgive myself and that will never happen.

When a person willfully takes another person's life in the name of politics, a stain is placed upon his soul that can never be erased. Not even death can remove the stain because the stained soul merely transits from this place to another in eternity.

Any attempt at describing the emotional trauma involved when you kill another human being cannot be done with words. Each person is endowed with individual senses and feelings that react differently when confronted with this personal act of tragedy.

Some may see it as a duty.

Some may see it as self-defense.

And some see it for what it is, the theft of a separate and unique life with its own destiny, a theft carried out in the name of ideology, race, religion or culture.

How irrational is the belief that justifies a system of national values that usurps the greater power of creation. Our world, threatened with enormous natural attrition, should never allow political considerations to determine who lives and who dies.

Reflections of a Mercenary

For many years, I held the naive belief that a patriot is someone who would give his life to defend his country against its enemies. Some of those enemies are foreign governments. Some are within our own government.

Now, I believe the patriot who dies in the defense of his country, at the hands of our foreign enemies, is a patriot who dies with some sense of honor. Not so the patriot who fights enemies within our government. This kind of patriot is never allowed to die with honor and is himself considered an enemy. He is publicly ridiculed and dishonored by those within the government who skillfully cut away his credibility and twist his good intentions.

Perhaps my feelings about what I did and why I did it can best be expressed in a letter I wrote, while in self-imposed exile in the Philippines, to one of few people in which I have any trust, Peter Dale Scott, an author, poet and University of California professor.

Peter is as educated as I am uneducated. He is as understanding as I am confused. Most of all, he is wise. That's why I can confide in him when I can't even confide in myself.

April 10, 1988

Dear Peter,
Thought I would write you today as I barely remember your call last night. I know the phone rang and it was you, but the sedatives had been in action for a few hours and I was unable to comprehend what you said. I am sorry that you wasted the call.

Yesterday I fought a mighty battle within my head. I had just received a call from a journalists about information dealing with the Barry Seal part of the Contra puzzle, when I asked him questions about progress, if any, on the sub-committee hearings. He related to me that some impressive things were coming out and that Sen. Kerry seemed to have information he was not releasing which appeared to have weight. I was not at all sure of exactly what he was talking about, but as he spoke I was reliving parts of past times in my mind. This journalist is a lightweight, but has often asked some primary questions. I have never seen any results of his writings, but he is persistent.

When I fall back into the period of time that I call my "uncertain era," my anxiety level begins to rise. I think back to the day when I was first interviewed by three journalist at the Center. The first story that came out, Village Voice, and how dismayed I felt over the accusations aimed at me. I guess my "loss of virginity" with the press wasn't easy. Articles that had appeared in Memphis were more general and undefined, but when I found that I was beginning to have my credibility questioned, I found that disturbing. It became something akin to drawing battle lines with the press and certain press personalities. The gauntlet was thrown down and I had to take up the challenge to prove that what I was saying was true, not for their benefit as much as for myself.

The one thing that sticks out in my mind is that I became full of self doubt about what I was saying and all the ways people tried to work in angles to break my statements and knowledge of events. Working for that one sentence in some newspaper that would say this guy is on target seemed to be a daily quest. I knew a few people believed what I said, but as one journalist told me, "I need you as a source, but the paper would never allow your name to appear with the information."

This was like being the carrier of a terrible disease and newspapers being afraid to name you as the carrier for fear of some associated stigma. This wasn't as bitter a pill to swallow as the ones that used the information as if it was delivered to them in a vision. It was hard seeing something you wrote for a journalist being printed under his byline and knowing he was only the conduit and never had an original thought in his life.

I would feel it was egotistical for me to think I could have broken any major news piece, much less have my name on it. The feeling was more like knowing you had the story and [were] freely giving it to a journalist, but seeing something somewhere, regardless of the size, that was a small piece of you there in print. Attribution meant I was getting through. It really never came.

Many people still wonder who I am and what I am. They wonder what I was doing in all the Contra mess and if I truly knew as much as I said I did. When I first interviewed with Scott Armstrong and felt like he was penetrating some holy recess of my mind, I felt a combination of new feelings. I knew what I knew in my mind, but I felt I was bound to guard many portions of my knowledge. I went on the defense because what I spoke about in general terms, to people I knew who understood the jargon, did not appear to have such a meaningful direction.

I almost felt like I was imposing on people, a beggar if you will, about information critical to a process I had come to know as flawed and transparent. I felt like a salesman, of a sort, trying to push a product on people suspect of my goods. I was asked to come and give this information. Now I immediately had to justify its meaning and substance to people who I knew had nearly no knowledge of the gift I could have bestowed on them.

In those days I seemed to be a ball bouncing between walls. Quick judgments were made of me and sides were chosen for the slaughter that would follow in the days to come. Little did I realize I was the pawn of both left and right. My knowledge served both sides well, but the recoil from the shocks started tearing away at my mind and soul.

Forty five years of my life were being run through a political autopsy with the findings more of a surprise to me than any other. My mindset in life was certain. I had always been in command of my senses and thought processes. I had no fear or conscience about the tasks and ideals I carried out on a day to day basis. Listening close to the pulses of thoughts behind the people claiming friendship while beckoning me to betray my beliefs, I was swayed to the course of change.

A kind of self righteousness set in like a palsy. I faced each joust from opposing foes with eagerness and the instinct to overcome their ability to quell my releases of information that was allowing the media to ride roughshod over sharp denials. Each and every crack in the armor of the now perceived enemy, brought a swell of pride to my heart. Hurting with words, hurting with knowledge had become a new and wondrous weapon. In my heart I felt these things, but outwardly I displayed an almost unconcerned attitude towards the dismantling of an 'enterprise' I help carry forth at one time.

During the days of my participation, there were few things I would not have done to see that the 'cause' survived and progressed. I cursed the liberals and demagogues who tried to muzzle the ways of the right. It was my nature to protect the vanquished rebels from any form of political action that may have brought it all to an end. I ate, slept and connived with those I now was trying expose, for reasons known only to myself. The guilt and the knowledge were hard to balance. I questioned myself on numerous occasions about why I had become the detractor of something I had elevated to lofty heights during my life. No answers came. I felt the doors close behind me and the footsteps of actions gaining on me. I was actually in a dead runaway from myself and the stains I could not wash off. Somehow justification had to be reached with my reasoning or I would surely succumb to the need to revert back to the old ways. A balance was struck and my determination was steadfast. Unlike a baptismal, I could not be born again into a new person or consciousness, because the past was alive in my heart and in my mind. I had to block out the will, the yearning and desire to step back into the past.

My course was plotted by my own actions and deeds. Lost in the mixed feelings was the reality that I was a fountain of unproven facts. I was a seer. I was a weaver of believable scenarios that came true. The ups and downs of the information battle, won or lost, kept me as an addict on the drug of survival and the need to be proven correct in my assertions.

Through it all I built a most fallible shield around my feelings. I had the perception that all would come out right. I had become accustomed to the feeling I could only be physically harmed, but never dealt a [death blow] to my emotional state of well being.

The re-enforcers of my drive to continue the hunt/kill pursuit, kept me [piqued] as to possible outcomes and glimpses of successful finality. This was the folly of it all. I had so swung my beliefs, trust and loyalty to a group of people as to be blinded by the fact they only served foolish masters as I had done.

I had made the quantum leap from plausible deniability to plausible political opportunism. I so wanted to be useful and looked upon with respect, I allowed my vision of life to become blurred. Somewhere in the fray I lost my identity. In the rush to deliver up more incriminating facets of a gem, now dislodged from its setting, I over ran a part of me I can no longer find. Lost in the shuffle (were) slivers of dignity, pride and self esteem.

Regardless of where I am or ever will be physically, an unseen part of me will be drifting in the darkness of self despair. I cast my lot with thieves from both worlds of opposition. I had friends, of a past nature, and I found friends for the future, from it all. These are the blessings of a time when I rode the carrousel of good versus evil.

I cannot say I will look back on those times, as I will forever live in "those times." I will always wonder if the price was worth the thankless duty to principles. In that some may benefit from all the bloodletting of Iran/Contra, I will file into my misgivings the possibility that change begets the whole, not the part.

In my far too dramatic outline of my feelings, the point to it all is, a singular question will forever haunt me. Will I ever believe I traded precious convictions for personal revenge?

At this point in my life I cannot come to grips with the undeniable facts that my contribution to a sordid part of the history of my country was the obsession of a zealot [Oliver North] which may have pushed him to disaster [with me] being the unnamed source who will always carry the shadow of doubt.

Miskito, Sumo, Rama Asla Takan ka_____
Wayah, Mayangna, Rama, Balna kakak aslah kalahna
Pacpa, Sumukitna, Rama Umusik_____

A QUIEN CONCIERNE

Sr:

    Esta carta representa la autorizacion al Coronel Flaco
nosotros hemos hablado sobre el beneficio que representa
ante el Estado Mayor MISURA y los Miembros del Consejo
de Ancianos.
    Esta autorizacion ha sido solamente con el, votando
este mandato no habra otra persona que intervenga agenos a la
Organizacion MISURA.
    En esta urgencia le extendemos la autorizacion legal de
la directiva del Estado Mayor MISURA y miembros del
Consejo de Ancianos de la Republica de MISURA.
    Esta autorizacion es para la negociacion del
mantenimiento de cualquier equipo; abastecimiento y para
el dinero designado para ser enviado directo a los MISURAS.
Para continuar esta larga trayectoria para la liberacion
de nuestro pueblo.

En concenso firmamos;

Fraternalmente.

Estado Mayor MISURA

A: _____
  Raul Tobias Mendez
B: _____
  Selso Wiggins
C: _____
  Hilton Fagoth
D: _____
  Eduardo Pantin
E: _____
  Alejo Theofilo. B

Miembros del Consejo de
Ancianos MISURA.

_____
Enrique Lopez
_____
Mirigildo Ramon
_____
Sifred Williams
_____
Rodolfo Rivera
_____
Genova Bell
_____
Cirilo Baptis

1. The letter in Spanish is from the Council of Elders of the Indian Confederation "MISURA" authorizing Colonel Flaco to represent them to acquire supplies and equipment for the "liberation of our people." MISURA tribes live on the East Coast of Nicaragua and Honduras.

```
Lt. Colonel Oliver North
NSC
OEOB 392
Washington, D.C.                      January 31, 1985

Ollie:

The following info came in while you were gone.  Thought it was
something you should know.

    o  Flacko is back in Miami. On Tuesday he met with Steadman
       Faggoth to work out an arrangement.  In essence, Flacko
       is to assume the responsibility of training the Indians
       at Rus Rus. Supposedly the Council of Elders will agree
       to this. There are 4 people in Miami ready to go back
       to Honduras on Monday with Flacko and his side kick
       Tieador. Another 11 are supposed to fly into Miami tonight
       and then they all will go south on Monday and then on to
       Rus Rus.

       Flacko has been working on getting the support of some
       of the Cuban community, including: the Cuban Legion and
       Joe Contine (sp?); the Brigade; the Cuban Independent
       Movement, which is Montos's group; and Alpha 66. He hopes
       this support will be both financial and manpower.

       Flacko's long term goal is to buildup the Miskito and train
       them to the point where they can start taking land.  The area
       he wants them to concentrate on is where there is a port and
       where one of the operating gold mines is.  The ultimate plan
       is to open the port and take the gold mine. Once the port is
       open a boat would sail from Miami directly to the port with
       men and supplies, drop them off and take out the gold which
       is captured.

       Flacko is also setting himself up to be the one who handles
       all financial support for the Miskitos. Thus everything
       going to them in terms of support from groups in the U.S.
       goes through him. He and his buddy Tieador then have an
       opportunity to make a little on the side. At least some of
       the funds are to go through a company called Delphi Corporation
       which has P.O. Boxes in Alabama and Texas.

       A Texas businessman named Mako Stewart, of Stewart Enterprises,
       provided Flacko with $25,000 for financing his last trip and
       to begin to help the Miskito.  Supposedly he is involved with
       the selling of bonds which supposedly just got approved by
       the SEC.  The $ from the sales of the bonds will be divided
       with 60% going to the FDN and 40% going to the Miskito.
       Mako will funnel the 40% through Flacko, who he thinks walks
       on water.

       Would seem a good idea to deal with Flacko as soon as possible.
       Probably will not be scared off as he believes he has done
       nothing to violate the neutrality act. If he is held probably
       will still move forward after he is let out, unless he can
       be locked up for a good long time. Best bet might be to dry
       up his funds, have someone talk to him about National Security
       and put the word out that he is not to be touched. But, if
       possible it might be wise to do this in someway that doesn't
       ruin whatever pr potential CMA has for the good of the cause.

       Posey has been doing the best he can to either sit on Flacko
       or deal him out, but that is not possible because right now
       Flacko knows too much and it would do no one any good if he
       went to the press. He has got to be finessed out.
```

2. Partial text of letter to Lieutenant Colonel Oliver North from Robert Owen, formerly an aide to Vice President Dan Quayle. Owen updates North on Colonel Flaco's progress with the Indians and on Flaco's financial support. Owen recommends that North "dry up" Flaco's funds and have someone talk to him about "national security."

U.S. Department of Justice

Federal Bureau of Investigation

Office of the Director

UNCLASSIFIED

JULY 18, 1986

JACK TERRELL   N 4589

WARNING NOTICE: Because of the extreme sensitivity of the
sources and the substance of the following, no disclosure can be
made of the information without the authorization of the
originator.

This document is classified "Secret" in its entirety.

Terrell was first interviewed by the FBI on March 5, 1986,
because he was described by a witness cooperating in a neutrality
investigation as knowledgeable on the matter. The investigation
concerned alleged activities of the Civilian Military Assistance
(CMA) including smuggling weapons from south Florida into Central
America on behalf of the "Contra" guerrillas, smuggling
narcotics, plotting the assassination of the U.S. Ambassador to
Costa Rica and discussing bombing the U.S. Embassy in Costa Rica.
Some of the subjects of the investigation were known to have
recruited, trained and transported over a dozen people from south
Florida to fight with the Anti-Sandinista "Contra " guerrillas in
the Nicaragua-Costa Rica border area.

At the time he was interviewed, Terrell acknowledged that
he was aware of the plot to assassinate U.S. Ambassador Tambs and
the CMA's plan to attack embassies. Although his knowledge of
the facts relating to the embassy attacks varied from other
information known to the FBI, he advised that they were planned
to implicate the Sandinistas. He also stated that it was his
opinion that the activities of the CMA were being coordinated by
the CIA.

The CIA advised the FBI that the subjects of the
neutrality investigation, Rene Corbo (also spelled Corvo,) Steven
P. Carr, Robert Thompson, Thomas Posey, and Jesus Garcia were not
CIA assets.

UNCLASSIFIED

This document contains neither
recommendations nor conclusions of
the FBI. It is the property of
the FBI and is loaned to your agency;
it and its contents are not to be
distributed outside your agency nor
duplicated within your agency.

Partially Declassified/Released on ___
Under provisions of E.O. 12356
by 3. Reger, National Security C

3. First page of FBI memo written by Oliver "Buck" Revell as part of a plan to portray Jack Terrell as a terrorist threat. The remainder of the memo was substantially censored and revised.

UNCLASSIFIED

Non-Log

NATIONAL SECURITY COUNCIL
WASHINGTON DC 20506

14042

July 17, 1986

ACTION

MEMORANDUM FOR JOHN M. POINDEXTER

N 45918

FROM: OLIVER L. NORTH

SUBJECT: Terrorist Threat: Terrel

Several months ago, a U.S. citizen named Jack Terrel became an active participant in the disinformation/active measures campaign against the Nicaraguan Democratic Resistance. Terrel's testimony was used in the Avirgan/Honey suit in Costa Rica and has been entered in the Florida law suit against Richard Secord, et al. Terrel has appeared on various television "documentaries" alleging corruption, human rights abuses, drug running, arms smuggling, and assassination attempts by the resistance and their supporters. Terrel has also been working closely with various Congressional staffs in preparing for hearings and inquiries regarding the role of U.S. Government officials in illegally supporting the Nicaraguan resistance.

After the "West 57th" piece by CBS two weeks ago, Project Democracy officials decided to use its security apparatus to attempt to determine how much Terrel actually knows about their operations. One of the security officers for Project Democracy met several times with Terrel and evaluated him as "extremely dangerous" and possibly working for the security services of another country.

This afternoon, Associate FBI Director, Oliver Revell, called and asked for any information which we might have regarding Terrel in order to assist them in investigating his offer to assassinate the President of the United States. ████████████████████ The FBI now believes that Terrel may well be a paid asset of the Nicaraguan Intelligence Service (DGSE) or another hostile security service.

Mr. Revell has asked to meet with the Project Democracy security officer who has been meeting with Terrel. A meeting has been arranged for this evening. The FBI has notified the Secret Service and is preparing a counter intelligence/counter-terrorism operations plan for review by OSG-TIWG tomorrow.

TOP SECRET
Declassify: OADR

TOP SECRET

UNCLASSIFIED

(1227)

4. First draft of Lieutenant Colonel Oliver North's memorandum for John Poindexter on the terrorist threat posed by Jack Terrell. Poindexter disapproved the draft and wrote back by hand, "Ollie, Give me another memo, for the President this time including the results of OSG [Operations Sub Group of the supersecret Terrorist Incident Working Group.] What to you want me to tell the AG [Attorney General]?"

TOP SECRET   2

N 45919

It is interesting to note that Terrel has been a part of what appears to be a much larger operation being conducted against our support for the Nicaraguan resistance. We have not pursued this investigation -- which includes threatening phone calls to the managing editor of the Washington Post -- because of its political implications. It would now appear that ▉▉▉▉▉▉ ▉▉▉▉▉ of Terrel's activities, this may well be much more than a political campaign.

RECOMMENDATION

That you discuss this matter with the Attorney General and the President, as appropriate.

Approve _____   Disapprove _J_

Ollie,

Give me another memo, for the President this time including the results of OSG.

What do you want me to tell AG?

J

TOP SECRET   UNCLASSIFIED

5. *Second page of North's memo to Poindexter dated July 17, 1986, with Poindexter's hand-written note and disapproval.*

THE WHITE
WASHINGTON

14035

INFORMATION

July 28, 1986

MEMORANDUM FOR THE PRESIDENT.

FROM: JOHN M. POINDEXTER

N 45896

SUBJECT: Terrorist Threat: Terrell

Issue

Anti-contra and anti-U.S. activities by U.S. citizen, Jack
Terrell.

Background

Several months ago, a U.S. citizen named Jack Terrell became an
active participant in the disinformation/active measures campaign
against the Nicaraguan Democratic Resistance. Terrell has
appeared on various television "documentaries" alleging corruption,
human rights abuses, drug running, arms smuggling, and assassination attempts by the resistance and their supporters. Terrell is
also believed to be involved with various Congressional staffs in
preparing for hearings and inquiries regarding the role of U.S.
Government officials in illegally supporting the Nicaraguan
resistance.

Terrell was first interviewed by the FBI on March 5, 1986, as a
cooperating witness in a neutrality investigation concerning
alleged activities of the Civilian Military Assistance (CMA)
group -- including weapons and narcotics smuggling, plotting the
assassination of the U.S. Ambassador to Costa Rica, Lew Tambs,
and bombing his embassy.

Discussion

The Operations Sub-Group (OSG) of the Terrorist Incident Working
Group (TIWG) has made available to the FBI all information on Mr.
Terrell from other U.S. Government agencies. Various government
agencies -- Customs, Secret Service, the Bureau of Alcohol,
Tobacco and Firearms -- have information on some of Terrell's
activities and the FBI is currently consolidating this information
for their investigation.

SECRET
Declassify: OADR

SECRETED

1226

Partially Declassified/Released on 28 Jan 1987
under provisions of E.O. 12356
by 9. Peltz, National Security Council

6. *Revised memorandum from Lieutenant Colonel Oliver North to John
Poindexter dated July 28, 1986. Note that President Ronald Reagan, who
claimed that he had no knowledge of the illegal support of the Contras,
initialled the memo at the upper right-hand corner. The memo notes that
Terrell was involved with various Congressional staffs in preparing for
hearings and inquiries into the Iran-Contra incidents.*

SECRET   2

The FBI reports that Terrell went to Miami, coincident with your
visit on Wednesday. The FBI, in concert with the Secret Service,
has Terrell under active surveillance.

The FBI has advised that the non-U.S. Government
supporters of the Nicaraguan resistance have been particularly
helpful in this investigation.   N 4589

It is important to note that Terrell has been a principal witness
against supporters of the Nicaraguan resistance both in and
outside the U.S. Government. Terrell's accusations have formed
the basis of a civil law suit in the U.S. District Court in Miami
and his charges are at the center of Senator Kerry's investigation in the Senate Foreign Relations Committee. Since it is
important to protect the knowledge that Terrell is the subject of
a criminal investigation, none of those with whom he has been in
contact on the Hill have been advised.

                                    Prepared by:
                                    Oliver L. North

SECRET

UNCLASSIFIED
SECRET

7. *Second page of North's memorandum. Note changes from draft,
including deletion of mention of the* Washington Post *and the addition
of concern about Senator Kerry's investigation.*

832

UNCLASSIFIED

15 July '86

Summary of Comments from Interviews-Jack Terrell
(His statements/comments)

-Jack Reynolds Terrell, 45 years of age, born in Alabama, 5'10"
165 lbs, slender build, brown/grey hair.

-Ran away from home at 14 years of age, conflicts with family/father,
family well-off, father worked with Southern Railway.

-Jack and 2 boys stole a Model A Ford, broke into a gas station and
took money for gas. He was 14 years of age, was sentenced to 18 years
in prison. Spent 6 years in Alabama and was released. Never returned
home. Hired by the Alabama prison system as to work with wayward
teenagers.

-Parents are now dead. Has 2 sisters - 1 in Alabama, 1 in Florida.

-He married and divorced. Gave his wife substantial money at time of
divorce as he was a millionaire by age 27. She is still unmarried
and in Alabama.

-He had 5 companies in the past. Has no income now. Gets no money
from Christic Institute or news interviews. Lives off of friends
such as the apartment in DC on Mass Ave.

-Christic handles causes and cases for fights against "big brother"
companies and governments." Sheehan is brilliant, Davis is a Jesuit
priest and lawyer. Sheehan studied for the priesthood. Sheehan and
wife live in a house near the monistary in DC owned by the Catholic
Church. The Church supports Christic financially.

-Jack gets no money from Sen Kerry - either by check or cash.

-Jack gets no money from anyone and is "hurting slightly."

-Jack does not want to align himself with any political group or
cause. Will help only if the cause is identifying with actions such
as the Government and CIA which hurts or is not helping the people
(Indians) in Nicaragua: Most all of the monies brought in were
actually skimmed off by the senior officers and very little ever
got down to the people needing food, medicines, etc.

-Hull is an agent for the CIA, has an 8,000 acre ranch with 5 air
strips. Strips were used for landings and transfer of military equipment but also drugs. TV News shots actually show officials helping
transfer boxes, etc.

UNCLASSIFIED

8. Original profile of Jack Terrell written by North's investigator, Glenn Robinette. Note Robinette's focus on Terrell's prison record and sources of income. Terrell, Robinette found, was a millionaire by age 27, (not the typical income bracket for a mercenary) and received no money from the Christic Institute or from Senator Kerry.

833

UNCLASSIFIED

-Sen Kerry introduced/arranged a meeting with financial investors
in the Boston area for the air services. They liked it and are
awaiting Jack's return to the area for more talks.
-Jack is a pilot of prop aircraft including choppers. No jets.
-Christic has a hundred witnesses and will win the suit now pending in Florida. Jack will testify for Avigan/Honey. The Americans
named in the suit are either employees of CIA or contract employees.
-The Senate plans very strong efforts to defeat the funding. Peace
groups plan large demonstrations throught the country. The approval
will be defeated. Christic has about 12 attorneys supporting them.
-Singlaub and North have provided secret funding in the past and it
was not distributed fairly.
-Jack has very good contacts in Costa Rica. He was there in February
and May '86. He has a valid US passport which was once taken from
him and stamped "Cancelled." by the US authorities when he was
forcibly removed by gunpoint from Nicaragua by direction of the CIA.
-Jack as an IQ of 180 and total recall of names and numbers from
many years ago.
-On Sat evening 12 July '86, Jack received a call from an Anchorage
newspaper reporter who asked what he knew about a local air company
named MockAir (sp?). What Jack said to the reporter is not known yet
He did tell me that "MockAir is owned by Zantoc in Chicago who is
owned by Evergreen who is owned by Air America, the largest airline
in the USA and has never carried a legitimate passenger. MockAir is
owned/connected with Maul Corporation, Maultrie, Georgia. They make
STOL aircraft. STOL aircraft were used by AF General Richard Secord
in covert air operations. He also used PV-1 Neptunes for the same
purpose." "He runs an 'under-airforce' for North.".
-George Dooley was the operator of Air America and recently died.
-News reporters Brian Berger, AP and Christopher Dickey, Washington
Post know a great deal about the Nicaraguan problem and have talked
with people involved down there and here in the US.
-Jack, as a convicted felon cannot get a job easily. He has limited
employed possiblities, not with Kerry or US Government. He must
travel on his own, be independent, create his own successes.

UNCLASSIFIED

9. Second page of Robinette's profile on Terrell. This document was reprinted in the transcript of the Iran-Contra hearings. Note that Robinette emphasizes Terrell's photographic memory and 180 IQ.

UNCLASSIFIED   17 July '86

Notes on J.Terrell -Operational Use/Threat   14043
                                                            N 45920

The comments are based upon about eight meetings and calls. It is believed that Jack has accepted me for what I said I am - a non-practicing attorney representing a group of investors who think that the subject of country conflics, Rambo, guns, escapes, small groups fighting for minorities, etc., is highly marketable at this time. Terrell was picked as "he has been highly visible in the news media and has been associated with these type activities, speaks well, etc."

Again, I believe that Terrell has accepted me. I would estimate a rating of about 75%. It is quite possible that I am being stroked for a period due to his personality and background.

Summary for Review and Next Step

Terrell is a Survivor.

Due to his running away from home at 13 - sentenced to prison at 14 for 6 years - being on his own - employment difficult due to his felony record - broken marriage.

Makes friends slowly - never fully commits himself to anyone - never volunteers too much personal information unless he has a reason - will never be tied to anything that he cannot leave easily - never commit himself to a group or cause unless it is popular and resonably beneficial to him and also, allows him some room to "waffle" later if necessary for his benefit.

He is articulate and soft spoken - gives an appearance of sincerity and speaks easily and convincingly. His statements usually contain a great variety of names and incidents. To dispute any of his questionable statements would require a great amount of time for subsequent interviews and fact finding.

To his listeners and readers, a little bit of truth from someone involved in a sensational matter results in the opinion that there must be some validity to most all of his statements.

UNCLASSIFIED   (1237)

10. Robinette's re-written analysis of Jack Terrell found in Lieutenant Colonel Oliver North's office safe at the National Security Council. Robinette admits that he was falsely misleading Terrell into believing that he represented a group of investors interested in making a film or publishing a book about his experiences.

Even if his statements are only factual 25 to 75% of the time,
his remaining false statements, lies, hearsays, blend in easily with
the rest of his other statements. There is little opportunity to dispute and actually confront him later about his previously spoken statements unless there is a filmed or taped record of exactly what he said.
He will always deny or explain what he said or meant when forced into
a position to do so.

N 45921

Terrell may actually possess enough information - either from
first-hand personal knowledge or from other sources - to be dangerous
to our objectives. A review of my notes made from meetings with Terrell
appear that what he knows - partially or fully, fact or hearsay -
could be embarrassing to RS and whoever, if he is in a situation where
he is telling stories to make his point covincingly. He is certainly
going to quote names and organizations - known or not-known - to show
his great and intimate knowledge of "secret operations."

Operational Decision Needed

If Terrell is considered to be a serious threat to us based
upon the foregoing paragraphs, I suggest the following actions:
1. Change the direction of the original "Sting" plan byreducing the
present to a lower-key effort and my interest (with him) in producing
a book, movie, TV, about him and his expeiences. He is certainly in
touch with enough news reporters and some film types to go on his own.
2. Increase the (my) interest in setting-up a chopper service or air
fright line in Costa Rica as proposed in Terrell's written outlines
given to me. The "investors" would require that he reduce or stop his
"political talking" as it would "affect our investment." Any activity
of this type would require "prior discussion and approval by me."
3. Through (2) above, I would have continous contact with him, his
obvious selfish interests to become involved in making money -- and,
his willingness to continue to talk about a number of things. Working
(1) and (2) together for a period of time would permit us (me) to
learn information which may be underway and critical to our current
programs, efforts - past, present or future.

Ultimately, the chopper or air freight service in Costa Rica
could be a winner - even connected to some future non-commerical work?
Terrell wants to go to Costa Rica - we would have him in hand and
somewhat in our control.

(2)  UNCLASSIFIED

**11. Second page of Robinette's investigative report. Robinette planned
a "sting" on Terrell concerning both investors for a book/movie deal and
for a helicopter service in Costa Rica.**

Notes

Chapter 1

1. "Copter," *Knight-Ridder* news wire, Sept. 12, 1984.
2. "Parker's death won't deter group's mission," *Huntsville News*, Sept. 6, 1984, p. 1.
3. *op. cit.*, "Copter."
4. "Journal of a Professional Adventurer," *Soldier of Fortune* magazine, January 1985, p. 76.
5. Jack Terrell interviews with FDN military commander Enrique Bermudez, November and December 1984.
6. "Nicaragua Victims Tied to Recruiting: U.S. Officials Say Insurgents Are Attracting Volunteers," the *New York Times*, Sept. 4, 1984, p. 1: and Jack Terrell interviews with FDN general staff members, Enrique Bermudez and CMA leader Tom Posey in late 1984 and early 1985 concerning the executions of Parker, Powell and Pozo.
7. "Mystery Involving Mercs," *Time* magazine, Sept. 17, 1984, p. 33.
8. "Families: U.S. unit has covert role," The *Miami Herald*, Dec. 17, 1984, p. 1.
9. Jack Terrell interviews with Enrique Bermudez concerning CIA plans for Nicaragua, November 1984.
10. "CIA counterterror chief reportedly being forced to retire," United Press International in the *Atlanta Journal-Constitution*, Sept. 13, 1987, p. 3-A.

Chapter 2

1. "Mercenaries bungled invasion of Dominica," *Los Angeles Times-Washington Post* News Service in the *Atlanta Journal-Constitution*, Aug. 9, 1981.
2. "FBI Holds 8 in Plot on Honduras: Killing of Leader, Seizure of Power Allegedly Planned," the *Washington Post*, Nov. 2, 1984, p. 1.
3. Affidavit of Gerard Latchinian, filed in connection with U.S. vs. Jose A. Bueso-Rosa, Case No. 84-2864-CIV, U.S. District Curt, Southern District of Florida.
4. *op. cit.*, "FBI Holds 8"
5. Jack Terrell interview with Gerard Latchinian, July 1986.
6. McNeil, Frank, *War and Peace in Central America: Reality and Illusion*, Charles Scribner's Sons, (New York: 1988), p. 230.
7. *Ibid.*, p. 229.

Chapter 3

1. Dickey, Christopher, *With the Contras: A Reporter in the Wilds of Nicaragua*, (New York: Simon and Shuster, 1983), pp. 82-84.

Chapter 12

1. "A C.I.A. Man in Nicaragua," *Life* magazine, February 1985, pp. 24-28.
2. Senate Committee on Foreign Relations, Subcommittee on Terrorism, Narcotics and International Operations report, "Drugs, Law Enforcement and Foreign Policy" (hereafter *The Kerry Report)*, *(Washington, D.C.: U.S. Government Printing Office, April 13, 1989)*, Vol. 1, p. 121.
3. FBI 302, Continental Bank Bombing, FBI Agent George Kiszynski, MM174A-1298, released in *U.S. v. Corbo*, Southern District of Florida, 1988, as cited in *The Kerry Report*, Vol. 2, pp. 203-212.

Chapter 14

1. "First American LRRP Into Nicaragua," *Eagle* magazine, September 1985.
2. Oliver North notebook of 5 January 1985, as contained in Motion to Dismiss the indictment on grounds of selective prosecution and request for evidentiary hearing, *U.S. vs. Jack Terrel, et al*, U.S. Distict Court Southern District of Florida, Case No. 88-6097-Cr-Judge Roettger, (hereafter Selective Prosecution Motion), exhibit 12.
3. Oliver North notebook of Nov. 27, 1984.
4. Robert Owen memo of January 31, 1985 (RWO-2), as contained in Selective Prosecution Motion, Exhibit 17.

Chapter 15

1. Pegasus/Frank Camper report to DIA, December 12, 1984, as contained in *The Kerry Report*, Vol. 2, pp. 350-357.
2. "Nicaragua Rebels Getting Advice From White House on Operations," the *New York Times*, Aug. 8, 1985, p. 1.
3. Robert Owen memo of April 1, 1985, Exhibit RWO-7 in Iran-Contra documents.

4. Bradlee, Ben Jr., *Guts and Glory*, Donald I. Fine, Inc., (New York: 1988), p. 302.

5. "La Penca: Report of an Investigation," by Martha Honey and Tony Avirgan, The Christic Institute (Washington D.C., undated), p. 33.

6. From Jack Terrell's personal field notes dated 11/29-12/13 (1984), pp. 1-2.

7. *The Kerry Report*, Vol. 1, p. 404.

8. Florida Aircraft Leasing Corp. air cargo manifest of March 6, 1985 as contained in *The Kerry Report*, Vol. 3, p. 274.

9. *The Kerry Report*, Vol. 1, p. 404.

10. Iran-Contra deposition of Jeffrey Feldman, Appendix B, Vol. 10, p. 70.

11. *Ibid.*, p. 79.

12. *Ibid.*, pp. 82-83.

13. Robert Owen memo of April 7, 1986, Exhibit RWO-15 in Iran-Contra documents.

14. *Ibid.*

Chapter 16

1. "Contra-gate," by James Ridgeway, the *Village Voice*, May 20, 1986.

2. Transcript of "All Things Considered," National Public Radio, May 5, 1986, as contained in *The Kerry Report*, Vol. 2, p. 271.

3. *Ibid.*, p. 270.

4. "Iran-Contra's Untold Story," by Robert Parry and Peter Kornbluh, Foreign Policy, NO. 72, Fall 1988, pp. 3-4.

5. *Ibid*, pp. 23-26.

6. FBI documents as contained in *Report of the Congressional Committees Investigating the Iran-Contra Affair*, (hereafter *Iran-Contra Report*), Government Printing Office, (Washington: 1987), Appendix A, pp. 798-800.

7. *La Penca: On Trial in Costa Rica, The CIA vs. The Press*, edited by Tony Avirgan and Martha Honey, Editorial Porvenir (Costa Rica: 1987), pp. 9-10.

8. *Ibid.*, p. 14.

9. *Ibid.*,

10. Cockburn, Leslie, *Out of Control*, Atlantic Monthly Press (New York: 1987), p. 236.

11. *Ibid.*

12. *Ibid.*, p. 237.

13. *Ibid.*, 238.

14. *Ibid.*

15. Glenn Robinette Deposition to Iran-Contra committee, Jan. 17, 1987, pp. 5-7.

16. *The Kerry Report*, Vol. 1, p. 424.

17. *Ibid.*

18. Selective Prosecution Motion, p. 32.

19. *Ibid.*

20. FBI Washington Field Office memorandum of interview with Glenn Robinette, July 25, 1986.

21. *Ibid.*

22. Scott, Peter Dale and Jonathan Marshall, *Cocaine Politics: Drugs, Armies and the CIA in Central America*, University of California Press, (Berkeley: 1991), p. 141.

23. Oliver Revell deposition to the Iran-Contra commitee, July 15, 1987, pp. 25-28.

24. *Iran-Contra Report*, p. 112.

25. *Cocaine Politics*, pp. 140-141.

26. Glenn Robinette deposition of April 27, 1988, p. 27, as contained in Defendant's Response to Government's Motion to Quash Subpoena to Oliver B. Revell, Executive Assistant Director, Federal Bureau of Investigation, U.S. vs. the LaRouche Campaign, U.S. District Court, District of Massachusetts, Criminal Case No. 86-323-K, April 1988, (hereafter Robinette-LaRouche deposition).

27. *Ibid.*

28. FBI Washington Field Office Memorandum of July 25, 1986 concerning interview with Glenn Robinette on July 17, 1986, p. 1.

29. FBI memorandum of July 25, 1986 concerning interview with Glenn Robinette on July 24, 1986, p. 1.

30. Robinette memo of July 15, 1986, *Iran-Contra Report*, Appendix A, Vol. 1, p. 832.

31. "Notes on J. Terrell — Operation Use/Threat," unaddressed memorandum from Glenn Robinette dated July 17, 1986.

32. *Ibid.*

33. Robinette-Larouche deposition, p. 27.

34. *Ibid.*

35. *Ibid.*

36. National Security Concil Memorandum of July 17, 1986 from Oliver L. North to John M. Poindexter, (Poindexter 44 in Iran-Contra documents.)

37. National Security Council Memorandum of July 25, 1986 from Oliver L. North to John M. Poindexter, (Poindexter 45 in Iran-Contra documents.)

38. National Security Council Memorandum of July 28, 1986 to Ronald Reagan from John M. Poindexter, (included in Poindexter 45 in Iran-Contra documents.)

39. FBI Miami Field Office report of July 28, 1986.

40. Oliver Revell Iran-Contra deposition, pp. 27-32.

Chapter 17

1. "Fortier, aide to Reagan, Dies," United Press International in the *New York Times*, Aug. 25, 1986, p. B-6.

2. *Ibid.*

3. Bradlee, *Guts and Glory* pp. 165-166; "North's NSC office reportedly being abolished," the *Atlanta Journal-Constitution*, Dec. 25, 1986, p. A-13.

4. "Iran Arms Cash Is Tied to CIA-Run Account Aiding Afghan Rebels," the *Washington Post*, Dec. 3, 1986, p. A-1.

5. "McFarlane says covert aid to contras was doomed to fail," the *Atlanta Constitution*. May 12, 1987, p. A-G.

6. "Schultz balks at forced polygraph," The Associated Press in the *Atlanta Constitution*, Dec. 20, 1985, p. A-1.

7. Scott, *Cocaine Politics*, pp. 127-128.

8. *Iran-Contra Report*, p. 77.

9. *Ibid.*

10. "Hasenfus tells court his role was to load supplies, drop them to contras," the *Atlanta Consistution*, Nov. 5, 1986, p. A-2.

11. *Iran-Contra Report*, p. 144.

12. Bradlee, *Guts and Glory*, p. 445.

13. *Iran-Contra Report*, p. 144.

14. "Who Killed Barry Seal," the *Village Voice*, July 1, 1986.

15. Shannon, Elaine, *Desparados: Latin Drug Lords, U.S. Lawmen, and the War America Can't Win*, Viking (New York: 1988), p. 161.

16. *Iran-Contra Report*, p. 145.

17. *Iran-Contra Report*, p. 40.

18. Robbins, Christopher, *The Ravens: Pilots of the Secret War of Laos*, Corgi Books, (London: 1989) p. 153.

19. *Ibid.*

20. Bradlee, *Guts and Glory*, p. 196.

21. *Ibid.*, p. 120.

22. *Ibid.*, p. 196-197.

23. *Ibid.*, p. 197.

24. *Iran-Contra Report*, p. 67.

25. "2 in Nicaragua crash linked to airline here," *Miami News*, Oct. 8, 1986.

26. *Iran-Contra Report*, p. 144.

27. FBI Washington Field Office secret memorandum 0055 of July 23, 1986, pp. 3-4.

28. "Latin Study Unit Target of Thieves: Files on Weapons Shipments Are Stolen in Washington," the *New York Times*, Dec. 2, 1986.

29. *Ibid.*

30. "Notes on J. Terrell—Operation Use/Threat," unaddressed meorandum from Glenn Robinette dated July 17, 1986.

Chapter 18

1. "Miami visitor's connections to contras are shadowy," Cox News Service, March 5, 1987.

2. *Iran-Contra Report*, p. 107.

3. Jensen deposition, pp. 54-55, *Iran-Contra Report*, Appendix B. Vol. 14, pp. 587-89.

4. Department of Justice routing slip of March 24, 1986 as contained in "Selective Prosecution Motion," exhibit 20.

5. John Mattes testimony as contained in *La Penca: On Trial in Costa Rica, The CIA vs. The Press*, edited by Tony Avirgan and Martha Honey, Editorial Porvenir (Costa Rica: 1987), pp. 25-32.

6. Authors' interview with John Mattes, June 20, 1992.

7. Feldman deposition, p. 79.

8. Feldman draft memo of May 14, 1986, *Iran-Contra Report*, Appendix A., Vol. 1, p. 774.

9. Feldman deposition, p. 102.

10. Feldman deposition, pp. 92-95.

11. "Anti-Contra witness said to fabricate story," the *Washington Times*, June 3, 1986, p. 1.

12. *Ibid.*

13. Kevin Currier Iran-Contra deposition, May 5, 1987, pp. 48-49.

14. Feldman deposition, p. 105.

15. Feldman deposition, p. 109.

16. Deposition of Jack Terrell taken February 12, 1988 from "Tony Avirgan and Martha Honey vs. John Hull, Rene Corbo, Felipe Vidal, el at," 86-1146-CIV-KING; and "Tony Avirgan and Martha Honey vs. Raul Villaverde, et al," 78-1545-CIV-KING, U.S. District Court, Southern District of Florida (hereafter Terrell Deposition), pp. 21-22.

17. "Illegal aid given by 7 to contras, indictments say," the *[Memphis] Commerical Appeal*, July 14, 1988, p. 1.

18. "Soldier Who Trained Contras Says Indictment Makes Him Scapegoat," the *Atlanta Journal-Constitution*, July 24, 1988, p. 1-A.

19. *U.S. vs. Jack Terrell, et al*, U.S. District Court, Southern District of Florida, Case No. 88-6097-Cr-Judge Roettger (hereafter Terrell Indictment), July 13, 1988.

20. "Contra mercenary: Actions approved by White House," the *Miami Herald*, July 26, 1988. p. 10-A.

21. *Ibid.*

22. "Motion to Dismiss Indictment for Failure to State a Criminal Violation as the United States is Not At Peace With Nicaragua and Request for Evidentiary Hearing" (hereafter "At Peace Motion"), U.S. District Court, Southern District of Florida, Case No. 88-6097-CR-Roettger, Aug. 12, 1988, p. 49.

23. Jack Terrell diary of Friday, Sept. 2, 1988.

24. Jack Terrell diary of Wednesday, Oct. 12, 1988.

25. "Order on Motions to Dismiss," *U.S. vs. Jack Terrell, et al*, U.S. District Court, Southern District of Florida, Case No. 88-6097-Cr-Roettger, July 12, 1989, p. 10.

26. *Cocaine Politics*, pp. 148-149; *The Kerry Report* p. 588; Leon Kellner deposition of Nov. 8, 1988 to Kerry subcommittee.

27. "Order on Motions to Dismiss," p. 8.

Chapter 19

1. Transcript of conversation between Raul Manglapus and Jack Terrell, provided by ABC-TV News, p. 4.

2. *Ibid.*, p. 3.

3, *Ibid.*, p. 7.

4. Report of Polygraph Examination of Jack Reynolds Terrell Re(garding) Alleged Assassination Conspiracy, Slattery Associates, Inc. file No. 91-533 (S), Oct. 16, 1991, p. 3.

5. *Ibid.*, p. 4.

6. *Ibid.*,. p. 5.

7 "The Secretary and the Spook," *Asiaweek*, Oct. 28, 1991.

8. "Terrell crime record in U.S. revealed," the *Philippine Star*, Oct. 31, 1991, p. 1.

9. *op. cit., Asiaweek.*

10. "Jack Terrell Pledges to Fight Contra Indictment," International Center for Development Policy press release, by Virginia Foote, July 25, 1988.

11. Letter of Oct 29, 1991 from Lindsay Mattison, executive director, International Center for Development Policy, to Raul Manglapus.

12. Letter of June 20, 1988 from Lindsay Mattison to Jack Terrell.

13. "Terrell placed on CID blacklist," the *Philippine Star*, Oct. 26, 1991.

14. "Manglapus refuses to testify in probe," *Daily Globe*, Nov. 9, 1991, p. 1.

15. *Ibid.*

16. "Maceda questions Terrell on assassination plot," *Manila Standard*, Nov. 13, 1991, p. 3.

17. *Ibid.*

A

ABC, 297, 322, 383, 395, 434-436
Abrams, Elliott, 73, 378
Achille Lauro, 357
ACLU (American Civil Liberties Union), 410-411
Adair, Jim, 28, 30, 148, 154-157, 260, 278, 286-287, 292, 306
Adams, Joe Sam "Tirador," 189, 191, 193, 198, 199, 211, 214-216, 218-221, 226, 228- 229, 231, 233, 237, 239, 240-242, 255-256, 260-263, 266-267, 272- 273, 279-280, 284, 286, 292-293, 300, 302, 306, 386, 389, 393, 410- 415, 430
Afghanistan, 348, 366, 451
Air America, 370-371, 373
Alabama Boys Industrial School 171-172
Alabama National Guard, 14, 20
Albright, Cliff, 20, 179
Alcuaz, Baby, 433
Alcuaz, Jose Luis "Lingoy," 432-435, 442-443
Alpha 66, 185, 192
Alvarez, Manny, 93, 98
Alzugarey, Dr. Manuel, 195, 197
ANC (African National Congress), 384
Applicano, Hector, 63
Aquino, Corazon, 370, 424-426, 431-433, 437, 442
Arana, Frank, 68, 140, 159, 162, 163
ARDE (Democratic Revolutionary Alliance), 193, 195, 204, 213, 225, 242
Argentina, 80, 131, 229, 232, 237, 270, 317
Armstrong, Scott, 327-330, 333-334, 457
Artolla, Ardan, 283
Asiaweek, 437
Associated Press, 322, 324, 336, 353, 364, 380, 401
Attica prison, 338
Australia, 28, 30
Avirgan, Tony, 317-318, 339, 343, 345-346, 359, 402, 409, 410, 450
AWACS (Airborne Warning and Control System), 375

B

Baldi, Alberto Rodriguez, 346
Ballesteros, Juan Matta, 216
Baltimore Sun, 380
Baptists, 231, 264

Barger, Brian, 297, 298, 322, 324, 336, 401
Bastian, James, 373
BATF (Bureau of Alcohol Tobacco and Firearms), 199
Batista, Fulgencio, 185, 243
Bay of Pigs, 16, 188, 371, 416
BCCI (Bank of Credit and Commerce International), 325
Beckwith, "Charging Charlie," 72
Beisner, David, 350-351, 355, 362
Benedicto, Lincoln V., 303
Bennett, Gary, 144
Bermudez, Enrique, 47, 76-80, 83-86, 88-91, 93, 94, 96-103, 105-111, 115, 117, 122, 142-145, 148-157, 160, 167, 211, 257
Bernstein, Carl, 329
Bevadra, Timmy, 384
Bibit, Billy, 427
Black, Roy, 414
Blanton, Walton "Cisco," 20, 30, 33, 34, 42, 48-50, 52-53, 55, 57, 59-68, 70, 74, 88, 93-97, 101-102, 106, 108, 110, 115-116, 122, 127
BLEF (Burma Expeditionary Force), 386
Blum, Jack, 328, 329, 333
Boland Amendment, 17, 21, 95, 153, 166, 194, 210, 297, 352, 369, 413, 420- 421
Bonnet, Charles, 92
Borge, Tomas, 32, 103
Boston Globe, 322, 399
Bradford, Bob "Traveler," 135, 137-139, 144, 158, 260, 278
Brazil, 117, 153, 247
Brigade 2506, 185, 186, 187, 189, 241
Brokaw, Tom, 96
Brookings Institution, 355
Bueso-Rosa, Jose A., 71, 73
Burma, 331, 385-386, 388-391, 393, 410, 419, 439
Burma Expeditionary Force (BLEF), 386
Bush, George, 186, 371, 398, 438
Buzenberg, Bill, 341-342

C

CAB (Civil Aeronautics Board), 373-374, 384
"Caballo," 260, 278, 303
Caldera, Juan, 93
Calero, Adolfo, 26, 31-32, 34, 53-54, 79-80, 93-100, 105-108, 122, 144, 157, 160, 167-168, 182-183, 188-199, 202-203, 205-207, 211-216, 225, 240-243, 253, 299, 317-

318, 339, 348, 408, 412, 438
Calero, Mario, 26-27, 29-34, 36, 41-45, 47, 52-53, 55, 58, 60, 63, 68, 78, 94, 105-106, 115-117, 122, 127-130, 134-135, 137-138, 140, 144, 159, 163, 166-167, 181-182, 188, 192, 239-240, 257, 307, 315, 342, 412
Calhoon, Charlie, 315, 322-323
Cambodia, 40, 49
Camper, Frank, 147, 252, 260, 287, 308, 318
Canada, 384
Cannon, "Big John," 137-138
Cardovo, Roberto Suazo, 73
Carr, Steve, 308, 315, 318-320, 343-345
Casey, William, 16-17, 299, 313-314, 374, 395, 412, 417, 422
Cassell, Carlos, 243-244
Cassil, Teri, 42, 167
Castillo, Donald (Pulmon), 60, 64, 66, 67-71, 75, 80, 87, 93, 101, 103, 104, 116-121, 123, 124, 160, 283, 284, 292, 300, 302
Castillo, Tomas (Joe Fernandez), 66, 323, 377
Castro, Fidel, 15, 54, 185-189, 192, 195, 197, 209, 243, 248, 412
Castro, Oto, 346, 347
Catholicism, 72, 85, 103, 135, 327
Cayman Islands, 373
CBS, 158, 316, 336-337, 343, 355, 360, 383, 408, 450
CDI (Center for Defense Information), 331
Cessnas, 14, 18, 182, 218
Chad, 313
Chaffard, Claude "Frenchy," 147, 308, 343
Chamarro, Edgar, 332
Chamorro, Fernando "El Negro," 193
Chanes, Francisco "Paco," 245-248, 319-320, 339
Chang, George, 221, 369-370
Channell, Carl "Spitz," 350
Chicago Tribune, 380
"Chico," 260, 278, 292
Chile, 71
China, 95, 100, 388, 423-425
Christic Institute, 338-340, 343, 348-349, 357-358, 374, 378, 402, 404, 408-411, 414, 416, 438
CIA (Central Intelligence Agency), 13, 16, 28, 34, 38, 40, 45, 51-52, 64, 71-73, 78, 80, 85,

89, 95, 103, 108-110, 125, 128,
131, 133, 149-153, 167, 176-177,
186, 192-194, 197-198, 206, 209-
210, 214, 216-219, 237, 241-244,
252, 258, 268, 270-271, 274, 276-
277, 299, 305-308, 313-315, 318,
339, 342, 345, 349, 350, 366-368,
371-378, 394-395, 401-402, 405,
408, 413, 417, 438, 450
Cirro, Commandante, 116, 284
Clarridge, Duane (Dewey), 16,
17, 32, 73, 413
Clines, Thomas, 339, 375
CMA (Civilian Military Assistance), 12-13, 20-30, 32, 34, 36-
39, 45-52, 92, 94, 106-107, 115,
122, 127-128, 134-137, 140-141,
147, 158-160, 166-167, 179-198,
204, 206, 210-216, 221, 237-238,
243-246, 250-251, 254, 299, 307-
308, 310, 312, 315, 321, 323, 333,
339, 368, 386, 397, 402-410
CNN (Cable News Network),
383
Cockburn, Leslie, 337, 343, 345,
347, 408
COE (Special Operations Company), 78, 93, 97, 100, 102-103,
105, 111, 143, 154-155
CoIntelPro, 352
Cojuangco, Eduardo "Danding,"
431
Cold War, 15, 158, 339
Colombia, 179, 182, 187, 203,
209, 295, 320, 372-373, 404
"Commandante 26," 71, 75, 79,
85, 101, 106, 110-111, 153, 155
Committee for a Free Afghanistan, 348
Communists, 10, 12, 14-16, 18,
23-26, 32, 35, 41, 53, 72, 130,
136, 138, 142-143, 149, 158, 169,
196, 204, 209, 222, 228, 241, 244,
248-249, 259, 267, 275, 324, 350-
352, 372, 383, 406, 428, 348
Contras, 11-13, 16-21, 28, 31, 33,
38, 43, 51-52, 69, 71, 74-76, 79,
81, 85, 87, 88-89, 91-96, 101-
112, 115, 121, 125, 128-136, 141,
143-149, 151-153, 155-159, 166,
169, 179, 192, 194, 198-199, 203,
204-210, 213, 217, 220-221, 236,
238, 241-242, 248, 251, 253-254,
264-265, 268, 271, 273, 294, 297,
307, 311, 315, 317, 319, 320-324,
328-338, 340-342, 345, 349-350,
352, 354-355, 358, 361, 364, 366,
368-369, 371, 374, 376-378, 380-
383, 387, 389, 395-397, 398, 401,

403-406, 408-414, 419, 421, 423,
425, 438, 451-455, 457
Cooper, Bill, 370, 373-374, 376,
451
Cooper, Nicklous T., 316
Cordero, Manuel, 316
Cordova, Roberto Suazo, 71, 72
CORU, 185, 192
Corvo, Rene "Ho Chi Minh,"
195, 244, 319, 347
Costa Rica, 16, 87, 192-196, 203-
204, 210-214, 225-226, 237, 241-
246, 295, 308, 315, 317-318, 320-
323, 326, 339, 343-348, 358-359,
377, 399, 400-402, 408-409
Courtney, William, 14, 20-21, 127
Coutin, Hilda, 187
Coutin, Jose "Joe," 185, 187, 189,
194-195, 211, 228, 239, 243, 250-
251, 260, 306, 413, 421
CRDB (Committee for the Res-
toration of Democracy in
Burma), 385, 388, 390, 393
Cruz, Miguel, 217, 218, 219, 220
Cruz, Romulo, 10
Cuba, 9, 11, 14, 16, 24, 54, 90, 93,
152, 160, 185-197, 209-210, 228-
229, 235, 237, 241, 243, 245, 251-
252, 259, 287, 295, 316, 318-319,
322, 351, 371, 373, 400, 412,
413
Cuban Legion, 185-187, 259
Currier, Kevin, 401, 403, 406-407
Curtis, Bill, 158

D
D'Aubuisson, Roberto, 87
D'Escoto, Miguel, 32
Davies, John, 320, 343
Davis, Burke, 172
DEA (Drug Enforcement
Admin.), 45, 72, 179, 187, 316,
372
Dean, John, 335
"Deep Throat," 367
Delphi Company, 226, 227
Delta Force, 72
Democrats, 43, 217, 322, 334, 352
Denton, Jeremiah, 294-298, 300,
312
Department of Corrections, 310
Department of Justice, 73, 418
Desert One, 72
DGSE (Nicaraguan Intelligence
Service), 360
DIA (Defense Intelligence Agen-
cy), 13-15, 21, 38, 73, 125, 147,
210, 308, 366, 368, 417
Diego, Wycliffe, 249
Doan, Harry, 372

Dogherty, Carroll, 316, 336-337
Dominican Republic, 31, 46, 198
DRA (Democratic Revolutionary
Alliance), 404
Draper Correctional Center, 174,
175, 177, 310
Drew, Chris, 380
Driscoll, Sue, 226
Drugs, 37, 116-117, 127, 185, 187,
189, 194-195, 211, 203, 209, 216,
244, 247, 250-251, 258, 295-296,
298, 316, 320, 323, 344, 352, 357,
361, 372, 395, 399, 400, 402, 405,
449-450
Duarte, Jose Napoleon, 87
Dutton, Robert, 376, 377
Ducy, Lanny "Doc Zorro," 129-
134, 139, 144, 145, 152, 153, 158,
159, 168, 181, 183, 190, 192, 193,
197-201, 203, 230, 231, 306-307
Duvalier, Eric, 419-420

E
Eagle magazine, 28, 148, 154, 260
EATSCO (Egyptian American
Transport and Services Co.), 375
El Salvador, 31, 57-62, 87, 91-92,
103, 116, 118, 120, 139, 144, 243,
280, 315, 319, 331, 354, 370, 372-
379
Engelberg, Steve, 380, 382
England, 57, 308, 318, 320, 343,
400
Enrile, Juan Ponce, 431
Escobar, Pablo, 372
Estorga, Nora, 32

F
Fadlallah, Mohammed Hussein,
313
Fagoth, Edna, 219-220, 226
Fagoth, Hilton, 221, 234
Fagoth, Steadman, 196-198, 216,
219, 221, 233, 236-237, 241, 248-
249, 258-259, 264, 275-276, 283
Fairburn, John (John Cattle), 196-
199, 206, 210, 214, 216
FBI (Federal Bureau of Investigation), 45, 71, 206, 210, 245, 248,
305, 308, 315, 317, 319, 321-324,
343, 350-352, 355, 357-362, 364,
372, 378, 398, 400-406, 410, 413,
418, 435, 438, 450
FDN (Nicaraguan Democratic -
Force), 11, 18, 26, 28-34, 41, 43,
46, 48, 53-56, 60, 64-65, 68, 73, 76-
80, 86-95, 101-102, 107-108, 110,
115, 117, 120, 122-131, 136 140,
143-144, 148, 151, 153-154, 158-
163, 166, 167, 168-169, 181, 183,

188-189, 192-200, 203, 210-217, 220, 222-223, 225, 226, 229, 232, 236-242, 247, 253-258, 262, 264, 266, 268, 271-274, 276, 279-285, 293-294, 303, 307, 310, 312, 315, 318, 321, 332-333, 338, 346, 359, 395, 402, 404, 409
Federal Law Enforcement Academy, 310
Feldman, Jeffrey, 322-324, 397, 401-407, 411-412, 414, 415, 417-419
Fernandez, Joe, 401
Ferria, Maria, 428-429, 436
Flores, Captain, 71, 123, 124, 150
Fonte, Michael, 327, 328, 330, 331
Foote, Virginia, 331, 425, 437
Foreign Relations Committee, 334
Fortier, Donald, 36-41, 46, 49-51, 106, 125, 162, 166, 240, 255, 298, 308, 311, 329, 365, 366
France, 92, 201, 415, 435
Francis, Fred, 93-98
Freedom of Information Act, 334
Front Line, 131

G
Gadd, Richard, 376-377
Galil, Amac, 211, 347-348
Garay, Edward de, 376
Garcia, Graciela, 59- 60, 118, 120, 123, 161, 217, 258, 303, 307, 309, 325, 348
Garcia, Jesus, 251, 315, 321-322, 343, 397, 398, 399, 401-402, 407
Gardner, Jim, 135, 142, 145
Gardner, Richard, 336
Garwood, Ellen, 350
Genesco, 28-29
Germany, 231
Ghadaffi, Moammar, 26, 374
Giap, Vo Nguyen, 92
Gillego, Baonifacio, 370
Glasser, Ellen, 350-351, 355, 358, 362
Glibbery, Peter, 308, 315, 318, 320, 343-345, 400
Gold, Walter, 354-355
Goldwater, Barry, 417
Gregg, Donald, 186, 371
Gregorie, Richard, 403, 407
Grothaus, Dan, 380
Guardia Nacionale, 16, 54, 64, 78-80, 87, 102, 104, 132
Guatemala, 80, 120, 276
"Gustavo," 102, 105, 143, 154

H
Hacienda Police, 59
Hakim, Albert, 241, 339, 375
Hall, Bill, 374
Hamilton, Lee, 438
Harvard Univerity, 340
Hasenfus, Eugene, 371-373, 376-378, 406, 407, 451
Heinz, Chris, 30, 47
Henning, Fred, 144
Heritage Foundation, 348-349
Herman, Roger, 200, 231, 239
Hesburgh, Theodore, 53
Hill, J.D., 178-180
Honasan, Gregorio "Gringo," 424, 426, 429, 431, 436
Honduras, 11-20, 26, 28-31, 33-34, 36-37, 40-41, 43, 47-48, 51-53, 55-63, 65-75, 77-81, 83, 87-89, 101, 104, 109-112, 116, 118-179, 181-189, 191, 193, 196-199, 202, 205, 210, 213-222, 225, 226, 227, 228, 233-252, 254, 255, 257, 262, 264, 271-272, 275, 278, 280, 283-284, 295, 297, 299, 301-303, 306-307, 309, 317, 320, 322, 324, 326, 336, 346, 350, 366, 387, 389, 399, 404, 412-413, 451
HonduTel, 116
Honey, Martha, 317, 339, 343, 345-346, 359, 402, 409, 410, 450
Hong Kong, 422-424
House Foreign Affairs Commit-tee, 365
Houston Post, 380
Hull, John, 194-198, 203-206, 211-214, 241-246, 250, 253, 298, 308, 312, 315, 317-318, 320-323, 339, 343-348, 357, 398-402, 408, 412, 450
Hume, John, 408-409, 411
Hunt, Meg, 294-298, 312

I
Imbeke, Tabo, 384
InComCon (Int. Command and Control), 314-316, 325, 329, 335, 337-338, 351, 354, 365-368, 376, 379, 381-382, 394
India, 386
Indonesia, 428
International Center for Develop-ment Policy, 328, 330, 331, 334-335, 337, 340-341, 350, 351, 362, 369, 370, 373-374, 378, 381, 383-385, 394, 408, 410, 416, 423, 425, 434, 437, 439, 440, 441
Iran, 375-376, 379, 381, 395-396, 438, 449
Iran Missiles Committee, 395
Iran-Contra scandal, 186, 270, 299, 335, 342, 355, 357, 366, 384, 395, 405, 423, 445, 459
Irish Republican Army, 313
Isham, Chris, 434-436
Israel, 69, 96, 191, 262, 302, 330, 354-355
Italy, 120

J
Jamaica, 165
Japan, 386, 387
Jensen, D. Lowell, 401
Jensen, Lowell, 401
"Jesus," 192, 211
JM Wave, 186
Johnson, Paul "Pablo," 242, 260, 261, 308
Jones, Bruce, 205, 242, 244-245, 247, 315, 317, 339
JSC (Joint Special Operations Command), 348, 376
Justice Department, 324, 375, 401, 404-406, 412-413, 418, 419

K
Kapunan, Eduardo "Red," 428
Karenni National Progressive Party, 388
Kellner, Leon, 323, 402-403, 405-407, 414, 418-421
Kelly, Mike, 380
Kennedy, John F., 339
Kerry, John, 322, 324-327, 330, 333-335, 343, 351, 352, 381, 394, 399, 403-405, 413, 419-421, 450
Keyes, James, 147, 308
KGB, 364
Khmer Rouge, 40
Kiszynski, George, 323, 410, 450
Klinghofer, Leon, 357
Kong, Colonel, 387, 389
Korea, 92, 176-177, 331, 369
Ku Klux Klan, 22, 26
Kurkjian, Stephen, 322, 399
Kyin, Nai Shwe, 392

L
La Barricada, 11
La Reforma Prison, 318, 324, 343, 345, 347, 399
La, Nai Non, 389
Lacey, Donald, 211, 317
Langton, William G., 373
Laos, 40, 49, 375, 387
Latchinian, Gerard, 72-73
Lau, Ricardo, 91

Laurel, Salvador, 431
Lebanon, 313, 378
Lee, Shinbom, 369
Lehtinen, Dexter, 414-415
Libya, 211, 367, 374
Life magazine, 205, 242, 244-245
Lima, Mike, 83
Lisker, Joel, 296-298
Livingston, Bob, 43-44
"Lobo," 260, 278, 287, 292
Lopez, Walter, 33
Love, Andrew, 408
Lugar, Richard, 352, 405
Lukey, Leonel, 63, 64, 123, 139, 117, 227

M
Maceda, Ernesto, 437, 442
MacMichael, David, 378, 379, 408, 419-420
Maestri, Ralph, 322, 399
Manglapus, Raul, 370, 424-442
Manila Bulletin, 430
"Marcel," 117, 140
Marcos, Ferdinand, 370, 424-425
Marcos, Imelda, 443
Marta, Dr. Em, 390, 393
Martin, Mary, 380
Martinez, Alex, 412
Matos, Hubert, 54, 188
Mattes, John, 321, 322, 343-345, 397-403, 405, 410, 411, 414-422
Mattison, Lindsay, 330-336, 339-341, 348, 353, 369-370, 378, 381, 385-386, 394, 408, 411, 416, 425, 434, 437, 438, 439
McCall, Dick, 322, 327, 328, 331, 333
McCoy, Jim, 31
McFarlane, Robert, 36, 365-366, 375
McKay, Karen, 348, 376
Meese, Edwin, 381, 382, 383, 384, 401, 406, 412-413
Memphis Commercial-Appeal, 135, 144, 158, 336
Messick, Rick, 404-405
Messing, Andy, 319
Mexico, 18, 22, 143
Miami Herald, 361
Miami News, 377, 380
Minh, Ho Chi, 92
Miskito Indians, 196, 198, 200, 202, 210, 217, 219-222, 225, 227-239, 249, 259, 261, 262-270, 272-274, 276-277, 279, 283-284, 288-290, 293, 294, 296, 299-302, 304, 308-313, 341, 358, 422
MISURA (Indian confederation), 131, 168, 195-196, 216, 219-222,

229, 232-234, 236-241, 248-259, 261-267, 269-271, 274-279, 282-286, 293, 296, 298, 300-301
Mitra, Ramon, 431
Mondale, Walter, 107
Montez, Oscar (Orlando Montelegre), 68, 239-240, 256-258, 264, 266, 273, 279-280, 283-285, 293-294, 303
Mujahadeen, 348, 451
Mullins, Jim, 411, 416
Mya, Bo, 388, 390, 392
"Mycroft," 147, 252, 260, 286, 292, 300

N
National Public Radio, 341
National Security Archive, 327, 334
National Training School for Boys, 176
NBC, 93-97
NDF (National Democratic Front), 388-391
Neutrality Act, 32, 196, 308, 324, 361, 412-413, 417, 421, 437
New York Times, 311, 353, 365, 368, 380
Newsweek, 395
Nicaragua *passim*
Nixon, Richard M., 329, 352, 369, 384
Noble, Alexander, 428
Noriega, Manuel, 102
North, Oliver, 17, 41, 73, 147, 203, 205-207, 211, 242, 246, 250, 296-299, 308, 311-314, 323-324, 343, 349-350, 353-367, 372, 374-377, 381, 393-395, 401, 404-405, 410-413, 422, 441, 445, 449-450
Notre Dame University, 53
Nottingham, Milton G., 38, 329-330, 176-178
NPA (Communist New Peoples Army) 428
NSC (National Security Council) 17, 36-38, 73, 125, 147, 203, 206, 210, 250, 252, 255, 298, 299-301, 308, 311, 313, 315, 321, 354, 359, 365-366, 368, 369, 373, 377-378, 395, 402, 410, 417

O
Oblando y Bravo, Miguel, 103
Ocean Hunter Seafood, 246-247, 319
October Surprise, 438
Odorizzi, Charles, 72
Office of Political-Military

Affairs, 366
Ohrman, Robert "Doc," 30, 34, 49, 135, 138-142, 145
OIJ (Costa Rican Organization of Jud. Investigation) 347
Omega 7, 185, 192
Operation Elephant Herd, 368
Operation Sea Spray, 31
Orion Pictures, 206
Ortega, Daniel, 32, 103, 260
OSG, (Operations Sub-Group), 357, 360
Owen, Robert, 203-206, 211-214, 242-246, 250, 298, 299, 312, 317-318, 324, 339, 354, 357, 374, 400, 401, 411-412

P
Palmer, Robert "Thom," 260, 286, 292
Pan Am, 59, 118, 120, 161
Panama, 20, 102, 198, 243-344, 373
Pantin, Eduardo, 277, 286, 290, 292
"Papillon," 284, 292, 300, 302
Pappas, Ike, 316
"Pappy," 147-148, 260, 286, 292
Park, Tsongun, 176, 329, 330, 333
Parker, Dana H., 12-23, 34-35, 66, 78, 104, 107, 109, 127, 159, 179, 206, 254, 368, 451
Parry, Bob, 322, 324, 336, 364, 380, 401
Passage, David, 374
Pastora, Eden, 192-193, 204, 211, 212-214, 225, 242, 254, 299, 317, 339, 343, 345, 346, 357, 404, 438
Pathot Lao, 40
"Pecos Bill," 86-90, 93, 97, 99, 104, 110, 112, 116, 142, 150, 284
Pegasus, 31-33, 41, 47, 49, 86, 101-106, 109, 115, 117, 122, 127-130, 134, 136, 143, 144, 147, 148, 150, 152, 157-161, 163, 168, 180, 182, 186-189, 191, 198, 200, 202, 210, 239, 240, 258, 286, 307, 308, 386
Philippine Star, 437
Philippines, 331, 352, 370, 386, 387, 389, 395, 407, 408, 411, 423-443 *passim*, 455
Phoenix Project, 31, 32
Poindexter, John, 73, 359-361, 366, 381, 401, 412, 413
Portocarrero, Felipe, 43, 44
Portugal, 373
Portuondo, Joseph J., 408
Posey, Patsy, 23, 24
Posey, Tom, 21-36, 42, 46, 48-50,

52, 104-106, 122, 127, 134-138, 144, 148, 157-160, 166, 181-183, 185, 189-191, 193, 195-196, 199, 206, 207, 209, 211-212, 214, 216, 225-226, 239, 242-246, 248, 250-251, 259, 291, 297, 308, 315, 318, 321, 323, 339, 342, 346, 397-398, 404, 410, 412
Potts, Ray, 20
Powell, James III, 12-23, 34-35, 66, 78, 104, 107, 109, 127, 159, 179, 206, 254, 368, 451
Pozo, Mario, 12, 19, 78
"Prairie Fire," 40
Project Democracy, 360

Q
Quayle, Dan, 203, 398
Quintero, Rafael "Chi," 339

R
Ramos, Fidel "Eddie," 251, 278, 281, 289, 291, 293, 431,
Rangoon, 385, 388
"Raoul," 228- 229, 234, 236-237, 259, 267, 276, 282, 284, 288, 302
Reagan, Ronald, 15, 17, 23, 26, 36, 80, 107- 108, 110, 112, 125-126, 131, 209, 210, 214, 217, 241, 301, 304, 323, 324, 333, 337, 352, 354, 357, 358, 360, 361, 364, 365, 367, 369, 374, 375-379, 382, 384, 394, 401, 405-407, 411, 417, 450, 451
Recondo School, 147, 252, 260, 287, 289, 308
Recondo, Caesar, 216
Redeker, Bill, 435, 436
Reh, Saw Maw, 388
Republicans, 112, 334
Revell, Oliver "Buck," 357, 359, 364, 402
Reymundo, Maria, 429
Reymundo, Melba, 429-430, 436
Rhodesia, 49
Rice University, 199
Richard, Mark, 402
Ridgeway, James, 335
Robbins, Dave, 226
Robelo, Alfonso, 193, 213, 242
Robinette, Glenn, 349, 354-360, 374, 394, 404
Robinson, Aubrey, 409
Robles, Rex, 428, 431
Rodriguez, Felix (Max Gomez), 186, 371, 376
Rodriguez, Luis, 246
Rodriguez, Masareno,

"Pedrico," 228, 229, 233, 237, 238, 259, 260, 261, 262, 263, 267, 268, 287, 291, 292, 300, 302
Rodriguez, Marcelino, 211
Roettger, David, 419, 420, 421
Roettger, Norman, 415
Roitan Island, 165, 166, 167, 168, 180, 181
Romero, Oscar Arnulfo, 91
Rorick, Melinda, 374
Rosenblatt, Maurice, 330, 335
Rosenblith, Ron, 326-327, 333, 399- 400
Rossi, Donald "Ramos," 147, 242,-243, 260-261, 302

S
Sa, Khun, 388, 389, 391
Sackowitz, Theodore, 402
Sanchez, Aristides, 86, 162, 163, 211, 258
Sanchez, Cheppie, 86, 97, 142
Sanchez, Nestor, 73
Sandinistas, 9-19, 26, 32, 47, 49, 54, 64, 70, 78, 80-81, 84-85, 87, 88, 95, 98-103, 106-107, 109-110, 112, 129-134, 142, 143, 149, 151, 152, 154, 156, 157, 160, 166, 179, 188- 189, 192-194, 196, 199, 201, 203- 204, 209-210, 212-213, 219, 221, 222, 230, 232-236, 241, 242, 245, 249, 252, 265, 267, 268, 270-272, 274-275, 277, 282, 286, 288, 291, 292, 295-297, 301, 302, 304, 316, 317, 320, 352, 357, 364, 370-372, 389, 404, 451
SATCO, 372-374
Saudi Arabia, 375
Saum, Alan, 398
Sawyer, Wallace Blaine "Buzz," 370, 373-374, 451
Scharf, Larry, 403
Schnapp, Mark, 414
School of the Americas, 102
Scott, Peter Dale, 455
Seal, Adler Berriman, 187
Seal, Barry, 179, 372, 404, 455
SEALs (Sea, Air and Land), 15, 201, 376, 420
Secord, Richard, 241, 339, 349, 354-59, 374, 375, 376, 377, 393, 394, 422
Secret Service, 27, 359, 362-363, 421, 450
Senate Foreign Relations

Committee, 39, 404, 405, 450
Seng, Brang, 385, 387-393
Seng, Zau, 387, 392
SETCO Airlines, 216-217, 258
Shackley, Theodore, 186, 339, 375
Shadoan, George, 408-409
Sheehan, Danny, 338-340, 343, 349, 402, 408-409
Sheehan, Sara, 339, 340
"Shooter," 160-161
Shultz, George, 367
Sikaffy, Faiz J., 71, 73
Silkwood, Karen, 338
Singapore, 428
Singlaub, John, 241, 339, 414, 422
Sistoso, Efrin, 429, 442
Slattery Associates, 436
Slattery, George B., 436
Smalley, J.B., 135, 138
Smith, "Mr.," 311-314, 316, 337, 338, 353, 354, 365, 367, 368, 373, 379-82, 393
Smith, William Kennedy, 414
Snow, Lurana, 414- 415, 419
Socialism, 248
SOG (Studies and Observations Group), 40, 49
Soldier of Fortune magazine, 24, 28, 290
Somoza, Anastasio, 54, 64, 79, 80, 83, 87, 110, 132, 179, 193, 212, 222, 451
Somoza, Luis, 54
South Africa, 331, 384, 385
South Korea, 186
Southern Air Transport, 370-371, 373, 377, 384
Southern Railroad, 170
Soviet Union, 15, 24, 71, 262, 371, 408
SOW (Special Operations Wing), 16
Special Forces, 179
Spivey, Loher H., 206, 207, 323
State Department, 13, 72, 140, 159, 285, 299, 301, 302, 365, 371, 405
Stearns, Clarence Louis, 377
Stewart Mott Foundation, 339
Stewart, Maco, 51, 129, 130, 134, 144, 159, 181, 183, 192, 198, 199, 200-203, 210, 216-217, 226-228, 231, 238, 239, 245, 246, 294, 306, 412, 415
Stone, Tom, 27, 30
Stuart, J.E.B., 172
Sullivan, L.B., 310, 311

T

TACA Airlines, 56, 57, 58, 61, 117-118, 139, 144
Tambs, Lewis, 321, 323. 324, 397, 400-401
Tan Sasha airlines, 118, 121, 139
Task Force 160, 19, 20, 215
TEA (Tropas Especiales del Atlantico), 132-134, 230, 231, 232, 233, 238, 259, 261, 263, 271, 272, 276, 277, 278, 279, 281, 282, 285, 286, 287, 288- 289, 293, 300-301
Terrell, Billy Reynolds, 170
Terrell, Peggy, 178
Terrell, Vivian, 170, 180, 454
Terrell, William Randolph, 178
Thailand, 375, 387-392, 403, 419
Theofilo, Alejo, 221-222, 228, 232-234, 264, 266-276, 281, 284, 288-294, 300
Thomas, Bill, 135, 142, 144, 158, 159, 161, 162, 181, 336
Thompson, Richard, 134-135, 139, 141, 142, 144, 146
Thompson, Robert "Pantera," 308, 319, 343, 345-347
Thu, Ye Kyaw, 385-386, 388-390
"Tigrillo," 83, 105, 143, 273
Time-Life, 92
TIWG (Terrorist Incident Working Group), 357, 360
Tobias, Raoul, 221
"Toro," 70-71
Trott, Steven, 402
Turney, Jim "Sailor", 25-26, 30, 46, 48- 49, 135-136, 138- 139, 145-146, 152, 158, 162, 216

U

UDT (Underwater Demolition team), 176
Uni-Prawn, 424
United Nations, 200, 436, 428
University of California, 455
University of Miami, 398
UNO (United Nicaraguan Opposition), 193, 213
UPI Television Network, 318

V

Vanderbilt University, 316
Vasquez, Daniel III, 319
Vaughn, Frederico, 372
Vega, Martin, 363
Venezuela, 151
Vidal, Felipe, 192, 194-195, 211, 213, 244, 250
Viet Cong, 31, 40

Vietnam, 10, 14-15, 22, 24, 25, 31, 34, 40, 92, 127, 129, 147, 152, 215, 294, 335, 348, 375
Village Voice, 335
Voice of America, 108

W

Wallace, George C., 20
Wallace, Jane, 337
Walsh, Lawrence, 407, 418-419
Warwick, Mal, 336, 355
Washington News Network, 354
Washington Post, 327, 329, 353, 360
Washington Times, 348, 372, 404
Watergate scandal, 186, 367, 368, 329, 384, 405
Watkins, John C., 174, 175, 310
Watson, Samuel, 371
"West 57th Street," 345, 354, 360
West Point, 375
West, Ty, 337
White, Robert, 331, 379-380
Wiggins, Selso, 221, 291
Wilson, Edwin, 374, 375
Win, Ne, 386, 389
Win, Tin Maung, 385
Winer, John, 327-328, 330-331, 333, 343, 345, 394
Woodward, Bob, 329, 367
World War II, 339, 386
Wounded Knee, 235, 338

Z

Zinn, U Thant, 389, 393